DI029385

THE EPISTLE TO THE ROMANS

Rev. W. SANDAY, D.D., LL.D., Litt.D.

AND

Rev. A. C. HEADLAM, D.D.

PRINTED IN GREAT BRITAIN BY
MORRISON AND GIBB LIMITED
FOR
T. & T. CLARK, EDINBURGH
NEW YORK: CHARLES SCRIBNER'S SONS

The Rights of Translation and of Reproduction are Reserved

A

CRITICAL AND EXEGETICAL COMMENTARY

ON

THE EPISTLE TO THE ROMANS

BY THE REV.

WILLIAM SANDAY, D.D., LL.D., LITT.D., F.B.A.

LADY MARGARET PROFESSOR OF DIVINITY, AND
CANON OF CHRIST CHURCH, OXFORD
CHAPLAIN IN ORDINARY TO THE KING

AND THE

REV. ARTHUR C. HEADLAM, D.D.

PRINCIPAL OF KING'S COLLEGE, LONDON

FIFTH EDITION

EDINBURGH
T. & T. CLARK, 38 GEORGE STREET

FIRST EDITION . . September 1895
FIFTH EDITION . . December 1902
„   „   . Latest Reprint 1955

PREFACE

THE commentaries on the Epistle to the Romans which already exist in English, unlike those on some other Books of the New Testament, are so good and so varied that to add to their number may well seem superfluous. Fortunately for the present editors the responsibility for attempting this does not rest with them. In a series of commentaries on the New Testament it was impossible that the Epistle to the Romans should not be included and should not hold a prominent place. There are few books which it is more difficult to exhaust and few in regard to which there is more to be gained from renewed interpretation by different minds working under different conditions. If it is a historical fact that the spiritual revivals of Christendom have been usually associated with closer study of the Bible, this would be true in an eminent degree of the Epistle to the Romans. The editors are under no illusion as to the value of their own special contribution, and they will be well content that it should find its proper level and be assimilated or left behind as it deserves.

Perhaps the nearest approach to anything at all distinctive in the present edition would be (1) the distribution of the subject-matter of the commentary, (2) the attempt to furnish an interpretation of the Epistle which might be described as historical.

Some experience in teaching has shown that if a difficult

Epistle like the Romans is really to be understood and grasped at once as a whole and in its parts, the argument should be presented in several different ways and on several different scales at the same time. And it is an advantage when the matter of a commentary can be so broken up that by means of headlines, headings to sections, summaries, paraphrases, and large and small print notes, the reader may not either lose the main thread of the argument in the crowd of details, or slur over details in seeking to obtain a general idea. While we are upon this subject, we may explain that the principle which has guided the choice of large and small print for the notes and longer discussions is not exactly that of greater or less importance, but rather that of greater or less directness of bearing upon the exegesis of the text. This principle may not be carried out with perfect uniformity : it was an experiment the effect of which could not always be judged until the commentary was in print; but when once the type was set the possibility of improvement was hardly worth the trouble and expense of resetting.

The other main object at which we have aimed is that of making our exposition of the Epistle historical, that is of assigning to it its true position in place and time—on the one hand in relation to contemporary Jewish thought, and on the other hand in relation to the growing body of Christian teaching. We have endeavoured always to bear in mind not only the Jewish education and training of the writer, which must clearly have given him the framework of thought and language in which his ideas are cast, but also the position of the Epistle in Christian literature. It was written when a large part of the phraseology of the newly created body was still fluid, when a number of words had not yet come to have a fixed meaning, when their origin and associations—to us obscure—were still fresh and vivid. The problem which a commentator ought to propose to himself in the first instance is not what answer

does the Epistle give to questions which are occupying
men's minds now, or which have occupied them in any
past period of Church history, but what were the questions
of the time at which the Epistle was written and what
meaning did his words and thoughts convey to the writer
himself.

It is in the pursuit of this original meaning that we have
drawn illustrations somewhat freely from Jewish writings,
both from the Apocryphal literature which is mainly the
product of the period between 100 B.C. and 100 A.D., and
(although less fully) from later Jewish literature. In the
former direction we have been much assisted by the
attention which has been bestowed in recent years on
these writings, particularly by the excellent editions of the
Psalms of Solomon and of the Book of Enoch. It is by
a continuous and careful study of such works that any
advance in the exegesis of the New Testament will be
possible. For the later Jewish literature and the teaching
of the Rabbis we have found ourselves in a position of
greater difficulty. A first-hand acquaintance with this
literature we do not possess, nor would it be easy for most
students of the New Testament to acquire it. Moreover
complete agreement among the specialists on the subject
does not as yet exist, and a perfectly trustworthy standard
of criticism seems to be wanting. We cannot therefore feel
altogether confident of our ground. At the same time we
have used such material as was at our disposal, and certainly to ourselves it has been of great assistance, partly as
suggesting the common origin of systems of thought which
have developed very differently, partly by the striking
contrasts which it has afforded to Christian teaching.

Our object is historical and not dogmatic. Dogmatics
are indeed excluded by the plan of this series of commentaries, but they are excluded also by the conception which
we have formed for ourselves of our duty as commentators.
We have sought before all things to understand St. Paul,

and to understand him not only in relation to his surroundings but also to those permanent facts of human
nature on which his system is based. It is possible that
in so far as we may succeed in doing this, data may be
supplied which at other times and in other hands may be
utilized for purposes of dogmatics ; but the final adjust-
ments of Christian doctrine have not been in our thoughts.

To this general aim all other features of the commentary
are subordinate. It is no part of our design to be in the
least degree exhaustive. If we touch upon the history of
exegesis it is less for the sake of that history in itself than
as helping to throw into clearer relief that interpretation
which we believe to be the right one. And in like manner
we have not made use of the Epistle as a means for
illustrating New Testament grammar or New Testament
diction, but we deal with questions of grammar and diction
just so far as they contribute to the exegesis of the text
before us. No doubt there will be omissions which are not
to be excused in this way. The literature on the Epistle
to the Romans is so vast that we cannot pretend to have
really mastered it. We have tried to take account of
monographs and commentaries of the most recent date,
but here again when we have reached what seemed to us
a satisfactory explanation we have held our hand. In
regard to one book in particular, Dr. Bruce's *St. Paul's
Conception of Christianity*, which came out as our own
work was far advanced, we thought it best to be quite
independent. On the other hand we have been glad to
have access to the sheets relating to Romans in Dr. Hort's
forthcoming *Introductions to Romans and Ephesians*, which,
through the kindness of the editors, have been in our
possession since December last.

The Commentary and the Introduction have been about
equally divided between the two editors ; but they have
each been carefully over the work of the other, and they
desire to accept a joint responsibility for the whole. The

editors themselves are conscious of having gained much by this co-operation, and they hope that this gain may be set off against a certain amount of unevenness which was inevitable.

It only remains for them to express their obligations and thanks to those many friends who have helped them directly or indirectly in various parts of the work, and more especially to Dr. Plummer and the Rev. F. E. Brightman of the Pusey House. Dr. Plummer, as editor of the series, has read through the whole of the Commentary more than once, and to his courteous and careful criticism they owe much. To Mr. Brightman they are indebted for spending upon the proof-sheets of one half of the Commentary greater care and attention than many men have the patience to bestow on work of their own.

The reader is requested to note the table of abbreviations on p. cx ff., and the explanation there given as to the Greek text made use of in the Commentary. Some additional references are given in the Index (p. 444 ff).

W. SANDAY.
A. C. HEADLAM.

Oxford, *Whitsuntide*, 1895.

PREFACE TO THE SECOND EDITION

We are indebted to the keen sight and disinterested care of friends for many small corrections. We desire to thank especially Professor Lock, Mr. C. H. Turner, the Revs. F. E. Brightman, W. O. Burrows, and R. B. Rackham. References have been inserted, where necessary, to the edition of 4 Ezra by the late Mr. Bensly, published in *Texts and Studies*, iii. 2. No more extensive recasting of the commentary has been attempted.

Oxford, *Lent*, 1896.

PREFACE TO THE THIRD EDITION

THE demand for a new Edition has come upon us so suddenly in the midst of other work, that we have again confined ourselves to small corrections, the knowledge of which we owe to the kindness of many friends and critics. We have especially to thank Dr. Carl Clemen of Halle, not only for a useful and helpful review in the *Theologische Literaturzeitung*, No. 26, Nov. 7, 1896, p. 590, but also for privately communicating to us a list of misprints. We have also to thank the Rev. H. T. Purchas of New Zealand, Mr. John Humphrey Barbour of the U.S.A., and the Rev. C. Plummer for corrections and suggestions. We should like also to refer to an article in the *Expositor* (Vol. IV, 1896, p. 124) by the late Rev. J. Barmby, on *The Meaning of the 'Righteousness of God' in the Epistle to the Romans,* in which he works out more fully the opinions to which we referred on p. 24. We are glad again to express our obligations to him and our sense of the loss of one who was a vigorous and original worker both in Church History and in New Testament Exegesis.

We can only now chronicle the appearance of the first volume of the elaborate *Einleitung in das N. T.* (Leipzig, 1897) of Dr. Zahn, which discusses the questions relating to the Epistle with the writer's accustomed thoroughness and learning, a new 'improved' edition of the *Einleitung* of Dr. B. Weiss, and an edition of the Greek text of the Pauline Epistles with concise commentary by the same author. Both these works have appeared during the present year. The volume of essays dedicated to Dr. B. Weiss on his seventieth birthday, *Theol. Studien &c.* (Göttingen, 1897), contains two papers which have a bearing upon the Epistle, *Zur paulinischen Théodicée* by Dr. Ernst Kühl, and *Beiträge zur paulin. Rhetorik* by Dr. Joh. Weiss. We should hope to take account of these and other works if at some future time we are permitted to undertake a fuller revision of our commentary.

W. S.

A. C. H.

OXFORD, *December,* 1897.

PREFACE TO THE FIFTH EDITION

ONCE more the call for a new edition has come upon us suddenly, and at a time when it would not be possible for either of us to devote much attention to it. But apart from this, it would be equally true of both of us that our thoughts and studies have of late travelled so far from the Epistle to the Romans that to come back to it would be an effort, and would require more leisure than we are likely to have for some years to come. We are well aware that much water has flowed under the bridge since we wrote, and that many problems would have to be faced afresh if a searching revision of our work were attempted.

As we cannot undertake this at present, it may be right that we should at least suggest to the reader where he may go for further information.

A very excellent and thorough survey of the whole subject will be found in the article ' Romans ' in Hastings' *Dictionary of the Bible* by Dr. A. Robertson. The corresponding article in the *Encyclopaedia Biblica* has not yet appeared. For more detailed exegesis the most important recent event is probably the appearance (in 1899) of the ninth edition of Meyer's Commentary by Dr. B. Weiss, who has done us the honour to include systematic reference to our own work. In any revision of this it would be our first duty to give to the points on which Dr. Weiss differs from us renewed consideration. In English the most considerable recent commentary is Dr. Denney's in the *Expositor's Greek Testament* (1900). There is also a thoughtful and useful little commentary in the *Century Bible* by A. E. Garvie.

Perhaps the most conspicuous of the problems raised by the Epistle, which have been or are being carried on beyond the point at which we had left them, would be

(i) the question as to the meaning of the 'righteousness of God' in i. 17, &c. Something was said on this subject in the New Testament portion of the article 'God' in Hastings' *Dictionary*, ii. 210–12, where reference is made to an interesting tract by Dalman, *Die richterliche Gerechtigkeit im A. T.* (Berlin, 1897), and to other literature. Something also was said in the *Journal of Theological Studies*, i. 486 ff., ii. 198 ff. And the question is again raised by Dr. James Drummond in the first number of the *Hibbert Journal*, pp. 83–95. This paper is to be continued; and the subject is sure to be heard of further. (ii) Another leading problem is that as to the relation of St. Paul to the Jewish Law, on which perhaps the most important recent contributions have been those by Sieffert ('Die Entwicklungslinie d. paulin. Gesetzeslehre nach den 4 Hauptbriefen d. Apost.') in the volume of Studies in honour of B. Weiss (Göttingen, 1897) and by P. Feine (*Das gesetzesfreie Evangelium d. Paulus*, Leipzig, 1899). (iii) A third deeply important question is being much agitated at the present time; viz. that as to the exact nature and significance of the 'Mystical Union' described in Rom. vi and viii. This is even more a question of Biblical and Dogmatic Theology than of Exegesis, and it is from this side that it is being discussed in such books as Dr. Moberly's *Atonement and Personality* (1901), Mr. Wilfrid Richmond's *Essay on Personality as a Philosophical Principle* (1900), and more incidentally in several works by Dr. W. R. Inge. (iv) Various questions raised in the Introduction are discussed in Dr. Moffatt's *Historical New Testament* (Edinburgh, 1901).

Two more general subjects are receiving special attention at the present time. One of these is the historical position and character of New Testament Greek, on which much new light is thrown by the study of inscriptions and of the mass of recently discovered papyri. We associate these studies especially with the names of G. A. Deissmann, whose *Bible Studies* have recently been published in English (Edinburgh, 1901), A. Thumb, K. Dieterich, and others. It is the less necessary to go into details about these, as an excellent account is given of all that has been done in a series of papers by H. A. A. Kennedy in the *Expository Times*, vol. xii (1901). Dr. Kennedy was himself a pioneer of the newer movement in England with his *Sources of New Testament Greek* (Edinburgh, 1895). We ought not however to forget the still earlier work of Dr. Hatch, *Essays in Biblical Greek* (Oxford, 1889), which was really at the time in advance of similar research on the Continent.

The other subject might be described as the Rhetoric of the New Testament. A comprehensive treatment of ancient rhetorical prose in general has been undertaken by Prof. E. Norden of Breslau in *Die antike Kunstprosa* (Leipzig, 1898). Dr. Norden devotes pp. 451–510 to an analysis of style in the New Testament, and also pays special attention to the later Christian writers, both Greek and Latin. The 'Rhetoric of St. Paul' in particular is the subject of a monograph by Dr. Johannes Weiss in the volume dedicated to his father. Nor should we close this survey without a special word of commendation for *The Relation of St. Paul to Contemporary Jewish Thought* by Mr. H. St. John Thackeray (London, 1900).

For the rest we must leave our book to take its place, such as it is, in the historical development of literature on the Epistle.

W. S.
A. C. H.

November, 1902.

CONTENTS

—————♦♦—————

INTRODUCTION

§ 1. ROME IN A.D. 58.

IT was during the winter 57–58, or early in the spring of the year 58, according to almost all calculations, that St. Paul wrote his Epistle to the Romans, and that we thus obtain the first trustworthy information about the Roman Church. Even if there be some slight error in the calculations, it is in any case impossible that this date can be far wrong, and the Epistle must certainly have been written during the early years of Nero's reign. It would be unwise to attempt a full account either of the city or the empire at this date, but for the illustration of the Epistle and for the comprehension of St. Paul's own mind, a brief reference to a few leading features in the history of each is necessary [1].

For certainly St. Paul was influenced by the name of Rome. In Rome, great as it is, and to Romans, he wishes to preach the Gospel: he prays for a prosperous journey that by the will of God he may come unto them: he longs to see them: the universality of the Gospel makes him desire to preach it in the universal city [2]. And the impression which we gain from the Epistle to the Romans is supported by our other sources of information. The desire to visit Rome dominates the close of the Acts of the Apostles: 'After I have been there, I must also see Rome.' 'As thou hast testified of me in Jerusalem, so must thou bear witness also at Rome [3].' The imagery of citizenship has impressed itself upon his language [4]. And this was the result both of his experience and of his birth. Wherever Christianity had been preached the Roman authorities had appeared as the power which restrained

---

[1] The main authorities used for this section are Furneaux, *The Annals of Tacitus*, vol. ii, and Schiller, *Geschichte des Römischen Kaisserreichs unter der Regierung des Nero*.

[2] Rom. i. 8–15.

[3] Acts xix. 21 ; xxiii. 11.

[4] Phil. i. 27 ; iii. 20 ; Eph. ii. 19 ; Acts xxiii. 1.

the forces of evil opposed to it[1]. The worst persecution of the Christians had been while Judaea was under the rule of a native prince. Everywhere the Jews had stirred up persecutions, and the imperial officials had interfered and protected the Apostle. And so both in this Epistle and throughout his life St. Paul emphasizes the duty of obedience to the civil government, and the necessity of fulfilling our obligations to it. But also St. Paul was himself a Roman citizen. This privilege, not then so common as it became later, would naturally broaden the view and impress the imagination of a provincial; and it is significant that the first clear conception of the universal character inherent in Christianity, the first bold step to carry it out, and the capacity to realize the importance of the Roman Church should come from an Apostle who was not a Galilaean peasant but a citizen of a universal empire. 'We cannot fail to be struck with the strong hold that Roman ideas had on the mind of St. Paul,' writes Mr. Ramsay, 'we feel compelled to suppose that St. Paul had conceived the great idea of Christianity as the religion of the Roman world; and that he thought of the various districts and countries in which he had preached as parts of the grand unity. He had the mind of an organizer; and to him the Christians of his earliest travels were not men of Iconium and of Antioch—they were a part of the Roman world, and were addressed by him as such[2].'

It was during the early years of Nero's reign that St. Paul first came into contact with the Roman Church. And the period is significant. It was what later times called the *Quinquennium* of Nero, and remembered as the happiest period of the Empire since the death of Augustus[3]. Nor was the judgement unfounded. It is

---

[1] 2 Thess. ii. 7 ὁ κατέχων, 6 τὸ κατέχον. It is well known that the commonest interpretation of these words among the Fathers was the Roman Empire (see the *Catena* of passages in Alford, iii. p. 56 ff.), and this accords most suitably with the time when the Epistle was written (*c.* 53 A.D.). The only argument of any value for a later date and the unauthentic character of the whole Epistle or of the eschatological sections (ii. 1–12) is the attempt to explain this passage of the return of Nero, but such an interpretation is quite unnecessary, and does not particularly suit the words. St. Paul's experience had taught him that there were lying restrained and checked great forces of evil which might at any time burst out, and this he calls the 'mystery of iniquity,' and describes in the language of the O. T. prophets. But everywhere the power of the civil government, as embodied in the Roman Empire (τὸ κατέχον) and visibly personified in the Emperor (ὁ κατέχων), restrained these forces. Such an interpretation, either of the eschatological passages of the Epistle or of the Apocalypse, does not destroy their deeper spiritual meaning; for the writers of the New Testament, as the prophets of the Old, reveal to us and generalize the spiritual forces of good and evil which underlie the surface of society.

[2] Ramsay, *The Church in the Roman Empire*, pp. 147, 148; cf. also pp. 60, 70, 158 n. See also Lightfoot, *Biblical Essays*, pp. 202–205.

[3] Aur. Victor, *Caes.* 5, *Epit.* 12, *Unde quidam prodidere, Traianum solitum dicere, procul distare cunctos principes a Neronis quinquennio.* The expression

probable that even the worst excesses of Nero, like the worst cruelty
of Tiberius, did little harm to the mass of the people even in Rome;
and many even of the faults of the Emperors assisted in working
out the new ideas which the Empire was creating. But at present
we have not to do with faults. Members of court circles might
have unpleasant and exaggerated stories to tell about the death of
Britannicus; tales might have been circulated of hardly pardon-
able excesses committed by the Emperor and a noisy band of
companions wandering at night in the streets; the more respectable of the Roman aristocracy would consider an illicit union
with a freedwoman and a taste for music, literature, and the drama,
signs of degradation, but neither in Rome nor in the provinces
would the populace be offended; more far-seeing observers might
be able to detect worse signs, but if any ordinary citizen, or
if any one acquainted with the provinces had been questioned, he
would certainly have answered that the government of the Empire
was good. This was due mainly to the gradual development of
the ideas on which the Empire had been founded. The structure
which had been sketched by the genius of Caesar, and built up
by the art of Augustus, if allowed to develop freely, guaranteed
naturally certain conditions of progress and good fortune. It was
due also to the wise administration of Seneca and of Burrus. It
was due apparently also to flashes of genius and love of popularity
on the part of the Emperor himself.

The provinces were well governed. Judaea was at this time
preparing for insurrection under the rule of Felix, but he was
a legacy from the reign of Claudius. The difficulties in Armenia
were met at once and vigorously by the appointment of Corbulo;
the rebellion in Britain was wisely dealt with; even at the end of
Nero's reign the appointment of Vespasian to Judaea, as soon as
the serious character of the revolt was known, shows that the
Emperor still had the wisdom to select and the courage to appoint
able men. During the early years a long list is given of trials
for *repetundae*; and the number of convictions, while it shows that
provincial government was not free from corruption, proves that
it was becoming more and more possible to obtain justice. It
was the corruption of the last reign that was condemned by
the justice of the present. In the year 56, Vipsanius Laenas,
governor of Sardinia, was condemned for extortion; in 57,
Capito, the 'Cilician pirate,' was struck down by the senate
'with a righteous thunderbolt.' Amongst the accusations against

---

quinquennium may have been suggested by the *certamen quinquennale* which
Nero founded in Rome, as Dio tells us, ὑπὲρ τῆς σωτηρίας τῆς τε διαμονῆς τοῦ
κράτους αὐτοῦ, Dio, *Epit.* lxi. 21; Tac. *Ann.* xiv. 20; Suet. *Nero* 12; cf. the
coins described, Eckhel, vi. 264; Cohen, i. p. 282, 47-65. CER. QUINQ.
ROM. CO.

Suillius in 58 was the misgovernment of Asia. And not only were the favourites of Claudius condemned, better men were appointed in their place. It is recorded that freedmen were never made procurators of imperial provinces. And the Emperor was able in many cases, in that of Lyons, of Cyrene, and probably of Ephesus, to assist and pacify the provincials by acts of generosity and benevolence [1].

We may easily, perhaps, lay too much stress on some of the measures attributed to Nero; but many of them show, if not the policy of his reign, at any rate the tendency of the Empire. The police regulations of the city were strict and well executed [2]. An attack was made on the exactions of publicans, and on the excessive power of freedmen. Law was growing in exactness owing to the influence of Jurists, and was justly administered except where the Emperor's personal wishes intervened [3]. Once the Emperor—was it a mere freak or was it an act of far-seeing political insight?—proposed a measure of free trade for the whole Empire. Governors of provinces were forbidden to obtain condonation for exactions by the exhibition of games. The proclamation of freedom to Greece may have been an act of dramatic folly, but the extension of Latin rights meant that the provincials were being gradually put more and more on a level with Roman citizens. And the provinces flourished for the most part under this rule. It seemed almost as if the future career of a Roman noble might depend upon the goodwill of his provincial subjects [4]. And wherever trade could flourish there wealth accumulated. Laodicea was so rich that the inhabitants could rebuild the city without aid from Rome, and Lyons could contribute 4,000,000 sesterces at the time of the great fire [5].

When, then, St. Paul speaks of the 'powers that be' as being 'ordained by God'; when he says that the ruler is a minister of God for good; when he is giving directions to pay 'tribute' and 'custom'; he is thinking of a great and beneficent power which has made travel for him possible, which had often interfered to protect him against an angry mob of his own countrymen, under which he had seen the towns through which he passed enjoying peace, prosperity and civilization.

[1] For the provincial administration of Nero see Furneaux, *op. cit.* pp. 56, 57; W. T. Arnold, *The Roman System of Provincial Administration*, pp. 135, 137; Tac. *Ann.* xiii. 30, 31, 33, 50, 51, 53–57.

[2] Suetonius, *Nero* 16. Schiller, p. 420.

[3] Schiller, pp. 381, 382: 'In dem Mechanismus des gerichtlichen Verfahrens, im Privatrecht, in der Ausbildung und Förderung der Rechtswissenschaft, selbst auf dem Gebiete der Appellation können gegründete Vorwürfe kaum erhoben werden. Die kaiserliche Regierung liess die Verhältnisse hier ruhig den Gang gehen, welchen ihnen frühere Regierungen angewiesen hatten.'

[4] Tac. *Ann.* xv. 20, 21.

[5] Arnold, p. 137.

But it was not only Nero, it was Seneca[1] also who was ruling in Rome when St. Paul wrote to the Church there. The attempt to find any connexions literary or otherwise between St. Paul and Seneca may be dismissed; but for the growth of Christian principles, still more perhaps for that of the principles which prepared the way for the spread of Christianity, the fact is of extreme significance. It was the first public appearance of Stoicism in Rome, as largely influencing politics, and shaping the future of the Empire. It is a strange irony that makes Stoicism the creed which inspired the noblest representatives of the old régime, for it was Stoicism which provided the philosophic basis for the new imperial system, and this was not the last time that an aristocracy perished in obedience to their own morality. What is important for our purpose is to notice that the humanitarian and universalist ideas of Stoicism were already beginning to permeate society. Seneca taught, for example, the equality in some sense of all men, even slaves; but it was the populace who a few years later (A. D. 61) protested when the slaves of the murdered Pedanius Secundus were led out to execution[2]. Seneca and many of the Jurists were permeated with the Stoic ideas of humanity and benevolence; and however little these principles might influence their individual conduct they gradually moulded and changed the law and the system of the Empire.

If we turn from the Empire to Rome, we shall find that just those vices which the moralist deplores in the aristocracy and the Emperor helped to prepare the Roman capital for the advent of Christianity. If there had not been large foreign colonies, there could never have been any ground in the world where Christianity could have taken root strongly enough to influence the surrounding population, and it was the passion for luxury, and the taste for philosophy and literature, even the vices of the court, which demanded Greek and Oriental assistance. The Emperor must have teachers in philosophy, and in acting, in recitation and in flute-playing, and few of these would be Romans. The statement of Chrysostom that St. Paul persuaded a concubine of Nero to accept Christianity and forsake the Emperor has probably little foundation[3], the conjecture that this concubine was Acte is worthless; but it may illustrate how it was through the non-Roman element of Roman society that Christianity spread. It is not possible to estimate the exact proportion of foreign elements in a Roman household, but a study of the names in any of the Columbaria of the imperial period

---

[1] See Lightfoot, *St. Paul and Seneca, Philippians*, p. 268. To this period of his life belong the ἀποκολοκύντωσις, the *De Clementia*, the *De Vita Beata*, the *De Beneficiis*, and the *De Constantia Sapientis*. See Teuffel, *History of Roman Literature*, translated by Warr, ii. 42.

[2] Tac. *Ann.* xiv. 42–45.

[3] Chrysostom, *Hom. in Act. App.* 46, 3.

will illustrate how large that element was. Men and women of every race lived together in the great Roman slave world, or when they had received the gift of freedom remained attached as clients and friends to the great houses, often united by ties of the closest intimacy with their masters and proving the means by which every form of strange superstition could penetrate into the highest circles of society [1].

And foreign superstition was beginning to spread. The earliest monuments of the worship of Mithras date from the time of Tiberius. Lucan in his *Pharsalia* celebrates the worship of Isis in Rome; Nero himself reverenced the Syrian Goddess, who was called by many names, but is known to us best as Astarte; Judaism came near to the throne with Poppaea Sabina, whose influence over Nero is first traced in this year 58; while the story of Pomponia Graecina who, in the year 57, was entrusted to her husband for trial on the charge of 'foreign superstition' and whose long old age was clouded with continuous sadness, has been taken as an instance of Christianity. There are not inconsiderable grounds for this view; but in any case the accusation against her is an illustration that there was a path by which a new and foreign religion like Christianity could make its way into the heart of the Roman aristocracy [2].

§ 2.   THE JEWS IN ROME [3].

There are indications enough that when he looked towards Rome St. Paul thought of it as the seat and centre of the Empire. But he had at the same time a smaller and a narrower object. His chief interest lay in those little scattered groups of Christians of whom he had heard through Aquila and Prisca, and probably

---

[1] We have collected the following names from the contents of one columbarium (*C. I. L.* vi. 2, p. 941). It dates from a period rather earlier than this. It must be remembered that the proportion of foreigners would really be larger than appears, for many of them would take a Roman name. Amaranthus 5180, Chrysantus 5183, Serapio (*bis*) 5187, Pylaemenianus 5188, Creticus 5197, Asclepiades 5201, Melicus 5217, Antigonus 5227, Cypare 5229, Lezbius 5221, Amaryllis 5258, Perseus 5279, Apamea 5287 a, Ephesia 5299, Alexandrianus 5316, Phyllidianus 5331, Mithres 5344, Diadumenus 5355, Philumenus 5401, Philogenes 5410, Graniae Nicopolinis 5419, Corinthus 5439, Antiochis 5437, Athenais 5478, Eucharistus 5477, Melitene 5490, Samothrace, Mystius 5527, Lesbus 5529. The following, contained among the above, seems to have a special interest: Ἥδυκος Εὐόδου πρεσβευτὴς Φαναγορείτων τῶν κατὰ Βώσπορον, and Ἀσπούργος Βιομάσου υἱὸς ἑρμηνεὺς Σαρμάτων βωσπορανός 5207.

[2] Tac. *Ann.* xiii. 32; Lightfoot, *Clement*, i. 30.

[3] Since this section was written the author has had access to Berliner, *Geschichte d. Juden in Rom* (Frankfurt a. M. 1893), which has enabled him to correct some current misconceptions. The facts are also excellently put together by Schürer, *Neutest. Zeitgesch.* ii. 505 ff.

through others whom he met on his travels. And the thought of the
Christian Church would at once connect itself with that larger
community of which it must have been in some sense or other an
offshoot, the Jewish settlement in the imperial city.

(1) *History.* The first relations of the Jews with Rome go back
to the time of the Maccabaean princes, when the struggling patriots
of Judaea had some interests in common with the great Republic
and could treat with it on independent terms. Embassies were
sent under Judas [1] (who died in 160 B.C.) and Jonathan [2] (who died
in 143), and at last a formal alliance was concluded by Simon
Maccabaeus in 140, 139 [3]. It was characteristic that on this last
occasion the members of the embassy attempted a religious
propaganda and were in consequence sent home by the praetor
Hispalus [4].

This was only preliminary contact. The first considerable
settlement of the Jews in Rome dates from the taking of Jerusalem
by Pompey in B.C. 63 [5]. A number of the prisoners were sold as
slaves; but their obstinate adherence to their national customs
proved troublesome to their masters and most of them were soon
manumitted. These released slaves were numerous and important enough to found a synagogue of their own [6], to which they
might resort when they went on pilgrimage, at Jerusalem. The
policy of the early emperors favoured the Jews. They passionately
bewailed the death of Julius, going by night as well as by day to
his funeral pyre [7]; and under Augustus they were allowed to form
a regular colony on the further side of the Tiber [8], roughly speaking opposite the site of the modern ' Ghetto.' The Jews' quarter
was removed to the left bank of the river in 1556, and has been
finally done away with since the Italian occupation.

[1] 1 Macc. viii. 17–32.　　　　　　　　[2] 1 Macc. xii. 1–4, 16.
[3] 1 Macc. xiv. 24 ; xv. 15–24.
[4] This statement is made on the authority of Valerius Maximus I. iii. 2
(Excerpt. Parid.) : *Judaeos qui Sabazi Jovis cultu Romanos inficere mores
conati sunt, repetere domos suas coegit.* Doubt is thrown upon it by Berliner
(p. 4), but without sufficient reason. Val. Max. wrote under Tiberius, and made
use of good sources. At the same time, what he says about Jupiter Sabazius
is very probably based on a misunderstanding ; nor need we suppose that the
action of some members of the embassy affected the relations of the two peoples.
[5] This too is questioned by Berliner (p. 5 ff.), who points out that Philo, *Leg.
ad Caium* 23, from which the statement is taken, makes no mention of Pompey.
But it is difficult to see what other occasion could answer to the description, as
this does very well. Berliner however is more probably right in supposing
that there must have been other and older settlers in Rome to account for the
language of Cicero so early as B. C. 59 (see below). These settlers may have
come for purposes of trade.
[6] It was called after them the ' synagogue of the Libertini' (Acts vi. 10).
[7] Sueton. *Caesar* 84.
[8] This was the quarter usually assigned to prisoners of war (*Beschreibung d.
Stadt Rom*, III. iii. 578).

Here the Jews soon took root and rapidly increased in numbers. It was still under the Republic (B.C. 59) that Cicero in his defence of Flaccus pretended to drop his voice for fear of them[1]. And when a deputation came from Judaea to complain of the misrule of Archelaus, no less than 8000 Roman Jews attached themselves to it[2]. Though the main settlement was beyond the Tiber it must soon have overflowed into other parts of Rome. The Jews had a synagogue in connexion with the crowded Subura[3] and another probably in the Campus Martius. There were synagogues of Αὐγουστήσιοι and Ἀγριππήσιοι (i. e. either of the household or under the patronage of Augustus[4] and his minister Agrippa), the position of which is uncertain but which in any case bespeak the importance of the community. Traces of Jewish cemeteries have been found in several out-lying regions, one near the Porta Portuensis, two near the Via Appia and the catacomb of S. Callisto, and one at Portus, the harbour at the mouth of the Tiber[5].

Till some way on in the reign of Tiberius the Jewish colony flourished without interruption. But in A.D. 19 two scandalous cases occurring about the same time, one connected with the priests of Isis, and the other with a Roman lady who having become a proselyte to Judaism was swindled of money under pretence of sending it to Jerusalem, led to the adoption of repressive measures at once against the Jews and the Egyptians. Four thousand were banished to Sardinia, nominally to be employed in putting down banditti, but the historian scornfully hints that if they fell victims to the climate no one would have cared[6].

The end of the reign of Caligula was another anxious and critical time for the Jews. Philo has given us a graphic picture of the reception of a deputation which came with himself at its head to beg for protection from the riotous mob of Alexandria. The half-crazy emperor dragged the deputation after him from one point to another of his gardens only to jeer at them and refuse any further

---

[1] The Jews were interested in this trial as Flaccus had laid hands on the money collected for the Temple at Jerusalem. Cicero's speech makes it clear that the Jews of Rome were a formidable body to offend.

[2] Joseph. *Ant.* XVII. xi. 1; *B. J.* II. vi. 1.

[3] There is mention of an ἄρχων Σιβουρησίων, *C. I. G.* 6447 (Schürer, *Gemeindeverfassung d. Juden in Rom*, pp. 16, 35; Berliner, p. 94). As synagogues were not allowed within the *pomoerium* (*ibid.* p. 16) we may suppose that the synagogue itself was without the walls, but that its frequenters came from the Subura.

[4] Berliner conjectures that the complimentary title may have been given as a sort of equivalent for emperor-worship (*op. cit.* p. 21).

[5] Data relating to the synagogues have been obtained from inscriptions, which have been carefully collected and commented upon by Schürer in the work quoted above (Leipzig, 1879), also more recently by Berliner (*op. cit.* p. 46 ff.).

[6] Tacitus, *Annal.* ii. 85 *si ob gravitatem caeli interissent, vile damnum.*

answer to their petition[1]. Caligula insisted on the setting up of his own bust in the Temple at Jerusalem, and his opportune death alone saved the Jews from worse things than had as yet befallen them (A.D. 41).

In the early part of the reign of Claudius the Jews had friends at court in the two Herod Agrippas, father and son. But a mysterious notice of which we would fain know more shows them once again subject to measures of repression. At a date which is calculated at about A.D. 52 we find Aquila and Prisca at Corinth 'because Claudius had commanded all the Jews to depart from Rome' (Acts xviii. 2). And Suetonius in describing what is probably the same event sets it down to persistent tumults in the Jewish quarter 'at the instigation of Chrestus[2].' There is at least a considerable possibility, not to say probability, that in this enigmatic guise we have an allusion to the effect of the early preaching of Christianity, in which in one way or another Aquila and Prisca would seem to have been involved and on that account specially singled out for exile. Suetonius and the Acts speak of a general edict of expulsion, but Dio Cassius, who is more precise, would lead us to infer that the edict stopped short of this. The clubs and meetings (in the synagogue) which Caligula had allowed, were forbidden, but there was at least no wholesale expulsion[3].

Any one of three interpretations may be put upon *impulsore Chresto assidue tumultuantes.* (i) The words may be taken literally as they stand. 'Chrestus' was a common name among slaves, and there may have been an individual of that name who was the author of the disturbances. This is the view of Meyer and Wieseler. (ii) Or it is very possible that there may be a confusion between 'Chrestus' and 'Christus.' Tertullian accuses the Pagans of pronouncing the name 'Christians' wrongly as if it were *Christiani,* and so bearing unconscious witness to the gentle and kindly character of those who owned it. *Sed et cum perperam Chrestianus pronunciatur a vobis (nam nec nominis certa est notitia penes vos) de suavitate vel benignitate compositum est (Apol.* 3; cf. Justin, *Apol.* i. § 4). If we suppose some such very natural confusion, then the disturbances may have had their origin in the excitement caused by the Messianic expectation which was ready to break out at slight provocation wherever Jews congregated. This is the view of Lange and others including in part Lightfoot (*Philippians,* p. 169). (iii) There remains the third possibility, for which some preference has been expressed above, that the disturbing cause was not the Messianic expectation in general but the particular form of it identified with Christianity. It is certain that Christianity must have been preached at Rome as early as this; and the preaching of it was quite as likely to lead to actual violence and riot as at Thessalonica or Antioch of Pisidia or Lystra (Acts xvii. 5; xiv. 19;

---

[1] *Leg. ad Caium* 44, 45.

[2] Sueton. *Claud.* 25 *Judaeos impulsore Chresto assidue tumultuantes Roma expulit.*

[3] Dio Cassius, lx. 6 τούς τε Ἰουδαίους, πλεονάσαντας αὖθις ὥστε χαλεπῶς ἂν ἄνευ ταραχῆς ὑπὸ τοῦ ὄχλου σφῶν τῆς πόλεως εἰρχθῆναι, οὐκ ἐξήλασε μέν, τῷ δὲ δὴ πατρίῳ νόμῳ βίῳ χρωμένους ἐκέλευσε μὴ συναθροίζεσθαι, τάς τε ἑταιρείας ἐπαναχθείσας ὑπὸ τοῦ Γαΐου διέλυσε.

xiii. 50). That it did so, and that this is the fact alluded to by Suetonius is the opinion of the majority of German scholars from Baur onwards. It is impossible to verify any one of the three hypotheses; but the last would fit in well with all that we know and would add an interesting touch if it were true [1].

The edict of Claudius was followed in about three years by his death (A. D. 54). Under Nero the Jews certainly did not lose but probably rather gained ground. We have seen that just as St. Paul wrote his Epistle Poppaea was beginning to exert her influence. Like many of her class she dallied with Judaism and befriended Jews. The mime Aliturus was a Jew by birth and stood in high favour [2]. Herod Agrippa II was also, like his father, a *persona grata* at the Roman court. Dio Cassius sums up the history of the Jews under the Empire in a sentence which describes well their fortunes at Rome. Though their privileges were often curtailed, they increased to such an extent as to force their way to the recognition and toleration of their peculiar customs [3].

(2) *Organization.* The policy of the emperors towards the Jewish nationality was on the whole liberal and judicious. They saw that they had to deal with a people which it was at once difficult to repress and useful to encourage; and they freely conceded the rights which the Jews demanded. Not only were they allowed the free exercise of their religion, but exceptional privileges were granted them in connexion with it. Josephus (*Ant.* XIV. x.) quotes a number of edicts of the time of Julius Caesar and after his death, some of them Roman and some local, securing to the Jews exemption from service in the army (on religious grounds), freedom of worship, of building synagogues, of forming clubs and collecting contributions (especially the *didrachma*) for the Temple at Jerusalem. Besides this in the East the Jews were largely permitted to have their own courts of justice. And the wonder is that in spite of all their fierce insurrections against Rome these rights were never permanently withdrawn. As late as the end of the second century (in the pontificate of Victor 189–199 A. D.)

[1] A suggestion was made in the *Church Quarterly Review* for Oct. 1894, which deserves consideration; viz. that the dislocation of the Jewish community caused by the edict of Claudius may explain 'why the Church of the capital did not grow to the same extent as elsewhere out of the synagogue. Even when St. Paul arrived there in bonds the chiefs of the restored Jewish organization professed to have heard nothing, officially or unofficially, of the Apostle, and to know about the Christian sect just what we may suppose the rioters ten years earlier knew, that it was "everywhere spoken against"' (p. 175).

[2] *Vit. Joseph.* 3; *Ant.* XX. viii. 11.

[3] Dio Cassius xxxvii. 17 ἔστι καὶ παρὰ τοῖς Ῥωμαίοις τὸ γένος τοῦτο, κολουσθὲν μὲν πολλάκις αὐξηθὲν δὲ ἐπὶ πλεῖστον, ὥστε καὶ εἰς παρρησίαν τῆς νομίσεως ἐκνικῆσαι.

Callistus, who afterwards himself became Bishop of Rome, was banished to the Sardinian mines for forcibly breaking up a Jewish meeting for worship (Hippol. *Refut. Haer.* ix. 12).

There was some natural difference between the East and the West corresponding to the difference in number and concentration of the Jewish population. In Palestine the central judicial and administrative body was the Sanhedrin; after the Jewish War the place of the Sanhedrin was taken by the Ethnarch who exercised great powers, the Jews of the Dispersion voluntarily submitting to him. At Alexandria also there was an Ethnarch, as well as a central board or senate, for the management of the affairs of the community. At Rome, on the other hand, it would appear that each synagogue had its own separate organization. This would consist of a ' senate' (γερουσία), the members of which were the ' elders' (πρεσβύτεροι). The exact relation of these to the ' rulers' (ἄρχοντες) is not quite clear : the two terms may be practically equivalent; or the ἄρχοντες may be a sort of committee within the larger body[1]. The senate had its ' president' (γερουσιάρχης); and among the rulers one or more would seem to have been charged with the conduct of the services in the synagogue (ἀρχισυνάγωγος, ἀρχισυνάγωγοι). Under him would be the ὑπηρέτης (*Chazan*) who performed the minor duties of giving out and putting back the sacred rolls (Luke iv. 20), inflicted scourging (Matt. x. 17), and acted as schoolmaster. The priests as such had no special *status* in the synagogue. We hear at Rome of wealthy and influential people who were called ' father' or ' mother of the synagogue' ; this would be an honorary title. There is also mention of a προστάτης or *patronus*, who would on occasion act for the synagogue in its relation to the outer world.

(3) *Social status and condition.* There were certainly Jews of rank and position at Rome. Herod the Great had sent a number of his sons to be educated there (the ill-fated Alexander and Aristobulus as well as Archelaus, Antipas, and Philip the tetrarch[2]). At a later date other members of the family made it their home (Herod the first husband of Herodias, the younger Aristobulus, and at one time Herod Agrippa I). There were also Jews attached in one way or another to the imperial household (we have had mention of the synagogues of the *Agrippesii* and *Augustesii*). These would be found in the more aristocratic quarters. The Jews'

---

[1] This is the view of Schürer (*Gemeindeverf.* p. 22). The point is not discussed by Berliner. Dr. Edersheim appears to regard the ' elders' as identical with the ' rulers,' and the ἀρχισυνάγωγος as chief of the body. He would make the functions of the γερουσιάρχης political rather than religious, and he speaks of this office as if it were confined to the Dispersion of the West (*Life and Times,* &c. i. 438). These are points which must be regarded as more or less open.

[2] Jos. *Ant.* XV. x. 1 ; XVII. i. 3.

quarter proper was the reverse of aristocratic. The fairly plentiful notices which have come down to us in the works of the Satirists lead us to think of the Jews of Rome as largely a population of beggars, vendors of small wares, sellers of lucifer matches, collectors of broken glass, fortune-tellers of both sexes. They haunted the Aventine with their baskets and wisps of hay [1]. Thence they would sally forth and try to catch the ear especially of the wealthier Roman women, on whose superstitious hopes and fears they might play and earn a few small coins by their pains [2].

Between these extremes we may infer the existence of a more substantial trading class, both from the success which at this period had begun to attend the Jews in trade and from the existence of the numerous synagogues (nine are definitely attested) which it must have required a considerable amount and some diffusion of wealth to keep up. But of this class we have less direct evidence.

In Rome, as everywhere, the Jews impressed the observer by their strict performance of the Law. The Jewish sabbath was proverbial. The distinction of meats was also carefully maintained [3]. But along with these external observances the Jews did succeed in bringing home to their Pagan neighbours the contrast of their purer faith to the current idolatries, that He whom they served did not dwell in temples made with hands, and that He was not to be likened to 'gold or silver or stone, graven by art and device of man.'

It is difficult to say which is more conspicuous, the repulsion or the attraction which the Jews exercised upon the heathen world. The obstinate tenacity with which they held to their own customs, and the rigid exclusiveness with which they kept aloof from all others, offended a society which had come to embrace all the varied national religions with the same easy tolerance and which passed from one to the other as curiosity or caprice dictated. They looked upon the Jew as a gloomy fanatic, whose habitual expression was a scowl. It was true that he condemned, as he had reason to condemn, the heathen laxity around him. And his neighbours, educated and populace alike, retaliated with bitter hatred and scorn.

At the same time all—and there were many—who were in search

---

[1] The purpose of this is somewhat uncertain: it may have been used to pack their wares.

[2] The passages on which this description is based are well known. *Small Trades*: Martial, *Epig.* I. xlii. 3–5 ; XII. lvii. 13, 14. *Mendicancy*: Juvenal, *Sat.* iii. 14 ; vi. 542 ff. *Proselytism*: Horace, *Sat.* I. iv. 142 f. ; Juvenal, *Sat.* xiv. 96 ff.

[3] Horace, *Sat.* I. ix. 69 f. ; Juvenal, *Sat.* xiv. 96 ff. (of proselytes) ; Persius, *Sat.* v. 184 ; Sueton. *Aug.* 76. The texts of Greek and Latin authors relating to Judaism have recently been collected in a complete and convenient form by Théodore Reinach (*Textes relatifs au Judaisme*, Paris, 1895).

of a purer creed than their own, knew that the Jew had something to give them which they could not get elsewhere. The heathen Pantheon was losing its hold, and thoughtful minds were 'feeling after if haply they might find' the one God who made heaven and earth. Nor was it only the higher minds who were conscious of a strange attraction in Judaism. Weaker and more superstitious natures were impressed by its lofty claims, and also as we may believe by the gorgeous apocalyptic visions which the Jews of this date were ready to pour out to them. The seeker wants to be told something that he can *do* to gain the Divine favour; and of such demands and precepts there was no lack. The inquiring Pagan was met with a good deal of tact on the part of those whom he consulted. He was drawn on little by little; there was a place for every one who showed a real sympathy for the faith of Israel. It was not necessary that he should at once accept circumcision and the whole burden of the Mosaic Law; but as he made good one step another was proposed to him, and the children became in many cases more zealous than their fathers [1]. So round most of the Jewish colonies there was gradually formed a fringe of Gentiles more or less in active sympathy with their religion, the 'devout men and women,' 'those who worshipped God' (εὐσεβεῖς, σεβόμενοι, σεβόμενοι τὸν Θεόν, φοβούμενοι τὸν Θεόν) of the Acts of the Apostles. For the student of the origin of the Christian Church this class is of great importance, because it more than any other was the seed plot of Christianity; in it more than in any other the Gospel took root and spread with ease and rapidity [2].

§ 3. The Roman Church.

(1) *Origin.* The most probable view of the origin of the Christian Church in Rome is substantially that of the commentator known as Ambrosiaster (see below, § 10). This fourth-century writer, himself probably a member of the Roman Church, does not claim for it an apostolic origin. He thinks that it arose among the Jews of Rome and that the Gentiles to whom they conveyed a knowledge of Christ had not seen any miracles or any of the Apostles [3]. Some such conclusion as this fits in well with

---

[1] Juvenal, *Sat.* xiv. 96 ff.

[2] See the very ample collection of material on this subject in Schürer, *Neutest. Zeitgesch.* ii. 558 ff.

[3] *Constat itaque temporibus apostolorum Iudaeos, propterea quod sub regno Romano agerent, Romae habitasse: ex quibus hi qui crediderant, tradiderunt Romanis ut Christum profitentes, Legem servarent ... Romanis autem irasci non debuit, sed et laudare fidem illorum; quia nulla insignia virtutum*

the phenomena of the Epistle. St. Paul would hardly have written as he does if the Church had really been founded by an Apostle. He clearly regards it as coming within his own province as Apostle of the Gentiles (Rom. i. 6, 14 f.); and in this very Epistle he lays it down as a principle governing all his missionary labours that he will not 'build upon another man's foundation' (Rom. xv. 20). If an Apostle had been before him to Rome the only supposition which would save his present letter from clashing with this would be that there were two distinct churches in Rome, one Jewish-Christian the other Gentile-Christian, and that St. Paul wrote only to the latter. But not only is there no hint of such a state of things, but the letter itself (as we shall see) implies a mixed community, a community not all of one colour, but embracing in substantial proportions both Jews and Gentiles.

At a date so early as this it is not in itself likely that the Apostles of a faith which grew up under the shadow of Jewish particularism would have had the enterprise to cast their glance so far west as Rome. It was but natural that the first Apostle to do this should be the one who both in theory and in practice had struck out the boldest line as a missionary; the one who had formed the largest conception of the possibilities of Christianity, the one who risked the most in the effort to realize them, and who as a matter of principle ignored distinctions of language and of race. We see St. Paul deliberately conceiving and long cherishing the purpose of himself making a journey to Rome (Acts xix. 21; Rom. i. 13; xv. 22-24). It was not however to *found* a Church, at least in the sense of first foundation, for a Church already existed with sufficient unity to have a letter written to it.

If we may make use of the data in ch. xvi—and reasons will be given for using them with some confidence—the origin of the Roman Church will be fairly clear, and it will agree exactly with the probabilities of the case. Never in the course of previous history had there been anything like the freedom of circulation and movement which now existed in the Roman Empire [1]. And this movement followed certain definite lines and set in certain definite directions. It was at its greatest all along the Eastern shores of the Mediterranean, and its general trend was to and from Rome. The constant coming and going of Roman officials, as one provincial governor succeeded another; the moving of troops

---

videntes, nec aliquem apostolorum, susceperant fidem Christi ritu licet Iudaico (S. Ambrosii *Opp.* iii. 373 f., ed. Ballerini). We shall see that Ambrosiaster exaggerates the strictly Jewish influence on the Church, but in his general conclusion he is more right than we might have expected.

[1] 'The conditions of travelling, for ease, safety, and rapidity, over the greater part of the Roman empire, were such as in part have only been reached again in Europe since the beginning of the present century' (Friedländer, *Sittengeschichte Roms,* ii. 3).

from place to place with the sending of fresh batches of recruits and the retirement of veterans; the incessant demands of an ever-increasing trade both in necessaries and luxuries; the attraction which the huge metropolis naturally exercised on the imagination of the clever young Orientals who knew that the best openings for a career were to be sought there; a thousand motives of ambition, business, pleasure drew a constant stream from the Eastern provinces to Rome. Among the crowds there would inevitably be some Christians, and those of very varied nationality and antecedents. St. Paul himself had for the last three years been stationed at one of the greatest of the Levantine *emporia*. We may say that the three great cities at which he had spent the longest time—Antioch, Corinth, Ephesus—were just the three from which (with Alexandria) intercourse was most active. We may be sure that not a few of his own disciples would ultimately find their way to Rome. And so we may assume that all the owners of the names mentioned in ch. xvi had some kind of acquaintance with him. In several cases he adds some endearing little expression which implies personal contact and interest: Epaenetus, Ampliatus, Stachys are all his 'beloved'; Urban has been his 'helper'; the mother of Rufus had been also as a mother to him; Andronicus and Junia (or Junias) and Herodion are described as his 'kinsmen'—i. e. perhaps his fellow-tribesmen, possibly like him natives of Tarsus. Andronicus and Junias, if we are to take the expression literally, had shared one of his imprisonments. But not by any means all were St. Paul's own converts. The same pair, Andronicus and Junias, were Christians of older standing than himself. Epaenetus is described as the first convert ever made from Asia: that may of course be by the preaching of St. Paul, but it is also possible that he may have been converted while on pilgrimage to Jerusalem. If the Aristobulus whose household is mentioned is the Herodian prince, we can easily understand that he might have Christians about him. That Prisca and Aquila should be at Rome is just what we might expect from one with so keen an eye for the strategy of a situation as St. Paul. When he was himself established and in full work at Ephesus with the intention of visiting Rome, it would at once occur to him what valuable work they might be doing there and what an excellent preparation they might make for his own visit, while in his immediate surroundings they were almost superfluous. So that instead of presenting any difficulty, that he should send them back to Rome where they were already known, is most natural.

In this way, the previous histories of the friends to whom St. Paul sends greeting in ch. xvi may be taken as typical of the circumstances which would bring together a number of similar groups of Christians at Rome. Some from Palestine, some from Corinth, some from Ephesus and other parts of proconsular Asia, possibly some from Tarsus and more from the Syrian Antioch, there was in the first instance, as we may believe, nothing concerted in their going ; but when once they arrived in the metropolis, the free-masonry common amongst Christians would soon make them known to each other, and they would form, not exactly an organized Church, but such a fortuitous assemblage of Christians as was only waiting for the advent of an Apostle to constitute one.

For other influences than those of St. Paul we are left to general probabilities. But from the fact that there was a synagogue specially assigned to the Roman 'Libertini' at Jerusalem and that this synagogue was at an early date the scene of public debates between Jews and Christians (Acts vi. 9), with the further fact that regular communication would be kept up by Roman Jews frequenting the feasts, it is equally clear that Palestinian Christianity could hardly fail to have its representatives. We may well believe that the vigorous preaching of St. Stephen would set a wave in motion which would be felt even at Rome. If coming from such a source we should expect the Jewish Christianity of Rome to be rather of the freer Hellenistic type than marked by the narrowness of Pharisaism. But it is best to abstain from anticipating, and to form our idea of the Roman Church on better grounds than conjecture.

If the view thus given of the origin of the Roman Church is correct, it involves the rejection of two other views, one of which at least has imposing authority ; viz. (i) that the Church was founded by Jewish pilgrims from the First Pentecost, and (ii) that its true founder was St. Peter.

(i) We are told expressly that among those who listened to St. Peter's address on the Day of Pentecost were some who came from Rome, both born Jews of the Dispersion and proselytes. When these returned they would naturally take with them news of the strange things which were happening in Palestine. But unless they remained for some time in Jerusalem, and unless they attended very diligently to the teaching of the Apostles, which would as yet be informal and not accompanied by any regular system of *Catechesis*, they would not know enough to make them in the full sense 'Christians' ; still less would they be in a position to evangelize others. Among this first group there would doubtless be some who would go back predisposed and prepared to receive fuller instruction in Christianity ; they might be at a similar stage to that of the disciples of St. John the Baptist at Ephesus (Acts xix. 2 ff.) ; and under the successive impact of later visits (their own or their neighbours') to Jerusalem, we could imagine that their faith would be gradually consolidated. But it would take more than they brought away from the Day of Pentecost to lay the foundations of a Church.

(ii) The traditional founder of the Roman Church is St. Peter. But it is only in a very qualified sense that this tradition can be made good. We may say at once that we are not prepared to go the length of those who would deny the connexion of St. Peter with the Roman Church altogether. It is true that there is hardly an item in the evidence which is not subject to some deduction. The evidence which is definite is somewhat late, and the evidence which is early is either too uncertain or too slight and vague to carry a clear conclusion [1]. Most decisive of all, if it held good, would be the allusion in St. Peter's own First Epistle if the 'Babylon' from which he writes (1 Pet. v. 13) is really a covert name for Rome. This was the view of the Early Church, and although perhaps not absolutely certain it is in accordance with all probability. The Apocalypse confessedly puts 'Babylon' for Rome (Rev. xiv. 8; xvi. 19, &c.), and when we remember the common practice among the Jewish Rabbis of disguising their allusions to the oppressor [2], we may believe that Christians also, when they had once become suspected and persecuted, might have fallen into the habit of using a secret language among themselves, even where there was less occasion for secresy. When once we adopt this view, a number of details in the Epistle (such as the mention of Silvanus and Mark, and the points of contact between 1 Peter and Romans) find an easy and natural explanation [3].

The genuine Epistle of Clement of Rome (c. 97 A.D.) couples together St. Peter and St. Paul in a context dealing with persecution in such a way as to lend some support to the tradition that both Apostles had perished there [4]; and the Epistle of Ignatius addressed to Rome (c. 115 A.D.) appeals to both Apostles as authorities which the Roman Church would be likely to recognize [5]; but at the utmost this proves nothing as to the origin of the Church. When we descend a step later, Dionysius of Corinth (c. 171 A.D.) does indeed couple the two Apostles as having joined in 'planting' the Church of Rome as they had done previously that of Corinth [6]. But this Epistle alone is proof that if St. Paul could be said to have 'planted' the Church, it could not be in the sense of first foundation; and a like consideration must be taken to qualify the statements of Irenaeus [7]. By the beginning of the third century we get in Tertullian [8] and Caius of Rome [9] explicit references to Rome as the scene of the double martyrdom. The latter writer points to the 'trophies' (τὰ τρόπαια [10]) of the two Apostles as existing in his day on the Vatican and by the Ostian Way. This is conclusive evidence as to the belief of the Roman Church about the year 200. And it is followed by another piece of evidence which is good and precise as far as it goes.

[1] The summary which follows contains only the main points and none of the indirect evidence. For a fuller presentation the reader may be referred to Lightfoot, *St. Clement* ii. 490 ff., and Lipsius, *Apokr. Apostelgesch.* ii. 11 ff.

[2] On this practice, see Biesenthal, *Trostschreiben an die Hebräer*, p. 3 ff.; and for a defence of the view that St. Peter wrote his First Epistle from Rome, Lightfoot, *St. Clement* ii. 491 f.; Von Soden in *Handcommentar* III. ii. 105 f. &c. Dr. Hort, who had paid special attention to this Epistle, seems to have held the same opinion (*Judaistic Christianity*, p. 155).

[3] There is a natural reluctance in the lay mind to take ἐν Βαβυλῶνι in any other sense than literally. Still it is certainly to be so taken in *Orac. Sibyll.* v. 159 (Jewish); and it should be remembered that the advocates of this view include men of the most diverse opinions, not only the English scholars mentioned above and Döllinger, but Renan and the Tübingen school generally.

[4] *Ad Cor.* v. 4 ff.　　　　　　　　　　[5] *Ad Rom.* iv. 3.

[6] Eus. *H. E.* II. xxv. 8.　　　　　　　[7] *Adv. Haer.* III. iii. 2, 3.

[8] *Scorp.* 15; *De Praescript.* 36.　　　[9] Eus. *H. E.* II. xxv. 6, 7.

[10] There has been much discussion as to the exact meaning of this word. The leading Protestant archaeologists (Lipsius, Erbes, V. Schultze) hold that it refers to some conspicuous mark of the place of martyrdom (a famous 'terebinth' near the *naumachium* on the Vatican (*Mart. Pet. et Paul.* 63) and a 'pine-tree' near the road to Ostia. The Roman Catholic authorities would refer it to the 'tombs' or 'memorial chapels' (*memoriae*). It seems to us probable that buildings of some kind were already in existence. For statements of the opposing views see Lipsius, *Apokr. Apostelgesch.* ii. 21; De Waal, *Die Apostelgruft ad Catacumbas*, p. 14 ff.

Two fourth-century documents, both in texts which have undergone some corruption, the *Martyrologium Hieronymianum* (ed. Duchesne, p. 84) and a *Depositio Martyrum* in the work of Philocalus, the so-called ' chronographer of the year 354,' connect a removal of the bodies of the two Apostles with the consulship of Tuscus and Bassus in the year 258. There is some ambiguity as to the localities from and to which the bodies were moved; but the most probable view is that in the Valerian persecution when the cemeteries were closed to Christians, the treasured relics were transferred to the site known as *Ad Catacumbas* adjoining the present Church of St. Sebastian [1]. Here they remained, according to one version, for a year and seven months, according to another for forty years. The later story of an attempt by certain Orientals to steal them away seems to have grown out of a misunderstanding of an inscription by Pope Damasus (366-384 A.D.) [2].

Here we have a chain of substantial proof that the Roman Church fully believed itself to be in possession of the mortal remains of the two Apostles as far back as the year 200, a tradition at that date already firmly established and associated with definite well-known local monuments. The tradition as to the twenty-five years' episcopate of St. Peter presents some points of resemblance. That too appears for the first time in the fourth century with Eusebius (c. 325 A.D.) and his follower Jerome. By skilful analysis it is traced back a full hundred years earlier. It appears to be derived from a list drawn up probably by Hippolytus [3]. Lipsius would carry back this list a little further, and would make it composed under Victor in the last decade of the second century [4], and Lightfoot seems to think it possible that the figures for the duration of the several episcopates may have been present in the still older list of Hegesippus, writing under Eleutherus (c. 175-190 A.D.) [5].

Thus we have the twenty-five years' episcopate of St. Peter certainly believed in towards the end of the first quarter of the third century, if not by the beginning of the last quarter of the second. We are coming back to a time when a continuous tradition is beginning to be possible. And yet the difficulties in the way of bringing St. Peter to Rome at a date so early as the year 42 (which seems to be indicated) are so great as to make the acceptance of this chronology almost impossible. Not only do we find St. Peter to all appearance still settled at Jerusalem at the time of the Council in A.D. 51, but we have seen that it is highly improbable that he had visited Rome when St. Paul wrote his Epistle to the Church there. And it is hardly less improbable that a visit had been made between this and the later Epistles (Phil., Col., Eph., Philem.). The relations between the two Apostles and of both to the work of missions in general, would almost compel some allusion to such a visit if it had taken place. Between the years 58 or 61-63 and 170 there is quite time for legend to grow up; and Lipsius has pointed out a possible way in which it might arise [6]. There is evidence that the tradition of our Lord's command to the Apostles to remain at Jerusalem for twelve years after His Ascension, was current towards the end of the second century. The travels of the Apostles are usually dated from the end of this period

---

[1] The best account of this transfer is that given by Duchesne, *Liber Pontificalis* i. cvi f.

[2] So Lipsius, after Erbes, *Apokr. Apostelgesch.* ii. 335 f., 391 ff. ; also Lightfoot, *Clement* ii. 500. The Roman Catholic writers, Kraus and De Waal, would connect the story with the jealousies of Jewish and Gentile Christians in the first century: see the latter's *Die Apostelgruft ad Catacumbas*, pp. 33 f., 49 ff. This work contains a full survey of the controversy with new archaeological details.

[3] Lightfoot, *op. cit.* i. 259 ff.; 333.

[4] *Ap.* Lightfoot, pp. 237, 333.   [5] *Ibid.* p. 333.

[6] *Apokr. Apostelgesch.* ii. 27, 69.

(i.e. about 41–42 A.D.). Then the traditional date of the death of St. Peter is 67 or 68; and subtracting 42 from 67 we get just the 25 years required. It was assumed that St. Peter's episcopate dated from his first arrival in Rome.

So far the ground is fairly clear. But when Lipsius goes further than this and denies the Roman visit *in toto*, his criticism seems to us too drastic[1]. He arrives at his result thus. He traces a double stream in the tradition. On the one hand there is the ' Petro-pauline tradition ' which regards the two Apostles as establishing the Church in friendly co-operation[2]. The outlines of this have been sketched above. On the other hand there is the tradition of the conflict of St. Peter with Simon Magus, which under the figure of Simon Magus made a disguised attack upon St. Paul[3]. Not only does Lipsius think that this is the earliest form of the tradition, but he regards it as the original of all other forms which brought St. Peter to Rome[4] : the only historical ground for it which he would allow is the visit of St. Paul. This does not seem to us to be a satisfactory explanation. The traces of the Petro-pauline tradition are really earlier than those of the Ebionite legend. The way in which they are introduced is free from all suspicion. They are supported by collateral evidence (St. Peter's First Epistle and the traditions relating to St. Mark) the weight of which is considerable. There is practically no conflicting tradition. The claim of the Roman Church to joint foundation by the two Apostles seems to have been nowhere disputed. And even the Ebionite fiction is more probable as a distortion of facts that have a basis of truth than as pure invention. The visit of St. Peter to Rome, and his death there at some uncertain date[5], seem to us, if not removed beyond all possibility of doubt, yet as well established as many of the leading facts of history.

(2) *Composition.* The question as to the origin of the Roman Church has little more than an antiquarian interest ; it is an isolated fact or series of facts which does not greatly affect either the picture which we form to ourselves of the Church or the sense in which we understand the Epistle addressed to it. It is otherwise with the question as to its composition. Throughout the Apostolic age the determining factor in most historical problems is the relative

---

[1] It is significant that on this point Weizsäcker parts company from Lipsius (*Apost. Zeitalt.* p. 485).

[2] *Op. cit.* p. 11 ff.   [3] *Ibid.* p. 28 ff.

[4] *Ibid.* p. 62 ff.

[5] There is no substantial reason for supposing the death of St. Peter to have taken place at the same time as that of St. Paul. It is true that the two Apostles are commemorated upon the same day (June 29), and that the Chronicle of Eusebius refers their deaths to the same year (A.D. 67 Vers. Armen. ; 68 Hieron.). But the day is probably that of the deposition or removal of the bodies to or from the Church of St. Sebastian (see above) ; and for the year the evidence is very insufficient. Professor Ramsay (*The Church in the Roman Empire,* p. 279 ff.) would place the First Epistle of St. Peter in the middle of the Flavian period, A.D. 75–80 ; and it must be admitted that the authorities are not such as to impose an absolute veto on this view. The fact that tradition connects the death of St. Peter with the Vatican would seem to point to the great persecution of A.D. 64 ; but the state of things implied in the Epistle does not look as if it were anterior to this. On the other hand, Professor Ramsay's arguments have greatly shaken the objections to the traditional date of the death of St. Paul.

preponderance of the Jewish element or the Gentile. Which of these two elements are we to think of as giving its character to the Church at Rome? Directly contrary answers have been given to the question and whole volumes of controversy have grown up around it; but in this instance some real advance has been made, and the margin of difference among the leading critics is not now very considerable.

Here as in so many other cases elsewhere the sharper statement of the problem dates from Baur, whose powerful influence drew a long train of followers after him; and here as so often elsewhere the manner in which Baur himself approaches the question is determined not by the minute exegesis of particular passages but by a broad and comprehensive view of what seems to him to be the argument of the Epistle as a whole. To him the Epistle seems to be essentially directed against Jewish Christians. The true centre of gravity of the Epistle he found in chaps. ix–xi. St. Paul there grapples at close quarters with the objection that if his doctrine held good, the special choice of Israel—its privileges and the promises made to it—all fell to the ground. At first there is no doubt that the stress laid by Baur on these three chapters in comparison with the rest was exaggerated and one-sided. His own disciples criticized the position which he took up on this point, and he himself gradually drew back from it, chiefly by showing that a like tendency ran through the earlier portion of the Epistle. There too St. Paul's object was to argue with the Jewish Christians and to expose the weakness of their reliance on formal obedience to the Mosaic Law.

The writer who has worked out this view of Baur's most elaborately is Mangold. It is not difficult to show, when the Epistle is closely examined, that there is a large element in it which is essentially Jewish. The questions with which it deals are Jewish, the validity of the Law, the nature of Redemption, the principle on which man is to become righteous in the sight of God, the choice of Israel. It is also true that the arguments with which St. Paul meets these questions are very largely such as would appeal specially to Jews. His own views are linked on directly to the teaching of the Old Testament, and it is to the Old Testament that he goes in support of them. It is fair to ask, what sort of relevance arguments of this character would have as addressed to Gentiles.

It was also possible to point to one or two expressions in detail which might seem to favour the assumption of Jewish readers. Such would be Rom. iv. 1 where Abraham is described (in the most probable text) as 'our forefather according to the flesh' (τὸν προπάτορα ἡμῶν κατὰ σάρκα). To that however it was obvious to reply that in 1 Cor. x. 1 St. Paul spoke of the Israelites in the

wilderness as 'our fathers,' though no one would maintain that the
Corinthian Christians were by birth Jews. There is more weight
—indeed there is real weight—in the argument drawn from the
section, Rom. vii. 1–6, where not only are the readers addressed
as ἀδελφοί μου (which would be just as possible if they were converts from heathenism) but a sustained contrast is drawn between
an earlier state under the Law (ὁ νόμος vv. 1, 4, 5, 6; not vv. 2, 3
where the force of the article is different) and a later state of freedom from the Law. It is true that this could not have been
written to a Church which consisted wholly of Gentiles, unless the
Apostle had forgotten himself for the moment more entirely than
he is likely to have done. Still such expressions should not be
pressed too far. He associates his readers with himself in a manner
somewhat analogous to that in which he writes to the Corinthians,
as if their spiritual ancestry was the same as his own. Nor was
this without reason. He regards the whole pre-Messianic period
as a period of Law, of which the Law of Moses was only the most
conspicuous example.

It is a minor point, but also to some extent a real one, that the
exhortations in chs. xiii, xiv are probably in part at least addressed
to Jews. That turbulent race, which had called down the inter-
ference of the civil power some six or seven years before, needed
a warning to keep the peace. And the party which had scruples
about the keeping of days is more likely to have been Jewish than
Gentile. Still that would only show that some members of the
Roman Church were Jews, not that they formed a majority. Indeed
in this instance the contrary would seem to be the case, because
their opponents seem to have the upper hand and all that St. Paul
asks for on their behalf is toleration.

We may take it then as established that there were Jews in the
Church, and that in substantial numbers; just as we also cannot
doubt that there was a substantial number of Gentiles. The direct
way in which St. Paul addresses the Gentiles in ch. xi. 13 ff. (ὑμῖν
δὲ λέγω τοῖς ἔθνεσιν κ.τ.λ.) would be proof sufficient of this. But it
is further clear that St. Paul regards the Church as broadly and in
the main a Gentile Church. It is the Gentile element which gives
it its colour. This inference cannot easily be explained away from
the passages, Rom. i. 5–7, 13–15; xv. 14–16. In the first St. Paul
numbers the Church at Rome among the Gentile Churches, and
bases on his own apostleship to the Gentiles his right to address
them. In the second he also connects the obligations he is under
to preach to them directly with the general fact that all Gentiles
without exception are his province. In the third he in like manner
excuses himself courteously for the earnestness with which he has
written by an appeal to his commission to act as the priest who
lays upon the altar the Church of the Gentiles as his offering.

This then is the natural construction to put upon the Apostle's language. The Church to which he is writing is Gentile in its general complexion; but at the same time it contains so many born Jews that he passes easily and freely from the one body to the other. He does not feel bound to measure and weigh his words, because if he writes in the manner which comes most naturally to himself he knows that there will be in the Church many who will understand him. The fact to which we have already referred, that a large proportion even of the Gentile Christians would have approached Christianity through the portals of a previous connexion with Judaism, would tend to set him still more at his ease in this respect. We shall see in the next section that the force which impels the Apostle is behind rather than in front. It is not to be supposed that he had any exact statistics before him as to the composition of the Church to which he was writing. It was enough that he was aware that a letter such as he has written was not likely to be thrown away.

If he had stayed to form a more exact estimate we may take the greetings in ch. xvi as a rough indication of the lines that it would follow. The collection of names there points to a mixture of nationalities. Aquila at least, if not also Prisca [1], we know to have been a Jew (Acts xviii. 2). Andronicus and Junias and Herodion are described as 'kinsmen' (συγγενεῖς) of the Apostle: precisely what this means is not certain—perhaps 'members of the same tribe'—but in any case they must have been Jews. Mary (Miriam) is a Jewish name; and Apelles reminds us at once of *Iudaeus Apella* (Horace, *Sat.* I. v. 100). And there is besides 'the household of Aristobulus,' some of whom—if Aristobulus was really the grandson of Herod or at least connected with that dynasty—would probably have the same nationality. Four names (Urbanus, Ampliatus, Rufus, and Julia) are Latin. The rest (ten in number) are Greek with an indeterminate addition in 'the household of Narcissus.' Some such proportions as these might well be represented in the Church at large.

(3) *Status and Condition.* The same list of names may give us some idea of the social status of a representative group of Roman Christians. The names are largely those of slaves and freedmen. In any case the households of Narcissus and Aristobulus would belong to this category. It is not inconceivable, though of course not proveable, that Narcissus may be the well-known freedman of Claudius, put to death in the year 54 A.D., and Aristobulus the scion of the house of Herod. We know that at the time when

---

[1] See the note on ch. xvi. 3, where reference is made to the view favoured by Dr. Hort (*Rom. and Eph.* p. 12 ff.), that Prisca was a Roman lady belonging to the well-known family of that name.

St. Paul wrote to the Philippians Christianity had penetrated into the retinue of the Emperor himself (Phil. iv. 22). A name like Philologus seems to point to a certain degree of culture. We should therefore probably not be wrong in supposing that not only the poorer class of slaves and freedmen is represented. And it must be remembered that the better sort of Greek and some Oriental slaves would often be more highly educated and more refined in manners than their masters. There is good reason to think that Pomponia Graecina, the wife of Aulus Plautius the conqueror of Britain, and that in the next generation Flavius Clemens and Domitilla, the near relations and victims of Domitian, had come under Christian influence [1]. We should therefore be justified in supposing that even at this early date more than one of the Roman Christians possessed a not inconsiderable social standing and importance. If there was any Church in which the 'not many wise men after the flesh, not many mighty, not many noble,' had an exception, it was at Rome.

When we look again at the list we see that it has a tendency to fall into groups. We hear of Prisca and Aquila, 'and the Church that is in their house,' of the household of Aristobulus and the Christian members of the household of Narcissus, of Asyncritus, &c. 'and the brethren that are with them,' of Philologus and certain companions 'and all the saints that are with them.' It would only be what we should expect if the Church of Rome at this time consisted of a number of such little groups, scattered over the great city, each with its own rendezvous but without any complete and centralized organization. In more than one of the incidental notices of the Roman Church it is spoken of as 'founded' (Iren. *Adv. Haer.* III. i. 1; iii. 3) or 'planted' (Dionysius of Corinth in Eus. *H. E.* II. xxv. 8) by St. Peter and St. Paul. It may well be that although the Church did not in the strict sense owe to these Apostles its origin, it did owe to them its first existence as an organized whole.

We must not however exaggerate the want of organization at the time when St. Paul is writing. The repeated allusions to 'labouring' (κοπιᾶν) in the case of Mary, Tryphaena and Tryphosa, and Persis—all, as we observe, women—points to some kind of regular ministry (cf. for the quasi-technical sense of κοπιᾶν 1 Thess. v. 12; 1 Tim. v. 17). It is evident that Prisca and Aquila took the lead which we should expect of them; and they were well trained in St. Paul's methods. Even without the help of an Apostle, the Church had evidently a life of its own; and where there is life there is sure to be a spontaneous tendency to definite articulation of function. When St. Paul and St. Peter arrived we

---

[1] Lightfoot, *Clement,* i. 30–39, &c.

may believe that they would find the work half done; still it would wait the seal of their presence, as the Church of Samaria waited for the coming of Peter and John (Acts viii. 14).

§ 4. The Time and Place, Occasion and Purpose, of the Epistle.

(1) *Time and Place.* The time and place at which the Epistle was written are easy to determine. And the simple and natural way in which the notes of both in the Epistle itself dovetail into the narrative of the Acts, together with the perfect consistency of the whole group of data—subtle, slight, and incidental as they are—in the two documents, at once strongly confirms the truth of the history and would almost alone be enough to dispose of the *doctrinaire* objections which have been brought against the Epistle.

St. Paul had long cherished the desire of paying a visit to Rome (Rom. i. 13; xv. 23), and that desire he hopes very soon to see fulfilled; but at the moment of writing his face is turned not westwards but eastwards. A collection has been made in the Greek Churches, the proceeds of which he is with an anxious mind about to convey to Jerusalem. He feels that his own relation and that of the Churches of his founding to the Palestinian Church is a delicate matter; the collection is no lightly considered act of passing charity, but it has been with him the subject of long and earnest deliberation; it is the olive-branch which he is bent upon offering. Great issues turn upon it; and he does not know how it will be received[1].

We hear much of this collection in the Epistles written about this date (1 Cor. xvi. 1 ff.; 2 Cor. viii. 1 ff.; ix. 1 ff.). In the Acts it is not mentioned before the fact; but retrospectively in the course of St. Paul's address before Felix allusion is made to it: 'after many years I came to bring alms to my nation and offerings' (Acts xxiv. 17). Though the collection is not mentioned in the earlier chapters of the Acts, the order of the journey is mentioned. When his stay at Ephesus was drawing to an end we read that 'Paul purposed in the spirit, when he had passed through Macedonia and Achaia, to go to Jerusalem, saying, After I have been there, I must also see Rome' (Acts xix. 21). Part of this programme has been accomplished. At the time of writing St. Paul seems to be at the capital of Achaia. The allusions

[1] On this collection see an excellent article by Mr. Rendall in *The Expositor*, 1893, ii. 321 ff.

which point to this would none of them taken separately be
certain, but in combination they amount to a degree of probability which is little short of certainty. The bearer of the
Epistle appears to be one Phoebe who is an active, perhaps an
official, member of the Church of Cenchreae, the harbour of
Corinth (Rom. xvi. 1). The house in which St. Paul is staying,
which is also the meeting-place of the local Church, belongs to
Gaius (Rom. xvi. 23); and a Gaius St. Paul had baptized at
Corinth (1 Cor. i. 14). He sends a greeting also from Erastus,
who is described as 'oeconomus' or 'treasurer' of the city. The
office is of some importance, and points to a city of some importance. This would agree with Corinth; and just at Corinth
we learn from 2 Tim. iv. 20 that an Erastus was left behind on
St. Paul's latest journey—naturally enough if it was his home.

The visit to Achaia then upon which these indications converge
is that which is described in Acts xx. 2, 3. It occupied three
months, which on the most probable reckoning would fall at
the beginning of the year 58. St. Paul has in his company at
this time Timothy and Sosipater (or Sopater) who join in the
greeting of the Epistle (Rom. xvi. 21) and are also mentioned
in Acts xx. 4. Of the remaining four who send their greetings
we recognize at least Jason of Thessalonica (Rom. xvi. 21; cf.
Acts xvii. 6). Just the lightness and unobtrusiveness of all these
mutual coincidences affixes to the works in which they occur
the stamp of reality.

The date thus clearly indicated brings the Epistle to the Romans into
close connexion with the two Epistles to Corinthians, and less certainly with
the Epistle to Galatians. We have seen how the collection for the Churches
of Judaea is one of the links which bind together the first three. Many
other subtler traces of synchronism in thought and style have been pointed
out between all four (especially by Bp. Lightfoot in *Journ. of Class. and
Sacr. Philol.* iii [1857], p. 289 ff.; also *Galatians*, p. 43 ff., ed. 2). The
relative position of 1 and 2 Corinthians and Romans is fixed and certain.
If Romans was written in the early spring of A.D. 58, then 1 Corinthians
would fall in the spring and 2 Corinthians in the autumn of A.D. 57 [1]. In
regard to Galatians the data are not so decisive, and different views are held.
The older opinion, and that which would seem to be still dominant in
Germany (it is maintained by Lipsius writing in 1891), is that Galatians
belongs to the early part of St. Paul's long stay at Ephesus, A.D. 54 or 55.
In England Bp. Lightfoot found a number of followers in bringing it into
closer juxtaposition with Romans, about the winter of A.D. 57-58. The
question however has been recently reopened in two opposite directions: on
the one hand by Dr. C. Clemen (*Chronologie der paulinischen Briefe*, Halle,
1893), who would place it after Romans; and on the other hand by

---

[1] Jülicher, in his recent *Einleitung*, p. 62, separates the two Epistles to the
Corinthians by an interval of eighteen months; nor can this opinion be at once
ruled out of court, though it seems opposed to 1 Cor. xvi. 8, from which we
gather that when he wrote the first Epistle St. Paul did not contemplate staying
in Ephesus longer than the next succeeding Pentecost.

Mr. F. Rendall in *The Expositor* for April, 1894 (p. 254 ff.), who would place it some years earlier.

Clemen, who propounds a novel view of the chronology of St. Paul's life generally, would interpose the Council of Jerusalem (which he identifies with the visit of Acts xxi and not with that of Acts xv) between Romans, which he assigns to the winter of A.D. 53-54, and Galatians, which he places towards the end of the latter year [1]. His chief argument is that Galatians represents a more advanced and heated stage of the controversy with the Judaizers, and he accounts for this by the events which followed the Council (Gal. ii. 12 ff.; i. 6 ff.). There is, however, much that is arbitrary in the whole of this reconstruction; and the common view seems to us far more probable that the Epistle to the Romans marks rather the gradual subsidence of troubled waters than their first disturbing. There is more to be said for Mr. Rendall's opinion that Galatians was written during the early part of St. Paul's first visit to Corinth in the year 51 (or 52). The question is closely connected with the controversy reopened by Professor Ramsay as to the identity of the Galatian Churches. For those who see in them the Churches of South Galatia (Antioch in Pisidia, Iconium, Lystra and Derbe) the earlier date may well seem preferable. If we take them to be the Churches of North Galatia (Pessinus, Ancyra, and Tavium), then the Epistle cannot be earlier than St. Paul's settlement at Ephesus on his third journey in the year 54. The argument which Bishop Lightfoot based on resemblances of thought and language between Galatians and Romans rests upon facts that are indisputable, but does not carry with it any certain inference as to date.

(2) *Occasion.* If the time and place of the Epistle are clear, the occasion of it is still clearer; St. Paul himself explains it in unmistakable language twice over. At the beginning of the Epistle (Rom. i. 10-15) he tells the Romans how much he has longed to pay them a visit; and now that the prospect has been brought near he evidently writes to prepare them for it. And at the end of the Epistle (ch. xv. 22-33) he repeats his explanation detailing all his plans both for the near and for the more distant future, and telling them how he hopes to make his stay with them the most important stage of his journey to Spain. We know that his intention was fulfilled in substance but not in the manner of its accomplishment. He went up to Jerusalem and then

---

[1] Dr. Clemen places St. Paul's long stay at Ephesus (2¼ years on his reckoning) in 50-52 A.D. In the course of it would fall our 1 Corinthians and two out of the three letters which are supposed to be combined in our 2 Corinthians (for this division there is really something of a case). He then inserts a third missionary journey, extending not over three months (as Acts xx. 3), but over some two years in Macedonia and Greece. To this he refers the last Corinthian letter (2 Cor. i-viii) and a genuine fragment of Ep. to Titus (Tit. iii. 12-14). Ep. to Romans is written from Corinth in the winter of A.D. 53-54. Then follow the Council at Jerusalem, the dispute at Antioch, Ep. to Galatians, and a fourth journey in Asia Minor, with another genuine fragment, 2 Tim. iv. 19-21. This fills the interval which ends with the arrest at Jerusalem in the year 58, Epp. to Phil., Col., Philem. and one or two more fragments of Past. Epp., the Apostle's arrival at Rome in A.D. 61 and his death in A.D. 64. The whole scheme stands or falls with the place assigned to the Council of Jerusalem, and the estimate formed of the historical character of the Acts.

to Rome, but only after two years' forcible detention, and as a prisoner awaiting his trial.

(3) *Purpose.* A more complicated question meets us when from the occasion or proximate cause of the Epistle to the Romans we pass to its purpose or ulterior cause. The Apostle's reasons for writing to Rome lie upon the surface; his reasons for writing the particular letter he did write will need more consideration. No doubt there is a providence in it. It was willed that such a letter should be written for the admonition of after-ages. But through what psychological channels did that providence work?

Here we pass on to much debated ground; and it will perhaps help us if we begin by presenting the opposing theories in as antithetical a form as possible.

When the different views which have been held come to be examined, they will be found to be reducible to two main types, which differ not on a single point but on a number of co-ordinated points. One might be described as primarily historical, the other primarily dogmatic; one directs attention mainly to the Church addressed, the other mainly to the writer; one adopts the view of a predominance of Jewish-Christian readers, the other pre-supposes readers who are predominantly Gentile Christians.

Here again the epoch-making impulse came from Baur. It was Baur who first worked out a coherent theory, the essence of which was that it claimed to be historical. He argued from the analogy of the other Epistles which he allowed to be genuine. The circumstances of the Corinthian Church are reflected as in a glass in the Epistles to the Corinthians; the circumstances of the Galatian Churches come out clearly from that to the Galatians. Did it not follow that the circumstances of the Roman Church might be directly inferred from the Epistle to the Romans, and that the Epistle itself was written with deliberate reference to them? Why all this Jewish-sounding argument if the readers were not Jews? Why these constant answers to objections if there was no one to object? The issues discussed were similar in many respects to those in the Epistle to the Galatians. In Galatia a fierce controversy was going on. Must it not therefore be assumed that there was a like controversy, only milder and more tempered, at Rome, and that the Apostle wished to deal with it in a manner correspondingly milder and more tempered?

There was truth in all this; but it was truth to some extent one-sided and exaggerated. A little reflexion will show that the cases of the Churches of Corinth and Galatia were not exactly parallel to that of Rome. In Galatia St. Paul was dealing with a perfectly definite state of things in a Church which he himself had founded, and the circumstances of which he knew from within and not merely by hearsay. At Corinth he had spent a still longer time; when he wrote he was not far distant; there had been frequent communications between the Church and the Apostle; and in the case of 1 Corinthians he had actually before him a letter containing a number of questions which he was requested to answer, while in that of 2 Corinthians he had a personal report brought to him by Titus. What could there be like this at Rome? The Church there St. Paul had not founded, had not even seen; and, if we are to believe Baur and the great majority of his followers, he had not even any recognizable correspondents to keep him informed about it. For by what may seem a strange inconsistency it was especially the school of Baur which denied the genuineness of ch. xvi, and so cut away a whole list of persons from one or other of whom St. Paul might have really learnt something about Roman Christianity.

These contradictions were avoided in the older theory which prevailed before the time of Baur and which has not been without adherents, of whom the most prominent perhaps is Dr. Bernhard Weiss, since his day. According to this theory the main object of the Epistle is doctrinal; it is rather a theological treatise than a letter; its purpose is to instruct the Roman Church in central principles of the faith, and has but little reference to the circumstances of the moment.

It would be wrong to call this view—at least in its recent forms —unhistorical. It takes account of the situation as it presented itself, but looks at another side of it from that which caught the eye of Baur. The leading idea is no longer the position of the readers, but the position of the writer: every thing is made to turn on the truths which the Apostle wished to place on record, and for which he found a fit recipient in a Church which seemed to have so commanding a future before it.

Let us try to do justice to the different aspects of the problem. The theories which have so far been mentioned, and others of which we have not yet spoken, are only at fault in so far as they are exclusive and emphasize some one point to the neglect of the rest. Nature is usually more subtle than art. A man of St. Paul's ability sitting down to write a letter on matters of weight would be likely to have several influences present to his mind at once, and his language would be moulded now by one and now by another.

Three factors may be said to have gone to the shaping of this letter of St. Paul's.

The first of these will be that which Baur took almost for the only one. The Apostle had some real knowledge of the state of the Church to which he was writing. Here we see the importance of his connexion with Aquila and Prisca. His intercourse with them would probably give the first impulse to that wish which he tells us that he had entertained for many years to visit Rome in person. When first he met them at Corinth they were newly arrived from the capital; he would hear from them of the state of things they left behind them; and a spark would be enough to fire his imagination at the prospect of winning a foothold for Christ and the Gospel in the seat of empire itself. We may well believe—if the speculations about Prisca are valid, and even without drawing upon these—that the two wanderers would keep up communication with the Christians of their home. And now, very probably at the instance of the Apostle, they had returned to prepare the way for his coming. We cannot afford to lose so valuable a link between St. Paul and the Church he had set his heart on visiting. Two of his most trusted friends are now on the spot, and they would not fail to report all that it was essential to the Apostle to know. He may have had other correspondents besides, but they would be the chief. To this source we may look for what there is of local colour in the Epistle. If the argument is addressed now to Gentiles by birth and now to Jews; if we catch a glimpse of parties in the Church, 'the strong' and 'the weak'; if there is a hint of danger threatening the peace and the faith of the community (as in ch. xvi. 17–20)—it is from his friends in Rome that the Apostle draws his knowledge of the conditions with which he is dealing.

The second factor which helps in determining the character of the Epistle has more to do with what it is not than with what it is: it prevents it from being as it was at one time described, 'a compendium of the whole of Christian doctrine.' The Epistle is not this, because like all St. Paul's Epistles it implies a common basis of Christian teaching, those παραδόσεις as they are called elsewhere (1 Cor. xi. 2; 2 Thess. ii. 15; iii. 6), which the Apostle is able to take for granted as already known to his readers, and which he therefore thinks it unnecessary to repeat without special reason. He will not 'lay again' a foundation which is already laid. He will not speak of the 'first principles' of a Christian's belief, but will 'go on unto perfection.' Hence it is that just the most fundamental doctrines—the Divine Lordship of Christ, the value of His Death, the nature of the Sacraments—are assumed rather than stated or proved. Such allusions as we get to these are concerned not with the rudimentary but with the more developed forms of the doctrines in question. They nearly always add something to the common stock of teaching, give to it a profounder significance, or apply it in new and unforeseen directions. The last charge that could be brought against the Epistle would be that it consisted of Christian commonplaces. It is one of the most original of writings. No Christian can have read it for the first time without feeling that he was introduced to heights and depths of Christianity of which he had never been conscious before.

For, lastly, the most powerful of all the influences which have shaped the contents of the Epistle is the experience of the writer. The main object which he has in view is really not far to seek. When he thought of visiting Rome his desire was to 'have some fruit' there, as in the rest of the Gentile world (Rom. i. 13). He longed to impart to the Roman Christians some 'spiritual gift,' such as he knew that he had the power of imparting (i. 11 ; xv. 29). By this he meant the effect of his own personal presence, but the gift was one that could be exercised also in absence. He has exercised it by this letter, which is itself the outcome of a πνευματικὸν χάρισμα, a word of instruction, stimulus, and warning, addressed in the first instance to the Church at Rome, and through it to Christendom for all time.

The Apostle has reached another turning-point in his career. He is going up to Jerusalem, not knowing what will befall him there, but prepared for the worst. He is aware that the step which he is taking is highly critical and he has no confidence that he will escape with his life [1]. This gives an added solemnity to his utterance ; and it is natural that he should cast back his glance over the years which had passed since he became a Christian and sum up the result as he felt it for himself. It is not exactly a conscious summing up, but it is the momentum of this past experience which guides his pen.

Deep in the background of all his thought lies that one great event which brought him within the fold of Christ. For him it had been nothing less than a revolution ; and it fixed permanently his conception of the new forces which came with Christianity into the world. 'To believe in Christ,' 'to be baptized into Christ,' these were the watchwords; and the Apostle felt that they were pregnant with intense meaning. That new personal relation of the believer to his Lord was henceforth the motive-power which dominated the whole of his life. It was also met, as it seemed, in a marvellous manner from above. We cannot doubt that from his conversion onwards St. Paul found himself endowed with extraordinary energies. Some of them were what we should call miraculous; but he makes no distinction between those which were miraculous and those which were not. He set them all down as miraculous in the sense of having a direct Divine cause. And when he looked around him over the Christian Church he saw that like endowments, energies similar in kind if inferior to his own in degree, were widely diffused. They were the characteristic mark of Christians. Partly they took a form which would be commonly described as supernatural, unusual powers of healing, unusual gifts of utterance, an unusual magnetic influence upon others; partly they consisted

---

[1] This is impressively stated in Hort, *Rom. and Eph.* p. 42 ff.

in a strange elation of spirit which made suffering and toil seem light and insignificant; but most of all the new impulse was moral in its working, it blossomed out in a multitude of attractive traits— 'love, joy, peace, longsuffering, kindness, goodness, faithfulness, meekness, temperance.'   These St. Paul called 'fruits of the Spirit.'   The act of faith on the part of man, the influence of the Spirit (which was only another way of describing the influence of Christ Himself[1]) from the side of God, were the two outstanding facts which made the lives of Christians differ from those of other men.

These are the postulates of Christianity, the forces to which the Apostle has to appeal for the solution of practical problems as they present themselves.   His time had been very largely taken up with such problems.   There had been the great question as to the terms on which Gentiles were to be admitted to the new society. On this head St. Paul could have no doubt.   His own ruling principles, 'faith' and 'the Spirit,' made no distinction between Jew and Gentile; he had no choice but to contend for the equal rights of both—a certain precedence might be yielded to the Jews as the chosen people of the Old Covenant, but that was all.

This battle had been fought and won.   But it left behind a question which was intellectually more troublesome—a question brought home by the actual effect of the preaching of Christianity, very largely welcomed and eagerly embraced by Gentiles, but as a rule spurned and rejected by the Jews—how it could be that Israel, the chosen recipient of the promises of the Old Testament, should be excluded from the benefit now that those promises came to be fulfilled.   Clearly this question belongs to the later reflective stage of the controversy relating to Jew and Gentile.   The active contending for Gentile liberties would come first, the philosophic or theological assignment of the due place of Jew and Gentile in the Divine scheme would naturally come afterwards.   This more advanced stage has now been reached ; the Apostle has made up his mind on the whole series of questions at issue; and he takes the opportunity of writing to the Romans at the very centre of the empire, to lay down calmly and deliberately the conclusions to which he has come.

The Epistle is the ripened fruit of the thought and struggles of the eventful years by which it had been preceded.   It is no merely abstract disquisition but a letter full of direct human interest in the persons to whom it is written ; it is a letter which contains here and there side-glances at particular local circumstances, and at least one emphatic warning (ch. xvi. 17–20) against a danger which had not reached the Church as yet, but any day might reach

---

[1] See the notes on ch. viii. 9–17 ; compare also ch. vi. 1–14.

it, and the full urgency of which the Apostle knew only too well;
but the main theme of the letter is the gathering in of the harvest,
at once of the Church's history since the departure of its Master,
and of the individual history of a single soul, that one soul which
under God had had the most active share in making the course of
external events what it was. St. Paul set himself to give the
Roman Church of his best; he has given it what was perhaps in
some ways too good for it—more we may be sure than it would be
able to digest and assimilate at the moment, but just for that very
reason a body of teaching which eighteen centuries of Christian
interpreters have failed to exhaust. Its richness in this respect is
due to the incomparable hold which it shows on the essential
principles of Christ's religion, and the way in which, like the
Bible in general, it pierces through the conditions of a particular
time and place to the roots of things which are permanent and
universal.

§ 5. The Argument.

In the interesting essay in which, discarding all tradition, he
seeks to re-interpret the teaching of St. Paul directly from the
standpoint of the nineteenth century, Matthew Arnold maps out the
contents of the Epistle as follows:—

'If a somewhat pedantic form of expression may be forgiven for
the sake of clearness, we may say that of the eleven first chapters
of the Epistle to the Romans—the chapters which convey Paul's
theology, though not . . . with any scholastic purpose or in any
formal scientific mode of exposition—of these eleven chapters, the
first, second, and third are, in a scale of importance, fixed by
a scientific criticism of Paul's line of thought, sub-primary; the
fourth and fifth are secondary; the sixth and eighth are primary;
the seventh chapter is sub-primary; the ninth, tenth, and eleventh
chapters are secondary. Furthermore, to the contents of the
separate chapters themselves this scale must be carried on, so far as
to mark that of the two great primary chapters, the sixth and
eighth, the eighth is primary down only to the end of the twenty-
eighth verse; from thence to the end it is, however, eloquent, yet
for the purpose of a scientific criticism of Paul's essential theology
only secondary' (*St. Paul and Protestantism*, p. 92 f.).

This extract may serve as a convenient starting-point for our
examination of the argument: and it may conduce to clearness of
apprehension if we complete the summary analysis of the Epistle
given by the same writer, with the additional advantage of presenting
it in his fresh and bright manner;—

'The first chapter is to the Gentiles—its purport is: You have not righteousness. The second is to the Jews—its purport is: No more have you, though you think you have. The third chapter assumes faith in Christ as the one source of right-eousness for all men. The fourth chapter gives to the notion of righteousness through faith the sanction of the Old Testament and of the history of Abraham. The fifth insists on the causes for thankfulness and exultation in the boon of righteousness through faith in Christ; and applies illustratively, with this design, the history of Adam. The sixth chapter comes to the all-important question: "What is that faith in Christ which I, Paul, mean?"— and answers it. The seventh illustrates and explains the answer. But the eighth down to the end of the twenty-eighth verse, develops and completes the answer. The rest of the eighth chapter expresses the sense of safety and gratitude which the solution is fitted to inspire. The ninth, tenth, and eleventh chapters uphold the second chapter's thesis—so hard to a Jew, so easy to us—that righteous-ness is not by the Jewish law; but dwell with hope and joy on a final result of things which is to be favourable to Israel' (*ibid.* p. 93).

Some such outline as this would be at the present stage of in-vestigation generally accepted. It is true that Baur threw the centre of gravity upon chapters ix–xi, and held that the rest of the Epistle was written up to these: but this view would now on almost all hands be regarded as untenable. The problem discussed in these chapters doubtless weighed heavily on the Apostle's mind; in the circumstances under which he was writing it was doubtless a problem of very considerable urgency; but for all that it is a problem which belongs rather to the circumference of St. Paul's thought than to the centre; it is not so much a part of his funda-mental teaching as a consequence arising from its collision with an unbelieving world.

On this head the scholarship of the present day would be on the side of Matthew Arnold. It points, however, to the necessity, in any attempt to determine what is primary and what is not primary in the argument of the Epistle, of starting with a clear understanding of the point of view from which the degrees of relative importance are to be assigned. Baur's object was historical—to set the Epistle in relation to the circumstances of its composition. On that assumption his view was partially—though still not more than partially—justified. Matthew Arnold's object on the other hand was what he calls 'a scientific criticism of Paul's thought'; by which he seems to mean (though perhaps he was not wholly clear in his own mind) an attempt to discriminate in it those elements which are of the highest permanent value. It was natural that he should attach the greatest importance to those elements in particular which seemed to be capable of direct personal verification. From this point of view we need not question his assignment of a primary significance to chapters vi and viii. His reproduction of the thought of these chapters is the best thing in his book, and we have drawn upon it ourselves in the commentary upon them (p. 163 f.). There is more in the same connexion that well deserves attentive study. But there are other portions of the Epistle which are not capable of verification precisely in the same manner, and yet were of primary importance to St. Paul himself and may be equally of primary importance to those of us who are willing to accept his testimony in spiritual things which lie beyond the reach of our personal experience. Matthew Arnold is limited by the method which he applies—and which others would no doubt join with him in applying—to the subjective side of Christianity, the emotions and efforts which it generates in Christians. But there is a further question how and why they came to be generated. And in the answer which St. Paul would give, and which the main body of Christians very largely on his authority would also give to that question, he and they alike are led up into regions where direct human verification ceases to be possible.

It is quite true that 'faith in Christ' means attachment to Christ, a strong emotion of love and gratitude. But that emotion is not confined, as we say, to 'the historical Christ,' it has for its object not only Him who walked the earth as 'Jesus of Nazareth'; it is directed towards the same Jesus 'crucified, risen and ascended to the right hand of God.' St. Paul believed, and we also believe, that His transit across the stage of our earth was accompanied by consequences in the celestial sphere which transcend our faculties. We cannot pretend to be able to verify them as we can verify that which passes in our own minds. And yet a certain kind of indirect verification there is. The thousands and tens of thousands of Christians who have lived and died in the firm conviction of the truth of these supersensual realities, and who upon the strength of them have reduced their lives to a harmonious unity superseding the war of passion, do really afford no slight presumption that the beliefs which have enabled them to do this are such as the Ruler of the universe approves, and such as aptly fit into the eternal order. Whatever the force of this presumption to the outer world, it is one which the Christian at least will cherish.

We therefore do not feel at liberty to treat as anything less than primary that which was certainly primary to St. Paul. We entirely accept the view that chapters vi and viii are primary, but we also feel bound to place by their side the culminating verses of chapter iii. The really fundamental passages in the Epistle we should say were, ch. i. 16, 17, which states the problem, and iii. 21-26, vi. 1-14, viii. 1-30 (rather than 1-28), which supply its solution. The problem is, How is man to become righteous in the sight of God?

And the answer is (1) by certain great redemptive acts on the part of God which take effect in the sphere above, though their consequences are felt throughout the sphere below; (2) through a certain ardent apprehension of these acts and of their Author Christ, on the part of the Christian; and (3) through his continued self-surrender to Divine influences poured out freely and unremittingly upon him.

It is superfluous to say that there is nothing whatever that is new in this statement. It does but reproduce the belief, in part implicit rather than explicit, of the Early Church; then further defined and emphasized more vigorously on some of its sides at the Reformation; and lastly brought to a more even balance (or what many would fain make a more even balance) by the Church of our own day. Of course it is liable to be impugned, as it is impugned by the attractive writer whose words have been quoted above, in the interest of what is thought to be a stricter science. But whatever the value in itself of the theory which is substituted for it, we may be sure that it does not adequately represent the mind of St. Paul. In the present commentary our first object is to do justice to this. How it is afterwards to be worked up into a complete scheme of religious belief, it lies beyond our scope to consider.

For the sake of the student it may be well to draw out the contents of the Epistle in a tabular analytical form. St. Paul, as Matthew Arnold rightly reminds us, is no Schoolman, and his method is the very reverse of all that is formal and artificial. But it is undoubtedly helpful to set before ourselves the framework of his thought, just as a knowledge of anatomy conduces to the better understanding of the living human frame.

I.—Introduction (i. 1-15).
    a. The Apostolic Salutation (i. 1-7).
    β. St. Paul and the Roman Church (i. 8-15).

II.—Doctrinal.
    THE GREAT THESIS. Problem: How is Righteousness to be attained? Answer: Not by man's work, but by God's gift, through Faith, or loyal attachment to Christ (i. 16, 17).

  A. Righteousness as a state or condition in the sight of God (Justification) (i. 18-v. 21).
    1. Righteousness not hitherto attained (i. 18-iii. 20).
      [Rather, by contrast, a scene which bespeaks impending Wrath].
    a. Failure of the Gentile (i. 18-32).
      (i.) Natural Religion (i. 18-20);
      (ii.) deserted for idolatry (i. 21-25);
      (iii.) hence judicial abandonment to abominable sins (26, 27), to every kind of moral depravity (28-31), even to perversion of conscience (32).
    β. [Transitional]. Future judgement without respect of persons such as Jew or Gentile (ii. 1-16).

B. Progressive Righteousness in the Christian (Sanctification) (vi–viii).
  1. Reply to further casuistical objection : ' If more sin means more
      grace, why not go on sinning ?'
      The immersion of Baptism carried with it a death to sin,
      and union with the risen Christ. The Christian there-
      fore cannot, must not, sin (vi. 1–14).
  2. The Christian's Release : what it is, and what it is not : shown by
      two metaphors.
    a. Servitude and emancipation (vi. 15–23).
    β. The marriage-bond (vii. 1–6).
      [The Christian's old self dead to the Law with Christ ; so that
      he is henceforth free to live with Him].
  3. Judaistic objection from seeming disparagement of Law : met by an
      analysis of the moral conflict in the soul. Law is impotent,
      and gives an impulse or handle to sin, but is not itself sinful
      (vii. 7–24). The conflict ended by the interposition of
      Christ (25).
  4. Perspective of the Christian's New Career (viii).
      The Indwelling Spirit.
    a. Failure of the previous system made good by Christ's Incarnation
      and the Spirit's presence (viii. 1–4).
    β. The new régime contrasted with the old—the régime of the Spirit
      with the weakness of unassisted humanity (viii. 5–9).
    γ. The Spirit's presence a guarantee of bodily as well as moral
      resurrection (viii. 10–13) ;
    δ. also a guarantee that the Christian enjoys with God a son's relation,
      and will enter upon a son's inheritance (viii. 14–17).
    ε. That glorious inheritance the object of creation's yearning (viii.
      18–22) ;
      and of the Christian's hope (viii. 23–25).
    η. Human infirmity assisted by the Spirit's intercession (viii. 26, 27) ;
    θ. and sustained by the knowledge of the connected chain by which
      God works out His purpose of salvation (viii. 28–30).
    ι. Inviolable security of the Christian in dependence upon God's
      favour and the love of Christ (viii. 31–39).

C Problem of Israel's Unbelief. The Gospel in history (ix, x, xi). The
      rejection of the Chosen People a sad contrast to its high destiny and
      privileges (ix. 1–5).
  1. Justice of the Rejection (ix. 6–29).
    a. The Rejection of Israel not inconsistent with the Divine promises
      (ix. 6–13) ;
    β. nor with the Divine Justice (ix. 14–29).
      (i.) The absoluteness of God's choice shown from the O. T. (ix.
      14–18).
      (ii.) A necessary deduction from His position as Creator (ix.
      19–23).
      (iii.) The alternate choice of Jews and Gentiles expressly reserved
      and foretold in Scripture (ix. 24–29).
  2. Cause of the Rejection.
    a. Israel sought righteousness by Works instead of Faith, in their own
      way and not in God's way (ix. 30–x. 4).
      And this although God's method was—
      (i.) Not difficult and remote but near and easy (x. 5–10) ;
      (ii.) Within the reach of all, Jew and Gentile alike (x. 11–13).
    β. Nor can Israel plead in defence want of opportunity or warning—
      (i.) The Gospel has been fully and universally preached (x. 14–18).

e

(ii.) Israel had been warned beforehand by the Prophet that they would reject God's Message (x. 19-21).

3. Mitigating considerations. The purpose of God (xi).
 α. The Unbelief of Israel is now as in the past only partial (xi. 1-10).
 β. It is only temporary—
   (i.) Their fall has a special purpose—the introduction of the Gentiles (xi. 11-15).
   (ii.) That Israel will be restored is vouched for by the holy stock from which it comes (xi. 16-24).
 γ. In all this may be seen the purpose of God working upwards through seeming severity, to a beneficent result — the final restoration of all (xi. 25-31).
   Doxology (xi. 33-36).

III.—Practical and Hortatory.
   (1) The Christian sacrifice (xii. 1, 2).
   (2) The Christian as a member of the Church (xii. 3-8).
   (3) The Christian in his relation to others (xii. 9-21).
   The Christian's vengeance (xii. 19-21).
   (4) Church and State (xiii. 1-7).
   (5) The Christian's one debt ; the law of love (xiii. 8-10).
   The day approaching (xiii. 11-14).
   (6) Toleration ; the strong and the weak (xiv. 1-xv. 6).
   The Jew and the Gentile (xv. 7-13).

IV.—Epilogue.
   α. Personal explanations. Motive of the Epistle. Proposed visit to Rome (xv. 14-33).
   β. Greetings to various persons (xvi. 1-16).
   A warning (xvi. 17-20).
   Postscript by the Apostle's companions and amanuensis (xvi. 21-23).
   Benediction and Doxology (xvi. 24-27).

It is often easiest to bring out the force and strength of an argument by starting from its conclusion, and we possess in the doxology at the end of the Epistle a short summary made by St. Paul himself of its contents. The question of its genuineness has been discussed elsewhere, and it has been shown in the commentary how clearly it refers to all the leading thoughts of the Epistle ; it remains only to make use of it to help us to understand the argument which St. Paul is working out and the conclusion to which he is leading us.

The first idea which comes prominently before us is that of ' the Gospel'; it meets us in the Apostolic salutation at the beginning, in the statement of the thesis of the Epistle, in the doxology at the end where it is expanded in the somewhat unusual form ' according to my Gospel and the preaching of Jesus Christ.' So again in xi. 28 it is incidentally shown that what St. Paul is describing is the method or plan of the Gospel. This idea of the Gospel then is a fundamental thought of the Epistle ; and it seems to mean this. There are two competing systems or plans of life or salvation before St. Paul's mind. The one is the old Jewish system, a knowledge of which is presupposed ; the other is the Christian system, a knowledge of which again is presupposed. St. Paul is not expounding the Christian religion, he is writing to Christians: what he aims at expounding is the meaning of the new system. This may perhaps explain the manner in which he varies between the expressions ' the Gospel,' or ' the Gospel of God,' or ' the Gospel of Jesus Christ,' and ' my Gospel.' The former represents the Christian religion as recognized and preached by all, the latter represents his own personal exposition of its plan and meaning. The main purpose of the argument then is an explanation of the meaning of the new Gospel of Jesus Christ, as succeeding to and taking the place of the old method, but also in a sense as embracing and continuing it.

St. Paul begins then with a theological description of the new method. He shows the need for it, he explains what it is—emphasizing its distinctive features in contrast to those of the old system, and at the same time proving that it is the necessary and expected outcome of that old system. He then proceeds to describe the working of this system in the Christian life; and lastly he vindicates for it its true place in history. The universal character of the new Gospel has been already emphasized, he must now trace the plan by which it is to attain this universality. The rejection of the Jews, the calling of the Gentiles, are both steps in this process and necessary steps. But the method and plan pursued in these cases and partially revealed, enable us to learn, if we have faith to do so, that ' mystery which has been hidden from the foundation of the world,' but which has always guided the course of human history—the purpose of God to ' sum up all things in Christ.'

If this point has been made clear, it will enable us to bring out the essential unity and completeness of the argument of the Epistle. We do not agree as we have explained above with the opinion of Baur, revived by Dr. Hort, that chap. ix–xi represent the essential part of the Epistle, to which all the earlier part is but an introduction. That is certainly a one-sided view. But Dr. Hort's examination of the Epistle is valuable as reminding us that neither are these chapters an appendix accidentally added which might be omitted without injuring St. Paul's argument and plan.

We can trace incidentally the various difficulties, partly raised by opponents, partly suggested by his own thought, which have helped to shape different portions of the Epistle. We are able to analyze and separate the different stages in the argument more accurately and distinctly than in any other of St. Paul's writings. But this must not blind us to the fact that the whole is one great argument; the purpose of which is to explain the Gospel of God in Jesus the Messiah, and to show its effects on human life, and in the history of the race, and thus to vindicate for it the right to be considered the ultimate and final revelation of God's purpose for mankind.

§ 6. LANGUAGE AND STYLE.

(1) *Language*[1]. It will seem at first sight to the uninitiated reader a rather strange paradox that a letter addressed to the capital of the Western or Latin world should be written in Greek. Yet there is no paradox, either to the classical scholar who is acquainted with the history of the Early Empire, or to the ecclesiastical historian who follows the fortunes of the Early Church. Both are aware that for fully two centuries and a half Greek was the predominant language if not of the city of Rome as a whole yet of large sections of its inhabitants, and in particular of those sections among which was to be sought the main body of the readers of the Epistle.

The early history of the Church of Rome might be said to fall into three periods, of which the landmarks would be (1) the appearance of the first Latin writers, said by Jerome[2] to be Apollonius who suffered under Commodus in the year 185, and whose Apology and Acts have been recently recovered in an Armenian Version and edited by Mr. Conybeare[3], and Victor, an African by birth, who became Bishop of Rome about 189 A.D. (2) Next would come in the middle of the third century a more considerable body of Latin literature, the writings of Novatian and the correspondence between the Church of Rome and Cyprian at Carthage. (3) Then, lastly, there would be the definite Latinizing of the capital of the West which followed upon the transference of the seat of empire to Constantinople dating from 330 A.D.

(1) The evidence of Juvenal and Martial refers to the latter half of the first century. Juvenal speaks with indignation of the extent to which Rome was being converted into 'a Greek city[4].' Martial regards ignorance of Greek as a mark of rusticity[5]. Indeed, there was a double tendency which embraced at once classes at both ends of the social scale. On the one hand among slaves and in the trading classes there were swarms of Greeks and Greek-speaking Orientals. On the other hand in the higher ranks it was the fashion to speak Greek; children were taught it by Greek nurses; and in after life the use of it was carried to the pitch of affectation[6].

For the Jewish colony we have the evidence of the inscriptions. Out of thirty-eight collected by Schürer[7] no less than thirty are Greek and eight only

---

[1] The question of the use of Greek at Rome has been often discussed and the evidence for it set forth, but the classical treatment of the subject is by the late Dr. C. P. Caspari, Professor at Christiania, in an Excursus of 200 pages to vol. iii. of his work *Quellen zur Geschichte des Taufsymbols* (Christiania, 1875).

[2] *De Vir. Ill.* liii. *Tertullianus presbyter nunc demum primus post Victorem et Apollonium Latinorum ponitur.*

[3] *Monuments of Early Christianity* (London, 1894), p. 29 ff.

[4] Juv. *Sat.* iii. 60 f.; cf. vi. 187 ff.   [5] *Epig.* xiv. 58.

[6] Caspari, *Quellen zum Taufsymbol*, iii. 286 f.

[7] *Gemeindeverfassung*, p. 33 ff. The inscriptions referred to are all from Roman sites. There is also one in Greek from Portus.

Latin; and if one of the Greek inscriptions is in Latin characters, conversely three of the Latin are in Greek characters. There do not seem to be any in Hebrew[1].

Of Christian inscriptions the proportion of Greek to Latin would seem to be about 1 : 2. But the great mass of these would belong to a period later than that of which we are speaking. De Rossi[2] estimates the number for the period between M. Aurelius and Septimius Severus at about 160, of which something like half would be Greek. Beyond this we can hardly go.

But as to the Christian Church there is a quantity of other evidence. The bishops of Rome from Linus to Eleutherus (c. 174–189 A.D.) are twelve in number: of these not more than three (Clement, Sixtus I = Xystus, Pius) bear Latin names. But although the names of Clement and Pius are Latin the extant Epistle of Clement is written in Greek; we know also that Hermas, the author of ' The Shepherd,' was the brother of Pius[3], and he wrote in Greek. Indeed all the literature that we can in any way connect with Christian Rome down to the end of the reign of M. Aurelius is Greek. Besides the works of Clement and Hermas we have still surviving the letter addressed to the Church at Rome by Ignatius; and later in the period, the letter written by Soter (c. 166–174 A.D.) to the Corinthian Church was evidently in Greek[4]. Justin and Tatian who were settled in Rome wrote in Greek; so too did Rhodon, a pupil of Tatian's at Rome who carried on their tradition[5]. Greek was the language of Polycarp and Hegesippus who paid visits to Rome of shorter duration. A number of Gnostic writers established themselves there and used Greek for the vehicle of their teaching: so Cerdon, Marcion, and Valentinus, who were all in Rome about 140 A.D. Valentinus left behind a considerable school, and the leading representatives of the 'Italic' branch, Ptolemaeus and Heracleon, both wrote in Greek. We may assume the same thing of the other Gnostics combated by Justin and Irenaeus. Irenaeus himself spent some time at Rome in the Episcopate of Eleutherus, and wrote his great work in Greek.

To this period may also be traced back the oldest form of the Creed of the Roman Church now known as the Apostles' Creed[6]. This was in Greek. And there are stray Greek fragments of Western Liturgies which ultimately go back to the same place and time. Such would be the *Hymnus angelicus* (Luke ii. 14) repeated in Greek at Christmas, the *Trishagion, Kyrie eleison* and *Christe eleison.* On certain set days (at Christmas, Easter, Ember days, and some others) lections were read in Greek as well as Latin; hymns were occasionally sung in Greek; and at the formal committal of the Creed to the candidates for baptism (the so-called *Traditio* and *Redditio Symboli*) both the Apostles' Creed (in its longer and shorter forms) and the Nicene were

---

[1] Comp. also Berliner, i. 54.   [2] *Ap.* Caspari, p. 303.

[3] Pius is described in the *Liber Pontificalis* as *natione Italus . . . de civitate Aquileia*; but there is reason to think that Hermas was a native of Arcadia. The assignments of nationality to the earliest bishops are of very doubtful value.

[4] It was to be kept in the archives and read on Sundays like the letter of Clement (Eus. *H. E.* IV. xxiii. 11).

[5] Eus. *H. E.* V. xiii. 1.

[6] It was in pursuit of the origin of this Creed that Caspari was drawn into his elaborate researches. It is generally agreed that it was in use at Rome by the middle of the second century. The main question at the present moment is whether it was also composed there, and if not whence it came. Caspari would derive it from Asia Minor and the circle of St. John. This is a problem which we may look to have solved by Dr. Kattenbusch of Giessen, who is continuing Caspari's labours (*Das Apostolische Symbol*, Bd. I. Leipzig, 1894).

recited and the questions put first in Greek and then in Latin[1]. These are all survivals of Roman usage at the time when the Church was bilingual.

(2) The dates of Apollonius and of Bp. Victor are fixed, but rather more uncertainty hangs over that of the first really classical Christian work in Latin, the *Octavius* of Minucius Felix. This has been much debated, but opinion seems to be veering round to the earlier date[2], which would bring him into near proximity to Apollonius, perhaps at the end of the reign of M. Aurelius. The period which then begins and extends from c. 180–250 A.D. shows a more even balance of Greek and Latin. The two prominent writers, Hippolytus and Caius, still make use of Greek. The grounds perhaps preponderate for regarding the Muratorian Fragment as a translation. But at the beginning of the period we have Minucius Felix and at the end Novatian, and Latin begins to have the upper hand in the names of bishops. The glimpse which we get of the literary activity of the Church of Rome through the letters and other writings preserved among the works of Cyprian shows us at last Latin in possession of the field.

(3) The Hellenizing character of Roman Christianity was due in the first instance to the constant intercourse between Rome and the East. In the troubled times which followed the middle of the third century, with the decay of wealth and trade, and Gothic piracies breaking up the *pax Romana* on the Aegean, this intercourse was greatly interrupted. Thus Greek influences lost their strength. The Latin Church, Rome reinforced by Africa, had now a substantial literature of its own. Under leaders like Tertullian, Cyprian, and Novatian it had begun to develop its proper individuality. It could stand and walk alone without assistance from the East. And a decisive impulse was given to its independent career by the founding of Constantinople. The stream set from that time onwards towards the Bosphorus and no longer towards the Tiber. Rome ceases to be the centre of the Empire to become in a still more exclusive sense the capital of the West.

(2) *Style.* The Epistles which bear the name of St. Paul present a considerable diversity of style. To such an extent is this the case that the question is seriously raised whether they can have had the same author. Of all the arguments urged on the negative side this from style is the most substantial; and whatever decision we come to on the subject there remains a problem of much complexity and difficulty.

It is well known that the Pauline Epistles fall into four groups which are connected indeed with each other, but at the same time stand out with much distinctness. These groups are: 1, 2 Thess.; Gal., 1, 2 Cor., Rom.; Phil., Col., Eph., Philem.; Past. Epp. The four Epistles of the second group hang very closely together; those of the third group subdivide into two pairs, Phil. Philem. on the one hand, and Eph. Col. on the other. It is hard to dissociate Col. from Philem.; and the very strong presumption in favour of the genuineness of the latter Epistle reacts upon the former. The tendency of critical inquiry at the present moment is in favour of Colossians and somewhat less decidedly in favour of Ephesians. It is, for instance, significant that Jülicher in his recent *Einleitung*

---

[1] More precise and full details will be found in Caspari's Excursus, *Op. cit.* p. 466 ff.

[2] Krüger, *Altchristl. Lit.* p. 88.

(Freiburg i. B. and Leipzig, 1894) sums up rather on this side of
the question than the other.   We believe that this points to what
will be the ultimate verdict.   But in the matter of style it must be
confessed that Col. and Eph.—and more especially Eph.—stand at
the furthest possible remove from Romans.   We may take Eph.
and Rom. as marking the extreme poles of difference within the
Epistles claimed for St. Paul[1].   Any other member of the second
group would do as well; but as we are concerned specially with
Rom., we may institute a comparison with it.

The difference is not so much a difference of ideas and of
vocabulary as a difference of structure and composition.   There are,
it is true, a certain number of new and peculiar expressions in the
later Epistle ; but these are so balanced by points of coincidence,
and the novel element has so much of the nature of simple addition rather than contrariety, that to draw a conclusion adverse to
St. Paul's authorship would certainly not be warranted.   The sense
of dissimilarity reaches its height when we turn from the materials
(if we may so speak) of the style to the way in which they are
put together.   The discrepancy lies not in the anatomy but in the
surface distribution of light and shade, in the play of feature, in
the temperament to which the two Epistles seem to give expression.
We will enlarge a little on this point, as the contrast may help us
to understand the individuality of the Epistle to the Romans.

This Epistle, like all the others of the group, is characterized
by a remarkable energy and vivacity.   It is calm in the sense
that it is not aggressive and that the rush of words is always well
under control.   Still there is a rush of words, rising repeatedly to
passages of splendid eloquence ; but the eloquence is spontaneous,
the outcome of strongly moved feeling ; there is nothing about it
of laboured oratory.   The language is rapid, terse, incisive ; the
argument is conducted by a quick cut and thrust of dialectic ; it
reminds us of a fencer with his eye always on his antagonist.

We shut the Epistle to the Romans and we open that to the
Ephesians ; how great is the contrast !   We cannot speak here of
vivacity, hardly of energy ; if there is energy it is deep down
below the surface.   The rapid argumentative cut and thrust is
gone.   In its place we have a slowly-moving onwards-advancing
mass, like a glacier working its way inch by inch down the valley.
The periods are of unwieldy length; the writer seems to stagger
under his load.   He has weighty truths to express, and he struggles
to express them—not without success, but certainly with little
flexibility or ease of composition.   The truths unfolded read like
abstract truths, ideal verities, 'laid up in the heavens' rather than
embodying themselves in the active controversies of earth.

[1] The difference between these Epistles on the side we are considering is
greater (e. g.) than that between Romans and the Pastorals.

There is, as we shall see, another side. We have perhaps exaggerated the opposition for the sake of making the difference clear. When we come to look more closely at the Epistle to the Romans we shall find in it not a few passages which tend in the direction of the characteristics of Ephesians; and when we examine the Epistle to the Ephesians we shall find in it much to remind us of characteristics of Romans. We will however leave the comparison as it has been made for the moment, and ask ourselves what means we have of explaining it. Supposing the two Epistles to be really the work of the same man, can the difference between them be adequately accounted for?

There is always an advantage in presenting proportions to the eye and reducing them to some sort of numerical estimate. This can be done in the present case without much difficulty by reckoning up the number of longer pauses. This is done below for the two Epistles, Romans and Ephesians. The standard used is that of the Revisers' Greek Text, and the estimate of length is based on the number of στίχοι or printed lines[1]. It will be worth while to compare the Epistles chapter by chapter:—

ROMANS.

	στίχοι.	(·)	(.)	(;)
Ch. I.	64	13	14	—
II.	51	14	7	8
III.	47	20	12	16
IV.	45	6	14	7
V.	47	6	15	—
VI.	42	8	14	8
VII.	49	16	20	5
VIII.	70	17	26	14
IX.	55	8	19	10
X.	37	6	16	9
XI.	63	16	27	11
Total for doctrinal portion	570	130	184	88
			402	
XII.	36	14	12	—
XIII.	29	11	15	1
XIV	41	11	27	3
XV.	63	8	24	—
XVI.	50	7	28	—
Total for the Epistle	789	181	290	92
			563	

Here the proportion of major points to στίχοι is for the doctrinal chapters 402 : 570 = (approximately) 1 in 1.4; and for the whole Epistle not very different, 563 : 789 = 1 in 1.418. The proportion of interrogative sentences is for the whole Epistle, 92 : 789, or 1 in 8.6; for the doctrinal chapters only, 88 : 570, or 1 in 6.5; and for the practical portion only, 4 : 219, or 1 in 55. This last item is instructive, because it shows how very

[1] The counting of these is approximate, anything over half a line being reckoned as a whole line, and anything less than half a line not reckoned.

greatly, even in the same Epistle, the amount of interrogation varies with the subject-matter. We also observe that in two even of the doctrinal chapters interrogative sentences are wanting. They lie indeed in patches or thick clusters, and are not distributed equally throughout the Epistle.

Now we turn to Ephesians, for which the data are as follows:—

EPHESIANS.

	στίχοι	(·)	(.)	(;)
Ch. I.	45	4	3	—
II.	40	9	6	—
III.	36	2	6	—
	[121	15	15	—]
IV.	55	8	13	1
V.	50	11	17	—
VI.	44	2	13	—
Total	270	36	58	1
			95	

This gives a very different result. The proportion of major points is for Eph. i–iii, roughly speaking, 1 in 4, as against 1 in 1.4 for Rom. i–xii, and for the whole Epistle rather more than 1 in 3, as against 1 in 1.418. The proportion of interrogations is 1 in 270 compared with 1 in 8.6 or 6.5.

In illustrating the nature of the difference in style between Romans and Ephesians we have left in suspense for a time the question as to its cause. To this we will now return, and set down some of the influences which may have been at work—which we may be sure were at work—and which would go a long way to account for it.

(1) First would be *the natural variation of style which comes from dealing with different subject-matter.* The Epistles of the second group are all very largely concerned with the controversy as to Circumcision and the relations of Jewish and Gentile Christians. In the later Epistle this controversy has retired into the background, and other topics have taken its place. Ideas are abroad as to the mediating agencies between God and man which impair the central significance of the Person of Christ; and the multiplication of new Churches with the growing organization of intercommunication between those of older standing, brings to the front the conception of the Church as a whole, and invests it with increased impressiveness.

These facts are reflected on the vocabulary of the two Epistles. The controversy with the Judaizers gives a marked colour to the whole group which includes the Epistle to the Romans. This will appear on the face of the statistics of usage as to the frequency with which the leading terms occur in these Epistles and in the rest of the Pauline *Corpus.* Of course some of the instances will be accidental, but by far the greater number are significant. Those which follow have a direct bearing on the Judaistic controversy. 'Elsewhere' means elsewhere in the Pauline Epistles.

[1] Ἀβραάμ Rom. 9, 2 Cor. 1, Gal. 9; not elsewhere in St. Paul. [σπέρμα
    Ἀβραάμ Rom. 2, 2 Cor. 1, Gal. 1.]
ἀκροβυστία Rom. 3, 1 Cor. 2, Gal. 3; elsewhere 3.
ἀποστολή Rom. 1, 1 Cor. 1, Gal. 1; not elsewhere in St. Paul.
δικαιοῦν Rom. 15, 1 Cor. 2, Gal. 3; elsewhere 2.
δικαίωμα Rom. 5; not elsewhere.
δικαίωσις Rom. 2; not elsewhere.
καταργεῖν Rom. 6, 1 Cor. 9, 2 Cor. 4, Gal. 3; elsewhere 4.
νόμος Rom. 76, 1 Cor. 8, Gal. 32; elsewhere 6.
περιτομή Rom. 15, 1 Cor. 1, Gal. 7; elsewhere 8.
σπέρμα Rom. 9, 1 Cor. 1, 2 Cor. 1, Gal. 5; elsewhere 1.
Connected with this controversy, though not quite so directly, would be :—
    ἀσθενής Rom. 1, 1 Cor. 10, 2 Cor. 1, Gal. 1; elsewhere 1.
    ἀσθενεῖς Rom. 4, 1 Cor. 2, 2 Cor. 6; elsewhere 2.
    ἀσθένεια Rom. 2, 1 Cor. 2, 2 Cor. 6, Gal. 1; elsewhere 1.
    ἀσθένημα Rom. 1; not elsewhere.
    ἐλεύθερος Rom. 2, 1 Cor. 6, Gal. 6; elsewhere 2.
    ἐλευθεροῦν Rom. 4, Gal. 1; not elsewhere.
    ἐλευθερία Rom. 1, 1 Cor. 1, 2 Cor. 1, Gal. 1; not elsewhere.
    καυχᾶσθαι Rom. 5, 1 Cor. 5 (1 v.l.), 2 Cor. 20, Gal. 2; elsewhere 3.
    καύχημα Rom. 1, 1 Cor. 3, 2 Cor. 3, Gal. 1; elsewhere 2.
    καύχησις Rom. 2, 1 Cor. 1, 2 Cor. 6; elsewhere 1.
    κατακαυχᾶσθαι Rom. 2; not elsewhere.
    ὀφειλέτης Rom. 3, Gal. 1; not elsewhere.
    ὀφείλημα Rom. 1; not elsewhere.
    σκάνδαλον Rom. 4, 1 Cor. 1, Gal. 1; not elsewhere. [σκανδαλίζειν
    1 Cor. 2, 2 Cor. 1, Rom. 1 v.l.]
    ὠφελεῖν Rom. 1, 1 Cor. 2, Gal. 1 : ὠφέλεια Rom. 1; neither elsewhere.
Two other points may be noticed, one in connexion with the large use of
the O.T. in these Epistles, and the other in connexion with the idea of
successive periods into which the religious history of mankind is divided :—
    γέγραπται Rom. 16, 1 Cor. 7, 2 Cor. 2, Gal. 4; not elsewhere in
    St. Paul.
    ἄχρις οὗ Rom. 1, 1 Cor. 2, Gal. 2 (1 v.l.); not elsewhere.
    ἐφ' ὅσον χρόνον Rom. 1, 1 Cor. 1, Gal. 1; not elsewhere
These examples stand out very distinctly; and their disappearance from
the later Epistle is perfectly intelligible : *cessante causa, cessat effectus.*

(2) But it is not only that the subject-matter of Ephesians differs
from that of Romans, *the circumstances* under which it is presented
also differ. Romans belongs to a period of controversy, and
although at the time when the Epistle is written the worst is over,
and the Apostle is able to survey the field calmly, and to state his
case uncontroversially, still the crisis through which he has passed
has left its marks behind. The echoes of war are still in his ears.
The treatment of his subject is concrete and not abstract. He
sees in imagination his adversary before him, and he argues much
as he might have argued in the synagogue, or in the presence of
refractory converts. The atmosphere of the Epistle is that of
personal debate. This acts as a stimulus, it makes the blood

---

[1] These examples are selected from the lists in Bishop Lightfoot's classical
essay 'On the Style and Character of the Epistle to the Galatians,' in *Journ. of
Class. and Sacr. Philol.* iii. (1857) 308 ff.

circulate more rapidly in the veins, and gives to the style a liveliness and directness which might be wanting when the pressure was removed. Between Romans, written to a definite Church and gathering up the result of a time of great activity, the direct outcome of prolonged discussion in street and house and school, and Ephesians, written in all probability not to a single Church but to a group of Churches, with its personal edge thus taken off, and written too under confinement after some three years of enforced inaction, it would be natural that there should be a difference.

(3) This brings us to a third point which may be taken with the last, the allowance which ought to be made for *the special temperament* of the Apostle. His writings furnish abundant evidence of a highly strung nervous organization. It is likely enough that the physical infirmity from which he suffered, the 'thorn in the flesh' which had such a prostrating effect upon him, was of nervous origin. But constitutions of this order are liable to great fluctuations of physical condition. There will be 'lucid moments,' and more than lucid moments—months together during which the brain will work not only with ease and freedom, but with an intensity and power not vouchsafed to other men. And times such as these will alternate with periods of depression when body and mind alike are sluggish and languid, and when an effort of will is needed to compel production of any kind. Now the physical conditions under which St. Paul wrote his letter to the Romans would as naturally belong to the first head as those under which he wrote the Epistle which we call 'Ephesians' would to the second. Once more we should expect antecedently that they would leave a strong impress upon the style.

The difference in style between Rom. and Eph. would seem to be very largely a difference in the amount of vital energy thrown into the two Epistles. Vivacity is a distinguishing mark of the one as a certain slow and laboured movement is of the other. We may trace to this cause the phenomena which have been already noted—the shorter sentences of Romans, the long involved periods of Ephesians, the frequency of interrogation on the one hand, its absence on the other. In Rom. we have the champion of Gentile Christendom with his sword drawn, prepared to meet all comers ; in Eph. we have 'such an one as Paul the aged, and now a prisoner also of Jesus Christ.'

Among the expressions specially characteristic of this aspect of Ep. to Romans would be the following :—

ἄρα, beginning a sentence, Rom. 9, 1 Cor. 1, 2 Cor. 2, Gal. 5 ; elsewhere Epp. Paul. 3, Heb. 2. [ἄρα οὖν Rom. 8 (or 9 v.l.), Gal. 1 ; elsewhere 3 : ἄρα without οὖν Rom. 1 (or 2 v.l.), 1 Cor. 1, Gal. 3, Heb. 2.]

[λέγω]

ἀλλὰ λέγω Rom. 2.

λέγω δέ Gal. 2.

λέγω οὖν Rom. 2.

λέγω δὲ τοῦτο ὅτι 1 Cor. 1.

πάλιν λέγω 2 Cor. 2.

τοῦτο δὲ λέγω Gal. 1.

ἐγὼ Παῦλος λέγω ὑμῖν ὅτι Gal. 1.

ποῦ; ποῦ οὖν; Rom. 1, 1 Cor. 8, Gal. 1; not elsewhere.

τί οὖν; τίς οὖν; Rom. 11, 1 Cor. 5, Gal. 1; not elsewhere. [τί οὖν ἐροῦμεν; Rom. 6; τί ἐροῦμεν; Rom 1.]

τί λέγω (λέγει, &c.) Rom. 3, Gal. 1; not elsewhere.

διατί Rom. 1, 1 Cor. 2, 2 Cor. 1; not elsewhere.

ὑπέρ, unusual compounds of—

    ὑπερεκτείνειν 2 Cor. 1.

    ὑπερλίαν 2 Cor. 2.

    ὑπερνικᾶν Rom. 1.

    ὑπερπερισσεύειν Rom. 1, 2 Cor. 1.

    ὑπερφρονεῖν Rom. 1.

(4) A last cause which we suspect may possibly have been at work, though this is more a matter of conjecture, is *the employment of different amanuenses.* We know that St. Paul did not as a rule write his own letters. But then the question arises, How were they written? It seems to us probable that they were in the first instance taken down in shorthand—much as our own merchants or public men dictate their correspondence to a shorthand writer—and then written out fair. We believe this to have been the case from the double fact that dictation was extremely common—so that even as early as Horace and Persius *dictare* had already come to mean ' to compose '—and from the wide diffusion of the art of shorthand. We know that Origen's lectures were taken down in this way, and that fair copies were made of them at leisure (Eus. *H. E.* VI. xxiii. 2). But we can well believe that if this were the case some scribes would be more expert than others, and would reproduce what was dictated to them more exactly. Tertius, we should suppose, was one of the best of those whom St. Paul employed for this purpose. An inferior scribe would get down the main words correctly, but the little connecting links he may have filled in for himself.

This is rather speculation, and we should not wish to lay stress upon it in any particular instance. It is however interesting to note that if we look below the superficial qualities of style at the inner tendencies of mind to which it gives expression the resemblance between Ephesians and Romans becomes more marked, so that we may well ask whether we have not before us in both the same hand. One of the most striking characteristics of St. Paul is the sort of telescopic manner, in which one clause is as it were drawn out of another, each new idea as it arises leading on to some further new idea, until the main thought of the paragraph is reached again often by a circuitous route and not seldom with a somewhat violent twist or turn at the end. This is specially noticeable in abstract doctrinal passages, just as a briefer, more broken, and more direct form of address is adopted in the exhortations relating to matters of practice. A certain laxity of grammatical structure is common to both.

We will place side by side one or two passages which may help to show the fundamental resemblance between the two Epistles. [For a defence of the punctuation of the extract from Romans reference may be made to the notes *ad loc.*]

ROM. iii. 21–26.

Νυνὶ δὲ χωρὶς νόμου δικαιοσύνη
Θεοῦ πεφανέρωται, μαρτυρουμένη ὑπὸ
τοῦ νόμου καὶ τῶν προφητῶν· δικαιοσύνη δὲ Θεοῦ διὰ πίστεως Ἰησοῦ
Χριστοῦ εἰς πάντας τοὺς πιστεύοντος·
οὐ γάρ ἐστι διαστολή· πάντες γὰρ
ἥμαρτον, καὶ ὑστεροῦνται τῆς δόξης
τοῦ Θεοῦ· δικαιούμενοι δωρεὰν τῇ
αὐτοῦ χάριτι διὰ τῆς ἀπολυτρώσεως
τῆς ἐν Χ. Ἰ., ὃν προέθετο ὁ Θεὸς
ἱλαστήριον διὰ τῆς πίστεως ἐν τῷ
αὐτοῦ αἵματι, εἰς ἔνδειξιν τῆς δικαιοσύνης αὐτοῦ, διὰ τὴν πάρεσιν τῶν
προγεγονότων ἁμαρτημάτων ἐν τῇ
ἀνοχῇ τοῦ Θεοῦ πρὸς τὴν ἔνδειξιν
τῆς δικαιοσύνης αὐτοῦ ἐν τῷ νῦν
καιρῷ, εἰς τὸ εἶναι αὐτὸν δίκαιον καὶ
δικαιοῦντα τὸν ἐκ πίστεως Ἰησοῦ.

EPH. iii. 1–7.

Τούτου χάριν ἐγὼ Παῦλος ὁ δέσμιος
τοῦ Χριστοῦ Ἰησοῦ ὑπὲρ ὑμῶν τῶν
ἐθνῶν,—εἴγε ἠκούσατε τὴν οἰκονομίαν
τῆς χάριτος τοῦ Θεοῦ τῆς δοθείσης μοι
εἰς ὑμᾶς, ὅτι κατὰ ἀποκάλυψιν ἐγνωρίσθη μοι τὸ μυστήριον, καθὼς προ-
έγραψα ἐν ὀλίγῳ, πρὸς ὃ δύνασθε ἀνα-
γινώσκοντες νοῆσαι τὴν σύνεσίν μου ἐν
τῷ μυστηρίῳ τοῦ Χ., ὃ ἑτέραις γενεαῖς
οὐκ ἐγνωρίσθη τοῖς υἱοῖς τῶν ἀνθρώπων,
ὡς νῦν ἀπεκαλύφθη τοῖς ἁγίοις ἀποστόλοις αὐτοῦ καὶ προφήταις ἐν Πνεύματι·
εἶναι τὰ ἔθνη συγκληρονόμα καὶ σύσσωμα
καὶ συμμέτοχα τῆς ἐπαγγελίας ἐν Χ. Ἰ.
διὰ τοῦ εὐαγγελίου οὗ ἐγενήθην διάκονος κατὰ τὴν δωρεὰν τῆς χάριτος τοῦ
Θεοῦ τῆς δοθείσης μοι κατὰ τὴν ἐνέργειαν τῆς δυνάμεως αὐτοῦ.

In the Romans passage we have first the revelation of the righteousness of
God, then a specification of the particular aspect of that righteousness with
a stress upon its universality, then the more direct assertion of this universality, followed in loose construction (see the note *ad loc.*) by an announcement of the free character of the redemption wrought by Christ, then a fuller
comment on the method of this redemption, its object, the cause which rendered
it necessary, its object again, and its motive. A wonderful series of contents
to come from a single sentence, like those Chinese boxes in which one box
is cunningly fitted within another, each smaller than the last.

The passage from Ephesians in like manner begins with a statement of the
durance which the Apostle is suffering for the Gentiles, then goes off to
explain why specially for the Gentiles, so leading on to the μυστήριον on
which that mission to the Gentiles is based, then refers back to the previous
mention of this μυστήριον, which the readers are advised to consult, then
gives a fuller description of its character, and at last states definitely its
substance. Dr. Gifford has pointed out (on Rom. iii. 26) how the argument works round in Eph. to the same word μυστήριον as in Rom. to the
same word ἔνδειξιν. And we have similar examples in Rom. ii. 16 and iii. 8,
where two distinct trains of thought and of construction converge upon
a clause which is made to do duty at the same time for both.

The particular passage of Ephesians was chosen as illustrating this pecu-
liarity. But the general tendency to the formation of periods on what we
have called the 'telescopic' method—not conforming to a plan of structure
deliberately adopted from the first, but linking on clause to clause, each suggested by the last—runs through the whole of the first three chapters of
Eph. and has abundant analogues in Rom. (i. 1–7, 18–24; ii. 5–16; iii. 21–
26; iv. 11–17; v. 12–14; ix. 22–29; xv. 14–28). The passages from
Rom. are as we have said somewhat more lively than those from Eph.;
they have a more argumentative cast, indicated by the frequent use of γάρ;
whereas those from Eph. are not so much argumentative as expository, and
consist rather of a succession of clauses connected by relatives. But the
difference is really superficial, and the underlying resemblance is great.

Just one other specimen may be given of marked resemblance of a somewhat different kind—the use of a quotation from the O.T. with running
comments. In this instance we may strengthen the impression by printing
for comparison a third passage from Ep. to Galatians.

ROM. x. 5-8.

Μωσῆς γὰρ γράφει ὅτι τὴν δικαιοσύνην τὴν ἐκ νόμου ὁ ποιήσας ἄνθρωπος ζήσεται ἐν αὐτῇ. ἡ δὲ ἐκ πίστεως δικαιοσύνη οὕτω λέγει, Μὴ εἴπῃς ἐν τῇ καρδίᾳ σου Τίς ἀναβήσεται εἰς τὸν οὐρανόν; (τοῦτ' ἔστι, Χριστὸν καταγαγεῖν·) ἤ, Τίς καταβήσεται εἰς τὴν ἄβυσσον; (τοῦτ' ἔστι, Χριστὸν ἐκ νεκρῶν ἀναγαγεῖν.) ἀλλὰ τί λέγει; Ἐγγύς σου τὸ ῥῆμά ἐστιν, ἐν τῷ στόματί σου καὶ ἐν τῇ καρδίᾳ σου· τοῦτ' ἔστι τὸ ῥῆμα τῆς πίστεως ὃ κηρύσσομεν.

EPH. iv. 7-11.

Ἑνὶ δὲ ἑκάστῳ ἡμῶν ἐδόθη ἡ χάρις κατὰ τὸ μέτρον τῆς δωρεᾶς τοῦ Χριστοῦ. διὸ λέγει, Ἀναβὰς εἰς ὕψος ᾐχμαλώτευσεν αἰχμαλωσίαν, καὶ ἔδωκε δόματα τοῖς ἀνθρώποις. (τὸ δὲ Ἀνέβη τί ἐστιν εἰ μὴ ὅτι καὶ κατέβη εἰς τὰ κατώτερα μέρη τῆς γῆς; ὁ καταβὰς αὐτός ἐστι καὶ ὁ ἀναβὰς ὑπεράνω πάντων τῶν οὐρανῶν, ἵνα πληρώσῃ τὰ πάντα.) καὶ αὐτὸς ἔδωκε τοὺς μὲν ἀποστόλους κ.τ.λ.

GAL. iv. 25-31.

Τὸ δὲ Ἄγαρ Σινᾶ ὄρος ἐστὶν ἐν τῇ Ἀραβίᾳ, συστοιχεῖ δὲ τῇ νῦν Ἱερουσαλήμ· δουλεύει γὰρ μετὰ τῶν τέκνων αὐτῆς. ἡ δὲ ἄνω Ἱερουσαλὴμ ἐλευθέρα ἐστίν, ἥτις ἐστὶ μήτηρ ἡμῶν. γέγραπται γάρ, Εὐφράνθητι, στεῖρα ἡ οὐ τίκτουσα ... ἡμεῖς δέ, ἀδελφοί, κατὰ Ἰσαὰκ ἐπαγγελίας τέκνα ἐσμέν. ἀλλ' ὥσπερ τότε ὁ κατὰ σάρκα γεννηθεὶς ἐδίωκε τὸν κατὰ Πνεῦμα, οὕτω καὶ νῦν. ἀλλὰ τί λέγει ἡ γραφή; Ἔκβαλε τὴν παιδίσκην καὶ τὸν υἱὸν αὐτῆς, οὐ γὰρ μὴ κληρονομήσῃ ὁ υἱὸς τῆς παιδίσκης μετὰ τοῦ υἱοῦ τῆς ἐλευθέρας. διό, ἀδελφοί, οὐκ ἐσμὲν παιδίσκης τέκνα, ἀλλὰ τῆς ἐλευθέρας.

It would be interesting to work out the comparison of this passage of Eph. with the earlier Epistles phrase by phrase (e. g. cp. Eph. iv. 7 with Rom. xii. 3, 6; 1 Cor. xii. 11; 2 Cor. x. 13); but to do this would be really endless and would have too remote a bearing on our present subject. Enough will have been said both to show the individuality of style in Ep. to Romans [1] and also to show its place in connexion with the range of style in the Pauline Epistles generally, as seen in a somewhat extreme example. It is usual, especially in Germany, to take Ep. to Romans with its companion Epistles as a standard of style for the whole of the *Corpus Paulinum*. But Bp. Lightfoot has pointed out that this is an error, this group of Epistles having been written under conditions of high tension which in no writer are likely to have been permanent. 'Owing to their greater length in proportion to the rest, it is probably from these Epistles that we get our general impression of St. Paul's style; yet their style is in some sense an exceptional one, called forth by peculiar circumstances, just as at a late period the style of the Pastoral Epistles is also exceptional though in a different way. The normal style of the Apostle is rather to be sought for in the Epistles to the Thessalonians and those of the Roman captivity [2].'

When we look back over the whole of the data the impression which they leave is that although the difference, taken at its extremes, is no doubt considerable, it is yet sufficiently bridged over. It does not seem to be anywhere so great as to necessitate the assumption of different authorship. Even though any single cause would hardly be enough to account for it, there may quite

---

[1] Besides the passages commented upon here, reference may be made to the marked coincidences between the doxology, Rom. xv. 25-27, and Ep. to Ephesians. These are fully pointed out *ad loc.*, and the genuineness of the doxology is defended in § 9 of this Introduction.

[2] *Journ. of Class. and Sacr. Philol., ut sup.,* p. 302.

well have been a concurrence of causes. And on the other hand the positive reasons for supposing that the two Epistles had really the same author, are weighty enough to support the conclusion. Between the limits thus set, it seems to us that the phenomena of style in the Epistles attributed to St. Paul may be ranged without straining.

§ 7. THE TEXT.

(1) *Authorities.* The authorities quoted for the various readings to the text of the Epistle are taken directly from Tischendorf's great collection (*Nov. Test. Graec.* vol. ii. ed. 8, Lipsiae, 1872), with some verification of the Patristic testimony. For a fuller account of these authorities the student must be referred to the *Prolegomena* to Tischendorf's edition (mainly the work of Dr. C. R. Gregory, 1884, 1890, 1894), and to the latest edition of Scrivener's *Introduction* (ed. Miller, London, 1894). They may be briefly enumerated as follows :

(1) GREEK MANUSCRIPTS.

Primary uncials.

א Cod. Sinaiticus, saec. iv. Brought by Tischendorf from the Convent of St. Catherine on Mt. Sinai ; now at St. Petersburg. Contains the whole Epistle complete.

Its correctors are

    א^a contemporary, or nearly so, and representing a second MS. of high value ;

    א^b attributed by Tischendorf to saec. vi ;

    א^c attributed to the beginning of saec. vii. Two hands of about this date are sometimes distinguished as א^{ca} and א^{cb}.

A. Cod. Alexandrinus, saec. v. Once in the Patriarchal Library at Alexandria ; sent by Cyril Lucar as a present to Charles I in 1628, and now in the British Museum. Complete.

B. Cod. Vaticanus, saec. iv. In the Vatican Library certainly since 1533 [1] (Batiffol, *La Vaticane de Paul iii a Paul v,* p. 86). Complete.

    The corrector B^2 is nearly of the same date and used a good copy, though not quite so good as the original. Some six centuries later the faded characters were re-traced, and a few new readings introduced by B^3.

C. Cod. Ephraemi Rescriptus, saec. v. In the National Library at Paris. Contains the whole Epistle, with the exception of the following passages : ii. 5 κα]τὰ δὲ τὴν . . . ὑπὸ τοῦ νόμου

---

[1] Dr. Gregory would carry back the evidence further, to 1521 (*Proleg.* p. 360), but M. Batiffol could find no trace of the MS. in the earlier lists.

iii. 21 ; ix. 6 οὐχ οἷον . . . ἐάν x. 15 : xi. 31 ἠπεί]θησαν τῷ
. . . πλήρωμα xiii. 10.

D. Cod. Claromontanus, saec. vi. Graeco-Latinus. Once at
Clermont, near Beauvais (if the statement of Beza is to be
trusted), now in the National Library at Paris. Contains the
Pauline Epistles, but Rom. i. 1, Παῦλος . . . ἀγαπητοῖς Θεοῦ
i. 7, is missing, and i. 27 ἐξεκαύθησαν . . . ἐφευρετὰς κακῶν i. 30
(in the Latin i. 24–27) is supplied by a later hand.

E. Cod. Sangermanensis, saec. ix. Graeco-Latinus. Formerly
at St. Germain-des-Prés, now at St. Petersburg. [This MS.
might well be allowed to drop out of the list, as it is nothing
more than a faulty copy of D.]

F. Cod. Augiensis, saec. ix. Graeco-Latinus. Bought by Bentley
in Germany, and probably written at Reichenau (*Augia
Major*); now in the Library of Trinity College, Cambridge.
Rom. i. 1 Παῦλος . . . ἐν τῷ νό[μῳ] iii. 19 is missing, both
in the Greek and Latin texts.

G. Cod. Boernerianus, saec. ix ex. Graeco-Latinus. Written at
St. Gall, now at Dresden. Rom. i. 1 ἀφωρισμένος . . . πίστεως
i. 5, and ii. 16 τὰ κρυπτὰ . . . νόμου ᾖς ii. 25 are missing.
Originally formed part of the same MS. with Δ (Cod. San-
gallensis) of the Gospels.

It has been suggested by Traube (Wattenbach, *Anleitung zur Griech.
Paläographie*, ed. 3, 1895, p. 41) that this MS. was written by the same
hand as a well-known Psalter in the library of the Arsenal at Paris which
bears the signature Σηδύλιος Σκόττος ἐγὼ ἔγραψα. The resemblance of the
handwriting is close, as may be seen by comparing the facsimile of the Paris
Psalter published by Omont in the *Mélanges Graux*, p. 313, with that of the
St. Gall Gospels in the Palaeographical Society's series (i. pl. 179). This
fact naturally raises the further question whether the writer of the MS. of
St. Paul's Epistles is not also to be identified with the compiler of the commentary entitled *Collectanea in omnes B. Pauli Epistolas* (Migne, *Patrol.
Lat.* ciii. 9–128), which is also ascribed to a ‘ Sedulius Scotus.’ The answer
must be in the negative. The commentary presents none of the characteristic readings of the MS., and appears to represent a higher grade of
scholarship. It is more probable that the scribe belonged to the *fratres
hellenici* who formed a sort of guild in the monastery of St. Gall (see the
authorities quoted in Caspari, *Quellen zum Taufsymbol*, iii. 475 n. and
compare Berger, *Histoire de la Vulgate*, p. 137). There are several instances
of the name ‘ Sedulius Scotus ’ (Migne, *P. L. ut sup.*).

It should be noted that of these MSS. ℵ A B C are parts of what
were once complete Bibles, and are designated by the same letter
throughout the LXX and Greek Testament; D E F G are all
Graeco-Latin, and are different MSS. from those which bear the
same notation on the Gospels and Acts. In Westcott and Hort's
Introduction they are distinguished as $D_2 E_3 F_2 G_3$. An important
MS., Cod. Coislinianus (H or H_2), which, however, exists only in
fragments, is unfortunately wanting for this Epistle : see below.

Secondary uncials.

K. Cod. Mosquensis, saec. ix. Brought to Moscow from the monastery ol St. Dionysius on Mount Athos. Contains Acts, Epp. Cath., Epp. Paul. Rom. x. 18 ἀλλὰ λέγω to the end is missing.

L. Cod. Angelicus, saec. ix. In the Angelican Library of the Augustinian monks at Rome. Contains Acts, Epp. Cath., Epp. Paul. Romans complete.

P. Cod. Porphyrianus, saec. ix in. A palimpsest brought from the East by Tischendorf and called after its present owner Bishop Porphyry. Contains Acts, Epp. Cath., Epp. Paul., Apoc. Rom. ii. 15 [ἀπολογου]μένων . . . ἡ ἀδικία ἡ[μῶν] iii. 5 ; viii. 35 Θεὸς ὁ δικαιῶν . . . ἵνα ἡ κα[τ᾽ ἐκλογήν] ix. 11 ; xi. 22 καὶ ἀποτομίαν . . . θυσίαν xii. 1 are missing.

S. Cod. Athous Laurae, saec. viii–ix. In the monastery Laura on Mount Athos. Contains Acts, Epp. Cath., Epp. Paul. Romans complete. This MS. has not yet been collated.

Σ. Cod. Patiriensis, saec. v. Formerly belonging to the Basilian monks of the abbey of Sta. Maria de lo Patire near Rossano, now in the Vatican. There is some reason to think that the MS. may have come originally from Constantinople (cf. Batiffol, *L'Abbaye de Rossano*, pp. 6, 79 and 62, 71–74). Twenty-one palimpsest leaves, containing portions of Acts, Epp. Cath., Epp. Paul. These include Rom. xiii. 4–xv. 9. A study of readings from this MS. is published in the *Revue Biblique* for April, 1895.

Minuscules.

A few only of the leading minuscules can be given,

5. (= Evv. 5, Act. 5), saec. xiv. At Paris ; at one time in Calabria.

17. (= Evv. 33, Act. 13), saec. ix (Omont, ix–x Gregory). At Paris. Called by Eichhorn ‘ the queen of cursives.’

31. (= Act. 25, Apoc. 7). Written 1087 A.D. Belonged to John Covell. English chaplain at Constantinople about 1675 ; now in the British Museum.

32. (= Act. 26), saec. xii. Has a similar history to the last.

37. (= Evv. 69, Act. 31, Apoc. 14), saec. xv. The well-known ‘ Leicester MS.’ ; one of the ‘ Ferrar group,’ the archetype of which was probably written in Calabria.

47. Saec. xi. Now in the Bodleian, but at one time belonged to the monastery of the Holy Trinity on the island of Chalcis.

67. (= Act. 66, Apoc. 34), saec. xi. Now at Vienna : at one time in the possession of Arsenius, archbishop of Monemvasia in Epidaurus. The marginal corrector (67**) drew from a MS. containing many peculiar and ancient readings akin to those of M Paul., which is not extant for Ep. to Romans.

71. Saec. x–xi. At Vienna. Thought to have been written in Calabria.

80. (= Act. 73), saec. xi. In the Vatican.

93. (= Act. 83, Apoc. 99), saec. xii (Gregory). At Naples. Said to have been compared with a MS. of Pamphilus, but as yet collated only in a few places.

137. (= Evv. 263, Act. 117), saec. xiii–xiv. At Paris.

252. (Gregory, 260 Scrivener = Evv. 489. Greg., 507 Scriv. ; Act. 195 Greg., 224 Scriv.). In the library of Trin. Coll., Cambridge. Written on Mount Sinai in the year 1316.

These MSS. are partly those which have been noticed as giving conspicuous readings in the commentary, partly those on which stress is laid by Hort (*Introd.* p. 166), and partly those which Bousset connects with his ‘ Codex Pamphili ’ (see below).

(2) Versions.

The versions quoted are the following:

> The Latin (Latt.).
> > The Vetus Latina (Lat. Vet.).
> > The Vulgate (Vulg.).
>
> The Egyptian (Aegypt.).
> > The Bohairic (Boh.).
> > The Sahidic (Sah.).
>
> The Syriac (Syrr.).
> > The Peshitto (Pesh.).
> > The Harclean (Harcl.).
>
> The Armenian (Arm.).
> The Gothic (Goth.).
> The Ethiopic (Aeth.).

Of these the Vetus Latina is very imperfectly preserved to us. We possess only a small number of fragments of MSS. These are:

> gue. Cod. Guelferbytanus, saec. vi, which contains fragments of Rom. xi. 33–xii. 5; xii. 17–xiii. 5; xiv. 9–20; xv. 3–13.
>
> r. Cod. Frisingensis, saec. v or vi, containing Rom. xiv. 10–xv. 13.
>
> r₃. Cod. Gottvicensis, saec. vi or vii, containing Rom. v. 16–vi. 4; vi. 6–19.

The texts of these fragments are, however, neither early (relatively to the history of the Version) nor of much interest. To supplement them we have the Latin versions of the bilingual MSS. D E F G mentioned above, usually quoted as d e f g, and quotations in the Latin Fathers. The former do not strictly represent the underlying Greek of the Version, as they are too much conformed to their own Greek. d (as necessarily e) follows an Old-Latin text not in all cases altered to suit the Greek; g is based on the Old Latin but is very much modified; f is the Vulgate translation, altered with the help of g or a MS. closely akin to g. For the Fathers we are mainly indebted to the quotations in Tertullian (saec. ii–iii), Cyprian (saec. iii), the Latin Irenaeus (saec. ii, or more probably iv), Hilary of Poitiers (saec. iv), and to the so-called *Speculum S. Augustini* (cited as m), a Spanish text also of the fourth century (see below, p. 124).

One or two specimens are given in the course of the commentary of the evidence furnished by the Old-Latin Version (see on i. 30; v. 3–5; viii. 36), which may also serve to illustrate the problems raised in connexion with the history of the Version. They have however more to do with the changes in the Latin diction of the Version than with its text. The fullest treatment of the *Vetus Latina* of St. Paul's Epistles will be found in Ziegler, *Die lateinischen Bibelübersetzungen vor Hieronymus*, München, 1879; but the subject has not as yet been sufficiently worked at for a general agreement to be reached.

For the Vulgate the following MSS. are occasionally quoted:

> am. Cod. Amiatinus c. 700 A.D.
>
> fuld. Cod. Fuldensis c. 546 A.D.
>
> harl. British Museum Harl. 1775. Saec. vi or vii.
>
> tol. Cod. Toletanus. Saec. x, or rather perhaps viii (see Berger, *Histoire de la Vulgate*, p. 14).

The Vulgate of St. Paul's Epistles is a revision of the Old Latin so slight and cursory as to be hardly an independent authority. It was however made

with the help of the Greek MSS., and we have the express statement of
St. Jerome himself that in Rom. xii. 11 he preferred to follow Greek MSS.
and to say *Domino servientes* for *tempori servientes* of the older Version
(*Ep.* xxvii. 3 *ad Marcellam*). And this reading is found in the text of the
Vulgate.

Of the Egyptian Versions, Bohairic is that usually known as Memphitic
(= 'me.' WH.) and cited by Tisch. as 'Coptic' ('cop.'). For the reasons
which make it correct to describe it as Bohairic see Scrivener, *Introd.* ii. 106,
ed. 4. It is usually cited according to Tischendorf (who appears in the
Epistles to have followed Wilkins; see Tisch. *N.T.* p. ccxxxiv, ed. 7), but
in some few instances on referring to the original it has become clear that
his quotations cannot always be trusted: see the notes on v. 6; viii. 28;
x. 5; xvi. 27. This suggests that not only a fresh edition of the text, but
also a fresh collation with the Greek, is much needed.

In the Sahidic (Thebaic) Version (= 'sah.' Tisch., 'the.' WH.) some
few readings have been added from the fragments published by Amélineau
in the *Zeitschrift für Aegypt. Sprache*, 1887. These fragments contain vi.
20-23; vii. 1-21; viii. 15-38; ix. 7-23; xi. 31-36; xii. 1-9.

The reader may be reminded that the Peshitto Syriac was certainly current
much in its present form early in the fourth century. How much earlier
than this it was in use, and what amount of change it had previously undergone, are questions still being debated. In any case, there is no other form
of the Version extant for the Pauline Epistles.

The Harclean Syriac (= 'syr. p[osterior]' Tisch., 'hl.' WH.) is a recension made by the Monophysite Thomas of Harkhel or Heraclea in 616
A.D., of the older Philoxenian Version of 508 A.D., which for this part
of the N.T. is now lost. A special importance attaches to the readings,
sometimes in the text but more often in the margin, which appear to be
derived from 'three (v. l. two) approved and accurate Greek copies' in the
monastery of the Enaton near Alexandria (WH. *Introd.* p. 156 f.).

The Gothic Version is also definitely dated at about the middle of the
fourth century, and the Armenian at about the middle of the fifth. The dates
of the two Egyptian Versions and of the Ethiopic are still uncertain
(Scrivener, *Introd.* ii. 105 f., 154, ed. 4). It is of more importance to know
that the types of text which they represent are in any case early, the
Egyptian somewhat the older.

The abbreviations in references to the Patristic writings are such as it is
hoped will cause no difficulty (but see p. cx).

(2) *Internal Grouping of Authorities.* The most promising and
successful of all the directions in which textual criticism is being
pursued at this moment is that of isolating comparatively small
groups of authorities, and investigating their mutual relations and
origin. For the Pauline Epistles the groups most affected by
recent researches are ℵB; ℵᶜH, Arm., Euthal., and in less degree
a number of minuscules; D[E]F G.

ℵ B.

The proofs seem to be thickening which connect these two great MSS.
with the library of Eusebius and Pamphilus at Caesarea. That is a view
which has been held for some time past (e. g. by the late Canon Cook,
Revised Version of the First Three Gospels, p. 159 ff.; and Dr. Scrivener,
Collation of Cod. Sinaiticus, p. xxxvii f.), but without resting upon any very
solid arguments. And it must always be remembered that so excellent
a palaeographer as Dr. Ceriani of Milan (*ap.* Scrivener, *Introd.* i. 121, ed. 4)
thought that B was written in Italy (Magna Graecia), and that Dr. Hort

also gives some reasons for ascribing an Italian origin to this MS. We are however confronted by the fact that there is a distinct probability that both MSS. if they were not written in the same place had at least in part the same scribes. It was first pointed out by Tischendorf (*N. T. Vat.*, Lipsiae, 1867, pp. xxi–xxiii), on grounds which seem to be sufficient, that the writer whom he calls the 'fourth scribe' of ℵ wrote also the N.T. portion of B. And, as it has been said, additional arguments are becoming available for connecting ℵ with the library at Caesarea (see Rendel Harris, *Stichometry*, p. 71 ff.; and the essay of Bousset referred to below).

The *provenance* of ℵ would only carry with it approximately and not exactly that of B. The conditions would be satisfied if it were possible, or not difficult, for the same scribe to have a hand in both. For instance, the view that ℵ had its origin in Palestine would not be inconsistent with the older view, recently revived and defended by Bousset, that B was an Egyptian MS. There would be so much coming and going between Palestine and Egypt, especially among the followers of Origen, that they would belong virtually to the same region. But when Herr Bousset goes further and maintains that the text of B represents the recension of Hesychius [1], that is another matter, and as it seems to us, at least *prima facie*. by no means probable. The text of B must needs be older than the end of the third century, which is the date assigned to Hesychius. If we admit that the MS. may be Egyptian, it is only as one amongst several possibilities. Nothing can as yet be regarded as proved.

Apart from such external data as coincidences of handwriting which connect the two MSS. as they have come down to us there can be no doubt that they had also a common ancestor far back in the past. The weight which their agreement carries does not depend on the independence of their testimony so much as upon its early date. That the date of their common readings is in fact extremely early appears to be proved by the number of readings in which they differ, these divergent readings being shared not by any means always by the same but by a great variety of other authorities. From this variety it may be inferred that between the point of divergence of the ancestors of the two MSS. and the actual MSS. the fortunes of each had been quite distinct. Not only on a single occasion, but on a number of successive occasions, new strains of text have been introduced on one or other of the lines. ℵ especially has received several side streams in the course of its history, now of the colour which we call 'Western' and now 'Alexandrian'; and B also (as we shall see) in the Pauline Epistles has a clear infusion of Western readings. It is possible that all these may have come in from a single copy; but it is less likely that all the 'Western' or all the 'Alexandrian' readings which are found in ℵ had a single origin. Indeed the history of ℵ since it was written does but reflect the history of its ancestry. We have only to suppose the corrections of ℵ^a embodied in the text of one MS., then those of ℵ^b first inserted in the margin and then embodied in the text of a succeeding MS., then those of ℵ^{ca} in a third and ℵ^{cb} in a fourth, to form a mental picture of the process by which our present MS. became what it is. It remains for critical analysis to reconstruct this process, to pick to pieces the different elements of which the text of the MS. consists, to arrange them in their order and determine their affinities. This analysis will doubtless be carried further than it has been.

ℵ^c H, Arm., Euthal.

A number of scholars working on ℵ have thrown out suggestions which would tend to group together these authorities, and possibly to bring them into some further connexion with ℵ B. The MS. H Paul. (unfortunately, as we have

---

[1] A similar view is held by Corssen. He regards the modern text based on ℵ B as *nur ein Spiegelbild einer willkürlich fixierten Recension des vierten Jahrhunderts* (*Der Cyprianische Text d. Acta Apostolorum*, Berlin, 1892, p. 24).

said, not extant for Romans) bears upon its face the traces of its connexion with the library of Caesarea, as the subscription to Ep. to Titus states expressly that the MS. was corrected ' with the copy at Caesarea in the library of the holy Pamphilus written with his own hand.' Now in June, 1893, Dr. Rendel Harris pointed out a connexion between this MS. H Paul. and Euthalius (*Stichometry*, p. 88). This had also been noticed by Dr. P. Corssen in the second of the two programmes cited below (p. 12). Early in 1894 Herr W. Bousset brought out in Gebhardt and Harnack's *Texte u. Unter-suchungen* a series of *Text-kritische Studien zum N. T.*, in the course of which (without any concert with Dr. Rendel Harris, but perhaps with some knowledge of Corssen) he not only adduced further evidence of this connexion, but also brought into the group the third corrector of א (א°). A note at the end of the Book of Esther said to be by his hand speaks in graphic terms of a MS. corrected by the Hexapla of Origen, com-pared by Antoninus a confessor, and corrected by Pamphilus 'in prison' (i. e. just before his death in the persecution of Diocletian). Attention had often been drawn to this note, but Herr Bousset was the first to make the full use of it which it deserved. He found on examination that the presump-tion raised by it was verified and that there was a real and close connexion between the readings of א° and those of H and Euthalius which were inde-pendently associated with Pamphilus[1]. Lastly, to complete the series of novel and striking observations, Mr. F. C. Conybeare comes forward in the current number of the *Journal of Philology* (no. 46, 1895) and maintains a further connexion of the group with the Armenian Version. These researches are at present in full swing, and will doubtless lead by degrees to more or less definite results. The essays which have been mentioned all contain some more speculative matter in addition to what has been mentioned, but it is also probable that they have a certain amount of solid nucleus. It is only just what we should have expected. The library founded by Pamphilus at Caesarea was the greatest and most famous of all the book-collections in the early Christian centuries; it was also the greatest centre of literary and copying activity just at the moment when Christianity received its greatest expansion ; the prestige not only of Eusebius and Pamphilus, but of the still more potent name (for some time yet to come) of Origen, attached to it. It would have been strange if it had not been consulted from far and wide and if the influence of it were not felt in many parts of Christendom.

D F G, Goth.

Not only is E a mere copy of D, but there is a very close relation between F and G, especially in the Greek. It is not as yet absolutely determined what that relation is. In an essay written in 1871 (reprinted in Lightfoot, *Biblical Essays*, p. 321 ff.) Dr. Hort states his opinion that F Greek is a direct copy of G, F Latin a Vulgate text partly assimilated to the Greek and with intrusive readings from the Latin of G. Later (*Introd.* p. 150) he writes that F is 'as certainly in its Greek text a transcript of G as E of D : if not it is an inferior copy of the same immediate exemplar.' This second alterna-tive is the older view, adopted by Scrivener (*Introd.* p. 181, ed. 3) and maintained with detailed arguments in two elaborate programmes by Dr. P. Corssen (*Epp. Paulin. Codd. Aug. Boern. Clarom.*, 1887 and 1889).

---

[1] Since the above was written all speculations on the subject of Euthalius have been superseded by Prof. Armitage Robinson's admirable essay in *Texts and Studies*, iii. 3. Both the text of Euthalius and that of the *Codex Pamphili* are shown to be as yet very uncertain quantities. Still it is probable that the authorities in question are really connected, and that there are elements in their text which may be traceable to Euthalius on the one hand and the Caesarean Library on the other.

We are not sure that the question can still be regarded as settled in this sense, and that Dr. Hort's original view is not to be preferred. Dr. Corssen admits that there are some phenomena which he cannot explain (1887, p. 13). These would fall naturally into their place if F Gk. is a copy of G; and the arguments on the other side do not seem to be decisive. In any case it should be remembered that F Gk. and G Gk. are practically one witness and not two.

Dr. Corssen reached a number of other interesting conclusions. Examining the common element in D F G he showed that they were ultimately derived from a single archetype (Z), and that this archetype was written *per cola et commata*, or in clauses corresponding to the sense (sometimes called στίχοι), as may be seen in the Palaeographical Society's facsimile of D (ser. i. pl. 63, 64). Here again we have another coincidence of independent workers, for in 1891 Dr. Rendel Harris carrying further a suggestion of Rettig's had thrown out the opinion, that not only did the same system of colometry lie behind Cod. Δ Evv. (the other half, as we remember, of G Paul.) and D Evv. Act. (Cod. Bezae, which holds a like place in the Gospel and Acts to D Paul.), but that it also extended to the other important Old-Latin MS. k (Cod. Bobiensis), and even to the Curetonian Syriac —to which we suppose may now be added the Sinai palimpsest. If that were so—and indeed without this additional evidence—Dr. Corssen probably puts the limit too late when he says that such a MS. is not likely to have been written before the time of St. Chrysostom, or 407 A. D.

Thus Dr. Corssen thinks that there arose early in the fifth century a 'Graeco-Latin edition,' the Latin of which was more in agreement with Victorinus Ambrosiaster and the Spanish *Speculum*. For the inter-connexion of this group he adduces a striking instance from 1 Cor. xiii. 1; and he argues that the locality in which it arose was more probably Italy than Africa. As to the place of origin we are more inclined to agree with him than as to the date, though the *Speculum* contains an African element. He then points out that this Graeco-Latin edition has affinities with the Gothic Version. The edition did not contain the Epistle to the Hebrews; and the Epistle to the Romans in it ended at Rom. xv. 14 (see § 9 below); it was entirely without the doxology (Rom. xvi. 25–27).

Dr. Corssen thinks that this Graeco-Latin edition has undergone some correction in D by comparison with Greek MSS. and therefore that it is in part more correctly preserved in G, which however in its turn can only be used for reconstructing it with caution.

Like all that Dr. Corssen writes this sketch is suggestive and likely to be fruitful, though we cannot express our entire agreement with it. We only regret that we cannot undertake here the systematic inquiry which certainly ought to be made into the history of this group. The lines which it should follow would be something of this kind. (i) It should reconstruct as far as possible the common archetype of D and G. (ii) It should isolate the peculiar element in both MSS. and distinguish between earlier and later readings. The instances in which the Greek has been conformed to the Latin will probably be found to be late and of little real importance. (iii) The peculiar and ancient readings in G g should be carefully collected and studied. An opportunity might be found of testing more closely the hypothesis propounded in § 9 of this Introduction. (iv) The relations of the Gothic Version to the group should be determined as accurately as possible. (v) The characteristics both of D and of the archetype of D G should be compared with those of Cod. Bezae and the Old-Latin MSS. of the Gospels and Acts.

(3) *The Textual Criticism of Epistle to Romans.* The textual criticism of the Pauline Epistles generally is inferior in interest to

that of the Historical Books of the New Testament. When this is said it is not meant that investigations such as those outlined above are not full of attraction, and in their way full of promise. Anything which throws new light on the history of the text will be found in the end to throw new light on the history of Christianity. But what is meant is that the textual phenomena are less marked, and have a less distinctive and individual character.

This may be due to two causes, both of which have really been at work. On the one hand, the latitude of variation was probably never from the first so great; and on the other hand the evidence which has come down to us is inferior both in quantity and quality, so that there are parts of the history—and those just the most interesting parts—which we cannot reconstruct simply for want of material. A conspicuous instance of both conditions is supplied by the state of what is called the 'Western Text.' It is probable that this text never diverged from the other branches so widely as it does in the Gospels and Acts; and just for that section of it which diverged most we have but little evidence. For the oldest forms of this text we are reduced to the quotations in Tertullian and Cyprian. We have nothing like the best of the Old-Latin MSS. of the Gospels and Acts; nothing like forms of the Syriac Versions such as the Curetonian and Sinaitic; nothing like the *Diatessaron*.

And yet when we look broadly at the variants to the Pauline Epistles we observe the same main lines of distribution as in the rest of the N.T. A glance at the *apparatus criticus* of the Epistle to the Romans will show the tendency of the authorities to fall into the groups D E F G; ℵ B; ℵ A C L P. These really correspond to like groups in the other Books: D E F G correspond to the group which, in the nomenclature of Westcott and Hort, is called 'Western'; ℵ B appear (with other leading MSS. added) to mark the line which they would call 'Neutral'; ℵ A C L P would *include*, but would not be identical with, the group which they call 'Alexandrian.' The later uncials generally (with accessions every now and then from the older ranks) would constitute the family which they designate as 'Syrian,' and which others have called 'Antiochene,' 'Byzantine,' 'Constantinopolitan,' or 'Ecclesiastical.'

Exception is taken to some of these titles, especially to the term 'Western,' which is only retained because of its long-established use, and no doubt gives but a very imperfect geographical description of the facts. It might be proposed to substitute names suggested in most cases by the leading MS. of the group, but generalized so as to cover other authorities as well. For instance, we might speak of the δ-text (='Western'), the β-text (='Neutral'), the α-text (='Alexandrian'), and the ε-text or σ-text (='Ecclesiastical' or 'Syrian'). Such terms would beg no questions; they would simply describe facts. It would be an advantage that the same term 'δ-text' would be equally suggested by the leading MS. in the Gospels and Acts, and in the Pauline Epistles; the term 'β-text,' while suggested by B, would carry with it no assumption of superiority; 'α-text' would recall equally 'Alexandrian' and 'Codex Alexandrinus'; and 'ϵ-text' or 'σ-text' would not imply any inherent inferiority, but would only describe the undoubted facts, either that the text in question was that generally accepted by the Church throughout the Middle Ages, or that in its oldest form it can be traced definitely to the region of Antioch and northern Syria. It is certain that this text (alike for Gospels, Acts, and Epistles) appears in the fourth century in this region, and spread from it; while as to the debated point of its previous history nothing would be either affirmed or denied.

If some such nomenclature as this were adopted a further step might be taken by distinguishing the earlier and later stages of the same text as δ^1, δ^2, &c., σ^1, σ^2, &c. It would also have to be noted that although in the vast majority of cases the group would include the MS. from which it took its name, still in some instances it would not include it, and it might even be ranged on the opposite side. This would occur most often with the α-text and A, but it would occur also occasionally with the β-text and B (as conspicuously in Rom. xi. 6).

Such being the broad outlines of the distribution of authorities on the Epistle to the Romans, we ask, What are its distinctive and individual features? These are for the most part shared with the rest of the Pauline Epistles. One of the advantages which most of the other Epistles possess. Romans is without: none of the extant fragments of Cod. H belong to it. This deprives us of one important criterion; but conclusions obtained for the other Epistles may be applied to this. For instance, the student will observe carefully the readings of $\aleph^c$ and Arm. Sufficient note has unfortunately not been taken of them in the commentary, as the clue was not in the writer's hands when it was written. In this respect the reader must be asked to supplement it. He should of course apply the new test with caution, and judge each case on its merits: only careful use can show to what extent it is valid. When we consider the mixed origin of nearly all ancient texts, sweeping propositions and absolute rules are seen to be out of place.

The specific characteristics of the textual apparatus of Romans may be said to be these : (i) the general inferiority in boldness and originality of the δ- (or Western) text ; (ii) the fact that there is a distinct Western element in B, which therefore when it is combined with authorities of the δ- or Western type is diminished in value; (iii) the consequent rise in importance of the group $\aleph$AC; (iv) the existence of a few scattered readings either of B alone or of B in combination with one or two other authorities which have considerable intrinsic probability and may be right.

We proceed to say a few words on each of these heads.

(i) The first must be taken with the reservations noted above. The Western or δ-text has not it is true the bold and interesting variations which are found in the Gospels and Acts. It has none of the striking interpolations which in those Books often bring in ancient and valuable matter. That may be due mainly to the fact that the interpolations in question are for the most part historical, and therefore would naturally be looked for in the Historical Books. In Ep. to Romans the more important δ-variants are not interpolations but omissions (as e. g. in the Gospel of St. Luke). Still these variants preserve some of the freedom of correction and paraphrase to which we are accustomed elsewhere.

E. g. iii. 9 τί προκατέχομεν πέρισσον ; D* G, Chrys. Orig.-lat. *al.* : τί οὖν ; προεχόμεθα ; *rel.*

    iv. 19 οὐ κατενόησεν D E F G, &c. Orig.-lat. Epiph. Ambrstr. *al.* : κατενόησεν ℵ A B C *al.*

    v. 14 ἐπὶ τοὺς ἁμαρτήσαντας 62, 63, 67**, Orig.-lat. *Codd. Lat. ap.* Aug., Ambrstr. : ἐπὶ τοὺς μὴ ἁμαρτήσαντας *rel.*

    vii 6 τοῦ θανάτου D E F G, *Codd. ap.* Orig.-lat. *al.* : ἀποθανόντες *rel.*

    xii. 11 τῷ καιρῷ δουλεύοντες D* F G, *Codd. Lat. ap.* Hieron. *ap.* Orig.-lat. Ambrstr. : τῷ Κυρίῳ δουλεύοντες *rel.*

    13 ταῖς μνείαις τῶν ἁγίων D* F G, *Codd. ap.* Theod. Mops. *ap.* Orig.-lat. Hil. Ambrstr. *al.* : ταῖς χρείαις τῶν ἁγίων *rel.* [These two readings were perhaps due in the first instance to accidental errors of transcription.]

    xv. 13 πληροφορήσαι B F G : πληρώσαι *rel.*

    22 πολλάκις B D E F G : τὰ πολλά *rel.*

    31 δωροφορία B D* F G, Ambrstr. : διακονία *rel.*

The most interesting aspect of this branch of the text is the history of its antecedents as represented by the common archetype of D G, and even more by the peculiar element in G. The most prominent of these readings are discussed below in § 9, but a still further investigation of them in connexion with allied phenomena in other Epistles is desirable.

(ii) It will have been seen that in the last three readings just given B joins with the unmistakably Western authorities. And this phenomenon is in point of fact frequently repeated. We have it also in the omission of †πρῶτον i. 16 ; om. γάρ iii. 2 ; om. τῇ πίστει v. 2 ; *ins. μέν vi. 21 ; διὰ τὸ ἐνοικοῦν αὐτοῦ Πνεῦμα viii. 11 (where however there is a great mass of other authorities) ; *om. Ἰησοῦς and *om. ἐκ νεκρῶν viii. 34 ; ἡ διαθήκη ix. 4 ; ins. οὖν ix. 19 ; *ὅτι after νόμου and *†ταὐτά ins. after ποιήσας x. 5 ; ἐν [τοῖς] x. 20 ; *om. γάρ xiv. 5 ; om. οὖν, ἀποδώσει, †om. τῷ Θεῷ xiv. 12 ; *add ἢ σκανδαλίζεται ἢ ἀσθενεῖ xiv. 21 ; ἡμᾶς xv. 7 ; τὴν [καύχησιν] xv. 17.

It is perhaps significant that in all the instances marked with * the group is joined by ℵͨ. It may be through a copy related to the 'Codex Pamphili' that these readings came into B. We also note that the latest and worst of all the readings found in B, the long addition in xi. 6 εἰ δὲ ἐξ ἔργων οὐκέτι (om. ἐστί B) χάρις· ἐπεὶ τὸ ἔργον οὐκέτι ἐστὶ χάρις (sic B ; ἔργον al.) is shared by B with ℵͨ L. In the instances marked with †, and in xv. 13 πληροφορῆσαι, B agrees not with D but with G ; but on the other hand in viii. 34 (om. Ἰησοῦς) and in xv. 7 it agrees with D against G ; so that the resemblance to the peculiar element in the latter MS. does not stand out quite clearly. In the other instances both D and G are represented.

(iii) When B thus goes over to the Western or δ-group the main support of the alternative reading is naturally thrown upon ℵ A C. This is a group which outside the Gospels and Acts and especially in Past. Epp. Heb. and Apoc. (with or without other support) has not seldom preserved the right reading. It becomes in fact the main group wherever B is not extant. The principal difficulty—and it is one of the chief of the not very numerous textual difficulties in Romans—is to determine whether these MSS. really retain the original text or whether their reading is one of the finer Alexandrian corrections. This ambiguity besets us (e. g.) in the very complex attestation of viii. 11. The combination is strengthened where ℵ A are joined with the Westerns as in iii. 28. In this instance, as in a few others, they are opposed by B C, a pair which do not carry quite as much weight in the Epistles as they would in the Gospels.

(iv) It may appear paradoxical, but the value of B seems to rise when it is deserted by all or nearly all other uncials. Appearances may be deceptive, but there is not a little reason for thinking that the following readings belong to the soundest innermost kernel of the MS.

iv. 1 om. εὑρηκέναι.

v. 6 εἴ γε.

vii. 25 χάρις τῷ Θεῷ.

viii. 24 ὃ γὰρ βλέπει, τίς ἐλπίζει ;

x. 9 τὸ ῥῆμα . . . ὅτι Κύριος Ἰησοῦς.

xiv. 13 om. πρόσκομμα . . . ἤ.

xv. 19 Πνεύματος without addition.

As all these readings have been discussed more or less fully in the commentary, they need only be referred to here. Two more readings present considerable attractions.

ix. 23 om. καί.

xvi. 27 om. ᾧ.

They are however open to some suspicion of being corrections to ease the construction. The question is whether or not they are valid exceptions to the rule that the more difficult reading is to be preferred. Such exceptions there undoubtedly are ; and it is at least a tenable view that these are among them.

Other singular, or subsingular, readings of B will be found in **xv. 4,** 13, **30, 32.** But these are less attractive and less important.

§ 8. LITERARY HISTORY.

The literary history of the Epistle to the Romans begins earlier than that of any other book of the N.T. Not only is it clearly and distinctly quoted in the writings of the Apostolic Fathers, but even within the N.T. canon there are very close resemblances both in thought and language between it and at least three other books ; these resemblances we must first consider.

We shall begin with the first Epistle of St. Peter. In the following table the passages in which there is a similarity between the two Epistles are compared :

Rom. ix. 25 καλέσω τὸν οὐ λαόν μου λαόν μου, καὶ τὴν οὐκ ἠγαπημένην ἠγαπημένην.

1 Peter ii. 10 οἱ ποτὲ οὐ λαός, νῦν δὲ λαὸς Θεοῦ, οἱ οὐκ ἠλεημένοι, νῦν δὲ ἐλεηθέντες.

Rom. ix. 32, 33 προσέκοψαν τῷ λίθῳ τοῦ προσκόμματος, καθὼς γέγραπται, Ἰδού, τίθημι ἐν Σιὼν λίθον προσκόμματος καὶ πέτραν σκανδάλου· καὶ ὁ πιστεύων ἐπ᾽ αὐτῷ οὐ καταισχυνθήσεται.

1 Peter ii. 6-8 Ἰδού, τίθημι ἐν Σιὼν λίθον ἀκρογωνιαῖον ἐκλεκτόν, ἔντιμον· καὶ ὁ πιστεύων ἐπ᾽ αὐτῷ οὐ μὴ καταισχυνθῇ . . . οὗτος ἐγενήθη εἰς κεφαλὴν γωνίας, 8 καὶ λίθος προσκόμματος καὶ πέτρα σκανδάλου, οἳ προσκόπτουσι τῷ λόγῳ ἀπειθοῦντες, εἰς ὃ καὶ ἐτέθησαν.

Rom. xii. 1 παραστῆσαι τὰ σώματα ὑμῶν θυσίαν ζῶσαν, ἁγίαν, εὐάρεστον τῷ Θεῷ, τὴν λογικὴν λατρείαν ὑμῶν.

1 Peter ii. 5 ἀνενέγκαι πνευματικὰς θυσίας εὐπροσδέκτους Θεῷ διὰ Ἰ. Χρ.

Rom. xii. 2 μὴ συσχηματίζεσθε τῷ αἰῶνι τούτῳ.

1 Peter i. 14 μὴ συσχηματιζόμενοι ταῖς πρότερον ἐν τῇ ἀγνοίᾳ ὑμῶν ἐπιθυμίαις.

The following passages seem to be modelled on St. Paul's thoughts and words:

Rom. xii. 3 ἀλλὰ φρονεῖν εἰς τὸ σωφρονεῖν ...

6 ἔχοντες δὲ χαρίσματα κατὰ τὴν χάριν τὴν δοθεῖσαν ἡμῖν διάφορα ... εἴτε διακονίαν, ἐν τῇ διακονίᾳ ...

3 ἑκάστῳ ὡς ὁ Θεὸς ἐμέρισε μέτρον πίστεως.

Cf. also Rom. xiii. 11–14; 8–10; xii. 9, 13.

1 Peter iv. 7–11 πάντων δὲ τὸ τέλος ἤγγικε· σωφρονήσατε οὖν καὶ νήψατε εἰς προσευχάς· πρὸ πάντων τὴν εἰς ἑαυτοὺς ἀγάπην ἐκτενῆ ἔχοντες, ὅτι ἀγάπη καλύπτει πλῆθος ἁμαρτιῶν· φιλόξενοι εἰς ἀλλήλους, ἄνευ γογγυσμοῦ· ἔκαστος καθὼς ἔλαβε χάρισμα, εἰς ἑαυτοὺς αὐτὸ διακονοῦντες, ὡς καλοὶ οἰκονόμοι ποικίλης χάριτος Θεοῦ· εἴ τις λαλεῖ, ὡς λόγια Θεοῦ· εἴ τις διακονεῖ, ὡς ἐξ ἰσχύος ἧς χορηγεῖ ὁ Θεός.

Rom. xii. 9 ἡ ἀγάπη ἀνυπόκριτος ... 10 τῇ φιλαδελφίᾳ εἰς ἀλλήλους φιλόστοργοι.

1 Peter i. 22 τὰς ψυχὰς ὑμῶν ἡγνικότες ... εἰς φιλαδελφίαν ἀνυπόκριτον ἐκ καρδίας ἀλλήλους ἀγαπήσατε ἐκτενῶς.

Rom. xii. 16 τὸ αὐτὸ εἰς ἀλλήλους φρονοῦντες· μὴ τὰ ὑψηλὰ φρονοῦντες, ἀλλὰ τοῖς ταπεινοῖς συναπαγόμενοι. μὴ γίνεσθε φρόνιμοι παρ' ἑαυτοῖς.

17 μηδενὶ κακὸν ἀντὶ κακοῦ ἀποδιδόντες· προνοούμενοι καλὰ ἐνώπιον πάντων ἀνθρώπων·

18 εἰ δυνατόν, τὸ ἐξ ὑμῶν, μετὰ πάντων ἀνθρώπων εἰρηνεύοντες.

Cf. also vv. 9, 14.

1 Peter iii. 8, 9 τὸ δὲ τέλος, πάντες ὁμόφρονες, συμπαθεῖς, φιλάδελφοι, εὔσπλαγχνοι, ταπεινόφρονες, μὴ ἀποδιδόντες κακὸν ἀντὶ κακοῦ ἢ λοιδορίαν ἀντὶ λοιδορίας, τοὐναντίον δὲ εὐλογοῦντες, ὅτι εἰς τοῦτο ἐκλήθητε ἵνα εὐλογίαν κληρονομήσητε ...

11 ἐκκλινάτω δὲ ἀπὸ κακοῦ, καὶ ποιησάτω ἀγαθόν· ζητησάτω εἰρήνην καὶ διωξάτω αὐτήν.

Rom. xiii. 1 πᾶσα ψυχὴ ἐξουσίαις ὑπερεχούσαις ὑποτασσέσθω· οὐ γάρ ἐστιν ἐξουσία εἰ μὴ ὑπὸ Θεοῦ, αἱ δὲ οὖσαι ὑπὸ Θεοῦ τεταγμέναι εἰσίν ...

3 οἱ γὰρ ἄρχοντες οὐκ εἰσὶ φόβος τῷ ἀγαθῷ ἔργῳ, ἀλλὰ τῷ κακῷ ...

4 Θεοῦ γὰρ διάκονός ἐστιν, ἔκδικος εἰς ὀργὴν τῷ τὸ κακὸν πράσσοντι ...

7 ἀπόδοτε πᾶσι τὰς ὀφειλάς· τῷ τὸν φόρον τὸν φόρον, τῷ τὸ τέλος τὸ τέλος, τῷ τὸν φόβον τὸν φόβον, τῷ τὴν τιμὴν τὴν τιμήν.

1 Peter ii. 13–17 ὑποτάγητε πάσῃ ἀνθρωπίνῃ κτίσει διὰ τὸν Κύριον, εἴτε βασιλεῖ, ὡς ὑπερέχοντι, εἴτε ἡγεμόσιν, ὡς δι' αὐτοῦ πεμπομένοις εἰς ἐκδίκησιν κακοποιῶν ἔπαινον δὲ ἀγαθοποιῶν· ὅτι οὕτως ἐστὶ τὸ θέλημα τοῦ Θεοῦ ... πάντας τιμήσατε· τὴν ἀδελφότητα ἀγαπᾶτε· τὸν Θεὸν φοβεῖσθε· τὸν βασιλέα τιμᾶτε.

Although equal stress cannot be laid on all these passages the resemblance is too great and too constant to be merely accidental. In 1 Pet. ii. 6 we have a quotation from the O.T. with the same variations from the LXX that we find in Rom. ix. 32 (see the note). Not only do we find the same thoughts, such as the metaphorical use of the idea of sacrifice (Rom. xii. 1; 1 Pet. ii. 5), and the same rare words, such as συσχηματίζεσθαι, ἀνυπόκριτος, but in one passage (Rom. xiii. 1–7; 1 Pet. ii. 13–17) we have what must be accepted as conclusive evidence, the same ideas occurring in the same order. Nor can there be any doubt that of the two the Epistle to the Romans is the earlier. St. Paul works out a thesis clearly and logically; St. Peter gives a series of maxims for which he is largely indebted to St. Paul. For example, in Rom. xiii. 7 we have a broad general principle laid down, St. Peter, clearly influenced by the phraseology of that passage, merely gives three rules of conduct. In St. Paul the language and ideas come out of the sequence of thought; in St. Peter they are adopted because they had already been used for the same purpose.

This relation between the two Epistles is supported by other independent evidence. The same relation which prevails between the First Epistle of St. Peter and the Epistle to the Romans is also found to exist between it and the Epistle to the Ephesians, and the same hypothesis harmonizes best with the facts in that case also. The three Epistles are all connected with Rome: one of them being written to the city, the other two in all probability being written from it. We cannot perhaps be quite certain as to the date of 1 Peter, but it must be earlier than the Apostolic Fathers who quote it; while it in its turn quotes as we see at least two Epistles of St. Paul and these the most important. We may notice that these conclusions harmonize as far as they go with the view taken in § 3, that St. Peter was not the founder of the Roman Church and had not visited it when the Epistle to the Romans was written. In early church history arguments are rarely conclusive; and the even partial coincidence of different lines of investigation adds greatly to the strength of each.

The writer of the Epistle to the Hebrews again was probably indebted to the Romans, the resemblance between Rom. iv. 17 and Heb. xi. 11 is very close and has been brought out in the notes, while in Rom. xii. 19, Heb. x. 30, we have the same passage of Deuteronomy quoted with the same marked divergences from the text of the LXX. This is not in itself conclusive evidence; there may have been an earlier form of the version current, in fact there are strong grounds for thinking so; but the hypothesis that the author of the Hebrews used the Romans is certainly the simplest. We again notice that the Hebrews is a book closely connected with the Roman Church, as is proved by its early use in that Church, and if it were, as is possible, written from Rome or Italy its indebtedness to this Epistle would be accounted for. The two passages referred to are quoted below; and, although no other passages resemble one another sufficiently to be quoted, yet it is quite conceivable that many other of the words and phrases in the Hebrews which are Pauline in character may have been derived from an acquaintance with this Epistle.

The passages referred to are the following :

Rom. iv. 17–21 κατέναντι οὗ ἐπίστευσε Θεοῦ τοῦ ζωοποιοῦντος τοὺς
νεκροὺς ... καὶ μὴ ἀσθενήσας τῇ
πίστει κατενόησε τὸ ἑαυτοῦ σῶμα
ἤδη νενεκρωμένον (ἑκατονταέτης
που ὑπάρχων), καὶ τὴν νέκρωσιν τῆς
μήτρας Σάρρας· εἰς δὲ τὴν ἐπαγγελίαν τοῦ Θεοῦ οὐ διεκρίθη τῇ
ἀπιστίᾳ, ἀλλ' ἐνεδυναμώθη τῇ
πίστει, δοὺς δόξαν τῷ Θεῷ, καὶ
πληροφορηθεὶς ὅτι ὃ ἐπήγγελται
δυνατός ἐστι καὶ ποιῆσαι.

Heb. xi. 11, 12 πίστει καὶ αὐτὴ Σάρρα
δύναμιν εἰς καταβολὴν σπέρματος
ἔλαβεν καὶ παρὰ καιρὸν ἡλικίας, ἐπεὶ
πιστὸν ἡγήσατο τὸν ἐπαγγειλά-
μενον· διὸ καὶ ἀφ' ἑνὸς ἐγεννήθησαν,
καὶ ταῦτα νενεκρωμένου ...
19 λογισάμενος ὅτι καὶ ἐκ νεκρῶν
ἐγείρειν δυνατὸς ὁ Θεός.

Rom. xii. 19 ἐμοὶ ἐκδίκησις, ἐγὼ
ἀνταποδώσω, λέγει Κύριος.

Heb. x. 30 ἐμοὶ ἐκδίκησις, ἐγὼ
ἀνταποδώσω*.

When we pass to the Epistle of St. James we approach a much
more difficult problem. The relation between it and the Epistle
to the Romans has been often and hotly debated ; for it is
a theological as well as a literary question. The passages which
resemble one another in the two Epistles are given at length by
Prof. Mayor in his edition of the Epistle of St. James, p. xciii, who
argues strongly in favour of the later date of the Romans. The
following are among the most important of these ; we have not
thought it necessary to repeat all his instances :

Rom. ii. 1 διὸ ἀναπολόγητος εἶ, ὦ
ἄνθρωπε πᾶς ὁ κρίνων· ἐν ᾧ γὰρ
κρίνεις τὸν ἕτερον, σεαυτὸν κατα-
κρίνεις· τὰ γὰρ αὐτὰ πράσσεις ὁ
κρίνων.

James iv. 11 μὴ καταλαλεῖτε ἀλλήλων, ἀδελφοί. ὁ καταλαλῶν ἀδελφοῦ, ἢ
κρίνων τὸν ἀδελφὸν αὐτοῦ, καταλαλεῖ
νόμου, καὶ κρίνει νόμον· εἰ δὲ νόμον κρίνεις, οὐκ εἶ ποιητὴς νόμου, ἀλλὰ κριτής.

Rom. ii. 13 οὐ γὰρ οἱ ἀκροαταὶ
νόμου δίκαιοι παρὰ [τῷ] Θεῷ ἀλλ' οἱ
ποιηταὶ νόμου δικαιωθήσονται.

James i. 22 γίνεσθε δὲ ποιηταὶ
λόγου, καὶ μὴ μόνον ἀκροαταὶ παρα-
λογιζόμενοι ἑαυτούς.

Rom. iv. 1 τί οὖν ἐροῦμεν εὑρηκέναι
Ἀβραὰμ τὸν προπάτορα ἡμῶν
κατὰ σάρκα ; εἰ γὰρ Ἀβραὰμ ἐξ
ἔργων ἐδικαιώθη, ἔχει καύχημα.

James ii. 21 Ἀβραὰμ ὁ πατὴρ
ἡμῶν οὐκ ἐξ ἔργων ἐδικαιώθη,
ἀνενέγκας Ἰσαὰκ τὸν υἱὸν αὐτοῦ ἐπὶ τὸ
θυσιαστήριον ;

Rom. iv. 20 εἰς δὲ τὴν ἐπαγγελίαν
τοῦ Θεοῦ οὐ διεκρίθη τῇ ἀπιστίᾳ,
ἀλλ' ἐνεδυναμώθη τῇ πίστει.

James i. 6 αἰτείτω δὲ ἐν πίστει
μηδὲν διακρινόμενος· ὁ γὰρ διακρινόμενος ἔοικε κλύδωνι θαλάσσης ἀνεμι-
ζομένῳ καὶ ῥιπιζομένῳ.

Rom. v. 3–5 καυχώμεθα ἐν ταῖς
θλίψεσιν, εἰδότες ὅτι ἡ θλῖψις ὑπομονὴν κατεργάζεται, ἡ δὲ ὑπομονὴ
δοκιμήν, ἡ δὲ δοκιμὴ ἐλπίδα· ἡ
δὲ ἐλπὶς οὐ καταισχύνει, ὅτι ἡ ἀγάπη
τοῦ Θεοῦ ἐκκέχυται.

James i. 2–4 πᾶσαν χαρὰν ἡγήσασθε
ὅταν πειρασμοῖς περιπέσητε ποικίλοις,
γινώσκοντες ὅτι τὸ δοκίμιον ὑμῶν τῆς
πίστεως κατεργάζεται ὑπομονήν. ἡ δὲ
ὑπομονὴ ἔργον τέλειον ἐχέτω, ἵνα ἦτε
τέλειοι.

* The LXX of Deut. xxxii. 35 reads ἐν ἡμέρᾳ ἐκδικήσεως ἀνταποδώσω, ὅταν
σφαλῇ ὁ πούς αὐτῶν.

Rom. vii. 23 βλέπω δὲ ἕτερον νόμον ἐν τοῖς μέλεσί μου, ἀντιστρατευόμενον τῷ νόμῳ τοῦ νοός μου, καὶ αἰχμαλωτίζοντά με ἐν τῷ νόμῳ τῆς ἁμαρτίας τῷ ὄντι ἐν τοῖς μέλεσί μου.

Rom. xiii. 12 ἀποθώμεθα οὖν τὰ ἔργα τοῦ σκότους, ἐνδυσώμεθα δὲ τὰ ὅπλα τοῦ φωτός.

James iv. 1 πόθεν πόλεμοι καὶ πόθεν μάχαι ἐν ὑμῖν; οὐκ ἐντεῦθεν, ἐκ τῶν ἡδονῶν ὑμῶν τῶν στρατευομένων ἐν τοῖς μέλεσιν ὑμῶν;

James i. 21 ἀποθέμενοι πᾶσαν ῥυπαρίαν καὶ περισσείαν κακίας ἐν πραΰτητι δέξασθε τὸν ἔμφυτον λόγον τὸν δυνάμενον σῶσαι τὰς ψυχὰς ὑμῶν.

We may be expressing an excessive scepticism, but these resemblances seem to us hardly close enough to be convincing, and the priority of St. James cannot be proved. The problem of literary indebtedness is always a delicate one; it is very difficult to find a definite objective standpoint; and writers of competence draw exactly opposite conclusions from the same facts. In order to justify our sceptical attitude we may point out that resemblances in phraseology between two Christian writers do not necessarily imply literary connexion. The contrast between ἀκροαταί and ποιηταί was not made by either St. Paul or St. James for the first time; metaphors like θησαυρίζεις, expressions like ἐν ἡμέρᾳ ὀργῆς compared with ἐν ἡμέρᾳ σφαγῆς (both occur in the O.T.), the phrase νόμος ἐλευθερίας might all have independent sources. Nor are there any passages where we find the same order of thought (as in 1 Peter) or the same passage of the O.T. quoted with the same variations—either of which would form stronger evidence. The resemblance is closest in Rom. v. 3–5 = James i. 2–4 and in Rom. vii. 23 = James iv. 1, but these are not sufficient by themselves to establish a case.

Again, if we turn to the polemical passages, we may admit that 'Paul betrays a consciousness that Abraham had been cited as an example of works and endeavours to show that the word λογίζομαι is inconsistent with this.' But the controversy must have been carried on elsewhere than in these writings, and it is equally probable that both alike may be dealing with the problem as it came before them for discussion or as it was inherited from the schools of the Rabbis (see further the note on p. 102). There is, we may add, no marked resemblance in style in the controversial passage further than would be the necessary result of dealing with the same subject-matter. There is nothing decisive to prove obligation on the part of either Epistle to the other or to prove the priority of either. The two Epistles were written in the same small and growing community which had inherited or created a phraseology of its own, and in which certain questions early acquired prominence. It is quite possible that the Epistle of St. James deals with the same controversy as does that to the Romans; it may even possibly be directed against St. Paul's teaching or the teaching of St. Paul's followers; but there is no proof that either Epistle was written with a knowledge of the other. There are no resemblances in style sufficient to prove literary connexion.

One other book of the N.T. may just be mentioned. If the doxology at the end of Jude be compared with that at the end of Romans it is difficult to believe that they are quite independent. It may be that they follow a common form derived from Jewish doxologies, but it is more probable that the concluding verses of the Romans formed a model which was widely adopted in the Christian Church. We certainly seem to find doxologies of the same type as these two in 1 Clem.-Rom. lxiv, lxv. 2 ; *Mart. Polyc.* xx ; it is followed also in Eph. iii. 20. The resemblance in form of the doxologies may be seen by comparing them with one another.

Rom. xvi. 25-27 τῷ δὲ δυναμένῳ ὑμᾶς στηρίξαι ... μόνῳ σοφῷ Θεῷ, διὰ Ἰησοῦ Χριστοῦ, [ᾧ] ἡ δόξα εἰς τοὺς αἰῶνας.

Jude 24, 25 τῷ δὲ δυναμένῳ φυλάξαι ὑμᾶς ἀπταίστους, καὶ στῆσαι ... ἀμώμους ... μόνῳ Θεῷ σωτῆρι ἡμῶν, διὰ Ἰησοῦ Χριστοῦ τοῦ Κυρίου ἡμῶν, δόξα, μεγαλωσύνη, κράτος καὶ ἐξουσία, πρὸ παντὸς τοῦ αἰῶνος καὶ νῦν καὶ εἰς πάντας τοὺς αἰῶνας. ἀμήν.

When we enter the sub-apostolic age the testimony to the use of the Epistle is full and ample. The references to it in Clement of Rome are numerous. We can go further than this, the discussions on πίστις and δικαιοσύνη (see p. 147) show clearly that Clement used this Epistle at any rate as a theological authority. Bishop Lightfoot has well pointed out how he appears as reconciling and combining four different types of Apostolic teaching. The Apostles belong to an older generation, their writings have become subjects of discussion. Clement is already beginning to build up, however inadequately, a Christian theology combining the teaching of the different writers of an earlier period. If we turn to Ignatius' letters what will strike us is that the words and ideas of the Apostle have become incorporated with the mind of the writer. It is not so much that he quotes as that he can never break away from the circle of Apostolic ideas. The books of the N.T. have given him his vocabulary and form the source of his thoughts. Polycarp quotes more freely and more definitely. His Epistle is almost a cento of N.T. passages, and among them are undoubted quotations from the Romans. As the quotations of Polycarp come from Rom., 1 Cor., 2 Cor., Gal., Eph., Phil., 1 Tim., 2 Tim., it is difficult not to believe that he possessed and made use of a collection of the Pauline Epistles. Corroborative evidence of this might be found in the desire he shows to make a collection of the letters of Ignatius. He would be more likely to do this if he already possessed collections of letters; and it is really impossible to maintain that the Ignatian letters were formed into one collection before those of St. Paul had been. Assuming then, as we are entitled to do, that the Apostolic Fathers represent the first quarter of the second century we find the Epistle to the Romans at that time widely read, treated as a standard authority on Apostolic teaching, and taking its place in a collection of Pauline letters.

The following are quotations and reminiscences of the Epistle in Clement of Rome:

Rom. i. 21 ἐσκοτίσθη ἡ ἀσύνετος αὐτῶν καρδία.

Clem. 36 διὰ τούτου ἡ ἀσύνετος καὶ ἐσκοτωμένη διάνοια ἡμῶν ἀναθάλλει εἰς τὸ θαυμαστὸν αὐτοῦ φῶς.
Clem. 51 διὰ τὸ σκληρυνθῆναι αὐτῶν τὰς ἀσυνέτους καρδίας.

Rom. ii. 24 τὸ γὰρ ὄνομα τοῦ Θεοῦ δι' ὑμᾶς βλασφημεῖται ἐν τοῖς ἔθνεσιν, καθὼς γέγραπται.

Clem. 47 ὥστε καὶ βλασφημίας ἐπιφέρεσθαι τῷ ὀνόματι Κυρίου διὰ τὴν ὑμετέραν ἀφροσύνην.

Rom. iv. 7 "Μακάριοι ὧν ἀφέθησαν αἱ ἀνόμιαι καὶ ὧν ἐπεκαλύφθησαν αἱ ἁμαρτίαι· 8 μακάριος ἀνὴρ ᾧ οὐ μὴ λογίσηται Κύριος ἁμαρτίαν." 9 ὁ μακαρισμὸς οὖν οὗτος ἐπὶ τὴν περιτομήν; ἢ καὶ ἐπὶ τὴν ἀκροβυστίαν;

Clem. 50 Μακάριοι ὧν ἀφέθησαν αἱ ἀνομίαι καὶ ὧν ἐπεκαλύφθησαν αἱ ἁμαρτίαι· μακάριος ἀνὴρ ᾧ οὐ μὴ λογίσηται Κύριος ἁμαρτίαν. οὐδέ ἐστιν ἐν τῷ στόματι αὐτοῦ δόλος. οὗτος ὁ μακαρισμὸς ἐγένετο ἐπὶ τοὺς ἐκλελεγμένους ὑπὸ τοῦ Θεοῦ κ.τ.λ.

Rom. vi. 1 τί οὖν ἐροῦμεν; ἐπιμένωμεν τῇ ἁμαρτίᾳ, ἵνα ἡ χάρις πλεονάσῃ; μὴ γένοιτο.

Clem. 33 τί οὖν ποιήσωμεν, ἀδελφοί; ἀργήσωμεν ἀπὸ τῆς ἀγαθοποιΐας καὶ ἐγκαταλείπωμεν τὴν ἀγάπην; μηθαμῶς τοῦτο ἐάσαι ὁ δεσπότης ἐφ' ἡμῖν γε γενηθῆναι.

Rom. i. 29 πεπληρωμένους πάσῃ ἀδικίᾳ, πονηρίᾳ, πλεονεξίᾳ, κακίᾳ, μεστοὺς φθόνου, φόνου, ἔριδος, δόλου, κακοηθείας, ψιθυριστάς. καταλάλους, θεοστυγεῖς, ὑβριστάς, ὑπερηφάνους, ἀλαζόνας, ἐφευρετὰς κακῶν, γονεῦσιν ἀπειθεῖς, ἀσυνέτους, ἀσυνθέτους, ἀστόργους, ἀνελεήμονας· οἵτινες, τὸ δικαίωμα τοῦ Θεοῦ ἐπιγνόντες, ὅτι οἱ τὰ τοιαῦτα πράσσοντες ἄξιοι θανάτου εἰσίν, οὐ μόνον αὐτὰ ποιοῦσιν, ἀλλὰ καὶ συνευδοκοῦσιν τοῖς πράσσουσιν.

Clem. 35 ἀπορρίψαντες ἀφ' ἑαυτῶν πᾶσαν ἀδικίαν καὶ ἀνομίαν, πλεονεξίαν, ἔρεις, κακοηθείας τε καὶ δόλους, ψιθυρισμούς τε καὶ καταλαλιάς, θεοστυγίαν, ὑπερηφανίαν τε καὶ ἀλαζονείαν, κενοδοξίαν τε καὶ ἀφιλοξενίαν. ταῦτα γὰρ οἱ πράσσοντες στυγητοὶ τῷ Θεῷ ὑπάρχουσιν· οὐ μόνον δὲ οἱ πράσσοντες αὐτά, ἀλλὰ καὶ οἱ συνευδοκοῦντες αὐτοῖς.

Rom. ix. 4, 5 ὧν...ἡ λατρεία καὶ αἱ ἐπαγγελίαι, ὧν οἱ πατέρες, καὶ ἐξ ὧν ὁ Χριστὸς τὸ κατὰ σάρκα.

Clem. 32 ἐξ αὐτοῦ γὰρ ἱερεῖς καὶ Λευῖται πάντες οἱ λειτουργοῦντες τῷ θυσιαστηρίῳ τοῦ Θεοῦ· ἐξ αὐτοῦ ὁ Κύριος Ἰησοῦς τὸ κατὰ σάρκα· ἐξ αὐτοῦ βασιλεῖς καὶ ἄρχοντες καὶ ἡγούμενοι κατὰ τὸν Ἰούδαν.

Rom. xiii. 1, 2 πᾶσα ψυχὴ ἐξουσίαις ὑπερεχούσαις ὑποτασσέσθω· οὐ γὰρ ἔστιν ἐξουσία εἰ μὴ ὑπὸ Θεοῦ, αἱ δὲ οὖσαι ὑπὸ Θεοῦ τεταγμέναι εἰσίν. ὥστε ὁ ἀντιτασσόμενος τῇ ἐξουσίᾳ

Clem. 61 σύ, δέσποτα, ἔδωκας τὴν ἐξουσίαν τῆς βασιλείας αὐτοῖς διὰ τοῦ μεγαλοπρεποῦς καὶ ἀνεκδιηγήτου κράτους σου, εἰς τὸ γινώσκοντας ἡμᾶς τὴν ὑπὸ σοῦ αὐτοῖς δεδομένην δόξαν καὶ

τῇ τοῦ Θεοῦ διαταγῇ ἀνθέστηκεν· οἱ
δὲ ἀνθεστηκότες ἑαυτοῖς κρῖμα λή-
ψονται.

τιμὴν ὑποτάσσεσθαι αὐτοῖς, μηδὲν ἐναν-
τιουμένους τῷ θελήματί σου.

References in the letters of Ignatius are the following :

Rom. i. 3 τοῦ γενομένου ἐκ σπέρματος Δαβὶδ κατὰ σάρκα, τοῦ
ὁρισθέντος υἱοῦ Θεοῦ ἐν δυνάμει.

Smyr. 1 ἀληθῶς ὄντα ἐκ γένους
Δαβὶδ κατὰ σάρκα, υἱὸν Θεοῦ
κατὰ θέλημα καὶ δύναμιν.

Rom. ii. 24.

Cf. Trall. 8 (both quote O. T.).

Rom. iii. 27 ποῦ οὖν ἡ καύχησις ;

Eph. 18 ποῦ καύχησις τῶν λεγο-
μένων συνετῶν ;
(Close to a quotation of 1 Cor. i. 20.)

Rom. vi. 4 οὕτω καὶ ἡμεῖς ἐν
καινότητι ζωῆς περιπατήσωμεν.

Eph. 19 Θεοῦ ἀνθρωπίνως φανερου-
μένου εἰς καινότητα ἀϊδίου ζωῆς.

Rom. vi. 5 ; viii. 17, 29.

Mag. 5 δι' οὗ ἐὰν μὴ αὐθαιρέτως
ἔχωμεν τὸ ἀποθανεῖν εἰς τὸ αὐτοῦ
πάθος, τὸ ζῆν αὐτοῦ οὐκ ἔστιν ἐν ἡμῖν.

Trall. 9 κατὰ τὸ ὁμοίωμα ὃς καὶ ἡμᾶς
τοὺς πιστεύοντας αὐτῷ οὕτως ἐγερεῖ ὁ
πατὴρ αὐτοῦ ἐν Χ. Ἰ., οὗ χωρὶς τὸ
ἀληθινὸν ζῆν οὐκ ἔχομεν.

Rom. vi. 17 εἰς ὃν παρεδόθητε
τύπον διδαχῆς.

Mag. 6 εἰς τύπον καὶ διδαχὴν
ἀφθαροίας.

Rom. vii. 6 ὥστε δουλεύειν ἡμᾶς
ἐν καινότητι πνεύματος καὶ οὐ παλαιότητι γράμματος.

Mag. 9 οἱ ἐν παλαιοῖς πράγμασιν
ἀναστραφέντες εἰς καινότητα ἐλπίδος
ἦλθον.

Rom. viii. 11 ὁ ἐγείρας Χ. Ἰ.
ἐκ νεκρῶν.

Trall. 9 ὃς καὶ ἀληθῶς ἠγέρθη ἀπὸ
νεκρῶν, ἐγείραντος αὐτὸν τοῦ
πατρὸς αὐτοῦ.

Rom. ix. 23 σκεύη ἐλέους ἃ προητοίμασεν εἰς δόξαν.

Eph. 9 προητοιμασμένοι εἰς οἰκοδομὴν Θεοῦ πατρός.

Rom. xiv. 17 οὐ γάρ ἐστιν ἡ
βασιλεία τοῦ Θεοῦ βρῶσις καὶ
πόσις.

Trall. 2 οὐ γὰρ βρωμάτων καὶ
ποτῶν εἰσιν διάκονοι.

Rom. xv. 5 τὸ αὐτὸ φρονεῖν ἐν
ἀλλήλοις κατὰ Χ. Ἰ.

Eph. 1 ὃν εὔχομαι κατὰ Ἰ. Χ. ὑμᾶς
ἀγαπᾶν, καὶ πάντας ὑμᾶς αὐτῷ ἐν ὁμοιό-
τητι εἶναι.

The following resemblances occur in the Epistle of Polycarp :

Rom. vi. 13 καὶ τὰ μέλη ὑμῶν
ὅπλα δικαιοσύνης.

Rom. xiii. 12 ἐνδυσώμεθα δὲ
τὰ ὅπλα τοῦ φωτός.

Pol. 4 ὁπλισώμεθα τοῖς ὅπλοις
τῆς δικαιοσύνης.

Rom. xii. 10 τῇ φιλαδελφίᾳ
εἰς ἀλλήλους φιλόστοργοι, τῇ
τιμῇ ἀλλήλους προηγούμενοι.

Pol. 10 *fraternitatis amatores
diligentes invicem,* in veritate sociati,
mansuetudinem Domini *alterutri
praestolantes,* nullum despicientes.

Rom. xiii. 8 ὁ γὰρ ἀγαπῶν τὸν
ἕτερον νόμον πεπλήρωκεν κ.τ.λ.

Pol. 3 ἐὰν γάρ τις τούτων ἐντὸς ᾖ
πεπλήρωκεν ἐντολὴν δικαιοσύνης· ὁ
γὰρ ἔχων ἀγάπην μακράν ἐστιν πάσης
ἁμαρτίας.

g

Rom. xiv. 10 πάντες γὰρ παραστησόμεθα τῷ βήματι τοῦ[1] Θεοῦ
...

12 ἄρα [οὖν] ἕκαστος ἡμῶν περὶ
ἑαυτοῦ λόγον δώσει[2] [τῷ Θεῷ][3].

Pol. 6 καὶ πάντας δεῖ παραστῆναι τῷ βήματι τοῦ Χριστοῦ,
καὶ ἕκαστον ὑπὲρ ἑαυτοῦ λόγον
δοῦναι.

It is hardly worth while to give evidence in detail from later
authors. We find distinct reminiscences of the Romans in Aristides
and in Justin Martyr [4]. Very interesting also is the evidence of the
heretical writers quoted by Hippolytus in the *Refutatio omnium
haeresium*; it would of course be of greater value if we could fix
with certainty the date of the documents he makes use of. We
find quotations from the Epistle in writings ascribed to the Naas-
senes [5], the Valentinians of the Italian school [6], and to Basileides [7].
In the last writer the use made of Rom. v. 13, 14 and viii. 19, 22
is exceedingly curious and interesting.

If we turn to another direction we find interesting evidence of
a kind which has not as yet been fully considered or estimated.
The series of quotations appended from the Testament of the
Twelve Patriarchs can hardly be explained on any other hypothesis than that the writer was closely acquainted with the Epistle
to the Romans. This is not the place to enter into the various
critical questions which have been or ought to be raised concerning that work, but it may be noticed here—

(1) That the writer makes use of a considerable number of
books of the N. T. The resemblances are not confined to the
writings of St. Paul.

(2) That the quotations occur over a very considerable portion
of the book, both in passages omitted in some MSS. and in
passages which might be supposed to belong to older works.

(3) The book is probably older than the time of Tertullian,
while the crude character of the Christology would suggest a considerably earlier date.

Rom. i. 4 τοῦ ὁρισθέντος υἱοῦ Θεοῦ
ἐν δυνάμει κατὰ πνεῦμα ἁγιωσύνης...

Test. Levi. 18 καὶ πνεῦμα ἁγιωσύνης ἔσται ἐπ᾽ αὐτοῖς....

Rom. ii. 13 οὐ γὰρ οἱ ἀκροαταὶ
νόμου δίκαιοι παρὰ τῷ Θεῷ.

Test. Aser. 4 οἱ γὰρ ἀγαθοὶ ἄνδρες
.... δίκαιοί εἰσι παρὰ τῷ Θεῷ.

---

[1] τοῦ Χριστοῦ Western and Syrian.
[2] ἀποδώσει B D F G.
[3] τῷ Θεῷ om. B F G.
[4] Rom. ii. 4 = Dial. 47; Rom. iii. 11–17 = Dial. 27; Rom. iv. 3 = Dial. 23;
Rom. ix. 7 = Dial. 44; Rom. ix. 27–29 = Dial. 32, 55, 64; Rom. x. 18 =
Apol. i. 40; Rom. xi. 2, 3 = Dial. 39.
[5] Hipp. *Ref.* v. 7, pp. 138. 64–140. 76 = Rom. i. 20–26
[6] Ibid. vi. 36, p. 286. 9–10 = Rom. viii. 11.
[7] Ibid. vii. 25, p. 370. 80 = Rom. v. 13, 14; ibid. p. 368. 75 = Rom. viii.
19, 22.

Rom. v. 6 ἔτι γὰρ Χριστὸς ὄντων ἡμῶν ἀσθενῶν ἔτι κατὰ καιρὸν ὑπὲρ ἀσεβῶν ἀπέθανε.

Test. Benj. 3 ἀναμάρτητος ὑπὲρ ἀσεβῶν ἀποθανεῖται.

Rom. vi. 1 ἐπιμένωμεν τῇ ἁμαρτίᾳ.

Test. Levi. 4 οἱ ἄνθρωποι ἀπιστοῦντες ἐπιμενοῦσιν ἐν ταῖς ἀδικίαις.

Rom. vi. 7 ὁ γὰρ ἀποθανὼν δεδικαίωται ἀπὸ τῆς ἁμαρτίας.

Test. Sym. 6 ὅπως δικαιωθῶ ἀπὸ τῆς ἁμαρτίας τῶν ψυχῶν ὑμῶν.

Rom. vii. 8 ἀφορμὴν δὲ λαβοῦσα ἡ ἁμαρτία διὰ τῆς ἐντολῆς κατειργάσατο ἐν ἐμοὶ πᾶσαν ἐπιθυμίαν.

Test. Neph. 8 καὶ δύο ἐντολαί εἰσι· καὶ εἰ μὴ γένωνται ἐν τάξει αὐτῶν, ἁμαρτίαν παρέχουσιν.

Rom. viii. 28 οἴδαμεν δὲ ὅτι τοῖς ἀγαπῶσι τὸν Θεὸν πάντα συνεργεῖ εἰς ἀγαθόν.

Test. Benj. 4 ὁ ἀγαθοποιῶν...τῷ ἀγαπῶντι τὸν Θεὸν συνεργεῖ.

Rom. ix. 21 ἢ οὐκ ἔχει ἐξουσίαν ὁ κεραμεὺς τοῦ πηλοῦ, ἐκ τοῦ αὐτοῦ φυράματος ποιῆσαι ὃ μὲν εἰς τιμὴν σκεῦος, ὃ δὲ εἰς ἀτιμίαν;

Test. Neph. 2 καθὼς γὰρ ὁ κεραμεὺς οἶδε τὸ σκεῦος, πόσον χωρεῖ, καὶ πρὸς αὐτὸν φέρει πηλόν, οὕτω καὶ ὁ Κύριος πρὸς ὁμοίωσιν τοῦ πνεύματος ποιεῖ τὸ σῶμα.

Rom. xii. 1 παραστῆσαι τὰ σώματα ὑμῶν θυσίαν ζῶσαν, ἁγίαν, εὐάρεστον τῷ Θεῷ, τὴν λογικὴν λατρείαν ὑμῶν.

Test. Levi 3 προσφέρουσι δὲ Κυρίῳ ὀσμὴν εὐωδίας λογικὴν καὶ ἀναίμακτον προσφοράν.

Rom. xii. 21 μὴ νικῶ ὑπὸ τοῦ κακοῦ, ἀλλὰ νίκα ἐν τῷ ἀγαθῷ τὸ κακόν.

Test. Benj. 4 οὕτως ὁ ἀγαθοποιῶν νικᾷ τὸ κακόν.

Rom. xiii. 12 ἀποθώμεθα οὖν τὰ ἔργα τοῦ σκότους, ἐνδυσώμεθα δὲ τὰ ὅπλα τοῦ φωτός.

Test. Neph. 2 οὕτως οὐδὲ ἐν σκότει δυνήσεσθε ποιῆσαι ἔργα φωτός.

Rom. xv. 33 ὁ δὲ Θεὸς τῆς εἰρήνης μετὰ πάντων ὑμῶν.

Test. Dan. 5 ἔχοντες τὸν Θεὸν τῆς εἰρήνης.

Rom. xvi. 20 ὁ δὲ Θεὸς τῆς εἰρήνης συντρίψει τὸν Σατανᾶν ὑπὸ τοὺς πόδας ὑμῶν ἐν τάχει.

Test. Aser. 7 καὶ ἐν ἡσυχίᾳ συντρίβων τὴν κεφαλὴν τοῦ δράκοντος δι' ὕδατος.

So far we have had no direct citation from the Epistle by name. Although Clement refers expressly to the First Epistle to the Corinthians, and Ignatius may refer to an Epistle to the Ephesians, neither they nor Polycarp, nor in fact any other writer, expressly mentions Romans. It is with Marcion (*c.* 140) that we obtain our first direct evidence. Romans was one of the ten Epistles he included in his *Apostolicon*, ascribing it directly to St. Paul. Nor have we any reason to think that he originated the idea of making a collection of the Pauline Epistles. The very fact, as Zahn points out, that he gives the same short titles to the Epistles that we find in our oldest MSS. (πρὸς ῥωμαίους) implies that these had formed part of a collection. Such a title would not be sufficient unless the books were included in a collection which had a distinguishing title of its own. In the *Apostolicon* of Marcion the Epistles were arranged in the following order: (1) Gal., (2) 1 Cor., (3) 2 Cor., (4) Rom., (5) 1 Thess., (6) 2 Thess., (7) Laodic. = Ephes., (8) Col., (9) Phil., (10) Philem. The origin of this arrangement we cannot conjecture with any certainty; but it may be noted that the Epistle placed first—the Galatians—is the one on which Marcion primarily rested his case and in which the anti-judaism of St. Paul is most prominent, while the four Epistles of the Captivity are grouped together at the conclusion. Another interesting point is the text of the Epistles used by Marcion. We need not stop to discuss the question whether the charge against Marcion of excising large portions of the Epistles is correct. That he did so is undoubted. In the Romans particularly he omitted chaps. i. 19–ii. 1; iii. 31–iv. 25; ix. 1–33; x. 5–xi. 32; xv.–xvi. Nor again can we doubt that he omitted and altered short passages in order to harmonize the teaching with his own. For instance, in x. 2, 3 he seems to have read ἀγνοοῦντες γὰρ τὸν Θεόν. Both these statements must be admitted. But two further questions remain : Can we in any case arrive at the text of the Epistles used by Marcion, and has Marcion's text influenced the variations of our MSS.? An interesting reading from this point of view is the omission of πρῶτον in i. 16 (see the notes, p. 24). Is this a case where his reading has influenced our MSS., or does he preserve an early variation or even the original text?

We need not pursue the history of the Epistle further. From the time of Irenaeus onwards we have full and complete citations in all the Church writers. The Epistle is recognized as being by St. Paul, is looked upon as canonical[1], and is a groundwork of Christian theology.

One more question remains to be discussed—its place in the collection of St. Paul's Epistles. According to the Muratorian fragment on the Canon the Epistles of St. Paul were early divided into two groups, those to churches and those to individuals; and this division permanently influenced the arrangement in the Canon, accounting of course incidentally for the varying place occupied by the Epistle to the Hebrews. It is with the former group only that we are concerned, and here we find that there is a very marked variation in the order. Speaking roughly the earlier lists all place the Epistle to the Romans at the end of the collection, whilst later lists, as for example the Canon of the received text, place it at the beginning.

For the earlier list our principal evidence is the Muratorian fragment on the Canon : *cum ipse beatus apostolus Paulus, sequens prodecessoris sui Iohannis ordinem, nonnisi nominatim septem ecclesiis scribat ordine tali : ad Corinthios (prima), ad Ephesios (secunda), ad Philippenses (tertia), ad Colossenses (quarta), ad Galatas (quinta), ad Thessalonicenses (sexta), ad Romanos (septima).* Nor does this

---

[1] On Harnack's theory that the Pauline Epistles had at the close of the second century less canonical authority than the Gospels, see Sanday, *Bampton Lectures*, pp. 20, 66.

stand alone. The same place apparently was occupied by Romans in the collection used by Tertullian, probably in that of Cyprian. It is suggested that it influenced the order of Marcion, who perhaps found in his copy of the Epistles Corinthians standing first, while the position of Romans at the end may be implied in a passage of Origen.

The later order (Rom., Cor., Gal., Eph., Phil., Col., Thess.) is that of all writers from the fourth century onwards, and, with the exception of changes caused by the insertion of the Epistle to the Hebrews, and of certain small variations which do not affect the point under discussion, of all Greek MSS., and of all MSS. of Versions. This widespread testimony implies an early date. But the arrangement is clearly not traditional. It is roughly based on the length of the Epistles, the Romans coming first as being the longer.

The origin of the early order is by no means clear. Zahn's conjecture, that it arose from the fact that the collection of Pauline Epistles was first made at Corinth, is ingenious but not conclusive, while Clem. Rom. 47, which he cites in support of his theory, will hardly prove as much as he wishes [1].

To sum up briefly. During the first century the Epistle to the Romans was known and used in Rome and perhaps elsewhere. During the first quarter of the second century we find it forming part of a collection of Pauline Epistles used by the principal Church writers of that time in Antioch, in Rome, in Smyrna, probably also in Corinth. By the middle of that century it had been included in an abbreviated form in Marcion's *Apostolicon*; by the end it appears to be definitely accepted as canonical.

§ 9. INTEGRITY OF THE EPISTLE.

The survey which has been given of the literary history of the Epistle to the Romans makes it perfectly clear that the external evidence in favour of its early date is not only relatively but absolutely very strong. Setting aside doubtful quotations, almost every Christian writer of the early part of the second century makes use of it; it was contained in Marcion's canon; and when Christian literature becomes extensive, the quotations are almost numerous enough to enable us to reconstruct the whole Epistle. So strong is this evidence and so clear are the internal marks of authenticity that the Epistle (with the exception of the last two chapters of which we shall speak presently) has been almost universally admitted to be a genuine work of St. Paul. It was accepted as such by Baur, and in consequence by all members of the Tübingen school; it is accepted at the present day by critics of every variety of opinion, by Hilgenfeld, Holtzmann, Weizsäcker, Lipsius, Harnack, as definitely as by those who are usually classed as conservative.

[1] On this subject see Zahn, *Geschichte*, &c., ii. p. 344.

To this general acceptance there have been few exceptions. The earliest writer who denied the genuineness of the Epistle appears to have been the Englishman Evanson (1792). The arguments on which he relied are mainly historical. The Epistle implies the existence of a Church in Rome, but we know from the Acts that no such Church existed. Equally impossible is it that St. Paul should have known such a number of persons in Rome, or that Aquila and Priscilla should have been there at this time. He interprets xvi. 13 literally, and asks why the aged mother of the Apostle should have wandered to Rome. He thinks that xi. 12, 15, 21, 22 must have been written after the fall of Jerusalem[1]. The same thesis was maintained by Bruno Bauer[2], and has been revived at the present day by certain Dutch and Swiss theologians, notably Loman and Steck.

Loman (1882) denied the historical reality of Christ, and considered that all the Pauline Epistles dated from the second century. Christianity itself was the embodiment of certain Jewish ideas. St. Paul was a real person who lived at the time usually ascribed to him, but he did not write the Epistles which bear his name. That he should have done so at such an early period in the history of Christianity would demand a miracle to account for its history; a statement which we need not trouble ourselves to refute. Loman's arguments appear to be the silence of the Acts, and in the case of the Romans the inconsistency of the various sections with one another; the differences of opinion which had arisen with regard to the composition of the Roman Church prove (he argues) that there is no clear historical situation implied[3]. Steck (1888) has devoted himself primarily to the Epistle to the Galatians which he condemns as inconsistent with the Acts of the Apostles, and as dependent upon the other leading Epistles, but he incidentally examines these also. All alike he puts in the second century, arranging them in the following order:—Romans, 1 Corinthians, 2 Corinthians, Galatians. All alike are he says built up under the influence of Jewish and Heathen writers, and he finds passages in the Romans borrowed from Philo, Seneca, and Jewish Apocryphal works to which he assigns a late date—such as the *Assumptio Mosis* and 4 Ezra[4]. Akin to these theories which deny completely the genuineness of the Epistle, are similar ones also having their origin for the most part in Holland, which find large interpolations in our present text and profess to distinguish different recensions. Earliest of these was Weisse (1867), who in addition to certain more reasonable theories with regard to the concluding chapters, professed to be able to distinguish by the evidence of style the genuine from the interpolated portions of the Epistle[5]. His example has been followed with greater indiscreetness by Pierson and Naber (1886), Michelsen (1886), Voelter (1889, 90), Van Manen (1891).

Pierson and Naber[6] basing their theory on some slight allusions in Josephus, consider that there existed about the beginning of the Christian era a school of elevated Jewish thinkers, who produced a large number of apparently fragmentary works distinguished by their lofty religious tone. These were made use of by a certain Paulus Episcopus, a Christian who incorporated them

[1] Evanson (Edward), *The Dissonance of the four generally received Evangelists examined*, Ed. 1, 1792, pp. 257–261; Ed. 2, 1805, pp. 306–312.

[2] Bruno Bauer, *Kritik der paul. Briefe*, 1852. *Christus und die Cäsaren*, p. 372.

[3] Loman (A. D.), *Quaestiones Paulinae, Theologisch Tijdschrift*, 1882, 1883, 1886.

[4] Steck (Rudolf), *Der Galaterbrief nach seiner Echtheit untersucht*. Berlin, 1888.

[5] Weisse (C. H.), *Beiträge zur Kritik der Paulinischen Briefe an die Galater, Römer, Philipper und Kolosser*. Leipzig, 1867.

[6] *Verisimilia, Laceram conditionem Novi Testamenti exhibentia*. A. Pierson, et S. A. Naber, Amstelodami, 1886.

in letters which he wrote in order to make up for his own poverty of religious and philosophical ideas. An examination of their treatment of a single chapter may be appended. The basis of ch. vi is a Jewish fragment (*admodum memorabile*) which extends from ver. 3 to ver. 11. This fragment Paulus Episcopus treated in his usual manner. He begins with the foolish question of ver. 2 which shows that he does not understand the argument that follows. He added interpolations in ver. 4. *Itidem odoramur manum eius* ver. 5. If we omit τῷ ὁμοιώματι in ver. 5 the difficulty in it vanishes. Ver. 8 again is feeble and therefore was the work of Paulus Episcopus: *non enim credimus nos esse victuros, sed novimus nos vivere* (ver. 11). vv. 11-23 with the exception apparently of ver. 14, 15 which have been misplaced, are the work of this interpolator who spoiled the Jewish fragment, and in these verses adapts what has preceded to the uses of the Church[1]. It will probably not be thought necessary to pursue this subject further.

Michelsen[2] basing his theory to a certain extent on the phenomena of the last two chapters considered that towards the end of the second century three recensions of the Epistle were in existence. The Eastern containing ch. i-xvi. 24; the Western ch. i-xiv and xvi. 25-27; the Marcionite ch. i-xiv. The redactor who put together these recensions was however also responsible for a considerable number of interpolations which Michelsen undertakes to distinguish. Völter's[3] theory is more elaborate. The original Epistle according to him contained the following portions of the Epistle. i. 1a, 7; 5, 6; 8-17; v. and vi. (except v. 13, 14, 20; vi. 14, 15); xii, xiii; xv. 14-32; xvi. 21-23. This bears all the marks of originality; its Christology is primitive, free from any theory of pre-existence or of two natures. To the first interpolator we owe i. 18; iii. 20 (except ii. 14, 15); viii. 1, 3-39; i. 1b-4. Here the Christology is different; Christ is the pre-existent Son of God. To the second interpolator we owe iii. 21—iv. 25; v. 13, 14, 20; vi. 14, 15; vii. 1-6; ix. x; xiv. 1—xv. 6. This writer who worked about the year 70 was a determined Antinomian, who could not see anything but evil in the Law. A third interpolator is responsible for vii. 7-25; viii. 2; a fourth for xi; ii. 14, 15; xv. 7-13; a fifth for xvi. 1-20; a sixth for xvi. 24; a seventh for xvi. 25-27.

Van Manen[4] is distinguished for his vigorous attacks on his predecessors; and for basing his own theory of interpolations on a reconstruction of the Marcionite text which he holds to be original.

It has been somewhat tedious work enumerating these theories, which will seem probably to most readers hardly worth while repeating; so subjective and arbitrary is the whole criticism. The only conclusion that we can arrive at is that if early Christian documents have been systematically tampered with in a manner which would justify any one of these theories, then the study of Christian history would be futile. There is no criterion of style or of language which enables us to distinguish a document from the interpolations, and we should be compelled to make use of a number of writings which we could not either trust or criticize. If the documents are not trustworthy, neither is our criticism.

But such a feeling of distrust is not necessary, and it may be worth while to conclude this subject by pointing out certain reasons which enable us to feel confident in most at any rate of the documents of early Christianity.

---

[1] *Op. cit.*, pp. 139-143.

[2] Michelsen (J. H. A.), *Theologisch Tijdschrift*, 1886, pp. 372 ff, 473 ff.; 1887, p. 163 ff.

[3] Voelter (Daniel), *Theologisch Tijdschrift*, 1889, p. 265 ff.; and *Die Composition der paul. Hauptbriefe, I. Der Römer- und Galaterbrief*, 1890.

[4] Van Manen (W. C.), *Theologisch Tijdschrift*, 1887. *Marcion's Brief van Paulus aan de Galatiës*, pp. 382-404, 451-533; and *Paulus II, De brief aan de Romeinen*. Leiden, 1891.

It has been pointed out that interpolation theories are not as absurd as they might *prima facie* be held to be, for we have instances of the process actually taking place. The obvious examples are the Ignatian letters. But these are not solitary, almost the whole of the Apocryphal literature has undergone the same process; so have the Acts of the Saints; so has the *Didache* for example when included in the Apostolic Constitutions. Nor are we without evidence of interpolations in the N. T.; the phenomenon of the Western text presents exactly the same characteristics. May we not then expect the same to have happened in other cases where we have little or no information? Now in dealing with a document which has come down to us in a single MS. or version, or on any slight traditional evidence this possibility must always be considered, and it is necessary to be cautious in arguing from a single passage in a text which may have been interpolated. Those who doubted the genuineness of the Armenian fragment of Aristides for example, on the grounds that it contained the word Theotokos, have been proved to be wrong, for that word as was suspected by many has now been shown to have been interpolated. But in the case of the N. T. we have so many authorities going back independently to such an early period, that it is most improbable that any important variation in the text could escape our knowledge. The different lines of text in St. Paul's Epistles must have separated as early as the beginning of the second century; and we shall see shortly that one displacement in the text, which must have been early, and may have been very early, has influenced almost all subsequent documents. The number, the variety, and the early character of the texts preserved to us in MSS., Versions, and Fathers, is a guarantee that a text formed on critical methods represents within very narrow limits the work as it left its author's hands.

A second line of argument which is used in favour of interpolation theories is the difficulty and obscurity of some passages. No doubt there are passages which are difficult; but it is surely very gratuitous to imagine that everything which is genuine is easy. The whole tendency of textual criticism is to prove that it is the custom of 'redactors' or 'correctors' or 'interpolators' to produce a text which is always superficially at any rate more easy than the genuine text. But on the other side, although the style of St. Paul is certainly not always perfectly smooth; although he certainly is liable to be carried away by a side issue, to change the order of his thoughts, to leap over intermediate steps in his argument, yet no serious commentators of whatever school would doubt that there is a strong sustained argument running through the whole Epistle. The possibility of the commentaries which have been written proves conclusively the improbability of theories implying a wide element of interpolation. But in the case of St. Paul we may go further. Even where there is a break in the argument, there is almost always a verbal connexion. When St. Paul passes for a time to a side issue there is a subtle connexion in thought as in words which would certainly escape an interpolator's observation. This has been pointed out in the notes on xi. 10; xv. 20, where the question of interpolation has been carefully examined; and if any one will take the trouble to go carefully through the end of ch. v and the beginning of ch. vi, he will see how each sentence leads on to the next. For instance, the first part of v. 20, which is omitted by some of these critics, leads on immediately to the second (πλεονάσῃ . . . ἐπλεόνασεν), that suggests ὑπερεπερίσσευσεν, then comes πλεονάσῃ in vi. 1; but the connexion of sin and death clearly suggests the words of ver. 2 and the argument that follows. The same process may be worked out through the whole Epistle. For the most part there is a clear and definite argument, and even where the logical continuity is broken there is always a connexion either in thought or words. The Epistles of St. Paul present for the most part a definite and compact literary unit.

If to these arguments we add the external evidence which is given in detail above, we may feel reasonably confident that the historical conditions under which the Epistle has come down to us make the theories of this new school of critics untenable [1].

We have laid great stress on the complete absence of any textual justifications for any of the theories which have been so far noticed. This absence is made all the more striking by the existence of certain variations in the text and certain facts reported on tradition with regard to the last two chapters of the Epistle. These facts are somewhat complex and to a certain extent conflicting, and a careful examination of them and of the theories suggested to explain them is necessary [2].

It will be convenient first of all to enumerate these facts:

(1) The words ἐν Ῥώμῃ in i. 7 and 15 are omitted by the bilingual MS. G both in the Greek and Latin text (F is here defective). Moreover the cursive 47 adds in the margin of ver. 7 τὸ ἐν Ῥώμῃ, οὔτε ἐν τῇ ἐξηγήσει οὔτε ἐν τῷ ῥητῷ μνημονεύει. Bp. Lightfoot attempted to find corroborative evidence for this reading in Origen, in the writer cited as Ambrosiaster, and in the reading of D ἐν ἀγάπῃ for ἀγαπητοῖς. That he is wrong in doing so seems to be shown by Dr. Hort; but it may be doubtful if the latter is correct in his attempt to explain away the variation. The evidence is slight, but it is hardly likely that it arose simply through transcriptional error. If it occurred only in one place this might be sufficient; if it occurred only in one MS. we might ascribe it to the delinquencies of a single scribe; as it is, we must accept it as an existing variation supported by slight evidence, but evidence sufficiently good to demand an explanation.

(2) There is considerable variation in existing MSS. concerning the place of the final doxology (xvi. 25-27).

a. In ℵ B C D E minusc. pauc. codd. ap. Orig.-lat., d e f Vulg. Pesh. Boh. Aeth., Orig.-lat. Ambrstr. Pelagius it occurs at the end of chap. xvi. and there only.

b. In L minusc. plus quam 200, codd. ap. Orig.-lat., Harcl., Chrys. Theodrt. Jo.-Damasc. it occurs at the end of chap. xiv and there only.

c. In A P 5. 17 Arm. codd. it is inserted in both places.

d. In Fᵍʳ. G codd. ap. Hieron. (in Eph. iii. 5), g, Marcion (vide infra) it is entirely omitted. It may be noted that G leaves a blank space at the end of chap. xiv, and that f is taken direct from the Vulgate, a space being left in F in the Greek corresponding to these verses. Indirectly D and Sedulius also attest the omission by placing the Benediction after ver. 24, a transposition which would be made (see below) owing to that verse being in these copies at the end of the Epistle.

In reviewing this evidence it becomes clear (i) that the weight of good authority is in favour of placing this doxology at the end of the Epistle, and there only. (ii) That the variation in position—a variation which must be explained—is early, probably earlier than the time of Origen, although we can never have complete confidence in Rufinus' translation. (iii) That the evidence for complete omission goes back to Marcion, and that very probably his excision of the words may have influenced the omission in Western authorities.

[1] The English reader will find a very full account of this Dutch school of critics in Knowling, The Witness of the Epistles, pp. 133-243. A very careful compilation of the results arrived at is given by Dr. Carl Clemen, Die Einheitlichkeit der Paulinischen Briefe. To both these works we must express our obligations, and to them we must refer any who wish for further information.

[2] The leading discussion on the last two chapters of the Romans is contained in three papers, two by Bp. Lightfoot, and one by Dr. Hort first published in the Journal of Philology, vols. ii, iii, and since reprinted in Lightfoot, Biblical Essays, pp. 287-374.

(3) There is very considerable evidence that Marcion omitted the whole of the last two chapters.

a. Origen (*int. Ruf.*) x. 43, vol. vii, p. 453, ed. Lomm. writes: *Caput hoc Marcion, a quo Scripturae Evangelicae atque Apostolicae interpolatae sunt, de hac epistola penitus abstulit ; et non solum hoc, sed et ab eo loco, ubi scriptum est:* omne autem quod non est ex fide, peccatum est : *usque ad finem cuncta dissecuit. In aliis vero exemplaribus, id est, in his quae non sunt a Marcione temerata, hoc ipsum caput diverse positum invenimus, in nonnullis etenim codicibus post eum locum, quem supra diximus hoc est:* omne autem quod non est ex fide, peccatum est: *statim coherens habetur:* ei autem, qui penitus est vos confirmare. *Alii vero codices in fine id, ut nunc est positum, continent.* This extract is quite precise, nor is the attempt made by Hort to emend it at all successful. He reads *in* for *ab*, having for this the support of a Paris MS., and then emends *hoc* into *hic* ; reading *et non solum hic sed et in eo loco*, &c., and translating 'and not only here but also,' at xiv. 23 'he cut out everything quite to the end.' He applies the words to the Doxology alone. The changes in the text are slight and might be justified, but with this change the words that follow become quite meaningless : *usque ad finem cuncta dissecuit* can only apply to the whole of the two chapters. If Origen meant the doxology alone they would be quite pointless.

b. But we have other evidence for Marcion's text. Tertullian, *Adv. Marc.* v. 14, quoting the words *tribunal Christi* (xiv. 10), states that they occur *in clausula* of the Epistle. The argument is not conclusive but the words probably imply that in Marcion's copy of the Epistle, if not in all those known to Tertullian, the last two chapters were omitted.

These two witnesses make it almost certain that Marcion omitted not only the doxology but the whole of the last two chapters.

(4) Some further evidence has been brought forward suggesting that an edition of the Epistle was in circulation which omitted the last two chapters.

a. It is pointed out that Tertullian, Marcion, Irenaeus, and probably Cyprian never quote from these last two chapters. The argument however is of little value, because the same may be said of 1 Cor. xvi. The chapters were not quoted because there was little or nothing in them to quote.

b. An argument of greater weight is found in certain systems of capitulations in MSS. of the Vulgate. In Codex Amiatinus the table of contents gives fifty-one sections, and the fiftieth section is described thus: *De periculo contristante fratrem suum esca sua, et quod non sit regnum Dei esca et potus sed iustitia et pax et gaudium in Spiritu Sancto ;* this is followed by the fifty-first and last section, which is described as *De mysterio Domini ante passionem in silentio habito, post passionem vero ipsius revelato.* The obvious deduction is that this system was drawn up for a copy which omitted the greater part at any rate of chaps. xv and xvi. This system appears to have prevailed very widely. In the Codex Fuldensis there are given in the table of contents fifty-one sections : of these the first twenty-three include the whole Epistle up to the end of chap. xiv, the last sentence being headed *Quod fideles Dei non debeant invicem iudicare cum unusquisque secundum regulas mandatorum ipse se debeat divino iudicio praeparare ut ante tribunal Dei sine confusione possit operum suorum praestare rationem.* Then follow the last twenty-eight sections of the Amiatine system, beginning with the twenty-fourth at ix. 1. Hence chaps. ix–xiv are described twice. The scribe seems to have had before him an otherwise unrecorded system which only embraced fourteen chapters, and then added the remainder from where he could get them in order to make up what he felt to be the right number of fifty-one.

Both these systems seem to exclude the last two chapters, whatever reason we may give for the phenomenon.

(5) Lastly, some critics have discovered a certain amount of significance in two other points,

a. The prayer at the end of chap. xv is supposed to represent, either with or without the ἀμήν (which is omitted in some MSS., probably incorrectly), a conclusion of the Epistle. As a matter of fact the formula does not represent any known form of ending, and may be paralleled from places in the body of the Epistle.

b. The two conclusions xvi. 20 and 24 of the T R are supposed to represent endings to two different recensions of the Epistle. But as will be seen by referring to the note on the passage, this is based upon a misreading. The reading of the T R is a late conflation of the two older forms of the text. The benediction stood originally at ver. 20 and only there, the verses that followed being a sort of postscript. Certain MSS. which were without the doxology (see above) moved it to their end of the Epistle after ver. 23, while certain others placed it after ver. 27. The double benediction of the T R arose by the ordinary process of conflation. The significance of this in corroborating the existence of an early text which omitted the doxology has been pointed out; otherwise these verses will not support the deductions made from them by Renan, Gifford, and others.

The above, stated as shortly as possible, are the diplomatic facts which demand explanation. Already in the seventeenth century some at any rate had attracted notice, and Semler (1769), Griesbach (1777) and others developed elaborate theories to account for them. To attempt to enumerate all the different views would be beside our purpose: it will be more convenient to confine ourselves to certain typical illustrations.

1. An hypothesis which would account for most (although not all) of the facts stated would be to suppose that the last two chapters were not genuine. This opinion was held by Baur[1], although, as was usual with him, on purely *a priori* grounds, and with an only incidental reference to the MS. evidence which might have been the strongest support of his theory. The main motive which induced him to excise them was the expression in xv. 8 that Christ was made 'a minister of circumcision,' which is inconsistent with his view of St. Paul's doctrine; and he supported his contention by a vigorous examination of the style and contents of these two chapters. His arguments have been noticed (so far as seemed necessary) in the commentary. But the consensus of a large number of critics in condemning the result may excuse our pursuing them in further detail. Doctrinally his views were only consistent with a one-sided theory of the Pauline position and teaching, and if that theory is given up then his arguments become untenable. As regards his literary criticism the opinion of Renan may be accepted: 'On est surpris qu'un critique aussi habile que Baur se soit contenté d'une solution aussi grossière. Pourquoi un faussaire aurait-il inventé de si insignificants détails? Pourquoi aurait-il ajouté à l'ouvrage sacré une liste de noms propres[2]?'.

But we are not without strong positive arguments in favour of the genuineness of at any rate the fifteenth chapter. In the first place a careful examination of the first thirteen verses shows conclusively that they are closely connected with the previous chapter. The break after xiv. 23 is purely arbitrary, and the passage that follows to the end of ver. 6 is merely a conclusion of the previous argument, without which the former chapter is incomplete, and which it is inconceivable that an interpolator could have either been able or desired to insert; while in vv. 7-13 the Apostle connects the special subject of which he has been treating with the general condition of the Church, and supports his main contention by a series of texts drawn from the O. T. Both in the appeal to Scripture and in the introduction of broad and general principles this conclusion may be exactly paralleled by the custom of St. Paul elsewhere in the Epistle. No theory therefore can be accepted which does not

---

[1] *Theologische Zeitung*, 1836, pp. 97, 144. *Paulus*, 1866, pp. 393 ff.

[2] *St. Paul*, p. lxxi, quoted by Lightfoot, *Biblical Essays*, p. 290.

recognize that xiv and xv. 13 form a single paragraph which must not be split up.

But further than this the remainder of chap. xv shows every sign of being a genuine work of the Apostle. The argument of Paley based upon the collection for the poor Christians at Jerusalem is in this case almost demonstrative (see p. xxxvi). The reference to the Apostle's intention of visiting Spain, to the circumstances in which he is placed, the dangers he is expecting, his hope of visiting Rome fulfilled in such a very different manner, are all inconsistent with spuriousness; while most readers will feel in the personal touches, in the combination of boldness in asserting his mission with consideration for the feelings of his readers, in the strong and deep emotions which are occasionally allowed to come to the surface, all the most characteristic marks of the Apostle's writing.

Baur's views were followed by Schwegler, Holsten, Zeller, and others, but have been rejected by Mangold, Hilgenfeld, Pfleiderer, Weizsäcker, and Lipsius. A modified form is put forward by Lucht [1], who considers that parts are genuine and part spurious: in fact he applies the interpolation theory to these two chapters (being followed to a slight extent by Lipsius). Against any such theory the arguments are conclusive. It has all the disadvantages of the broader theory and does not either solve the problem suggested by the manuscript evidence or receive support from it. For the rejection of the last two chapters as a whole there is some support, as we have seen; for believing that they contain interpolations (except in a form to be considered immediately) there is no external evidence. There is no greater need for suspecting interpolations in chap. xv than in chap. xiv.

2. We may dismiss then all such theories as imply the spuriousness of the last two chapters and may pass on to a second group which explains the phenomena of the MSS. by supposing that our Epistle has grown up through the combination of different letters or parts of letters either all addressed to the Roman Church, or addressed partly to the Roman Church, partly elsewhere. An elaborate and typical theory of this sort, and one which has the merit of explaining all the facts, is that of Renan [2]. He supposes that the so-called Epistle to the Romans was a circular letter and that it existed in four different forms:

(i) A letter to the Romans. This contained chap. i–xi and chap. xv.

(ii) A letter to the Ephesians. Chap. i–xiv and xvi. 1–20.

(iii) A letter to the Thessalonians. Chap. i–xiv and xvi. 21–24.

(iv) A letter to an unknown church. Chap. i–xiv and xvi. 25–27.

In the last three letters there would of course be some modifications in chap. i, of which we have a reminiscence in the variations of the MS. G.

This theory is supported by the following amongst other arguments:

(i) We know, as in the case of the Epistle to the Ephesians, that St. Paul wrote circular letters. (ii) The Epistle as we have it has four endings, xv. 33, xvi. 20, 24, 25–27. Each of these really represented the ending of a separate Epistle. (iii) There are strong internal grounds for believing that xvi. 1–20 was addressed to the Ephesian Church. (iv) The Macedonian names occurring in xvi. 21–24 suggest that these verses were addressed to a Macedonian church. (v) This explains how it came to be that such an elaborate letter was sent to a church of which St. Paul had such little knowledge as that of Rome.

This theory has one advantage, that it accounts for all the facts; but there are two arguments against it which are absolutely conclusive. One is that there are not four endings in the Epistle at all; xv. 33 is not like any of the

---

[1] Lucht, *Über die beiden letzten Capitel des Römerbriefs,* 1871.

[2] Renan, *St. Paul,* pp. lxiii ff. This theory is examined at great length by Bp. Lightfoot, *op. cit.* pp. 293 ff.

endings of St. Paul's Epistles; while, as is shown above, the origin of the duplicate benediction, xvi. 20 and 24, must be explained on purely textual grounds. If Renan's theory had been correct then we should not have both benedictions in the late MSS. but in the earlier. As it is, it is clear that the duplication simply arose from conflation. A second argument, in our opinion equally conclusive against this theory, is that it separates chap. xiv from the first thirteen verses of chap. xv. The arguments on this subject need not be repeated, but it may be pointed out that they are as conclusive against Renan's hypothesis as against that of Baur.

3. Renan's theory has not received acceptance, but there is one portion of it which has been more generally held than any other with regard to these final chapters; that namely which considers that the list of names in chap. xvi belongs to a letter addressed to Ephesus and not to one addressed to Rome. This view, first put forward by Schulz (1829), has been adopted by Ewald, Mangold, Laurent, Hitzig, Reuss, Ritschl, Lucht, Holsten, Lipsius, Krenkel, Kneucker, Weiss, Weizsäcker, Farrar. It has two forms; some hold ver. 1, 2 to belong to the Romans, others consider them also part of the Ephesian letter. Nor is it quite certain where the Ephesian fragment ends. Some consider that it includes vv. 17-21, others make it stop at ver. 16.

The arguments in favour of this view are as follows: 1. It is pointed out that it is hardly likely that St. Paul should have been acquainted with such a large number of persons in a church like that of Rome which he had never visited, and that this feeling is corroborated by the number of personal details that he adds; references to companions in captivity, to relations, to fellow-labourers. All these allusions are easily explicable on the theory that the Epistle is addressed to the Ephesian Church, but not if it be addressed to the Roman. 2. This opinion is corroborated, it is said, by an examination of the list itself. Aquila and Priscilla and the church that is in their house are mentioned shortly before this date as being at Ephesus, and shortly afterwards they are again mentioned as being in the same city (1 Cor. xvi. 19; 2 Tim. iv. 19). The very next name Epaenetus is clearly described as a native of the province of Asia. Of the others many are Jewish, many Greek, and it is more likely that they should be natives of Ephesus than natives of Rome. 3. That the warning against false teachers is quite inconsistent with the whole tenor of the letter, which elsewhere never refers to false teachers as being at work in Rome.

In examining this hypothesis we must notice at once that it does not in any way help us to solve the textual difficulties, and receives no assistance from them. The problems of the concluding doxology and of the omission of the last two chapters remain as they were. It is only if we insert a benediction both at ver. 20 and at ver. 24 that we get any assistance. In that case we might explain the duplicate benediction by supposing that the first was the conclusion of the Ephesian letter, the second the conclusion of the Roman. As we have seen, the textual phenomena do not support this view. The theory therefore must be examined on its own merits, and the burden of proof is thrown on the opponents of the Roman destination of the Epistle, for as has been shown the only critical basis we can start from, in discussing St. Paul's Epistles, is that they have come down to us substantially in the form in which they were written unless very strong evidence is brought forward to the contrary.

But this evidence cannot be called very strong. It is admitted by Weiss and Mangold, for instance, that the *a priori* arguments against St. Paul's acquaintance with some twenty-four persons in the Roman community are of slight weight. Christianity was preached amongst just that portion of the population of the Empire which would be most nomadic in character. It is admitted again that it would be natural that, in writing to a strange church, St. Paul should lay special stress on all those with whom he was acquainted or of whom he had heard, in order that he might thus commend himself to them. Again, when we come to examine the names, we find that those actually connected with Ephesus are only three, and of these persons two are known to have originally come from Rome, while the third alone can hardly be considered sufficient support for this theory. When again we come to examine the warning against heretics, we find that after all it is perfectly consistent with the body of the Epistle. If we conceive it to be a warning against false teachers whom St. Paul fears may come but who have not yet done so, it exactly suits the situation, and helps to explain the motives he had in writing the Epistle. He definitely states that he is only warning them that they may be wise if occasion arise.

The arguments against these verses are not strong. What is the value of the definite evidence in their favour? This is of two classes. (i) The archaeological evidence for connecting the names in the Epistle with Rome. (ii) The archaeological and literary evidence for connecting any of the persons mentioned here with the Roman Church.

(i) In his commentary on the Philippians, starting from the text Phil. iv. 22 ἀσπάζονται ὑμᾶς ... μάλιστα οἱ ἐκ τοῦ Καίσαρος οἰκίας, Bp. Lightfoot proceeds to examine the list of names in Rom. xvi in the light of Roman inscriptions. We happen to have preserved to us almost completely the funereal inscriptions of certain *columbaria* in which were deposited the ashes of members of the imperial household. Some of these date a little earlier than the Epistle to the Romans, some of them are almost contemporary. Besides these we have a large number of inscriptions containing names of freedmen and others belonging to the imperial household. Now examples of almost every name in Rom. xvi. 3-16 may be found amongst these, and the publication of the sixth volume of the *Corpus* of Latin Inscriptions has enabled us to add to the instances quoted. Practically every name may be illustrated in Rome, and almost every name in the Inscriptions of the household, although some of them are uncommon.

Now what does this prove? It does not prove of course that these are the persons to whom the Epistle was written; nor does it give overwhelming evidence that the names are Roman. It shows that such a combination of names was possible in Rome: but it shows something more than this. Mangold asks what is the value of this investigation as the same names are found outside Rome? The answer is that for the most part they are very rare. Lipsius makes various attempts to illustrate the names from Asiatic inscriptions, but not very successfully; nor does Mangold help by showing that the two common names Narcissus and Hermas may be paralleled elsewhere. We have attempted to institute some comparison, but it is not very easy and will not be until we have more satisfactory collections of Greek inscriptions. If we take the Greek *Corpus* we shall find that in the inscriptions of Ephesus only three names out of the twenty-four in this list occur; if we extend our survey to the province of Asia we shall find only twelve. Now what this comparison suggests is that such a combination of names—Greek, Jewish, and Latin—could as a matter of fact only be found in the mixed population which formed the lower and middle classes of Rome. This evidence is not conclusive, but it shows that there is no *a priori* improbability in the names being Roman, and that it would be difficult anywhere else to illustrate such an heterogeneous collection.

To this we may add the further evidence afforded by the explanation given by Bishop Lightfoot and repeated in the notes, of the households of Narcissus and Aristobulus: evidence again only corroborative but yet of some weight.

(ii) The more direct archaeological evidence is that for connecting the names of Prisca, Amplias, Nereus, and Apelles definitely with the early history of Roman Christianity. These points have been discussed sufficiently in the notes, and it is only necessary to say here that it would be an excess of scepticism to look upon such evidence as worthless, although it might not weigh much if there were strong evidence on the other side.

To sum up then. There is no external evidence against this section, nor does the exclusion of it from the Roman letter help in any way to solve the problems presented by the text. The arguments against the Roman destination are purely *a priori*. They can therefore have little value. On being examined they were found not to be valid ; while evidence not conclusive but considerable has been brought forward in favour of the Roman destination. For these reasons we have used the sixteenth chapter without hesitation in writing an account of the Roman Church, and any success we have had in the drawing of the picture which we have been able to present must be allowed to weigh in the evidence.

4. Reiche (in 1833) suggested that the doxology was not genuine, and his opinion has been largely followed, combined in some cases with theories as to the omission of other parts, in some cases not. It is well known that passages which did not originally form part of the text are inserted in different places in different texts ; for instance, the *pericope adulterae* is found in more than one place. It would still be difficult to find a reason for the insertion of the doxology in the particular place at the end of chap. xiv, but at the same time the theory that it is not genuine will account for its omission altogether in some MSS. and its insertion in different places in others. We ask then what further evidence there is for this omission, and are confronted with a large number of arguments which inform us that it is clearly unpauline because it harmonizes in style, in phraseology, and in subject-matter with non-pauline Epistles—that to the Ephesians and the Pastoral Epistles. This argument must tell in different ways to different critics. It will be very strong, if not conclusive, to those who consider that these Epistles are not Pauline. To those however who accept them as genuine these arguments will rather confirm their belief in the Pauline authorship.

5. But there is an alternative hypothesis which may demand more careful consideration from us, that although it comes from St. Paul it belongs to rather a later period in his life. It is this consideration amongst others which forms the basis of the theory put forward by Dr. Lightfoot. He considers that the original Epistle to the Romans written by St. Paul contained all our present Epistle except xvi. 25-27; that at a somewhat later period—the period perhaps of his Roman imprisonment, St. Paul turned this into a circular letter; he cut off the last two chapters which contained for the most part purely personal matter, he omitted the words ἐν 'Ρώμῃ in i. 7 and 15; and then added the doxology at the end because he felt the need of some more fitting conclusion. Then, at a later date, in order to make the original Epistle complete the doxology was added from the later recension to the earlier.

Dr. Lightfoot points out that this hypothesis solves all the problems. It explains the existence of a shorter recension, it explains the presence of the doxology in both places, it explains the peculiar style of the doxology. We may admit this, but there is one point it does not explain; it does not explain how or why St. Paul made the division at the end of chap. xiv. There is nothing in the next thirteen verses which unfits them for general circulation. They are in fact more suitable for an encyclical letter than is chap. xiv. It is to us inconceivable that St. Paul should have himself mutilated his own argument by cutting off the conclusion of it. This consideration therefore seems to us decisive against Dr. Lightfoot's theory.

6. Dr. Hort has subjected the arguments of Dr. Lightfoot to a very close examination. He begins by a careful study of the doxology and has shown clearly first of all that the parallels between it and passages in the four acknowledged Epistles are much commoner and nearer than was thought to be the case; and secondly that it exactly reproduces and sums up the whole argument of the Epistle. On his investigation we have based our commentary, and we

must refer to that and to Dr. Hort's own essay for the reasons which make us accept the doxology as not only a genuine work of St. Paul, but also as an integral portion of the Epistle. That at the end he should feel compelled once more to sum up the great ideas of which the Epistle is full and put them clearly and strongly before his readers is quite in accordance with the whole mind of the Apostle. He does so in fact at the conclusion of the Galatian letter, although not in the form of a doxology.

Dr. Hort then proceeds to criticize and explain away the textual phenomena. We have quoted his emendation of the passage in Origen and pointed out that it is to us most unconvincing. No single argument in favour of the existence of the shorter recension may be strong, but the combination of reasons is in our opinion too weighty to be explained away.

Dr. Hort's own conclusions are: (1) He suggests that as the last two chapters were considered unsuitable for public reading, they might be omitted in systems of lectionaries while the doxology—which was felt to be edifying—was appended to chap. xiv, that it might be read. (2) Some such theory as this might explain the capitulations. 'The analogy of the common Greek capitulations shows how easily the personal or local and as it were temporary portions of an epistle might be excluded from a schedule of chapters or paragraphs.' (3) The omission of the allusions to Rome is due to a simple transcriptional accident. (4) 'When all is said, two facts have to be explained, the insertion of the Doxology after xiv and its omission.' This latter is due to Marcion, which must be explained to mean an omission agreeing with the reading in Marcion's copy. 'On the whole it is morally certain that the omission is his only as having been transmitted by him, in other words that it is a genuine ancient reading.' Dr. Hort finally concludes that though a genuine reading it is incorrect and perhaps arises through some accident such as the tearing off of the end of a papyrus roll or the last sheet in a book.

While admitting the force of some of Hort's criticisms on Lightfoot, and especially his defence of the genuineness of the doxology, we must express our belief that his manner of dealing with the evidence is somewhat arbitrary, and that his theory does not satisfactorily explain all the facts.

7. We ourselves incline to an opinion suggested first we believe by Dr. Gifford.

As will have already become apparent, no solution among those offered has attempted to explain what is really the most difficult part of the problem, the place at which the division was made. We know that the doxology was in many copies inserted at the end of chap. xiv; we have strong grounds for believing that in some editions chaps. xv and xvi were omitted; why is it at this place, certainly not a suitable one, that the break occurs? As we have seen, a careful examination of the text shows that the first thirteen verses of chap. xv are linked closely with chap. xiv—so closely that it is impossible to believe that they are not genuine, or that the Apostle himself could have cut them off from the context in publishing a shorter edition of his Epistle intended for a wide circulation. Nor again is it probable that any one arranging the Epistle for church services would have made the division at this place. The difficulty of the question is of course obscured for us by the division into chapters. To us if we wished to cut off the more personal part of the Epistle, a rough and ready method might suggest itself in the excision of the last two chapters, but we are dealing with a time before the present or probably any division into chapters existed.

Now if there were no solution possible, we might possibly ascribe this division to accident; but as a matter of fact internal evidence and external testimony alike point to the same cause. We have seen that there is considerable testimony for the fact that Marcion excised the last two chapters, and if we examine the beginning of chap. xv we shall find that as far as regards the first thirteen verses hardly any other course was possible for him, if he held the opinions which are ascribed to him. To begin with, five of these verses contain quotations from the O. T.; but further ver. 8 contains an expression λέγω γὰρ Χριστὸν διάκονον γεγενῆσθαι περιτομῆς ὑπὲρ ἀληθείας Θεοῦ, which he most certainly could not have used. Still more is this the case with regard to ver. 4, which directly contradicts the whole of his special teaching. The words at the end of chap. xiv might seem to make a more suitable ending than either of the next two verses, and at this place the division was drawn. The remainder of these two chapters could be omitted simply because they were useless for the definite dogmatic purpose Marcion had in view, and the Doxology which he could not quite like would go with them.

If we once assume this excision by Marcion it may perhaps explain the phenomena. Dr. Hort has pointed out against Dr. Lightfoot's theory of a shorter recension with the doxology that all the direct evidence for omitting the last two chapters is also in favour of omitting the Doxology. 'For the omission of xv, xvi, the one direct testimony, if such it be, is that of Marcion: and yet the one incontrovertible fact about him is that he omitted the Doxology. If G is to be added on the strength of the blank space after xiv, yet again it leaves out the Doxology.' We may add also the capitulations of Codex Fuldensis which again, as Dr. Hort points out, have no trace of the Doxology. Our evidence therefore points to the existence of a recension simply leaving out the last two chapters.

Now it is becoming more generally admitted that Marcion's *Apostolicon* had some—if not great—influence on variations in the text of the N. T. His edition had considerable circulation, especially at Rome, and therefore presumably in the West, and it is from the West that our evidence mostly comes. When in adapting the text for the purposes of church use it was thought advisable to omit the last portions as too personal and not sufficiently edifying, it was natural to make the division at a place where in a current edition the break had already been made. The subsequent steps would then be similar to those suggested by Dr. Hort. It was natural to add the Doxology in order to give a more suitable conclusion, or to preserve it for public reading at this place, and subsequently it dropped out at the later place. That is the order suggested by the manuscript evidence. All our best authorities place it at the end; A P Arm.—representing a later but still respectable text—have it in both places; later authorities for the most part place it only at xiv. 23.

It remains to account for the omission of any reference to Rome in the first chapter of G. This may of course be a mere idiosyncracy of that MS., arising either from carelessness of transcription (a cause which we can hardly accept) or from a desire to make the Epistle more general in its character. But it does not seem to us at all improbable that this omission may also be due to Marcion. His edition was made with a strongly dogmatic purpose. Local and personal allusions would have little interest to him. The words ἐν 'Ρώμῃ could easily be omitted without injuring the context. The opinion is perhaps corroborated by the character of the MS. in which the omission occurs. Allusion has been made (p. lxix) to two dissertations by Dr. Corssen on the allied MSS. D F G. In the second of these, he suggests that the archetype from which these MSS. are derived (Z) ended at xv. 13. Even if his argument were correct, it would not take away from the force of the other facts which have been mentioned. We should still have to explain how it was that the Doxology was inserted at the end of chap. xiv, and the previous discussion would stand as it is: only a new fact would have to be accounted for. When, however, we come to examine Dr. Corssen's arguments they hardly seem to support his contention. It may be admitted indeed, that the capitulations of the Codex Amiatinus might have been made for a copy which ended at xv. 13, but they present no solid argument for the existence of such a copy. Dr. Corssen points out that in the section xv. 14—xvi. 23, there are a considerable number of variations in the text, and suggests that that implies a different source for the text of that portion of the epistle. The number of variations in the *pericope adulterae* are, it is well known, considerable; and in the same way he would argue that this portion which has all these variations must come from a separate source. But the facts do not support his contention. It is true that in forty-three verses he is able to enumerate twenty-four variations; but if we examine the twenty-three verses of chap. xiv we shall find fourteen variations, a still larger proportion. Moreover, in xiv. 13 there are as numerous and as important variations as in any of the following verses. Dr. Corssen's arguments do not bear out his conclusion. As a matter of fact, as Dr. Hort pointed out against Dr. Lightfoot, the text of D F G presents exactly the same phenomena throughout the Epistle, and that suggests, although it does not perhaps prove, that the archetype contained the last two chapters. The scribe however was probably acquainted with a copy which omitted them. This archetype is alone or almost alone amongst our sources for the text in omitting the Doxology. It also omits as we have seen ἐν Ῥώμῃ in both places. We would hazard the suggestion that all these variations were due directly or indirectly to the same cause, the text of Marcion.

In our opinion then the text as we have it represents substantially the Epistle that St. Paul wrote to the Romans, and it remains only to explain briefly the somewhat complicated ending. At xv. 13 the didactic portion of it is concluded, and the remainder of the chapter is devoted to the Apostle's personal relations with the Roman Church, and a sketch of his plans. This paragraph ends with a short prayer called forth by the mingled hopes and fears which these plans for the future suggest. Then comes the commendation of Phoebe, the bearer of the letter (xvi. 1, 2); then salutations (3–16). The Apostle might now close the Epistle, but his sense of the danger to which the Roman Church may be exposed, if it is visited by false teachers, such as he is acquainted with in the East, leads him to give a final and direct warning against them. We find a not dissimilar phenomenon in the Epistle to the Philippians. There in iii. 1 he appears to be concluding, but before he concludes he breaks out into a strong, even indignant warning against false teachers (iii. 2–21), and even after that dwells long and feelingly over his salutations. The same difficulty of ending need not therefore surprise us when we meet it in the Romans. Then comes (xvi. 20) the concluding benediction. After this a postscript with salutations from the companions of St. Paul. Then finally the Apostle, wishing perhaps, as Dr. Hort suggests, to raise the Epistle once more to the serene tone which has characterized it throughout, adds the concluding Doxology, summing up the whole argument of the Epistle. There is surely nothing unreasonable in supposing that there would be an absence of complete sameness in the construction of the different letters. It is not likely that all would exactly correspond to the same model. The form in each case would be altered and changed in accordance with the feelings of the Apostle, and there is abundant proof throughout the Epistle that the Apostle felt earnestly the need of preserving the Roman Church from the evils of disunion and false teaching.

§ 10. COMMENTARIES.

A very complete and careful bibliography of the Epistle to the Romans was added by the editor, Dr. W. P. Dickson, to the English translation of Meyer's *Commentary*. This need not be repeated here. But a few leading works may be mentioned, especially such as have been most largely used in the preparation

of this edition. One or two which have not been used are added
as links in the historical chain. Some conception may be formed
of the general characteristics of the older commentators from the
sketch which is given of their treatment of particular subjects; e.g.
of the doctrine of δικαίωσις at p. 147 ff., and of the interpretation of
ch. ix. 6–29 on p. 269 ff. The arrangement is, roughly speaking,
chronological, but modern writers are grouped rather according to
their real affinities than according to dates of publication which
would be sometimes misleading.

1. *Greek Writers.*

ORIGEN (Orig.); ob. 253: *Comment. in Epist. S. Pauli ad
Romanos* in *Origenis Opera* ed. C. H. E. Lommatzsch, vols. vi, vii :
Berolini, 1836, 1837. The standard edition, on which that of
Lommatzsch is based, is that begun by Charles Delarue, Bene-
dictine of the congregation of St. Maur in 1733, and completed after
his death by his nephew Charles Vincent Delarue in 1759. The
Commentary on Romans comes in Tom. iv, which appeared in
the latter year. A new edition—for which the beginnings have
been made, in Germany by Dr. P. Koetschau, and in England by
Prof. Armitage Robinson and others—is however much needed.

The Commentary on our Epistle belongs to the latter part of
Origen's life when he was settled at Caesarea. A few fragments of
the original Greek have come down to us in the *Philocalia* (ed.
Robinson, Cambridge, 1893), and in Cramer's *Catena*, Tom. iv.
(Oxon. 1844); but for the greater part we are dependent upon the
condensed translation of Rufinus (hence ' Orig.-lat.'). There is no
doubt that Rufinus treated the work before him with great freedom.
Its text in particular is frequently adapted to that of the Old-Latin
copy of the Epistles which he was in the habit of using ; so that
' Orig.-lat.' more often represents Rufinus than Origen. An admirable account of the Commentary, so far as can be ascertained,
in both its forms is given in Dr. Westcott's article ORIGENES in
Dict. Chr. Biog. iv. 115–118.

This work of Origen's is unique among commentaries. The
reader is astonished not only at the command of Scripture but at
the range and subtlety of thought which it displays. The questions
raised are often remarkably modern. If he had been as successful
in answering as he is in propounding them Origen would have left
little for those who followed him. As it is he is hampered by
defects of method and especially by the fatal facility of allegory;
the discursiveness and prolixity of treatment are also deterrent to
the average reader.

CHRYSOSTOM (Chrys.); ob. 407: *Homil. in Epist. ad Romanos,*
ed. Field : Oxon. 1849; a complete critical edition. A translation

(not of this but of Savile's text which is superior to Montfaucon's),
by the Rev. J. B. Morris, was given in the *Library of the Fathers*,
vol. vii: Oxford, 1841. The Homilies were delivered at Antioch
probably between 387–397 A.D. They show the preacher at his
best and are full of moral enthusiasm and of sympathetic human
insight into the personality of the Apostle; they are also the work
of an accomplished scholar and orator, but do not always sound the
depths of the great problems with which the Apostle is wrestling.
They have at once the merits and the limitations of Antiochene
exegesis.

THEODORET (Theodrt., Thdrt.) played a well-known moderating
part in the controversies of the fifth century. He died in 458 A.D.
As a commentator he is a *pedisequus*—but one of the best of the
many *pedisequi*—of St. Chrysostom. His Commentary on the Ep.
to the Romans is contained in his *Works*, ed. Sirmond: Paris,
1642, Tom. iii. 1–119; also ed. Schulze and Noesselt, Halle,
1769–1774.

JOANNES DAMASCENUS (Jo.-Damasc.); died before 754 A.D. His
commentary is almost entirely an epitome of Chrysostom; it is
printed among his works (ed. Lequien: Paris, 1712, tom. ii.
pp. 1–60). The so-called *Sacra Parallela* published under his
name are now known to be some two centuries earlier and
probably in great part the work of Leontius of Byzantium (see the
brilliant researches of Dr. F. Loofs: *Studien über die dem Johannes
von Damascus zugeschriebenen Parallelen*, Halle, 1892).

OECUMENIUS (Oecum.); bishop of Tricca in Thessaly in the
tenth century. The Commentary on Romans occupies pp. 195–
413 of his *Works* (ed. Joan. Hentenius: Paris, 1631). It is practically a Catena with some contributions by Oecumenius himself;
it includes copious extracts from Photius (Phot.), the eminent
patriarch of Constantinople (*c.* 820–*c.* 891); these are occasionally
noted.

THEOPHYLACT (Theoph.); archbishop of Bulgaria under Michael
VII Ducas (1071–1078), and still living in 1118. His Commentary
is one of the best specimens of its kind (*Opp.* ed. Venet., 1754–
1763, tom. ii. 1–118).

EUTHYMIUS ZIGABENUS (Euthym.-Zig.); living after 1118; monk
in a monastery near Constantinople and in high favour with the
emperor Alexius Comnenus. His Commentaries on St. Paul's
Epistles were not published until 1887 (ed. Calogeras: Athens);
and as for that reason they have not been utilized in previous
editions we have drawn upon them rather largely. They deserve
citation by their terseness, point, and general precision of thought,
but like all the writers of this date they follow closely in the foot-
steps of Chrysostom.

2. *Latin Writers.*

AMBROSIASTER (Ambrstr.). The Epistle to the Romans heads
a series of Commentaries on thirteen Epistles of St. Paul, which in
some (though not the oldest) MSS. bear the name of St. Ambrose,
and from that circumstance came to be included in the printed
editions of his works. The Benedictines, Du Frische and Le
Nourry in 1690, argued against their genuineness, which has been
defended with more courage than success by the latest editor,
P. A. Ballerini (*S. Ambrosii Opera*, tom. iii, p. 350 ff. ; Mediolani,
1877). The real authorship of this work is one of the still open
problems of literary criticism. The date and place of composition
are fairly fixed. It was probably written at Rome, and (unless
the text is corrupt) during the Episcopate of Damasus about the
year 380 A. D. The author was for some time supposed to be
a certain Hilary the Deacon, as a passage which appears in the
commentary is referred by St. Augustine to *sanctus Hilarius*
(*Contra duas Epp. Pelag.* iv. 7). The commentary cannot really
proceed from the great Hilary (of Poitiers), but however the fact is
to be explained it is probably he who is meant. More recently an
elaborate attempt has been made by the Old-Catholic scholar,
Dr. Langen, to vindicate the work for Faustinus, a Roman presbyter of the required date. [Dr. Langen first propounded his
views in an address delivered at Bonn in 1880, but has since given
the substance of them in his *Geschichte d. röm. Kirche*, pp. 599–
610.] A case of some strength seemed to be made out, but it
was replied to with arguments which appear to preponderate by
Marold in Hilgenfeld's *Zeitschrift* for 1883, pp. 415–470. Unfortunately the result is purely negative, and the commentary is still
without an owner. It has come out in the course of discussion
that it presents a considerable resemblance, though not so much
as to imply identity of authorship, with the *Quaestiones ex utroque
Testamento*, printed among the works of St. Augustine. The commentator was a man of intelligence who gives the best account we
have from antiquity of the origin of the Roman Church (see above,
p. xxv), but it has been used in this edition more for its interesting
text than for the permanent value of its exegesis.

PELAGIUS (Pelag.). In the Appendix to the works of St. Jerome
(ed. Migne xi. [*P. L.* xxx.], col. 659 ff.) there is a series of Commentaries on St. Paul's Epistles which is now known to proceed
really from the author of Pelagianism. The Commentary was
probably written before 410. It consists of brief but well written
scholia rather dexterously turned so as not to clash with his
peculiar views. But it has not come down to us as Pelagius left it.
Cassiodorus, and perhaps others, made excisions in the interests
of orthodoxy.

HUGH OF ST. VICTOR (Hugo a S. Victore, Hugh of Paris);
c. 1097–1141. Amongst the works of the great mystic of the
twelfth century are published *Allegoriae in Novum Testamentum*,
Lib. VI. *Allegoriae in Epistolam Pauli ad Romanos* (Migne,
P. L. clxxv, col. 879), and *Quaestiones et Decisiones in Epistolas
D. Pauli.* 1. *In Epistolam ad Romanos* (Migne, clxxv, col. 431).
The authenticity of both these is disputed. St. Hugh was a typical
representative of the mystical as opposed to the rationalizing
tendency of the Middle Ages.

PETER ABELARD, 1079–1142. *Petri Abaelardi commentariorum
super S. Pauli Epistolam ad Romanos libri quinque* (Migne, *P. L.*
clxxviii. col. 783). The commentary is described as being 'literal,
theological, and moral. The author follows the text exactly,
explains each phrase, often each part of a phrase separately, and
attempts (not always very successfully) to show the connexion of
thought. Occasionally he discusses theological or moral questions,
often with great originality, often showing indications of the opinions
for which he was condemned' (Migne, *op. cit.* col. 30). So far as
we have consulted it, we have found it based partly on Origen partly
on Augustine, and rather weak and indecisive in its character.

THOMAS AQUINAS, *c.* 1225–1274, called Doctor Angelicus. His
Expositio in Epistolas omnes Divi Pauli Apostoli (*Opp.* Tom. xvi.
Venetiis, 1593) formed part of the preparation which he made for
his great work the *Summa Theologiae*—a preparation which consisted
in the careful study of the sentences of Peter Lombard, the Scriptures
with the comments of the Fathers, and the works of Aristotle. His
commentary works out in great detail the method of exegesis started
by St. Augustine. No modern reader who turns to it can fail to
be struck by the immense intellectual power displayed, and by the
precision and completeness of the logical analysis. Its value is
chiefly as a complete and methodical exposition from a definite
point of view. That in attempting to fit every argument of
St. Paul into the form of a scholastic syllogism, and in making
every thought harmonize with the Augustinian doctrine of grace,
there should be a tendency to make St. Paul's words fit a precon-
ceived system is not unnatural.

3. *Reformation and Post-Reformation Periods.*

COLET, John (*c.* 1467–1519); Dean of St. Paul's. Colet, the
friend of Erasmus, delivered a series of lectures on the Epistle to
the Romans about the year 1497 in the University of Oxford.
These were published in 1873 with a translation by J. H. Lupton,
M.A., Sur-Master of St. Paul's School. They are full of interest
as an historical memorial of the earlier English Reformation.

ERASMUS, Desiderius. 1466–1536. Erasmus' Greek Testament

with a new translation and annotations was published in 1516;
his *Paraphrasis Novi Testamenti*, a popular work, in 1522. He
was greater always in what he conceived and planned than in the
manner in which he accomplished it. He published the first
edition of the Greek New Testament, and the first commentary on
it which made use of the learning of the Renaissance, and edited
for the first time many of the early fathers. But in all that he did
there are great defects of execution, defects even for his own time.
He was more successful in raising questions than in solving them;
and his commentaries suffer as much from timidity as did those of
Luther from excessive boldness. His aim was to reform the Church
by publishing and interpreting the records of early Christianity—an
aim which harmonized ill with the times in which he lived. His
work was rather to prepare the way for future developments.

LUTHER, Martin, 1483–1546. Luther's contribution to the
literature of the Romans was confined to a short Preface, published
in 1523. But as marking an epoch in the study of St. Paul's
writings, the most important place is occupied by his Commentary
on the Galatians. This was published in a shorter form, *In epist.
P. ad Galatas Mart. Lutheri comment.* in 1519; in a longer form,
*In epist. P. ad Gal. commentarius ex praelectionibus Mart. Lutheri
collectus*, 1535. Exegesis was not Luther's strong point, and his
commentaries bristle with faults. They are defective, and prolix;
full of bitter controversy and one-sided. The value of his contribution to the study of St. Paul's writings was of a different character.
By grasping, if in a one-sided way, some of St. Paul's leading
ideas, and by insisting upon them with unwearied boldness and
persistence, he produced conditions of religious life which made
the comprehension of part of the Apostle's teaching possible. His
exegetical notes could seldom be quoted, but he paved the way for
a correct exegesis.

MELANCHTHON, Philip (1497–1560), was the most scholarly of
the Reformers. His *Adnotationes in ep. P. ad Rom.* with a preface
by Luther was published in 1522, his *Commentarii in Ep. ad Rom.*
in 1540.

CALVIN, John (1509–1564). His *Commentarii in omnes epistolas
Pauli Apost.* was first published at Strassburg in 1539. Calvin was
by far the greatest of the commentators of the Reformation. He
is clear, lucid, honest, and straightforward.

As the question is an interesting one, how far Calvin brought his peculiar
views ready-made to the study of the Epistle and how far he derived them
from it by an uncompromising exegesis, we are glad to place before the
reader a statement by one who is familiar with Calvin's writings (Dr. A. M.
Fairbairn, Principal of Mansfield College). 'The first edition of the
Institutes was published in 1536. It has hardly any detailed exposition of
the higher Calvinistic doctrine, but is made up of six parts: Expositions
(i) of the Decalogue; (ii) of the Apostolic Creed; (iii) of the Lord's Prayer;

(iv) of the Sacraments; (v) of the Roman or false doctrine of Sacraments, and (vi) of Christian Liberty or Church Polity.   There is just a single paragraph on Election.   In 1539 he published two things, the *Commentary on Romans* and the 2nd edition of the *Institutes*.   And the latter are greatly expanded with all his distinctive doctrines fully developed.   Two things are, I think, certain: this development was due to his study (1) of Augustine, especially the Anti-Pelagian writings, and (2) of St. Paul.   But it was St. Paul read through Augustine.   The exegetical stamp is peculiarly distinct in the doctrinal parts of the *Institutes*; and so I should say that his ideas were not so much philosophical as theological and exegetical in their basis. I ought to add however as indicating his philosophical bent that his earliest studies—before he became a divine—were on Seneca, *De Clementia.*'

BEZA, Theodore (1519–1605).   His edition of the Greek Testament with translation and annotations was first published by H. Stephanus in 1565, his *Adnotationes majores in N. T.* at Paris in 1594.

ARMINIUS (Jakob Harmensen), 1560–1609, Professor at Leyden, 1603.   As a typical example of the opposite school of interpretation to that of Calvin may be taken Arminius.   His works were comparatively few, and he produced few commentaries.   Two tracts of his however were devoted to explaining Romans vii and ix.   He admirably illustrates the statement of Hallam that 'every one who had to defend a cause, found no course so ready as to explain the Scriptures consistently with his own tenets.'

The two principal Roman Catholic commentators of the seventeenth century were Estius and Cornelius a Lapide.

CORNELIUS A LAPIDE (van Stein), ob. 1637, a Jesuit, published his *Commentaria in omnes d. Pauli epistolas* at Antwerp in 1614.

ESTIUS (W. van Est), ob. 1613, was Provost and Chancellor of Douay.   His *In omnes Pauli et aliorum apostolor. epistolas commentar.* was published after his death at Douay in 1614–1616.

GROTIUS (Huig van Groot), 1583–1645.   His *Annotationes in N. T.* were published at Paris in 1644.   This distinguished publicist and statesman had been in his younger days a pupil of J. J. Scaliger at Leyden, and his Commentary on the Bible was the first attempt to apply to its elucidation the more exact philological methods which he had learnt from his master.   He had hardly the philological ability for the task he had undertaken, and although of great personal piety was too much destitute of dogmatic interest.

The work of the philologists and scholars of the sixteenth and the first half of the seventeenth century on the Old and New Testament was summed up in *Critici Sacri*, first published in 1660.   It contains extracts from the leading scholars from Valla and Erasmus to Grotius, and represents the point which philological study in the N. T. had up to that time attained.

Two English commentators belonging to the seventeenth century deserve notice

HAMMOND, Henry (1605–1660), Fellow of Magdalen College, Oxford, and Canon of Christ Church. Hammond was well known as a royalist. He assisted in the production of Walton's *Polyglott*. His *Paraphrase and Annotations of the New Testament* appeared in 1653, a few years before his death, at a time when the disturbances of the Civil War compelled him to live in retirement. He has been styled the father of English commentators, and certainly no considerable exegetical work before his time had appeared in this country. But he has a further title to fame. His commentary undoubtedly deserves the title of 'historical.' In his interpretation he has detached himself from the dogmatic struggles of the seventeenth century, and throughout he attempts to expound the Apostle in accordance with his own ideas and those of the times when he lived.

LOCKE, John (1662–1704), the well-known philosopher, devoted his last years to the study of St. Paul's Epistles, and in 1705–1707 were published *A Paraphrase and Notes to the Epistle of St. Paul to the Galatians, the first and second Epistles to the Corinthians, and the Epistles to the Romans and Ephesians*. Appended is an *Essay for the understanding of St. Paul's Epistles by consulting St. Paul himself*. A study of this essay is of great interest. It is full of acute ideas and thoughts, and would amply vindicate the claim of the author to be classed as an 'historical' interpreter. The commentaries were translated into German, and must have had some influence on the future development of Biblical Exegesis.

BENGEL, J. A. (Beng.), 1687–1752; a Lutheran prelate in Würtemberg. His *Gnomon Novi Testamenti* (1742) stands out among the exegetical literature not only of the eighteenth century but of all centuries for its masterly terseness and precision and for its combination of spiritual insight with the best scholarship of his time.

WETSTEIN (or Wettstein), J. J., 1693–1754; after being deposed from office at Basel on a charge of heterodoxy he became Professor in the Remonstrants' College at Amsterdam. His Greek Testament appeared 1751, 1752. Wetstein was one of those indefatigable students whose first-hand researches form the base of other men's labours. In the history of textual criticism he deserves to be named by the side of John Mill and Richard Bentley; and besides his collation of MSS. he collected a mass of illustrative matter on the N. T. from classical, patristic, and rabbinical sources which is still of great value.

4. *Modern Period*.

THOLUCK, F. A. G., 1799–1877; Professor at Halle. Tholuck was a man of large sympathies and strong religious character, and both personally and through his commentary (which came out first in 1824 and has been more than once translated) exercised a wide influence outside Germany ; this is specially marked in the American exegetes.

FRITZSCHE, C. F. A. (Fri.), 1801–1846, Professor at Giessen. Fritzsche on Romans (3 vols. 1836–1843), like Lücke on St. John and Bleek on Hebrews, is a vast quarry of materials to which all subsequent editors have been greatly indebted. Fritzsche was one of those philologists whose researches did most to fix the laws of N. T. Greek, but his exegesis is hard and rationalizing. He engaged in a controversy with Tholuck the asperity of which he regretted before his death. He was however no doubt the better scholar and stimulated Tholuck to self-improvement in this respect.

MEYER, H. A. W. (Mey.), 1800–1873; Consistorialrath in the kingdom of Hanover. Meyer's famous commentaries first began to appear in 1832, and were carried on with unresting energy in a succession of new and constantly enlarged editions until his death. There is an excellent English translation of the Commentary on Romans published by Messrs. T. and T. Clark under the editorship of Dr. W. P. Dickson in 1873, 1874. Meyer and De Wette may be said to have been the founders of the modern style of commenting, at once scientific and popular : scientific, through its rigorous—at times too rigorous—application of grammatical and philological laws, and popular by reason of its terseness and power of presenting the sifted results of learning and research. Since Meyer's death the Commentary on Romans has been edited with equal conscientiousness and thoroughness by Dr. Bernhard Weiss, Professor at Berlin (hence ' Mey.-W.'). Dr. Weiss has not all his predecessor's vigour of style and is rather difficult to follow, but especially in textual criticism marks a real advance.

DE WETTE, W. M. L. (De W.), 1780–1849; Professor for a short time at Berlin, whence he was dismissed, afterwards at Basel. His *Kurzgefasstes exegetisches Handbuch zum Neuen Testament* first appeared in 1836–1848. De Wette was an ardent lover of freedom and rationalistically inclined, but his commentaries are models of brevity and precision.

STUART, Moses, 1780–1852; Professor at Andover, Mass. *Comm. on Romans* first published in 1832 (British edition with preface by Dr. Pye-Smith in 1833). At a time when Biblical exegesis was not being very actively prosecuted in Great Britain two works of solid merit were produced in America. One of these was by Moses Stuart, who did much to naturalize German methods. He expresses large obligations to Tholuck, but is independent as a commentator and modified considerably the Calvinism of his surroundings.

HODGE, Dr. C., 1797–1878; Professor at Princeton, New Jersey.

His *Comm. on Romans* first published in 1835, rewritten in 1864, is a weighty and learned doctrinal exposition based on the principles of the Westminster Confession. Like Moses Stuart, Dr. Hodge also owed much of his philological equipment to Germany where he had studied.

ALFORD, Dr. H. (Alf.), 1810–1871; Dean of Canterbury. His *Greek Testament* (1849–1861, and subsequently) was the first to import the results of German exegesis into many circles in England. Nonconformists (headed by the learned Dr. J. Pye-Smith) had been in advance of the Established Church in this respect. Dean Alford's laborious work is characterized by vigour, good sense, and scholarship, sound as far as it goes; it is probably still the best complete Greek Testament by a single hand.

WORDSWORTH, Dr. Christopher, 1809–1885; Bishop of Lincoln. Bishop Wordsworth's *Greek Testament* (1856–1860, and subsequently) is of an older type than Dean Alford's, and chiefly valuable for its patristic learning. The author was not only a distinguished prelate but a literary scholar of a high order (as may be seen by his *Athens and Attica, Conjectural Emendations of Ancient Authors*, and many other publications) but he wrote at a time when the reading public was less exigent in matters of higher criticism and interpretation.

JOWETT, B., 1817–1893; widely known as Master of Balliol College and Regius Professor of Greek in the University of Oxford. His edition of *St. Paul's Epistles to the Thessalonians, Galatians, and Romans* first appeared in 1855; second edition 1859; recently re-edited by Prof. L. Campbell. Professor Jowett's may be said to have been the first attempt in England at an entirely modern view of the Epistle. The essays contain much beautiful and suggestive writing, but the exegesis is loose and disappointing.

VAUGHAN, Dr. C. J. (Va.); Dean of Llandaff. Dr. Vaughan's edition first came out in 1859, and was afterwards enlarged; the edition used for this commentary has been the 4th (1874). It is a close study of the Epistle by a finished scholar with little further help than the *Concordance* to the Septuagint and Greek Testament: its greatest value lies in the careful selection of illustrative passages from these sources.

KELLY, W.; associated at one time with the textual critic Tregelles. His *Notes on the Epistle to the Romans* (London, 1873), are written from a detached and peculiar standpoint; but they are the fruit of sound scholarship and of prolonged and devout study, and they deserve more attention than they have received.

BEET, Dr. J. Agar; Tutor in the Wesleyan College, Richmond. Dr. Beet's may be described as the leading Wesleyan commentary: it starts from a very careful exposition of the text, but is intended throughout as a contribution to systematic theology. The first edition appeared in 1877, the second in 1881, and there have been several others since.

GODET, Dr. F. (Go.), Professor at Neuchatel. *Commentaire sur l'Epître aux Romains*, Paris, &c., 1879, English translation in T. and T. Clark's series, 1881. Godet and Oltramare are both Franco-Swiss theologians with a German training; and their commentaries are somewhat similar in character. They are extremely full, giving and discussing divergent interpretations under the names of their supporters. Both are learned and thoughtful works, strongest in exegesis proper and weakest in textual criticism.

OLTRAMARE, Hugues (Oltr.), 1813–1894; Professor at Geneva. *Commentaire sur l'Epître aux Romains*, published in 1881, 1882 (a volume on chaps. i.–v. 11 had appeared in 1843). Resembling Godet in many particulars, Oltramare seems to us to have the stronger grip and greater individuality in exegesis, though the original views of which he is fond do not always commend themselves as right.

MOULE, Rev. H. C. G. (Mou.); Principal of Ridley Hall, Cambridge. Mr. Moule's edition (in the *Cambridge Bible for Schools*) appeared in 1879. It reminds us of Dr. Vaughan's in its elegant scholarship and seeming independence of other commentaries, but it is fuller in exegesis. The point of view approaches as nearly as an English Churchman is likely to approach to Calvinism. Mr. Moule has also commented on the Epistle in *The Expositor's Bible*.

GIFFORD, Dr. E. H. (Gif.); sometime Archdeacon of London. The Epistle to the Romans in *The Speaker's Commentary* (1881) was contributed by Dr. Gifford, but is also published separately. We believe that this is on the whole the best as it is the most judicious of all English commentaries on the Epistle. There are few difficulties of exegesis which it does not fully face, and the solution which it offers is certain to be at once scholarly and well considered: it takes account of previous work both ancient and modern, though the pages are not crowded with names and references. Our obligations to this commentary are probably higher than to any other.

LIDDON, Dr. H. P. (Lid.); *Explanatory Analysis of St. Paul's Epistle to the Romans*, published posthumously in 1893, after being in an earlier form circulated privately among Dr. Liddon's pupils during his tenure of the Ireland Chair (1870–1882). The *Analysis* was first printed in 1876, but after that date much enlarged. It is what its name implies, an analysis of the argument with very full notes, but not a complete edition. It is perhaps true that the analysis is somewhat excessively divided and subdivided; in exegesis it is largely based on Meyer, but it shows everywhere the hand of a most lucid writer and accomplished theologian.

BARMBY, Dr. James; formerly Principal of Bishop Hatfield's Hall, Durham. Dr. Barmby contributed Romans to the *Pulpit Commentary* (London, 1890); a sound, independent and vigorous exposition.

LIPSIUS, Dr. R. A. (Lips.), 1830–1892; Professor at Jena. This most unwearied worker won and maintained his fame in other fields than exegesis. He had however written a popular commentary on Romans for the *Protestantenbibel* (English translation, published by Messrs. Williams & Norgate in 1883), and he edited the same Epistle along with Galatians and Philippians in the *Handcommentar zum Neuen Testament* (Freiburg i. B., 1891). This is a great improvement on the earlier work, and is perhaps in many respects the best, as it is the latest, of German commentaries; especially on the side of historical criticism and Biblical theology it is unsurpassed. No other commentary is so different from those of our own countrymen, or would serve so well to supplement their deficiencies.

SCHAEFER, Dr. A.; Professor at Münster. Dr. Schaefer's *Erklärung d. Briefes an die Römer* (Münster i. W., 1891) may be taken as a specimen of Roman Catholic commentaries. It is pleasantly and clearly written, with fair knowledge of exegetical literature, but seems to us often just to miss the point of the Apostle's thought. Dr. Schanz, the ablest of Roman Catholic commentators, has not treated St. Paul's Epistles.

We are glad to have been able to refer, through the kindness of a friend, to a Russian commentary.

THEOPHANES, ob. 1893; was Professor and Inspector in the St. Petersburgh Ecclesiastical Academy and afterwards Bishop of Vladimir and Suzdal. He early gave up his see and retired to a life of learning and devotion. His commentary on the Romans was published in 1890. He is described as belonging to an old and to a certain extent antiquated school of exegesis. His commentary is based mainly on that of Chrysostom. Theophanes has both the strength and weakness of his master. Like him he is often historical in his treatment, like him he sometimes fails to grasp the more profound points in the Apostle's teaching.

ABBREVIATIONS

———◆———

Ecclesiastical Writers (see p. xcviii ff.).

Amb.	Ambrose.
Ambrstr.	Ambrosiaster.
Ath.	Athanasius.
Aug.	Augustine.
Bas.	Basil.
Chrys.	Chrysostom.
Clem.-Alex.	Clement of Alexandria.
Clem.-Rom.	Clement of Rome.
Cypr.	Cyprian.
Cyr.-Alex.	Cyril of Alexandria.
Cyr.-Jerus.	Cyril of Jerusalem.
Epiph.	Epiphanius.
Eus.	Eusebius.
Euthym.-Zig.	Euthymius Zigabenus.
Hippol.	Hippolytus.
Ign.	Ignatius.
Jer. (Hieron.)	Jerome.
Jos.	Josephus.
Method.	Methodius.
Novat.	Novatian.
Oecum.	Oecumenius.
Orig.	Origen.
Orig.-lat.	Latin Version of Origen.
Pelag.	Pelagius.
Phot.	Photius.
Ruf.	Rufinus.
Sedul.	Sedulius.
Tert.	Tertullian.
Theod.-Mops.	Theodore of Mopsuessia.
Theodrt.	Theodoret.
Theoph.	Theophylact.

Versions (see p. lxvi f.).

Aegyptt.	Egyptian.
Boh.	Bohairic.
Sah.	Sahidic.
Aeth.	Ethiopic.
Arm.	Armenian.
Goth.	Gothic.
Latt.	Latin.
Lat. Vet.	Vetus Latina.
Vulg.	Vulgate.
Syrr.	Syriac.
Pesh.	Peshitto.
Harcl.	Harclean.
Cov.	Coverdale.
Genev.	Geneva.
Rhem.	Rheims (or Douay).
Tyn.	Tyndale.
Wic.	Wiclif.
AV.	Authorized Version.
RV.	Revised Version.

Editors (see p. cv ff.).

T. R.	Textus Receptus.
Tisch.	Tischendorf.
Treg.	Tregelles.
WH.	Westcott and Hort.
Alf.	Alford.
Beng.	Bengel.
Del.	Delitzsch.
De W.	De Wette.
Ell.	Ellicott.
Fri.	Fritzsche (C. F. A.).
Gif.	Gifford.
Go.	Godet.
Lft.	Lightfoot.
Lid.	Liddon.
Lips.	Lipsius.
Mey.	Meyer.
Mey.-W.	Meyer-Weiss.
Oltr.	Oltramare.
Va.	Vaughan.

C.I.G.	. . .	*Corpus Inscriptionum Graecarum.*
C.I.L.	. . .	*Corpus Inscriptionum Latinarum.*
Grm.-Thay.	. . .	Grimm-Thayer's *Lexicon.*
Trench, *Syn.*	. . .	Trench on *Synonyms.*
Win.	. . .	Winer's *Grammar.*
Exp.	. . .	*Expositor.*
JBExeg.	. . .	*Journal of the Society of Biblical Literature and Exegesis.*
ZwTh.	. . .	*Zeitschrift für wissenschaftliche Theologie.*
add.	. . .	addit, addunt, &c.
al.	. . .	alii, alibi.
cat. (*caten.*)	. . .	catena.
codd.	. . .	codices.
edd.	. . .	editores.
edd. pr.	. . .	editores priores (older editors).
om.	. . .	omittit, omittunt, &c.
pauc.	. . .	pauci.
pler.	. . .	plerique.
plur.	. . .	plures.
praem.	. . .	praemittit, praemittunt, &c.
rel.	. . .	reliqui.
2/3, 4/5, &c.	. . .	twice out of three times, four out of five times, &c.

In text-critical notes adverbs (*bis, semel,* &c.), statistics ($^2/_3$, $^4/_5$) and *cod. codd., ed. edd.,* &c., always qualify the word which precedes, not that which follows: 'Vulg. *codd.*' = some MSS. of the Vulgate, Epiph. *cod.* or Epiph. *ed.* = a MS. or some printed edition of Epiphanius.

N.B.—The text commented upon is that commonly known as the Revisers' Greek Text (i. e. the Greek Text presupposed in the Revised Version of 1881) published by the Clarendon Press. The few instances in which the editors dissent from this text are noted as they occur.

THE
EPISTLE TO THE ROMANS

—•—

THE APOSTOLIC SALUTATION.

I. 1, 7. * *Paul, a divinely chosen and accredited Apostle,
gives Christian greeting to the Roman Church, itself also
divinely called.*

¹Paul, a devoted servant of Jesus Christ, an Apostle called
by divine summons as much as any member of the original
Twelve, solemnly set apart for the work of delivering God's
message of salvation; ⁷Paul, so authorized and commissioned,
gives greeting to the whole body of Roman Christians (whether
Jewish or Gentile), who as Christians are special objects of the
Divine love, called out of the mass of mankind into the inner
society of the Church, consecrated to God, like Israel of old, as
His own peculiar people. May the free unmerited favour of
God and the peace which comes from reconciliation with Him be
yours! May God Himself, the heavenly Father, and the Lord
Jesus Messiah, grant them to you!

I. 2-6. *I preach, in accordance with our Jewish Scriptures, Jesus the Son of David and Son of God, whose
commission I bear.*

²The message which I am commissioned to proclaim is no
startling novelty, launched upon the world without preparation,
but rather the direct fulfilment of promises which God had
inspired the prophets of Israel to set down in Holy Writ. ³It
relates to none other than His Son, whom it presents in a twofold
aspect; on the one hand by physical descent tracing His lineage

* In this one instance we have ventured to break up the long and heavily-
weighted sentence in the Greek, and to treat its two main divisions separately.
But the second of these is not in the strict sense a parenthesis: the construction
of the whole paragraph is continuous.

B

to David, as the Messiah was to do, [4]and on the other hand, in virtue of the Holiness inherent in His spirit, visibly designated or declared to be Son of God by the miracle of the Resurrection. He, I say, is the sum and substance of my message, Jesus, the Jew's Messiah, and the Christian's Lord. [5]And it was through Him that I, like the rest of the Apostles, received both the general tokens of God's favour in that I was called to be a Christian and also the special gifts of an Apostle. [6]My duty as an Apostle is among all Gentile peoples, and therefore among you too at Rome, to win men over to the willing service of loyalty to Him; and the end to which all my labours are directed is the honour of His Holy Name.

1-7. In writing to the Church of the imperial city, which he had not yet visited, St. Paul delivers his credentials with some solemnity, and with a full sense of the magnitude of the issues in which they and he alike are concerned. He takes occasion at once to define (i) his own position, (ii) the position of his readers, (iii) the central truth in that common Christianity which unites them.

The leading points in the section may be summarized thus: (i) I, Paul, am an Apostle by no act of my own, but by the deliberate call and in pursuance of the long-foreseen plan of God (vv. 1, 7). (ii) You, Roman Christians, are also special objects of the Divine care. You inherit under the New Dispensation the same position which Israel occupied under the Old (vv. 6, 7). (iii) The Gospel which I am commissioned to preach, though new in the sense that it puts forward a new name, the Name of Jesus Christ, is yet indissolubly linked to the older dispensation which it fulfils and supersedes (vv. 2, 7; see note on κλητοῖς ἁγίοις). (iv) Its subject is Jesus, Who is at once the Jewish Messiah and the Son of God (vv. 3, 4). (v) From Him, the Son, and from the Father, may the blessedness of Christians descend upon you (ver. 7).

This opening section of the Epistle affords a good opportunity to watch the growth of a Christian Theology, in the sense of reflection upon the significance of the Life and Death of Christ and the relation of the newly inaugurated order of things to the old. We have to remember (1) that the Epistle was written about the year 58 A.D., or within thirty years of the Ascension; (2) that in the interval the doctrinal language of Christianity has had to be built up from the foundations. We shall do well to note which of the terms used are old and which new, and how far old terms have had a new face put upon them. We will return to this point at the end of the paragraph.

1. δοῦλος Ἰησοῦ Χριστοῦ : δοῦλος Θεοῦ or Κυρίου is an Old Testament phrase, applied to the prophets in a body from Amos onwards (Am. iii. 7; Jer. vii. 25 and repeatedly; Dan. ix. 6; Ezra ix. 11); also with slight variations to Moses (θεράπων Josh. i. 2), Joshua (Josh. xxiv. 29; Jud. ii. 8), David (title of Ps. xxxvi. [xxxv.]; Pss. lxxviii. [lxxvii.] 70; lxxxix. [lxxxviii.] 4, 21; also παῖς κυρίου, title of Ps. xviii. [xvii.]), Isaiah (παῖς Is. xx. 3); but applied also to worshippers generally (Pss. xxxiv. [xxxiii.] 23; cxiii. [cxii.] 1 παῖδες; cxxxvi. [cxxxv.] 22 of Israel, &c.).

This is the first instance of a similar use in the New Testament; it is found also in the greetings of Phil., Tit., Jas., Jude, 2 Pet., showing that as the Apostolic age progressed the assumption of the title became established on a broad basis. But it is noticeable how quietly St. Paul steps into the place of the prophets and leaders of the Old Covenant, and how quietly he substitutes the name of His own Master in a connexion hitherto reserved for that of Jehovah.

Ἰησοῦ Χριστοῦ. A small question of reading arises here, which is perhaps of somewhat more importance than may appear at first sight. In the opening verses of most of St. Paul's Epistles the MSS. vary between Ἰησοῦ Χριστοῦ and Χριστοῦ Ἰησοῦ. There is also evidently a certain method in the variation. The evidence stands thus (where that on one side only is given it may be assumed that all remaining authorities are on the other) :—

1 Thess. i. 1 Ἰησοῦ Χριστῷ unquestioned.
2 Thess. i. 1 Ἰησοῦ Χριστῷ Edd.; Χριστῷ Ἰησοῦ D E Fᵍʳ G, Ambrstr. (*sic* ed. Ballerini).
Gal. i. 1 Ἰησοῦ Χριστοῦ unquestioned.
1 Cor. i. 1 Χριστοῦ Ἰησοῦ B D E F G 17 *al. pauc.*, Vulg. *codd.*, Chrys. Ambrstr. Aug. *semel*, Tisch., WH. *marg.*
2 Cor. i. 1 Χριστοῦ Ἰησοῦ ℵ B M P 17 *marg.*, Harcl., Euthal. *cod.* Theodrt. Tisch. WH. RV.
Rom. i. 1 Χριστοῦ Ἰησοῦ B, Vulg. *codd.*, Orig. *bis* (*contra* Orig.-lat. *bis*) Aug. *semel* Amb. Ambrstr. *al. Lat.*, Tisch. WH. *marg.*
Phil. i. 1 Χριστοῦ Ἰησοῦ ℵ B D E, Boh., Tisch. WH. RV.
Eph. i. 1 Χριστοῦ Ἰησοῦ B D E P 17, Vulg. *codd.* Boh. Goth. Harcl., Orig. (*ex Caten.*) Jo.-Damasc. Ambrstr., Tisch. WH. RV.
Col. i. 1 Χριστοῦ Ἰησοῦ ℵ A B F G L P 17, Vulg. *codd.* Boh. Harcl., Euthal. *cod.* Jo.-Damasc. Ambrstr. Hieron. *al.*. Tisch. WH. RV.
Philem. i. 1 Χρ.στοῦ Ἰησοῦ ℵ A Dᶜ F G K P (*def.* B), &c., Boh., Hieron. (*ut vid.*) Ambrstr. *al.*, Tisch. WH. RV.
1 Tim. i. 1 Χριστοῦ Ἰησοῦ ℵ D F G P (*def.* B), Vulg. *codd.* Boh. Harcl., Jo.-Damasc. Ambrstr., Tisch. WH. RV.
2 Tim. i. 1 Χριστοῦ Ἰησοῦ ℵ D E F G K P (*def.* B) 17 *al.*, Vulg. *codd.* Boh. Sah. Harcl., Euthal. *cod.* Jo.-Damasc. Ambrstr. *al.*, Tisch. WH. RV.
Tit. i. 1 Ἰησοῦ Χριστοῦ ℵ Dᶜ E F G &c., Vulg. *codd.* Goth. Pesh. Arm. Aeth., Chrys. Euthal. *cod.* Ambrstr. (ed. Ballerin.) *al.*, Tisch. WH. (*sed* Χριστοῦ [Ἰησοῦ] *marg.*) RV.; Χριστοῦ Ἰησοῦ A *minusc. tres*, Vulg. *codd.* Boh. Harcl., Cassiod.; Χριστοῦ *tantum* Dᵍ⁻*.

It will be observed that the Epistles being placed in a roughly chronological order, those at the head of the list read indubitably Ἰησοῦ Χριστοῦ (or Χριστῷ), while those in the latter part (with the single exception of Tit., which is judiciously treated by WH.) as indubitably read Χριστοῦ Ἰησοῦ.

Just about the group 1 and 2 Cor. Rom. there is a certain amount of doubt.

Remembering the Western element which enters into B in Epp. Paul., it looks as if the evidence for χῡ ῑῡ in Cor. Rom. might be entirely Western; but that is not quite clear, and the reading may possibly be right. In any case it would seem that just about this time St. Paul fell into the habit of writing Χριστὸς 'Ιησοῦς. The interest of this would lie in the fact that in Χριστὸς 'Ιησοῦς the first word would seem to be rather more distinctly a proper name than in 'Ιησοῦς Χριστός. No doubt the latter phrase is rapidly passing into a proper name, but Χριστός would seem to have a little of its sense as a title still clinging to it : the phrase would be in fact transitional between Χριστός or ὁ Χριστός of the Gospels and the later Χριστὸς 'Ιησοῦς or Χριστός simply as a proper name (see Sanday, *Bampton Lectures*, p. 289 f., and an article by the Rev. F. Herbert Stead in *Expos.* 1888, i. 386 ff.). The subject would repay working out on a wider scale of induction.

κλητὸς ἀπόστολος. κλῆσις is another idea which has its roots in the Old Testament. Eminent servants of God become so by an express Divine summons. The typical examples would be Abraham (Gen. xii. 1–3), Moses (Ex. iii. 10), the prophets (Isa. vi. 8, 9; Jer. i. 4, 5, &c.). The verb καλεῖν occurs in a highly typical passage, Hos. xi. 1 ἐξ Αἰγύπτου μετεκάλεσα τὰ τέκνα μου. For the particular form κλητός we cannot come nearer than the 'guests' (κλητοί) of Adonijah (1 Kings i. 41, 49). By his use of the term St. Paul places himself on a level at once with the great Old Testament saints and with the Twelve who had been 'called' expressly by Christ (Mark i. 17; ii. 14 ‖). The same combination κλητὸς ἀπόστ. occurs in 1 Cor. i. 1, but is not used elsewhere by St. Paul or any of the other Apostles. In these two Epistles St. Paul has to vindicate the parity of his own call (on the way to Damascus, cf. also Acts xxvi. 17) with that of the elder Apostles.

On the relation of κλητός to ἐκλεκτός see Lft. on Col. iii. 12. There is a difference between the usage of the Gospels and Epistles. In the Gospels κλητοί are all who are invited to enter Christ's kingdom, whether or not they accept the invitation ; the ἐκλεκτοί are a smaller group, selected to special honour (Matt. xxii. 14). In St. Paul both words are applied to the same persons; κλητός implies that the call has been not only given but obeyed.

ἀπόστολος. It is well known that this word is used in two senses ; a narrower sense in which it was applied by our Lord Himself to the Twelve (Luke vi. 13; Mark iii. 14 v.l.), and a wider in which it includes certainly Barnabas (Acts xiv. 4, 14) and probably James, the Lord's brother (Gal. i. 19), Andronicus and Junias (Rom. xvi. 7), and many others (cf. 1 Cor. xii. 28; Eph. iv. 11; *Didaché* xi, xii, &c.; also esp. Lightfoot, *Gal.* p. 92 ff.; Harnack in *Texte u. Untersuch.* ii. 111 ff.). Strictly speaking St. Paul could only claim to be an Apostle in the wider acceptation of the term ; he lays stress, however, justly on the fact that he is κλητὸς ἀπόστολος, i. e. not merely an Apostle by virtue of possessing such qualifications as are described in Acts i. 21, 22, but through a direct intervention of Christ. At the same time it should be remembered that St. Paul lays stress on this fact not with a view to personal aggrandizement, but only with a view to commend his Gospel with the weight which he knows that it deserves.

ἀφωρισμένος: in a double sense, by God (as in Gal. i. 15) and by man (Acts xiii. 2). The first sense is most prominent here ; or rather it includes the second, which marks the historic fulfilment of the Divine purpose. The free acceptance of the human commission may enable us to understand how there is room for free will even in the working out of that which has been pre-ordained by God (see below on ch. xi). And yet the three terms, δοῦλος, κλητός, ἀφωρισμένος, all serve to emphasize the essentially Scriptural doctrine that human ministers, even Apostles, are but instruments in the hand of God, with no initiative or merit of their own.

This conception is not confined to the Canonical Books : it is found also in *Assump. Moys.* i. 14 *itaque excogitavit et invenit me, qui ab initio orbis terrarum praeparatus sum, ut sim arbiter testamenti illius.*

εἰς εὐαγγέλιον Θεοῦ. The particular function for which St. Paul is 'set apart' is to preach the Gospel of God. The Gospel is sometimes described as ' of God' and sometimes ' of Christ' (e. g. Mark i. 1). Here, where the thought is of the gradual unfolding in time of a plan conceived in eternity, ' of God' is the more appropriate. It is probably a mistake in these cases to restrict the force of the gen. to one particular aspect ('the Gospel of which God is the author,' or ' of which Christ is the subject'): all aspects are included in which the Gospel is in any way related to God and Christ.

εὐαγγέλιον. The fundamental passage for the use of this word appears to be Mark i. 14, 15 (cf. Matt. iv. 23). We cannot doubt that our Lord Himself described by this term (or its Aramaic equivalent) His announcement of the arrival of the Messianic Time. It does not appear to be borrowed directly from the LXX (where the word occurs in all only two [or three] times, and once for ' the reward of good tidings' ; the more common form is εὐαγγελία). It would seem, however, that there was some influence from the rather frequent use (twenty times) of εὐαγγελίζειν, εὐαγγελίζεσθαι, especially in Second Isaiah and the Psalms in connexion with the news of the Great Deliverance or Restoration from the Captivity. A conspicuous passage is Isa. lxi. 1, which is quoted or taken as a text in Luke iv. 18. The group of words is well established in Synoptic usage (εὐαγγέλιον, Matthew four times, Mark eight, Acts two ; εὐαγγελίζεσθαι, Matthew one, Luke ten, Acts fifteen). It evidently took a strong hold on the imagination of St. Paul in connexion with his own call to missionary labours (εὐαγγέλιον sixty

times in Epp. Paul, besides in Epp. and Apoc. only twice; εὐαγγελίζεσθαι twenty times in Epp. Paul., besides once mid. seven times
pass.). The disparity between St. Paul and the other N. T. writers
outside Evv. Synopt. Acts is striking. The use of εὐαγγέλιον for
a Book lies beyond our limits (Sanday, *Bamp. Lect.* p. 317 *n.*);
the way is prepared for it by places like Mark i. 1 ; Apoc. xiv. 6.

2. προεπηγγείλατο. The words ἐπαγγελία, ἐπαγγέλλεσθαι occur
several times in LXX, but not in the technical sense of the great
'promises' made by God to His people. The first instance of
this use is *Ps. Sol.* xii. 8 καὶ ὅσιοι κυρίου κληρονομήσαιεν ἐπαγγελίας
κυρίου: cf. vii. 9 τοῦ ἐλεῆσαι τὸν οἶκον Ἰακὼβ εἰς ἡμέραν ἐν ᾗ ἐπηγγείλω
αὐτοῖς, and xvii. 6 οἷς οὐκ ἐπηγγείλω, μετὰ βίας ἀφείλοντο : a group of
passages which is characteristic of the attitude of wistful expectation in the Jewish people during the century before the Birth of
Christ. No wonder that the idea was eagerly seized upon by the
primitive Church as it began to turn the pages of the O. T. and to
find one feature after another of the history of its Founder and of
its own history foretold there.

> We notice that in strict accordance with what we may believe to have been
> the historical sequence, neither ἐπαγγελία nor ἐπαγγέλλεσθαι (in the technical
> sense) occur in the Gospels until we come to Luke xxiv. 49, where ἐπαγ-
> γελία is used of the promised gift of the Holy Spirit ; but we no sooner cross
> over to the Acts than the use becomes frequent. The words cover (i) the
> promises made by Christ, in particular the promise of the Holy Spirit (which
> is referred to the Father in Acts i. 4); so ἐπαγγελία three times in the Acts,
> Gal. iii. 14, and Eph. i. 13; (ii) the promises of the O. T. fulfilled in Chris-
> tianity; so ἐπαγγελία four times in Acts (note esp. Acts xiii. 32, xxvi. 6),
> some eight times each in Rom. and Gal., both ἐπαγγελία and ἐπαγγέλλεσθαι
> repeatedly in Heb., &c.; (iii) in a yet wider sense of promises, whether as yet
> fulfilled or unfulfilled, e.g. 2 Cor. i. 20 ὅσαι γὰρ ἐπαγγελίαι Θεοῦ (cf. vii. 1) ;
> 1 Tim. iv. 8 ; 2 Tim. i. 1 ; 2 Pet. iii. 4 ἡ ἐπαγγελία τῆς παρουσίας αὐτοῦ.

ἐν γραφαῖς ἁγίαις : perhaps the earliest extant instance of the use
of this phrase (Philo prefers ἱεραὶ γραφαί, ἱεραὶ βίβλοι, ὁ ἱερὸς λόγος :
cf. Sanday, *Bamp. Lect.* p. 72); but the use is evidently well established, and the idea of a collection of authoritative books goes
back to the prologue to Ecclus. In γραφαῖς ἁγίαις the absence of
the art. throws the stress on ἁγίαις ; the books are 'holy' as containing the promises of God Himself, written down by inspired
men (διὰ τῶν προφητῶν αὐτοῦ).

3. γενομένου. This is contrasted with ὁρισθέντος, γενομένου denoting, as usually, 'transition from one state or mode of subsistence
to another' (*Sp. Comm.* on 1 Cor. i. 30) ; it is rightly paraphrased
'[Who] was born,' and is practically equivalent to the Johannean
ἐλθόντος εἰς τὸν κόσμον.

ἐκ σπέρματος Δαβίδ. For proof that the belief in the descent of
the Messiah from David was a living belief see Mark xii. 35 ff.
πῶς λέγουσιν οἱ γραμματεῖς ὅτι ὁ Χριστὸς υἱός ἐστι Δαβίδ; (cf. Mark

xi. 10 and x. 47 f.) : also *Ps. Sol.* xvii. 23 ff. ἴδε, κύριε, καὶ ἀνάστησον
αὐτοῖς τὸν βασιλέα αὐτῶν υἱὸν Δαυὶδ εἰς τὸν καιρὸν ὃν οἶδας σύ, ὁ Θεός, τοῦ
βασιλεῦσαι ἐπὶ Ἰσραὴλ παῖδά σου κ.τ.λ. ; 4 Ezra xii. 32 (in three of the
extant versions, Syr. Arab. Armen.); and the Talmud and Targums
(passages in Weber, *Altsyn. Theol.* p. 341). Our Lord Himself
appears to have made little use of this title : he raises a difficulty
about it (Mark xii. 35–37 ‖). But this verse of Ep. to Romans
shows that Christians early pointed to His descent as fulfilling one
of the conditions of Messiahship ; similarly 2 Tim. ii. 8 (where the
assertion is made a part of St. Paul's ' Gospel '); Acts ii. 30 ; Heb.
vii. 14 'it is evident that our Lord hath sprung out of Judah' (see
also Eus. *H. E.* I. vii. 17, Joseph and Mary from the same tribe).
Neither St. Paul nor the Acts nor Epistle to Hebrews defines more
nearly how the descent is traced. For this we have to go to
the First and Third Gospels, the early chapters of which embody
wholly distinct traditions, but both converging on this point. There
is good reason to think that St. Luke i, ii had assumed substantially its present shape before A.D. 70 (cf. Swete, *Apost. Creed*,
p. 49).

In *Test. XII. Patriarch.* we find the theory of a double descent from Levi
and from Judah (Sym. 7 ἀναστήσει γὰρ Κύριος ἐκ τοῦ Λευεὶ ὡς ἀρχιερέα καὶ ἐκ
τοῦ Ἰούδα ὡς βασιλέα, Θεὸν καὶ ἄνθρωπον : Gad. 8 ὅπως τιμήσωσιν Ἰούδαν καὶ
Λευεί· ὅτι ἐξ αὐτῶν ἀνατελεῖ Κύριος, σωτὴρ τῷ Ἰσραήλ, &c. ; cf. Harnack's
note, *Patr. Apost.* i. 52). This is no doubt an inference from the relationship
of the Mother of our Lord to Elizabeth (Luke i. 36).

κατὰ σάρκα . . . κατὰ πνεῦμα are opposed to each other, not as
' human ' to ' divine,' but as ' body' to ' spirit,' both of which in
Christ are human, though the Holiness which is the abiding property of His Spirit is something more than human. See on κατὰ
πνεῦμ. ἁγιωσ. below.

4. ὁρισθέντος : ' designated.' It is usual to propose for this
word an alternative between (i) 'proved to be,' ' marked out as
being ' (δειχθέντος, ἀποφανθέντος Chrys.), and (ii) 'appointed,' ' instituted,' ' installed,' in fact and not merely in idea. For this latter
sense (which is that adopted by most modern commentators) the
parallels are quoted, Acts x. 42 οὗτός ἐστιν ὁ ὡρισμένος ὑπὸ τοῦ Θεοῦ
κριτὴς ζώντων καὶ νεκρῶν, and xvii. 31 μέλλει κρίνειν . . . ἐν ἀνδρὶ ᾧ
ὥρισε. The word itself does not determine the meaning either
way : it must be determined by the context. But here the particular
context is also neutral ; so that we must look to the wider context
of St. Paul's teaching generally. Now it is certain that St. Paul
did not hold that the Son of God *became* Son by the Resurrection.
The undoubted Epistles are clear on this point (esp. 2 Cor. iv. 4 ;
viii. 9 ; cf. Col. i. 15–19). At the same time he *did* regard the
Resurrection as making a difference—if not in the transcendental
relations of the Father to the Son (which lie beyond our cogni-

sance), yet in the visible manifestation of Sonship as addressed to the understanding of men (cf. esp. Phil. ii. 9 διὸ καὶ ὁ Θεὸς αὐτὸν ὑπερύψωσε, καὶ ἐχαρίσατο αὐτῷ τὸ ὄνομα τὸ ὑπὲρ πᾶν ὄνομα). This is sufficiently expressed by our word 'designated,' which might perhaps with advantage also be used in the two places in the Acts. It is true that Christ *becomes* Judge in a sense in which He does not become Son ; but He is Judge too not wholly by an external creation but by an inherent right. The Divine declaration, as it were, endorses and proclaims that right.

The Latin versions are not very helpful. The common rendering was *praedestinatus* (so expressly Rufinus [Orig.-lat.] *ad loc.*; cf. Introd. § 7). Hilary of Poitiers has *destinatus*, which Rufinus also prefers. Tertullian reads *definitus*.

υἱοῦ Θεοῦ. 'Son of God,' like 'Son of Man,' was a recognized title of the Messiah (cf. *Enoch* cv. 2 ; 4 Ezra vii. 28, 29 ; xiii. 32, 37, 52 ; xiv. 9, in all which places the Almighty speaks of the Messiah as 'My Son,' though the exact phrase 'Son of God' does not occur). It is remarkable that in the Gospels we very rarely find it used by our Lord Himself, though in face of Matt. xxvii. 43, John x. 36, cf. Matt. xxi. 37 f. *al.*, it cannot be said that He did not use it. It is more often used to describe the impression made upon others (e. g. the demonized, Mark iii. 11, v. 7 ‖ ; the centurion, Mark xv. 39 ‖), and it is implied by the words of the Tempter (Matt. iv. 3, 6 ‖) and the voice from heaven (Mark i. 11 ‖, ix. 7 ‖). The crowning instance is the confession of St. Peter in the version which is probably derived from the *Logia*, ' Thou art the Christ, the Son of the living God,' Matt. xvi. 16. It is consistent with the whole of our Lord's method that He should have been thus reticent in putting forward his own claims, and that He should have left them to be inferred by the free and spontaneous working of the minds of His disciples. Nor is it surprising that the title should have been chosen by the Early Church to express its sense of that which was transcendent in the Person of Christ : see esp. the common text of the Gospel of St. Mark, i. 1 (where the words, if not certainly genuine, in any case are an extremely early addition), and this passage, the teaching of which is very direct and explicit. The further history of the term, with its strengthening addition μονογενής, may be followed in Swete, *Apost. Creed*, p. 24 ff., where recent attempts to restrict the Sonship of Christ to His earthly manifestation are duly weighed and discussed. In this passage we have seen that the *declaration* of Sonship dates from the Resurrection : but we have also seen that St. Paul regarded the Incarnate Christ as existing before His Incarnation ; and it is as certain that when he speaks of Him as ὁ ἴδιος υἱός (Rom. viii. 32), ὁ ἑαυτοῦ υἱός (viii. 3), he intends to cover the period of pre-existence, as that St. John identifies the μονογενής with the pre-existent Logos. There is no sufficient reason to think that the Early Church, so far as it reflected upon these terms, understood them differently.

There are three moments to each of which are applied with variations the words of Ps. ii. 7 'Thou art my Son; this day have I begotten thee.' They are (i) the Baptism (Mark i. 11 ‖); (ii) the Transfiguration (Mark ix. 7 ‖); (iii) the Resurrection (Acts xiii. 33). We can see here the origin of the Ebionite idea of progressive exaltation, which is however held in check by the doctrine of the Logos in both its forms, Pauline (2 Cor. iv. 4, &c., *ut sup.*) and Johannean (John i. 1 ff.). The moments in question are so many steps in the passage through an earthly life of One who came forth from God and returned to God, not stages in the gradual deification of one who began his career as ψιλὸς ἄνθρωπος.

ἐν δυνάμει: not with υἱοῦ Θεοῦ, as Weiss, Lips. and others, 'Son of God *in power*,' opposed to the present state of humiliation, but rather adverbially, qualifying ὁρισθέντος, 'declared with might to be Son of God.' The Resurrection is regarded as a 'miracle' or 'signal manifestation of Divine Power.' Comp. esp. 2 Cor. xiii. 4 ἐσταυρώθη ἐξ ἀσθενείας, ἀλλὰ ζῇ ἐκ δυνάμεως Θεοῦ. This parallel determines the connexion of ἐν δυν.

κατὰ πνεῦμα ἁγιωσύνης: not (i) = Πνεῦμα Ἅγιον, the Third Person in the Trinity (as the Patristic writers generally and some moderns), because the antithesis of σάρξ and πνεῦμα requires that they shall be in the same person; nor (ii), with Beng. and other moderns (even Lid.) = the Divine Nature in Christ as if the Human Nature were coextensive with the σάρξ and the Divine Nature were coextensive with the πνεῦμα, which would be very like the error of Apollinaris; but (iii) the human πνεῦμα, like the human σάρξ, distinguished however from that of ordinary humanity by an exceptional and transcendent Holiness (cf. Heb. ii. 17; iv. 15 'it behoved Him in all things to be made like unto His brethren .. yet without sin').

ἁγιωσύνη, not found in profane literature, occurs three times in LXX of the Psalms, not always in agreement with Heb. (Pss. xcv. 6 [xcvi. 6 'strength']; xcvi. 12 [xcvii. 12 'holy name,' lit. 'memorial']; cxlv. 5 [cxlv. 5 'honour']). In all three places it is used of the Divine attribute; but in 2 Macc. iii. 12 we have ἡ τοῦ τόπου ἁγιωσύνη. In *Test. XII. Patr.* Levi 18 the identical phrase πνεῦμ. ἁγιωσ. occurs of the saints in Paradise. The passage is Christian in its character, but may belong to the original work and is in any case probably early. If so, the use of the phrase is so different from that in the text, that the presumption would be that it was not coined for the first time by St. Paul. The same instance would show that the phrase does not of itself and alone necessarily imply divinity. The πνεῦμα ἁγιωσύνης, though not the Divine nature, is that in which the Divinity or Divine Personality resided. The clear definition of this point was one of the last results of the Christological controversies of the fifth and sixth centuries (Loofs, *Dogmengesch.* § 39, 3). For ἁγιωσ. see on ἅγιοι ver. 7.

ἐξ ἀναστάσεως νεκρῶν: a remarkable phrase as applied to Christ. His was not a 'resurrection of dead persons' ('aȝenrisynge of dead

men' Wic.) but of a single dead person. We might expect rather
νεκροῦ or ἐκ νεκρῶν (as in 1 Pet. i. 3); and it is probable that this
form is only avoided because of ἐξ ἀναστάσεως coming just before.
But νεκρῶν coalesces closely in meaning with ἀναστ., so as to give it
very much the force of a compound word, 'by a dead-rising'
(*Todtenauferstehung*), 'a resurrection such as that when dead persons rise.' Christ is 'the first-born from the dead' (Col. i. 18).

τοῦ Κυρίου ἡμῶν. Although in O. T. regularly applied to God
as equivalent of *Adonai*, *Jahveh*, this word does not in itself
necessarily involve Divinity. The Jews applied it to their Messiah
(Mark xii. 36, 37 ‖; *Ps. Sol.* xvii. 36 βασιλεὺς αὐτῶν χριστὸς κύριος)
without thereby pronouncing Him to be 'God'; they expressly
distinguished between the Messiah and the *Memra* or 'Word' of
Jehovah (Weber, *Altsyn. Theol.* p. 178). On the lips of Christians
Κύριος denotes the idea of 'Sovereignty,' primarily over themselves
as the society of believers (Col. i. 18, &c.), but also over all creation
(Phil. ii. 10, 11; Col. i. 16, 17). The title was given to our Lord
even in His lifetime (John xiii. 13 'Ye call me, Master (ὁ διδά-
σκαλος), and, Lord (ὁ Κύριος): and ye say well; for so I am'), but
without a full consciousness of its significance: it was only after
the Resurrection that the Apostles took it to express their central
belief (Phil. ii. 9 ff., &c.).

5. ἐλάβομεν. The best explanation of the plur. seems to be that
St. Paul associates himself with the other Apostles.

χάρις is an important word with a distinctively theological use
and great variety of meaning: (1) objectively, 'sweetness,' 'at-
tractiveness,' a sense going back to Homer (*Od.* viii. 175); Ps. xlv.
(xliv.) 3 ἐξεχύθη χάρις ἐν χείλεσί σου: Eccl. x. 12 λόγοι στόματος
σοφοῦ χάρις: Luke iv. 22 λόγοι χάριτος : (2) subjectively 'favour,'
'kindly feeling,' 'good will,' especially as shown by a superior
towards an inferior. In Eastern despotisms this personal feeling
on the part of the king or chieftain is most important : hence
εὑρεῖν χάριν is the commonest form of phrase in the O. T. (Gen.
vi. 8; xviii. 3, &c.) ; in many of these passages (esp. in anthropo-
morphic scenes where God is represented as holding colloquy
with man) it is used of 'finding favour' in the sight of God. Thus
the word comes to be used (3) of the 'favour' or 'good will'
of God; and that (a) generally, as in Zech. xii. 10 ἐκχεῶ . . πνεῦμα
χάριτος καὶ οἰκτιρμοῦ, but far more commonly in N. T. (Luke ii. 40;
John i. 14, 16, &c.); (β) by a usage which is specially characteristic
of St. Paul (though not confined to him), with opposition to
ὀφείλημα, 'debt' (Rom. iv. 4), and to ἔργα, 'works' (implying merit,
Rom. xi. 6), '*unearned* favour'—with stress upon the fact that
it is unearned, and therefore as bestowed not upon the righteous
but on sinners (cf. esp. Rom. v. 6 with v. 2). In this sense the
word takes a prominent place in the vocabulary of Justification.

(4) The cause being put for the effect χάρις denotes (a) 'the state
of grace or favour' which the Christian enjoys (Rom. v. 2), or
(β), like χάρισμα, any particular gift or gifts of grace (πλήρης χάριτος
Acts vi. 8). We note however that the later technical use, esp.
of the Latin *gratia*, for the Divine prompting and help which
precedes and accompanies right action does not correspond exactly
to the usage of N. T.   (5) As χάρις or 'kindly feeling' in the
donor evokes a corresponding χάρις or 'gratitude' in the recipient,
it comes to mean simply 'thanks' (1 Cor. x. 30).

χάριν here = that general favour which the Ap. shares with all
Christians and by virtue of which he is one ; ἀποστολήν = the more
peculiar gifts of an Apostle.

We observe that St. Paul regards this spiritual endowment as
conferred upon him by Christ (δι' οὖ)—we may add, acting through
His Spirit, as the like gifts are described elsewhere as proceeding
from the Spirit (1 Cor. xii, &c.).

εἰς ὑπακοὴν πίστεως : may be rendered with Vulg. *ad obediendum
fidei* provided that πίστ. is not hardened too much into the sense
which it afterwards acquired of a 'body of doctrine' (with art.
τῇ πίστει Jude 3). At this early date a body of formulated doctrine,
though it is rapidly coming to exist, does not still exist : πίστις
is still, what it is predominantly to St. Paul, the lively act or impulse
of adhesion to Christ. In confessing Christ the lips 'obey' this
impulse of the heart (Rom. x. 10). From another point of view,
going a step further back, we may speak of 'obeying the Gospel'
(Rom. x. 16). Faith is the act of assent by which the Gospel is
appropriated. See below on ver. 17.

ἐν πᾶσι τοῖς ἔθνεσιν. Gif. argues for the rendering 'among all
nations' on the ground that a comprehensive address is best suited
to the opening of the Epistle, and to the proper meaning of the
phrase πάντα τὰ ἔθνη (cf. Gen. xviii. 18, &c.). But St. Paul's commission as an Apostle was specially to the *Gentiles* (Gal. ii. 8), and it
is more pointed to tell the Roman Christians that they thus belong
to his special province (ver. 6), than to regard them merely as one
among the mass of nations. This is also clearly the sense in which
the word is used in ver. 13. Cf. Hort, *Rom. and Eph.* p. 21 f.

ὑπὲρ τοῦ ὀνόματος αὐτοῦ. This is rather more than simply 'for
His glory.' The idea goes back to the O. T. (Ps. cvi. [cv.] 8 ;
Ezek. xx. 14 ; Mal. i. 11). The Name of God is intimately
connected with the revelation of God. Israel is the instrument or
minister of that revelation ; so that by the fidelity of Israel the
revelation itself is made more impressive and commended in the
eyes of other nations. But the Christian Church is the new Israel :
and hence the gaining of fresh converts and their fidelity when
gained serves in like manner to commend the further revelation
made of God in Christ (αὐτοῦ, cf. Acts v. 41 ; Phil. ii. 9).

6. ἐν οἷς: not merely in a geographical sense of a Jewish community among Gentiles, but clearly numbering the Roman Church
among Gentile communities.

κλητοὶ Ἰησοῦ Χριστοῦ: 'called ones of Jesus Christ': gen. of
possession.

7. ἐν Ῥώμῃ: om. G g, *schol. cod.* 47 (τὸ ἐν Ῥώμῃ οὔτε ἐν τῇ ἐξηγήσει
οὔτε ἐν τῷ ῥητῷ μνημονεύει, i. e. some commentator whom the Scholiast
had before him). G reads πᾶσι τοῖς οὖσιν ἐν ἀγάπῃ Θεοῦ (similarly
d* Vulg. *codd.* and the commentary of Ambrstr. seem to imply
πᾶσι τοῖς οὖσιν ἐν Ῥώμῃ ἐν ἀγάπῃ Θεοῦ). The same MS. omits τοῖς
ἐν Ῥώμῃ in ver. 15. These facts, taken together with the fluctuating position of the final doxology, xvi. 25–27, would seem
to give some ground for the inference that there were in circulation
in ancient times a few copies of the Epistle from which all local
references had been removed. It is however important to notice
that the authorities which place the doxology at the end of ch. xiv
are quite different from those which omit ἐν Ῥώμῃ here and in
ver. 15. For a full discussion of the question see the Introduction,
§ 9.

κλητοῖς ἁγίοις. Κλητὴ ἁγία represents consistently in LXX the
phrase which is translated in AV. and RV. 'an holy convocation'
(so eleven times in Lev. xxiii and Ex. xii. 16). The rendering appears to be due to a misunderstanding, the Heb. word used being one
with which the LXX translators were not familiar. Whereas in
Heb. the phrase usually runs, '*on* such a day there shall be a holy
convocation,' the LXX treat the word translated convocation as an
adj. and make 'day' the subject of the sentence, 'such a day
(or feast) shall be κλητὴ ἁγία, i. e. specially appointed, chosen,
distinguished, holy (day).' This is a striking instance of the way
in which St. Paul takes a phrase which was clearly in the first
instance a creation of the LXX and current wholly through
it, appropriating it to Christian use, and recasts its meaning, substituting a theological sense for a liturgical. Obviously
κλητοῖς has the same sense as κλητός in ver. 1: as he himself was
'called' to be an Apostle, so all Christians were 'called' to be
Christians; and they personally receive the consecration which
under the Old Covenant was attached to 'times and seasons.'

For the following detailed statement of the evidence respecting κλητὴ ἁγία
we are indebted to Dr. Driver:—

κλητή corresponds to מִקְרָא, from קָרָא *to call*, a technical term almost
wholly confined to the Priests' Code, denoting apparently a special religious
meeting, or 'convocation,' held on certain sacred days.

It is represented by κλητή, Ex. xii. 16 b; Lev. xxiii. 7, 8, 27, 35, 36;
Num. xxviii. 25. Now in all these passages, where the Heb. has '*on* such
a day there shall be a holy convocation,' the LXX have 'such a day shall
be κλητὴ ἁγία,' i.e. they alter the form of the sentence, make *day* subject,
and use κλητή with its proper force as an adj. 'shall be a *called* (i.e.

a specially appointed, chosen, distinguished*), *holy* (day)'; cf. κλ. in *Il.* ix.
165 and Rom. i. 1.   They read analogously with מִקְרָא in Lev. xxiii. 2 αἱ
ἑορταὶ κυρίου, ἃς καλέσετε αὐτὰς κλητὰς ἁγίας (cf. v. 37), 21 καὶ καλέσετε
ταύτην τὴν ἡμέραν κλητήν· ἁγία ἔσται ὑμῖν.   In Lev. xxiii. 3 (cf. v. 24),
κλητὴ ἁγία seems to be in apposition with ἀνάπαυσις.   The usage of κλητή
in Lev. xxiii is, however, such as to suggest that it was probably felt to
have the form of a subst. (sc. ἡμέρα) ; cf. ἐπίκλητος.

This view of κλ. is supported by their rendering of מִקְרָא elsewhere.   In
Ex. xii. 16 a, Lev. xxiii. 4 they also alter the form of the sentence, and
render it by a verb, κληθήσεται ἁγία, and ἁγίας καλέσετε respectively.

In Num. xxviii. 18, 26 (καὶ τῇ ἡμέρᾳ τῶν νέων . . . . ἐπίκλητος ἁγία ἔσται
ὑμῖν: similarly xxix. 1, 7, 12), they express it by ἐπίκλητος (the same word
used (ἡ ἡμέρα ἡ πρώτη ἐπίκλητος ἁγία ἔσται ὑμῖν) *ib.* i. 16; xxvi. 9, for the
ordinary partic. *called, summoned*), i.e. I suppose in the same sense of
specially appointed (cf. Josh. xx. 9 αἱ πόλεις αἱ ἐπίκλητοι τοῖς υἱοῖς Ἰσραήλ).

Is. i. 13 'the calling of a convocation' is represented in LXX by ἡμέραν
μεγάλην, and iv. 5 'all her convocations' by τὰ περικίκλῳ αὐτῆς.

From all this, it occurs to me that the LXX were not familiar with the term
מקרא, and did not know what it meant.   I think it probable that they pronounced it not as a subst. מִקְרָא, but as a *participle* מְקֹרָא ('called').

ἁγίοις.   The history of this word would seem to be very parallel
to that of κλητοῖς.   It is more probable that its meaning developed
by a process of deepening from without inwards than by extension
from within outwards.   Its connotation would seem to have been
at first physical and ceremonial, and to have become gradually
more and more ethical and spiritual.   (1) The fundamental idea
appears to be that of 'separation.'   So the word 'holy' came
to be applied in all the Semitic languages, (2) to that which was
'set apart' for the service of God, whether things (e. g. 1 Kings vii.
51 [37]) or persons (e. g. Ex. xxii. 31 [29]).   But (3) inasmuch as
that which was so 'set apart' or 'consecrated' to God was required
to be free from blemish, the word would come to denote 'freedom
from blemish, spot, or stain'—in the first instance physical, but
by degrees, as moral ideas ripened, also moral.   (4) At first the
idea of 'holiness,' whether physical or moral, would be directly
associated with the service of God, but it would gradually become
detached from this connexion and denote 'freedom from blemish,
spot, or stain,' in itself and apart from any particular destination.
In this sense it might be applied even to God Himself, and we
find it so applied even in the earliest Hebrew literature (e. g.
1 Sam. vi. 20).   And in proportion as the conception of God itself
became elevated and purified, the word which expressed this
central attribute of His Being would contract a meaning of more
severe and awful purity, till at last it becomes the culminating
and supreme expression for the very essence of the Divine Nature.
When once this height had been reached the sense so acquired

---

* Biel (*Lex. in LXX.*) cites from Phavorinus the gloss, κλ., ἡ καλεστὴ καὶ ἡ
ἐξοχωτάτη.

would be reflected back over all the lower uses, and the tendency
would be more and more to assimilate the idea of holiness in
the creature to that of holiness in the Creator. This tendency
is formulated in the exhortation, 'Ye shall be holy; for I, the
Lord your God, am holy' (Lev. xix. 2, &c.).

Such would appear to have been the history of the word up to
the time when St. Paul made use of it. He would find a series of
meanings ready to his hand, some lower and some higher; and he
chooses on this occasion not that which is highest but one rather
midway in the scale. When he describes the Roman Christians as
ἅγιοι, he does not mean that they reflect in their persons the attributes of the All-Holy, but only that they are 'set apart' or 'consecrated' to His service. At the same time he is not content to rest
in this lower sense, but after his manner he takes it as a basis or
starting-point for the higher. Because Christians are 'holy' in the
sense of 'consecrated,' they are to become daily more fit for the
service to which they are committed (Rom. vi. 17, 18, 22), they are
to be 'transformed by the renewing' of their mind (Rom. xii. 2).
He teaches in fact implicitly if not explicitly the same lesson as
St. Peter, 'As He which called you is holy, be ye yourselves also
holy in all manner of living (AV. conversation); because it is
written, Ye shall be holy, for I am holy' (1 Pet. i. 15, 16).

We note that *Ps. Sol.* had already described the Messianic
people as λαὸς ἅγιος (καὶ συνάξει λαὸν ἅγιον, οὗ ἀφηγήσεται ἐν δικαιοσύνῃ
xvii. 28; cf. Dan. vii. 18–27; viii. 24). Similarly *Enoch* ciii. 2;
cviii. 3, where 'books of the holy ones = the roll of the members
of the Kingdom' (Charles). The same phrase had been a designation for Israel in O. T., but only in Deut. (vii. 6; xiv. 2, 21; xxvi.
19; xxviii. 9, varied from Ex. xix. 6 ἔθνος ἅγιον). We have thus
another instance in which St. Paul transfers to Christians a title
hitherto appropriated to the Chosen People. But in this case the
Jewish Messianic expectation had been beforehand with him.

There is a certain element of conjecture in the above sketch, which is
inevitable from the fact that the earlier stages in the history of the word had
been already gone through when the Hebrew literature begins. The instances
above given will show this. The main problem is how to account for the
application of the same word at once to the Creator and to His creatures,
both things and persons. The common view (accepted also by Delitzsch) is
that in the latter case it means 'separated' or 'set apart' for God, and in
the former case that it means 'separate from evil' (*sejunctus ab omni vitio,
labis expers*). But the link between these two meanings is little more than
verbal; and it seems more probable that the idea of holiness in God, whether
in the sense of exaltedness (Baudissin) or of purity (Delitzsch), is derivative
rather than primary. There are a number of monographs on the subject, of
which perhaps the best and the most accessible is that by Fr. Delitzsch
in Herzog's *Real-Encyklopädie*, ed. 2, s. v. 'Heiligkeit Gottes.' Instructive discussions will be found in Davidson, *Ezekiel*, p. xxxix. f.; Robertson
Smith, *Religion of the Semites*, pp. 132 ff., 140 (140 ff., 150 ed. 2); Schultz,
Theology of the Old Testament, ii. 131, 167 ff. A treatise by Dr. J. Agar

Beet is on a good method, but is somewhat affected by critical questions as to the sequence of the documents.

There is an interesting progression in the addresses of St. Paul's Epp.: 1, 2 Thess. Gal. τῇ ἐκκλησίᾳ (ταῖς ἐκκλησίαις); 1, 2 Cor. τῇ ἐκκλ.+τοῖς ἁγίοις; 1 Cor. Rom. κλητοῖς ἁγίοις; Rom. Phil. πᾶσι τοῖς ἁγίοις; Eph. Col. τοῖς ἁγίοις καὶ πιστοῖς.

The idea of the local Church, as a unit in itself, is more prominent in the earlier Epp.; that of individual Christians forming part of the great body of believers (the Church Catholic) is more prominent in the later. And it would be natural that there should be some such progression of thought, as the number of local churches multiplied, and as the Apostle himself came to see them in a larger perspective. It would however be a mistake to argue at once from this that the use of ἐκκλησία for the local Church necessarily came first in order of time. On the other side may be urged the usage of the O. T., and more particularly of the Pentateuch, where ἐκκλησία constantly stands for the religious assembly of the whole people, as well as the saying of our Lord Himself in Matt. xvi. 18. But the question is too large to be argued as a side issue.

Rudolf Sohm's elaborate *Kirchenrecht* (Leipzig, 1892) starts from the assumption that the prior idea is that of the Church as a whole. But just this part of his learned work has by no means met with general acceptance.

χάρις καὶ εἰρήνη. Observe the combination and deepened religious significance of the common Greek salutation χαίρειν, and the common Heb. salutation *Shalom*, 'Peace.' χάρις and εἰρήνη are both used in the full theological sense: χάρις = the favour of God, εἰρήνη = the cessation of hostility to him and the peace of mind which follows upon it.

There are four formulae of greeting in N. T.: the simple χαίρειν in St. James; χάρις καὶ εἰρήνη in Epp. Paul. (except 1, 2 Tim.) and in 1, 2 St. Peter; χάρις, ἔλεος, εἰρήνη in the Epistles to Timothy and 2 St. John; ἔλεος καὶ εἰρήνη καὶ ἀγάπη in St. Jude.

εἰρήνη. We have seen how χάρις had acquired a deeper sense in N. T. as compared with O. T.; with εἰρήνη this process had taken place earlier. It too begins as a phrase of social intercourse, marking that stage in the advance of civilization at which the assumption that every stranger encountered was an enemy gave place to overtures of friendship (Εἰρήνη σοι Jud. xix. 20, &c.). But the word soon began to be used in a religious sense of the cessation of the Divine anger and the restoration of harmony between God and man (Ps. xxix. [xxviii.] 11 Κύριος εὐλογήσει τὸν λαὸν αὐτοῦ ἐν εἰρήνῃ: lxxxv. [lxxxiv.] 8 λαλήσει εἰρήνην ἐπὶ τὸν λαὸν αὐτοῦ: *ibid.* 10 δικαιοσύνη καὶ εἰρήνη κατεφίλησαν: cxix. [cxviii.] 165 εἰρήνη πολλὴ τοῖς ἀγαπῶσι τὸν νόμον: Is. liii. 5 παιδεία εἰρήνης ἡμῶν ἐπ' αὐτόν: Jer. xiv. 13 ἀλήθειαν καὶ εἰρήνην δώσω ἐπὶ τῆς γῆς: Ezek xxxiv. 25 διαθήσομαι τῷ Δαυὶδ διαθήκην εἰρήνης [cf. xxxvii. 26]. Nor is this use confined to the Canonical Scriptures: cf. *Enoch* v. 4 (other reff. in Charles, *ad loc.*); *Jubilees* i. 15, 29; xxii. 9; xxxiii. 12, 30, &c.; it was one of the functions of the Messiah to bring 'peace' (Weber, *Allsyn. Theol.* p. 362 f.).

The nearest parallel for the use of the word in a salutation as here is Dan. iii. 98 [31]; iv. 34 (LXX); iii. 98 [31]; vi. 25 (Theodot.) εἰρήνη ὑμῖν πληθυνθείη.

ἀπὸ Θεοῦ πατρὸς ἡμῶν καὶ Κυρίου Ἰησοῦ Χριστοῦ. The juxta-position of God as Father and Christ as Lord may be added to the proofs already supplied by vv. 1, 4, that St. Paul, if not formally enunciating a doctrine of the Divinity of Christ, held a view which cannot really be distinguished from it. The assignment of the respective titles of 'Father' and 'Lord' represents the first begin-ning of Christological speculation. It is stated in precise terms and with a corresponding assignment of appropriate prepositions in 1 Cor. viii. 6 ἀλλ' ἡμῖν εἷς Θεὸς ὁ πατήρ, ἐξ οὗ τὰ πάντα, καὶ ἡμεῖς εἰς αὐτόν, καὶ εἷς Κύριος Ἰησοῦς Χριστός, δι' οὗ τὰ πάντα, καὶ ἡμεῖς δι' αὐτοῦ. The opposition in that passage between the gods of the heathen and the Christians' God seems to show that ἡμῶν = at least primarily, ' us Christians ' rather than ' us men.'

Not only does the juxtaposition of ' Father ' and ' Lord ' mark a stage in the doctrine of the Person of Christ ; it also marks an important stage in the history of the doctrine of the Trinity. It is found already some six years before the composition of Ep. to Romans at the time when St. Paul wrote his earliest extant Epistle (1 Thess. i. 1 ; cf. 2 Thess. i. 2). This shows that even at that date (A. D. 52) the definition of the doctrine had begun. It is well also to remember that although in this particular verse of Ep. to Romans the form in which it appears is incomplete, the triple formula concludes an Epistle written a few months earlier (2 Cor. xiii. 14). There is nothing more wonderful in the history of human thought than the silent and imperceptible way in which this doctrine, to us so difficult, took its place without struggle and without controversy among accepted Christian truths.

πατρὸς ἡμῶν. The singling out of this title must be an echo of its constant and distinctive use by our Lord Himself. The doctrine of the Fatherhood of God was taught in the Old Testament (Ps. lxviii. 5 ; lxxxix. 26 ; Deut. xxxii. 6 ; Is. lxiii. 16 ; lxiv. 8 ; Jer. xxxi. 9 ; Mal. i. 6 ; ii. 10) ; but there is usually some restriction or qualification—God is the Father of Israel, of the Messianic King, of a particular class such as the weak and friendless. It may also be said that the doctrine of Divine Fatherhood is implicitly contained in the stress which is laid on the ' loving-kindness ' of God (e. g. in such fundamental passages as Ex. xxxiv. 6, 7 compared with Ps. ciii. 13). But this idea which lies as a partially developed germ in the Old Testament breaks into full bloom in the New. It is placed by our Lord Himself in the fore-front of the conception of God. It takes however a two-fold ramification : ὁ πατὴρ ὑμῶν [ἡμῶν, σου, αὐτῶν] (e. g. twenty times in St. Matt.), and ὁ πατήρ μου [ὁ πατήρ] (e. g. twenty-three times in St. Matt.). In particular this second phrase marks the distinction between the Son and the Father ; so that when the two are placed in juxtaposition, as in the greeting of this and other Epistles, ὁ Πατήρ is the natural term to use. The mere fact of juxtaposition sufficiently suggests the πατὴρ τοῦ Κυρίου ἡμῶν Ἰησοῦ Χριστοῦ (which is expressed in full in 2 Cor. i. 3; Eph. i. 3; Col. i. 3 ; cf. Rom. xv. 6; 2 Cor. xi. 31, but not Eph. iii. 14; Col. ii. 2); so that the Apostle widens the reference by throwing in ἡμῶν, to bring out the connexion between the source of ‘ grace and peace ’ and its recipients.

It is no doubt true that πατήρ is occasionally used in N. T. in the more general sense of ‘ Creator ’ (James i. 17 ‘Father of lights,’ i. e. in the first instance, Creator of the heavenly bodies; Heb. xii. 9 ‘ Father of spirits ’; cf. Acts xvii. 28, but perhaps not Eph. iv. 6 πατὴρ πάντων, where πάντων may be masc.). It is true also that ὁ πατὴρ τῶν ὅλων in this sense is common in Philo, and that similar phrases occur in the early post-apostolic writers (e. g. Clem. Rom. *ad Cor.* xix. 2 ; Justin, *Apol.* i. 36, 61 ; Tatian, *Or. c. Graec.* 4). But when Harnack prefers to give this interpretation to *Pater* in the earliest creeds (*Das Apost. Glaubensbekenntniss*, p. 20), the immense preponderance of N. T. usage, and the certainty that the Creed is based upon that usage (e. g. in 1 Cor. viii. 6) seem to be decisive against him. On the early history of the term see esp. Swete, *Apost. Creed*, p. 20 ff.

The Theological Terminology of Rom. i. 1–7.

In looking back over these opening verses it is impossible not to be struck by the definiteness and maturity of the theological teaching contained in them. It is remarkable enough, and characteristic of this primitive Christian literature, especially of the Epistles of St. Paul, that a mere salutation should contain so much weighty teaching of any kind ; but it is still more remarkable when we think what that teaching is and the early date at which it was penned. There are no less than five distinct groups of ideas all expressed with deliberate emphasis and precision: (1) A complete set of ideas as to the commission and authority of an Apostle ; (2) A complete set of ideas as to the status in the sight of God of a Christian community ; (3) A clear apprehension of the relation of the new order of things to the old; (4) A clear assertion of what we should call summarily the Divinity of Christ, which St. Paul regarded both in the light of its relation to the expectations of his countrymen, and also in its transcendental reality, as revealed by or inferred from the words and acts of Christ Himself; (5) A some-what advanced stage in the discrimination of distinct Persons in the Godhead. We observe too how St. Paul connects together these groups of ideas, and sees in them so many parts of a vast Divine plan which covers the whole of human history, and indeed stretches back beyond its beginning. The Apostle has to the full that sense which is so impressive in the Hebrew prophets that he himself is only an instrument, the place and function of which are clearly foreseen, for the accomplishment of God's gracious pur-poses (compare e. g. Jer. i. 5 and Gal. i. 15). These purposes are working themselves out, and the Roman Christians come within their range.

When we come to examine particular expressions we find that a large proportion of them are drawn from the O. T. In some cases an idea which has been hitherto fluid is sharply formulated (κλητός, ἀφωρισμένος); in other cases an old phrase has been adopted with comparatively little modification (ὑπὲρ τοῦ ὀνόματος αὐτοῦ, and perhaps εἰρήνη); in others the transference involves a larger modification (δοῦλος Ἰησοῦ Χριστοῦ, χάρις, κλητοὶ ἅγιοι, Κύριος, Θεὸς πατήρ); in others again we have a term which has ac-quired a significance since the close of the O. T. which Christianity appropriates (ἐπαγγελία [προεπηγγείλατο], γραφαὶ ἅγιαι, ἀνάστασις νεκρῶν, ἅγιοι); in yet others we have a new coinage (ἀπόστολος, εὐαγγέλιον), which however in these instances is due, not to St. Paul or the other Apostles, but to Christ Himself.

ST. PAUL AND THE ROMAN CHURCH.

I. 8-15. *God knows how long I have desired to see you —a hope which I trust may at last be accomplished—and to deliver to you, as to the rest of the Gentile world, my message of salvation.*

[8] In writing to you I must first offer my humble thanks to God, through Him Who as High Priest presents all our prayers and praises, for the world-wide fame which as a united Church you bear for your earnest Christianity. [9] If witness were needed to show how deep is my interest in you, I might appeal to God Himself Who hears that constant ritual of prayer which my spirit addresses to Him in my work of preaching the glad tidings of His Son. [10] He knows how unceasingly your Church is upon my lips, and how every time I kneel in prayer it is my petition, that at some near day

I may at last, in the course which God's Will marks out for me, really have my way made clear to visit you. [11] For I have a great desire to see you and to impart to you some of those many gifts (of instruction, comfort, edification and the like) which the Holy Spirit has been pleased to bestow upon me, and so to strengthen your Christian character. [12] I do not mean that I am above receiving or that you have nothing to bestow,—far from it,—but that I myself may be cheered by my intercourse with you (ἐν ὑμῖν), or that we may be mutually cheered by each other's faith, I by yours and you by mine. [13] I should be sorry for you to suppose that this is a new resolve on my part. The fact is that I often intended to visit you—an intention until now as often frustrated —in the hope of reaping some spiritual harvest from my labours among you, as in the rest of the Gentile world. [14] There is no limit to this duty of mine to preach the Gospel. To all without distinction whether of language or of culture, I must discharge the debt which Christ has laid upon me. [15] Hence, so far as the decision rests with me, I am bent on delivering the message of salvation to you too at Rome.

8. διά. *Agere autem Deo gratias, hoc est sacrificium laudis offerre: et ideo addit* per Jesum Christum; *velut per Pontificem magnum* Orig.

ἡ πίστις ὑμῶν. For a further discussion of this word see below on ver. 17. Here it is practically equivalent to 'your Christianity,' the distinctive act which makes a man a Christian carrying with it the direct consequences of that act upon the character. Much confusion of thought would be saved if wherever 'faith' was mentioned the question were always consciously asked, Who or what is its object? It is extremely rare for faith to be used in the N. T. as a mere abstraction without a determinate object. In this Epistle 'faith' is nearly always 'faith *in Christ*.' The object is expressed in iii. 22, 26 but is left to be understood elsewhere. In the case of Abraham 'faith' is not so much 'faith in God' as 'faith in the *promises* of God,' which promises are precisely those which are fulfilled in Christianity. Or it would perhaps be more strictly true to say that the *immediate* object of faith is in most cases Christ or the promises which pointed to Christ. At the same time there is always in the background the Supreme Author of that whole 'economy' of which the Incarnation of Christ formed a part. Thus it is God Who justifies though the moving cause of justification is usually defined as 'faith in Christ.' And inasmuch as it is He Who both promised that Christ should come and also

Himself brought about the fulfilment of the promise, even justifying faith may be described as 'faith in God.' The most conspicuous example of this is ch. iv. 5 τῷ δὲ μὴ ἐργαζομένῳ, πιστεύοντι δὲ ἐπὶ τὸν δικαιοῦντα τὸν ἀσεβῆ, λογίζεται ἡ πίστις αὐτοῦ εἰς δικαιοσύνην.

9. λατρεύω connected with λάτρις, 'hired servant,' and λάτρον, 'hire': (i) already in classical Gk. applied to the service of a higher power (διὰ τὴν τοῦ θεοῦ λατρείαν Plato, *Apol.* 23 B); (ii) in LXX always of the service either of the true God or of heathen divinities. Hence Augustine: Λατρεία . . . *aut semper aut tam frequenter ut fere semper, ea dicitur servitus quae pertinet ad colendum Deum* (Trench, *Syn.* p. 120 f.).

> Λατρεύειν is at once somewhat wider and somewhat narrower in meaning than λειτουργεῖν: (i) it is used only (or almost wholly) of the service of God where λειτουργεῖν (λειτουργός) is used also of the service of men (Josh. i. 1 v. l.; 1 Kings i. 4, xix. 21; 2 Kings iv. 43, vi. 15, &c.); (ii) but on the other hand it is used of the service both of priest and people, esp. of the service rendered to Jahveh by the whole race of Israel (Acts xxvi. 7 τὸ δωδεκάφυλον ἐν ἐκτενείᾳ λατρεῦον, cf. Rom. ix. 4); λειτουργεῖν is appropriated to the ministrations of priests and Levites (Heb. x. 11, &c.). Where λειτουργεῖν (λειτουργός) is not strictly in this sense, there is yet more or less conscious reference to it (e. g. in Rom. xiii. 6 and esp. xv. 16).

ἐν τῷ πνεύματί μου. The πνεῦμα is the organ of service; the εὐαγγέλιον (= τὸ κήρυγμα τοῦ εὐαγγελίου) the sphere in which the service is rendered.

ἐπὶ τῶν προσευχῶν μου: 'at my prayers,' at all my times of prayer (cf. 1 Thess. i. 2 ; Eph. i. 16; Philem. 4).

10. εἴπως. On the construction see Burton, *Moods and Tenses,* § 276.

ἤδη ποτέ: a difficult expression to render in English; 'now at length' (AV. and RV.) omits ποτέ, just as 'in ony maner sumtyme' (Wic.) omits ἤδη; 'sometime at the length' (Rhem.) is more accurate, 'some near day at last.' In contrast with νῦν (which denotes present time simply) ἤδη denotes the present or near future in relation to the process by which it has been reached, and with a certain suggestion of surprise or relief that it has been reached so soon as it has. So here ἤδη = 'now, after all this waiting': ποτέ makes the moment more indefinite. On ἤδη see Bäumlein, *Griech. Partikeln,* p. 138 ff.

εὐοδωθήσομαι. The word has usually dropped the idea of ὁδός and means 'to be prospered' in any way (e. g. 1 Cor. xvi. 2 ὅ τι ἂν εὐοδῶται, where it is used of profits gained in trade; similarly in LXX and *Test. XII. Patr.* Jud. 1, Gad 7); and so here Mey. Gif. RV., &c. It does not, however, follow that because a metaphor is often dropped, it may not be recalled where it is directly suggested by the context. We are thus tempted to render with the earlier English Versions and Vulg. *prosperum iter habeam* ('I have a spedi wey' Wic.).

ἐν τῷ θελήματι τοῦ Θεοῦ. St. Paul has a special reason for laying stress on the fact that all his movements are in the hands of God. He has a strong sense of the risks which he incurs in going up to Jerusalem (Rom. xv. 30 f.), and he is very doubtful whether anything that he intends will be accomplished (Hort, *Rom. and Eph.* p. 42 ff.).

ἐλθεῖν : probably for ὥστε ἐλθεῖν (Burton, § 371 *c*).

11. ἐπιποθῶ : ἐπι- marks the direction of the desire, 'to you-ward' ; thus by laying stress on the personal object of the verb it rather strengthens its emotional character.

χάρισμα πνευματικόν. St. Paul has in his mind the kind of gifts —partly what we should call natural and partly transcending the ordinary workings of nature—described in 1 Cor. xii–xiv ; Rom. xii. 6 ff. Some, probably most, of these gifts he possessed in an eminent degree himself (1 Cor. xiv. 18), and he was assured that when he came to Rome he would be able to give the Christians there the fullest benefit of them (Rom. xv. 29 οἶδα δὲ ὅτι ἐρχόμενος πρὸς ὑμᾶς ἐν πληρώματι εὐλογίας Χριστοῦ ἐλεύσομαι). His was con-spicuously a case which came under the description of John vii. 38 'He that believeth on Me, as the scripture hath said, out of his belly shall flow rivers of living water,' i. e. the believer in Christ should himself become a centre and abounding source of spiritual influence and blessing to others.

εἰς τὸ στηριχθῆναι : εἰς τό with Infin. expressing purpose 'is employed with special frequency by Paul, but occurs also in Heb. 1 Pet. and Jas.' (Burton, § 409).

12. συμπαρακληθῆναι : the subject is ἐμέ, which, from the συν- in συμπαρακλ. and ἐν ὑμῖν, is treated in the latter part of the sentence as equivalent to ἡμεῖς. We note of course the delicacy with which the Apostle suddenly checks himself in the expression of his desire to impart from his own fulness to the Roman Christians : he will not assume any airs of superiority, but meets them frankly upon their own level : if he has anything to confer upon them they in turn will confer an equivalent upon him.

13. οὐ θέλω : οὐκ οἴομαι (D*) G, *non arbitror* d e g Ambrstr. ; an instance of Western paraphrase.

σχῶ, 'I may *get*.'

14. Ἕλλησί τε καὶ βαρβάροις : a resolution into its parts of πάντα τὰ ἔθνη, according to (i) divisions of language, (ii) degrees of culture.

15. τὸ κατ' ἐμέ. It is perhaps best, with Gif. Va. Mou., to take τὸ κατ' ἐμέ as subject, πρόθυμον as predicate : so g Vulg. *quod in me promtum est.* In that case τὸ κατ' ἐμέ will = 'I, so far as it rests with me,' i. e. 'under God'—*L'homme propose, Dieu dispose* ; cf. ἐν τῷ θελήματι τοῦ Θεοῦ above. Differently Orig.-lat. (Rufinus) who

makes τὸ κατ' ἐμέ adverbial, *quod in me est promtus sum*: so too
d e Ambrstr. The objection to this is that St. Paul would have
written πρόθυμός εἰμι. Mey. Lips. and others take τὸ κατ' ἐμὲ πρόθυμον together as subject of [ἐστιν] εὐαγγελίσασθαι, 'hence the eagerness on my part (is) to preach.' In Eph. vi. 21; Phil. i. 12; Col.
iv. 7 τὰ κατ' ἐμέ = ' my affairs.'

THESIS OF THE EPISTLE: THE RIGHTEOUSNESS
OF GOD BY FAITH.

I. 16, 17. *That message, humble as it may seem, casts
a new light on the righteousness of God: for it tells how
His righteousness flows forth and embraces man, when it is
met by Faith, or loyal adhesion to Christ.*

[16] Even there, in the imperial city itself, I am not ashamed of my
message, repellent and humiliating as some of its features may
seem. For it is a mighty agency, set in motion by God Himself,
and sweeping on with it towards the haven of Messianic security
every believer—first in order of precedence the Jew, and after him
the Gentile. [17] Do you ask how this agency works and in what it
consists? It is a revelation of the righteousness of God, manifested
in a new method by which righteousness is acquired by man,—
a method, the secret of which is Faith, or ardent loyalty to Jesus
as Messiah and Lord; which Faith is every day both widening its
circles and deepening its hold. It was such an attitude as this
which the prophet Habakkuk meant when, in view of the desolating
Chaldaean invasion, he wrote: 'The righteous man shall save his
life by his faith, or loyalty to Jehovah, while his proud oppressors
perish.'

16. ἐπαισχύνομαι. St. Paul was well aware that his Gospel was
'unto Jews a stumbling-block and unto Gentiles foolishness'
(1 Cor. i. 23). How could it be otherwise, as Chrysostom says, he
was about to preach of One who 'passed for the son of a carpenter,
brought up in Judaea, in the house of a poor woman . . . and who
died like a criminal in the company of robbers?' It hardly needed
the contrast of imperial Rome to emphasize this. On the attraction
which Rome had for St. Paul see the Introduction, § 1; also Hicks
in *Studia Biblica*, iv. 11.

We have an instance here of a corruption coming into the Greek text
through the Latin: ἐπαισχ. ἐπὶ εὐαγγέλιον G, *erubesco super evangelium* g,

confundor de evangelio Aug. The Latin renderings need not imply any various reading. The barbarism in G, which it will be remembered has an interlinear version, arose from the attempt to find a Greek equivalent for every word in the Latin. This is only mentioned as a clear case of a kind of corruption which doubtless operated elsewhere, as notably in Cod. Bezae. It is to be observed, however, that readings of this kind are necessarily quite late.

δύναμις is the word properly used of the manifestations of Divine power. Strictly indeed δύναμις is the inherent attribute or faculty, ἐνέργεια is the attribute or faculty in operation. But the two words are closely allied to each other and δύναμις is so often used for exerted power, especially Divine superhuman power, that it practically covers ἐνέργεια. St. Paul might quite well have written ἐνέργεια here, but the choice of δύναμις throws the stress rather more on the *source* than on the *process*. The word δύναμις in a context like this is one of those to which modern associations seem to give a greater fulness and vividness of meaning. We shall not do wrong if we think of the Gospel as a 'force' in the same kind of sense as that in which science has revealed to us the great 'forces' of nature. It is a principle operating on a vast and continually enlarging scale, and taking effect in a countless number of individuals. This conception only differs from the scientific conception of a force like 'heat' or 'electricity' in that whereas the man of science is too apt to abstract his conception of force from its origin, St. Paul conceives of it as essentially a mode of personal activity; the Gospel has all God's Omnipotence behind it. As such it is before all things a *real* force, not a sham force like so many which the Apostle saw around him; its true nature might be misunderstood, but that did not make it any less powerful : ὁ λόγος γὰρ ὁ τοῦ σταυροῦ τοῖς μὲν ἀπολλυμένοις μωρία ἐστί, τοῖς δὲ σωζομένοις ἡμῖν δύναμις Θεοῦ ἐστί 1 Cor. i. 18 ; cf. 1 Cor. ii. 4, iv. 20 ; 1 Thess. i. 5.

εἰς σωτηρίαν. The fundamental idea contained in σωτηρία is the removal of dangers menacing to life and the consequent placing of life in conditions favourable to free and healthy expansion. Hence, as we might expect, there is a natural progression corresponding to the growth in the conception of life and of the dangers by which it is threatened. (i) In the earlier books of the O. T. σωτ. is simply deliverance from physical peril (Jud. xv. 18 ; 1 Sam. xi. 9, 13, &c.). (ii) But the word has more and more a tendency to be appropriated to the great deliverances of the nation (e. g. Ex. xiv. 13, xv. 2, the Passage of the Red Sea ; Is. xlv. 17, xlvi. 13, lii. 10, &c., the Return from Exile). (iii) Thus by a natural transition it is associated with the Messianic deliverance ; and that both (*a*) in the lower forms of the Jewish Messianic expectation (*Ps. Sol.* x. 9 ; xii. 7 ; cf. *Test. XII. Patr.* Sym. 7 ; Jud. 22 ; Benj. 9, 10 [the form used in all these passages is σωτήριον] ; Luke i. 69, 71, 77), and (β) in the higher form of the Christian hope (Acts iv. 12 ; xiii. 26, &c.).

In this latter sense σωτηρία covers the whole range of the Messianic deliverance, both in its negative aspect as a rescuing from the Wrath under which the whole world is lying (ver. 18 ff.) and in its positive aspect as the imparting of 'eternal life' (Mark x. 30 ‖ ; John iii. 15, 16, &c.). Both these sides are already combined in the earliest extant Epistle (ὅτι οὐκ ἔθετο ἡμᾶς ὁ Θεὸς εἰς ὀργήν, ἀλλ' εἰς περιποίησιν σωτηρίας διὰ τοῦ Κυρίου ἡμῶν Ἰησοῦ Χριστοῦ, τοῦ ἀποθανόντος ὑπὲρ ἡμῶν, ἵνα εἴτε γρηγορῶμεν εἴτε καθεύδωμεν ἅμα σὺν αὐτῷ ζήσωμεν 1 Thess. v. 9, 10).

πρῶτον: om. B G g, Tert. adv. Marc. Lachmann Treg. WH. bracket, because of the combination of B with Western authorities, but they do no more than bracket because in Epp. Paul. B has a slight Western element, to which this particular reading may belong. In that case it would rest entirely upon Western authority. Marcion appears to have omitted πρῶτον as well as the quotation from Habakkuk, and it is possible that the omission in this small group of Western MSS. may be due to his influence.

For the precedence assigned to the Jew comp. Rom. iii. 1, ix. 1 ff., xi. 16 ff., xv. 9; also Matt. xv. 24; Jo. iv. 22; Acts xiii. 46. The point is important in view of Baur and his followers who exaggerate the opposition of St. Paul to the Jews. He defends himself and his converts from their attacks; but he fully concedes the priority of their claim and he is most anxious to conciliate them (Rom. xv. 31 ; cf. ix. 1 ff., x. 1 ff.; xv. 8, &c.: see also Introduction § 4).

17. δικαιοσύνη Θεοῦ. For some time past it has seemed to be almost an accepted exegetical tradition that the 'righteous-ness of God' means here 'a righteousness of which God is the author and man the recipient,' a righteousness not so much 'of God' as 'from God,' i.e. a state or condition of righteousness bestowed by God upon man. But quite recently two protests have been raised against this view, both English and both, as it happens, associated with the University of Durham, one by Dr. Barmby in the Pulpit Commentary on Romans, and the other by Dr. A. Robertson in The Thinker for Nov. 1893 *; comp. also a concise note by Dr. T. K. Abbott ad loc. There can be little doubt that the protest is justified; not so much that the current view is wrong as that it is partial and incomplete.

The 'righteousness of God' is a great and comprehensive idea which embraces in its range both God and man; and in this fundamental passage of the Epistle neither side must be lost sight of. (1) In proof that the righteousness intended here is primarily 'the righteousness of God Himself' it may be urged: (i) that this is consistently the sense of the righteousness of God in the Old Testament and more particularly in passages closely resembling the present, such as Ps. xcviii. [xcvii.] 2, 'The Lord hath made

* The point is, however, beginning to attract some attention in Germany.

known His *salvation* : His *righteousness* hath He *revealed* (ἀπεκάλυψεν) in the sight of the nations,' which contains the three key-
words of the verse before us ; (ii) that elsewhere in the Epistle
δικ. Θεοῦ = 'the righteousness of God Himself' (several of the
passages, e. g. iii. 21, 22, x. 3, have the same ambiguity as the
text, but iii. 5, 25, 26 are quite clear) ; (iii) that the marked
antithesis ἀποκαλύπτεται γὰρ ὀργὴ Θεοῦ in ver. 18 compared with
δικαιοσύνη γὰρ Θεοῦ ἀποκαλύπτεται in ver. 17 requires that the gen.
Θεοῦ shall be taken in the same sense in both places. These are
arguments too strong to be resisted.

(2) But at the same time those which go to prove that δικ. Θεοῦ is
a gift of righteousness bestowed upon man are hardly less convincing. (i) The righteousness in question is described as being
revealed ἐκ πίστεως εἰς πίστιν ; and in the parallel passage iii. 22 it is
qualified as δικ. Θεοῦ διὰ πίστεως Ἰησοῦ Χριστοῦ εἰς πάντας τοὺς πιστεύοντας, where its relation to the human recipient is quite unmistakable. (ii) This relation is further confirmed by the quotation from
Habakkuk where the epithet δίκαιος is applied not to God but to
man. Observe the logical connexion of the two clauses, δικαιοσύνη
γὰρ Θεοῦ ἀποκαλύπτεται . . . καθὼς γέγραπται, Ὁ δὲ δίκαιος ἐκ πίστεως
ζήσεται. (iii) Lastly, in the parallel Phil. iii. 9 the thought of the
Apostle is made quite explicit : μὴ ἔχων ἐμὴν δικαιοσύνην τὴν ἐκ νόμου,
ἀλλὰ τὴν διὰ πίστεως Χριστοῦ, τὴν ἐκ Θεοῦ δικαιοσύνην ἐπὶ τῇ πίστει. The
insertion of the preposition ἐκ transfers the righteousness from
God to man, or we may say traces the process of extension by
which it passes from its source to its object.

For (3) the very cogency of the arguments on both sides is
enough to show that the two views which we have set over against
each other are not mutually exclusive but rather inclusive. The
righteousness of which the Apostle is speaking not only proceeds
from God but *is* the righteousness of God Himself : it is this, however, not as inherent in the Divine Essence but as going forth and
embracing the personalities of men. It is righteousness active and
energizing ; the righteousness of the Divine Will as it were projected and enclosing and gathering into itself human wills. St. Paul
fixes this sense upon it in another of the great key-verses of the
Epistle, ch. iii. 26 εἰς τὸ εἶναι αὐτὸν δίκαιον καὶ δικαιοῦντα τὸν ἐκ πίστεως
Ἰησοῦ. The second half of this clause is in no way opposed to the
first, but follows from it by natural and inevitable sequence : God
attributes righteousness to the believer because He is Himself
righteous. The whole scheme of things by which He gathers to
Himself a righteous people is the direct and spontaneous expression
of His own inherent righteousness : a necessity of His own Nature
impels Him to make them like Himself. The story how He has
done so is the burden of the 'Gospel.' For a fuller development
of the idea contained in ' the righteousness of God' see below.

ἐκ πίστεως. This root-conception with St. Paul means in the
first instance simply the acceptance of Jesus of Nazareth as Messiah
and Son of God ; the affirmation of that primitive Christian Creed
which we have already had sketched in vv. 3, 4. It is the 'Yes' of
the soul when the central proposition of Christianity is presented to
it. We hardly need more than this one fact, thus barely stated, to
explain why it was that St. Paul attached such immense importance
to it. It is so characteristic of his habits of mind to go to the root
of things, that we cannot be surprised at his taking for the centre of
his system a principle which is only less prominent in other writers
because they are content, if we may say so, to take their section of
doctrine lower down the line and to rest in secondary causes instead
of tracing them up to primary. Two influences in particular seem
to have impelled the eager mind of St. Paul to his more penetrative
view. One was his own experience. He dated all his own spiritual triumphs from the single moment of his vision on the road to
Damascus. Not that they were all actually won there, but they
were all *potentially* won. That was the moment at which he was
as a brand plucked from the burning : anything else that came to
him later followed in due sequence as the direct and inevitable outcome of the change that was then wrought in him. It was then
that there flashed upon him the conviction that Jesus of Nazareth,
whom he had persecuted as a pretender and blasphemer, was really
exalted to the right hand of God, and really charged with infinite
gifts and blessings for men. The conviction then decisively won
sank into his soul, and became the master-key which he applied to
the solution of all problems and all struggles ever afterwards.

But St. Paul was a Jew, an ardent Jew, a Pharisee, who had
spent his whole life before his conversion in the study of the Old
Testament. And it was therefore natural to him, as soon as he
began to reflect on this experience of his that he should go back to
his Bible, and seek there for the interpretation of it. When he
did so two passages seemed to him to stand out above all others.
The words πίστις, πιστεύω are not very common in the LXX, but
they occurred in connexion with two events which were as much
turning-points in the history of Israel as the embracing of Christianity had been a turning-point for himself. The Jews were in
the habit of speculating about Abraham's faith, which was his
response to the promise made to him. The leading text which
dealt with this was Gen. xv. 6: and there it was distinctly laid
down that this faith of Abraham's had consequences beyond itself :
another primary term was connected with it : 'Abraham believed
God and it (his belief) was reckoned unto him for righteousness.'
Again just before the beginning of the great Chaldaean or Baby-
lonian invasion, which was to take away their 'place and nation'
from the Jews but which was at the same time to purify them in

the furnace of affliction, the Prophet Habakkuk had announced that
one class of persons should be exempted on the ground of this
very quality, 'faith.' 'The just or righteous man shall live by
faith.' Here once more faith was brought into direct connexion
with righteousness. When therefore St. Paul began to interrogate
his own experience and to ask why it was that since his conversion,
i. e. since his acceptance of Jesus as Messiah and Lord, it had
become so much easier for him to do right than it had been before;
and when he also brought into the account the conclusion, to which
the same conversion had led him, as to the significance of the Life
and Death of Jesus for the whole Church or body of believers; what
could lie nearer at hand than that he should associate faith and
righteousness together, and associate them in the way of referring
all that made the condition of righteousness so much more possible
under Christianity than it had been under Judaism, objectively to
the work of the Messiah, and subjectively to the appropriation of
that work by the believer in the assent which he gave to the one
proposition which expressed its value?

It will be seen that there is more than one element in this conception which has to be kept distinct. As we advance further in
the Epistle, and more particularly when we come to the great
passage iii. 21–26, we shall become aware that St. Paul attached to
the Death of Christ what we may call a sacrificial efficacy. He
regarded it as summing up under the New Covenant all the functions that the Mosaic Sacrifices had discharged under the Old. As
they had the effect, as far as anything outward could have the
effect, of placing the worshipper in a position of fitness for approach to God; so once for all the sacrifice of Christ had placed
the Christian worshipper in this position. That was a fact objective and external to himself of which the Christian had the benefit
simply by being a Christian; in other words by the sole act of
faith. If besides this he also found by experience that in following
with his eye in loyal obedience (like the author of Ps. cxxiii) his
Master Christ the restraint of selfishness and passion became far
easier for him than it had been, that was indeed a different matter;
but that too was ultimately referable to the same cause; it too
dated from the same moment, the moment of the acceptance of
Christ. And although in this case more might be said to be done
by the man himself, yet even there Christ was the true source of
strength and inspiration; and the more reliance was placed on this
strength and inspiration the more effective it became; so much so
that St. Paul glories in his infirmities because they threw him back
upon Christ, so that when he was weak, then he became strong.

On this side the influence of Christ upon the Christian life was
a continuous influence extending as long as life itself. But even
here the critical moment was the first, because it established the

relation. It was like magnetism which begins to act as soon as the connexion is complete. Accordingly we find that stress is constantly laid upon this first moment—the moment of being 'baptized into Christ' or 'putting on Christ,' although it is by no means implied that the relation ceases where it began, and on the contrary it is rather a relation which should go on strengthening. Here too the beginning is an act of faith, but the kind of faith which proceeds ἐκ πίστεως εἰς πίστιν. We shall have the process described more fully when we come to chapters vi–viii.

ἐκ πίστεως εἰς πίστιν. The analogy of Ps. lxxxiii. 8 (lxxxiv. 7) ἐκ δυνάμεως εἰς δύναμιν, and of 2 Cor. ii. 16 ἐκ θανάτου εἰς θάνατον ... ἐκ ζωῆς εἰς ζωήν, seems to show that this phrase should be taken as widely as possible. It is a mistake to limit it either to the deepening of faith in the individual or to its spread in the world at large (*ex fide predicantium in fidem credentium* Sedulius): both are included: the phrase means 'starting from a smaller quantity of faith to produce a larger quantity,' at once intensively and extensively, in the individual and in society.

ὁ δίκαιος ἐκ πίστεως. Some take the whole of this phrase together. 'The man whose righteousness is based on faith,' as if the contrast (not expressed but implied) were between the man whose righteousness is based on faith and one whose righteousness is based on works. It is true that this is quite in harmony with St. Paul's teaching as expressed more fully in Rom. iii. 22, 25; Gal. ii. 16: but it was certainly not the meaning of Habakkuk, and if St. Paul had intended to emphasize the point here it lay very near at hand to write ὁ δὲ ἐκ πίστεως δίκαιος, and so remove all ambiguity. It is merely a question of emphasis, because in the ordinary way of taking the verse it is implied that the ruling motive of the man, the motive which gives value to his righteousness and gains for him the Divine protection, is his faith.

A few authorities (C*, Vulg. *codd. non opt.* Harcl., Orig.-lat. Hieron.) insert μου (ὁ δὲ δίκ. μου ἐκ πίστεως, or ὁ δὲ δίκ. ἐκ πίστεως μου ζήσεται) from the LXX. Marcion, as we should expect, seems to have omitted not only πρῶτον but the quotation from Habakkuk; this would naturally follow from his antipathy to everything Jewish, though he was not quite consistent in cutting out all quotations from the O. T. He retains the same quotation (not, however, as a quotation) in Gal. iii. 4, the context of which he is able to turn against the Jews. For the best examination of Marcion's text see Zahn, *Gesch. d. Neutest. Kanons*, ii. 515 ff.

The word δίκαιος and its cognates.

δίκαιος, δικαιοσύνη. In considering the meaning and application of these terms it is important to place ourselves at the right point of view—at the point of view, that is, of St. Paul himself, a Jew of the Jews, and not either Greek or mediaeval or modern. Two main facts have to be borne in mind in regard to the history of the words δίκαιος and δικαιοσύνη. The first is that although there was a sense in which the Greek words covered the whole range of right action (*Eth. Nic.* V. i. 15 δικαιοσύνη = τελεία ἀρετή with the single qualification that it is πρὸς ἕτερον, the duty to one's neighbour*), yet in practice it was far more commonly used in the narrower sense of Justice (distributive or corrective *ibid.* 2 ff.). The Platonic designation of δικαιοσύνη as one of the four cardinal virtues (Wisdom, Temperance, and Courage or Fortitude, being the others) had a decisive and lasting influence on the whole subsequent history of the word in the usage of Greek philosophy, and of all those moral systems which have their roots in that fertile soil. In giving a more limited scope to the word Plato was only following the genius of his people. The real standard of Greek morals was rather τὸ καλόν—that which was morally noble, impressive, admirable—than τὸ δίκαιον. And if there was this tendency to throw the larger sense of δικαιοσύνη into the background in Greek morals, that tendency was still more intensified when the scene was changed from Greece to Rome. The Latin language had no equivalent at all for the wider meaning of δικαιοσύνη. It had to fall back upon *justitia*, which in Christian circles indeed could not help being affected by the dominant use in the Bible, but which could never wholly throw off the limiting conditions of its origin. This is the second fact of great and outstanding significance. We have to remember that the Middle Ages derived one half of its list of virtues through Cicero from the Stoics and Plato, and that the four Pagan virtues were still further thrown into the shade by the Christian triad.

Happily for ourselves we have in English two distinct words for the two distinct conceptions, 'justice' and 'righteousness.' And so especially from the time of the translation of the Bible into the vernacular, the conception 'righteousness' has gone far to recover its central importance. The same may perhaps be said of the Teutonic nations generally, through the strength of the Biblical influence, though the German branch has but the single word *Gerechtigkeit* to express the two ideas. With them it is probably true that the wider sense takes precedence of the narrower. But at the time when St. Paul wrote the Jew stood alone in maintaining the larger sense of the word full and undiminished.

It is a subordinate question what was the origin of the fundamental idea. A recent writer (Smend, *Alttest. Religionsgesch.* p. 410 ff.) puts forward the view that this was the 'being in the right,' as a party to a suit in a court of law. It may well be true that as δίκη meant in the first instance 'usage,' and then came to mean 'right' because usage was the earliest standard of right, in like manner the larger idea of 'righteousness' may have grown up out of the practice of primitive justice. It may have been first applied to the litigant who was adjudged to be 'in the right,' and to the judge, who awarded 'the right' carefully and impartially.

This is matter, more or less, of speculation. In any case the Jew of St. Paul's day, whatever his faults, assigned no inadequate place to Righteousness. It was with him really the highest moral ideal, the principle of all action, the goal of all effort.

If the Jew had a fault it was not that righteousness occupied an inadequate place in his thoughts; it was rather that he went a wrong way to attain to it. Ἰσραὴλ δὲ διώκων νόμον δικαιοσύνης εἰς νόμον οὐκ ἔφθασε, is St. Paul's mournful verdict (Rom. ix. 31). For a Jew the whole sphere of righteousness was taken up by the Mosaic Law. His one idea of righteousness was that of conformity to this Law. Righteousness was for him essentially obedience to the law. No doubt it was this in the first instance out of regard to the law as the expressed Will of God. But the danger lay in resting too much in the code as a code and losing sight of the personal Will of a holy and good God behind it. The Jew made this mistake; and the consequence was that his view of obedience to the law became formal and mechanical. It was impossible for an impartial mind not to be deeply touched by the spectacle

* Aristotle quotes the proverb ἐν δὲ δικαιοσύνῃ συλλήβδην πᾶσ' ἀρετὴ ἔνι.

of the religious leaders of a nation devoting themselves with so much earnestness and zeal to the study of a law which they believed to come, and which
in a certain sense and measure really did come, from God, and yet failing so
disastrously as their best friends allow that they did fail in grasping the
law's true spirit. No one felt more keenly than St. Paul himself the full
pathos of the situation. His heart bleeds for them (Rom. ix. 2); he cannot
withhold his testimony to their zeal, though unhappily it is not a zeal
according to knowledge (Rom. x. 2).

Hence it was that all this mass—we must allow of honest though ill-
directed effort—needed reforming. The more radical the reformation the
better. There came One Who laid His finger upon the weak place and
pointed out the remedy—at first as it would seem only in words in which the
Scripture-loving Rabbis had been before Him: 'Thou shalt love the Lord
thy God with all thy heart and with all thy soul and with all thy mind . . .
and . . . Thou shalt love thy neighbour as thyself' (Matt. xxii. 37, 39 ∥),
and then more searchingly and with greater fulness of illustration and
application, 'There is nothing from without the man that going into him
can defile him: but the things which proceed out of the man are those that
defile the man' (Mark vii. 15 ∥); and then yet again more searchingly still,
'Come unto me all ye that labour and are heavy laden . . . Take My yoke
upon you and learn of Me . . . For My yoke is easy, and My burden is light'
(Matt. xi. 28–30).

So the Master; and then came the disciple. And he too seized the heart
of the secret. He too saw what the Master had refrained from putting with
a degree of emphasis which might have been misunderstood (at least the
majority of His reporters might leave the impression that this had been the
case, though one, the Fourth Evangelist, makes Him speak more plainly).
The later disciple saw that, if there was to be a real reformation, the first
thing to be done was to give it a personal ground, to base it on a personal
relationship. And therefore he lays down that the righteousness of the
Christian is to be a 'righteousness *of faith*.' Enough will have been said in
the next note and in those on ἐκ πίστεως and δικαιοσύνη Θεοῦ as to the
nature of this righteousness. It is sharply contrasted with the Jewish conception of righteousness as obedience to law, and of course goes far deeper
than any Pagan conception as to the motive of righteousness. The specially
Pauline feature in the conception expressed in this passage is that the
'declaration of righteousness' on the part of God, the Divine verdict of
acquittal, runs *in advance* of the actual practice of righteousness, and comes
forth at once on the sincere embracing of Christianity.

δικαιοῦν, δικαιοῦσθαι. The verb δικαιοῦν means properly 'to pronounce
righteous.' It has relation to a verdict pronounced by a judge. In so far as
the person 'pronounced righteous' is not really righteous it has the sense of
'amnesty' or 'forgiveness.' But it cannot mean to 'make righteous.'
There may be other influences which go to make a person righteous, but
they are not contained, or even hinted at, in the word δικαιοῦν. That word
means 'to declare righteous,' 'to treat as righteous'; it may even mean 'to
prove righteous'; but whether the person so declared, treated as, or proved
to be righteous is really so, the word itself neither affirms nor denies.

This rather sweeping proposition is made good by the following considerations:—

(i) By the nature of verbs in -όω: comp. *Sp. Comm.* on 1 Cor. vi. 11
'How can δικαιοῦν possibly signify "to *make righteous*?"' Verbs indeed of
this ending from adjectives of *physical* meaning may have this use, e. g.
τυφλοῦν, "to make blind." But when such words are derived from adjectives
of *moral* meaning, as ἀξιοῦν, ὁσιοῦν, δικαιοῦν, they do by usage and must
from the nature of things signify to *deem*, to *account*, to *prove*, or to *treat
as* worthy, holy, righteous.'

(ii) By the regular use of the word. Godet (p. 199) makes a bold assertion, which he is hardly likely to have verified, but yet which is probably right, that there is no example in the whole of classical literature where the word = 'to *make* righteous.' The word however is not of frequent occurrence.

(iii) From the constant usage of the LXX (O. T. and Apocr.), where the word occurs some forty-five times, always or almost always with the forensic or judicial sense.

In the great majority of cases this sense is unmistakable. The nearest approach to an exception is Ps. lxxiii [lxxii] 13 ἄρα ματαίως ἐδικαίωσα τὴν καρδίαν μου, where, however, the word seems to = 'pronounced righteous,' in other words, 'I called my conscience clear.' In Jer. iii. 11 ; Ezek. xvi. 51, 52 δικ. = 'prove righteous.'

(iv) From a like usage in the Pseudepigraphic Books: e. g. *Ps. Sol.* ii. 16 ; iii. 5 ; iv. 9 ; viii. 7, 27, 31 ; ix. 3 (in these passages the word is used consistently of 'vindicating' the character of God) ; *justifico* 4 Ezr. iv. 18 ; x. 16 ; xii. 7 ; 5 Ezr. ii. 20 (*Libb. Apocr.* ed. O. F. Fritzsche, p. 643)—all these passages are forensic ; *Apoc. Baruch.* (in Ceriani's translation from the Syriac) xxi. 9, 11 ; xxiv. 1—where the word is applied to those who are 'declared innocent' as opposed to 'sinners.'

(v) From the no less predominant and unmistakable usage of the N. T. : Matt. xi. 19 ; xii. 37 ; Luke vii. 29, 35 ; x. 29 ; xvi. 15 ; xviii. 14 ; Rom. ii. 13 ; iii. 4 ; 1 Cor. iv. 4 ; 1 Tim. iii. 16—to quote only passages which are absolutely unambiguous.

(vi) The meaning is brought out in full in ch. iv. 5 τῷ δὲ μὴ ἐργαζομένῳ, πιστεύοντι δὲ ἐπὶ τὸν δικαιοῦντα τὸν ἀσεβῆ, λογίζεται ἡ πίστις αὐτοῦ εἰς δικαιοσύνην. Here it is expressly stated that the person justified has nothing to show in the way of meritorious acts ; his one asset (so to speak) is faith, and this faith is taken as an 'equivalent for righteousness.'

We content ourselves for the present with stating this result as a philological fact. What further consequences it has, and how it fits into the teaching of St. Paul, will appear later: see the notes on δικαιοσύνη Θεοῦ above and below.

δικαίωμα. For the force of the termination -μα reference should be made to a note by the late T. S. Evans in *Sp. Comm.* on 1 Cor. v. 6, part of which is quoted in this commentary on Rom. iv. 2. δικαίωμα is the definite concrete expression of the act of δικαίωσις : we might define it as 'a declaration that a thing is δίκαιον, or that a person is δίκαιος.' From the first use we get the common sense of 'ordinance,' 'statute,' as in Luke i. 6 ; Rom. i. 32, ii. 26, and practically viii. 4 ; from the second we get the more characteristically Pauline use in Rom. v. 16, 18. For the special shades of meaning in these passages see the notes upon them.

δικαίωσις. This word occurs only twice in this Epistle (iv. 25, v. 18), and not at all besides in the N. T. Its place is taken by the verb δικαιοῦν, just as in the Gospel of St. John the verb πιστεύειν occurs no less than ninety-eight times, while the substantive πίστις is entirely absent. In meaning δικαίωσις preserves the proper force of the termination -σις : it denotes the 'process or act of pronouncing righteous,' in the case of sinners, 'the act of acquittal.'

The Meaning of Faith in the New Testament and in some Jewish Writings.

The word πίστις has two leading senses, (1) fidelity and (2) belief. The second sense, as we have said, has its more exact significance determined by its object : it may mean, (i) belief in God ; (ii) belief in the promises of God ; (iii) belief in Christ ; (iv) belief in some particular utterance, claim, or promise of God or Christ.

The last of these senses is the one most common in the Synoptic Gospels. 'Faith' is there usually 'belief in the miracle-working power of Christ or of God through Christ.' It is (*a*) the response of the applicant for relief— whether for himself or another—to the offer expressed or implied of that relief by means of miracles (Mark v. 34 ‖ ; x. 52 ‖). The effect of the miracle is usually proportioned to the strength of this response (Matt. ix. 29 κατὰ τὴν πίστιν ὑμῶν γενηθήτω ὑμῖν : for degrees of faith see Matt. viii. 10, 26 ; Luke xvii. 5, &c.). In Acts iii. 16 the faith which has just before been described as 'faith in the Name' (of Christ) is spoken of as 'faith brought into being by Christ' (ἡ πίστις ἡ δι᾽ αὐτοῦ). Faith is also (β) the confidence of the disciple that he can exercise the like miracle-working power when expressly conferred upon him (Mark xi. 22–24 ‖). This kind of faith our Lord in one place calls 'faith in God' (Mark xi. 22). There is one instance of 'faith' used in a more general sense. When the Son of Man asks whether when He comes He shall find faith on the earth (Luke xviii. 8) He means 'faith in Himself.'

Faith in the performance of miracles is a sense which naturally passes over into the Acts (Acts iii. 16 ; xiv. 9). We find in that book also '*the* faith' (ἡ πίστις Acts vi. 7 ; xiii. 8 ; xiv. 22 ; xvi. 5 ; xxiv. 24), i.e. 'the faith distinctive of Christians,' belief that Jesus is the Son of God. 'A door of faith' (Acts xiv. 27) means 'an opening for the spread of this belief.' When πίστις is used as an attribute of individuals (πλήρης πίστεως Acts vi. 5 of Stephen ; xi. 24 of Barnabas) it has the Pauline sense of the enthusiasm and force of character which come from this belief in Jesus.

In the Epistle of St. James πίστις is twice applied to prayer (Jas. i. 6 ; v. 15), where it means the faith that God will grant what is prayed for. Twice it means 'Christian faith' (Jas. i. 3 ; ii. 1). In the controversial passage, Jas. ii. 14–26, where Faith is contrasted with Works, the faith intended is 'faith in God.' One example of it is the 'belief that God is One' (Jas. ii. 19) ; another is the trust in God which led Abraham to sacrifice Isaac (Jas. ii. 21), and to believe in the promise of his birth (Jas. ii. 23). Faith with St. James is more often the faith which is common to Jew and Christian ; even where it is Christian faith, it stops short of the Christian enthusiasm.

In St. Jude, whose Epistle must on that account be placed late in the Apostolic age, faith has got the concrete sense of a 'body of belief'—not necessarily a large or complete body, but, as we should say, 'the essentials of Christianity.' As the particular point *against* which the saints are to contend is the denial of Christ, so the faith for which they are to contend would be the (full) confession of Christ (Jude 3 f., 20).

In the two Epistles of St. Peter faith is always Christian faith (1 Pet. i. 5, 7–9 ; ii. 6 ; 2 Pet. i. 1, 5), and usually faith as the foundation of character. When St. Peter speaks of Christians as 'guarded through faith unto salvation' (1 Pet. i. 5) his use approaches that of St. Paul ; faith is treated as the 'one thing needful.'

St. John, as we have seen, very rarely uses the word πίστις (1 Jo. v. 4), though he makes up by his fondness for πιστεύω. With him too faith is a very fundamental thing ; it is the 'victory which overcometh the world.' It is defined to be the belief 'that Jesus is the Son of God' (1 Jo. v. 5). Compared with St. Paul's conception we may say that faith with St. John is rather contemplative and philosophic, where with St. Paul it is active and enthusiastic. In the Apocalypse faith comes nearer to fidelity ; it is belief steadfastly held (Rev. ii. 13, 19 ; xiii. 10 ; xiv. 12 ; cf. also πιστός i. 5 ; ii. 10, &c.).

The distinctive use of 'faith' in the Epistle to the Hebrews is for faith in the fulfilment of God's promises, a firm belief of that which is still future and unseen (ἐλπιζομένων ὑπόστασις, πραγμάτων ἔλεγχος οὐ βλεπομένων Heb. xi. 1). This use not only runs through ch. xi, but is predominant in all the places where the word occurs (Heb. iv. 2 ; vi. 1 ; x. 22 f. ; xii. 2 ; xiii. 7) : it is not found in St. Paul of promises the fulfilment of which is still future (for this he prefers ἐλπίς : cf. Rom. viii. 25 εἰ δὲ ὃ οὐ βλέπομεν ἐλπίζομεν, δι' ὑπομονῆς ἀπεκδεχόμεθα). St. Paul does however use ' faith' for the confidence of O.T. saints in the fulfilment of particular promises made to them (so of Abraham in Rom. iv).

Going outside the N. T. it is natural that the use of 'faith' should be neither so high nor so definite. Still the word is found, and frequently enough to show that the idea ' was in the air' and waiting only for an object worthy of it. ' Faith' enters rather largely into the eschatological teaching respecting the Messianic time. Here it appears to have the sense of 'fidelity to the O. T. religion.' In the *Psalms of Solomon* it is characteristic of the Messiah Himself : *Ps. Sol.* xvii. 45 ποιμαίνων τὸ ποίμνιον Κυρίου ἐν πίστει καὶ δικαιοσύνῃ. In the other Books it is characteristic of His subjects. Thus 4 Ezr. vi. 28 *florebit autem fides et vincetur corruptela*; vii. 34 *veritas stabit et fides convalescet*; 44 (114) *soluta est intemperantia, abscissa est incredulitas* (=ἀπιστία). In *Apoc. Baruch.* and *Assump. Moys.* the word has this sense, but not quite in the same connexion : *Apoc. Bar.* liv. 5 *revelas abscondita immaculatis qui in fide subiecerunt se tibi et legi tuae*; 21 *glorificabis fideles iuxta fidem eorum*; lix. 2 *incredulis tormentum ignis reservatum*; *Ass. Moys.* iv. 8 *duae autem tribus permanebunt in praeposita fide.* In *Apoc. Bar* lvii. 2 we have it in the sense of faith in the prophecy of coming judgement : *fides iudicii futuri tunc gignebatur.* Several times, in opposition to the use in St. Paul, we find *opera et fides* combined, still in connexion with the ' last things ' but retrospectively with reference to the life on earth. So 4 Ezra ix. 7, 8 *et erit, omnis qui salvus factus fuerit et qui poterit effugere per opera sua vel per fidem in qua credidit, is relinquetur de praedictis periculis et videbit salutare meum in terra mea et in finibus meis*; xiii. 23 *ipse custodibit qui in periculo inciderint, hi sunt qui habent opera et fidem ad Fortissimum.* We might well believe that both these passages were suggested, though perhaps somewhat remotely, by the verse of Habakkuk which St. Paul quotes. The same may be said of 5 Ezr. xv. 3, 4 *nec turbent te incredulitates dicentium, quoniam omnis incredulus in incredulitate sua morietur* (*Libb. Apocr.* p. 645, ed. O. F. Fritzsche).

Among all these various usages, in Canonical Books as well as Extracanonical, the usage of St. Paul stands out markedly. It forms a climax to them all with the single exception of St. John. There is hardly one of the ordinary uses which is not represented in the Pauline Epistles. To confine ourselves to Ep. to Romans; we have the word (i) clearly used in the sense of 'fidelity' or 'faithfulness' (the faithfulness of God in performing His promises), Rom. iii. 3 ; also (ii) in the sense of a faith which is practically that of the miracle-worker, faith as the foundation for the exercise of spiritual gifts, Rom. xii. 3, 6. We have it (iii) for a faith like that of Abraham in the fulfilment of the promises of which he was the chosen recipient, Rom. iv. *passim.* The faith of Abraham however becomes something more than a particular attitude in regard to particular promises; it is (iv) a standing attitude, deliberate faith in God, the key-note of his character; in ch. iv. the last sense is constantly gliding into this. A faith like Abraham's is typical of the Christian's faith, which has however both a lower sense and a higher : sometimes (v) it is in a general sense the acceptance of Christianity, Rom. i. 5 ; x. 8, 17 ; xvi. 26; but it is also (vi) that specially strong and confident acceptance, that firm planting of the character upon the service of Christ, which enables a man to disregard small scruples, Rom. xiv. 1, 22 f.; cf. i. 17. The centre and mainspring of this higher form of faith is (vii) defined more exactly as 'faith in Jesus Christ,' Rom. iii. 22 q. v., 26. This is the crowning and characteristic sense with St. Paul ; and it is really this which he has in view wherever he ascribes to faith the decisive significance which he does ascribe to it, even though the object is not expressed (as in i. 17 ; iii.

27 ff.; v. 1, 2). We have seen that it is not merely assent or adhesion but *enthusiastic* adhesion, personal adhesion; the highest and most effective motive-power of which human character is capable. It is well to remember that St. Paul has all these meanings before him; and he glances from one to another as the hand of a violin-player runs over the strings of his violin.

The Righteousness of God.

The idea of the righteousness of God, imposing as it is in the development given to it in this Epistle, is by no means essentially a new one. It is one of those fundamental Biblical ideas which run through both Testaments alike and appear in a great variety of application. The Hebrew prophets were as far as possible from conceiving of the Godhead as a metaphysical abstraction. The I AM THAT I AM of the Book of Exodus is very different from the ὄντως ὄν, the Pure Being, without attributes because removed from all contact with matter, of the Platonizing philosophers. The essential properties of Righteousness and Holiness which characterized the Lord of all spirits contained within themselves the springs of an infinite expansiveness. Having brought into existence a Being endowed with the faculty of choice and capable of right and wrong action they could not rest until they had imparted to that Being something of themselves. The Prophets and Psalmists of the Old Testament seized on this idea and gave it grand and far-reaching expression. We are apt not to realize until we come to look to what an extent the leading terms in this main proposition of the Epistle had been already combined in the Old Testament. Reference has been made to the triple combination of 'righteousness,' 'salvation' and 'revelation' in Ps. xcviii. [xcvii.] 2: similarly Is. lvi. 1 'My salvation is near to come, and My righteousness to be revealed.' The double combination of 'righteousness' and 'salvation' is more common. In Ps. xxiv. [xxiii.] 5 it is slightly obscured in the LXX: 'He shall receive a blessing from the Lord and righteousness (ἐλεημοσύνην) from the God of his salvation (παρὰ Θεοῦ σωτῆρος αὐτοῦ).' In the Second Part of Isaiah it occurs frequently: Is. xlv. 21-25 'There is no God beside Me ; a just God and a Saviour (δίκαιος καὶ σωτήρ). Look unto Me and be ye saved . . . the word is gone forth from My mouth in righteousness and shall not return (*or* righteousness is gone forth from My mouth, a word which shall not return R. V. *marg.*) . . . Only in the Lord shall one say unto Me is righteousness and strength. . . . In the Lord shall all the seed of Israel be justified (ἀπὸ Κυρίου δικαιωθήσονται), and shall glory': Is. xlvi. 13 'I bring near My righteousness; it shall not be far off, and My salvation shall not tarry: and I will place salvation in Zion for Israel My glory': Is. li. 5, 6 'My righteousness is near, My salvation is gone forth . . .

My salvation shall be for ever, and My righteousness shall not be abolished.'

In all these passages the righteousness of God is conceived as 'going forth,' as projected from the Divine essence and realizing itself among men. In Is. liv. 17 it is expressly said, 'Their righteousness [which] is of Me'; and in Is. xlv. 25 the process is described as one of justification ('in the Lord shall all the seed of Israel be justified': see above). In close attendance on the righteousness of God is His salvation; where the one is the other immediately follows.

These passages seem to have made a deep impression upon St. Paul. To him too it seems a necessity that the righteousness of God should be not only inherent but energizing, that it should impress and diffuse itself as an active force in the world.

According to St. Paul the manifestation of the Divine righteousness takes a number of different forms. Four of these may be specified. (1) It is seen in the fidelity with which God fulfils His promises (Rom. iii. 3, 4). (2) It is seen in the punishment which God metes out upon sin, especially the great final punishment, the ἡμέρα ὀργῆς καὶ ἀποκαλύψεως δικαιοκρισίας τοῦ Θεοῦ (Rom. ii. 5). Wrath is only the reaction of the Divine righteousness when it comes into collision with sin. (3) There is one signal manifestation of righteousness, the nature of which it is difficult for us wholly to grasp, in the Death of Christ. We are going further than we have warrant for if we set the Love of God in opposition to His Justice; but we have the express warrant of Rom. iii. 25, 26 for regarding the Death on Calvary as a culminating exhibition of the Divine righteousness, an exhibition which in some mysterious way explains and justifies the apparent slumbering of Divine resentment against sin. The inadequate punishment hitherto inflicted upon sin, the long reprieve which had been allowed mankind to induce them to repent, all looked forward as it were to that culminating event. Without it they could not have been; but the shadow of it was cast before, and the prospect of it made them possible. (4) There is a further link of connexion between what is said as to the Death of Christ on Calvary and the leading proposition laid down in these verses (i. 16, 17) as to a righteousness of God apprehended by faith. The Death of Christ is of the nature of a sacrifice (ἐν τῷ αὐτοῦ αἵματι) and acts as an ἱλαστήριον (iii. 25 q. v.) by virtue of which the Righteousness of God which reaches its culminating expression in it becomes capable of wide diffusion amongst men. This is the great 'going forth' of the Divine Righteousness, and it embraces in its scope all believers. The essence of it, however, is—at least at first, whatever it may be ultimately—that it consists not in making men actually righteous but in 'justifying' or treating them as if they were righteous.

Here we reach a fundamental conception with St. Paul, and one which dominates all this part of the Epistle to the Romans, so that it may be well to dwell upon it in some detail.

We have seen that a process of transference or conversion takes place ; that the righteousness of which St. Paul speaks, though it issues forth from God, ends in a state or condition of man. How could this be? The name which St. Paul gives to the process is δικαίωσις (iv. 25, v. 18). More often he uses in respect to it the verb δικαιοῦσθαι (iii. 24, 28, v. 1, 9, viii. 30, 33). The full phrase is δικαιοῦσθαι ἐκ πίστεως : which means that the believer, by virtue of his faith, is ʻaccounted or treated as if he were righteousʼ in the sight of God. More even than this: the person so ʻaccounted righteousʼ may be, and indeed is assumed to be, not actually righteous, but ἀσεβής (Rom. iv. 5), an offender against God.

There is something sufficiently startling in this. The Christian life is made to have its beginning in a fiction. No wonder that the fact is questioned, and that another sense is given to the words —that δικαιοῦσθαι is taken to imply not the attribution of righteousness in idea but an imparting of actual righteousness. The facts of language, however, are inexorable : we have seen that δικαιοῦν, δικαιοῦσθαι have the first sense and not the second; that they are rightly said to be ʻforensicʼ; that they have reference to a judicial verdict, and to nothing beyond. To this conclusion we feel bound to adhere, even though it should follow that the state described is (if we are pressed) a fiction, that God is regarded as dealing with men rather by the ideal standard of what they may be than by the actual standard of what they are. What this means is that when a man makes a great change such as that which the first Christians made when they embraced Christianity, he is allowed to start on his career with a clean record; his sin-stained past is not reckoned against him. The change is the great thing; it is that at which God looks. As with the Prodigal Son in the parable the breakdown of his pride and rebellion in the one cry, ʻFather, I have sinnedʼ is enough. The father does not wait to be gracious. He does not put him upon a long term of probation, but reinstates him at once in the full privilege of sonship. The justifying verdict is nothing more than the ʻbest robeʼ and the ʻringʼ and the ʻfatted calfʼ of the parable (Luke xv. 22 f.).

When the process of Justification is thus reduced to its simplest elements we see that there is after all nothing so very strange about it. It is simply Forgiveness, Free Forgiveness. The Parable of the Prodigal Son is a picture of it which is complete on two of its sides, as an expression of the attitude of mind required in the sinner, and of the reception accorded to him by God. To

insist that it must also be complete in a negative sense, and that
it excludes any further conditions of acceptance, because no such
conditions are mentioned, is to forget the nature of a parable.
It would be as reasonable to argue that the father would be
indifferent to the future conduct of the son whom he has recovered
because the curtain falls upon the scene of his recovery and is
not again lifted. By pressing the argument from silence in this
way we should only make the Gospels inconsistent with themselves, because elsewhere they too (as we shall see) speak of
further conditions besides the attitude and temper of the sinner.

We see then that at bottom and when we come to the essence of
things the teaching of the Gospels is not really different from the
teaching of St. Paul. It may be said that the one is tenderly and
pathetically human where the other is a system of Jewish Scholasticism. But even if we allow the name it is an encouragement
to us to seek for the simpler meaning of much that we may be
inclined to call 'scholastic.' And we may also by a little inspection
discover that in following out lines of thought which might come
under this description St. Paul is really taking up the threads of
grand and far-reaching ideas which had fallen from the Prophets
of Israel and had never yet been carried forwards to their legitimate
issues. The Son of Man goes straight, as none other, to the
heart of our common humanity; but that does not exclude the
right of philosophizing or theologizing on the facts of religion, and
that is surely not a valueless theology which has such facts as its
foundation.

What has been thus far urged may serve to mitigate the apparent
strangeness of St. Paul's doctrine of Justification. But there is
much more to be said when we come to take that doctrine with
its context and to put it in its proper place in relation to the whole
system.

In the first place it must be remembered that the doctrine belongs
strictly speaking only to the beginning of the Christian's career.
It marks the initial stage, the entrance upon the way of life. It
was pointed out a moment ago that in the Parable of the Prodigal
Son the curtain drops at the readmission of the prodigal to his
home. We have no further glimpse of his home life. To isolate
the doctrine of Justification is to drop the curtain at the same
place, as if the justified believer had no after-career to be recorded.

But St. Paul does not so isolate it. He takes it up and follows
every step in that after-career till it ends in the final glory (οὓς δὲ
ἐδικαίωσε, τούτους καὶ ἐδόξασε viii. 30). We may say roughly that
the first five chapters of the Epistle are concerned with the doctrine
of Justification, in itself (i. 16—iii. 30), in its relation to leading
features of the Old Covenant (iii. 31—iv. 25) and in the conse-

quences which flowed from it (v. 1–21). But with ch. vi another factor is introduced, the Mystical Union of the Christian with the Risen Christ. This subject is prosecuted through three chapters, vi–viii, which really cover (except perhaps the one section vii. 7–25)—and that with great fulness of detail—the whole career of the Christian subsequent to Justification. We shall speak of the teaching of those chapters when we come to them.

It is no doubt an arguable question how far these later chapters can rightly be included under the same category as the earlier. Dr. Liddon for instance summarizes their contents as 'Justification considered subjectively and in its effects upon life and conduct. Moral consequences of Justification. (A) The Life of Justification and sin (vi. 1–14). (B) The Life of Justification and the Mosaic Law (vi. 15—vii. 25). (C) The Life of Justification and the work of the Holy Spirit (viii.).' The question as to the legitimacy of this description hangs together with the question as to the meaning of the term Justification. If Justification=*Justitia infusa* as well as *imputata*, then we need not dispute the bringing of chaps. vi–viii under that category. But we have given the reasons which compel us to dissent from this view. The older Protestant theologians distinguished between Justification and Sanctification; and we think that they were right both in drawing this distinction and in referring chaps. vi–viii to the second head rather than to the first. On the whole St. Paul does keep the two subjects separate from each other; and it seems to us to conduce to clearness of thought to keep them separate.

At the same time we quite admit that the point at issue is rather one of clearness of thought and convenience of thinking than anything more material. Although separate the two subjects run up into each other and are connected by real links. There is an organic unity in the Christian life. Its different parts and functions are no more really separable than the different parts and functions of the human body. And in this respect there is a true analogy between body and soul. When Dr. Liddon concludes his note (p. 18) by saying, 'Justification and sanctification may be distinguished by the student, as are the arterial and nervous systems in the human body; but in the living soul they are coincident and inseparable,' we may cordially agree. The distinction between Justification and Sanctification or between the subjects of chaps. i. 16—v, and chaps. vi–viii is analogous to that between the arterial and nervous systems; it holds good as much and no more—no more, but as much.

A further question may be raised which the advocates of the view we have just been discussing would certainly answer in the affirmative, viz. whether we might not regard the whole working out of the influences brought to bear upon the Christian in chaps.

vi–viii, as yet a fifth great expression of the Righteousness of God as energizing amongst men. We too think that it might be so regarded. It stands quite on a like footing with other manifestations of that Righteousness. All that can be said to the contrary is that St. Paul himself does not explicitly give it this name.

THE UNIVERSAL NEED: FAILURE OF THE GENTILES.

I. 18-32. *This revelation of Righteousness, issuing forth from God and embracing man, has a dark background in that other revelation of Divine Wrath at the gross wickedness of men* (ver. 18).

There are three stages: (1) *the knowledge of God which all might have from the character imprinted upon Creation* (vv. 19–20); (2) *the deliberate ignoring of this knowledge and idle speculation ending in idolatry* (vv. 21–23); (3) *the judicial surrender of those who provoke God by idolatry to every kind of moral degradation* (vv. 24–32).

[18] This message of mine is the one ray of hope for a doomed world. The only other revelation, which we can see all around us, is a revelation not of the Righteousness but of the Wrath of God breaking forth—or on the point of breaking forth—from heaven, like the lightning from a thundercloud, upon all the countless offences at once against morals and religion of which mankind are guilty. They stifle and suppress the Truth within them, while they go on still in their wrong-doing (ἐν ἀδικ.). [19] It is not merely ignorance. All that may be known of God He has revealed in their hearts and consciences. [20] For since the world has been created His attributes, though invisible in themselves, are traced upon the fabric of the visible creation. I mean, His Power to which there is no beginning and those other attributes which we sum up under the common name of Divinity.

So plain is all this as to make it impossible to escape the responsibility of ignoring it. [21] The guilt of men lay not in their ignorance; for they had a knowledge of God. But in spite of that knowledge, they did not pay the homage due to Him as

God: they gave Him no thanks; but they gave the rein to futile speculations; they lost all intelligence of truth, and their moral sense was obscured. [22] While they boasted of their wisdom, they were turned to folly. [23] In place of the majesty of the Eternal God, they worshipped some fictitious representation of weak and perishable man, of bird, of quadruped or reptile.

[24] Such were the beginnings of idolatry. And as a punishment for it God gave them up to moral corruption, leaving them to follow their own depraved desires wherever they might lead, even to the polluting of their bodies by shameful intercourse. [25] Reprobates, who could abandon the living and true God for a sham divinity, and render divine honours and ritual observance to the creature, neglecting the Creator (Blessed be His name for ever!).

[26] Because of this idolatry, I repeat, God gave them up to the vilest passions. Women behaved like monsters who had forgotten their sex. [27] And men, forsaking the natural use, wrought shame with their own kind, and received in their physical degradation a punishment such as they deserved.

[28] They refused to make God their study: and as they rejected Him, so He rejected them, giving them over to that abandoned mind which led them into acts disgraceful to them as men: [29] replete as they were with every species of wrong-doing; with active wickedness, with selfish greed, with thorough inward depravity: their hearts brimming over with envy, murderous thoughts, quarrelsomeness, treacherous deceit, rank ill-nature; backbiters, [30] slanderers; in open defiance of God, insolent in act, arrogant in thought, braggarts in word towards man; skilful plotters of evil, bad sons, [31] dull of moral apprehension, untrue to their word, void of natural duty and of humanity: [32] Reprobates, who, knowing full well the righteous sentence by which God denounces death upon all who act thus, are not content with doing the things which He condemns themselves but abet and applaud those who practise them.

18. There is general agreement as to the structure of this part of the Epistle. St. Paul has just stated what the Gospel is; he now goes on to show the necessity for such a Gospel. The world is lost without it. Following what was for a Jew the obvious division, proof is given of a complete break-down in regard to righteousness (i) on the part of the Gentiles, (ii) on the

part of the Jews. The summary conclusion of the whole section
i. 18—iii. 20 is given in the two verses iii. 19, 20 : it is that the
whole world, Gentile and Jew alike, stands guilty before God.
Thus the way is prepared for a further statement of the means of
removing that state of guilt offered in the Gospel.

Marcion retained ver. 18, omitting Θεοῦ, perhaps through some accident
on his own part or in the MS. which he copied (Zahn, *ut sup.* p. 516; the
rather important cursive 47 has the same omission). The rest of the chapter
with ii. 1 he seems to have excised. He may have been jealous of this
trenchant attack upon the Gentiles.

Ἀποκαλύπτεται. How is this revelation made ? Is the reference
to the Final Judgement, or to the actual condition, as St. Paul
saw it, of the heathen world? Probably not to either exclusively,
but to both in close combination. The condition of the world
seems to the Apostle ripe for judgement; he sees around him
on all hands signs of the approaching end. In the latter half
of this chapter St. Paul lays stress on these signs : he develops
the ἀποκαλύπτεται, present. In the first half of the next chapter
he brings out the final doom to which the signs are pointing.
Observe the links which connect the two sections : ἀποκαλύπτεται
i. 18 = ἀποκάλυψις ii. 5; ὀργή i. 18, ii. 5, 8; ἀναπολόγητος i. 20,
ii. 1.

ὀργὴ Θεοῦ. (1) In the O. T. the conception of the Wrath of
God has special reference to the Covenant-relation. It is inflicted
either (*a*) upon Israelites for gross breach of the Covenant (Lev.
x. 1, 2 Nadab and Abihu; Num. xvi. 33, 46 ff. Korah; xxv. 3
Baal-peor), or (*β*) upon non-Israelites for oppression of the Chosen
People (Jer. l. 11–17; Ezek. xxxvi. 5). (2) In the prophetic
writings this infliction of 'wrath' is gradually concentrated upon
a great Day of Judgement, the Day of the Lord (Is. ii. 10–22, &c.;
Jer. xxx. 7, 8; Joel iii. 12 ff. ; Obad. 8 ff.; Zeph. iii. 8 ff.). (3) Hence
the N. T. use seems to be mainly, if not altogether, eschatological :
cf. Matt. iii. 7 ; 1 Thess. i. 10; Rom. ii. 5, v. 9; Rev. vi. 16, 17.
Even 1 Thess. ii. 16 does not seem to be an exception : the state
of the Jews seems to St. Paul to be only a foretaste of the final
woes. See on this subject esp. Ritschl, *Rechtfertigung u. Versöh-
nung*, ii. 124 ff. ed. 2.

Similarly Euthym.-Zig. Ἀποκαλύπτεται κ.τ.λ. ἐν ἡμέρᾳ δηλονότι κρίσεως.
We must remember however that St. Paul regarded the Day of Judgement as
near at hand.

ἐν ἀδικίᾳ, 'living in unrighteousness *the while*' Moule.

κατεχόντων. κατέχειν = (i) 'to hold fast' Lk. viii. 15; 1 Cor. xi. 2,
xv. 2, &c.; (ii) 'to hold down,' 'hold in check' 2 Thess. ii. 6, 7,
where τὸ κατέχον, ὁ κατέχων = the force of [Roman] Law and Order
by which Antichrist is restrained : similarly here but in a bad

sense; it is the truth which is 'held down,' hindered, thwarted, checked in its free and expansive operation.

19. διότι: *always* in Gk. Test. = 'because.' There are three uses: (i) for δι' ὅ τι = *propter quod, quamobrem*, 'wherefore,' introducing a consequence; (ii) for διὰ τοῦτο ὅτι = *propterea quod*, or *quia*, 'because,' giving a reason for what has gone before; (iii) from Herod. downwards, but esp. in later Gk. = ὅτι, 'that.'

τὸ γνωστόν. This is a similar case to that of εὐοδωθήσομαι above: γνωστός in Scripture generally (both LXX and N. T.) means as a rule 'known' (e. g. Acts i. 19, ii. 14, xv. 18, &c.); but it does not follow that it may not be used in the stricter sense of 'knowable,' 'what may be known' ('the intelligible nature' T. H. Green, *The Witness of God*, p. 4) where the context favours that sense: so Orig. Theoph. Weiss. Gif., against Chrys. Mey. De W. Va. There is the more room for this stricter use here as the word does not occur elsewhere in St. Paul and the induction does not cover his writings.

ἐν αὐτοῖς, 'within them.' St. Paul repeatedly uses this preposition where we might expect a different one (cf. Gal. i. 16; Rom. ii. 15): any revelation must pass through the human consciousness: so Mey. Go. Oltr. Lips., not exactly as Gif. ('in their very nature and constitution as men') or Moule ('*among* them).'

Compare also Luther, *Table Talk*, Aph. dxlix: 'Melanchthon discoursing with Luther touching the prophets, who continually boast thus: "Thus saith the Lord," asked whether God in person spoke with them or no. Luther replied: "They were very holy, spiritual people, who seriously contemplated upon holy and divine things: therefore God spake with them in their consciences, which the prophets held as sure and certain revelations."'

It is however possible that allowance should be made for the wider Hebraistic use of ἐν, as in the phrase λαλεῖν ἔν τινι (Habak. ii. 1 ἀποσκοπεύσω τοῦ ἰδεῖν τί λαλήσει ἐν ἐμοί: cf. Zech. i. 9, 13, 14, 19; ii. 3; iv. 4, 5; v. 5, 10; vi. 4; also 4 Ezr. v. 15 *angelus qui loquebatur in me*. In that case too much stress must not be laid on the preposition as describing an internal process. At the same time the analogy of λαλεῖν ἐν does not cover the very explicit φανερόν ἐστιν ἐν αὐτοῖς: and we must remember that St. Paul is writing as one who had himself an 'abundance of revelations' (2 Cor. xii. 7), and uses the language which corresponded to his own experience.

20. ἀπὸ κτίσεως κόσμου. Gif. is inclined to translate this 'from the created universe,' 'creation' (in the sense of 'things created') being regarded as the *source* of knowledge: he alleges Vulg. *a creatura mundi*. But it is not clear that Vulg. was intended to have this sense; and the parallel phrases ἀπ' ἀρχῆς κόσμου (Matt. xxiv. 21), ἀπὸ καταβολῆς κόσμου (Matt. xxv. 34; Luke xi. 50; Rev. xiii. 8; xvii. 8), ἀπ' ἀρχῆς κτίσεως (Mark x. 6; xiii. 19; 2 Pet. iii. 4), seem to show that the force of the prep. is rather *temporal*, '*since* the creation of the universe' (ἀφ' οὗ χρόνου ὁ ὁρατὸς ἐκτίσθη κόσμος Euthym.-Zig.). The idea of knowledge being derived from the fabric of the created world is in any case contained in the context.

κτίσεως: see Lft. *Col.* p. 214. κτίσις has three senses: (i) the act of creating (as here); (ii) the result of that act, whether (a) the aggregate of created things (Wisd. v. 18; xvi. 24; Col. i. 15 and probably Rom. viii. 19 ff.); or (β) a creature, a single created thing (Heb. iv. 13, and perhaps Rom. viii. 39, q. v.).

καθορᾶται: commonly explained to mean 'are clearly seen' (κατά with intensive force, as in καταμανθάνειν, κατανοεῖν); so Fri. Grm.-Thay. Gif. &c. It may however relate rather to the direction of sight, 'are surveyed,' 'contemplated' ('are under observation' Moule). Both senses are represented in the two places in which the word occurs in LXX: (i) in Job x. 4 ἢ ὥσπερ βροτὸς ὁρᾷ καθορᾷς; (ii) in Num. xxiv. 2 Βαλαὰμ ... καθορᾷ τὸν Ἰσραὴλ ἐστρατοπεδευκότα κατὰ φυλάς.

ἀίδιος: ἀιδιότης is a Divine attribute in Wisd. ii. 23 (v. l., see below); cf. also Wisd. vii. 26 φωτὸς ἀιδίου, Jude 6.

The argument from the nature of the created world to the character of its Author is as old as the Psalter, Job and Isaiah: Pss. xix. 1; xciv. 9; cxliii. 5; Is. xlii. 5; xlv. 18; Job xii. 9; xxvi. 14; xxxvi. 24 ff.; Wisd. ii. 23; xiii. 1, 5, &c. It is common to Greek thought as well as Jewish: Arist. *De Mundo* 6 ἀθεώρητος ἀπ' αὐτῶν τῶν ἔργων θεωρεῖται [ὁ Θεός] (Lid.). This argument is very fully set forth by Philo, *De Praem. et Poen.* 7 (Mang. ii. 415). After describing the order and beauty of Nature he goes on: 'Admiring and being struck with amazement at these things, they arrived at a conception consistent with what they had seen, that all these beauties so admirable in their arrangement have not come into being spontaneously (οὐκ ἀπαυτοματισθέντα γέγονεν), but are the work of some Maker, the Creator of the world, and that there must needs be a Providence (πρόνοιαν); because it is a law of nature that the Creative Power (τὸ πεποιηκός) must take care of that which has come into being. But these admirable men superior as they are to all others, as I said, advanced from below upwards as if by a kind of celestial ladder guessing at the Creator from His works by probable inference (οἷα διά τινος οὐρανίου κλίμακος ἀπὸ τῶν ἔργων εἰκότι λογισμῷ στοχασάμενοι τὸν δημιουργόν).

θειότης: θεότης = Divine Personality, θειότης = Divine nature and properties: δύναμις is a single attribute, θειότης is a summary term for those other attributes which constitute Divinity: the word appears in Biblical Gk. first in Wisd. xviii. 9 τὸν τῆς θειότητος νόμον ἐν ὁμονοίᾳ διέθεντο.

Didymus (*Trin.* ii. 11; Migne, *P. G.* xxxix. 664) accuses the heretics of reading θεότης here, and it is found in one MS., P.

It is certainly somewhat strange that so general a term as θειότης should be combined with a term denoting a particular attribute like δύναμις. To meet this difficulty the attempt has been made to narrow down θειότης to the signification of δόξα, the divine glory or splendour. It is suggested that this word was not used because it seemed inadequate to describe the uniqueness of the Divine Nature (Rogge, *Die Anschauungen d. Ap. Paulus von d. religiös-sittl. Charakt. d. Heidentums*, Leipzig, 1888, p. 10 f.)

εἰς τὸ εἶναι : εἰς τό denotes here not direct and primary purpose but indirect, secondary or conditional purpose. God did not design that man should sin ; but He did design that if they sinned they should be without excuse : on His part all was done to give them a sufficient knowledge of Himself. Burton however (*Moods and Tenses*, § 411) takes εἰς τό here as expressing not purpose but result, because of the causal clause which follows. ' This clause could be forced to an expression of purpose only by supposing an ellipsis of some such expression as καὶ οὕτως εἰσίν, and seems therefore to require that εἰς τὸ εἶναι be interpreted as expressing result.' There is force in this reasoning, though the use of εἰς τό for mere result is not we believe generally recognized.

21. ἐδόξασαν.   δοξάζω is one of the words which show a deepened significance in their religious and Biblical use. In classical Greek in accordance with the slighter sense of δόξα it merely = ' to form an opinion about ' (δοξαζόμενος ἄδικος, ' held to be unrighteous,' Plato, *Rep.* 588 B); then later with a gradual rise of signification ' to do honour to ' or ' praise ' (ἐπ᾽ ἀρετῇ δεδοξασμένοι ἄνδρες Polyb. VI. liii. 10). And so in LXX and N. T. with a varying sense according to the subject to whom it is applied : (i) Of the honour done by man to man (Esth. iii. 1 ἐδόξασεν ὁ βασιλεὺς 'Αρταξέρξης 'Αμάν); (ii) Of that which is done by man to God (Lev. x. 3 ἐν πάσῃ τῇ συναγωγῇ δοξασθήσομαι) ; (iii) Of the glory bestowed on man by God (Rom. viii. 30 οὓς δὲ ἐδικαίωσε, τούτους καὶ ἐδόξασε) ; (iv) In a sense specially characteristic of the Gospel of St. John, of the visible manifestation of the glory, whether of the Father by His own act (Jo. xii. 28), or of the Son by His own act (Jo. xi. 4), or of the Son by the act of the Father (Jo. vii. 39; xii. 16, 23, &c.), or of the Father by the Incarnate Son (Jo. xiii. 31 ; xiv. 13 ; xvii. 1, 4, &c.).

ἐματαιώθησαν, ' were frustrated,' ' rendered futile.' In LXX τὰ μάταια = ' idols ' as ' things of nought.' The two words occur together in 2 Kings xvii. 15 καὶ ἐπορεύθησαν ὀπίσω τῶν ματαίων καὶ ἐματαιώθησαν.

διαλογισμοῖς : as usually in LXX and N. T. in a bad sense of ' perverse, self-willed, reasonings or speculations' (cf. Hatch, *Ess. in Bibl. Gk.* p. 8).

Comp. *Enoch* xcix. 8, 9 ' And they will become godless by reason of the foolishness of their hearts, and their eyes will be blinded through the fear of their hearts and through visions in their dreams. Through these they will become godless and fearful, because they work all their works in a lie and they worship a stone.'

καρδία : the most comprehensive term for the human faculties,

the seat of feeling (Rom. ix. 2 ; x. 1); will (1 Cor. iv. 5 ; vii. 37 ;
cf. Rom. xvi. 18); thoughts (Rom. x. 6, 8).   Physically καρδία
belongs to the σπλάγχνα (2 Cor. vi. 11, 12); the conception of its
functions being connected with the Jewish idea that life resided in
the blood : morally it is neutral in its character, so that it may be
either the home of lustful desires (Rom. i. 24), or of the Spirit
(Rom. v. 5).

23. ἤλλαξαν ἐν : an imitation of a Heb. construction : cf. Ps.
cvi. (cv.) 20 ; also for the expression Jer. ii. 11 (Del. *ad loc.*) &c.
δόξαν = 'manifested perfection.'   See on iii. 23.

Comp. with this verse Philo, *Vit. Mos.* iii. 20 (Mang. ii. 161) οἱ τὸν
ἀληθῆ θεὸν καταλιπόντες τοὺς ψευδωνύμους ἐδημιούργησαν, φθαρταῖς καὶ γενηταῖς
οὐσίαις τὴν τοῦ ἀγενήτου καὶ ἀφθάρτου πρόσρησιν ἐπιφημίσαντες : also *De Ebriet.*
28 (Mang. i. 374) παρ' ὃ καὶ θεοπλαστεῖν ἀρξάμενος ἀγαλμάτων καὶ ξοάνων καὶ
ἄλλων μυρίων ἀφιδρυμάτων ὕλαις διαφόροις τετεχνιτευμένων κατέπλησε τὴν
οἰκουμένην . . . κατειργάσατο τὸ ἐναντίον οὗ προσεδόκησεν, ἀντὶ ὁσιότητος
ἀσέβειαν—τὸ γὰρ πολύθεον ἐν ταῖς τῶν ἀφρόνων ψυχαῖς ἀθεότης, καὶ θεοῦ τιμῆς
ἀλογοῦσιν οἱ τὰ θνητὰ θειώσαντες—οἷς οὐκ ἐξήρκεσεν ἡλίου καὶ σελήνης . . .
εἰκόνας διαπλάσασθαι, ἀλλ' ἤδη καὶ ἀλόγοις ζῴοις καὶ φυτοῖς τῆς τῶν ἀφθάρτων
τιμῆς μετέδοσαν.

24. παρέδωκεν : three times repeated, here, in ver. 26 and in
ver. 28.   These however do not mark so many distinct stages in
the punishment of the heathen ; it is all one stage.   Idolatry leads
to moral corruption which may take different forms, but in all is
a proof of God's displeasure.   Gif. has proved that the force of
παρέδωκεν is not merely *permissive* (Chrys. Theodrt. Euthym.-Zig.*),
through God permitting men to have their way ; or *privative*,
through His withdrawing His gracious aid ; but *judicial*, the appropriate punishment of their defection : it works automatically, one
evil leading to another by natural sequence.

This is a Jewish doctrine : *Pirqê Aboth*, iv. 2 ' Every fulfilment of duty is
rewarded by another, and every transgression is punished by another' ; *Shab-
bath* 104ᵃ ' Whosoever strives to keep himself pure receives the power to do
so, and whosoever will be impure to him is it [the door of vice] thrown
open' ; Jerus. Talmud, ' He who erects a fence round himself is fenced, and
he who gives himself over is given over' (from Delitzsch, Notes on Heb.
Version of Ep. to Rom.).   The Jews held that the heathen because of their
rejection of the Law were wholly abandoned by God : the Holy Spirit was
withdrawn from them (Weber, *Altsyn. Theol.* p. 66).

ἐν αὐτοῖς ℵ A BCD*, several cursives ; ἐν ἑαυτοῖς DᶜEFGKLP,
&c., printed editions of Fathers, Orig. Chrys. Theodrt., Vulg. (*ut
contumeliis adficiant corpora sua in ipsis*).   The balance is strongly

* Similarly Adrian, an Antiochene writer (c. 440 A.D.) in his Εἰσαγωγὴ εἰς
τὰς θείας γραφάς, a classified collection of figures and modes of speech employed in Holy Scripture, refers this verse to the head Τὴν ἐπὶ τῶν ἀνθρωπίνων
κακῶν συγχώρησιν τοῦ Θεοῦ ὡς πρᾶξιν αὐτοῦ λέγει· ἐπειδὴ κωλῦσαι δυνάμενος,
τοῦτο οὐ ποιεῖ.

in favour of αὐτοῖς. With this reading ἀτιμάζεσθαι is pass., and ἐν αὐτοῖς = 'among them': with ἐν ἑαυτοῖς, ἀτιμ. is mid. (as Vulg.).

On the forms, αὐτοῦ, αὑτοῦ and ἑαυτοῦ see Buttmann, *Gr. of N. T. Gk.* (tr. Thayer) p. 111; Hort, *Introd.*, Notes on Orthography. p. 144.

In N. T. Greek there is a tendency to the disuse of strong reflexive forms. Simple possession is most commonly expressed by αὐτοῦ, αὐτῆς, &c.: only where the reflexive character is emphasized (not merely *suum*, but *suum ipsius*) is ἑαυτοῦ used (hence the importance of such phrases as τὸν ἑαυτοῦ υἱὸν πέμψας Rom. viii. 3). Some critics have denied the existence in the N. T. of the aspirated αὑτοῦ: and it is true that there is no certain proof of aspiration (such as the occurrence before it of οὐχ or an elided preposition; in early MSS. breathings are rare), but in a few strong cases, where the omission of the aspirate would be against all Greek usage, it is retained by WH. (e.g. in Jo. ii. 24; Lk. xxiii. 12).

25. οἵτινες: ὅστις, often called 'rel. of quality,' (i) denotes a single object with reference to its kind, its nature, its capacities, its character ('one who,' 'being of such a kind as that'); and thus (ii) it frequently makes the adjectival sentence assign a cause for the main sentence: it is used like *qui*, or *quippe qui*, with subj.

τὴν ἀλήθειαν ... τῷ ψεύδει: abstr. for concrete, for τὸν ἀληθινὸν Θεόν ... τοῖς ψεύδεσι θεοῖς, cf. 1 Thess. i. 9.

ἐσεβάσθησαν. This use of σεβάζεσθαι is an ἅπαξ λεγόμενον; the common form is σέβεσθαι (see Va.).

παρὰ τὸν κτίσαντα = not merely '*more than* the Creator' (a force which the preposition might bear), but '*passing by* the Creator altogether,' 'to the neglect of the Creator.'

Cf. Philo, *De Mund. Opif.* 2 (Mangey, i. 2) τινὲς γὰρ τὸν κόσμον μᾶλλον ἢ τὸν κοσμοποιὸν θαυμάσαντες (Loesner).

ὅς ἐστιν εὐλογητός. Doxologies like this are of constant occurrence in the Talmud, and are a spontaneous expression of devout feeling called forth either by the thought of God's adorable perfections or sometimes (as here) by the forced mention of that which reverence would rather hide.

27. ἀπολαμβάνοντες: ἀπολ.= (i) 'to receive *back*' (as in Luke vi. 34); (ii) 'to receive *one's due*' (as in Luke xxiii. 41); and so here.

28. ἐδοκίμασαν: δοκιμάζω = (i) 'to test' (1 Cor. iii. 13, &c.); (ii) 'to approve after testing' (so here; and ii. 18; xiv. 22, &c.); similarly ἀδόκιμον = 'rejected after testing,' 'reprobate.'

ἐν ἐπιγνώσει: ἐπίγνωσις = '*after* knowledge': hence (i) recognition (vb. = 'to recognize,' Matt. vii. 16; xvii. 12, &c.); (ii) 'advanced' or 'further knowledge,' 'full knowledge.' See esp. *Sp. Comm.* on 1 Cor. xiii. 12; Lft. on Phil. i. 9.

νοῦν = the reasoning faculty, esp. as concerned with moral action, the intellectual part of conscience: νοῦς and συνείδησις are combined in Tit. i. 15: νοῦς may be either bad or good; for the good sense see Rom. xii. 2; Eph. iv. 23.

τὰ καθήκοντα: a technical term with the Stoics, 'what is morally fitting'; cf. also 2 Macc. vi. 4.

29. We must beware of attempting to force the catalogue which follows into a logical order, though here and there a certain amount of grouping is noticeable. The first four are general terms for wickedness; then follows a group headed by the alliterative φθόνου, φόνου, with other kindred vices; then two forms of backbiting; then a group in descending climax of sins of arrogance; then a somewhat miscellaneous assortment, in which again alliteration plays a part.

ἀδικίᾳ: a comprehensive term, including all that follows.

πορνείᾳ: om. אABCK; probably suggested by similarity in sound to πονηρίᾳ.

πονηρίᾳ: contains the idea of '*active* mischief' (Hatch, *Bibl. Gk.* p. 77 f.; Trench, *Syn.* p. 303). Dr. T. K. Abbott (*Essays*, p. 97) rather contests the assignment of this specific meaning to πονηρία; and no doubt the use of the word is extremely wide: but where definition is needed it is in this direction that it must be sought.

κακίᾳ: as compared with πονηρία denotes rather inward viciousness of disposition (Trench, *Syn.* p. 36 f.).

The MSS. vary as to the order of the three words πονηρίᾳ, πλεονεξίᾳ, κακίᾳ, WH. *text* RV. retain this order with BL, &c., Harcl. Arm., Bas. Greg.-Nyss. *al.*: Tisch. WH. *marg.* read πονηρ. κακ. πλεον. with אA, Pesh. *al.*: WH. *marg.* also recognizes κακ. πονηρ. πλεον. with C, Boh. *al.*

πλεονεξίᾳ. On the attempt which is sometimes made to give to this word the sense of 'impurity' see Lft. on Col. iii. 5. The word itself means only 'selfish greed,' which may however be exhibited under circumstances where impurity lies near at hand: e.g. in 1 Thess. iv. 6 πλεονεκτεῖν is used of adultery, but rather as a wrong done to another than as a vice.

κακοηθείας: the tendency to put the worst construction upon everything (Arist. *Rhet.* ii. 13; cf. Trench, *Syn.* p. 38). The word occurs several times in 3 and 4 Maccabees.

30. ψιθυριστάς, καταλάλους. The idea of secresy is contained in the first of these words, not in the second: ψιθ. susurratores Cypr. Lucif. Ambrstr. susurrones Aug. Vulg.; καταλ. detractores Cypr. Aug. Vulg., detrectatores (detract-) Lucif. Ambrstr. *al.*

θεοστυγεῖς: may be either (i) passive, Deo odibiles Vulg.: so Mey. Weiss Fri. Oltr. Lips. Lid.; on the ground that this is the constant meaning in class. Gk., where the word is not uncommon; or (ii) active, Dei osores = abhorrentes Deo Cypr.: so Euthym.-Zig. (τοὺς τὸν Θεὸν μισοῦντας), Tyn. and other English versions not derived from Vulg., also Gif. Go. Va., with some support from Clem. Rom. ad Cor. xxxv. 5, who in paraphrasing this passage uses θεοστυγία clearly with an active signification, though he follows it by στυγητοὶ τῷ Θεῷ. As one among a catalogue of vices this would give the more pointed sense, unless we might suppose that θεοστυγεῖς had come to have a meaning like our 'desperadoes.' The three terms

which follow remind us of the bullies and braggarts of the Eliza-
bethan stage.   For the distinction between them see Trench, *Syn.*
p. 95 ff.

It is well preserved in the Cyprianic Latin, *iniuriosi, superbi, iactantes sui.*
For the last phrase Lucif. has *gloriantes* ; either would be better than the
common rendering *elatos* (Cod. Clarom. Cod. Boern. Ambrstr. Aug. Vulg.).

ὑπερήφανος. Mayor (on Jas. iv. 6) derives this word from the adjectival
form ὕπερος (rather than ὑπέρ Trench) and φαίνω, comparing ἐλαφηβόλος from
ἔλαφος and βάλλω : he explains it as meaning ' conspicuous beyond others,'
' outshining them,' and so ' proud,' ' haughty ' : see his note, and the exx.
there quoted from Ecclus. and *Pss. Sol.*

31. ἀσυνέτους: ἀσυνειδήτους (' without conscience ') Euthym.-Zig. How
closely the two words σύνεσις and συνείδησις are related will appear from
Polyb. XVIII. xxvi. 13 οὐδεὶς οὕτως οὔτε μάρτυς ἐστὶ φοβερὸς οὔτε κατήγορος
δεινὸς ὡς ἡ σύνεσις ἡ ἐγκατοικοῦσα ταῖς ἑκάστων ψυχαῖς. [But is not this
a gloss. on the text of Polyb. ?   It is found in the margin of Cod. Urbin.]

ἀσυνθέτους, ' false to their engagements ' (συνθῆκαι) ; cf. Jer. iii. 7,
LXX.

ἀσπόνδους after ἀστόργους (Trench, *Syn.* p. 95 ff.) is added
from 2 Tim. iii. 3 [C K L P].

32. οἵτινες : see on ver. 25 above.

τὸ δικαίωμα : prob. in the first instance (i) a declaration that
a thing is δίκαιον [τὸ δικαίωμα τοῦ νόμου = ' that which the Law lays
down as right,' Rom. viii. 4]; hence, ' an ordinance ' (Luke i. 6 ;
Rom. ii. 26 ; Heb. ix. 1, 10) ; or (ii) ' a declaration that a person
is δίκαιος,' ' a verdict of not guilty,' ' an acquittal ' : so esp. in
St. Paul (e. g. Rom. v. 16).   But see also note on p. 31.

ἐπιγνόντες : ἐπιγινώσκοντες (B) 80, WH. *marg.*

ποιοῦσιν . . . συνευδοκοῦσιν.   There has been some disturbance of
the text here : B, and apparently Clem. Rom., have ποιοῦντες . . .
συνευδοκοῦντες ; and so too D E Vulg. (am. fuld.) Orig.-lat. Lucif.
and other Latin Fathers, but inserting, *non intellexerunt* (οὐκ
ἐνόησαν D).   WH. obelize the common text as prob. corrupt : they
think that it involves an anticlimax, because to applaud an action
in others is not so bad as to do it oneself ; but from another point
of view to set up a public opinion in favour of vice is worse than
to yield for the moment to temptation (see the quotation from
Apollinaris below).   If the participles are wrong they have probably
been assimilated mechanically to πράσσοντες.   Note that ποιεῖν =
facere, to produce a certain result ; πράσσειν = *agere*, to act as
moral agent : there may be also some idea of repeated action.

συνευδοκοῦσι denotes ' hearty approval ' (Rendall on Acts xxii.
20, in *Expos.* 1888, ii. 209) ; cf. 1 Macc. i. 57 συνευδοκεῖ τῷ νόμῳ :
the word occurs four times besides in N. T. (Luke, Epp. Paul.).

ἀμφότεροι δὲ πονηροί, καὶ ὁ κατάρξας, καὶ ὁ συνδραμών. τοῦ δὲ ποιεῖν
τὸ συνευδοκεῖν χεῖρον τίθησι κατὰ τὸ λεγόμενον, εἰ ἐθεώρεις κλέπτην,

συνέτρεχες αὐτῷ. ὁ μὲν γὰρ ποιῶν, μεθύων τῷ πάθει, ἡττᾶται τῆς πράξεως·
ὁ δὲ συνευδοκῶν, ἐκτὸς ὢν τοῦ πάθους, πονηρίᾳ χρώμενος, συντρέχει τῷ κακῷ
(Apollinaris in Cramer's *Catena*).

St. Paul's Description of the Condition of the Heathen World.

It would be wrong to expect from St. Paul an investigation of
the origin of different forms of idolatry or a comparison of the
morality of heathen religions, such as is now being instituted in the
Comparative Science of Religion.   For this it was necessary to
wait for a large and comprehensive collection of data which has
only become possible within the present century and is still far from
complete.   St. Paul looks at things with the insight of a religious
teacher ; he describes facts which he sees around him ; and he connects these facts with permanent tendencies of human nature and
with principles which are apparent in the Providential government
of the world.

The Jew of the Dispersion, with the Law of Moses in his hand,
could not but revolt at the vices which he found prevailing among
the heathen.   He turned with disgust from the circus and the
theatre (Weber, *Altsyn. Theol.* pp. 58, 68).   He looked upon the
heathen as given over especially to sins of the flesh, such as those
which St. Paul recounts in this chapter.   So far have they gone as
to lose their humanity altogether and become like brute beasts
(*ibid.* p. 67 f.).   The Jews were like a patient who was sick but
with hope of recovery.   Therefore they had a law given to them to
be a check upon their actions.   The Heathen were like a patient
who was sick unto death and beyond all hope, on whom therefore
the physician put no restrictions (*ibid.* p. 69).

The Christian teacher brought with him no lower standard, and
his verdict was not less sweeping.   'The whole world,' said St.
John, 'lieth in wickedness,' rather perhaps, 'in [the power of] the
Wicked One' (1 Jo. v. 19).   And St. Paul on his travels must
have come across much to justify the denunciations of this chapter.
He saw that idolatry and licence went together.   He knew that
the heathen myths about their gods ascribed to them all manner
of immoralities.   The lax and easy-going anthropomorphism of
Hellenic religion and the still more degraded representations, with
at times still more degraded worship, of the gods of Egypt and the

E

East, were thrown into dark relief by his own severe conception of the Divine Holiness. It was natural that he should give the account he does of this degeneracy. The lawless fancies of men invented their own divinities. Such gods as these left them free to follow their own unbridled passions. And the Majesty on High, angered at their wilful disloyalty, did not interfere to check their downward career.

It is all literally true. The human imagination, following its own devices, projects even into the Pantheon the streak of evil by which it is itself disfigured. And so the mischief is made worse, because the worshipper is not likely to rise above the objects of his worship. It was in the strict sense due to supernatural influence that the religion of the Jew and of the Christian was kept clear of these corrupt and corrupting features. The state of the Pagan world betokened the absence, the suspension or withholding, of such supernatural influence; and there was reason enough for the belief that it was judicially inflicted.

At the same time, though in this passage, where St. Paul is measuring the religious forces in the world, he speaks without limitation or qualification, it is clear from other contexts that condemnation of the insufficiency of Pagan creeds did not make him shut his eyes to the good that there might be in Pagan characters. In the next chapter he distinctly contemplates the case of Gentiles who being without law are a law unto themselves, and who find in their consciences a substitute for external law (ii. 14, 15). He frankly allows that the ‘uncircumcision which is by nature’ put to shame the Jew with all his greater advantages (ii. 26-29). We therefore cannot say that *a priori* reasoning or prejudice makes him untrue to facts. The Pagan world was not wholly bad. It had its scattered and broken lights, which the Apostle recognizes with the warmth of genuine sympathy. But there can be equally little doubt that the moral condition of Pagan civilization was such as abundantly to prove his main proposition, that Paganism was unequal to the task of reforming and regenerating mankind.

There is a monograph on the subject, which however does not add much beyond what lies fairly upon the surface: Rogge, *Die Anschauungen d. Ap. Paulus von d. religiös-sittlichen Charakter d. Heidentums*, Leipzig, 1888.

If the statements of St. Paul cannot be taken at once as supplying the place of scientific inquiry from the side of the Comparative History of Religion, so neither can they be held to furnish data which can be utilized just as they stand by the historian. The standard which St. Paul applies is not that of the historian but of the preacher. He does not judge by the average level of moral attainment at different epochs but by the ideal standard of that which ought to be attained. A calm and dispassionate weighing of the facts, with due allowance for the nature of the authorities, will be found in Friedländer, *Sittengeschichte Roms*, Leipzig, 1869–1871.

Use of the Book of Wisdom in Chapter I.

i. 18–32. In two places in Epist. to Romans, ch. i and ch. ix, there are clear indications of the use by the Apostle of the Book of Wisdom. Such indications are not wanting elsewhere, but we have thought it best to call attention to them especially at the points where they are most continuous and most striking. We begin by placing side by side the language of St. Paul and that of the earlier work by which it is illustrated.

Romans.

i. 20. τὰ γὰρ ἀόρατα αὐτοῦ ἀπὸ κτίσεως κόσμου τοῖς ποιήμασι νοούμενα καθορᾶται,

ἥ τε ἀΐδιος αὐτοῦ δύναμις καὶ θειότης·

εἰς τὸ εἶναι αὐτοὺς ἀναπολογήτους·

21. ἐματαιώθησαν ἐν τοῖς διαλογισμοῖς αὐτῶν, καὶ ἐσκοτίσθη ἡ ἀσύνετος αὐτῶν καρδία.
22. φάσκοντες εἶναι σοφοὶ ἐμωράνθησαν·

23. καὶ ἤλλαξαν τὴν δόξαν τοῦ ἀφθάρτου Θεοῦ ἐν ὁμοιώματι εἰκόνος φθαρτοῦ ἀνθρώπου καὶ πετεινῶν καὶ τετραπόδων καὶ ἑρπετῶν.

Wisdom.

xiii. 1. καὶ ἐκ τῶν ὁρωμένων ἀγαθῶν οὐκ ἴσχυσαν εἰδέναι τὸν ὄντα οὔτε τοῖς ἔργοις προσέχοντες ἐπέγνωσαν τὸν τεχνίτην.

xiii. 5. ἐκ γὰρ μεγέθους καὶ καλλονῆς κτισμάτων ἀναλόγως ὁ γενεσιουργὸς αὐτῶν θεωρεῖται.

ii. 23. [ὁ Θεὸς ἔκτισε ... τὸν ἄνθρωπον ... εἰκόνα τῆς ἰδίας ἀϊδιότητος * (Cod. 248 *al.*, Method. Athan. Epiph.; ἰδιότητος ℵAB, Clem.-Alex. &c.) ἐποίησεν.]
xviii. 9. τὸν τῆς θειότητος νόμον.
xiii. 8. πάλιν δὲ οὐδ' αὐτοὶ συγγνωστοί.

xiii. 1. μάταιοι γὰρ πάντες ἄνθρωποι φύσει, οἷς παρῆν θεοῦ ἀγνωσία †.

xii. 24. καὶ γὰρ τῶν πλάνης ὁδῶν μακρότερον ἐπλανήθησαν θεοὺς ὑπολαμβάνοντες τὰ καὶ ἐν ζῴοις τῶν ἐχθρῶν ἄτιμα, νηπίων δίκην ἀφρόνων ψευσθέντες.
xii. 1. τὸ ἄφθαρτόν σου πνεῦμα.
xiv. 8. τὸ δὲ φθαρτὸν Θεὸς ὠνομάσθη.
xiii. 10. ταλαίπωροι δὲ καὶ ἐν νεκροῖς αἱ ἐλπίδες αὐτῶν, οἵτινες ἐκάλεσαν θεοὺς ἔργα χειρῶν ἀνθρώπων.

* The more recent editors as a rule read ἰδιότητος with the uncials and Gen. i. 26 f.; but it is by no means clear that they are right: Cod. 248 embodies very ancient elements and the context generally favours ἀϊδιότητος. It still would not be certain that St.

Paul had this passage in his mind.
† The parallel here is not quite exact. St. Paul says, 'They did know but relinquished their knowledge,' Wisd. 'They ought to have known but did not.'

25. οἵτινες μετήλλαξαν τὴν ἀλήθειαν
τοῦ Θεοῦ ἐν τῷ ψεύδει, καὶ ἐσεβάσθησαν καὶ ἐλάτρευσαν τῇ κτίσει παρὰ τὸν
κτίσαντα.

24. διὸ παρέδωκεν κ. τ. λ.
26. διὰ τοῦτο παρέδωκεν κ. τ. λ.

29. πεπληρωμένους πάσῃ ἀδικίᾳ, πονηρίᾳ, πλεονεξίᾳ, κακίᾳ, μεστοὺς φθόνου,
φόνου, ἔριδος, δόλου, κακοηθείας, ψιθυριστάς, καταλάλους, θεοστυγεῖς, ὑβριστάς, ὑπερηφάνους, ἀλαζόνας, ἐφευρετὰς
κακῶν, γονεῦσιν ἀπειθεῖς, ἀσυνέτους,
ἀσυνθέτους, ἀστόργους, ἀνελεήμονας.

xiii. 13, 14. ἀπείκασεν αὐτὸ εἰκόνι
ἀνθρώπου, ἢ ζῴῳ τινὶ εὐτελεῖ ὡμοίωσεν
αὐτό.

xiii. 17 sqq. οὐκ αἰσχύνεται τῷ
ἀψύχῳ προσλαλῶν· καὶ περὶ μὲν ὑγιείας
τὸ ἀσθενὲς ἐπικαλεῖται, περὶ δὲ ζωῆς τὸ
νεκρὸν ἀξιοῖ κ. τ. λ.

xiv. 11. διὰ τοῦτο καὶ ἐν εἰδώλοις
ἐθνῶν ἐπισκοπὴ ἔσται, ὅτι ἐν κτίσματι
Θεοῦ εἰς βδέλυγμα ἐγενήθησαν.

xiv. 21. τὸ ἀκοινώνητον ὄνομα λίθοις
καὶ ξύλοις περιέθεσαν.

xiv. 12. ἀρχὴ γὰρ πορνείας ‡ ἐπίνοια
εἰδώλων, εὑρέσεις δὲ αὐτῶν φθορὰ ζωῆς.

xiv. 16. εἶτα ἐν χρόνῳ κρατυνθὲν τὸ
ἀσεβὲς ἔθος ὡς νόμος ἐφυλάχθη.

xiv. 22. εἶτ' οὐκ ἤρκεσε τὸ πλανᾶ-
σθαι περὶ τὴν τοῦ Θεοῦ γνῶσιν, ἀλλὰ καὶ
ἐν μεγάλῳ ζῶντες ἀγνοίας πολέμῳ τὰ
τοσαῦτα κακὰ εἰρήνην προσαγορεύουσιν,
23. ἢ γὰρ τεκνοφόνους τελετὰς ἢ κρύφια
μυστήρια ἢ ἐμμανεῖς ἐξάλλων θεσμῶν
κώμους ἄγοντες, 24. οὔτε βίους οὔτε
γάμους καθαροὺς ἔτι φυλάσσουσιν, ἕτερος δ' ἕτερον ἢ λοχῶν ἀναιρεῖ ἢ νοθεύων
ὀδυνᾷ.

25. πάντα δὲ ἐπιμὶξ ἔχει αἷμα καὶ
φόνος κλοπὴ καὶ δόλος, φθορά, ἀπιστία,
τάραχος, ἐπιορκία, θόρυβος ἀγαθῶν,
26. χάριτος ἀμνησία, ψυχῶν μιασμός,
γενέσεως (sex) ἐναλλαγή, γάμων ἀταξία,
μοιχεία καὶ ἀσέλγεια.

27. ἡ γὰρ τῶν ἀνωνύμων εἰδώλων
θρησκεία παντὸς ἀρχὴ κακοῦ καὶ αἰτία
καὶ πέρας ἐστίν.

It will be seen that while on the one hand there can be no question of
direct quotation, on the other hand the resemblance is so strong both as to
the main lines of the argument (i. Natural religion discarded, ii. idolatry,
iii. catalogue of immorality) and in the details of thought and to some
extent of expression as to make it clear that at some time in his life St. Paul
must have bestowed upon the Book of Wisdom a considerable amount of
study.

[Compare the note on ix. 19–29 below, also an essay by E. Grafe in
Theol. Abhandlungen C. von Weizsäcker gewidmet, Freiburg, i. B. 1892,
p. 251 ff. In this essay will be found a summary of previous discussions of
the question and an estimate of the extent of St. Paul's indebtedness which
agrees substantially with that expressed above. It did not extend to any of
the leading ideas of Christianity, and affected the form rather than the
matter of the arguments to which it did extend. Rom. i. 18–32, ix. 19–23
are the most conspicuous examples.]

‡ A.V. expands this as ' [spiritual]
fornication'; and so most moderns.
But even so the phrase might have
had something to do in suggesting the
thought of St. Paul.

TRANSITION FROM GENTILE TO JEW. BOTH
ALIKE GUILTY.

II. 1–16. *This state of things puts out of court the [Jewish]
critic who is himself no better than the Gentile. He can
claim no exemption, but only aggravates his sin by im-
penitence* (vv. 1–5). *Strict justice will be meted out to all—
the Jew coming first then the Gentile* (vv. 6–11). *The Jew,
will be judged by the Law of Moses, the Gentile by the Law
of Conscience, at the Great Assize which Christ will hold*
(vv. 12–16).

¹ The Gentile sinner is without excuse; and his critic—whoever he may be—is equally without excuse, even though [like
the Jew] he imagines himself to be on a platform of lofty superiority.
No such platform really exists. In fact the critic only passes
sentence upon himself, for by the fact of his criticism he shows that
he can distinguish accurately between right and wrong, and his
own conduct is identical with that which he condemns. ² And we
are aware that it is at his *conduct* that God will look. The
standard of His judgement is reality, and not a man's birth or
status as either Jew or Gentile. ³ Do you suppose—you Jewish
critic, who are so ready to sit in judgement on those who copy your
own example—do you suppose that a special exemption will be
made in your favour, and that you personally (σύ emphatic) will
escape? ⁴ Or are you presuming upon all that abundant goodness,
forbearance, and patience with which God delays His punishment
of sin? If so, you make a great mistake. The object of that long-
suffering is not that you may evade punishment but only to induce
you to repent. ⁵ While you with that callous impenitent heart of
yours are heaping up arrears of Wrath, which will burst upon you
in the Day of Wrath, when God will stand revealed in His character
as the Righteous Judge. ⁶ The principle of His judgement is clear
and simple. He will render to every man his due, by no fictitious
standard (such as birth or status) but strictly according to what
he has done. ⁷ To those who by steady persistence in a life-work
of good strive for the deathless glories of the Messianic Kingdom,

He will give that for which they strive, viz. eternal life. [8] But to those mutinous spirits who are disloyal to the right and loyal only to unrighteousness, for such there is in store anger and fury, [9] galling, nay crushing, pain: for every human being they are in store, who carries out to the end his course of evil, whether he be Jew or whether he be Gentile—the Jew again having precedence. [10] On the other hand the communicated glory of the Divine Presence, the approval of God and the bliss of reconciliation with Him await the man who labours on at that which is good—be he Jew or Gentile; here too the Jew having precedence, but only precedence : [11] for God regards no distinctions of race.

[12] Do not object that the Jew has a position of privilege which will exempt him from this judgement, while the Gentile has no law by which he can be judged. The Gentiles, it is true, have no law; but as they have sinned, so also will they be punished without one [see vv. 14, 15]. The Jews live under a law, and by that law they will be judged. [13] For it is not enough to hear it read in the synagogues. That does not make a man righteous before God. His verdict will pronounce righteous only those who have *done* what the Law commands. [14] I say that Gentiles too, although they have no written law, will be judged. For whenever any of them instinctively put in practice the precepts of the Law, their own moral sense supplies them with the law they need. [15] Because their actions give visible proof of commandments written not on stone but on the tables of the heart. These actions themselves bear witness to them; and an approving conscience also bears them witness; while in their dealings with one another their inward thoughts take sometimes the side of the prosecution and sometimes (but more rarely) of the defence. [16] These hidden workings of the conscience God can see; and therefore He will judge Gentile as well as Jew, at that Great Assize which I teach that He will hold through His Deputy, Jesus Messiah.

1. The transition from Gentile to Jew is conducted with much rhetorical skill, somewhat after the manner of Nathan's parable to David. Under cover of a general statement St. Paul sets before himself a typical Jew. Such an one would assent cordially to all that had been said hitherto (p. 49, *sup.*). It is now turned against himself, though for the moment the Apostle holds in suspense the direct affirmation, ' Thou art the man.'

There is evidence that Marcion kept vv. 2, 12–14, 16, 20 (from ἔχοντα)–29; for the rest evidence fails. We might suppose that Marcion would omit vv. 17–20, which record (however ironically) the privileges of the Jew; but the retention of the last clause of ver. 20 is against this.

διό links this section closely to the last; it is well led up to by i. 32, but ἀναπολ. pointing back to i. 20 shows that the Apostle had more than this in his mind.

2. οἴδαμεν δέ ABD &c., Harcl.,Orig.-lat. Tert. Ambrstr. Theodrt. *al.* WH. *text* RV. *text*: οἴδαμεν γάρ ℵ C 17 *al. pauc.* Latt. (*exc.* g) Boh. Arm., Chrys., Tisch. WH. *marg.* RV. *marg.* An even balance of authorities, both sides drawing their evidence from varied quarters. A more positive decision than that of WH. RV. would hardly be justified.

οἴδαμεν: οἶδα = to know for a fact, by external testimony; γιγνώσκω = to know by inner personal experience and appropriation: see *Sp. Comm.* iii. 299; Additional note on 1 Cor. viii. 1.

3. σύ emphatic; 'thou, of all men.' There is abundant illustration of the view current among the Jews that the Israelite was secure simply as such by virtue of his descent from Abraham and of his possession of the Law: cf. Matt. iii. 8, 9 'Think not to say within yourselves, We have Abraham to our father'; Jo. viii. 33; Gal. ii. 15; the passages quoted by Gif.; Weber, *Altsyn. Theol.* p. 69 f.

There may be an element of popular misunderstanding, there is certainly an element of inconsistency, in some of these passages. The story of Abraham sitting at the gate of Paradise and refusing to turn away even the wicked Israelite can hardly be a fair specimen of the teaching of the Rabbis, for we know that they insisted strenuously on the performance of the precepts of the Law, moral as well as ceremonial. But in any case there must have been a strong tendency to rest on supposed religious privileges apart from the attempt to make practice conform to them.

4. χρηστότητος: *bonitatis* Vulg., in Tit. iii. 4 *benignitas*: see Lft. on Gal. v. 22. χρηστότης = 'kindly disposition'; μακροθυμία = 'patience,' opp. to ὀξυθυμία a 'short' or 'quick temper,' 'irascibility' (cf. βραδὺς εἰς ὀργήν Jas. i. 19); ἀνοχή = 'forbearance,' 'delay of punishment,' cf. ἀνέχομαι to hold one's hand.

Comp. Philo, *Leg. Allegor.* i. 13 (Mang. i. 50) Ὅταν γὰρ ὕῃ μὲν κατὰ θαλάττης, πηγὰς δὲ ἐν τοῖς ἐρημοτάτοις ἐπομβρῇ . . . τί ἕτερον παρίστησιν ἢ τὴν ὑπερβολὴν τοῦ τε πλούτου καὶ τῆς ἀγαθότητος αὐτοῦ;

With μακροθυμίας comp. a graphic image in *Apoc. Baruch.* xii. 4 *Evigilabit contra te furor qui nunc in longanimitate tanquam in frenis retinetur.*

The following is also an impressive statement of this side of the Divine attributes: 4 Ezr. vii. 62–68 (132–138) *Scio, Domine, quoniam* (= ὅτι 'that') *nunc vocatus est Altissimus misericors, in eo quod misereatur his qui nondum in saeculo advenerunt; et miserator in eo quod miseretur illis qui conversionem faciunt in lege eius; et longanimis, quoniam longanimitatem praestat his qui peccaverunt quasi suis operibus; et munificus, quoniam quidem donare*

*vult pro exigere; et multae misericordiae, quoniam multiplicat magis miseri-
cordias his qui praesentes sunt et qui praeterierunt et qui futuri sunt: si
enim non multiplicaverit, non vivificabitur saeculum cum his qui inhabitant
in eo; et donator, quoniam si non donaverit de bonitate sua ut alleventur hi
qui iniquitatem fecerunt de suis iniquitatibus, non poterit decies millesima
pars vivificari hominum.*

καταφρονεῖς: cf. *Apoc. Baruch.* xxi. 20 *Innotescat potentia tua illis qui
putant longanimitatem tuam esse infirmitatem.*

εἰς μετάνοιάν σε ἄγει : its purpose or tendency is to induce you
to repent.

'The Conative Present is merely a species of the Progressive Present. A
verb which of itself suggests effort when used in a tense which implies action
in progress, and hence incomplete, naturally suggests the idea of attempt'
(Burton, § 11).

'According to R. Levi the words [Joel ii. 13] mean: God removes to
a distance His Wrath. Like a king who had two fierce legions. If these,
thought he, encamp near me in the country they will rise against my subjects
when they provoke me to anger. Therefore I will send them far away.
Then if my subjects provoke me to anger before I send for them (the legions)
they may appease me and I shall be willing to be appeased. So also said
God: Anger and Wrath are the messengers of destruction. I will send them
far away to a distance, so that when the Israelites provoke Me to anger, they
may come, before I send for them, and repent, and I may accept their
repentance (cf. Is. xiii. 5). And not only that, said R. Jizchak, but he
locks them up (Anger and Wrath) out of their way; see Jer. l. 25, which
means: Until He opens His treasure-chamber and shuts it again, man
returns to God and He accepts him' (*Tract. Thaanith* ii. 1 *ap.* Winter u.
Wünsche, *Jüd. Litt.* i. 207).

5. κατά: 'in accordance with,' *secundum duritiam tuam* Vulg.

ὀργήν : see on i. 18 above.

ὀργὴν ἐν ἡμέρᾳ ὀργῆς : to be taken closely together, ' wrath (to
be inflicted) in a day of wrath.'

The doctrine of a 'day of the Lord' as a day of judgement is taught by
the Prophets from Amos onwards (Amos v. 18; Is. ii. 12 ff.; xiii. 6 ff.; xxiv.
21; Jer. xlvi. 10; Joel ii. 1 ff.; Zeph. i. 7 ff.; Ezek. vii. 7 ff.; xxx. 3 ff.; Zech.
xiv. 1; Mal. iii. 2; iv. 1. It also enters largely into the pseudepigraphic
literature : *Enoch* xlv. 2 ff. (and the passages collected in Charles' Note);
Ps. Sol. xv. 13 ff.; 4 Ezr. vi. 18 ff., 77 ff. [vii. 102 ff. ed. Bensly]; xii. 34;
Apoc. Baruch. li. 1; lv. 6, &c.

δικαιοκρισίας : not quite the same as δικαίας κρίσεως 2 Thess. i. 5
(cf. *justi judicii* Vulg.), denoting not so much the character of the
judgement as the character of the Judge (δικαιοκριτής 2 Macc. xii.
41; cf. ὁ δίκαιος κριτής 2 Tim. iv. 8).

The word occurs in the *Quinta* (the fifth version included in Origen's
Hexapla) of Hos. vi. 5; it is also found twice in *Test. XII Patriarch.* Levi 3
ὁ δεύτερος ἔχει πῦρ, χιόνα, κρύσταλλον ἕτοιμα εἰς ἡμέραν προστάγματος Κυρίου
ἐν τῇ δικαιοκρισίᾳ τοῦ Θεοῦ. *Ibid.* 15 λήψεσθε ὀνειδισμὸν καὶ αἰσχύνην αἰώνιον
παρὰ τῆς δικαιοκρισίας τοῦ Θεοῦ.

6. ὃς ἀποδώσει: Prov. xxiv. 12 (LXX). The principle here laid
down, though in full accord with the teaching of the N. T.

generally (Matt. xvi. 27; 2 Cor. v. 10; Gal. vi. 7; Eph. vi. 8;
Col. iii. 24, 25; Rev. ii. 23; xx. 12; xxii. 12), may seem at first
sight to conflict with St. Paul's doctrine of Justification by Faith.
But Justification is a past act, resulting in a present state: it
belongs properly to the beginning, not to the end, of the Christian's
career (see on δικαιωθήσονται in ver. 13). Observe too that there is
no real antithesis between Faith and Works in themselves. Works
are the evidence of Faith, and Faith has its necessary outcome in
Works. The true antithesis is between *earning* salvation and
receiving it as a gift of God's bounty. St. Paul himself would
have allowed that there might have been a question of earning
salvation if the Law were really kept (Rom. x. 5; Gal. iii. 12).
But as a matter of fact the Law was not kept, the works were not
done.

7. καθ' ὑπομονὴν ἔργου ἀγαθοῦ: collective use of ἔργον, as in
ver. 15, 'a lifework,' the sum of a man's actions.

8. τοῖς δὲ ἐξ ἐριθείας: 'those whose motive is factiousness,' opp.
to the spirit of single-minded unquestioning obedience, those who
use all the arts of unscrupulous faction to contest or evade commands which they ought to obey. From ἔριθος 'a hired labourer'
we get ἐριθεύω 'to act as a hireling,' ἐριθεύομαι a political term
for 'hiring paid canvassers and promoting party spirit:' hence
ἐριθεία = the spirit of faction, the spirit which substitutes factious
opposition for the willing obedience of loyal subjects of the kingdom of heaven. See Lft. and Ell. on Gal. v. 20, but esp. Fri.
ad loc.

The ancients were strangely at sea about this word. Hesychius (cent. 5)
derived ἔριθος from ἔρα 'earth'; the *Etymologicum Magnum* (a compilation
perhaps of the eleventh century) goes a step further, and derives it from ἔρα
θής *agricola mercede conductus*; Greg. Nyssen. connects it with ἔριον 'wool'
(ἔριθος was used specially of woolworkers); but most common of all is the
connexion with ἔρις (so Theodrt. on Phil. ii. 3; cf. Vulg. *his qui ex contentione [per contentionem* Phil. ii. 3; *rixae* Gal. v. 20]). There can be
little doubt that the use of ἐριθεία was affected by association with ἔρις,
though there is no real connexion between the two words (see notes on
ἐπωρώθησαν xi. 7, κατανύξεως xi. 8).

ὀργὴ . . . θυμός: see Lft. and Ell. on Gal. v. 20; Trench, *Syn.*
p. 125: ὀργή is the settled feeling, θυμός the outward manifestation,
'outbursts' or 'ebullitions of wrath.'

ὀργὴ δέ ἐστιν ὁ ἐπόμενος τοῖς ἁμαρτάνουσιν ἐπὶ τιμωρίᾳ πόνος. θυμὸν δὲ
ὁρίζονται ὀργὴν ἀναθυμιωμένην καὶ διοιδαίνουσαν Orig. (in Cramer's *Catena*).

9. θλῖψις καὶ στενοχωρία: *tribulatio* (*pressura* in the African form
of the Old Latin) *et angustia* Vulg., whence our word 'anguish':
στενοχωρία is the stronger word = 'torturing confinement' (cf. 2 Cor.
iv. 8). But the etymological sense is probably lost in usage;
calamitas et angustiae h. e. summa calamitas Fri. p. 196.

For similar combinations ('day of tribulation and pain,' 'of tribulation and great shame,' 'of suffering and tribulation,' 'of anguish and affliction,' &c.) see Charles' note on *Enoch* xlv. 2.

κατεργαζομένου = 'carry to the end'; κατά either strengthening the force of the simple vb., as *per* in *perficere*, or giving it a bad sense, as in *perpetrare* Fri. p. 107.

11. προσωποληψία: peculiar to Biblical and Ecclesiastical Greek (Eph. vi. 9; Col. iii. 25; Jas. ii. 1; cf. προσωπολήπτης Acts x. 34; προσωπολημπτεῖν Jas. ii. 9; ἀπροσωπολήπτως 1 Pet. i. 17): πρόσωπον λαμβάνειν = (i) to give a gracious reception to a suppliant or suitor (Lev. xix. 15); and hence (ii) to show partiality, give corrupt judgement. In N. T. always with a bad sense.

The idea goes back to Deut. **x.** 17 ὁ Θεὸς . . . οὐ θαυμάζει πρόσωπον οὐδ' οὐ μὴ λάβῃ δῶρον, which is adopted in *Ps. Sol.* ii. 19 ὁ Θεὸς κριτὴς δίκαιος καὶ οὐ θαυμάσει πρόσωπον, and explained in *Jubilees* v. 15 'And He is not one who will regard the person (of any) nor receive gifts; when He says that He will execute judgement on each: if one gave him everything that is on the earth, He will not regard the gifts or the person (of any), nor accept anything at his hands, for he is a Righteous Judge'; cf. *Apoc. Baruch.* xiii. 7, *Pirqê Aboth* iv. 31 'He is about to judge with whom there is no iniquity, nor forgetfulness, nor respect of persons, nor taking of a bribe.'

12, 13. νόμος and ὁ νόμος. The distinction between these two forms did not escape the scholarship of Origen, whose comment on Rom. iii. 21 reads thus in Rufinus' translation (ed. Lommatzsch, vi. 201): *Moris est apud Graecos nominibus ἄρθρα praeponi, quae apud nos possunt articuli nominari. Si quando igitur Mosis legem nominat, solitum nomini praemittit articulum: si quando vero naturalem vult intelligi, sine articulo nominat legem.* This distinction however, though it holds good generally, does not cover all the cases. There are really three main uses: (1) ὁ νόμος = the Law of Moses; the art. denotes something with which the readers are familiar, '*their own law*,' which Christians in some sense inherited from the Jews through the O. T. (2) νόμος = law in general (e. g. ii. 12, 14; iii. 20 f.; iv. 15; v. 13, &c.). (3) But there is yet a third usage where νόμος without art. really means the Law of Moses, but the absence of the art. calls attention to it not as proceeding from Moses, but in its quality *as law*; *non quia Mosis sed quia lex* as Gif. expresses it in his comment on Gal. ii. 19 (p. 46). St. Paul regards the Pre-Messianic period as essentially a period of Law, both for Jew and for Gentile. Hence when he wishes to bring out this he uses νόμος without art. even where he is referring to the Jews; because his main point is that they were under 'a legal system'—who gave it and what name it bore was a secondary consideration. The Law of the Jews was only a typical example of a state of things that was universal. This will explain passages like Rom. v. 20, x. 4.

There will remain a few places, which do not come under any of these heads, where the absence of the art. is accounted for by the influence of the context, usually acting through the law of grammatical sympathy by which when one word in a phrase drops the article another also drops it; some of these passages involve rather nice points of scholarship (see the notes on ii. 25; iii. 31; xiii. 8). On the whole subject compare esp. Gif. p. 47 ff.; also a monograph by Grafe, *Die paulinische Lehre von Gesetz*, Freiburg i. B. 1884, ed. 2, 1893. Dr. Grafe goes rather too far in denying the distinction between νόμος and ὁ νόμος, but his paper contains many just remarks and criticisms.

12. ἀνόμως. The heathen are represented as deliberately rejecting not only the Law of Moses but even the Noachic ordinances. Thus they have become enemies of God and as such are doomed to destruction (Weber, *Altsyn. Theol.* p. 65).

ἥμαρτον. Burton (§ 54) calls this a 'collective Aorist,' represented in English by the Perfect. 'From the point of view from which the Apostle is speaking, the sin of each offender is simply a past fact, and the sin of all a series or aggregate of facts together, constituting a past fact. But inasmuch as this series is not separated from the time of speaking we must as in iii. 23 employ an English Perfect in translation.' Prof. Burton suggests an alternative possibility that the aor. may be *proleptic*, as if it were spoken looking backwards from the Last Judgement of the sins which will then be past; but the parallels of iii. 23, v. 12 are against this.

13. οἱ ἀκροαταὶ νόμου : cf. κατηχούμενος ἐκ τοῦ νόμου ver. 18; also *Pereq R. Meir* 6 (*Sayings of the Jewish Fathers*, ed. Taylor, p. 115) 'Thorah is acquired ... by learning, by a listening ear,' &c. It is interesting to note that among the sayings ascribed to Simeon, very possibly St. Paul's own class-mate and son of Gamaliel his teacher, is this : 'not learning but doing is the groundwork; and whoso multiplies words occasions sin' (*Pirqê Aboth.* i. 18, ed. Taylor; reff. from Delitzsch).

νόμου *sine artic. bis* ℵABDG. The absence of the art. again (as in the last verse) generalizes the form of statement, 'the hearers and the doers of law' (whatever that law may be); cf. vii. 1.

δικαιωθήσονται. The word is used here in its universal sense of 'a judicial verdict,' but the fut. tense throws forward that verdict to the Final Judgement. This use must be distinguished from that which has been explained above (p. 30 f.), the special or, so to speak, technical use of the term Justification which is characteristic of St. Paul. It is not that the word has any different sense but that it is referred to the past rather than to the future (δικαιωθέντες aor. cf. v. 1, 9); the acquittal there dates from the moment at which the man becomes a Christian; it marks the initial step in his career, his right to approach the presence of God as if he were righteous. See on ver. 6 above.

14. ἔθνη : τὰ ἔθνη would mean all or most Gentiles, ἔθνη means only some Gentiles ; the number is quite indefinite, the prominent point being their character as Gentiles.

Cf. 4 Ezr. iii. 36 *homines quidem per nomina invenies servasse mandata tua, gentes autem non invenies.*

τὰ μὴ νόμον ἔχοντα, the force of μή is 'who *ex hypothesi* have not a law,' whom we conceive of as not having a law; cf. τὰ μὴ ὄντα 1 Cor. i. 28 (*quae pro nihilo habentur* Grimm).

ἑαυτοῖς εἰσι νόμος : *ubi legis impletio, ibi lex* P. Ewald.

The doctrine of this verse was liberal doctrine for a Jew. The Talmud recognizes no merit in the good deeds of heathen unless they are accompanied by a definite wish for admission to the privileges of Judaism. Even if a heathen were to keep the whole law it would avail him nothing without circumcision (*Debarim Rabba* 1). If he prays to Jehovah his prayer is not

heard (*ibid.*). If he commits sin and repents, that too does not help him
(*Pesikta* 156ᵃ). Even for his alms he gets no credit (*Pesikta* 12ᵇ). 'In
their books' (i.e. in those in which God sets down the actions of the
heathen) 'there is no desert' (*Shir Rabba* 86ᶜ). See Weber, *Altsyn. Theol.*
p. 66 f. Christian theologians have expressed themselves much to the same
effect. Their opinions are summed up concisely by Mark Pattison, *Essays*,
ii. 61. 'In accordance with this view they interpreted the passages in
St. Paul which speak of the religion of the heathen; e.g. Rom. ii. 14.
Since the time of Augustine (*De Spir. et Lit.* § 27) the orthodox interpretation had applied this verse, either to the Gentile converts, or to the favoured
few among the heathen who had extraordinary divine assistance. The
Protestant expositors, to whom the words "do by nature the things contained
in the law" could never bear their literal force, sedulously preserved the
Augustinian explanation. Even the Pelagian Jeremy Taylor is obliged to
gloss the phrase "by nature," thus: "By fears and secret opinions which the
Spirit of God, who is never wanting to men in things necessary, was pleased
to put into the hearts of men" (*Duct. Dubit.* Book II. ch. 1, § 3). The
rationalists, however, find the expression "by nature," in its literal sense,
exactly conformable to their own views (John Wilkins [1614–1672], *Of Nat.
Rel.* II. c. 9), and have no difficulty in supposing the acceptableness of those
works, and the salvation of those who do them. Burnet, on Art. XVIII.,
in his usual confused style of eclecticism, suggests both opinions without
seeming to see that they are incompatible relics of divergent schools of
doctrine.'

15, οἵτινες: see on i. 25.

ἐνδείκνυνται: ἔνδειξις implies an appeal to facts; *demonstratio
rebus gestis facta* (P. Ewald, *De Vocis* Συνειδήσεως, &c., p. 16 n.).

τὸ ἔργον τοῦ νόμου: 'the work, course of conduct belonging to'
(i.e. in this context 'required by' or 'in accordance with') 'the
Law': collective use of ἔργον as in ver. 7 above.

[Probably not as Ewald *op. cit.* p. 17 after Grotius, *opus legis est id, quod
lex in Judaeis efficit, nempe cognitio liciti et illiciti.*]

συμμαρτυρούσης αὐτῶν τῆς συνειδήσεως. This phrase is almost
exactly repeated in ch. ix. 1 συμμαρτ. μοι τῆς συνειδ. μου. In both
cases the conscience is separated from the self and personified as
a further witness standing over against it. Here the quality of the
acts themselves is one witness, and the approving judgement passed
upon them by the conscience is another concurrent witness.

συνειδήσεως. Some such distinction as this is suggested by the original
meaning and use of the word συνείδησις, which = 'co-knowledge,' the knowledge or reflective judgement which a man has *by the side of* or *in conjunction
with* the original consciousness of the act. This second consciousness is easily
projected and personified as confronting the first.
   The word is quoted twice from Menander (342–291 B.C.), *Monost.* 597
(cf. 654) ἅπασιν ἡμῖν ἡ συνείδησις θεός (ed. Didot, pp. 101, 103). It is significant that both the word and the idea are completely absent from Aristotle.
They rise into philosophical importance in the more introspective moral
teaching of the Stoics. The two forms, τὸ συνειδός and ἡ συνείδησις appear
to be practically convertible. Epictetus (*Fragm.* 97) compares the conscience to a παιδαγωγός in a passage which is closely parallel to the comment
of Origen on this verse of Ep. Rom. (ed. Lommatzsch, vi. 107) *spiritus . . .*

velut paedagogus ei [sc. *animae*] *quidam sociatus et rector ut eam de melioribus moneat vel de culpis castiget et arguat.*

In Biblical Greek the word occurs first with its full sense in Wisd. xvii. 10. [11] ἀεὶ δὲ προσείληφε τὰ χαλεπὰ [πονηρία] συνεχομένη τῇ συνειδήσει. In Philo τὸ συνειδός is the form used. In N. T. the word is mainly Pauline (occurring in the speeches of Acts xxiii. 1, xxiv. 16; Rom. 1 and 2 Cor., Past. Epp., also in Heb.); elsewhere only in 1 Pet. and the *peric. adult.* John viii. 9. It is one of the few technical terms in St. Paul which seem to have Greek rather than Jewish affinities.

The 'Conscience' of St. Paul is a natural faculty which belongs to all men alike (Rom. ii. 15), and pronounces upon the character of actions, both their own (2 Cor. i. 12) and those of others (2 Cor. iv. 2, v. 11). It can be over-scrupulous (1 Cor. x. 25), but is blunted or 'seared' by neglect of its warnings (1 Tim. iv. 2).

The usage of St. Paul corresponds accurately to that of his Stoic contemporaries, but is somewhat more restricted than that which obtains in modern times. Conscience, with the ancients, was the faculty which passed judgment upon actions *after they were done* (in technical language the *conscientia consequens moralis*), not so much the general source of moral obligation. In the passage before us St. Paul speaks of such a source (ἑαυτοῖς εἰσι νόμος); but the law in question is rather generalized from the dictates of conscience than antecedent to them. See on the whole subject a treatise by Dr. P. Ewald, *De Vocis* Συνειδήσεως *apud script. N. T. vi ac potestate* (Lipsiae, 1883).

μεταξὺ ἀλλήλων. This clause is taken in two ways: (i) of the 'thoughts,' as it were, personified, Conscience being in debate with itself, and arguments arising now on the one side, and now on the other (cf. Shakspeare's 'When to the sessions of sweet silent thought, I summon up remembrance of things past'); in this case μεταξὺ ἀλλήλων almost = 'alternately,' 'in mutual debate'; (ii) taking the previous part of the verse as referring to the decisions of Conscience when in private it passes in review a man's own acts, and this latter clause as dealing rather with its judgements on the acts of the others; then μεταξὺ ἀλλήλων will = 'between one another,' 'between man and man,' 'in the intercourse of man with man'; and λογισμῶν will be the 'arguments' which now take one side and now the other. The principal argument in favour of this view (which is that of Mey. Gif. Lips.) is the emphatic position of μεταξὺ ἀλλήλων, which suggests a contrast between the two clauses, as if they described two different processes and not merely different parts or aspects of the same process.

There is a curious parallel to this description in *Assump. Moys.* i. 13 *Creavit enim orbem terrarum propter plebem suam, et non coepit eam inceptionem creaturae . . . palam facere, ut in ea gentes arguantur et humiliter inter se disputationibus arguant se.*

τῶν λογισμῶν: the λογισμοί are properly 'thoughts' conceived in the mind, not 'arguments' used in external debate. This appears from the usage of the word, which is frequently combined with καρδία (πολλοὶ λογισμοὶ ἐν καρδίᾳ ἀνδρός Prov. xix. 21; cf. Ps. xxxii. 11; Prov. vi. 18): it is used of secret 'plots' (Jer. xviii. 18 δεῦτε

λογισώμεθα ἐπὶ Ἰερεμίαν λογισμόν, 'devise devices'), and of the Divine
intentions (Jer. xxix [xxxvi] 11 λογιοῦμαι ἐφ' ὑμᾶς λογισμὸν εἰρήνης).
in the present passage St. Paul is describing an internal process,
though one which is destined to find external expression; it is the
process by which are formed the moral judgements of men upon
their fellows.

'The conscience' and 'the thoughts' both belong to the same persons.
This is rightly seen by Klöpper, who has written at length on the passage
before us (*Paulinische Studien*, Königsberg, 1887, p. 10); but it does not
follow that both the conscience and the thoughts are exercised upon the same
objects, or that μεταξὺ ἀλλήλων must be referred to the thoughts in the
sense that influences from without are excluded. The parallel quoted in
support of this (Matt. xviii. 15 μεταξὺ σοῦ καὶ αὐτοῦ μόνου) derives that part
of its meaning from μόνου, not from μεταξύ.

ἢ καί: 'or even,' 'or it may be,' implying that ἀπολ. is the exception, κατηγ. the rule.

16. The best way to punctuate is probably to put (in English)
a colon after ver. 13, and a semi-colon at the end of ver. 15: ver.
16 goes back to δικαιωθήσονται in ver. 13, or rather forms a conclusion to the whole paragraph, taking up again the ἐν ἡμέρᾳ of ver. 5.
The object of vv. 13-15 is to explain how it comes about that
Gentiles who have no law may yet be judged as if they had one:
they have a second inferior kind of law, if not any written precepts
yet the law of conscience; by this law they will be judged when
quick and dead are put upon their trial.

Orig., with his usual acuteness, sees the difficulty of connecting ver. 16 with
ver. 15, and gives an answer which is substantially right. The 'thoughts
accusing and condemning' are not conceived as rising up at the last day but
now. They leave however marks behind, *velut in ceris, ita in corde nostro.*
These marks God can see (ed. Lomm. p. 109).

ἐν ἡμέρᾳ ὅτε (*et* WH. *marg.*): ἐν ᾗ ἡμέρᾳ B, WH. *text*: ἐν ἡμέρᾳ ᾗ A,
Pesh. Boh. *al.,* WH. *marg.*

διὰ Ἰησοῦ Χριστοῦ (*et* WH. *marg.*): διὰ Χριστοῦ Ἰησοῦ ℵB, Orig., Tisch.
WH. *text.*

κρινεῖ: might be κρίνει, as RV. *marg.,* fut. regarded as certain.

κατὰ τὸ εὐαγγέλιόν μου. The point to which St. Paul's Gospel,
or habitual teaching, bears witness is, not that God will judge the
world (which was an old doctrine), but that He will judge it *through
Jesus Christ* as His Deputy (which was at least new in its application, though the Jews expected the Messiah to act as Judge, *Enoch*
xlv, xlvi, with Charles' notes).

The phrase κατὰ τὸ εὐαγγ. μου occurs Rom. xvi. 25, of the specially
Pauline doctrine of 'free grace'; 2 Tim. ii. 8, (i) of the resurrection of
Christ from the dead, (ii) of His descent from the seed of David.
We note in passing the not very intelligent tradition (introduced by φασὶ
δέ, Eus. *H. E.* III. iv. 8), that wherever St. Paul spoke of 'his Gospel' he
meant the Gospel of St. Luke.

FAILURE OF THE JEWS.

II. 17-29. *The Jew may boast of his possession of a special Revelation and a written Law, but all the time his practice shows that he is really no better than the Gentile* (vv. 17-24). *And if he takes his stand on Circumcision, that too is of value only so far as it is moral and spiritual. In this moral and spiritual circumcision the Gentile also may share* (vv. 25-29).

¹⁷ Do you tell me that you bear the proud name of Jew, that you repose on a written law as the charter of your salvation? Do you boast that Jehovah is your God, ¹⁸ that you are fully acquainted with His revealed Will, that you adopt for yourself a high standard and listen to the reading of the Law every Sabbath-day? ¹⁹ Do you give yourself out with so much assurance as a guide to the poor blind Gentile, a luminary to enlighten his darkness? ²⁰ Do you call your pupils dullards and yourself their schoolmaster? Are they mere infants and you their teacher? You, who have all knowledge and all truth visibly embodied for you in the Law? ²¹ Boastful Jew! How does your practice comport with your theory? So ready to teach others, do you need no teaching yourself? The eighth ²² and seventh commandments which you hold up to others—do you yourself keep them? You profess to loathe and abhor idols; but do you keep your hands from robbing their temples? ²³ You vaunt the possession of a law; and by the violation of that law you affront and dishonour God Who gave it. ²⁴ As Isaiah wrote that the Gentiles held the Name of God in contempt because they saw His people oppressed and enslaved, so do they now for a different reason—because of the gross inconsistency in practice of those who claim to be His people.

²⁵ True it is that behind the Law you have also the privilege of Circumcision, which marks the people of Promise. And Circumcision has its value if you are a law-performer. But if you are a law-breaker you might as well be uncircumcised. ²⁶ Does it not follow that if the uncircumcised Gentile keeps the weightier statutes of the Moral Law, he will be treated as if he were circumcised? ²⁷ And uncircumcised as he is, owing to his Gentile birth, yet if he

fulfils the Law, his example will (by contrast) condemn you who with the formal advantages of a written law and circumcision, only break the law of which you boast. ²⁸ For it is not he who has the outward and visible marks of a Jew who is the true Jew; neither is an outward and bodily circumcision the true circumcision. ²⁹ But he who is inwardly and secretly a Jew is the true Jew; and the moral and spiritual circumcision is that which really deserves the name. The very word ' Jew '—descendant of Judah—means ' praise ' (Gen. xxix. 35). And such a Jew has his ' praise,' not from man but from God.

17. εἰ δέ ℵ A B D* *al.*, Latt. Pesh. Boh. Arm. Aeth., &c.: *Ἴδε D° L al.*, Harcl., Chrys. *al.* The authorities for εἰ δέ include all the oldest MSS., all the leading versions, and the oldest Fathers : ἴδε is an itacism favoured by the fact that it makes the construction slightly easier. Reading εἰ δέ the apodosis of the sentence begins at ver. 21.

Ἰουδαῖος: here approaches in meaning (as in the mouth of a Jew it would have a tendency to do) to Ἰσραηλίτης, a member of the Chosen People, opposed to the heathen.

Strictly speaking, Ἑβραῖος, opp. Ἑλληνιστής, calls attention to language; Ἰουδαῖος, opp. Ἕλλην, calls attention to nationality ; Ἰσραηλίτης = a member of the theocracy, in possession of full theocratic privileges (Trench, *Syn.* § xxxix, p. 132 ff.). The word Ἰουδαῖος does not occur in LXX (though Ἰουδαϊσμός is found four times in 2 Macc.), but at this date it is the common word ; Ἑβραῖος and Ἰσραηλίτης are terms reserved by the Jews themselves, the one to distinguish between the two main divisions of their race (the Palestinian and Greek-speaking), the other to describe their esoteric status.

For the Jew's pride in his privileges comp. 4 Ezra vi. 55 f. *haec autem omnia dixi coram te, Domine, quoniam dixisti eas* (sc. *gentes*) *nil esse, et quoniam salivae assimilatae sunt, et quasi stillicidium de vase similasti habundantiam eorum.*

ἐπονομάζῃ: ' bearest the name ': ἐπονομάζειν = ' to *impose* a name,' pass. ' to have a name imposed.'

ἐπαναπαύῃ νόμῳ: ' have a law to lean upon ': so (without art.) ℵ A B D*; but it is not surprising that the later MSS. should make the statement more definite, ' lean upon *the* Law.' For ἐπαν. (*requiescis* Vulg.) cf. Mic. iii. 11 ; Ezek. xxix. 7 : the word implies at once the sense of support and the saving of ill-directed labour which resulted to the Jew from the possession of a law.

καυχᾶσαι ἐν Θεῷ: suggested by Jer. ix. 24 ' let him that glorieth glory in this, that he understandeth and knoweth Me, that I am the Lord.'

καυχᾶσαι: for καυχᾷ, stopping at the first step in the process of con-traction (καυχάεσαι, καυχᾶσαι, καυχᾷ). This is one of the forms which used to be called 'Alexandrine,' but which simply belong to the popular Greek current at the time (Hort, *Introd.* p. 304). καυχᾶσαι occurs also in 1 Cor. iv. 7, κατακαυχᾶσαι Rom. xi. 18; comp. ὀδυνᾶσαι Luke xvi. 25, and from un-contracted verbs, φάγεσαι . . . πίεσαι Luke xvii. 8, δύνασαι Matt. v. 36 (but δύνῃ Mark ix. 22); see Win. *Gr.* xiii. 2 *b* (p. 90).

18. τὸ θέλημα. Bp. Lightfoot has shown that this phrase was so constantly used for 'the Divine Will' that even without the art. it might have that signification, as in 1 Cor. xvi. 12 (*On Revision*, p. 106 ed. 1, p. 118 ed. 2).

δοκιμάζεις τὰ διαφέροντα : *probas utiliora* Cod. Clarom. Rufin. Vulg.; *non modo prae malis bona sed in bonis optima* Beng. on Phil. i. 10, where the phrase recurs exactly. Both words are ambiguous : δοκιμάζειν = (i) 'to test, assay, discern'; (ii) 'to approve after testing' (see on i. 28); and τὰ διαφέροντα may be either 'things which differ,' or 'things which stand out, or excel.' Thus arise the two interpretations represented in RV. and RV. *marg.*, with a like division of commentators. The rendering of RV. *marg.* ('provest the things that differ,' 'hast experience of good and bad' Tyn.) has the support of Euthym.-Zig. (διακρίνεις τὰ διαφέροντα ἀλλήλων· οἷον καλὸν καὶ κακόν, ἀρετὴν καὶ κακίαν), Fri. De W. Oltr. Go. Lips. Mou. The rendering of RV. ('approvest the things that are excellent') is adopted by Latt. Orig. (*ita ut non solum quae sint bona scias, verum etiam quae sint meliora et utiliora discernas*), most English Versions, Mey. Lft. Gif. Lid. (Chrys. does not distinguish; Va is undecided). The second rendering is the more pointed.

κατηχούμενος ἐκ τοῦ νόμου : cf. Acts xv. 21.

19. πέποιθας κ.τ.λ. The common construction after πέποιθας is ὅτι : acc. and infin. is very rare. It seems better, with Vaughan, to take σεαυτόν closely with πέποιθας, 'and art persuaded as to thyself that thou art,' &c.

ὁδηγὸν . . . τυφλῶν. It is natural to compare Matt. xv. 14 τυφλοί εἰσιν ὁδηγοὶ τυφλῶν κ.τ.λ.; also xxiii. 16, 24. Lips. thinks that the first saying was present to the mind of the Apostle. It would not of course follow that it was current in writing, though that too is possible. On the other hand the expression may have been more or less proverbial : comp. Wünsche, *Erläut. d. Evang.* on Matt. xxiii. 16. The same epithet was given by a Galilaean to R. Chasda, *Baba Kama* fol. 52 a. 'When the Shepherd is angry with the sheep he blinds their leader; i.e. when God determines to punish the Israelites, He gives them unworthy rulers.'

20. παιδευτήν : 'a schoolmaster,' with the idea of discipline, correction, as well as teaching; cf. Heb. xii. 9.

νηπίων : 'infants,' opp. to τέλειοι, 'adults,' as in Heb. v. 13, 14.

μόρφωσιν : 'outline,' 'delineation,' 'embodiment.' As a rule σχῆμα = outward form as opp. to inward substance, while μορφή = outward form as determined by inward substance; so that σχῆμα is the variable, μορφή the permanent, element in things : see Lft. *Phil.* p. 125 ff.; *Sp. Comm.* on 1 Cor. vii. 31. Nor does the present passage conflict with this distinction. The Law was a real

expression of Divine truth, so far as it went. It is more difficult to
account for 2 Tim. iii. 5 ἔχοντες μόρφωσιν εὐσεβείας τὴν δὲ δύναμιν
αὐτῆς ἠρνημένοι.

See however Lft. in *Journ. of Class. and Sacr. Philol.* (1857) iii. 115
'They will observe that in two passages where St. Paul does speak of that
which is unreal or at least external, and does not employ σχῆμα, he still
avoids using μορφή as inappropriate, and adopts μόρφωσις instead (Rom. ii.
20; 2 Tim. iii. 5), where the termination -ωσις denotes "the aiming after or
affecting the μορφή."' Can this quite be made good?

21. οὖν: resumptive, introducing the apodosis to the long protasis in vv. 17–20. After the string of points, suspended as it were
in the air, by which the Apostle describes the Jew's complacency,
he now at last comes down with his emphatic accusation. Here
is the 'Thou art the man' which we have been expecting since
ver. 1.

κλέπτειν: infin. because κηρύσσων contains the idea of command.

22. βδελυσσόμενος: used of the expression of physical disgust,
esp. of the Jew's horror at idolatry.

Note the piling up of phrases in Deut. vii. 26 καὶ οὐκ εἰσοίσεις βδέλυγμα
[here of the gold and silver plates with which idols were overlaid] εἰς
τὸν οἶκόν σου, καὶ ἔσῃ ἀνάθημα ὥσπερ τοῦτο, προσοχθίσματι προσοχθιεῖς καὶ
βδελύγματι βδελύξῃ, ὅτι ἀνάθημά ἐστιν. Comp. also Dan. xii. 11 ; Matt. xxiv.
15, &c. One of the ignominies of captivity was to be compelled to carry
the idols of the heathen : *Assump. Moys.* viii. 4 *cogentur palam baiulare idola
eorum inquinata.*

ἱεροσυλεῖς. The passage just quoted (Deut. vii. 26 with 25),
Joseph. *Ant.* IV. viii. 10, and Acts xix. 37 (where the town-clerk
asserts that St. Paul and his companions were ' *not* ἱερόσυλοι') show
that the robbery of temples was a charge to which the Jews were
open in spite of their professed horror of idol-worship.

There were provisions in the Talmud which expressly guarded against
this : everything which had to do with an idol was a βδέλυγμα to him unless
it had been previously desecrated by Gentiles. But for this the Jew might
have thought that in depriving the heathen of their idol he was doing a good
work. See the passages in Delitzsch *ad loc.*; also on ἱεροσυλία, which must
not be interpreted too narrowly, Lft., *Ess. on Supern. Rel.* p. 299 f.;
Ramsay, *The Church in the Roman Empire,* p. 144 n., where it is noted
that ἱεροσυλία was just one of the crimes which a provincial governor could
proceed against by his own *imperium.*
The Eng. Versions of ἱεροσυλεῖς group themselves thus: 'robbest God of
his honour' Tyn. Cran. Genev.; 'doest sacrilege' (or equivalent) Wic.
Rhem. AV. RV. *marg.*; 'dost rob temples' RV.

23. It is probably best not to treat this verse as a question.
The questions which go before are collected by a summary accusation. Gif., with a delicate sense of Greek composition, sees
a hint of this in the change from participles to the relative and
indic. (ὁ διδάσκων ... ὃς καυχᾶσαι).

24. A free adaptation of Is. lii. 5 (LXX). Heb. 'And con-tinually all the day long My Name is blasphemed': LXX adds to this δι' ὑμᾶς and ἐν τοῖς ἔθνεσιν. St. Paul omits διαπαντός and changes μου to τοῦ Θεοῦ.

The original meant that the Name of God was reviled by the tyrants and oppressors of Israel: St. Paul, following up a suggestion in the LXX (δι' ὑμᾶς), traces this reviling to the scandal caused by Israel's inconsistency. The fact that the formula of quotation is thrown to the end shows that he is conscious of applying the passage freely: it is almost as if it were an after-thought that the language he has just used is a quotation at all. See the longer note on ch. x, below.

25. νόμον πράσσῃς. On the absence of the art. see especially the scholarly note in Va.: 'It is almost as if νόμον πράσσειν and νόμον παραβάτης were severally like νομοθετεῖν, νομοφυλακεῖν, &c., νομοθέτης, νομοδιδάσκαλος, &c., one compound word: *if thou be a law-doer ... if thou be a law-transgressor*, &c., indicating the *character* of the person, rather than calling attention to the particular *form* or *designation* of the law, which claims obedience.'

γέγονεν: 'is by that very fact become.' Del. quotes the realistic ex-pression given to this idea in the Jewish fancy that God would send his angel to remove the marks of circumcision on the wicked

26. εἰς περιτομὴν λογισθήσεται: λογίζεσθαι εἴς τι = λογίζεσθαι εἰς τὸ εἶναί τι, εἰς denoting result, 'so as to be in place of,' 'reckoned as a substitute or equivalent for' (Fri., Grm.-Thay. s. v. λογίζομαι 1 a).

Of the synonyms τηρεῖν, φυλάσσειν, τελεῖν; τηρεῖν = 'to keep an eye upon,' 'to observe carefully' (and then do); φυλάσσειν = 'to guard as a deposit,' 'to preserve intact' against violence from without or within; τελεῖν = 'to bring (a law) to its proper fulfilment' in action; τηρεῖν and φυλάσσειν are both from the point of view of the agent, τελεῖν from that of the law which is obeyed. See Westcott on Jo. xvii. 12; 1 Jo. ii. 3.

27. κρινεῖ: most probably categorical and not a question as AV. and RV.; = 'condemn' by comparison and contrast, as in Matt. xii. 41, 42 'the men of Nineveh shall stand up in the judge-ment with this generation and shall condemn it,' &c. Again we are pointed back to vv. 1-3; the judge of others shall be himself judged.

ἡ ἐκ φύσεως ἀκροβυστία: uncircumcision which physically re-mains as it was born. The order of the words seems opposed to Prof. Burton's rendering, 'the uncircumcision which by nature fulfils the law' (ἐκ φύσ. = φύσει v. 14).

διά of 'attendant circumstances' as in iv. 11, viii. 25, xiv. 20; Anglicè 'with,' with all your advantages of circumcision and the possession of a written law.

The distinction between the literal Israel which is after the flesh and the true spiritual Israel is a leading idea with St. Paul and is worked out at length in ix. 6 ff.; see also pp. 2, 14 *sup*. We may

compare Phil. iii. 3, where St. Paul claims that Christians represent
the true circumcision.

28. ὁ ἐν τῷ φανερῷ. The Greek of this and the next verse is elliptical,
and there is some ambiguity as to how much belongs to the subject and how
much to the predicate. Even accomplished scholars like Dr. Gifford and
Dr. Vaughan differ. The latter has some advantage in symmetry, making
the missing words in both clauses belong to the subject ('Not he who is
[a Jew] outwardly is a Jew ... but he who is [a Jew] in secret is a Jew');
but it is a drawback to this view of the construction that it separates περιτομή
and καρδίας: Gif., as it seems to us rightly, combines these ('he which is
inwardly a Jew [is truly a Jew], and circumcision of heart ... [is true
circumcision']). Similarly Lips. Weiss (but not Mey.).

29. περιτομὴ καρδίας. The idea of a spiritual (heart-) circumcision goes back to the age of Deuteronomy; Deut. x. 16 περιτε-
μεῖσθε τὴν σκληροκαρδίαν ὑμῶν: Jer. iv. 4 περιτμήθητε τῷ Θεῷ ὑμῶν, καὶ
περιτέμεσθε τὴν σκληροκαρδίαν ὑμῶν: cf. Jer. ix. 26; Ezek. xliv. 7;
Acts vii. 51. Justin works out elaborately the idea of the Christian
circumcision, *Dial. c. Tryph* 114.

ὁ ἔπαινος. We believe that Dr. Gifford was the first to point
out that there is here an evident play on the name 'Jew': Judah
='Praise' (cf. Gen. xxix. 35; xlix. 8).

CASUISTICAL OBJECTIONS ANSWERED.

III. 1-8. *This argument may suggest three objections:*
(i) *If the moral Gentile is better off than the immoral Jew,
what becomes of the Jew's advantages?*—ANSWER. *He still
has many. His (e.g.) are the promises* (vv. 1-2). (ii) *But
has not the Jews' unbelief cancelled those promises?*—
ANSWER. *No unbelief on the part of man can affect the
pledged word of God: it only serves to enhance His faithfulness* (vv. 3, 4). (iii) *If that is the result of his action, why
should man be judged?*—ANSWER. *He certainly will be
judged: we may not say (as I am falsely accused of saying),
Do evil that good may come* (vv. 5-8).

¹ If the qualifications which God requires are thus inward and
spiritual, an objector may urge, What becomes of the privileged
position of the Jew, his descent from Abraham, and the like?
What does he gain by his circumcision? ² He does gain much
on all sides. The first gain is that to the Jews were committed

the prophecies of the Messiah. [Here the subject breaks off; a fuller enumeration is given in ch. ix. 4, 5.]

³ You say, But the Jews by their unbelief have forfeited their share in those prophecies. And I admit that some Jews have rejected Christianity, in which they are fulfilled. What then? The promises of God do not depend on man. He will keep His word, whatever man may do. ⁴ To suggest otherwise were blasphemy. Nay, God must be seen to be true, though all mankind are convicted of falsehood. Just as in Ps. li the Psalmist confesses that the only effect of his own sin will be that (in forensic metaphor) God will be ' declared righteous ' in His sayings [the promises just mentioned], and gain His case when it is brought to trial.

⁵ A new objection arises. If our unrighteousness is only a foil to set off the righteousness of God would not God be unjust who punishes men for sin? (Speaking of God as if He were man can hardly be avoided.) ⁶ That too were blasphemy to think ! If any such objection were sound, God could not judge the world. But we know that He will judge it. Therefore the reasoning must be fallacious.

⁷ If, you say, as in the case before us, the truthfulness of God in performing His promises is only thrown into relief by my infidelity, which thus redounds to His glory, why am I still like other offenders (καί) brought up for judgement as a sinner?

⁸ So the objector. And I know that this charge of saying ' Let us do evil that good may come ' is brought with slanderous exaggeration against me—as if the stress which I lay on faith compared with works meant, Never mind what your actions are, provided only that the end you have in view is right.

All I will say is that the judgement which these sophistical reasoners will receive is richly deserved.

1 ff. It is characteristic of this Epistle that St. Paul seems to imagine himself face to face with an opponent, and that he discusses and answers arguments which an opponent might bring against him (so iii. 1 ff., iv. 1 ff., vi. 1 ff., 15 ff., vii. 7 ff.). No doubt this is a way of presenting the dialectical process in his own mind. But at the same time it is a way which would seem to have been suggested by actual experience of controversy with Jews and the narrower Jewish Christians. We are told expressly that the charge of saying 'Let us do evil that good may come' was brought as a matter of fact against the Apostle (ver. 8). And vi. 1, 15 restate this charge in Pauline language. The Apostle as it were takes it up and gives it out again as if it came in the logic of his own thought. And the other charge of levelling down all the Jew's privileges, of ignoring the Old Testament and disparaging its saints, was one which must as inevitably have been brought against St. Paul as the like charges were brought against St. Stephen (Acts vi. 13 f.). It is probable however that St. Paul had himself wrestled with this question long before it was pointed against him as a weapon in controversy; and he propounds it in the order in which it would naturally arise in that stress of reasoning, pro and con., which went to the shaping of his own system. The modified form in which the question comes up the second time (ver. 9) shows—if our interpretation is correct—that St. Paul is there rather following out his own thought than contending with an adversary.

1. τὸ περισσόν. That which encircles a thing necessarily lies outside it. Hence περί would seem to have a latent meaning 'beyond,' which is appropriated rather by πέρα, πέραν, but comes out in περισσός, 'that which is in excess,' 'over and above.'

2. πρῶτον μέν: intended to be followed by ἔπειτα δέ, but the line of argument is broken off and not resumed. A list of privileges such as might have followed here is given in ch. ix. 4.

πρῶτον μὲν γάρ: om. γάρ B D* E G *minusc. pauc., verss. plur.,* Chrys. Orig.-lat. *al.,* [γάρ] WH.

ἐπιστεύθησαν. πιστεύω, in the sense of 'entrust,' 'confide,' takes acc. of the thing entrusted, dat. of the person; e. g. Jo. ii. 24 ὁ δὲ Ἰησοῦς οὐκ ἐπίστευεν ἑαυτὸν [rather αὑτὸν or αὑτόν] αὐτοῖς. In the passive the dat. becomes nom., and the acc. remains unchanged (Buttmann, pp. 175, 189, 190; Winer, xxxii. 5 [p. 287]; cf. 1 Cor. ix. 17; Gal. ii. 7).

τὰ λόγια. St. Paul might mean by this the whole of the O. T. regarded as the Word of God, but he seems to have in view rather those utterances in it which stand out as most unmistakably Divine; the Law as given from Sinai and the promises relating to the Messiah.

The old account of λόγιον as a dimin. of λόγος is probably correct, though Mey.-W. make it neut. of λόγιος on the ground that λογίδιον is the proper dimin. The form λογίδιον is rather a strengthened dimin., which by a process common in language took the place of λόγιον when it acquired the special sense of 'oracle.' From Herod. downwards λόγιον = 'oracle' as a brief condensed saying; and so, it came to = any 'inspired, divine utterance': e. g. in Philo of the 'prophecies' and of the 'ten commandments' (περὶ τῶν δέκα λογίων is the title of Philo's treatise). So in LXX the expression is used of the 'word of the Lord' five times in Isaiah and frequently in the Psalms (no less than seventeen times in Ps. cxix [cxviii]). From this usage it was natural that it should be transferred to the 'sayings' of the Lord Jesus (Polyc. *ad Phil.* vii. 1 ὃς ἂν μεθοδεύῃ τὰ λόγια τοῦ Κυρίου: cf. Iren.

Adv. Haer. I praef.; also Weiss, *Einl.* § 5. 4). But from the time of Philo onwards the word was used of any sacred writing, whether discourse or narrative; so that it is a disputed point whether the λόγια τοῦ Κυρίου which Papias ascribes to St. Matthew, as well as his own λογίων κυριακῶν ἐξηγήσεις (Eus. *H. E.* III. xxxix. 16 and 1) were or were not limited to discourse (see especially Lightfoot, *Ess. on Supern. Rel.* p. 172 ff.).

3. ἠπίστησαν . . . ἀπιστία. Do these words refer to 'unbelief' (Mey. Gif. Lid. Oltr. Go.) or to 'unfaithfulness' (De W. Weiss Lips. Va.)? Probably, on the whole, the former: because (i) the main point in the context is the disbelief in the promises of the O. T. and the refusal to accept them as fulfilled in Christ; (ii) chaps. ix–xi show that the problem of Israel's unbelief weighed heavily on the Apostle's mind; (iii) 'unbelief' is the constant sense of the word (ἀπιστέω occurs seven times, in which the only apparent exception to this sense is 2 Tim. ii. 13, and ἀπιστία eleven times, with no clear exception); (iv) there is a direct parallel in ch. xi. 20 τῇ ἀπιστίᾳ ἐξεκλάσθησαν, σὺ δὲ τῇ πίστει ἔστηκας. At the same time the one sense rather suggests than excludes the other; so that the ἀπιστία of man is naturally contrasted with the πίστις of God (cf. Va.).

πίστιν: 'faithfulness' to His promises; cf. Lam. iii. 23 πολλὴ ἡ πίστις σου: *Ps. Sol.* viii. 35 ἡ πίστις σου μεθ' ἡμῶν.

καταργήσει. καταργεῖν (from κατά causative and ἀργός = ἀεργός) = 'to render inert or inactive': a characteristic word with St. Paul, occurring twenty-five times in his writings (including 2 Thess. Eph. 2 Tim.), and only twice elsewhere (Lk. Heb.); = (i) in a material sense, 'to make sterile or barren,' of soil Lk. xiii. 7, cf. Rom. vi. 6 ἵνα καταργηθῇ τὸ σῶμα τῆς ἁμαρτίας, 'that the body as an instrument of sin may be paralysed, rendered powerless'; (ii) in a figurative sense, 'to render invalid,' 'abrogate,' 'abolish' (τὴν ἐπαγγελίαν Gal. iii. 17; νόμον Rom. iii. 31).

4. μὴ γένοιτο: a formula of negation, repelling with horror something previously suggested. 'Fourteen of the fifteen N. T. instances are in Paul's writings, and in twelve of them it expresses the Apostle's abhorrence of an inference which he fears may be falsely drawn from his argument' (Burton, *M. and T.* § 177; cf. also Lft. on Gal. ii. 17).

It is characteristic of the vehement impulsive style of this group of Epp. that the phrase is confined to them (ten times in Rom., once in 1 Cor., twice in Gal.). It occurs five times in LXX, not however standing alone as here, but worked into the body of the sentence (cf. Gen. xliv. 7, 17; Josh. xxii. 29, xxiv. 16; 1 Kings xx [xxi]. 3).

γινέσθω: see on i. 3 above; the transition which the verb denotes is often from a latent condition to an apparent condition, and so here, 'prove to be,' 'be seen to be.'

ἀληθής: as keeping His plighted word.

ψεύστης : in asserting that God's promises have not been fulfilled. καθὼς γέγραπται : ' *Even* as it stands written.' The quotation is exact from LXX of Ps. li [1]. 6. Note the mistranslations in LXX (which St. Paul adopts), νικήσῃς (or νικήσεις) for *insons sis*, ἐν τῷ κρίνεσθαι (pass.) for *in iudicando* or *dum iudicas*. The sense of the original is that the Psalmist acknowledges the justice of God's judgement upon him. The result of his sin is that God is pronounced righteous in His sentence, free from blame in His judging. St. Paul applies it as if the Most High Himself were put upon trial and declared guiltless in respect to the promises which He has fulfilled, though man will not believe in their fulfilment.

ὅπως ἄν : ἄν points to an unexpressed condition, ' in case a decision is given.'

δικαιωθῇς : ' that thou mightest be pronounced righteous ' by the judgement of mankind ; see p. 30 f. above, and compare Matt. xi. 19 καὶ ἐδικαιώθη ἡ σοφία ἀπὸ τῶν ἔργων (v. l. τέκνων : cf. Lk. vii. 35) αὐτῆς. *Test. XII Patr.* Sym. 6 ὅπως δικαιωθῶ ἀπὸ τῆς ἁμαρτίας τῶν ψυχῶν ὑμῶν. *Ps. Sol.* ii. 16 ἐγὼ δικαιώσω σε ὁ Θεός. The usage occurs repeatedly in this book ; see Ryle and James *ad loc.*

ἐν τοῖς λόγοις σου : not ' pleadings ' (Va.) but ' sayings,' i. e. the λόγια just mentioned. Heb. probably = ' judicial sentence.'

νικήσῃς : like *vincere*, of ' gaining a suit,' opp. to ἡττᾶσθαι : the full phrase is νικᾶν τὴν δίκην (Eur. *El.* 955, &c.).

νικήσῃς, B G K L &c. ; νικήσεις ℵ A D E, *minusc. aliq.* Probably νικήσεις is right, because of the agreement of ℵ A with the older types of Western Text, thus representing two great families. The reading νικήσῃς in B apparently belongs to the small Western element in that MS., which would seem to be allied to that in G rather than to that in D. There is a similar fluctuation in MSS. of the LXX : νικήσῃς is the reading of ℵ B (*def.* A), νικήσεις of some fourteen cursives. The text of LXX used by St. Paul differs not seldom from that of the great uncials.

κρίνεσθαι : probably not mid. (' to enter upon trial,' ' go to law,' lit. ' get judgment for oneself ') as Mey. Go. Va. Lid., but pass. as in ver. 7 (so Vulg. Weiss Kautzsch, &c. ; see the arguments from the usage of LXX and Heb. in Kautzsch, *De Vet. Test. Locis a Paulo allegatis*, p. 24 n.).

5. ἡ ἀδικία ἡμῶν : a general statement, including ἀπιστία. In like manner Θεοῦ δικαιοσύνην is general, though the particular instance which St. Paul has in his mind is the faithfulness of God to His promises.

συνίστησι : συνίστημι (συνιστάνω) has in N. T. two conspicuous meanings : (i) ' to bring together ' as two persons, ' to introduce ' or ' commend ' to one another (e. g. Rom. xvi. 1 ; 2 Cor. iii. 1 ; iv. 2 ; v. 12, &c. ; cf. συστατικαὶ ἐπιστολαί 2 Cor. iii. 1) ; (ii) ' to put together ' or ' make good ' by argument, ' to prove,' ' establish ' (*compositis collectisque quae rem contineant argumentis aliquid doceo* Fritzsche), as in Rom. v. 8; 2 Cor. vii. 11; Gal. ii. 18 (where see Lft. and Ell.).

Both meanings are recognized by Hesych. (συνιστάνειν· ἐπαινεῖν, φανεροῦν, βεβαιοῦν, παρατιθέναι); but it is strange that neither comes out clearly in the uses of the word in LXX; the second is found in Susann. 61 ἀνέστησαν ἐπὶ τοὺς δύο πρεσβύτας, ὅτι συνέστησεν αὐτοὺς Δανιὴλ ψευδομαρτυρήσαντας (Theod.).

τί ἐροῦμεν: another phrase, like μὴ γένοιτο, which is characteristic of this Epistle, where it occurs seven times; not elsewhere in N.T.

μὴ ἄδικος: the form of question shows that a negative answer is expected (μή originally meant 'Don't say that,' &c.).

ὁ ἐπιφέρων τὴν ὀργήν: most exactly, 'the inflicter of the anger' (Va.). The reference is to the Last Judgement: see on i. 18, xii. 19.

Burton however makes ὁ ἐπιφέρων strictly equivalent to a relative clause, and like a relative clause suggest a reason ('Who visiteth'='because He visiteth') *M. and T.* § 428.

κατὰ ἄνθρωπον λέγω: a form of phrase which is also characteristic of this group of Epistles, where the eager argumentation of the Apostle leads him to press the analogy between human and divine things in a way that he feels calls for apology. The exact phrase recurs only in Gal. iii. 15; but comp. also 1 Cor. ix. 8 μὴ κατὰ ἄνθρωπον ταῦτα λαλῶ; 2 Cor. xi. 17 ὃ λαλῶ, οὐ κατὰ Κύριον λαλῶ.

6. ἐπεὶ πῶς κρινεῖ: St. Paul and his readers alike held as axiomatic the belief that God would judge the world. But the objection just urged was inconsistent with that belief, and therefore must fall to the ground.

ἐπεί: 'since, if that were so, if the inflicting of punishment necessarily implied injustice.' Ἐπεί gets the meaning 'if so,' 'if not' ('or else'), from the context, the clause to which it points being supposed to be repeated: here ἐπεί sc. εἰ ἄδικος ἔσται ὁ ἐπιφέρων τὴν ὀργήν (cf. Buttmann, *Gr. of N. T. Gk.* p. 359).

τὸν κόσμον: all mankind.

7. The position laid down in ver. 5 is now discussed from the side of man, as it had just been discussed from the side of God.

εἰ δέ ℵ A *minusc. pauc.*, Vulg. *cod.* Boh., Jo.-Damasc., Tisch. WH. *text.* RV. *text.*; εἰ γάρ B D E G K L P &c., Vulg. Syrr., Orig.-lat. Chrys. *al.*, WH. *marg.* RV. *marg.* The second reading *may* be in its origin Western.

ἀλήθεια: the truthfulness of God in keeping His promises; ψεῦσμα, the falsehood of man in denying their fulfilment (as in ver. 4).

κἀγώ: 'I too,' as well as others, though my falsehood thus

redounds to God's glory. St. Paul uses the first person from motives of delicacy, just as in 1 Cor. iv. 6 he ʻtransfers by a fiction' (Dr. Field's elegant rendering of μετεσχημάτισα) to himself and his friend Apollos what really applied to his opponents.

8. There are two trains of thought in the Apostle's mind: (i) the excuse which he supposes to be put forward by the unbeliever that evil may be done for the sake of good; (ii) the accusation brought as a matter of fact against himself of saying that evil might be done for the sake of good. The single clause ποιήσωμεν τὰ κακὰ ἵνα ἔλθῃ τὰ ἀγαθά is made to do duty for both these trains of thought, in the one case connected in idea and construction with τί ... μή, in the other with λέγουσιν ὅτι. This could be brought out more clearly by modern devices of punctuation: τί ἔτι κἀγὼ ὡς ἁμαρτωλός, κρίνομαι; καὶ [τί] μὴ—καθὼς βλασφημούμεθα, καὶ καθώς φασί τινες ἡμᾶς λέγειν ὅτι—ποιήσωμεν κ.τ.λ. There is a very similar construction in vv. 25, 26, where the argument works up twice over to the same words, εἰς [πρὸς] τὴν ἔνδειξιν τῆς δικαιοσύνης αὐτοῦ, and the words which follow the second time are meant to complete both clauses, the first as well as the second. It is somewhat similar when in ch. ii. ver. 16 at once carries on and completes vv. 15 and 13.

St. Paul was accused (no doubt by actual opponents) of Antinomianism. What he said was, ʻThe state of righteousness is not to be attained through legal works; it is the gift of God.' He was represented as saying ʻtherefore it does not matter what a man does'—an inference which he repudiates indignantly, not only here but in vi. 1 ff., 15 ff.

ὧν τὸ κρίμα κ.τ.λ. This points back to τί ἔτι κἀγὼ κρίνομαι; the plea which such persons put in will avail them nothing; the judgement (of God) which will fall upon them is just. St. Paul does not argue the point, or say anything further about the calumny directed against himself; he contents himself with brushing away an excuse which is obviously unreal.

UNIVERSAL FAILURE TO ATTAIN TO RIGHTEOUSNESS.

III. 9–20. *If the case of us Jews is so bad, are the Gentiles any better? No. The same accusation covers both. The Scriptures speak of the universality of human guilt, which is laid down in* Ps. xiv *and graphically described in* Pss. **v**, cxl, x, *in* Is. lix, *and again in* Ps. xxxvi. *And if*

*the Jew is equally guilty with the Gentile, still less can he
escape punishment; for the Law which threatens him with
punishment is his own. So then the whole system of Law
and works done in fulfilment of Law, has proved a failure.
Law can reveal sin, but not remove it.*

⁹To return from this digression. What inference are we to
draw? Are the tables completely turned? Are we Jews not only
equalled but surpassed (προεχόμεθα passive) by the Gentiles? Not at
all. There is really nothing to choose between Jews and Gentiles.
The indictment which we have just brought against both (in i. 18–
32, ii. 17–29) proves that they are equally under the dominion
of sin. ¹⁰The testimony of Scripture is to the same effect. Thus
in Ps. xiv [here with some abridgment and variation], the Psalmist
complains that he cannot find a single righteous man, ¹¹that there is
none to show any intelligence of moral and religious truth, none to
show any desire for the knowledge of God. ¹²They have all (he
says) turned aside from the straight path. They are like milk
that has turned sour and bad. There is not so much as a single
right-doer among them. ¹³This picture of universal wickedness
may be completed from such details as those which are applied
to the wicked in Ps. v. 9 [exactly quoted]. Just as a grave stands
yawning to receive the corpse that will soon fill it with corruption,
so the throat of the wicked is only opened to vent forth depraved
and lying speech. Their tongue is practised in fraud. Or in
Ps. cxl. 3 [also exactly quoted]: the poison-bag of the asp lies
under their smooth and flattering lips. ¹⁴So, as it is described in
Ps. x. 7, throat, tongue, and lips are full of nothing but cursing
and venom. ¹⁵Then of Israel it is said [with abridgment from LXX
of Is. lix. 7, 8]: They run with eager speed to commit murder.
¹⁶Their course is marked by ruin and misery. ¹⁷With smiling
paths of peace they have made no acquaintance. ¹⁸To sum up the
character of the ungodly in a word [from Ps. xxxvi (xxxv). 1 LXX]:
The fear of God supplies no standard for their actions.

¹⁹Thus all the world has sinned. And not even the Jew can
claim exemption from the consequences of his sin. For when the
Law of Moses denounces those consequences it speaks especially
to the people to whom it was given. By which it was designed

that the Jew too might have his mouth stopped from all excuse, and that all mankind might be held accountable to God.

²⁰ This is the conclusion of the whole argument. By works of Law (i. e. by an attempted fulfilment of Law) no mortal may hope to be declared righteous in God's sight. For the only effect of Law is to open men's eyes to their own sinfulness, not to enable them to do better. That method, the method of works, has failed. A new method must be found.

9. τί οὖν; 'What then [follows]?' Not with προεχόμεθα, because that would require in reply οὐδὲν πάντως, not οὐ πάντως.

προεχόμεθα is explained in three ways: as intrans. in the same sense as the active προέχω, as trans. with its proper middle force, and as passive. (i) προεχόμεθα mid. = προέχομεν (*praecellimus eos* Vulg.; and so the majority of commentators, ancient and modern, Ἄρα περισσὸν ἔχομεν παρὰ τοὺς Ἕλληνας; Euthym.-Zig. ἔχομέν τι πλέον καὶ εὐδοκιμοῦμεν οἱ Ἰουδαῖοι; Theoph. 'Do we think ourselves better?' Gif.). But no examples of this use are to be found, and there seems to be no reason why St. Paul should not have written προέχομεν, the common form in such contexts. (ii) προεχόμεθα trans. in its more ordinary middle sense, 'put forward as an excuse or pretext' ('Do we excuse ourselves?' RV. *marg.*, 'Have we any defence?' Mey. Go.). But then the object must be expressed, and as we have just seen τί οὖν cannot be combined with προεχόμεθα because of οὐ πάντως. (iii) προεχόμεθα passive, 'Are we excelled?' 'Are we Jews worse off (than the Gentiles)?' a rare use, but still one which is sufficiently substantiated (cf. Field, *Ot. Norv. III ad loc.*). Some of the best scholars (e. g. Lightfoot, Field) incline to this view, which has been adopted in the text of RV. The principal objection to it is from the context. St. Paul has just asserted (ver. 2) that the Jew has an advantage over the Gentile: how then does he come to ask if the Gentile has an advantage over the Jew? The answer would seem to be that a different kind of 'advantage' is meant. The superiority of the Jew to the Gentile is *historic*, it lies in the possession of superior privileges; the practical equality of Jew and Gentile is in regard to their present moral condition (ch. ii. 17–29 balanced against ch. i. 18–32). In this latter respect St. Paul implies that Gentile and Jew might really change places (ii. 25–29). A few scholars (Olsh. Va.Lid.) take προεχόμεθα as pass., but give it the same sense as προέχομεν, 'Are we (Jews) preferred (to the Gentiles) in the sight of God?'

προεχόμεθα: v. l. προκατέχομεν περισσόν D* G, 31; Antiochene Fathers (Chrys. [ed. Field] Theodt. Severianus), also Orig.-lat. Ambrstr. (some MSS. but not the best, *tenemus amplius*): a gloss explaining προεχ. in the same way as Vulg. and the later Greek commentators quoted above. A L read προεχώμεθα.

οὐ πάντως. Strictly speaking οὐ should qualify πάντως, 'not altogether,' 'not entirely,' as in 1 Cor. v. 10 οὐ πάντως τοῖς πόρνοις τοῦ κόσμου τούτου: but in some cases, as here, πάντως qualifies οὐ, 'altogether not,' 'entirely not,' i. e. 'not at all' (nequaquam Vulg., οὐδαμῶς Theoph.). Compare the similar idiom in οὐ πάνυ; and see Win. Gr. lxi. 5.

προῃτιασάμεθα : in the section i. 18–ii. 29.

ὑφ' ἁμαρτίαν. In Biblical Greek ὑπό with dat. has given place entirely to ὑπό with acc. Matt. viii. 9 ἄνθρωπός εἰμι ὑπὸ ἐξουσίαν is a strong case. The change has already taken place in LXX; e.g Deut. xxxiii. 3 πάντες οἱ ἡγιασμένοι ὑπὸ τὰς χεῖράς σου, καὶ οὗτοι ὑπὸ σέ εἰσι.

10. The long quotation which follows, made up of a number of passages taken from different parts of the O. T., and with no apparent break between them, is strictly in accordance with the Rabbinical practice. ' A favourite method was that which derived its name from the stringing together of beads (Charaz), when a preacher having quoted a passage or section from the Pentateuch, strung on to it another and like-sounding, or really similar, from the Prophets and the Hagiographa' (Edersheim, Life and Times, &c. i. 449). We may judge from this instance that the first quotation did not always necessarily come from the Pentateuch —though no doubt there is a marked tendency in Christian as compared with Jewish writers to equalize the three divisions of the O. T. Other examples of such compounded quotations are Rom. ix. 25 f.; 27 f.; xi. 26 f.; 34 f.; xii. 19 f.; 2 Cor. vi. 16. Here the passages are from Pss. xiv [xiii]. 1–3 (=Ps. liii. 1–3 [lii. 2–4]), ver. 1 free, ver. 2 abridged, ver. 3 exact; v. 9 [10] exact; cxl. 3 [cxxxix. 4] exact: x. 7 [ix. 28] free; Is. lix. 7, 8 abridged; Ps. xxxvi [xxxv]. 1. The degree of relevance of each of these passages to the argument is indicated by the paraphrase : see also the additional note at the end of ch. x.

As a whole this conglomerate of quotations has had a curious history. The quotations in N.T. frequently react upon the text of O.T., and they have done so here: vv. 13–18 got imported bodily into Ps. xiv [xiii LXX] as an appendage to ver. 4 in the ' common ' text of the LXX (ἡ κοινή, i.e. the unrevised text current in the time of Origen). They are still found in Codd. ℵ* B R U and many cursive MSS. of LXX (om. ℵ^c^aA), though the Greek commentators on the Psalms do not recognize them. From interpolated MSS. such as these they found their way into Lat.-Vet., and so into Jerome's first edition of the Psalter (the ' Roman '), also into his second edition (the ' Gallican,' based upon Origen's Hexapla), though marked with an obelus after the example of Origen. The obelus dropped out, and they are commonly printed in the Vulgate text of the Psalms, which is practically the Gallican. From the Vulgate they travelled into Coverdale's Bible (A.D. 1535); from thence into Matthew's (Rogers') Bible, which in the

Psalter reproduces Coverdale (A. D. 1537), and also into the 'Great Bible'
(first issued by Cromwell in 1539, and afterwards with a preface by Cranmer,
whence it also bears the name of Cranmer's Bible, in 1540). The Psalter of
the Great Bible was incorporated in the Book of Common Prayer, in which
it was retained as being familiar and smoother to sing, even in the later
revision which substituted elsewhere the Authorized Version of 1611. The
editing of the Great Bible was due to Coverdale, who put an * to the
passages found in the Vulgate but wanting in the Hebrew. These marks
however had the same fate which befell the obeli of Jerome. They were
not repeated in the Prayer-Book; so that English Churchmen still read the
interpolated verses in Ps. xiv with nothing to distinguish them from the rest
of the text. Jerome himself was well aware that these verses were no part
of the Psalm. In his commentary on Isaiah, lib. xvi, he notes that St. Paul
quoted Is. lix. 7, 8 in Ep. to Rom., and he adds, *quod multi ignorantes, de
tertio decimo psalmo sumptum putant, qui versus* [στίχοι] *in editione Vulgata*
[i. e. the κοινή of the LXX] *additi sunt et in Hebraico non habentur* (Hieron.
Opp. ed. Migne, iv. 601; comp. the preface to the same book, *ibid.* col. 568 f.;
also the newly discovered *Commentarioli in Psalmos,* ed. Morin, 1895, p. 24 f.).

10. Some have thought that this verse was not part of the
quotation, but a summary by St. Paul of what follows. It does
indeed present some variants from the original, δίκαιος for ποιῶν
χρηστότητα and οὐδὲ εἷς for οὐκ ἔστιν ἕως ἑνός. In the LXX this clause
is a kind of refrain which is repeated exactly in ver. 3. St. Paul
there keeps to his text; but we cannot be surprised that in the
opening words he should choose a simpler form of phrase which
more directly suggests the connexion with his main argument.
The δίκαιος 'shall live by faith'; but till the coming of Christianity
there was no true δίκαιος and no true faith. The verse runs too
much upon the same lines as the Psalm to be other than a
quotation, though it is handled in the free and bold manner which
is characteristic of St. Paul.

11. οὐκ ἔστιν ὁ συνιῶν: *non est qui intelligat* (rather than *qui
intelligit*); Anglicè, 'there is none to understand.' [But ABG,
and perhaps Latt. Orig.-lat. Ambrstr., WH. *text* read συνιῶν, as also
(B)C WH. *text* ἐκζητῶν, without the art. after LXX. This would =
non est intelligens, non est requirens Deum (Vulg.) 'There is
no one of understanding, there is no inquirer after God.']

ὁ συνιῶν: on the form see Win. *Gr.* § xiv, 16 (ed. 8; xiv, 3 E. T.); Hort,
Intr. Notes on Orthog. p. 167; also for the accentuation, Fri. p. 174 f.
Both forms, συνιέω and συνίω, are found, and either accentuation, συνιῶν or
συνίων, may be adopted: probably the latter is to be preferred; cf. ἥφιε from
ἀφίω Mk. i. 34, xi. 16.

12. ἅμα: 'one and all.'

ἠχρειώθησαν: Heb. = 'to go bad,' 'become sour,' like milk;
comp. the ἀχρεῖος δοῦλος of Matt. xxv. 30.

ποιῶν (*sine artic.*) A B G &c. WH. *text*.

χρηστότητα = 'goodness' in the widest sense, with the idea of
'utility' rather than specially of 'kindness,' as in ii. 4.

ἕως ἑνός: cp. the Latin idiom *ad unum omnes* (Vulg. literally *usque ad unum*). B 67**, WH. *marg.* omit the second οὐκ ἔστιν [οὐκ ἔστιν ποιῶν χρηστότητα ἕως ἑνός]. The readings of B and its allies in these verses are open to some suspicion of assimilating to a text of LXX. In ver. 14 B 17 add αὐτῶν (ὧν τὸ στόμα αὐτῶν) corresponding to αὐτοῦ in B's text of Ps. x. 7 [ix. 28].

13. τάφος . . . ἐδολιοῦσαν. The LXX of Ps. v. 9 [10] corresponds pretty nearly to Heb. The last clause = rather *linguam suam blandam reddunt* (*poliunt*), or perhaps *lingua sua blandiuntur* (Kautzsch, p. 34): 'their tongue do they make smooth' Cheyne; 'smooth speech glideth from their tongue' De Witt.

ἐδολιοῦσαν: Win. *Gr.* § xiii, 14 (ed. 8; xiii, 2 f. E. T.). The termination -σαν, extended from imperf. and 2nd aor. of verbs in -μι to verbs in -ω, is widely found; it is common in LXX and in Alexandrian Greek, but by no means confined to it; it is frequent in Boeotian inscriptions, and is called by one grammarian a ' Boeotian ' form, as by others ' Alexandrian.'

ἰὸς ἀσπίδων: Ps. cxl. 3 [cxxxix. 4]. The position of the poison-bag of the serpent is rightly described. The venom is more correctly referred to the bite (as in Num. xxi. 9; Prov. xxiii. 32), than to the forked tongue (Job xx. 16): see art. 'Serpent' in *D. B.*

14. Ps. x. 7 somewhat freely from LXX [ix. 28]: οὗ ἀρᾶς τὸ στόμα αὐτοῦ γέμει καὶ πικρίας καὶ δόλου. St. Paul retains the rel. but changes it into the plural: στόμα αὐτῶν B 17, Cypr., WH. *marg.*

πικρία: Heb. more lit. = *fraudes.*

15-17. This quotation of Is. lix. 7, 8 is freely abridged from the LXX; and as it is also of some interest from its bearing upon the text of the LXX used by St. Paul, it may be well to give the original and the quotation side by side.

Rom. iii. 15-17.

ὀξεῖς οἱ πόδες αὐτῶν ἐκχέαι αἷμα· σύντριμμα καὶ ταλαιπωρία ἐν ταῖς ὁδοῖς αὐτῶν, καὶ ὁδὸν εἰρήνης οὐκ ἔγνωσαν.

Is. lix. 7, 8.

οἱ δὲ πόδες αὐτῶν [ἐπὶ πονηρίαν τρέχουσι] ταχινοὶ ἐκχέαι αἷμα [καὶ οἱ διαλογισμοὶ αὐτῶν διαλογισμοὶ ἀπὸ φόνων]. σύντριμμα καὶ ταλαιπωρία ἐν ταῖς ὁδοῖς αὐτῶν καὶ ὁδὸν εἰρήνης οὐκ οἴδασι [καὶ οὐκ ἔστι κρίσις ἐν ταῖς ὁδοῖς αὐτῶν].

αἷμα ἀναίτιον Theodotion, and probably also Aquila and Symmachus. [From the *Hexapla* this reading has got into several MSS. of LXX.] ἀφρόνων (for ἀπὸ φόνων) A ℵ: οἴδασι ℵ¹ B Q*, &c.: ἔγνωσαν A Q¹ *marg.* (Q = Cod. Marchalianus, XII Holmes) *minusc. aliq.*

19. What is the meaning of this verse? Does it mean that the passages just quoted are addressed to Jews (ὁ νόμος = O. T.;

νόμον τὴν παλαιὰν γραφὴν ὀνομάζει, ἧς μέρος τὰ προφητικά Euthym.-
Zig.), and therefore they are as much guilty before God as the
Gentiles? So most commentators. Or does it mean that the
guilt of the Jews being now proved, as they sinned they must also
expect punishment, the Law (ὁ νόμος = the Pentateuch) affirming
the connexion between sin and punishment. So Gif. Both interpretations give a good sense. [For though (i) does not strictly prove
that *all* men are guilty but only that the Jews are guilty, this was
really the main point which needed proving, because the Jews were
apt to explain away the passages which condemned them, and held
that—whatever happened to the Gentiles—they would escape.]
The question really turns upon the meaning of ὁ νόμος. It is
urged, (i) that there is only a single passage in St. Paul where
ὁ νόμος clearly = O. T. (1 Cor. xiv. 21, a quotation of Is. xxviii. 11):
compare however Jo. x. 34 (= Ps. lxxxii. 6), xv. 25 (= Ps.
xxxv. 19); (ii) that in the corresponding clause, τοῖς ἐν τῷ νόμῳ
must = the Law, in the narrower sense; (iii) that in ver. 21 the
Law is expressly distinguished from the Prophets.

Yet these arguments are hardly decisive: for (i) the evidence is
sufficient to show that St. Paul might have used ὁ νόμος in the wider
sense; for this one instance is as good as many; and (ii) we must
not suppose that St. Paul always rigidly distinguished which sense
he was using; the use of the word in one sense would call up the
other (cf. Note on ὁ θάνατος in ch. **v. 12**).

Oltr. also goes a way of his own, but makes ὁ νόμος = Law in the
abstract (covering at once for the Gentile the law of conscience, and for the
Jew the law of Moses), which is contrary to the use of ὁ νόμος.

λέγει . . . λαλεῖ: λέγειν calls attention to the substance of what
is spoken, λαλεῖν to the outward utterance; cf. esp. McClellan,
Gospels, p. 383 ff.

φραγῇ: cf. ἀναπολόγητος i. **20**, ii. **1**; the idea comes up at each
step in the argument.

ὑπόδικος: not exactly 'guilty before God,' but 'answerable to
God.' ὑπόδικος takes gen. of the penalty; dat. of the person injured
to whom satisfaction is due (τῶν διπλασίων ὑπόδικος ἔστω τῷ βλαφθέντι
Plato, *Legg.* 846 B). So here: all mankind has offended against
God, and owes Him satisfaction. Note the use of a forensic
term.

20. διότι: 'because,' not 'therefore,' as AV. (see on i. **19**).
Mankind is liable for penalties as against God, because there is
nothing else to afford them protection. Law can open men's
eyes to sin, but cannot remove it. Why this is so is shown in
vii. **7** ff.

δικαιωθήσεται: 'shall be pronounced righteous,' certainly not
'shall be made righteous' (Lid.); the whole context (ἵνα πᾶν στόμα

φραγῇ, ὑπόδικος, ἐνώπιον αὐτοῦ) has reference to à judicial trial and verdict.

πᾶσα σάρξ : man in his weakness and frailty (1 Cor. i. 29 ; 1 Pet. i. 24).

ἐπίγνωσις : 'clear knowledge'; see on i. 28, 32.

THE NEW SYSTEM.

III. 21-26. *Here then the new order of things comes in. In it is offered a Righteousness which comes from God but embraces man, by no deserts of his but as a free gift on the part of God. This righteousness, (i) though attested by the Sacred Books, is independent of any legal system (ver. 21) ; (ii) it is apprehended by faith in Christ, and is as wide as man's need (vv. 22, 23) ; (iii) it is made possible by the propitiatory Sacrifice of Christ (vv. 24, 25) ; which Sacrifice at once explains the lenient treatment by God of past sin and gives the most decisive expression to His righteousness (vv. 25, 26).*

[21] It is precisely such a method which is offered in Christianity. We have seen what is the state of the world without it.   But now, since the coming of Christ, the righteousness of God has asserted itself in visible concrete form, but so as to furnish at the same time a means of acquiring righteousness to man — and that in complete independence of law, though the Sacred Books which contain the Law and the writings of the Prophets bear witness to it.   [22] This new method of acquiring righteousness does not turn upon works but on faith, i. e. on ardent attachment and devotion to Jesus Messiah.   And it is therefore no longer confined to any particular people like the Jews, but is thrown open without distinction to all, on the sole condition of believing, whether they be Jews or Gentiles.   [23] The universal gift corresponds to the universal need. All men alike have sinned ; and all alike feel themselves far from the bright effulgence of God's presence.   [24] Yet estranged as they are God accepts them as righteous for no merit or service of theirs, by an act of His own free favour, the change in their relation to Him being due to the Great Deliverance wrought at the price of the Death of Christ Jesus.   [25] When the Messiah suffered upon the

Cross it was God Who set Him there as a public spectacle, to
be viewed as a Mosaic sacrifice might be viewed by the crowds assembled in the courts of the Temple.   The shedding of His Blood
was in fact a sacrifice which had the effect of making propitiation
or atonement for sin, an effect which man must appropriate through
faith.   The object of the whole being by this public and decisive
act to vindicate the righteousness of God.   In previous ages the
sins of mankind had been passed over without adequate punishment
or atonement : ²⁶ but this long forbearance on the part of God had in
view throughout that signal exhibition of His Righteousness which
He purposed to enact when the hour should come as now it has
come, so as to reveal Himself in His double character as at once
righteous Himself and pronouncing righteous, or accepting as
righteous, the loyal follower of Jesus.

21. νυνὶ δέ : ' now,' under the Christian dispensation.   Mey. De
W. Oltr. Go. and others contend for the rendering ' as it is,' on the
ground that the opposition is between two *states*, the state under
Law and the state without Law.   But here the two states or
relations correspond to two periods succeeding each other in order
of time ; so that νυνί may well have its first and most obvious
meaning, which is confirmed by the parallel passages, Rom. xvi.
25, 26 μυστηρίου . . . φανερωθέντος . . . νῦν, Eph. ii. 12, 13 νυνὶ
δὲ . . . ἐγενήθητε ἐγγύς, Col. i. 26, 27 μυστήριον τὸ ἀποκεκρυμμένον . . .
νῦν δὲ ἐφανερώθη, 2 Tim. i. 9, 10 χάριν τὴν δοθεῖσαν . . . πρὸ χρόνων
αἰωνίων φανερωθεῖσαν δὲ νῦν, Heb. ix. 26 νυνὶ δὲ ἅπαξ ἐπὶ συντελείᾳ
τῶν αἰώνων . . . πεφανέρωται.   It may be observed (i) that the N. T.
writers constantly oppose the pre-Christian and the Christian
dispensations to each other as periods (comp. in addition to the
passages already enumerated Acts xvii. 30; Gal. iii. 23, 25,
iv. 3, 4 ; Heb. i. 1) ; and (ii) that φανεροῦσθαι is constantly used
with expressions denoting time (add to passages above Tit. i. 3
καιροῖς ἰδίοις, 1 Pet. i. 20 ἐπ' ἐσχάτου τῶν χρόνων).   The leading
English commentators take this view.

An allusion of Tertullian's makes it probable that Marcion retained this
verse; evidence fails as to the rest of the chapter, and it is probable that he
cut out the whole of ch. iv, along with most other references to the history
of Abraham (Tert. on Gal. iv. 21-26, *Adv. Marc.* v. 4).

χωρὶς νόμου : 'apart from law,' 'independently of it,' not as
a subordinate system growing out of Law, but as an alternative for
Law and destined ultimately to supersede it (Rom. x. 4).

δικαιοσύνη Θεοῦ : see on ch. i. 17. St. Paul goes on to define
his meaning. The righteousness which he has in view is essentially

the righteousness of God; though the aspect in which it is regarded is as a condition bestowed upon man, that condition is the direct outcome of the Divine attribute of righteousness, working its way to larger realization amongst men. One step in this realization, the first great objective step, is the Sacrificial Death of Christ for sin (ver. 25); the next step is the subjective apprehension of what is thus done for him by faith on the part of the believer (ver. 22). Under the old system the only way laid down for man to attain to righteousness was by the strict performance of the Mosaic Law; now that heavy obligation is removed and a shorter but at the same time more effective method is substituted, the method of attachment to a Divine Person.

πεφανέρωται. Contrast the completed φανέρωσις in Christ and the continued ἀποκάλυψις in the Gospel (ch. i. 16): the verb φανεροῦσθαι is regularly used for the Incarnation with its accompaniments and sequents as outstanding facts of history prepared in the secret counsels of God and at the fitting moment 'manifested' to the sight of men; so, of the whole process of the Incarnation, 1 Tim. iii. 16; 2 Tim. i. 10; 1 Pet. i. 20; 1 Jo. iii. 5, 8: of the Atonement, Heb. ix. 26: of the risen Christ, Mark xvi. 12, 14; John xxi. 14: of the future coming to Judgement, 1 Pet. v. 4; 1 Jo. ii. 28. The nearest parallels to this verse which speaks of the manifestation of Divine 'righteousness' are 2 Tim. i. 10, which speaks of a like manifestation of Divine 'grace,' and 1 Jo. i. 2, which describes the Incarnation as the appearing on earth of the principle of 'life.'

μαρτυρουμένη κ. τ. λ.: another instance of the care with which St. Paul insists that the new order of things is in no way contrary to the old, but rather a development which was duly foreseen and provided for: cf. Rom. i. 2, iii. 31, the whole of ch. iv, ix. 25–33; x. 16–21; xi. 1–10, 26–29; xv. 8–12; xvi. 26 &c.

22. δέ turns to the particular aspect of the Divine righteousness which the Apostle here wishes to bring out; it is righteousness apprehended by faith in Christ and embracing the body of believers. The particle thus introduces a nearer definition, but in itself only marks the transition in thought which here (as in ch. ix. 30; 1 Cor. ii. 6; Gal. ii. 2; Phil. ii. 8) happens to be from the general to the particular.

πίστεως Ἰησοῦ Χριστοῦ: gen. of object, 'faith in Jesus Christ.' This is the hitherto almost universally accepted view, which has however been recently challenged in a very carefully worked out argument by Prof. Haussleiter of Greifswald (*Der Glaube Jesu Christi u. der christliche Glaube*, Leipzig, 1891).

Dr. Haussleiter contends that the gen. is subjective not objective, that like the 'faith of Abraham' in ch. iv. 16, it denotes the faith (in God) which Christ Himself maintained even through the ordeal of the Crucifixion, that this faith is here put forward as the central feature of the Atonement, and that it is to be grasped or appropriated by the Christian in a similar manner to that in which he reproduces the faith of Abraham. If this view held good, a number of other passages (notably i. 17) would be affected by it. But, although ably carried out, the interpretation of some of these passages seems to us forced; the theory brings together things, like the πίστις Ἰησοῦ Χριστοῦ here with the πίστις Θεοῦ in iii. 3, which are really disparate; and it has so far, we believe, met with no acceptance.

Ἰησοῦ Χριστοῦ. B, and apparently Marcion as quoted by Tertullian, drop Ἰησοῦ (so too WH. marg.); A reads ἐν Χριστῷ Ἰησοῦ.

καὶ ἐπὶ πάντας om. ℵ* A B C, 47. 67**, Boh. Aeth. Arm., Clem.-Alex. Orig. Did. Cyr.-Alex. Aug.: ins. D E F G K L &c. ἐπὶ πάντας alone is found in Jo. Damasc. Vulg. codd., so that εἰς πάντας καὶ ἐπὶ πάντας would seem to be a conflation, or combination of two readings originally alternatives. If it were the true reading εἰς would express 'destination for' all believers, ἐπί 'extension to' them.

23. οὐ γάρ ἐστι διαστολή. The Apostle is reminded of one of his main positions. The Jew has (in this respect) no real advantage over the Gentile; both alike need a righteousness which is not their own; and to both it is offered on the same terms.

ἥμαρτον. In English we may translate this 'have sinned' in accordance with the idiom of the language, which prefers to use the perfect where a past fact or series of facts is not separated by a clear interval from the present: see note on ii. 12.

ὑστεροῦνται: see Monro, Homeric Grammar, § 8 (3); mid. voice = 'feel want.' Gif. well compares Matt. xix. 20 τί ἔτι ὑστερῶ; (objective, 'What, as a matter of fact, is wanting to me?') with Luke xv. 14 καὶ αὐτὸς ἤρξατο ὑστερεῖσθαι (subjective, the Prodigal begins to feel his destitution).

τῆς δόξης. There are two wholly distinct uses of this word: (1) = 'opinion' (a use not found in N. T.) and thence in particular 'favourable opinion,' 'reputation' (Rom. ii. 7, 10; John xii. 43 &c.); (2) by a use which came in with the LXX as translation of Heb. כָּבוֹד = (i) 'visible brightness or splendour' (Acts xxii. 11; 1 Cor. xv. 40 ff.); and hence (ii) the brightness which radiates from the presence of God, the visible glory conceived as resting on Mount Sinai (Ex. xxiv. 16), in the pillar of cloud (Ex. xvi. 10), in the tabernacle (Ex. xl. 34) or temple (1 Kings viii. 11; 2 Chron. v. 14), and specially between the cherubim on the lid of the ark (Ps. lxxx. 1; Ex. xxv. 22; Rom. ix. 4 &c.); (iii) this visible splendour symbolized the Divine perfections, 'the majesty or goodness of God as manifested to men' (Lightfoot on Col. i. 11; comp. Eph. i. 6, 12, 17; iii. 16); (iv) these perfections are in a measure communicated to man through Christ (esp. 2 Cor. iv. 6, iii. 18). Both morally and physically a certain transfiguration takes place in the Christian, partially here, completely hereafter (comp. e.g. Rom. viii. 30 ἐδόξασεν with Rom. v. 2 ἐπ' ἐλπίδι τῆς

δόξης τοῦ Θεοῦ, viii. 18 τὴν μέλλουσαν δόξαν ἀποκαλυφθῆναι, 2 Tim.
ii. 10 δόξης αἰωνίου). The Rabbis held that Adam by the Fall lost
six things, 'the glory, life (immortality), his stature (which was
above that of his descendants), the fruit of the field, the fruits of
trees, and the light (by which the world was created, and which
was withdrawn from it and reserved for the righteous in the world
to come).' It is explained that 'the glory' was a reflection from
the Divine glory which before the Fall brightened Adam's face
(Weber, *Altsyn. Theol.* p. 214). Clearly St. Paul conceives of this
glory as in process of being recovered: the physical sense is also
enriched by its extension to attributes that are moral and
spiritual.

> The meaning of δόξα in this connexion is well illustrated by 4 Ezr. vii. 42
> [ed. Bensly = vi. 14 O. F. Fritzsche, p. 607], where the state of the blessed
> is described as *neque meridiem, neque noctem, neque ante lucem* [perh. for
> *antelucium*; vid. Bensly *ad loc.*], *neque nitorem, neque claritatem, neque
> lucem, nisi solummodo splendorem claritatis Altissimi* [perh. = ἀπαύγασμα
> δόξης Ὑψίστου]. In quoting this passage Ambrose has *sola Dei fulgebit
> claritas; Dominus enim erit lux omnium* (cf. Rev. xxi. 24). The blessed
> themselves shine with a brightness which is reflected from the face of God:
> *ibid.* vv. 97, 98 [Bensly = 71, 72 O. F. Fritzsche] *quomodo incipiet* (μέλλει)
> *vultus eorum fulgere sicut sol, et quomodo incipient stellarum adsimilari
> lumini . . . festinant enim videre vultum [eius] cui serviunt viventes et
> a quo incipient gloriosi mercedem recipere* (cf. Matt. xiii. 43).

24. δικαιούμενοι. The construction and connexion of this word
are difficult, and perhaps not to be determined with certainty.
(i) Many leading scholars (De W. Mey. Lips. Lid. Win. *Gr.* § xlv.
6 b) make δικαιούμενοι mark a detail in, or assign a proof of, the
condition described by ὑστεροῦνται. In this case there would be
a slight stress on δωρεάν: men are far from God's glory, *because* the
state of righteousness has to be given them; they do nothing for
it. But this is rather far-fetched. No such proof or further
description of ὑστεροῦνται is needed. It had already been proved
by the actual condition of Jews as well as Gentiles; and to prove
it by the gratuitousness of the justification would be an inversion
of the logical order. (ii) ὑστεροῦνται δικαιούμενοι is taken as = ὑστεροῦνται καὶ δικαιοῦνται (Fri.) or = ὑστερούμενοι δικαιοῦνται (Tholuck).
But this is dubious Greek. (iii) δικαιούμενοι is not taken with what
precedes, but is made to begin a new clause. In that case there is
an anacoluthon, and we must supply some such phrase as πῶς
καυχώμεθα; (Oltr.). But that would be harsh, and a connecting
particle seems wanted. (iv) Easier and more natural than any of
these expedients seems to be, with Va. and Ewald, to make οὐ γάρ
. . . ὑστεροῦνται practically a parenthesis, and to take the nom.
δικαιούμενοι 'as *suggested* by πάντες in ver. 23, but in sense referring
rather to τοὺς πιστεύοντας in ver. 22.' No doubt such a construction
would be irregular, but it may be questioned whether it is too

irregular for St. Paul. The Apostle frequently gives a new turn to
a sentence under the influence of some expression which is really
subordinate to the main idea. Perhaps as near a parallel as any
would be 2 Cor. viii. 18, 19 συνεπέμψαμεν δὲ τὸν ἀδελφὸν . . . οὗ
ὁ ἔπαινος ἐν τῷ εὐαγγελίῳ . . . οὐ μόνον δέ, ἀλλὰ καὶ χειροτονηθείς (as if
ὃς ἐπαινεῖται had preceded).

δωρεὰν τῇ αὐτοῦ χάριτι. Each of these phrases strengthens the
other in a very emphatic way, the position of αὐτοῦ further laying
stress on the fact that this manifestation of free favour on the part
of God is unprompted by any other external cause than the one
which is mentioned (διὰ τῆς ἀπολυτρώσεως).

ἀπολυτρώσεως. It is contended, esp. by Oltramare, (i) that
λυτρόω and ἀπολυτρόω in classical Greek = not 'to pay a ransom,'
but 'to take a ransom,' 'to put to ransom,' or 'release on ransom,'
as a conqueror releases his prisoners (the only example given of
ἀπολύτρωσις is Plut. *Pomp*. 24 πολέων αἰχμαλώτων ἀπολυτρώσεις, where
the word has this sense of 'putting to ransom'); (ii) that in LXX
λυτροῦσθαι is frequently used of the Deliverance from Egypt, the
Exodus, in which there is no question of ransom (so Ex. vi. 6,
xv. 13; Deut. vii. 8; ix. 26; xiii. 5, &c.: cf. also ἀπολυτρώσει
Ex. xxi. 8, of the 'release' of a slave by her master). The subst.
ἀπολύτρωσις occurs only in one place, Dan. iv. 30 [29 or 32], LXX
ὁ χρόνος μου τῆς ἀπολυτρώσεως ἦλθε of Nebuchadnezzar's recovery
from his madness. Hence it is inferred (cf. also Westcott, *Heb*.
p. 296, and Ritschl, *Rechtfert. u. Versöhn*. ii. 220 ff.) that here and
in similar passages ἀπολύτρωσις denotes 'deliverance' simply without
any idea of 'ransom.' There is no doubt that this part of the
metaphor might be dropped. But in view of the clear resolution of
the expression in Mark x. 45 (Matt. xx. 28) δοῦναι τὴν ψυχὴν αὐτοῦ
λύτρον ἀντὶ πολλῶν, and in 1 Tim. ii. 6 ὁ δοὺς ἑαυτὸν ἀντίλυτρον ὑπὲρ
πάντων, and in view also of the many passages in which Christians
are said to be 'bought,' or 'bought with a price' (1 Cor. vi. 20,
vii. 23; Gal. iii. 13; 2 Pet. ii. 1; Rev. v. 9: cf. Acts xx. 28;
1 Pet. i. 18, 19), we can hardly resist the conclusion that the idea
of the λύτρον retains its full force, that it is identical with the τιμή,
and that both are ways of describing the Death of Christ. The
emphasis is on the *cost* of man's redemption. We need not press
the metaphor yet a step further by asking (as the ancients did) to
whom the ransom or price was paid. It was required by that
ultimate necessity which has made the whole course of things what
it has been; but this necessity is far beyond our powers to grasp
or gauge.

τῆς ἐν Χριστῷ Ἰησοῦ. We owe to Haussleiter (*Der Glaube Jesu Christi*,
p. 116) the interesting observation that wherever the phrase ἐν Χριστῷ or ἐν
Χριστῷ Ἰησοῦ occurs there is no single instance of the variants ἐν Ἰησοῦ or
ἐν Ἰησοῦ Χριστῷ. This is significant, because in other combinations the

variants are frequent. It is also what we should expect, because ἐν Χριστῷ
and ἐν Χριστῷ Ἰησ. always relate to the glorified Christ, not to the historic
Jesus.

25. προέθετο may = either (i) 'whom God proposed to Himself,'
'purposed,' 'designed' (Orig. Pesh.); or (ii) 'whom God set forth
publicly' (*proposuit* Vulg.). Both meanings would be in full accordance with the teaching of St. Paul both elsewhere and in this
Epistle. For (i) we may compare the idea of the Divine πρόθεσις
in ch. ix. 11 (viii. 28); Eph. iii. 11 (i. 11); 2 Tim. i. 9; also
1 Pet. i. 20. For (ii) compare esp. Gal. iii. 1 οἷς κατ' ὀφθαλμοὺς
Ἰησοῦς Χριστὸς προεγράφη ἐσταυρωμένος. But when we turn to the
immediate context we find it so full of terms denoting publicity
(πεφανέρωται, εἰς ἔνδειξιν, πρὸς τὴν ἔνδειξιν) that the latter sense seems
preferable. The Death of Christ is not only a manifestation of the
righteousness of God, but a *visible* manifestation and one to which
appeal can be made.

ἱλαστήριον: usually subst. meaning strictly 'place or vehicle of
propitiation,' but originally neut. of adj. ἱλαστήριος (ἱλαστήριον
ἐπίθεμα Ex. xxv. 16 [17], where however Gif. takes the two words
as substantives in apposition). In LXX of the Pentateuch, as in
Heb. ix. 5, the word constantly stands for the 'lid of the ark,' or
'mercy-seat,' so called from the fact of its being sprinkled with the
blood of the sacrifices on the Day of Atonement. A number of
the best authorities (esp. Gif. Va. Lid. Ritschl, *Rechtfert. u. Versöhn.*
ii. 169 ff. ed. 2) take the word here in this sense, arguing (i) that
it suits the emphatic αὐτοῦ in ἐν τῷ αὐτοῦ αἵματι; (ii) that through
LXX it would be by far the most familiar usage; (iii) that the
Greek commentators (as Gif. has shown in detail) unanimously give
it this sense; (iv) that the idea is specially appropriate inasmuch as
on Christ rests the fulness of the Divine glory, 'the true Shekinah,'
and it is natural to connect with His Death the culminating rite in
the culminating service of Atonement. But, on the other hand,
there is great harshness, not to say confusion, in making Christ at
once priest and victim and place of sprinkling. Origen it is true
does not shrink from this; he says expressly *invenies igitur . . . esse
ipsum et propitiatorium et pontificem et hostiam quae offertur pro
populo* (*in Rom.* iii. 8, p. 213 Lomm.). But although there is
a partial analogy for this in Heb. ix. 11-14, 23-x. 22, where
Christ is both priest and victim, it is straining the image yet further
to identify Him with the ἱλαστήριον. The Christian ἱλαστήριον, or
'place of sprinkling,' in the literal sense, is rather the Cross. It is
also something of a point (if we are right in giving the sense of
publicity to προέθετο) that the sprinkling of the mercy-seat was just
the one rite which was withdrawn from the sight of the people.
Another way of taking ἱλαστήριον is to supply with it θῦμα on the
analogy of σωτήριον, τελεστήριον, χαριστήριον. This too is strongly

supported (esp. by the leading German commentators, De W. Fri.
Mey. Lips.).   But there seems to be no clear instance of ἱλαστήριον
used in this sense.   Neither is there satisfactory proof that ἱλαστ.
(subst.) = in a general sense 'instrument or means of propitiation.'
It appears therefore simplest to take it as adj. accus. masc. added
as predicate to ὅν.   There is evidence that the word was current as
an adj. at this date (ἱλαστήριον μνῆμα Joseph. Antt. XVI. vii. 1;
ἱλαστηρίου θανάτου 4 Macc. xvii. 22 *, and other exx.).   The
objection that the adj. is not applied properly to persons counts
for very little, because of the extreme rarity of the sacrifice of
a person.   Here however it is just this personal element which is
most important.   It agrees with the context that the term chosen
should be rather one which generalizes the character of propitiatory
sacrifice than one which exactly reproduces a particular feature of
such sacrifice.

The Latin versions do not help us: they give all three renderings, *propitiatorium*, *propitiatorem*, and *propitiationem*.   Syr. is also ambiguous.
The Coptic clearly favours the masc. rendering adopted above.

It may be of some interest to compare the Jewish teaching on the subject
of Atonement.   'When a man thinks, I will just go on sinning and repent
later, no help is given him from above to make him repent.   He who
thinks, I will but just sin and the Day of Atonement will bring me forgiveness, such an one gets no forgiveness through the Day of Atonement.
Offences of man against God the Day of Atonement can atone; offences of
man against his fellow-man the Day of Atonement cannot atone until he has
given satisfaction to his fellow-man'; and more to the same effect (Mishnah,
Tract. Joma, viii. 9, *ap.* Winter u. Wünsche, *Jüd. Lit.* p. 98).   We get
a more advanced system of casuistry in Tosephta, *Tract. Joma*, v: 'R. Ismael
said, Atonement is of four kinds.   He who transgresses a positive command
and repents is at once forgiven according to the Scripture, "Return, ye back-
sliding children, I will heal your backslidings" (Jer. iii. 23 [22]).   He who
transgresses a negative command or prohibition and repents has the atonement held in suspense by his repentance, and the Day of Atonement makes
it effectual, according to the Scripture, "For on this day shall atonement be
made for you" (Lev. xvi. 30).   If a man commits a sin for which is decreed
extermination or capital punishment and repents, his repentance and the
Day of Atonement together keep the atonement in suspense, and suffering
brings it home, according to the Scripture, "I will visit their transgression
with the rod and their iniquity with stripes" (Ps. lxxxix. 33 [32]).   But
when a man profanes the Name of God and repents, his repentance has not
the power to keep atonement in suspense, and the Day of Atonement has
not the power to atone, but repentance and the Day of Atonement atone
one third, sufferings on the remaining days of the year atone one third, and
the day of death completes the atonement according to the Scripture,
"Surely this iniquity shall not be expiated by you till you die" (Is. xxii. 14).
This teaches that the day of death completes the atonement.   Sin-offering
and trespass-offering and death and the Day of Atonement all being no
atonement without repentance, because it is written in Lev. xxiii. 21 (?)
"Only," i.e. when he turns from his evil way does he obtain atonement,
otherwise he obtains no atonement' (*op. cit.* p. 154).

* Some MSS. read here διὰ . . . τοῦ ἱλαστηρίου τοῦ θανάτου αὐτῶν (O. F.
Fritzsche *ad loc.*).

διὰ τῆς πίστεως: διὰ πίστεως אC*D*FG 67** al., Tisch. WH. *text.* The art. seems here rather more correct, pointing back as it would do to διὰ πίστεως 'I. X. in ver. 22; it is found in B and the mass of later authorities, but there is a strong phalanx on the other side; B is not infallible in such company (cf. xi. 6).

ἐν τῷ αὐτοῦ αἵματι : not with πίστεως (though this would be a quite legitimate combination ; see Gif. *ad loc.*), but with προέθετο ἱλαστήριον: the shedding and sprinkling of the blood is a principal idea, not secondary.

The significance of the Sacrificial Bloodshedding was twofold. The blood was regarded by the Hebrew as essentially the seat of life (Gen. ix. 4; Lev. xvii. 11 ; Deut. xii. 23). Hence the death of the victim was not only a death but a setting free of life ; the application of the blood was an application of life ; and the offering of the blood to God was an offering of life. In this lay more especially the virtue of the sacrifice (Westcott, *Ep. Jo.* p. 34 ff.; *Heb.* p. 293 f.).

For the prominence which is given to the Bloodshedding in connexion with the Death of Christ see the passages collected below.

εἰς ἔνδειξιν : εἰς denotes the final and remote object, πρός the nearer object. The whole plan of redemption from its first conception in the Divine Mind aimed at the exhibition of God's Righteousness. And the same exhibition of righteousness was kept in view in a subordinate part of that plan, viz. the forbearance which God displayed through long ages towards sinners. For the punctuation and structure of the sentence see below. For ἔνδειξιν see on ch. ii. 15: here too the sense is that of ' proof by an appeal to fact.'

εἰς ἔνδειξιν τῆς δικαιοσύνης αὐτοῦ. In what sense can the Death of Christ be said to demonstrate the righteousness of God? It demonstrates it by showing the impossibility of simply passing over sin. It does so by a great and we may say cosmical act, the nature of which we are not able wholly to understand, but which at least presents analogies to the rite of sacrifice, and to that particular form of the rite which had for its object propitiation. The whole Sacrificial system was symbolical; and its wide diffusion showed that it was a mode of religious expression specially appropriate to that particular stage in the world's development. Was it to lapse entirely with Christianity? The writers of the New Testament practically answer, No. The necessity for it still existed; the great fact of sin and guilt remained; there was still the same bar to the offering of acceptable worship. To meet this fact and to remove this bar, there had been enacted an Event which possessed the significance of sacrifice. And to that event the N. T. writers appealed as satisfying the conditions which the righteousness of God required. See the longer Note on 'The Death of Christ considered as a Sacrifice' below.

διὰ τὴν πάρεσιν: not 'for the remission,' as AV., which gives a somewhat unusual (though, as we shall see on iv. 25, not impossible) sense to διά, and also a wrong sense to πάρεσιν, but 'because of the pretermission, or passing over, of foregone sins.' For the difference between πάρεσις and ἄφεσις see Trench, *Syn.* p. 110 ff.: πάρεσις = 'putting *aside*,' temporary suspension of punishment which may at some later date be inflicted; ἄφεσις = 'putting *away*,' complete and unreserved forgiveness.

It is possible that the thought of this passage may have been suggested by Wisd. xi. 23 [24] καὶ παρορᾷς ἁμαρτήματα ἀνθρώπων εἰς μετάνοιαν. There will be found in Trench, *op. cit.* p. 111, an account of a controversy which arose out of this verse in Holland at the end of the sixteenth and beginning of the seventeenth centuries.

ἁμαρτημάτων: as contrasted with ἁμαρτία, ἁμάρτημα = the single act of sin, ἁμαρτία = the permanent principle of which such an act is the expression.

ἐν τῇ ἀνοχῇ: ἐν either (i) denotes *motive*, as Mey., &c. (Grimm, *Lex.* s. v. ἐν, 5 e); or (ii) it is temporal, '*during* the forbearance of God.' Of these (i) is preferable, because the whole context deals with the scheme as it lay in the Divine Mind, and the relation of its several parts to each other.

ἀνοχῇ: see on ii. 4, and note that ἀνοχή is related to πάρεσις as χάρις is related to ἄφεσις.

26. πρὸς τὴν ἔνδειξιν: to be connected closely with the preceding clause: the stop which separates this verse from the last should be wholly removed, and the pause before διὰ τὴν πάρεσιν somewhat lengthened; we should represent it in English by a dash or semi-colon. We may represent the various pauses in the passage in some such way as this: 'Whom God set forth as propitiatory—through faith—in His own blood—for a display of His righteousness; because of the passing-over of foregone sins in the forbearance of God with a view to the display of His righteousness at the present moment, so that He might be at once righteous (Himself) and declaring righteous him who has for his motive faith in Jesus.' Gif. seems to be successful in proving that this is the true construction : (i) otherwise it is difficult to account for the change of the preposition from εἰς to πρός; (ii) the art. is on this view perfectly accounted for, 'the same display' as that just mentioned ; (iii) τῶν προγεγονότων ἁμαρτημάτων seems to be contrasted with ἐν τῷ νῦν καιρῷ ; (iv) the construction thus most thoroughly agrees with St. Paul's style elsewhere : see Gifford's note and compare the passage quoted Eph. iii. 3–5, also Rom. iii. 7, 8, ii. 14–16.

δίκαιον καὶ δικαιοῦντα. This is the key-phrase which establishes the connexion between the δικαιοσύνη Θεοῦ, and the δικαιοσύνη ἐκ πίστεως. It is not that ' God is righteous *and yet* declares righteous the believer in Jesus,' but that ' He is righteous *and also*, we might almost say *and therefore*, declares righteous the believer.' The words indicate no opposition between justice and mercy. Rather that which seems to us and which really is an act of mercy is the direct outcome of the ' righteousness' which is a wider and more adequate name than justice. It is the essential righteousness of God which impels Him to set in motion that sequence of events in the sphere above and in the sphere below which leads to the free forgiveness of the believer and starts him on his way with a clean page to his record.

τὸν ἐκ πίστεως: ' him whose ruling motive is faith'; contrast οἱ ἐξ ἐριθείας ch. ii. 8 ; ὅσοι ἐξ ἔργων νόμου (' as many as depend on works of law ') Gal. iii. 10.

The Death of Christ considered as a Sacrifice.

It is impossible to get rid from this passage of the double idea (1) of a sacrifice ; (2) of a sacrifice which is propitiatory. In any case the phrase ἐν τῷ αὐτοῦ αἵματι carries with it the idea of sacrificial bloodshedding. And whatever sense we assign to ἱλαστήριον— whether we directly supply θῦμα, or whether we supply ἐπίθεμα and regard it as equivalent to the mercy-seat, or whether we take it as an adj. in agreement with ὅν—the fundamental idea which underlies the word must be that of propitiation. And further, when we ask, Who is propitiated ? the answer can only be ' God.' Nor is it possible to separate this propitiation from the Death of the Son.

Quite apart from this passage it is not difficult to prove that these two ideas of sacrifice and propitiation lie at the root of the teaching not only of St. Paul but of the New Testament generally. Before considering their significance it may be well first to summarize this evidence briefly.

(1) As in the passage before us, so elsewhere, the stress which is laid on αἷμα is directly connected with the idea of sacrifice. We have it in St. Paul, in Rom. v. 9 ; Eph. i. 7, ii. 13 ; Col. i. 20 (διὰ τοῦ αἵματος τοῦ σταυροῦ). We have it for St. Peter in 1 Pet. i. 2 (ῥαντισμὸν αἵματος) and 19 (τιμίῳ αἵματι ὡς ἀμνοῦ ἀμώμου καὶ ἀσπίλου). For St. John we have it in 1 Jo. i. 7, and in v. 6, 8. It also comes out distinctly in several places in the Apocalypse (i. 5, v. 9, vii. 14, xii. 11, xiii. 8). It is a leading idea very strongly represented in Ep. to Hebrews (especially in capp. ix, x, xiii). There is also the strongest reason to think that this Apostolic teaching was suggested by words of our Lord Himself, who spoke of His approaching death in terms proper to a sacrifice such as that by which the First Covenant had been inaugurated (comp. 1 Cor. xi. 25 with Matt. xxvi. 28 ; Mark xiv. 24 [perhaps not Luke xxii. 20]).

Many of these passages besides the mention of bloodshedding and the death of the victim (Apoc. v. 6, 12, xiii. 8 ἀρνίου ἐσφαγμένου: cf. v. 9) call attention to other details in the act of sacrifice (e. g. the sprinkling of the blood, ῥαντισμός 1 Pet. i. 2; Heb. xii. 24; cf. Heb. ix. 13, 19, 21).

We observe also that the Death of Christ is compared not only to one but to several of the leading forms of Levitical sacrifice: to the Passover (John i. 29, xix. 36; 1 Cor. v. 8, and the passages which speak of the 'lamb' in 1 Pet. and Apoc.); to the sacrifices of the Day of Atonement (so apparently in the passage from which we start, Rom. iii. 25, also in Heb. ii. 17; ix. 12, 14, 15, and perhaps 1 Jo. ii. 2, iv. 10; 1 Pet. ii. 24); to the ratification of the Covenant (Matt. xxvi. 28, &c.; Heb. ix. 15–22); to the sin-offering (Rom. viii. 3; Heb. xiii. 11; 1 Pet. iii. 18, and possibly if not under the earlier head, 1 Jo. ii. 2, iv. 10).

(2) In a number of these passages as well as in others, both from the Epistles of St. Paul and from other Apostolic writings, the Death of Christ is directly connected with the forgiveness of sins (e. g. Matt. xxvi. 28; Acts v. 30 f., apparently; 1 Cor. xv. 3; 2 Cor. v. 21; Eph. i. 7; Col. i. 14 and 20; Tit. ii. 14; Heb. i. 3, ix. 28, x. 12 al.; 1 Pet. ii. 24, iii. 18; 1 Jo. ii. 2, iv. 10; Apoc. i. 5). The author of Ep. to Hebrews generalizes from the ritual system of the Old Covenant that sacrificial bloodshedding is necessary in every case, or nearly in every case, to place the worshipper in a condition of fitness to approach the Divine Presence (Heb. ix. 22 καὶ σχεδὸν ἐν αἵματι πάντα καθαρίζεται κατὰ τὸν νόμον, καὶ χωρὶς αἱματεκχυσίας οὐ γίνεται ἄφεσις). The use of the different words denoting 'propitiation' is all to the same effect (ἱλαστήριον Rom. iii. 25; ἱλασμός 1 Jo. ii. 2, iv. 10; ἱλάσκεσθαι Heb. ii. 17).

This strong convergence of Apostolic writings of different and varied character seems to show that the idea of Sacrifice as applied to the Death of Christ cannot be put aside as a merely passing metaphor, but is interwoven with the very weft and warp of primitive Christian thinking, taking its start (if we may trust our traditions) from words of Christ Himself. What it all amounts to is that the religion of the New Testament, like the religion of the Old, has the idea of sacrifice as one of its central conceptions, not however scattered over an elaborate ceremonial system but concentrated in a single many-sided and far-reaching act.

It will be seen that this throws back a light over the Old Testament sacrifices—and indeed not only over them but over the sacrifices of ethnic religion—and shows that they were something more than a system of meaningless butchery, that they had a real spiritual significance, and that they embodied deep principles of religion in forms suited to the apprehension of the age to which they were given and capable of gradual refinement and purification,

In this connexion it may be worth while to quote a striking passage from a writer of great, if intermittent, insight, who approaches the subject from a thoroughly detached and independent standpoint. In his last series of Slade lectures delivered in Oxford (*The Art of England*, 1884, p. 14 f.), Mr. Ruskin wrote as follows: ' None of you, who have the least acquaintance with the general tenor of my own teaching, will suspect me of any bias towards the doctrine of vicarious Sacrifice, as it is taught by the modern Evangelical Preacher. But the great mystery of the idea of Sacrifice itself, which has been manifested as one united and solemn instinct by all thoughtful and affectionate races, since the world became peopled, is founded on the secret truth of benevolent energy which all men who have tried to gain it have learned—that you cannot save men from death but by facing it for them, nor from sin but by resisting it for them . . . Some day or other —probably now very soon—too probably by heavy afflictions of the State, we shall be taught . . . that all the true good and glory even of this world—not to speak of any that is to come, must be bought still, as it always has been, with our toil, and with our tears.'

After all the writer of this and the Evangelical Preacher whom he repudiates are not so very far apart. It may be hoped that the Preacher too may be willing to purify his own conception and to strip it of some quite unbiblical accretions, and he will then find that the central verity for which he contends is not inadequately stated in the impressive words just quoted.

The idea of Vicarious Suffering is not the whole and not perhaps the culminating point in the conception of Sacrifice, for Dr. Westcott seems to have sufficiently shown that the centre of the symbolism of Sacrifice lies not in the death of the victim but in the offering of its life. This idea of Vicarious Suffering, which is nevertheless in all probability the great difficulty and stumbling-block in the way of the acceptance of Bible teaching on this head, was revealed once and for all time in Isaiah liii. No one who reads that chapter with attention can fail to see the profound truth which lies behind it—a truth which seems to gather up in one all that is most pathetic in the world's history, but which when it has done so turns upon it the light of truly prophetic and divine inspiration, gently lifts the veil from the accumulated mass of pain and sorrow, and shows beneath its unspeakable value in the working out of human redemption and regeneration and the sublime consolations by which for those who can enter into them it is accompanied.

I said that this chapter gathers up in one all that is most pathetic in the world's history. It gathers it up as it were in a single typical Figure. We look at the lineaments of that Figure, and then we transfer our gaze and we recognize them all translated from idea into reality, and embodied in marvellous perfection upon Calvary.

Following the example of St. Paul and St. John and the Epistle to the Hebrews we speak of something in this great Sacrifice, which we call 'Propitiation.' We believe that the Holy Spirit spoke through these writers, and that it was His Will that we should use this word. But it is a word which we must leave it to Him to interpret. We drop our plummet into the depth, but the line attached to it is too short, and it does not touch the bottom. The awful processes of the Divine Mind we cannot fathom. Sufficient for us to know that through the virtue of the One Sacrifice our sacrifices are accepted, that the barrier which Sin places between us and God is removed, and that there is a 'sprinkling' which makes us free to approach the throne of grace.

This, it may still be objected, is but a 'fiction of mercy.' All mercy, all forgiveness, is of the nature of fiction. It consists in treating men better than they deserve. And if we 'being evil' exercise the property of mercy towards each other, and exercise it not rarely out of consideration for the merit of someone else than the offender, shall not our Heavenly Father do the same?

CONSEQUENCES OF THE NEW SYSTEM.

III. 27-31. *Hence it follows* (1) *that no claim can be made on the ground of human merit, for there is no merit in Faith* (vv. 27, 28); (2) *that Jew and Gentile are on the same footing, for there is but one God, and Faith is the only means of acceptance with Him* (vv. 29, 30).

An objector may say that Law is thus abrogated. On the contrary its deeper principles are fulfilled, as the history of Abraham will show (ver. 31).

[27] There are two consequences which I draw, and one that an objector may draw, from this. The first is that such a method of obtaining righteousness leaves no room for human claims or merit. Any such thing is once for all shut out. For the Christian system is not one of works—in which there might have been room for merit—but one of Faith. [28] Thus (οὖν, but see *Crit. Note*) we believe that Faith is the condition on which a man is pronounced righteous, and not a round of acts done in obedience to law.

[29] The second consequence [already hinted at in ver. 22] is that

Jew and Gentile are on the same footing. If they are not, then God must be God of the Jews in some exclusive sense in which He is not God of the Gentiles. ³⁰ Is that so? Not if I am right in affirming that there is but one God, Who requires but one condition—Faith, on which He is ready to treat as 'righteous' alike the circumcised and the uncircumcised—the circumcised with whom Faith is the moving cause, and the uncircumcised with whom the same Faith is both moving cause and sole condition of their acceptance.

³¹ The objector asks: Does not such a system throw over Law altogether? Far from it. Law itself (speaking through the Pentateuch) lays down principles (Faith and Promise) which find their true fulfilment in Christianity.

27. ἐξεκλείσθη : an instance of the 'summarizing' force of the aorist; 'it is shut out once for all,' 'by one decisive act.'

St. Paul has his eye rather upon the decisiveness of the act than upon its continued result. In English it is more natural to us to express decisiveness by laying stress upon the result—'*is* shut out.'

διὰ ποίου νόμου : νόμου here may be paraphrased 'system,' 'Law' being the typical expression to the ancient mind of a 'constituted order of things.'—Under what kind of system is this result obtained? Under a system the essence of which is Faith.

Similar metaphorical uses of νόμος would be ch. vii. 21, 23 ; viii. 2 ; x. 31, on which see the Notes.

28. οὖν recapitulates and summarizes what has gone before. The result of the whole matter stated briefly is that God declares righteous, &c. But it must be confessed that γάρ gives the better sense. We do not want a summary statement in the middle of an argument which is otherwise coherent. The alternative reading, λογιζόμεθα γάρ, helps that coherence. [The Jew's] boasting is excluded, *because* justification turns on nothing which is the peculiar possession of the Jew but on Faith. And so Gentile and Jew are on the same footing, as we might expect they would be, seeing that they have the same God.

οὖν B C Dᶜ K L P &c. ; Syrr. (Pesh.-Harcl.) ; Chrys. Theodrt. *al.* ; Weiss RV. WH. *marg.* : γάρ א A D* E F G *al. plur.* ; Latt. (Vet.-Vulg.) Boh. Arm. ; Orig.-lat. Ambrst. Aug. ; Tisch. WH. *text* RV. *marg.* The evidence for γάρ is largely Western, but it is combined with an element (א A, Boh.) which in this instance is probably not Western ; so that the reading would be carried back beyond the point of divergence of two most ancient lines of text. On the other hand B admits in this Epistle some comparatively late readings (cf. xi. 6) and the authorities associated with it are inferior (B C in *Epp.* is not so strong a combination as B C in *Gospp.*). We prefer the reading γάρ.

δικαιοῦσθαι: we must hold fast to the rendering 'is *declared*
righteous,' not 'is *made* righteous'; cf. on i. 17.

ἄνθρωπον: any human being.

29. ἤ presents, but only to dismiss, an alternative hypothesis on
the assumption of which the Jew might still have had something to
boast of. In rejecting this, St. Paul once more emphatically
asserts his main position. There is but one law (Faith), and there
is but one Judge to administer it. Though faith is spoken of in
this abstract way it is of course Christian faith, faith in Christ.

μόνον: μόνων B *al. plur.*, WH. *marg.*; perhaps assimilated to Ἰουδαίων
... καὶ ἐθνῶν.

30. εἴπερ : decisively attested in place of ἐπείπερ. The old distinction
drawn between εἰ περ and εἰ γε was that εἰ περ is used of a condition which
is assumed without implying whether it is rightly or wrongly assumed, εἰ γε
of a condition which carries with it the assertion of its own reality (Hermann
on Viger, p. 831; Bäumlein, *Griech. Partikeln*, p. 64). It is doubtful
whether this distinction holds in Classical Greek; it can hardly hold for
N.T. But in any case both εἰ περ and εἰ γε lay some stress on the condition,
as a condition: cf. Monro, *Homeric Grammar*, §§ 353, 354 'The Particle
πέρ is evidently a shorter form of the Preposition πέρι, which in its adverbial
use has the meaning *beyond, exceedingly*. Accordingly πέρ is *intensive*,
denoting that the word to which it is subjoined is true in a high degree, in
its fullest sense, &c. ... γε is used like πέρ to emphasize a particular word
or phrase. It does not however *intensify* the meaning, or insist on the fact
as *true*, but only calls attention to the word or fact. ... In a Conditional
Protasis (with ὅς, ὅτε, εἰ, &c.), γε emphasizes the condition as such: hence
εἰ γε *if only, always supposing that.* On the other hand εἰ περ means
supposing ever so much, hence *if really* (Lat. *si quidem*).'

ἐκ πίστεως ... διὰ τῆς πίστεως : ἐκ denotes 'source,' διά 'attendant circumstances.' The Jew is justified ἐκ πίστεως διὰ περιτομῆς :
the force at work is faith, the channel through which it works is
circumcision. The Gentile is justified ἐκ πίστεως καὶ διὰ τῆς πίστεως :
no special channel, no special conditions are marked out; faith is
the one thing needful, it is itself 'both law and impulse.'

διὰ τῆς πίστεως = 'the same faith,' 'the faith just mentioned.'

31. καταργοῦμεν: see on ver. 3 above.

νόμον ἱστῶμεν. If, as we must needs think, ch. iv contains the
proof of the proposition laid down in this verse, νόμον must = ultimately and virtually the Pentateuch. But it = the Pentateuch not
as an isolated Book but as the most conspicuous and representative
expression of that great system of Law which prevailed everywhere
until the coming of Christ.

The Jew looked at the O. T., and he saw there Law, Obedience
to Law or Works, Circumcision, Descent from Abraham. St. Paul
said, Look again and look deeper, and you will see—not Law but
Promise, not works but Faith—of which Circumcision is only the
seal, not literal descent from Abraham but spiritual descent. All
these things are realized in Christianity.

And then further, whereas Law (all Law and any kind of Law) was only an elaborate machinery for producing right action, there too Christianity stepped in and accomplished, as if with the stroke of a wand, all that the Law strove to do without success (Rom. xiii. 10 πλήρωμα οὖν νόμου ἡ ἀγάπη compared with Gal. **v. 6** πίστις δι' ἀγάπης ἐνεργουμένη).

THE FAITH OF ABRAHAM.

IV. 1–8. *Take the crucial case of Abraham. He, like the Christian, was declared righteous, not on account of his works—as something earned, but by the free gift of God in response to his faith. And David describes a similar state of things. The happiness of which he speaks is due, not to sinlessness but to God's free forgiveness of sins.*

[1] OBJECTOR. You speak of the history of Abraham. Surely he, the ancestor by natural descent of our Jewish race, might plead privilege and merit. [2] If we Jews are right in supposing that God accepted him as righteous for his works—those illustrious acts of his—he has something to boast of.

ST. PAUL. Perhaps he has before men, but not before God. [3] For look at the Word of God, that well-known passage of Scripture, Gen. xv. 6. What do we find there? Nothing about works, but 'Abraham put faith in God,' and it (i. e. his faith) was credited to him as if it were righteousness.

[4] This proves that there was no question of works. For a workman claims his pay as a debt due to him; it is not an act of favour. [5] But to one who is not concerned with works but puts faith in God Who pronounces righteous not the actually righteous (in which there would be nothing wonderful) but the ungodly—to such an one his faith is credited for righteousness.

[6] Just as again David in Ps. xxxii describes how God 'pronounces happy' (in the highest sense) those to whom he attributes righteousness without any reference to works: [7] 'Happy they,' he says,—not 'who have been guilty of no breaches of law,' but 'whose breaches of law have been forgiven and whose sins are veiled from sight. [8] A happy man is he whose sin Jehovah will not enter in His book.'

H

1 ff. The main argument of this chapter is quite clear but
the opening clauses are slightly embarrassed and obscure, due
as it would seem to the crossing of other lines of thought with
the main lines. The proposition which the Apostle sets himself to prove is that Law, and more particularly the Pentateuch,
is not destroyed but fulfilled by the doctrine which he preaches.
But the way of putting this is affected by two thoughts, which still
exert some influence from the last chapter, (i) the question as to
the advantage of the Jew, (ii) the pride or boasting which was
a characteristic feature in the character of the Jew but which
St. Paul held to be 'excluded.' Hitherto these two points have
been considered in the broadest and most general manner, but
St. Paul now narrows them down to the particular and crucial case
of Abraham. The case of Abraham was the centre and stronghold of the whole Jewish position. If therefore it could be shown
that this case made for the Christian conclusion and not for the
Jewish, the latter broke down altogether. This is what St. Paul
now undertakes to prove; but at the outset he glances at the two
side issues—main issues in ch. iii which become side issues in
ch. iv—the claim of 'advantage,' or special privilege, and the pride
which the Jewish system generated. For the sake of clearness we
put these thoughts into the mouth of the objector. He is of course
still a *supposed* objector; St. Paul is really arguing with himself;
but the arguments are such as he might very possibly have met
with in actual controversy (see on iii. 1 ff.).

1. The first question is one of reading. There is an important
variant turning upon the position or presence of εὑρηκέναι. (1)
K L P, &c., Theodrt. and later Fathers (the Syriac Versions which
are quoted by Tischendorf supply no evidence) place it after τὸν
προπάτορα ἡμῶν. It is then taken with κατὰ σάρκα: 'What shall we
say that A. has gained by his natural powers unaided by the grace
of God?' So Bp. Bull after Theodoret. [Euthym.-Zig. however,
even with this reading, takes κατὰ σάρκα with πατέρα: ὑπερβατὸν γὰρ
τὸ κατὰ σάρκα]. But this is inconsistent with the context. The
question is not, what Abraham had gained by the grace of God or
without it, but whether the new system professed by St. Paul left
him any gain or advantage at all. (2) ℵ A C D E F G, some cursives, Vulg. Boh. Arm. Aeth., Orig.-lat. Ambrstr. and others, place
after ἐροῦμεν. In that case κατὰ σάρκα goes not with εὑρηκέναι but
with τὸν προπάτορα ἡμῶν which it simply defines, 'our natural pro-
genitor.' (3) But a small group, B, 47*, and apparently Chrysostom
from the tenor of his comment, though the printed editions give it
in his text, omit εὑρηκέναι altogether. Then the idea of 'gain'
drops out and we translate simply 'What shall we say as to
Abraham our forefather?' &c. The opponents of B will say that
the sense thus given is suspiciously easy: it is certainly more

satisfactory than that of either of the other readings. The point is not what Abraham got by his righteousness, but how he got his righteousness—by the method of works or by that of faith. Does the nature of A.'s righteousness agree better with the Jewish system, or with St. Paul's? The idea of 'gain' was naturally imported from ch. iii. 1, 9. There is no reason why a right reading should not be preserved in a small group, and the fluctuating position of a word often points to doubtful genuineness. We therefore regard the omission of εὑρηκέναι as probable with WH. *text* Tr. RV. *marg.* For the construction comp. John i. 15 οὗτος ἦν ὃν εἶπον.

1–5. One or two small questions of form may be noticed. In ver. 1 προπάτορα (אֲ* et c A B C* *al.*) is decisively attested for πατέρα, which is found in the later MSS. and commentators. In ver. 3 the acute and sleepless critic Origen thinks that St. Paul wrote Ἀβράμ (with Heb. of Gen. xv; cf. Gen. xvii. 5), but that Gentile scribes who were less scrupulous as to the text of Scripture substituted Ἀβραάμ. It is more probable that St. Paul had before his mind the established and significant name throughout : he quotes Gen. xvii. 5 in ver. 17. In ver. 5 a small group (א D* F G) have ἀσεβῆν, on which form see WH. *Introd.* App. p. 157 f. ; Win. *Gr.* ed. 8, § ix. 8 ; Tisch. on Heb. vi. 19. In this instance the attestation may be wholly Western, but not in others.

τὸν προπάτορα ἡμῶν. This description of Abraham as ' our forefather ' is one of the arguments used by those who would make the majority of the Roman Church consist of Jews. St. Paul is not very careful to distinguish between himself and his readers in such a matter. For instance in writing to the Corinthians, who were undoubtedly for the most part Gentiles, he speaks of ' *our* fathers ' as being under the cloud and passing through the sea (1 Cor. x. 1). There is the less reason why he should discriminate here as he is just about to maintain that Abraham is the father of *all* believers, Jew and Gentile alike,—though it is true that he would have added ' not after the flesh but after the spirit.' Gif. notes the further point, that the question is put as proceeding from a Jew : along with Orig. Chrys. Phot. Euthym.-Zig. Lips. he connects τὸν προπάτ. ἡμ. with κατὰ σάρκα. It should be mentioned, however, that Dr. Hort (*Rom. and Eph.* p. 23 f.) though relegating εὑρηκέναι to the margin, still does not take κατὰ σάρκα with τὸν προπάτορα ἡμῶν.

2. καύχημα : ' Not *materies gloriandi* as Meyer, but rather *gloriatio*, as Bengel, who however might have added *facta* ' (T. S. Evans in *Sp. Comm.* on 1 Cor. v. 6). The termination -μα denotes not so much the *thing done* as the completed, determinate, act ; for other examples see esp. Evans *ut sup.* It would not be wrong to translate here ' has a ground of boasting,' but the idea of ' ground ' is contained in ἔχει, or rather in the context.

ἀλλ' οὐ πρὸς τὸν Θεόν. It seems best to explain the introduction of this clause by some such ellipse as that which is supplied in the

paraphrase. There should be a colon after καύχημα. St. Paul
does not question the supposed claim that Abraham has a καύχημα
absolutely—before man he might have it and the Jews were not
wrong in the veneration with which they regarded his memory,—
but it was another thing to have a καύχημα before God. There is
a stress upon τὸν Θεόν which is taken up by τῷ Θεῷ in the quotation. 'A. could not boast before *God.* He might have done so
if he could have taken his stand on works ; but works did not
enter into the question at all. In *God* he put faith.' On the
history and application of the text Gen. xv. 6, see below.

3. ἐλογίσθη : metaphor from accounts, ' was set down,' here ' on
the credit side.' Frequently in LXX with legal sense of imputation
or non-imputation of guilt, e.g. Lev. vii. 8 ἐὰν δὲ φαγὼν φάγῃ . . . οὐ
λογισθήσεται αὐτῷ, xvii. 4 λογισθήσεται τῷ ἀνθρώπῳ ἐκείνῳ αἷμα, &c.
The notion arises from that of the ' book of remembrance ' (Mal.
iii. 16) in which men's good or evil deeds, the wrongs and
sufferings of the saints, are entered (Ps. lvi. 8 ; Is. lxv. 6). Oriental
monarchs had such a record by which they were reminded of the
merit or demerit of their subjects (Esth. vi. 1 ff.), and in like
manner on the judgement day Jehovah would have the ' books '
brought out before Him (Dan. vii. 10; Rev. xx. 12 ; comp. also
' the books of the living,' ' the heavenly tablets,' a common expression in the Books of *Enoch, Jubilees,* and *Test. XII Patr.,* on which
see Charles on *Enoch* xlvii. 3 ; and in more modern times,
Cowper's sonnet ' There is a book . . . wherein the eyes of God
not rarely look ').

The idea of imputation in this sense was familiar to the Jews
(Weber, *Altsyn. Theol.* p. 233). They had also the idea of the
transference of merit and demerit from one person to another
(*ibid.* p. 280 ff. ; Ezek. xviii. 2 ; John ix. 2). That however is not
in question here ; the point is that one quality faith is set down, or
credited, to the individual (here to Abraham) in place of anothei
quality—righteousness.

ἐλογίσθη αὐτῷ εἰς δικαιοσύνην : was reckoned as equivalent to, as
standing in the place of, ' righteousness.' The construction is
common in LXX : cf. 1 Reg. (Sam.) i. 13 ; Job xli. 23 (24); Is.
xxix. 17 (=xxxii. 15); Lam. iv. 2 ; Hos. viii. 12. The exact
phrase ἐλογίσθη αὐτῷ εἰς δικαιοσ. recurs in Ps. cv [cvi]. 31 of the
zeal of Phinehas. On the grammar cf. Win. § xxix. 3 *a.* (p. 229,
ed. Moulton).

On the righteousness of Abraham see esp. Weber, *Altsyn. Paläst.
Theologie,* p. 255 ff. Abraham was the only righteous man of his
generation ; therefore he was chosen to be ancestor of the holy
People. He kept all the precepts of the Law which he knew
beforehand by a kind of intuition. He was the first of seven
righteous men whose merit brought back the Shekinah which had

retired into the seventh heaven, so that in the days of Moses it could take up its abode in the Tabernacle (*ibid.* p. 183). According to the Jews the original righteousness of Abraham, who began to serve God at the age of three (*ibid.* p. 118) was perfected (1) by his circumcision, (2) by his anticipatory fulfilment of the Law. But the Jews also (on the strength of Gen. xv. 6) attached a special importance to Abraham's *faith*, as constituting merit (see *Mechilta* on Ex. xiv. 31, quoted by Delitzsch *ad loc.* and by Lightfoot in the extract given below).

4, 5. An illustration from common life. The workman earns his pay, and can claim it as a right. Therefore when God bestows the gift of righteousness, of His own bounty and not as a right, that is proof that the gift must be called forth by something other than works, viz. by faith.

5. ἐπὶ τὸν δικαιοῦντα: ' on Him who pronounces righteous ' or ' acquits,' i. e. God. It is rather a departure from St. Paul's more usual practice to make the object of faith God the Father rather than God the Son. But even here the Christian scheme is in view, and faith in God is faith in Him as the alternative Author of that scheme. See on i. 8, **17**, above.

We must not be misled by the comment of Euthym.-Zig. τουτέστι πιστεύοντι ὅτι δύναται ὁ Θεὸς τὸν ἐν ἀσεβείᾳ βεβιωκότα, τοῦτον ἐξαίφνης οὐ μόνον ἐλευθερῶσαι κολάσεως, ἀλλὰ καὶ δίκαιον ποιῆσαι (comp. the same writer on ver. 25 ἵνα δικαίους ἡμᾶς ποιήσῃ). The evidence is too decisive (p. 30 f. *sup.*) that δικαιοῦν = not ' to make righteous ' but ' to declare righteous as a judge.' It might however be inferred from ἐξαίφνης that δίκαιον ποιῆσαι was to be taken somewhat loosely in the sense of ' treat as righteous.' The Greek theologians had not a clear conception of the doctrine of Justification.

τὸν ἀσεβῆ : not meant as a description of Abraham, from whose case St. Paul is now generalizing and applying the conclusion to his own time. The strong word ἀσεβῆ is probably suggested by the quotation which is just coming from Ps. xxxii. 1.

6. Δαβίδ (Δαυείδ). Both Heb. and LXX ascribe Ps. xxxii to David. In two places in the N. T., Acts iv. 25, 26 (= Ps. ii. 1, 2), Heb. iv. 7 (= Ps. xcv. 7) Psalms are quoted as David's which have no title in the Hebrew (though Ps. xcv [xciv] bears the name of David in the LXX), showing that by this date the whole Psalter was known by his name. Ps. xxxii was one of those which Ewald thought might really be David's : see Driver, *Introduction*, p. 357.

τὸν μακαρισμόν: not ' blessedness,' which would be μακαριότης but a ' *pronouncing* blessed '; μακαρίζειν τινα = ' to call a person blessed or happy ' (τούς τε γὰρ θεοὺς μακαρίζομεν . . . καὶ τῶν ἀνδρῶν τοὺς θειοτάτους μακαρίζομεν Arist. *Eth. Nic.* I. xii. 4; comp. Euthym.-Zig. ἐπίτασις δὲ καὶ κορυφὴ τιμῆς καὶ δόξης ὁ μακαρισμός, ' Felicitation is the strongest and highest form of honour and praise '). St. Paul uses the word again Gal. iv. 15. Who is it who thus *pronounces* a man blessed ? God. The Psalm describes how He does so.

7, 8. Μακάριοι, κ.τ.λ. This quotation of Ps. xxxii. 1, 2 is the same in Heb. and LXX. It is introduced by St. Paul as confirming his interpretation of Gen. xv. 6.

μακάριοι is, as we have seen, the highest term which a Greek could use to describe a state of felicity. In the quotation just given from Aristotle it is applied to the state of the gods and those nearest to the gods among men.

ᾧ οὐ μή. So Nᵒ A C Dᵒ F K L &c.: οὗ οὐ μή א B D E (?) G, 67**. οὗ is also the reading of LXX (ᾧ אᶜᵃ Rᵃ). The authorities for οὗ are superior as they combine the oldest evidence on the two main lines of transmission (א B + D) and it is on the whole more probable that ᾧ has been assimilated to the construction of λογίζεσθαι in vv. 3, 4, 5, 6 than that οὗ has been assimilated to the preceding ὧν or to the O.T. or that it has been affected by the following οὐ: ᾧ naturally established itself as the more euphonious reading.

οὐ μὴ λογίσηται. There is a natural tendency in a declining language to the use of more emphatic forms; but here a real emphasis appears to be intended, ' Whose sin the Lord will in no wise reckon': see Ell. on 1 Thess. iv. 15 [p. 154], and Win. § lvi. 3, p. 634 f.

The History of Abraham as treated by St. Paul and by St. James.

It is at first sight a remarkable thing that two New Testament writers should use the same leading example and should quote the same leading text as it would seem to directly opposite effect. Both St. Paul and St. James treat at some length of the history of Abraham; they both quote the same verse, Gen. xv. 6, as the salient characterization of that history; and they draw from it the conclusion—St. Paul that a man is accounted righteous πίστει χωρὶς ἔργων (Rom. iii. 28; cf. iv. 1-8), St. James as expressly, that he is accounted righteous ἐξ ἔργων καὶ οὐκ ἐκ πίστεως μόνον (Jas. ii. 24).

We notice at once that St. Paul keeps more strictly to his text. Gen. xv. 6 speaks only of faith. St. James supports his contention of the necessity of works by appeal to a later incident in Abraham's life, the offering of Isaac (Jas. ii. 21). St. Paul also appeals to particular incidents, Abraham's belief in the promise that he should have a numerous progeny (Rom. iv. 18), and in the more express prediction of the birth of Isaac (Rom. iv. 19-21). The difference is that St. Paul makes use of a more searching exegesis. His own spiritual experience confirms the unqualified affirmation of the Book of Genesis; and he is therefore able to take it as one of the foundations of his system. St. James, occupying a less exceptional standpoint, and taking words in the average sense put upon them, has recourse to the context of Abraham's life, and so harmonizes the text with the requirements of his own moral sense.

The fact is that St. James and St. Paul mean different things by 'faith,' and as was natural they impose these different meanings on the Book of Genesis, and adapt the rest of their conclusions to them. When St. James heard speak of ' faith,' he understood by it what the letter of the Book of Genesis allowed him to understand by it, a certain belief. It is what a Jew would consider the fundamental belief, belief in God, belief that God was One (Jas. ii. 19). Christianity is with him so much a supplement to the Jews' ordinary creed that it does not seem to be specially present to his mind when he is speaking of Abraham. Of course he too believes in the 'Lord Jesus Christ, the Lord of Glory' (Jas. ii. 1). He takes that belief for granted ; it is the *substratum* or basement of life on which are not to be built such things as a wrong or corrupt partiality (προσωπολημψία). If he were questioned about it, he would put it on the same footing as his belief in God. But St. James was a thoroughly honest, and, as we should say, a 'good' man; and this did not satisfy his moral sense. What is belief unless proof is given of its sincerity ? Belief must be followed up by action, by a line of conduct conformable to it. St. James would have echoed Matthew Arnold's proposition that 'Conduct is three-fourths of life.' He therefore demands—and from his point of view rightly demands—that his readers shall authenticate their beliefs by putting them in practice.

St. Paul's is a very different temperament, and he speaks from a very different experience. With him too Christianity is something added to an earlier belief in God; but the process by which it was added was nothing less than a convulsion of his whole nature. It is like the stream of molten lava pouring down the volcano's side. Christianity is with him a tremendous over-mastering force. The crisis came at the moment when he confessed his faith in Christ; there was no other crisis worth the name after that. Ask such an one whether his faith is not to be proved by action, and the question will seem to him trivial and superfluous. He will almost suspect the questioner of attempting to bring back under a new name the old Jewish notion of religion as a round of legal observance. Of course action will correspond with faith. The believer in Christ, who has put on Christ, who has died with Christ and risen again with him, must needs to the very utmost of his power endeavour to live as Christ would have him live. St. Paul is going on presently to say this (Rom. vi. 1, 12, 15), as his opponents compel him to say it. But to himself it appears a truism, which is hardly worth definitely enunciating. To say that a man is a Christian should be enough.

If we thus understand the real relation of the two Apostles, it will be easier to discuss their literary relation. Are we to suppose that either was writing with direct reference to the other? Did St. Paul mean to controvert St. James, or did St. James mean to controvert St. Paul? Neither hypothesis seems probable. If St. Paul had had before him the Epistle of St. James, when once he looked beneath the language to the ideas signified by the language, he would have found nothing to which he could seriously object. He would have been aware that it was not his own way of putting things; and he might have thought that such teaching was not intended for men at the highest level of spiritual attainment; but that would have been all. On the other hand, if St. James had seen the Epistle to the Romans and wished to answer it, what he has written would have been totally inadequate. Whatever value his criticism might have had for those who spoke of 'faith' as a mere matter of formal assent, it had no relevance to a faith such as that conceived by St. Paul. Besides, St. Paul had too effectually guarded himself against the moral hypocrisy which he was condemning.

It would thus appear that when it is examined the real meeting-ground between the two Apostles shrinks into a comparatively narrow compass. It does not amount to more than the fact that both quote the same verse, Gen. xv. 6, and both treat it with reference to the antithesis of Works and Faith.

Now Bp. Lightfoot has shown (*Galatians*, p. 157 ff., ed. 2) that Gen. xv. 6 was a standing thesis for discussions in the Jewish schools. It is referred to in the First Book of Maccabees: 'Was not Abraham found faithful in temptation, and it was imputed unto him for righteousness' (1 Macc. ii. 52)? It is repeatedly quoted and commented upon by Philo (no less than ten times, Lft.). The whole history of Abraham is made the subject of an elaborate allegory. The Talmudic treatise *Mechilta* expounds the verse at length: ' Great is faith, whereby Israel believed on Him that spake and the world was. For as a reward for Israel's having believed in the Lord, the Holy Spirit dwelt in them . . . In like manner thou findest that Abraham our father inherited this world and the world to come solely by the merit of faith, whereby he believed in the Lord; for it is said, " and he believed in the Lord, and He counted it to him for righteousness "' (quoted by Lft. *ut sup.* p. 160). Taking these examples with the lengthened discussions in St. Paul and St. James, it is clear that attention was being very widely drawn to this particular text: and it was indeed inevitable that it should be so when we consider the place which Abraham held in the Jewish system and the minute study which was being given to every part of the Pentateuch.

It might therefore be contended with considerable show of reason

that the two New Testament writers are discussing independently
of each other a current problem, and that there is no ground for
supposing a controversial relation between them. We are not sure
that we are prepared to go quite so far as this. It is true that the
bearing of Gen. xv. 6 was a subject of standing debate among the
Jews; but the same thing cannot be said of the antithesis of
Faith and Works. The controversy connected with this was
essentially a Christian controversy; it had its origin in the special
and characteristic teaching of St. Paul. It seems to us therefore
that the passages in the two Epistles have a real relation to that
controversy, and so at least indirectly to each other.

It does not follow that the relation was a literary relation. We
have seen that there are strong reasons against this *. We do not
think that either St. Paul had seen the Epistle of St. James, or
St. James the Epistle of St. Paul. The view which appears to us
the most probable is that the argument of St. James is directed not
against the writings of St. Paul, or against him in person, but
against hearsay reports of his teaching, and against the perverted
construction which might be (and perhaps to some slight extent
actually was) put upon it. As St. James sate in his place in the
Church at Jerusalem, as yet the true centre and metropolis of
the Christian world; as Christian pilgrims of Jewish birth were
constantly coming and going to attend the great yearly feasts,
especially from the flourishing Jewish colonies in Asia Minor and
Greece, the scene of St. Paul's labours; and as there was always
at his elbow the little *coterie* of St. Paul's fanatical enemies, it would
be impossible but that versions, scarcely ever adequate (for how
few of St. Paul's hearers had really understood him!) and often more
or less seriously distorted, of his brother Apostle's teaching, should
reach him. He did what a wise and considerate leader would
do. He names no names, and attacks no man's person. He does
not assume that the reports which he has heard are full and true
reports. At the same time he states in plain terms his own view
of the matter. He sounds a note of warning which seems to him
to be needed, and which the very language of St. Paul, in places
like Rom. vi. 1 ff., 15 ff., shows to have been really needed. And
thus, as so often in Scripture, two complementary sets of truths,
suited to different types of mind and different circumstances, are
stated side by side. We have at once the deeper principle of
action, which is also more powerful in proportion as it is deeper,
though not such as all can grasp and appropriate, and the plainer

---

* Besides what is said above, see Introduction § 8. It is a satisfaction to
find that the view here taken is substantially that of Dr. Hort, *Judaistic
Christianity*, p. 148, 'it seems more natural to suppose that a misuse or
misunderstanding of St. Paul's teaching on the part of others gave rise to
St. James's carefully guarded language.'

practical teaching pitched on a more every-day level and appealing to larger numbers, which is the check and safeguard against possible misconstruction.

FAITH AND CIRCUMCISION.

IV. 9-12. *The declaration made to Abraham did not depend upon Circumcision. For it was made before he was circumcised ; and Circumcision only came in after the fact, to ratify a verdict already given. The reason being that Abraham might have for his spiritual descendants the un-circumcised as well as the circumcised.*

⁹ Here we have certain persons pronounced ' happy.' Is this then to be confined to the circumcised Jew, or may it also apply to the uncircumcised Gentile? Certainly it may. For there is no mention of circumcision. It is his *faith* that we say was credited to Abraham as righteousness. ¹⁰ And the historical circumstances of the case prove that Circumcision had nothing to do with it. Was Abraham circumcised when the declaration was made to him? No: he was at the time uncircumcised. ¹¹ And circumcision was given to him afterwards, like a seal affixed to a document, to authenticate a state of things already existing, viz. the righteousness based on faith which was his before he was circumcised. The reason being that he might be the spiritual father alike of two divergent classes : at once of believing Gentiles, who though uncircumcised have a faith like his, that they too might be credited with righteousness; ¹² and at the same time of believing Jews who do not depend on their circumcision only, but whose files march duly in the steps of Abraham's faith—that faith which was his before his circumcision.

10. St. Paul appeals to the historic fact that the Divine recognition of Abraham's faith came in order of time before his circumcision : the one recorded in Gen. xv. 6, the other in Gen. xvii. 10 ff. Therefore although it might be (and was) confirmed by circumcision, it could not be due to it or conditioned by it.

11. σημεῖον περιτομῆς. Circumcision at its institution is said to be ἐν σημείῳ διαθήκης (Gen. xvii. 11), between God and the circumcised. The gen. περιτομῆς is a genitive of apposition or identity, a sign ' *consisting* in circumcision,' 'which *was* circumcision.' Some authorities (A C* *al.*) read περιτομήν.

σφραγῖδα. The prayer pronounced at the circumcising of a child runs thus : ' Blessed be He who sanctified His beloved from the womb, and put His ordinance upon His flesh, and sealed His offspring with the sign of a holy covenant.' Comp. Targum *Cant.* iii. 8 ' The seal of circumcision is in your flesh as it was sealed in the flesh of Abraham ' ; *Shemoth R.* 19 ' Ye shall not eat of the passover unless the seal of Abraham be in your flesh.' Many other parallels will be found in Wetstein *ad loc.* (cf. also Delitzsch).

At a very early date the same term σφραγίς was transferred from the rite of circumcision to Christian baptism. See the passages collected by Lightfoot on 2 Clem. vii. 6 (*Clem. Rom.* ii. 226), also Gebhardt and Harnack *ad loc.*, and Hatch, *Hibbert Lectures*, p. 295. Dr. Hatch connects the use of the term with ' the mysteries and some forms of foreign cult ' ; and it may have coalesced with language borrowed from these ; but in its origin it appears to be Jewish. A similar view is taken by Anrich, *Das antike Mysterienwesen in seinem Einfluss auf das Christentum* (Göttingen, 1894), p. 120 ff., where the Christian use of the word σφραγίς is fully discussed.

Barnabas (ix. 6) seems to refer to, and refute, the Jewish doctrine which he puts in the mouth of an objector : ἀλλ' ἐρεῖς· Καὶ μὴν περιτέτμηται ὁ λαὸς εἰς σφραγῖδα. ἀλλὰ πᾶς Σύρος καὶ Ἄραψ καὶ πάντες οἱ ἱερεῖς τῶν εἰδώλων. ἆρα οὖν κἀκεῖνοι ἐκ τῆς διαθήκης αὐτῶν εἰσίν ; ἀλλὰ καὶ οἱ Αἰγύπτιοι ἐν περιτομῇ εἰσίν. The fact that so many heathen nations were circumcised proved that circumcision could not be the seal of a special covenant.

εἰς τὸ εἶναι, κ.τ.λ. Even circumcision, the strongest mark of Jewish separation, in St. Paul's view looked beyond its immediate exclusiveness to an ultimate inclusion of Gentiles as well as Jews. It was nothing more than a ratification of Abraham's faith. Faith was the real motive power ; and as applied to the present condition of things, Abraham's faith in the promise had its counterpart in the Christian's faith in the fulfilment of the promise (i. e. in Christ). Thus a new division was made. The true descendants of Abraham were not so much those who imitated his circumcision (i. e. all Jews whether believing or not), but those who imitated his faith (i. e. believing Jews *and* believing Gentiles). εἰς τό denotes that all this was contemplated in the Divine purpose.

πατέρα πάντων τῶν πιστευόντων. Delitzsch (*ad loc.*) quotes one of the prayers for the Day of Atonement in which Abraham is called ' the first of my faithful ones.' He also adduces a passage, Jerus. Gemara on *Biccurim*, i. 1, in which it is proved that even the proselyte may claim the patriarchs as his אֲבוֹתַי because

Abram became Abraham, 'father of many nations,' lit. 'a great multitude'; 'he was so,' the Glossator adds, 'because he taught them to believe.'

δι' ἀκροβυστίας: 'though in a state of uncircumcision.' διά of attendant circumstances as in διὰ γράμματος καὶ περιτομῆς ii. 27, τῷ διὰ προσκόμματος ἐσθίοντι xiv. 20.

12. τοῖς στοιχοῦσι. As it stands the art. is a solecism: it would make those who are circumcised one set of persons, and those who follow the example of Abraham's faith another distinct set, which is certainly not St. Paul's meaning. He is speaking of Jews who are *both* circumcised *and* believe. This requires in Greek the omission of the art. before στοιχοῦσιν. But τοῖς στ. is found in all existing MSS. We must suppose therefore either (1) that there has been some corruption. WH. think that τοῖς may be the remains of an original αὐτοῖς: but that would not seem to be a very natural form of sentence. Or (2) we may think that Tertius made a slip of the pen in following St. Paul's dictation, and that this remained uncorrected. If the slip was not made by Tertius himself, it must have been made in some very early copy, the parent of all our present copies.

στοιχοῦσι. στοιχεῖν is a well-known military term, meaning strictly to 'march in file': Pollux viii. 9 τὸ δὲ βάθος στοῖχος καλεῖται, καὶ τὸ μὲν ἐφεξῆς εἶναι κατὰ μῆκος ζυγεῖν· τὸ δὲ ἐφεξῆς κατὰ βάθος στοιχεῖν, 'the technical term for marching abreast is ζυγεῖν, for marching in depth or in file, στοιχεῖν' (Wets.).

On οὐ μόνον rather than μὴ μόνον in this verse and in ver. 16 see Burton, *M. and T.* § 481.

Jewish Teaching on Circumcision.

The fierce fanaticism with which the Jews insisted upon the rite of Circumcision is vividly brought out in the *Book of Jubilees* (xv. 25 ff.): 'This law is for all generations for ever, and there is no circumcision of the time, and no passing over one day out of the eight days; for it is an eternal ordinance, ordained and written on the heavenly tables. And every one that is born, the flesh of whose foreskin is not circumcised on the eighth day, belongs not to the children of the covenant which the Lord made with Abraham, for he belongs to the children of destruction; nor is there moreover any sign on him that he is the Lord's, but (he is destined) to be destroyed and slain from the earth, and to be rooted out of the earth, for he has broken the covenant of the Lord our God. . . . And now I will announce unto thee that the children of Israel will not keep true to this ordinance, and they will not circumcise their sons according to all this law; for in the flesh of their circumcision they will omit this circumcision of their sons, and all of them, sons of Belial, will have their sons uncircumcised as they were born. And there shall be great wrath from the Lord against the children of Israel, because they have forsaken His covenant and turned away from His word, and provoked and blasphemed, according as they have not observed the ordinance of this law; for they treat their members like the Gentiles, so that they may be removed and rooted out of the land. And there will be no pardon or forgiveness for them, so that there should be pardon and release from all the sin of this error for ever.'

So absolute is Circumcision as a mark of God's favour that if an Israelite has practised idolatry his circumcision must first be removed before he can go down to Gehenna (Weber, *Altsyn. Theol.* p. 51 f.). When Abraham was circumcised God Himself took a part in the act (*ibid.* p. 253). It was his circumcision and anticipatory fulfilment of the Law which qualified Abraham to be the 'father of many nations' (*ibid.* p. 256). Indeed it was just through his circumcision that Isaac was born of a 'holy seed.' This was the current doctrine. And it was at the root of it that St. Paul strikes by showing that Faith was prior to Circumcision, that the latter was wholly subordinate to the former, and that just those privileges and promises which the Jew connected with Circumcision were really due to Faith.

PROMISE AND LAW.

IV. 13–17. *Again the declaration that was made to Abraham had nothing to do with Law. For it turned on Faith and Promise which are the very antithesis of Law. The reason being that Abraham might be the spiritual father of all believers, Gentiles as well as Jews, and that Gentiles might have an equal claim to the Promise.*

[13] Another proof that Gentiles were contemplated as well as Jews. The promise made to Abraham and his descendants of world-wide Messianic rule, as it was not dependent upon Circumcision, so also was not dependent upon Law, but on a righteousness which was the product of Faith. [14] If this world-wide inheritance really depended upon any legal system, and if it was limited to those who were under such a system, there would be no place left for Faith or Promise: Faith were an empty name and Promise a dead letter. [15] For Law is in its effects the very opposite of Promise. It only

serves to bring down God's wrath by enhancing the guilt of sin.
Where there is no law, there is no transgression, which implies
a law to be transgressed. Law and Promise therefore are mutually
exclusive; the one brings death, the other life. ¹⁶Hence it is that
the Divine plan was made to turn, not on Law and obedience to
Law, but on Faith. For faith on man's side implies Grace, or free
favour, on the side of God. So that the Promise depending as it
did not on Law but on these broad conditions, Faith and Grace,
might hold good equally for all Abraham's descendants—not only
for those who came under the Mosaic Law, but for all who could
lay claim to a faith like his. ¹⁷Thus Abraham is the true ancestor
of all Christians (ἡμῶν), as it is expressly stated in Gen. xvii. 5
'A father' (i.e. in spiritual fatherhood) 'of many nations have
I made thee *.'

13–17. In this section St. Paul brings up the key-words of his
own system Faith, Promise, Grace, and marshals them in array
over against the leading points in the current theology of the
Jews—Law, Works or performance of Law, Merit. Because the
working of this latter system had been so disastrous, ending only
in condemnation, it was a relief to find that it was not what God
had really intended, but that the true principles of things held out
a prospect so much brighter and more hopeful, and one which
furnished such abundant justification for all that seemed new in
Christianity.

13. οὐ γάρ, κ.τ.λ. The immediate point which this paragraph
is introduced to prove is that Abraham might be, in a true though
spiritual sense, the father of Gentiles as well as Jews. The ulterior
object of the whole argument is to show that Abraham himself
is rightly claimed not as the Jews contended by themselves but
by Christians.

διὰ νόμου: without art., any system of law.

ἡ ἐπαγγελία: see on ch. i. 2 (προεπηγγείλατο), where the uses of
the word and its place in Christian teaching are discussed. At the
time of the Coming of Christ the attention of the whole Jewish race
was turned to the promises contained in the O. T.; and in
Christianity these promises were (so to speak) brought to a head
and definitely identified with their fulfilment.

The following examples may be added to those quoted on ch. i. 2 to
illustrate the diffusion of this idea of 'Promise' among the Jews in the first
century A.D.: 4 Ezra iv. 27 *non capiet portare quae in temporibus iustis*

* There is a slight awkwardness in making our break in the middle of
a verse and of a sentence. St. Paul glides after his manner into a new subject,
suggested to him by the verse which he quotes in proof of what has gone before.

repromissa sunt; vii. 14 *si ergo non ingredientes ingressi fuerint qui vivunt angusta et vana haec, non poterunt recipere quae sunt reposita* (=τὰ ἀπο-κείμενα Gen. xlix. 10); *ibid.* 49 (119) ff. *quid enim nobis prodest si promissum est nobis immortale tempus, nos vero mortalia opera egimus?* &c. *Apoc. Baruch.* xiv. 13 *propter hoc etiam ipsi sine timore relinquunt mundum istum, et fidentes in laetitia sperant se recepturos mundum quem promisisti eis.* It will be observed that all these passages are apocalyptic and eschatological. The Jewish idea of Promise is vague and future; the Christian idea is definite and associated with a state of things already inaugurated.

τὸ κληρονόμον αὐτὸν εἶναι κόσμου. What Promise is this? There is none in these words. Hence (1) some think that it means the possession of the Land of Canaan (Gen. xii. 7; xiii. 14 f.; xv. 18; xvii. 8; cf. xxvi. 3; Ex. vi. 4) taken as a type of the world-wide Messianic reign; (2) others think that it must refer to the particular promise faith in which called down the Divine blessing—that A. should have a son and descendants like the stars of heaven. Probably this is meant in the first instance, but the whole series of promises goes together and it is implied (i) that A. should have a son; (ii) that this son should have numerous descendants; (iii) that in One of those descendants the whole world should be blessed; (iv) that through Him A.'s seed should enjoy world-wide dominion.

διὰ δικαιοσύνης πίστεως: this 'faith-righteousness' which St. Paul has been describing as characteristic of the Christian, and before him of Abraham.

14. οἱ ἐκ νόμου: 'the dependants of law,' 'vassals of a legal system,' such as were the Jews.

κληρονόμοι. If the right to that universal dominion which will belong to the Messiah and His people is confined to those who are subject to a law, like that of Moses, what can it have to do either with the Promise originally given to Abraham, or with Faith to which that Promise was annexed? In that case Faith and Promise would be pushed aside and cancelled altogether. But they cannot be cancelled; and therefore the inheritance must depend upon them and not upon Law.

15. This verse is parenthetic, proving that Law and Promise cannot exist and be in force side by side. They are too much opposed in their effects and operation. Law presents itself to St. Paul chiefly in this light as entailing punishment. It increases the guilt of sin. So long as there is no commandment, the wrong act is done as it were accidentally and unconsciously; it cannot be called by the name of transgression. The direct breach of a known law is a far more heinous matter. On this disastrous effect of Law see iii. 20, v. 13, 20, vii. 7 ff.

οὗ δέ for οὗ γάρ is decisively attested (א A B C &c.).

παράβασις is the appropriate word for the direct violation οι a code. It means to overstep a line clearly defined: *peccare est transilire lineas* Cicero, *Parad.* 3 (*ap.* Trench, *Syn.* p. 236).

16. ἐκ πίστεως. In his rapid and vigorous reasoning St. Paul contents himself with a few bold strokes, which he leaves it to the reader to fill in. It is usual to supply with ἐκ πίστεως either ἡ κληρονομία ἐστίν from v. 14 (Lips. Mey.) or ἡ ἐπαγγελία ἐστιν from v. 13 (Fri.), but as τὴν ἐπαγγελίαν is defined just below it seems better to have recourse to some wider thought which shall include both these. 'It was'='The Divine plan was, took its start, from faith.' The bold lines of God's plan, the Providential ordering of things, form the background, understood if not directly expressed, to the whole chapter.

εἰς τὸ εἶναι. Working round again to the same conclusion as before; the object of all these pre-arranged conditions was to do away with old restrictions, and to throw open the Messianic blessings to all who in any true sense could call Abraham 'father,' i.e. to believing Gentile as well as to believing Jew.

ABRAHAM'S FAITH A TYPE OF THE CHRISTIAN'S.

IV. 17-22. *Abraham's Faith was remarkable both for its strength and for its object: the birth of Isaac in which Abraham believed might be described as a 'birth from the dead.'*

23-25. *In this it is a type of the Christian's Faith, to which is annexed a like acceptance and which also has for its object a 'birth from the dead'—the Death and Resurrection of Christ.*

[17]In this light Abraham is regarded by God before whom he is represented as standing—that God who infuses life into the dead (as He was about to infuse it into Abraham's dead body), and who issues His summons (as He issued it then) to generations yet unborn.

[18]In such a God Abraham believed. Against all ordinary hope of becoming a father he yet had faith, grounded in hope, and enabling him to become the father not of Jews only but of widespread nations, to whom the Promise alluded when it said (Gen. xv. 5) 'Like the stars of the heaven shall thy descendants be.'

[19]Without showing weakness in his faith, he took full note of the fact that at his advanced years (for he was now about a hundred years old) his own vital powers were decayed; he took

full note of the barrenness of Sarah his wife; [20] and yet with the promise in view no impulse of unbelief made him hesitate; his faith endowed him with the power which he seemed to lack; he gave praise to God for the miracle that was to be wrought in him, [21] having a firm conviction that what God had promised He was able also to perform. [22] And for this reason that faith of his was credited to him as righteousness.

[23] Now when all this was recorded in Scripture, it was not Abraham alone who was in view [24] but we too—the future generations of Christians, who will find a like acceptance, as we have a like faith. Abraham believed on Him who caused the birth of Isaac from elements that seemed as good as dead: and we too believe on the same God who raised up from the dead Jesus our Lord, [25] who was delivered into the hands of His murderers to atone for our sins, and rose again to effect our justification (i. e. to put the crown and seal to the Atonement wrought by His Death, and at the same time to evoke the faith which makes the Atonement effectual).

17. πατέρα, κ.τ.λ. Exactly from LXX of Gen. xvii. 5. The LXX tones down somewhat the strongly figurative expression of the Heb., *patrem frementis turbae*, i. e. *ingentis multitudinis populorum* (Kautzsch, p. 25).

κατέναντι οὗ ἐπίστευσε Θεοῦ : attraction for κατέναντι Θεοῦ ᾧ ἐπίστευσε : κατέναντι describing the posture in which Abraham is represented as holding colloquy with God (Gen. xvii. 1 ff.).

ζωοποιοῦντος : 'maketh alive.' St. Paul has in his mind the two acts which he compares and which are both embraced under this word, (1) the Birth of Isaac, (2) the Resurrection of Christ. On the Hellenistic use of the word see Hatch, *Ess. in Bibl. Greek*, p. 5.

καλοῦντος [τὰ μὴ ὄντα ὡς ὄντα]. There are four views: (i) καλ.= 'to name, speak of, or describe, things non-existent as if they existed' (Va.); (ii) = 'to call into being, issue His creative fiat' (most commentators); (iii) = 'to call, or summon,' 'issue His commands to' (Mey. Gif.); (iv) in the dogmatic sense = 'to call, or invite to life and salvation' (Fri.). Of these (iv) may be put on one side as too remote from the context; and (ii) as Mey. rightly points out, seems to be negatived by ὡς ὄντα. The choice remains between (i) and (iii). If the former seems the simplest, the latter is the more forcible rendering, and as such more in keeping with the imaginative grasp of the situation displayed by St. Paul. In favour of this view may also be quoted *Apoc. Bar.* xxi. 4 *O qui fecisti terram audi me . . . qui vocasti ab initio mundi quod nondum erat, et*

obediunt tibi. For the use of καλεῖν see also the note on ix. ̔̍
below.

18. εἰς τὸ γενέσθαι = ὥστε γενέσθαι: 'his faith enabled him to
become the father,' but with the underlying idea that his faith in
this was but carrying out the great Divine purpose which ordered
all these events.

οὕτως ἔσται: = Gen. xv. 5 (LXX).

19. μὴ ἀσθενήσας. Comp. Lft. in *Journ. of Class. and Sac. Philol.*
iii. 106 n.: 'The New Testament use of μή with a participle ... has a much
wider range than in the earlier language. Yet this is no violation of
principle, but rather an extension of a particular mode of looking at the
subordinate event contained in the participial clause. It is viewed as an
accident or condition of the principal event described by the finite verb, and
is therefore negatived by the dependent negative μή and not by the absolute οὐ.
Rom. iv. 19 ... is a case in point whether we retain οὐ or omit it with
Lachm. In the latter case the sense will be, "he so considered his own
body now dead, *as not to be* weak in the (?) faith."' This is well expressed
in RV. '*without being* weakened,' except that 'being weakened' should be
rather 'showing weakness' or 'becoming weak.' See also Burton, *M. and T.*
§ 145.

κατενόησε ℵ A B C some good cursives, some MSS. of Vulg.
(including *am.*), Pesh. Boh., Orig.-lat. (which probably here preserves
Origen's Greek), Chrys. and others; οὐ κατενόησε D E F G K L P
&c., some MSS. of Vulg. (including *fuld*, though it is more probable that the negative has come in from the Old Latin and that
it was not recognized by Jerome), Syr.-Harcl., Orig.-lat. *bis*, Epiph.
Ambrstr. *al.*

Both readings give a good sense: κατενόησε, 'he *did* consider, and
yet did not doubt'; οὐ κατενόησε, 'he did *not* consider, and *therefore*
did not doubt.' Both readings are also early: but the negative
οὐ κατενόησε is clearly of Western origin, and must probably be set
down to Western laxity: the authorities which omit the negative
are as a rule the most trustworthy.

ὑπάρχων: 'being *already* about a hundred years old.' May we not say
that εἶναι denotes a present state simply as present, but that ὑπάρχειν denotes
a present state as a product of past states, or at least a state in present time
as related to past time ('*vorhandensein, dasein,* Lat. *existere, adesse, praesto
esse*' Schmidt)? See esp. T. S. Evans in *Sp. Comm.* on 1 Cor. vii. 26 : 'the
last word (ὑπάρχειν) is difficult; it seems to mean sometimes "to be originally," "to be substantially or fundamentally," or, as in Demosthenes, "to be
stored in readiness." An idea of *propriety* sometimes attaches to it: comp.
ὕπαρξις, "property" or "substance." The word however asks for further
investigation.' Comp. Schmidt, *Lat. u. gr. Synonymik,* § 74. 4.

20. οὐ διεκρίθη: 'did not hesitate' (τουτέστιν οὐδὲ ἐνεδοίασεν οὐδὲ ἀμφέ-
βαλε Chrys.). διακρίνειν act. = *diiudicare,* (i) to 'discriminate,' or 'distinguish'
between two things (Matt. xvi. 3 ; cf. 1 Cor. xi. 29, 31) or persons (Acts xv. 9;
1 Cor. iv. 7); (ii) to 'arbitrate' between two parties (1 Cor. vi. 5). δια-
κρίνεσθαι mid. (and pass.) = (i) 'to get a decision,' 'litigate,' 'dispute,' or
'contend' (Acts xi. 2 ; Jas. ii. 4 ; Jude 9); (ii) to 'be divided against oneself,' 'waver,' 'doubt.' The other senses are all found in LXX (where the
word occurs some thirty times), but this is wanting. It is however well

established for N.T., where it appears as the proper opposite of πίστις
πιστεύω. So Matt. xxi. 21 ἐὰν ἔχητε πίστιν, καὶ μὴ διακριθῆτε : Mark xi. 23 ὃς
ἂν εἴπῃ ... καὶ μὴ διακριθῇ ἐν τῇ καρδίᾳ αὐτοῦ ἀλλὰ πιστεύῃ : Rom. xiv. 23 ὁ δὲ
διακρινόμενος, ἐὰν φάγῃ, κατακέκριται, ὅτι οὐκ ἐκ πίστεως : Jas. i. 6 αἰτείτω δὲ
ἐν πίστει μηδὲν διακρινόμενος : also probably Jude 22. A like use is found in
Christian writings of the second century and later: e.g. *Protev. Jac.* 11
ἀκούσασα δὲ Μαριὰμ διεκρίθη ἐν ἑαυτῇ λέγουσα, κ.τ.λ. (quoted by Mayor on
Jas. i. 6) : *Clem. Homil.* i. 20 περὶ τῆς παραδοθείσης σοι ἀληθείας διακριθῇση :
ii. 40 περὶ τοῦ μόνου καὶ ἀγαθοῦ Θεοῦ διακριθῆναι. It is remarkable that a use
which (except as an antithesis to πιστεύειν) there is no reason to connect
specially with Christianity should thus seem to be traceable to Christian
circles and the Christian line of tradition. It is not likely to be in the strict
sense a Christian coinage, but appears to have had its beginning in near
proximity to Christianity. A parallel case is that of the word δίψυχος (St.
James, Clem. Rom., Herm., *Didaché*, &c.). The two words seem to belong
to the same cycle of ideas.

ἐνεδυναμώθη τῇ πίστει. τῇ πίστει is here usually taken as dat. of
respect, 'he was strengthened in his faith,' i.e. 'his faith was
strengthened, or confirmed.' In favour of this would be μὴ ἀσθενήσας
τῇ πίστει above ; and the surrounding terms (διεκρίθη, πληροφορηθείς)
might seem to point to a mental process. But it is tempting to
make τῇ πίστει instrumental or causal, like τῇ ἀπιστίᾳ to which it
stands in immediate antithesis : ἐνεδ. τῇ πίστ. would then = 'he was
endowed with power by means of his faith' (sc. τὸ νενεκρωμένον
αὐτοῦ σῶμα ἐνεδυναμώθη). According to the Talmud, *Abraham wurde
in seiner Natur erneuert, eine neue Creatur (Bammidbar Rabba* xi),
um die Zeugung zu vollbringen (Weber, p. 256). And we can
hardly doubt that the passage was taken in this way by the author
of Heb., who appears to have had it directly in mind : comp. Heb.
xi. 11, 12 πίστει καὶ αὐτὴ Σάρρα δύναμιν εἰς καταβολὴν σπέρματος ἔλαβε
καὶ παρὰ καιρὸν ἡλικίας ... διὸ καὶ ἀφ' ἑνὸς ἐγεννήθησαν, καὶ ταῦτα
νενεκρωμένου, καθὼς τὰ ἄστρα τοῦ οὐρανοῦ τῷ πλήθει (observe esp. δύναμιν
ἔλαβε, νενεκρωμένου). This sense is also distinctly recognized by
Euthym.-Zig. (ἐνεδυναμώθη εἰς παιδογονίαν τῇ πίστει· ἢ ἐνεδυναμώθη
πρὸς τὴν πίστιν). The other (common) interpretation is preferred by
Chrys., from whom Euthym.-Zig. seems to get his ὁ πίστιν
ἐπιδεικνύμενος δυνάμεως δεῖται πλείονος.

The Talmud lays great stress on the Birth of Isaac. In the
name of Isaac was found an indication that with him the history
of Revelation began. With him the people of revealed Religion
came into existence : with him 'the Holy One began to work
wonders' (*Beresh. Rabba* liii, *ap.* Weber, *Altsyn. Theol.* p. 256).
But it is of course a wholly new point when St. Paul compares the
miraculous birth of Isaac with the raising of Christ from the dead.
The parallel consists not only in the nature of the two events—
both a bringing to life from conditions which betokened only
death—but also in the faith of which they were the object.

δοὺς δόξαν: a Hebraism : cf. Josh. vii. 19 ; 1 Sam. vi. 5 ; 1
Chron. xvi. 28, &c.

21. πληροφορηθείς: πληροφορία = 'full assurance,' 'firm conviction,' 1 Thess. i. 5; Col. ii. 2; a word especially common amongst the Stoics.   Hence πληροφορεῖσθαι, as used of persons, = 'to be fully assured or convinced,' as here, ch. xiv. 5; Col. iv. 12.   As used of things the meaning is more doubtful: cf. 2 Tim. iv. 5, 17 and Luke i. 1, where some take it as = 'fully or satisfactorily proved,' others as = 'accomplished' (so Lat.-Vet. Vulg. RV. *text* Lft. *On Revision*, p. 142): see note *ad loc.*

23. δι᾽ αὐτὸν μόνον.   *Beresh. R.* xl. 8 'Thou findest that all that is recorded of Abraham is repeated in the history of his children' (Wetstein, who is followed by Meyer, and Delitzsch *ad loc.*). Wetstein also quotes *Taanith* ii. 1 *Fratres nostri, de Ninevitis non dictum est*: et respexit Deus saccum eorum.

24. τοῖς πιστεύουσιν: 'to us who believe.'   St. Paul asserts that his readers are among the class of believers.   Not 'if we believe,' which would be πιστεύουσιν (*sine artic.*).

25. διά with acc. is primarily retrospective, = 'because of': but inasmuch as the idea or motive precedes the execution, διά may be retrospective with reference to the idea, but prospective with reference to the execution.   Which it is in any particular case must be determined by the context.

Here διὰ τὰ παραπτ. may be retrospective, = 'because of our trespasses' (which made the death of Christ necessary); or it may be prospective, as Gif. 'because of our trespasses,' i. e. 'in order to atone for them.'

In any case διὰ τὴν δικαίωσιν is prospective, 'with a view to our justification,' 'because of our justification' conceived as a motive, i. e. to bring it about.   See Dr. Gifford's two excellent notes pp. 108, 109.

The manifold ways in which the Resurrection of Christ is connected with justification will appear from the exposition below. It is at once the great source of the Christian's faith, the assurance of the special character of the object of that faith, the proof that the Sacrifice which is the ground of justification is an accepted sacrifice, and the stimulus to that moral relation of the Christian to Christ in which the victory which Christ has won becomes his own victory. See also the notes on ch. vi. 5–8.

The Place of the Resurrection of Christ in the teaching of St. Paul.

The Resurrection of Christ fills an immense place in the teaching of St. Paul, and the fact that it does so accounts for the emphasis and care with which he states the evidence for it (**1 Cor. xv. 1–11**).

(i) The Resurrection is the most conclusive proof of the Divinity of Christ (Acts xvii. 31; Rom. i. 4; 1 Cor. xv. 14, 15).

(ii) As proving the Divinity of Christ the Resurrection is also the most decisive proof of the atoning value of His Death. But for the Resurrection, there would have been nothing to show—at least no clear and convincing sign to show—that He who died upon the Cross was more than man. But if the Victim of the Cross had been man and nothing more, there would have been no sufficient reason for attaching to His Death any peculiar efficacy; the faith of Christians would be 'vain,' they would be 'yet in their sins' (1 Cor. xv. 17).

(iii) In yet another way the Resurrection proved the efficacy of the Death of Christ. Without the Resurrection the Sacrifice of Calvary would have been incomplete. The Resurrection placed upon that Sacrifice the stamp of God's approval; it showed that the Sacrifice was accepted, and that the cloud of Divine Wrath— the ὀργή so long suspended and threatening to break (Rom. iii. 25, 26)—had passed away. This is the thought which lies at the bottom of Rom. vi. 7-10.

(iv) The Resurrection of Christ is the strongest guarantee for the resurrection of the Christian (1 Cor. xv. 20-23; 2 Cor. iv 14; Rom. viii. 11; Col. i. 18).

(v) But that resurrection has two sides or aspects: it is not only physical, a future rising again to physical life, but it is also moral and spiritual, a present rising from the death of sin to the life of righteousness. In virtue of his union with Christ, the close and intimate relation of his spirit with Christ's, the Christian is called upon to repeat in himself the redeeming acts of Christ. And this moral and spiritual sense is the only sense in which he can repeat them. We shall have this doctrine fully expounded in ch. vi. 1-11.

A recent monograph on the subject of this note (E. Schäder, *Die Bedeutung des lebendigen Christus für die Rechtfertigung nach Paulus*, Gütersloh, 1893) has worked out in much careful detail the third of the above heads. Herr Schäder (who since writing his treatise has become Professor at Königsberg) insists strongly on the personal character of the redemption wrought by Christ; that which redeems is not merely the act of Christ's Death but His Person (ἐν ᾧ ἔχομεν τὴν ἀπολύτρωσιν Eph. i. 7; Col. i. 14). It is as a Person that He takes the place of the sinner and endures the Wrath of God in his stead (Gal. iii. 13; 2 Cor. v. 21). The Resurrection is proof that this 'Wrath' is at an end. And therefore in certain salient passages (Rom. iv. 25; vi. 9, 10; viii. 34) the Resurrection is even put before the Death of Christ as the cause of justification. The treatise is well deserving of study.

It may be right also to mention, without wholly endorsing, Dr. Hort's significant aphorism: 'Reconciliation or Atonement is one aspect of redemption, and redemption one aspect of resurrection, and resurrection one aspect of life' (*Hulsean Lectures*, p. 210). This can more readily be accepted if 'one aspect' in each case is not taken to exclude the validity of other aspects. At the same time such a saying is useful as a warning, which is especially needed where the attempt is being made towards more exact definitions, that all definitions of great doctrines have a relative rather than an absolute value. They are partial symbols of ideas which the human mind cannot grasp in their entirety. If we could see as God sees we should doubtless find them running up into large and broad laws of His working. We desire to make this reserve in regard to our own attempts to define. Without it exact exegesis may well seem to lead to a revived Scholasticism.

BLISSFUL CONSEQUENCES OF JUSTIFICATION.

V. 1–11. *The state which thus lies before the Christian should have consequences both near and remote. The nearer consequences, peace with God and hope which gives courage under persecution* (vv. 1–4): *the remoter consequence, an assurance, derived from the proof of God's love, of our final salvation and glory. The first step (our present acceptance with God) is difficult; the second step (our ultimate salvation) follows naturally from the first* (vv. 5–11).

[1] We Christians then ought to enter upon our privileges. By that strong and eager impulse with which we enroll ourselves as Christ's we may be accepted as righteous in the sight of God, and it becomes our duty to enjoy to the full the new state of peace with Him which we owe to our Lord Jesus Messiah. [2] He it is whose Death and Resurrection, the object of our faith (iv. 25), have brought us within the range of the Divine favour. Within the sheltered circle of that favour we stand as Christians, in no merely passive attitude, but we exult in the hope of one day participating as in the favour of God so also in His glory. [3] Yes, and this exultation of ours, so far from being shaken by persecutions is actually founded upon them. For persecution only generates fortitude, or resolute endurance under trials: [4] and then fortitude leads on to the approved courage of the veteran; and that in turn strengthens the hope out of which it originally sprang.

[5] More: our hope is one that cannot prove illusory; because (and here a new factor is introduced, for the first time in this connexion) the Holy Spirit, through whom God is brought into personal contact with man—that Holy Spirit which we received when we became Christians, floods our hearts with the conscious-

ness of the Love of God for us. ⁶ Think what are the facts to which we can appeal. When we were utterly weak and prostrate, at the moment of our deepest despair, Christ died for us—not as righteous men, but as godless sinners ! ⁷ What a proof of love was there ! For an upright or righteous man it would be hard to find one willing to die; though perhaps for a good man (with the loveable qualities of goodness) one here and there may be brave enough to face death. ⁸ But God presses home the proof of His unmerited Love towards us, in that, sinners as we still were, Christ died for us.

⁹ Here then is an *a fortiori* argument. The fact that we have been actually declared 'righteous' by coming within the influence of Christ's sacrificial Blood—this fact which implies a stupendous change in the whole of our relations to God is a sure pledge of what is far easier—our escape from His final judgement. ¹⁰ For there is a double contrast. If God intervened for us while we were His enemies, much more now that we are reconciled to Him. If the first intervention cost the Death of His Son, the second costs nothing, but follows naturally from the share which we have in His Life. ¹¹ And not only do we look for this final salvation, but we are buoyed up by an exultant sense of that nearness to God into which we have been brought by Christ to whom we owe that one great step of our reconciliation.

1–11. Every line of this passage breathes St. Paul's personal experience, and his intense hold upon the objective facts which are the grounds of a Christian's confidence. He believes that the ardour with which he himself sought Christian baptism was met by an answering change in the whole relation in which he stood to God. That change he attributes ultimately, it is clear throughout this context, not merely in general terms to Christ ($\delta\iota\acute{a}$ v. 1, 2, 11 *bis*) but more particularly to the Death of Christ ($\pi\alpha\rho\epsilon\delta\acute{o}\theta\eta$ iv. 25; $\dot{a}\pi\acute{\epsilon}\theta\alpha\nu\epsilon$ v. 6, 8; $\dot{\epsilon}\nu \tau\hat{\wp} \alpha\emph{i}\mu\alpha\tau\iota$ v. 9 ; $\delta\iota\grave{a} \tau o\hat{v} \theta\alpha\nu\acute{a}\tau o\upsilon$ v. 10). He conceives of that Death as operating by a sacrificial blood-shedding ($\dot{\epsilon}\nu \tau\hat{\wp} \alpha\emph{i}\mu\alpha\tau\iota$: cf. iii. 25 and the passages referred to in the Note on the Death of Christ considered as a Sacrifice). The Blood of that Sacrifice is as it were sprinkled round the Christian, and forms a sort of hallowed enclosure, a place of sanctuary, into which he enters. Within this he is safe, and from its shelter he looks out exultingly over the physical dangers which threaten him ; they may strengthen his firmness of purpose, but cannot shake it.

1. The word $\delta\iota\kappa\alpha\acute{\iota}\omega\sigma\iota\nu$ at the end of the last chapter recalls St. Paul to his main topic. After expounding the nature of his new

method of obtaining righteousness in iii. 21–26, he had begun to draw some of the consequences from this (the deathblow to Jewish pride, and the equality of Jew and Gentile) in iii. 27–31. This suggested the digression in ch. iv, to prove that notwithstanding there was no breach of God's purposes as declared in the O. T. (strictly the Legal System which had its charter in the O. T.), but rather the contrary. Now he goes back to 'consequences' and traces them out for the individual Christian. He explains why it is that the Christian faces persecution and death so joyfully : he has a deep spring of tranquillity at his heart, and a confident hope of future glory.

ἔχωμεν. The evidence for this reading stands thus : ἔχωμεν א * A B* C D E K L, cursives, Vulg. Syrr. Boh. Arm. Aeth., Orig.·lat. repeatedly Chrys. Ambrstr. and others : ἔχομεν correctors of א B, F G (duplicate MSS. it will be remembered) in the Greek though not in the Latin, P and many cursives, Did. Epiph. Cyr.-Alex. in three places out of four. Clearly overwhelming authority for ἔχωμεν. It is argued however (i) that exhortation is here out of place: 'inference not exhortation is the Apostle's purpose' (Scrivener, *Introd.* ii. 380 ed. 4); (ii) that o and ω are frequently interchanged in the MSS., as in this very word Gal. vi. 10 (cf. 1 Cor. xv. 49); (iii) it is possible that a mistake might have been made by Tertius in copying or in some very early MS. from which the mass of the uncials and versions now extant may have descended. But these reasons seem insufficient to overthrow the weight of direct testimony. (i) St. Paul is apt to pass from argument to exhortation; so in the near context vi. (1), 12, (15); viii. 12 ; (ii) in ἔχωμεν inference and exhortation are really combined : it is a sort of light exhortation, 'we *should* have' (T. S. Evans).

As to the meaning of ἔχωμεν it should be observed that it does not = '*make* peace,' 'get' or 'obtain peace' (which would be σχῶμεν), but rather 'keep' or 'enjoy peace' (οὐ γάρ ἐστιν ἴσον μὴ οὖσαν εἰρήνην λαβεῖν καὶ δοθεῖσαν κατασχεῖν Chrys.; cf. Acts ix. 31 ἡ μὲν οὖν ἐκκλησία . . . εἶχεν εἰρήνην, 'continued in a state of peace '). The aor. part. δικαιωθέντες marks the initial moment of the state εἰρήνην ἔχωμεν. The declaration of 'not guilty,' which the sinner comes under by a heartfelt embracing of Christianity, at once does away with the state of hostility in which he had stood to God, and substitutes for it a state of peace which he has only to realize. This declaration of ' not guilty ' and the peace which follows upon it are not due to himself, but are διὰ τοῦ Κυρίου ἡμῶν Ἰησοῦ Χριστοῦ : *how* is explained more fully in iii. 25 ; also in vv. 9, 10 below.

Dr. J. Agar Beet (Comm. *ad loc.*) discusses the exact shade of meaning conveyed by the aor. part. δικαιωθέντες in relation to εἰρήνην ἔχωμεν. He contends that it denotes not so much the *reason* for entering upon the state in question as the *means* of entering upon it. No doubt this is perfectly tenable on the score of grammar; and it is also true that 'justification necessarily involves peace with God.' But the argument goes too much upon the assumption that εἰρ. ἔχ. = 'obtain peace,' which we have seen to be erroneous. The sense is exactly that of εἶχεν εἰρήνην in the passage quoted from the Acts, and δικαιωθ., as we have said, marks the initial moment in the state.

2. τὴν προσαγωγήν. Two stages only are described in vv. **1, 2** though different language is used about them: δικαιωθέντες = ἡ προσαγωγή, εἰρήνη = χάρις; the καύχησις is a characteristic of the state of χάρις, at the same time that it points forward to a future state of δόξα. The phrase ἡ προσαγ., 'our introduction,' is a connecting link between this Epistle and Ephesians (cp. Eph. ii. 18; iii. 12): the idea is that of introduction to the presence-chamber of a monarch. The rendering 'access' is inadequate, as it leaves out of sight the fact that we do not come in our own strength but need an 'introducer'—Christ.

ἐσχήκαμεν: not 'we have had' (Va.), but 'we have got or obtained,' aor. and perf. in one.

'Both grammar and logic will run in perfect harmony together if we render, "through whom we have by faith got or obtained our access into this grace wherein we stand." This rendering will bring to view two causes of getting the access or obtaining the introduction into the state of grace; one cause objective, Christ: the other subjective, faith; Christ the door, faith the hand which moves the door to open and to admit' (T. S. Evans in *Exp.* 1882, i. 169).

τῇ πίστει om. B D E F G, Lat. Vet., Orig.-lat. *bis.* The weight of this evidence depends on the value which we assign to B. All the other evidence is Western; and B also (as we have seen) has a Western element; so that the question is whether the omission here in B is an independent corroboration of the Western group or whether it simply belongs to it (does the evidence = β + δ, or δ only?). There is the further point that omissions in the Western text deserve more attention than additions. Either reading can be easily enough accounted for, as an obvious gloss on the one hand or the omission of a superfluous phrase on the other. The balance is sufficiently represented by placing τῇ πίστει in brackets as Treg. WH. RV. *marg.* (Weiss omits).

εἰς τὴν χάριν ταύτην: the 'state of grace' or condition of those who are objects of the Divine favour, conceived of as a space fenced in (Mey. Va. &c.) into which the Christian enters: cf. Gal. v. 4; 1 Pet. v. 12 (Va. and Grm.-Thay. s. v. χάρις 3. a).

ἑστήκαμεν: 'stand fast or firm' (see Va. and Grm.-Thay. s. v. ἵστημι ii. 2. d).

ἐπ' ἐλπίδι: as in iv. 18.

τῆς δόξης. See on iii. 23. It is the Glory of the Divine Presence (Shekinah) communicated to man (partially here, but) in full measure when he enters into that Presence; man's whole being will be transfigured by it.

Is the Society or the Individual the proper object of Justification?

It is well known to be a characteristic feature of the theology of Ritschl that he regards the proper object of Justification as the Christian Society as a collective whole, and not the individual as such. This view is based upon two main groups of arguments. (1) The first is derived from the analogy of the O. T. The great sacrifices of the O. T. were undoubtedly meant in the first instance for 'the congregation.' So in regard to the Passover it is laid down expressly that no alien is to eat of it, but all the congregation of Israel are to keep it (Ex. xii. 43 ff., 47). And still more distinctly as to the ritual of the Day of Atonement: the high priest is to 'make atonement for the holy place, because of the un-cleannesses of the children of Israel, and because of their trans-gressions, even all their sins'; he is to lay both his hands on the head of the goat, and 'confess over him all the iniquities of the children of Israel, and all their transgressions, even all their sins' (Lev. xvi. 16, 21, also 33 f.). This argument gains in force from the concentration of the Christian Sacrifice upon a single event, accomplished once for all. It is natural to think of it as having also a single and permanent object. (2) The second argument is derived from the exegesis of the N. T. generally (most clearly perhaps in Acts xx. 28 τὴν ἐκκλησίαν τοῦ Θεοῦ [v. l. Κυρίου], ἣν περιεποιήσατο διὰ τοῦ αἵματος τοῦ ἰδίου : but also in 1 Jo. ii. 2; iv. 10; 1 Pet. iii. 18; Apoc. i. 5 f.; v. 9 f.), and more particularly in the Epistles of St. Paul. The society is, it is true, most clearly indicated in the later Epp.; e. g. Tit. ii. 14 σωτῆρος ἡμῶν Ἰ. Χ., ὃς ἔδωκεν ἑαυτὸν ὑπὲρ ἡμῶν, ἵνα λυτρώσηται ἡμᾶς ... καὶ καθαρίσῃ ἑαυτῷ λαὸν περιούσιον : Eph. v. 25 f. ὁ Χριστὸς ἠγάπησε τὴν ἐκκλησίαν, καὶ ἑαυτὸν παρέδωκεν ὑπὲρ αὐτῆς· ἵνα αὐτὴν ἁγιάσῃ καθαρίσας κ.τ.λ. (cf. also Eph. ii. 18; iii. 12; Col. i. 14). But Ritschl also claims the support of the earlier Epp.: e. g. Rom. viii. 32 ὑπὲρ ἡμῶν πάντων παρέδωκεν αὐτόν : iii. 22 δικαιοσύνη δὲ Θεοῦ ... εἰς πάντας τοὺς πιστεύοντας : and the repeated ἡμεῖς in the contexts of three passages (Comp. *Recht-fert. u. Versöhn.* ii. 216 f., 160).

In reply the critics of Ritschl appeal to the distinctly in-dividualistic cast of such expressions as Rom. iii. 26 δικαιοῦντα τὸν ἐκ πίστεως Ἰησοῦ : iv. 5 ἐπὶ τὸν δικαιοῦντα τὸν ἀσεβῆ, with the context : x. 4 εἰς δικαιοσύνην παντὶ τῷ πιστεύοντι (Schäder, *op. cit.* p. 29 n. ; cf. also Gloël, *Der Heilige Geist*, p. 102 n.; Weiss, *Bibl. Theol.* § 82 b, referred to by Schäder).

It is undoubtedly true that St. Paul does use language which points to the direct justification of the individual believer. This

perhaps comes out most clearly in Rom. iv, where the personal
faith and personal justification of Abraham are taken as typical of
the Christian's. But need we on that account throw over the other
passages above quoted, which seem to be quite as unambiguous?
That which brings benefit to the Church collectively of necessity
brings benefit to the individuals of which it is composed. We
may if we like, as St. Paul very often does, leave out of sight the
intervening steps; and it is perhaps the more natural that he
should do so, as the Church is in this connexion an ideal entity.
But this entity is prior in thought to the members who compose
it; and when we think of the Great Sacrifice as consummated
once for all and in its effects reaching down through the ages, it is
no less natural to let the mind dwell on the conception which
alone embraces past, present, and future, and alone binds all the
scattered particulars into unity.

We must remember also that in the age and to the thought of
St. Paul the act of faith in the individual which brings him within
the range of justification is inseparably connected with its ratification in baptism. But the significance of baptism lies in the fact
that whoever undergoes it is made thereby member of a society,
and becomes at once a recipient of the privileges and immunities
of that society. St. Paul is about (in the next chapter) to lay
stress on this point. He there, as well as elsewhere, describes the
relation of spiritual union into which the Christian enters with
Christ as established by the same act which makes him also
member of the society. And therefore when at the beginning of
the present chapter he speaks of the entrance of the Christian into
the state of grace in metaphors which present that state under the
figure of a fenced-off enclosure, it is natural to identify the area
within which grace and justification operate with the area of the
society, in other words with the Church. The Church however in
this connexion can have no narrower definition than 'all baptized
persons.' And even the condition of baptism is introduced as an
inseparable adjunct to faith; so that if through any exceptional
circumstances the two were separated, the greater might be taken
to include the less. The Christian theologian has to do with what
is normal; the abnormal he leaves to the Searcher of hearts.

It is thus neither in a spirit of exclusiveness nor yet in that of
any hard and fast Scholasticism, but only in accordance with the
free and natural tendencies of the Apostle's thought, that we speak
of Justification as normally mediated through the Church. St.
Paul himself, as we have seen, often drops the intervening link,
especially in the earlier Epistles. But in proportion as his maturer
insight dwells more and more upon the Church as an organic
whole he also conceives of it as doing for the individual believer
what the 'congregation' did for the individual Israelites under the

older dispensation. The Christian Sacrifice with its effects, like the sacrifices of the Day of Atonement by which it is typified, reach the individual through the community.

3-5. The two leading types of the Old-Latin Version of the Epistle stand out distinctly in these verses. We are fortunately able to compare the Cyprianic text with that of Tertullian (*non solum . . . confundit*) and the European text of Cod. Clarom. with that of Hilary (*tribulatio . . . confundit*). The passage is also quoted in the so-called *Speculum* (m), which represents the Bible of the Spaniard Priscillian (*Classical Review*, iv. 416 f.).

CYPRIAN.	COD. CLAROM.
Non solum autem, sed et gloriamur in pressuris, scientes quoniam pressura tolerantiam operatur, tolerantia autem probationem, probatio autem spem; spes autem non confundit, quia dilectio Dei infusa est cordibus nostris per Spiritum Sanctum qui datus est nobis.	*Non solum autem, sed et gloriamur in tribulationibus, scientes quod tribulatio patientiam operatur, patientia autem probationem, probatio autem spem; spes autem non confundit, quia caritas Dei diffusa est in cordibus nostris per Spiritum Sanctum qui datus est nobis.*
verum etiam exultantes Tert.; *certi quod* Tert.; *perficiat* Tert. (ed. Vindob.); *tol. vero* Tert.; *spes vero* Tert.	*perficit* Hil.; *prob. vero* m Hil.; *spes vero* Hil. (Cod. Clarom. = m).

Here, as elsewhere in Epp. Paul., there is a considerable amount of matter common to all forms of the Version, enough to give colour to the supposition that a single translation lies at their root. But the salient expressions are changed; and in this instance Tertullian goes with Cyprian, as Hilary with the European texts. The renderings *tolerantia* and *pressura* are verified for Tertullian elsewhere (*tolerantia* Luke xxi. 19; 1 Thess. i. 4: *pressura* Rom. viii. 35; xii. 12; 1 Cor. vii. 28; 2 Cor. i. 8; iv. 17; vi. 4; vii. 4; Col. i. 24; 2 Thess. i. 4; Apoc. ii. 22; vii. 14), as also *dilectio* (to which the quotation does not extend in this passage, but which is found in Luke xi. 42; John xiii. 35; Rom. viii. 35, 39; 1 Cor. xiii. 1 ff., &c.). We note however that Hilary and Tertullian agree in *perficit* (*perficiat*), though in another place Hilary has allusively *tribulatio patientiam operatur.* Perhaps this coincidence may point to an older rendering.

3. οὐ μόνον δέ (ἐστήκαμεν ἀλλὰ καὶ καυχώμεθα, or ἐστηκότες ἀλλὰ καὶ καυχώμενοι): in this elliptical form characteristic of St. Paul and esp. of this group of Epistles (cf. v. 11; viii. 23; ix. 10; 2 Cor. viii. 19).

καυχώμενοι B C, Orig. *bis* and others: a good group, but open to suspicion of conforming to ver. 11 (q. v.); we have also found a similar group, on the whole inferior, in iii. 28. If καυχώμενοι were right it would be another example of that broken and somewhat inconsecutive structure which is doubtless due, as Va. suggests, to the habit of dictating to an amanuensis.

Note the contrast between the Jewish καύχησις which 'is excluded' (iii. 27) and this Christian καύχησις. The one rests on supposed human privileges and merit; the other draws all its force from the assurance of Divine love.

The Jewish writers know of another καύχησις (besides the empty boasting which St. Paul reprehends), but it is reserved for the blest in Paradise: 4 Ezr. vii. 98 [Bensly = vi. 72 O. F. Fritzsche] *exultabunt cum fiducia et . . . confidebunt non confusi, et gaudebunt non reverentes.*

ἐν ταῖς θλίψεσι. The θλίψεις are the physical hardships and sufferings that St. Paul regards as the inevitable portion of the Christian; cf. Rom. viii. 35 ff.; 1 Cor. iv. 11–13; vii. 26–32; xv. 30–32; 2 Cor. i. 3–10; xi. 23–27. Such passages give us glimpses of the stormy background which lies behind St. Paul's Epistles. He is so absorbed in his ' Gospel' that this makes very little impression upon him. Indeed, as this chapter shows, the overwhelming sense of God's mercy and love fills him with such exultation of spirit that bodily suffering not only weighs like dust in the balance but positively serves to strengthen his constancy. The same feeling comes out in the ὑπερνικῶμεν of viii. 37: the whole passage is parallel.

ὑπομονήν: not merely a passive quality but a 'masculine constancy in holding out under trials' (Waite on 2 Cor. vi. 4), 'fortitude.' See on ii. 7 above.

4. δοκιμή: the character which results from the process of trial, the temper of the veteran as opposed to that of the raw recruit; cf. James i. 12, &c. The exact order of ὑπομονή and δοκιμή must not be pressed too far : in St. James i. 3 τὸ δοκίμιον τῆς πίστεως produces ὑπομονή. If St. James had seen this Epistle (which is doubtful) we might suppose that he had this passage in his mind. The conception is that of 2 Tim. ii. 3 (in the revised as well as the received text).

ἡ δὲ δοκιμὴ ἐλπίδα. It is quite intelligible as a fact of experience that the hope which is in its origin doctrinal should be strengthened by the hardening and bracing of character which come from actual conflict. Still the ultimate basis of it is the overwhelming sense of God's love, brought home through the Death of Christ; and to this the Apostle returns.

5. οὐ καταισχύνει : ' does not disappoint,' ' does not prove illusory.' The text Is. xxviii. 16 (LXX) caught the attention of the early Christians from the Messianic reference contained in it ('Behold, I lay in Zion,' &c.), and the assurance by which this was followed ('he that believeth shall not be put to shame') was confirmed to them by their own experience: the verse is directly quoted Rom. ix. 33 q. v.; 1 Pet. ii. 6.

ἡ ἀγάπη τοῦ Θεοῦ: certainly ' the love of God for us,' not ' our love for God' (Theodrt. Aug. and some moderns): ἀγάπη thus comes to mean, ' our *sense* of God's love,' just as εἰρήνη = ' our sense of peace with God.'

ἐκκέχυται. The idea of spiritual refreshment and encouragement is usually conveyed in the East through the metaphor of *watering*. St. Paul seems to have had in his mind Is. xliv. 3 'I will pour water upon him that is thirsty, and streams upon the dry ground: I will *pour My Spirit* upon thy seed,' &c.

διὰ Πνεύματος Ἁγίου: without the art., for the Spirit *as imparted*.

St. Paul refers all his conscious experience of the privileges of Christianity to the operation of the Holy Spirit, dating from the time when he definitively enrolled himself as a Christian, i. e. from his baptism.

6. ἔτι γάρ. There is here a difficult, but not really very important, variety of reading, the evidence for which may be thus summarized :—

> ἔτι γάρ at the beginning of the verse with ἔτι also after ἀσθενῶν, the mass of MSS.

> ἔτι at the beginning of the verse only, some inferior MSS. (later stage of the Ecclesiastical text).

> εἰς τί γάρ (possibly representing ἵνα τί γάρ, *ut quid enim*), the Western text (Latin authorities).

> εἰ γάρ few authorities, partly Latin.

> εἴ γε B.

It is not easy to select from these a reading which shall account for all the variants. That indeed which has the best authority, the double ἔτι, does not seem to be tenable, unless we suppose an accidental repetition of the word either by St. Paul or his amanuensis. It would not be difficult to get ἔτι γάρ from ἵνα τί γάρ, or *vice versa*, through the doubling or dropping of ιν from the preceding word ημιν; nor would it be difficult to explain ἔτι γάρ from εἰ γάρ, or *vice versa*. We might then work our way back to an alternative εἰ γάρ or εἴ γε, which might be confused with each other through the use of an abbreviation. Fuller details are given below. We think on the whole that it is not improbable that here, as in iv. 1, B has preserved the original reading εἴ γε. For the meaning of εἴ γε (' so surely as ' Va.) see T. S. Evans in *Exp.* 1882, i. 176 f.; and the note on iii. 30 above.

In more detail the evidence stands thus: ἔτι γάρ here with ἔτι also after ἀσθενῶν א A C D* *al.*: ἔτι here only Dᶜ E K L P &c. : εἰς τί γάρ Dᵇ F G : *ut quid enim* Lat.-Vet. Vulg., Iren.-lat. Faustin: εἰ γάρ 104 Greg. (= h Scriv.), fuld., Isid.-Pelus. Aug. *bis*: εἰ γὰρ... ἔτι Boh. ('For if, we being still weak,' &c.): εἰ δέ Pesh. : εἴ γε B. [The readings are wrongly given by Lips., and not quite correctly even by Gif., through overlooking the commas in Tisch. The statement which is at once fullest and most exact will be found in WH.] It thus appears: (1) that the reading most strongly supported is ἔτι γάρ, with double ἔτι, which is impossible unless we suppose a *lapsus calami* between St. Paul and his amanuensis. (2) The Western reading is εἰς τί γάρ, which may conceivably be a paraphrastic equivalent for an original ἵνα τί γάρ (Gif., from *ut quid enim* of Iren.-lat. &c.): this is no doubt a very early reading. (3) Another sporadic reading is εἰ γάρ. (4) B alone gives εἴ γε. So far as sense goes this is the best, and there are not a few cases in N. T. where the reading of B alone strongly commends itself (cf. iv. 1 above). But the problem is, how to account for the other readings? It would not be difficult palaeographically from εἰ γάρ to get ἔτι γάρ by dittography of ι (ειγαρ, ειιγαρ, ετιγαρ), or from this again to get εἰς τί γάρ through dittography of ε and confusion with ϲ (εϲτιγαρ) ; or we might take the alternative ingeniously suggested by Gif., of supposing that the original reading was ἵνα

-ί γάρ, of which the first two letters had been absorbed by the previous ἡμῖν (ημιν[ιν]ατιγαρ). There would thus be no great difficulty in accounting for the origin either of ἔτι γάρ or of the group of Western readings; and the primitive variants would be reduced to the two, ει ϝαρ and ει ϝε. Dr. Hort proposed to account for these by a conjectural ει περ, which would be a conceivable root for all the variations—partly through paraphrase and partly through errors of transcription. We might however escape the necessity of resorting to conjecture by supposing confusion between ϝε and the abbreviation ϝϸ. [For this form see T. W. Allen, *Notes on Abbreviations in Greek MSS.* (Oxford, 1889), p. 9 and pl. iii; Lehmann, *Die tachygraphischen Abkürzungen d. griech. Handschriften* (Leipzig, 1880), p. 91 f. taf. 9. We believe that the oldest extant example is in the *Fragmentum Mathematicum Bobiense* of the seventh century (Wattenbach, *Script. Graec. Specim.* tab. 8), where the abbreviation appears in a corrupt form. But we know that shorthand was very largely practised in the early centuries (cf. Eus. *H. E.* VI. xxiii. 2), and it may have been used by Tertius himself.] Where we have such a tangled skein to unravel as this it is impossible to speak very confidently; but we suspect that εἴ γε, as it makes the best sense, may also be the original reading.

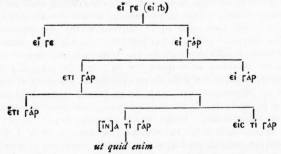

ut quid enim

ἀσθενῶν: 'incapable' of working out any righteousness for ourselves.

κατὰ καιρόν. St. Paul is strongly impressed with the fitness of the moment in the world's history which Christ chose for His intervention in it. This idea is a striking link of connexion between the (practically) acknowledged and the disputed Epistles; compare on the one hand Gal. iv. 4; 2 Cor. vi. 2; Rom. iii. 26; and on the other hand Eph. i. 10; 1 Tim. ii. 6; vi. 15; Tit. i. 3.

7. μόλις γάρ. The γάρ explains how this dying for sinners is a conspicuous proof of love. A few may face death for a good man, still fewer for a righteous man, but in the case of Christ there is more even than this; He died for declared enemies of God.

For μόλις the first hand of ℵ and Orig. read μόγις, which has more attestation in Luke ix. 39. The two words were easily confused both in sense and in writing.

ὑπὲρ δικαίου. There is clearly in this passage a contrast between ὑπὲρ δικαίου and ὑπὲρ τοῦ ἀγαθοῦ. They are not expressions which may be taken as roughly synonymous (Mey.-W. Lips. &c.). but it is implied that it is an easier thing to die for the ἀγαθός than for the δίκαιος. Similarly the Gnostics drew a distinction between the God of the O. T. and the God of the N. T., calling the one δίκαιος and the other ἀγαθός (Iren. *Adv. Haer.* I. xxvii. 1; comp. other passages and authorities quoted by Gif. p. 123). The δίκαιος keeps to the 'letter of his bond'; about the ἀγαθός there is something warmer and more genial such as may well move to self-sacrifice and devotion.

In face of the clear and obvious parallel supplied by Irenaeus, not to speak of others, it should not be argued as it is by Weiss and Lips. (who make τοῦ ἀγαθοῦ neut.) and even by Mey. and Dr. T. K. Abbott (*Essays*, p. 75) that there is no substantial difference between δίκαιος and ἀγαθός. We ourselves often use 'righteous' and 'good' as equivalent without effacing the distinction between them when there is any reason to emphasize it. The stumbling-block of the art. before ἀγαθοῦ and not before δικαίου need not stand in the way. This is sufficiently explained by Gif., who points out that the clause beginning with μόλις is virtually negative, so that δικαίου is indefinite and does not need the art., while the affirmative clause implies a definite instance which the art. indicates.

We go therefore with most English and American scholars (Stuart, Hodge, Gif. Va. Lid.) against some leading Continental names in maintaining what appears to be the simple and natural sense of the passage.

8. συνίστησι: see on iii. 5.

τὴν ἑαυτοῦ ἀγάπην: 'His *own* love,' emphatic, prompted from within not from without. Observe that the death of Christ is here referred to the will of the Father, which lies behind the whole of what is commonly (and not wrongly) called the 'scheme of re-demption.' Gif. excellently remarks that the 'proof of God's love towards us drawn from the death of Christ is strong in proportion to the closeness of the union between God and Christ.' It is the death of One who is nothing less than 'the Son.'

τὴν ἑαυτοῦ ἀγάπην εἰς ἡμᾶς ὁ Θεός ℵACKP &c.: ὁ Θεὸς εἰς ἡμᾶς DEFGL: om. ὁ Θεός B. There is no substantial difference of meaning, as εἰς ἡμᾶς in any case goes with συνίστησι, not with ἀγάπην.

ὑπὲρ ἡμῶν ἀπέθανε. St. Paul uses emphatic language, 1 Cor. xv. 1–3, to show that this doctrine was not confined to himself but was a common property of Christians.

9. St. Paul here separates between 'justification,' the pronouncing 'not guilty' of sinners in the past and their final salvation from the wrath to come. He also clearly connects the act of justification with the bloodshedding of Christ: he would have said with the author of Heb. ix. 22 χωρὶς αἱματεκχυσίας οὐ γίνεται ἄφεσις, see p. 92 above.

No clearer passage can be quoted for distinguishing the spheres of justification and sanctification than this verse and the next—the one an objective fact accomplished without us, the other a change operated within us. Both, though in different ways, proceed from Christ.

δι' αὐτοῦ : explained by the next verse ἐν τῇ ζωῇ αὐτοῦ. That which saves the Christian from final judgement is his union with the living Christ.

10. κατηλλάγημεν. The natural *prima facie* view is that the reconciliation is mutual ; and this view appears to verify itself on examination : see below.

ἐν τῇ ζωῇ αὐτοῦ. For the full meaning of this see the notes on ch. vi. 8–11 ; viii. 10, 11.

11. καυχώμενοι (א B C D, &c.) is decisively attested for καυχώμεθα, which was doubtless due to an attempt to improve the construction. The part. is loosely attached to what precedes, and must be taken as in sense equivalent to καυχώμεθα. In any case it is present and not future (as if constructed with σωθησόμεθα). We may compare a similar loose attachment of δικαιούμενοι in ch. iii. 24.

The Idea of Reconciliation or Atonement.

The καταλλαγή described in these verses is the same as the εἰρήνη of ver. 1; and the question necessarily meets us, What does this εἰρήνη or καταλλαγή mean? Is it a change in the attitude of man to God or in that of God to man? Many high authorities contend that it is only a change in the attitude of man to God.

Thus Lightfoot on Col. i. 21 : ' ἐχθρούς, " *hostile* to God," as the consequence of ἀπηλλοτριωμένους not "*hateful* to God," as it is taken by some. The active rather than the passive sense of ἐχθρούς is required by the context, which (as commonly in the N. T.) speaks of the sinner as reconciled to God, not of God as reconciled to the sinner . . . It is the mind of man, not the mind of God, which must undergo a change, that a reunion may be effected.'

Similarly Westcott on 1 Jo. ii. 2 (p. 85) : ' Such phrases as " propitiating God " and " God being reconciled " are foreign to the language of the N. T. Man is reconciled (2 Cor. v. 18 ff. ; Rom. v. 10 f.). There is " propitiation " in the matter of sin or of the sinner. The love of God is the same throughout; but He " cannot " in virtue of His very nature welcome the impenitent and sinful: and more than this, He " cannot " treat sin as if it were not sin. This being so, the ἱλασμός, when it is applied to the sinner, so to speak, neutralizes the sin.' [A difficult and it may be thought hardly tenable distinction. The relation of God to sin is not merely passive but active ; and the term ἱλασμός is properly

used in reference to a personal agent. *Some one* is 'propitiated':
and who can this be, but God?]

The same idea is a characteristic feature in the theology of
Ritschl (*Recht. u. Vers.* ii. 230 ff.).

No doubt there are passages where ἐχθρός denotes the hostility
and καταλλαγή the reconciliation of man to God; but taking the
language of Scripture as a whole, it does not seem that it can be
explained in this way.

(1) In the immediate context we have τὴν καταλλαγὴν ἐλάβομεν,
implying that the reconciliation comes to man from the side of
God, and is not directly due to any act of his own. We may
compare the familiar χάρις καὶ εἰρήνη, to which is usually added ἀπὸ
Θεοῦ in the greetings of the Epistles.

(2) In Rom. xi. 28 ἐχθροί is opposed to ἀγαπητοί, where ἀγαπητοί
must be passive ('beloved by God'), so that it is hardly possible
that ἐχθροί can be entirely active, though it may be partly so: it
seems to correspond to our word 'hostile.'

(3) It is difficult to dissociate such words as ἱλαστήριον (Rom. iii.
25), ἱλασμός (1 Jo. ii. 2) from the idea of propitiating a person.

(4) There is frequent mention of the Anger of God as directed
against sinners, not merely at the end of all things, but also at this
present time (Rom. i. 18, &c.). When that Anger ceases to be
so directed there is surely a change (or what we should be compelled to call a change) on the part of God as well as of man.

We infer that the natural explanation of the passages which
speak of enmity and reconciliation between God and man is that
they are not on one side only, but are mutual.

At the same time we must be well aware that this is only our
imperfect way of speaking: κατὰ ἄνθρωπον λέγω must be written
large over all such language. We are obliged to use anthropo-
morphic expressions which imply a change of attitude or relation
on the part of God as well as of man; and yet in some way which
we cannot wholly fathom we may believe that with Him there is
'no variableness, neither shadow of turning.'

THE FALL OF ADAM AND THE WORK OF CHRIST.

V. 12-14. *What a contrast does this last description
suggest between the Fall of Adam and the justifying Work
of Christ! There is indeed parallelism as well as contrast.
For it is true that as Christ brought righteousness and life,
so Adam's Fall brought sin and death. If death prevailed
throughout the pre-Mosaic period, that could not be due solely*

to the act of those who died. Death is the punishment of
sin; but they had not sinned against law as Adam had.
The true cause then was not their own sin, but Adam's;
whose fall thus had consequences extending beyond itself, like
the redeeming act of Christ.

[12] The description just given of the Work of Christ, first justifying
and reconciling the sinner, and then holding out to him the hope
of final salvation, brings out forcibly the contrast between the
two great Representatives of Humanity—Adam and Christ. The
act by which Adam fell, like the act of Christ, had a far-reaching
effect upon mankind. Through his Fall, Sin, as an active principle,
first gained an entrance among the human race; and Sin brought
with it the doom of (physical) Death. So that, through Adam's
Fall, death pervaded the whole body of his descendants, because
they one and all fell into sin, and died as he had died. [13] When
I say 'they sinned' I must insert a word of qualification. In the
strict sense of full responsibility, they could not sin: for that
attaches only to sin against law, and they had as yet no law to
sin against. [14] Yet they suffered the full penalty of sin. All
through the long period which intervened between Adam and the
Mosaic legislation, the tyrant Death held sway; even though
those who died had not sinned, as Adam had, in violation of
an express command. This proved that something deeper was
at work: and that could only be the transmitted effect of Adam's
sin. It is this transmitted effect of a single act which made Adam
a type of the coming Messiah.

12. διὰ τοῦτο : points to the logical connexion with what precedes. It has been argued, at somewhat disproportionate length,
whether this refers to ver. 11 only (Fricke, *De Mente dogmatica loci*
Paulini ad Rom. v. 12 sq., Lipsiae, 1880, Mey., Philippi, Beet), or
to vv. 9–11 (Fri.), or to vv. 1–11 (Rothe, Hofmann), or to the
whole discussion from i. 17 onwards (Beng., Schott, Reiche,
Rückert). We cannot lay down so precisely how much was
consciously present to the mind of the Apostle. But as the leading idea of the whole section is the comparison of the train of
consequences flowing from the Fall of Adam with the train of
consequences flowing from the Justifying Act of Christ, it seems
natural to include at least as much as contains a brief outline of
that work, i. e. as far as vv. 1–11.

That being so, we cannot with Fricke infer from ver. 11 that St. Paul only wishes to compare the result of *death* in the one case with that of *life* in the other. Fricke, however, is right in saying that his object is not to inquire into the origin of death or sin. The origin of both is assumed, not propounded as anything new. This is important for the understanding of the bearings of the passage. All turns on this, that the effects of Adam's Fall were transmitted to his descendants; but St. Paul nowhere says *how* they were transmitted; nor does he even define in precise terms *what* is transmitted. He seems, however, to mean (1) the liability to sin, (2) the liability to die as the punishment of sin.

ὥσπερ. The structure of the paragraph introduced by this word (to the end of ver. 14) is broken in a manner very characteristic of St. Paul. He begins the sentence as if he intended it to run: ὥσπερ δι᾽ ἑνὸς ἀνθρώπου ἡ ἁμαρτία εἰς τὸν κόσμον εἰσῆλθε, καὶ διὰ τῆς ἁμαρτίας ὁ θάνατος . . . οὕτω καὶ δι᾽ ἑνὸς ἀνθρώπου ἡ δικαιοσύνη εἰσῆλθε, καὶ διὰ τῆς δικαιοσύνης ἡ ζωή. But the words διὰ τῆς ἁμαρτίας ὁ θάνατος bring up the subject which St. Paul is intending to raise, viz. the connexion of sin and death with the Fall of Adam: he goes off upon this, and when he has discussed it sufficiently for his purpose, he does not return to the form of sentence which he had originally planned, but he attaches the clause comparing Christ to Adam by a relative (ὅς ἐστι τύπος τοῦ μέλλοντος) to the end of his digression: and so what should have been the main apodosis of the whole paragraph becomes merely subordinate. It is a want of finish in style due to eagerness and intensity of thought; but the meaning is quite clear. Compare the construction of ii. 16; iii. 8, 26.

ἡ ἁμαρτία: Sin, as so often, is personified: it is a malignant force let loose among mankind: see the fuller note at the end of the chapter.

εἰς τὸν κόσμον εἰσῆλθε: a phrase which, though it reminds us specially of St. John (John i. 9, 10; iii. 17, 19; vi. 14; ix. 5, 39; x. 36, &c.), is not peculiar to him (cf. 1 Tim. i. 15; Heb. x. 5). St. John and the author of Heb. apply it to the personal incarnation of the Logos; here it is applied to the impersonal self-diffusion of evil.

ὁ θάνατος. Some have taken this to mean 'eternal death,' chiefly on the ground of vv. 17, 21, where it seems to be opposed to 'eternal life.' Oltr. is the most strenuous supporter of this view. But it is far simpler and better to take it of 'physical death': because (1) this is clearly the sense of ver. 14; (2) it is the sense of Gen. ii. 17; iii. 19; to which St. Paul is evidently alluding. It seems probable that even in vv. 17, 21, the idea is in the first instance physical. But St. Paul does not draw the

marked distinction that we do between this life and the life to
come. The mention of death in any sense is enough to suggest
the contrast of life in all its senses. The Apostle's argument
is that the gift of life and the benefits wrought by Christ are
altogether wider in their range than the penalty of Adam's sin;
ὑπερεπερίσσευσεν ἡ χάρις is the keynote of the passage. It is not
necessary that the two sides of the antithesis should exactly correspond. In each particular the scale weighs heavily in favour
of the Christian.

The Western text (D E F G, &c.) omits this word altogether. Aug.
makes the subject of the vb. not death but sin : he makes it a charge against
the Pelagians that they understood in the second place ὁ θάνατος.

διῆλθεν: contains the force of distribution; 'made its way to
each individual member of the race': καθάπερ τις κλῆρος πατρὸς
διαβὰς ἐπὶ τοὺς ἐγγόνους ('like a father's inheritance divided among
his children'), Euthym.-Zig.

ἐφ' ᾧ. Though this expression has been much fought over,
there can now be little doubt that the true rendering is 'because.'
(1) Orig. followed by the Latin commentators Aug. and Ambrstr.
took the rel. as masc. with antecedent Ἀδάμ: 'in whom,' i. e. 'in
Adam.' But in that case (i) ἐπί would not be the right preposition ; (ii) ᾧ would be too far removed from its antecedent.
(2) Some Greeks quoted by Photius also took the rel. as masc.
with antecedent θάνατος : 'in which,' i. e. 'in death,' which is
even more impossible. (3) Some moderns, taking ᾧ as neut. and
the whole phrase as equivalent to a conjunction, have tried to
get out of it other meanings than 'because.' So (i) 'in like
manner as' ('all died, *just as* all sinned'), Rothe, De Wette;
(ii) (= ἐφ' ὅσον) 'in proportion as,' 'in so far as' ('all died, *in so
far as* all sinned'), Ewald, Tholuck (ed. 1856) and others. But
the Greek will not bear either of these senses. (4) ᾧ is rightly
taken as neut., and the phrase ἐφ' ᾧ as conj.='because' ('for
that' AV. and RV.) by Theodrt. Phot. Euthym.-Zig. and the mass
of modern commentators. This is in agreement with Greek
usage and is alone satisfactory.

ἐφ' ᾧ in classical writers more often means 'on condition that': cf.
Thuc. i. 113 σπονδὰς ποιησάμενοι ἐφ' ᾧ τοὺς ἄνδρας κομιοῦνται, ' on condition of getting back their prisoners,' &c. The plural ἐφ' οἷς is more
common, as in ἀνθ' ὧν, ἐξ ὧν, δι' ὧν. In N. T. the phrase occurs three
times, always as it would seem=*propterea quod*, 'because': cf. 2 Cor. v. 4
στενάζομεν βαρούμενοι· ἐφ' ᾧ οὐ θέλομεν ἐκδύσασθαι κ.τ.λ.; Phil. iii. 12
ἐφ' ᾧ καὶ κατελήφθην ὑπὸ Χ. Ἰ. (where 'seeing that' or 'because' appears
to be the more probable rendering). So Phavorinus (d. 1537; a lexico-
grapher of the Renaissance period, who incorporated the contents of older
works, but here seems to be inventing his examples) ἐφ' ᾧ ἀντὶ τοῦ διότι
λέγουσιν Ἀττικοί, οἶον ἐφ' ᾧ τὴν κλοπὴν εἰργάσω ('because you committed the theft') κ.τ.λ.

ἐφ' ᾧ πάντες ἥμαρτον. Here lies the *crux* of this difficult passage. In what sense did 'all sin'? (1) Many, including even Meyer, though explaining ἐφ' ᾧ as neut. rather than masc., yet give to the sentence as a whole a meaning practically equivalent to that which it has if the antecedent of ᾧ is Ἀδάμ. Bengel has given this classical expression: *omnes peccarunt, Adamo peccante*, 'all sinned implicitly in the sin of Adam,' his sin involved theirs. The objection is that the words supplied are far too important to be left to be understood. If St. Paul had meant this, why did he not say so? The insertion of ἐν Ἀδάμ would have removed all ambiguity. (2) The Greek commentators for the most part supply nothing, but take ἥμαρτον in its usual sense: 'all sinned in their own persons, and on their own initiative.' So Euthym.-Zig.: διότι πάντες ἥμαρτον ἀκολουθήσαντες τῷ προπάτορι κατά γε τὸ ἁμαρτῆσαι. The objection to this is that it destroys the parallelism between Adam and Christ: besides, St. Paul goes on to show in the same breath that they could not sin in the same way that Adam did. Sin implies law; but Adam's descendants had no law. (3) It is possible however to take ἥμαρτον in its ordinary sense without severing the connexion between Adam and his posterity. If they sinned, their sin was due in part to tendencies inherited from Adam. So practically Stuart, Fricke, Weiss, &c. There still remains the difficulty as to the connexion of this clause with what follows: see the next note.

> It is a further argument in favour of the view taken above that a very similar sequence of thought is found in 4 Ezra. Immediately after laying down that the sin of Adam's descendants is due to that *malignitas radicis* which they inherit from their forefather (see the passage quoted in full below), the writer goes on to describe this sin as a repetition of Adam's due to the fact that they too had within them the *cor malignum* as he had: *Et deliquerunt qui habitabant civitatem, in omnibus facientes sicut fecit Adam et omnes generationes eius, utebantur enim et ipsi corde maligno* (4 Ezra iii. 25 f.). Other passages may be quoted both from 4 Ezra and from *Apoc. Baruch.* which lay stress at once on the inherited tendency to sin and on the freedom of choice in those who give way to it : see the fuller note below.

13. ἄχρι γὰρ νόμου κ.τ.λ. At first sight this seems to give a reason for just the opposite of what is wanted: it seems to prove not that πάντες ἥμαρτον, but that however much men might sin they had not at least the full guilt of sin. This is really what St. Paul aims at proving. There is an under-current all through the passage, showing how there was something else at work besides the guilt of individuals. That 'something' is the effect of Adam's Fall. The Fall gave the predisposition to sin; and the Fall linked together sin and death.

St. Paul would not say that the absence of written law did away with all responsibility. He has already laid down most distinctly that Gentiles, though without such written law, have law enough to be judged by (ii. 12–16); and Jews before the time of Moses were only in the position of Gentiles. But the degree of their guilt could not be the same either as that of Adam, or as that of the Jews after the Mosaic legislation. Perhaps it might be regarded as an open question whether, apart from Adam, pre-Mosaic sins would have been punishable with death. What St. Paul wishes to bring out is that prior to the giving of the Law, the fate of mankind, to an extent and in a way which he does not define, was directly traceable to Adam's Fall.

ἁμαρτία δὲ οὐκ ἐλλογεῖται κ.τ.λ. The thought is one which had evidently taken strong hold on St. Paul: see on iv. 15, and the parallels there quoted.

ἐλλογεῖται: 'brought into account' (Gif.), as of an entry made in a ledger. The word also occurs in Philem. 18, where see Lightfoot's note.

ἐλλογεῖται (or ἐνλογεῖται) N°BCDEFGKLP, &c., ἐλλογᾶται N^d : ἐνελογεῖτο N*, ἐλλογᾶτο A 52 108; *imputabatur* Vulg. *codd.* Ambrstr. *al.* The imperf. appears to be a (mistaken) correction due to the context. As to the form of the verb: ἐλλόγα is decisively attested in Philem. 18; but it would not follow that the same form was used here where St. Paul is employing a different amanuensis: however, as the tendency of the MSS. is rather to obliterate vernacular forms than to introduce them, there is perhaps a slight balance of probability in favour of ἐλλογᾶται: see Westcott and Hort, *Notes on Orthography* in Appendix to *Introd.* p. 166 ff.

14. ἐβασίλευσεν ὁ θάνατος. St. Paul appeals to the universal prevalence of death, which is personified, as sin had been just before, under the figure of a grim tyrant, in proof of the mischief wrought by Adam's Fall. Nothing but the Fall could account for that universal prevalence. Sin and death had their beginnings together, and they were propagated side by side.

On the certainty and universality of Death, regarded as a penalty, comp. Seneca, *Nat. Quaest.* ii. 59 *Eodem citius tardiusve veniendum est . . . In omnes constitutum est capitale supplicium et quidem constitutione iustissima. nam quod magnum solet esse solatium extrema passuris, quorum eadem causa et sors eadem est.* Similarly Philo speaks of τὸν συμφυᾶ νεκρὸν ἡμῶν, τὸ σῶμα (*De Gigant.* 3 ; ed. Mang. i. 264). Elsewhere he goes a step further and asserts ὅτι παντὶ γεννητῷ . . . συμφυὲς τὸ ἁμαρτάνειν. For parallels in 4 Ezra and *Apoc. Baruch.* see below.

ἐπὶ τοὺς μὴ ἁμαρτήσαντας. A number of authorities, mostly Latin Fathers, but including also the important margin of Cod. 67 with three other cursives, the first hand of d, and the Greek of Orig. at least once, omit the negative, making the reign of death extend only over those who had sinned after the likeness of Adam. So Orig.-lat. (Rufinus) repeatedly and expressly, Latin MSS. known to Aug., the 'older Latin MSS.' according to Ambrstr. and Sedulius. The comment of Ambrstr. is interesting as showing a certain grasp of critical principles, though it was difficult for any one in those days to have sufficient command of MSS. to know the real state of the evidence. Ambrstr. prefers in this case the evidence of the Latin MSS., because those with which he is acquainted are older than the Greek, and represent, as he thinks, an older form of text. He claims that this form has the support of Tertullian,

Cyprian and Victorinus—a statement which we are not at present able to verify. He accounts for the Greek reading by the usual theory of heretical corruption. There is a similar question of the insertion or omission of a negative in Rom. iv. 19 (q.v.), Gal. ii. 5. In two out of the three cases the Western text omits the negative, but in ch. iv. 19 it inserts it.

τύπος (τύπτω): (1) the 'impression' left by a sharp blow (τὸν τύπον τῶν ἥλων John xx. 25), in particular the 'stamp' struck by a die; (2) inasmuch as such a stamp bears the figure on the face of the die, 'copy,' 'figure,' or 'representation'; (3) by a common transition from effect to cause, 'mould,' 'pattern,' 'exemplar'; (4) hence in the special sense of the word type, which we have adopted from the Greek of the N.T., 'an event or person in history corresponding in certain characteristic features to another event or person.' That which comes first in order of time is properly the type, that which comes afterwards the antitype (ἀντίτυπος 1 Pet. iii. 21). These correspondences form a part of the Divine economy of revelation: see esp. Cheyne, *Isaiah*, ii. 170 ff. (Essay III, 'On the Christian Element in the Book of Isaiah').

τοῦ μέλλοντος. (1) The entirely personal nature of the whole comparison prevents us from taking τοῦ μέλλ. as neut. = 'that which was to come' (Beng., Oltramare). If St. Paul had intended this, he would have written τοῦ μέλλοντος αἰῶνος. (2) Neither is it probable that we have here a direct allusion to the Rabbinical designation of the Messiah as ὁ δεύτερος or ὁ ἔσχατος Ἀδάμ (1 Cor. xv. 45, 47). If St. Paul had intended this, he would have written τοῦ μέλλοντος Ἀδάμ. (3) The context makes it clear enough who is intended. The first representative of the human race as such prefigured its second Great Representative, whose coming lay in the future: this is sufficiently brought out by the expression 'of Him who was to be.' ὁ μέλλων thus approximates in meaning to ὁ ἐρχόμενος (Matt. xi. 3; Luke vii. 19; Heb. x. 37), which however appears not to have been, as it is sometimes regarded, a standing designation for the Messiah *. In any case τοῦ μέλλοντος = 'Him who *was* to come' when Adam fell, not 'who *is* (still) to come' (Fri. De W.).

The Effects of Adam's Fall in Jewish Theology.

Three points come out clearly in these verses: (1) the Fall of Adam brought death not only to Adam himself but to his descendants; (2) the Fall of Adam also brought sin and the tendency to sin; (3) and yet in spite of this the individual does not lose his responsibility. All three propositions receive some partial illustration from Jewish sources, though the Talmud does

---

* 'The designation "The Coming One" (*Habba*), though a most truthful expression of Jewish expectancy, was not one ordinarily used of the Messiah.' Edersheim, *L. & T.* i. p. 668.

not seem to have had any consistent doctrine on the subject.
Dr. Edersheim says expressly: 'So far as their opinions can be
gathered from their writings the great doctrines of Original Sin and
of the sinfulness of our whole nature, were not held by the ancient
Rabbis' (*Life and Times*, &c. i. 165). Still there are approximations, especially in the writings on which we have drawn so freely
already, the Fourth Book of Ezra and the Apocalypse of Baruch.

(1) The evidence is strongest as to the connexion between Adam's sin and
the introduction of death. 'There were,' says Dr. Edersheim, 'two divergent
opinions—the one ascribing death to personal, the other to Adam's guilt'
(*op. cit.* i. 166). It is however allowed that the latter view greatly pre-
ponderated. Traces of it are found as far back as the Sapiential Books:
e.g. Wisd. ii. 23 f. ὁ Θεὸς ἔκτισεν τὸν ἄνθρωπον ἐπ' ἀφθαρσίᾳ . . . φθόνῳ δὲ
διαβόλου θάνατος εἰσῆλθεν εἰς τὸν κόσμον, where we note the occurrence of
St. Paul's phrase; Ecclus. xxv. 24 [33] δι' αὐτὴν (sc. τὴν γυναῖκα) ἀποθνή-
σκομεν πάντες. The doctrine is also abundantly recognized in 4 Ezra and
Apoc. Baruch.: 4 Ezr. iii. 7 *et huic* (sc. *Adamo*) *mandasti diligere viam
tuam, et praeterivit eam; et statim instituisti in eum mortem et in
nationibus* (= *generationibus*) *eius*: *Apoc. Baruch.* xvii. 3 (*Adam*) *mortem
attulit et abscidit annos eorum qui ab eo geniti fuerunt*: *ibid.* xxiii. 4
Quando peccavit Adam et decreta fuit mors contra eos qui gignerentur.

(2) We are warned (by Dr. Edersheim in *Sp. Comm. Apocr. ad loc.*) not
to identify the statement of Ecclus. xxv. 24 [33] ἀπὸ γυναικὸς ἀρχὴ ἁμαρτίας
with the N. T. doctrine of Original Sin: still it points in that direction; we
have just seen that the writer deduces from Eve the death of all mankind,
and in like manner he also seems to deduce from her (ἀπὸ γυν.) the *initium
peccandi*. More explicit are 4 Ezra iii. 21 f. *Cor enim malignum baiulans
primus Adam transgressus et victus est, sed et omnes qui de eo nati sunt:
et facta est permanens infirmitas, et lex cum corde populi, cum malignitate
radicis; et discessit quod bonum est, et mansit malignum*: *ibid.* iv. 30
*Quoniam granum seminis mali seminatum est in corde Adam ab initio, et
quantum impietatis generavit usque nunc, et generat usque dum veniat area*:
ibid. vii. 48 (118) *O tu quid fecisti Adam? Si enim tu peccasti, non est factus
solius tuus casus, sed et nostrum qui ex te advenimus.*

(3) And yet along with all this we have the explicit assertion of responsibility on the part of all who sin. This appears in the passage quoted above
on ver. 12 (*ad fin.*). To the same effect are 4 Ezr. viii. 59 f. *Non enim
Altissimus voluit hominem disperdi, sed ipsi qui creati sunt coinquinaverunt
nomen eius qui fecit eos*: *ibid.* ix. 11 *qui fastidierunt legem meam cum adhuc
erant habentes libertatem.* But the classical passage is *Apoc. Baruch.*
liv. 15, 19 *Si enim Adam prior peccavit, et attulit mortem super omnes
immaturam; sed etiam illi qui ex eo nati sunt, unusquisque ex eis praepa-
ravit animae suae tormentum futurum: et iterum unusquisque ex eis
elegit sibi gloriam futuram* . . . *Non est ergo Adam causa, nisi animae suae
tantum; nos vero unusquisque fuit animae suae Adam.*

The teaching of these passages does not really conflict with that of the
Talmud. The latter is thus summarized by Weber (*Altsyn. Theol.* p. 216):
'By the Fall man came under a curse, is guilty of death, and his right
relation to God is rendered difficult. More than this cannot be said. Sin,
to which the bent and leaning had already been planted in man by creation,
had become a fact; the "evil impulse" (= *cor malignum*) gained the mastery
over mankind, who can only resist it by the greatest efforts; before the Fall
it had had power over him, but no such ascendancy (*Uebermacht*).' Hence
when the same writer says a little further on that according to the Rabbis
'there is such a thing as transmission of guilt, but not such a thing as trans-

mission of sin (*Es gibt eine Erbschuld, aber keine Erbsünde*),' the negative proposition is due chiefly to the clearness with which the Rabbis (like *Apoc. Baruch.*) insist upon free-will and direct individual responsibility.

It seems to us a mistake to place the teaching of St. Paul in too marked opposition to this. There is no fundamental inconsistency between his views and those of his contemporaries. He does not indeed either affirm or deny the existence of the *cor malignum* before the Fall, nor does he use such explicit language as *nos vero unusquisque fuit animae suae Adam* : on the other hand he does define more exactly than the Rabbis the nature of human responsibility both under the Law (ch. vii. 7 ff.) and without it (ii. 12-15). But here, as elsewhere in dealing with this mysterious subject (see p. 267 below), he practically contents himself with leaving the two complementary truths side by side. Man inherits his nature; and yet he must not be allowed to shift responsibility from himself: there is that within him by virtue of which he is free to choose ; and on that freedom of choice he must stand or fall.

ADAM AND CHRIST.

V. 15-21. *So far the parallelism: but note also the contrast. How superior the Work of Christ!* (1) *How different in quality: the one act all sin, the other act all bounty or grace!* (ver. 15). (2) *How different in quantity, or mode of working: one act tainting the whole race with sin, and a multitude of sins collected together in one only to be forgiven!* (ver. 16). (3) *How different and surpassing in its whole character and consequences: a reign of Death and a reign of Life!* (ver. 17). *Summarizing: Adam's Fall brought sin: Law increased it: but the Work of Grace has cancelled, and more than cancelled, the effect of Law* (vv. 18-21).

[15] In both cases there is a transmission of effects: but there the resemblance ends. In all else the false step (or Fall, as we call it) of Adam and the free gift of God's bounty are most unlike. The fall of that one representative man entailed death upon the many members of the race to which he belonged. Can we then be surprised if an act of such different quality—the free unearned favour of God, and the gift of righteousness bestowed through

the kindness of that other Representative Man, Jesus Messiah
—should have not only cancelled the effect of the Fall, but
also brought further blessings to the whole race? [16] There is
a second difference between this boon bestowed through Christ
and the ill effects of one man's sinning. The sentence pronounced upon Adam took its rise in the act of a single man, and
had for its result a sweeping verdict of condemnation. But the
gift bestowed by God inverts this procedure. It took its rise in
many faults, and it had for its result a verdict declaring sinners
righteous. [17] Yet once more. Through the single fault of the one
man Adam the tyrant Death began its reign through that one
sole agency. Much more then shall the Christian recipients of
that overflowing kindness and of the inestimable gift of righteousness—much more shall they also reign, not in death but in life,
through the sole agency of Jesus Messiah.

[18] To sum up. On one side we have the cause, a single Fall;
and the effect, extending to all men, condemnation. On the other
side we have as cause, a single absolving act; and as effect, also
extending to all, a like process of absolution, carrying with it life.
[19] For as through the disobedience of the one man Adam all
mankind were placed in the class and condition of 'sinners,' so
through the obedience (shown in His Death upon the Cross) of the
one man, Christ, the whole multitude of believers shall be placed
in the class and condition of 'righteous.' [20] Then Law came in,
as a sort of 'afterthought,' a secondary and subordinate stage,
in the Divine plan, causing the indefinite multiplication of sins
which, like the lapse or fall of Adam, were breaches of express
command. Multiplied indeed they were, but only with the result
of calling forth a still more abundant stream of pardoning grace.
[21] Hitherto Sin has sat enthroned in a kingdom of the dead;
its subjects have been sunk in moral and spiritual death. But this
has been permitted only in order that the Grace or Goodwill of
God might also set up its throne over a people fitted for its sway
by the gift of righteousness, and therefore destined not for death
but for eternal life—through the mediation of Jesus Messiah, our
Lord.

15. παράπτωμα: lit. 'a slip or fall sideways,' 'a false step,'
'a lapse': hence metaph. in a sense not very dissimilar to ἁμάρτημα

(which is prop. 'missing a mark'). It is however appropriate
that παράπτ. should be used for a 'fall' or first deflection from
uprightness, just as ἁμάρτ. is used of the failure of efforts towards
recovery.   On the word see Trench, *Syn.* p. 237 f.

τοῦ ἑνός : '*the* one man,' *i.e.* Adam.

οἱ πολλοί : 'the many,' practically = πάντας ver. 12 ; πάντας ἀνθρώ-
πους in ver. 18, 'all mankind.'   It is very misleading to translate
as AV., ignoring the article, if 'through the offence of *one, many*
be dead, by the obedience of *one* shall *many* be made righteous.'
Redemption like the Fall proceeds not from any chance member of
the human race, and its effects extend not only to 'many' but to
'all'—to 'all,' that is potentially, if they embrace the redemption
which is offered them.

See Bentley, quoted by Lft. *On Revision*, p. 97, 'By this accurate version
some hurtful mistakes about partial redemption and absolute reprobation
had been happily prevented. Our English readers had then seen, what
several of the Fathers saw and testified, that οἱ πολλοί, *the many*, in an antithesis to *the one*, are equivalent to πάντες, *all*, in ver. 12, and comprehend the
whole multitude, the entire species of mankind, exclusive only of *the one.*'

πολλῷ μᾶλλον.   What we know of the character of God as displayed in Christ makes us more certain of the good result than of
the evil.

ἡ δωρεά is more fully defined below (ver. 17) as ἡ δωρεὰ τῆς
δικαιοσύνης : the gift is the condition of righteousness into which
the sinner enters.   δωρεά, 'boon,' like δῶρον contrasted with δόμα,
is reserved for the highest and best gifts ; so Philo, *Leg. Alleg.* iii.
70 ἔμφασιν μεγέθους τελείων ἀγαθῶν δηλοῦσιν (Lft. *Rev.* p. 77) ; comp.
also the ascending scale of expression in Jas. i. 17.

ἐν χάριτι goes closely with ἡ δωρεά.   In classical Greek we should
have had the art. ἡ ἐν χάριτι, but in Hellenistic Greek a qualifying
phrase is attached to a subst. without repetition of the art.   Mey.
however and some others (including Lid.) separate ἐν χάριτι from ἡ
δωρεά and connect it with ἐπερίσσευσε.

χάρις is more often applied to God the Father, and is exhibited in the
whole scheme of salvation. As applied to Christ it is (1) that active favour
towards mankind which moved Him to intervene for their salvation (cf. esp.
2 Cor. viii. 9) ; (2) the same active favour shown to the individual by the
Father and the Son conjointly (Rom. i. 7 q. v.).

16.   The absence of verbs is another mark of compressed anti-
thetic style.   With the first clause we may supply ἐστί, with the
second ἐγένετο : 'And not as through one man's sinning, so is the
boon.   For the judgement sprang from one to condemnation, but
the free gift sprang from many trespasses (and ended in) a declaration of righteousness.'   In the one case there is expansion outwards, from one to many : in the other case there is contraction

inwards; the movement originates with many sins which are all embraced in a single sentence of absolution.

δικαίωμα : usually the decision, decree, or ordinance by which a thing is declared δίκαιον (that which gives a thing the force of 'right'); here the decision or sentence by which persons are declared δίκαιοι. The sense is determined by the antithesis to κατά-κριμα. δικαίωμα bears to δικαίωσις the relation of an act completed to an act in process (see p. 31 *sup.*).

17. πολλῷ μᾶλλον. Here the *a fortiori* argument lies in the nature of the two contrasted forces : God's grace must be more powerful in its working than man's sin.

τὴν περισσείαν... τῆς δωρεᾶς τῆς δικαιοσύνης λαμβάνοντες. Every term here points to that gift of righteousness here described as something objective and external to the man himself, not wrought within him but coming to him, imputed not infused. It has its source in the overflow of God's free favour; it is a gift which man *receives* : see pp. 25, 30 f., 36 above.

βασιλεύσουσι. The metaphor is present to St. Paul's mind; and having used it just before of the prevalence of Death, he naturally recurs to it in the sense more familiar to a Christian of his share in the Messianic blessings, of which the foremost was a heightened and glorified vitality, that ' eternal life' which is his already in germ.

διὰ τοῦ ἑνὸς Ἰησοῦ Χριστοῦ. The διά here covers the whole media-tion of the Son in reference to man : it is through His Death that the sinner on embracing Christianity enters upon the state of righteous-ness, and through the union with Him which follows that his whole being is vitalized and transfigured through time into eternity.

18. This and the three following verses, introduced by the strongly illative particles ἄρα οὖν, sum up the results of the whole comparison between Adam and Christ : the resemblance is set forth in vv. 18, 19 ; the difference and vast preponderance of the scale of blessing in vv. 20, 21.

Again we have a condensed antithesis—the great salient strokes confronting each other without formal construction : origin, extent, issue, alike parallel and alike opposed. ' As then, through one lapse, to all men, unto condemnation—so also, through one justifying act, to all men, unto justification of life.' There are two difficulties, the interpretation of δι' ἑνὸς δικαιώματος and of δικαίωσιν ζωῆς.

δι' ἑνὸς δικαιώματος. Does δικαίωμα here mean the same thing as in ver. 16? If so, it is the sentence by which God declares men righteous on account of Christ's Death. Or is it the merit of that Death itself, the 'righteous act,' or ὑπακοή, of Christ? A number of scholars (Holsten, Va. Lips. Lid.) argue that it must be the latter in order to correspond with δι' ἑνὸς παραπτώματος. So too Euthym.-Zig. δι' ἑνὸς δικαιώματος τοῦ Χ. τὴν ἄκραν δικαιοσύνην πεπληρωκότος. But it seems better, with Mey. Gif. and others, to give the same sense to δικαίωμα as in ver. 16. We saw that there the sense was fixed by κατάκριμα, which is repeated in the present verse. On the other hand it is doubtful whether δικαίωμα can quite ='a righteous act.' God's sentence and the act of Christ are so inseparable that the one may be used in the antithesis as naturally as the other.

It is best also to follow the natural construction of the Greek and make ἑνός neut. in agreement with δικαιώμ. (Mey.-W. Va. Gif.) rather than masc. (Lips.).

δικαίωσιν ζωῆς. 'Life' is both the immediate and ultimate result of that state of things into which the Christian enters when he is declared ' righteous ' or receives his sentence of absolution.

19. διὰ τῆς παρακοῆς . . . διὰ τῆς ὑπακοῆς. It is natural that this aspect of the Fall as παρακοή should be made prominent in a context which lays stress on the effect of law or express command in enhancing the heinousness of sin. It is natural also that in antithesis to this there should be singled out in the Death of Christ its special aspect as ὑπακοή: cf. Heb. v. 8, 9; Matt. xxvi. 39; Phil. ii. 8. On the word παρακοή ('a failing to hear,' *incuria*, and thence *inobedientia*) see Trench, *Syn.* p. 234.

κατεστάθησαν . . . κατασταθήσονται: 'were constituted' . . . 'shall be constituted.' But in what sense ' constituted'? The Greek word has the same ambiguity as the English. If we define further, the definition must come from the context. Here the context is sufficiently clear: it covers on the one hand the whole result of Adam's Fall for his descendants prior to and independently of their own deliberate act of sin; and it covers on the other hand the whole result of the redeeming act of Christ so far as that too is accomplished objectively and apart from active concurrence on the part of the Christian. The fut. κατασταθήσονται has reference not to the Last Judgement but to future generations of Christians; to all in fact who reap the benefit of the Cross.

When St. Paul wrote in Gal. ii. 15 ἡμεῖς φύσει Ἰουδαῖοι, καὶ οὐκ ἐξ ἐθνῶν ἁμαρτωλοί, he implied (speaking for the moment from the stand-point of his countrymen) that Gentiles would be regarded as φύσει ἁμαρτωλοί: they belonged 'to the class' of sinners; just as we might speak of a child as belonging to the 'criminal class' before it had done anything by its own act to justify its place in that class. The meaning of the text is very similar: so far as it relates to the effects of the Fall of Adam it must be interpreted by vv. 12-14; and so far as it relates to the effects of the Death of Christ it is parallel to vv. 1, 2 δικαιωθέντες οὖν [ἐκ πίστεως] εἰρήνην ἔχομεν (contained in ἔχωμεν) πρὸς τὸν Θεὸν διὰ τοῦ Κυρίου ἡμῶν Ἰ. Χ., δι' οὗ καὶ τὴν προσαγωγὴν ἐσχήκαμεν εἰς τὴν χάριν ἐν ᾗ ἐστήκαμεν. For the use of καθίστασθαι there is a good parallel in Xen. *Mem.* ii. 1. 9 Ἐγὼ οὖν τοὺς μὲν βουλομένους πολλὰ πράγματα ἔχειν . . . εἰς τοὺς ἀρχικοὺς καταστήσαιμι, where κατασт. = εἰς τοὺς ἀρχικοὺς τάττομεν (*sup.*) and ἐμαυτὸν τάττω εἰς τοὺς βουλομένους (*inf.*).

20. παρεισῆλθεν : ‘come in to the side of a state of things already existing.’ St. Paul regarded Law as a ‘parenthesis’ in the Divine plan : it did not begin until Moses, and it ended with Christ (cp. iv. 13–16; x. 4). Here however he has in view only its late beginning : it is a sort of ‘after-thought’ (see the Paraphrase).

‘Why did he not say the Law *was given*, but *the Law entered by the way ?* It was to show that the need of it was temporary and not absolute or claiming precedence’ (πρόσκαιρον αὐτοῦ δεικνὺς τὴν χρείαν οὖσαν, καὶ οὐ κυρίαν οὐδὲ προηγουμένην) Chrys.

ἵνα πλεονάσῃ. For the force of ἵνα comp. εἰς τὸ εἶναι αὐτοὺς ἀναπολογήτους i. 20 : the multiplication of transgression is not the first and direct object of law, but its second and contingent object : law only multiplies trangression because it is broken and so converts into deliberate sin acts which would not have had that character if they had not been so expressly forbidden.

Τὸ δὲ ἵνα ἐνταῦθα οὐκ αἰτιολογίας πάλιν ἀλλ’ ἐκβάσεώς ἐστιν. Οὐ γὰρ διὰ τοῦτο ἐδόθη ἵνα πλεονάσῃ, ἀλλ’ ἐδόθη μὲν ὥστε μειῶσαι καὶ ἀνελεῖν τὸ παράπτωμα· ἐξέβη δὲ τοὐναντίον, οὐ παρὰ τὴν τοῦ νόμου φύσιν, ἀλλὰ παρὰ τὴν τῶν δεξαμένων ῥαθυμίαν (Chrys.) : a note which shows that the ancients were quite aware of the ecbatic sense of ἵνα (see on xi. 11).

πλεονάσῃ, as Va. remarks, might be transitive, but is more probably intransitive, because of ἐπλεόνασεν ἡ ἁμαρτ. which follows.

τὸ παράπτωμα : seems expressly chosen in order to remind us that all sins done in defiance of a definite command are as such repetitions of the sin of Adam.

21. ἐν τῷ θανάτῳ. Sin reigns, as it were, over a charnel-house ; the subjects of its empire are men as good as dead, dead in every sense of the word, dead morally and spiritually, and therefore doomed to die physically (see on vi. 8 below).

διὰ δικαιοσύνης. The reign of grace or Divine favour is made possible by the gift of righteousness which the Christian owes to the mediation of Christ, and which opens up for him the prospect of eternal life.

St. Paul's Conception of Sin and of the Fall.

St. Paul uses Greek words, and some of those which he uses cannot be said to have essentially a different meaning from that which attached to them on their native soil; and yet the different relations in which they are placed and the different associations which gather round them, convey what is substantially a different idea to the mind.

The word ἁμαρτία with its cognates is a case in point. The corresponding term in Hebrew has much the same original sense of 'missing a mark.' Both words are used with a higher and a lower meaning; and in both the higher meaning belongs to the sphere of religion. So that the difference between them is not in the words themselves but in the spirit of the religions with which they are connected.

This appears upon the face of it from the mere bulk of literary usage. In classical Greek ἁμαρτία, ἁμαρτάνειν are common enough in the lighter senses of 'missing an aim,' of 'error in judgement or opinion'; in the graver sense of serious wrong-doing they are rare. When we turn to the Bible, the LXX and the N.T. alike, this proportion is utterly reversed. The words denote nearly always religious wrong-doing, and from being in the background they come strongly to the front; so much so that in the *Concordance* to the LXX this group of words fills some thirteen columns, averaging not much less than eighty instances to the column.

This fact alone tells its own story. And along with it we must take the deepening of meaning which the words have undergone through the theological context in which they are placed. 'How can I do this great wickedness, and sin against God?' (Gen. xxxix. 9). 'Against Thee, Thee only, have I sinned, and done that which is evil in Thy sight' (Ps. li. 4). 'Behold, all souls are Mine; as the soul of the father, so also the soul of the son is Mine: the soul that sinneth, it shall die' (Ezek. xviii. 4). We have travelled a long way from Hellenic religion in such utterances as these.

It is impossible to have an adequate conception of sin without an adequate conception of God. The Hebrew in general, and St. Paul in particular, had this; and that is why Sin is such an intense reality to them. It is not a mere defect, the coming short of an ideal, the mark of an imperfect development. It is something more than a negation; it is a positive quality, calling forth a positive reaction. It is a personal offence against a personal God. It is an injury or wound—if the reaction which it involves may be described in such human terms as 'injury' or 'wound'— directed against the Holy One whose love is incessantly going forth towards man. It causes an estrangement, a deep gulf of separation, between God and man.

The guilt of sin is proportioned to the extent to which it is conscious and deliberate. Wrong actions done without the knowledge that they are wrong are not imputed to the doer (ἁμαρτία δὲ οὐκ ἐλλογεῖται μὴ ὄντος νόμου Rom. v. 13: cf. iv. 15). But as a matter of fact few or none can take advantage of this because everywhere— even among the heathen—there is some knowledge of God and of right and wrong (Rom. i. 19 f.; ii. 12, 14 f.), and the extent of that knowledge determines the degree of guilt. Where there is a written law like that of the Jews stamped with Divine authority, the guilt is at its height. But this is but the climax of an ascending scale in

which the heinousness of the offence is proportioned to advantages
and opportunities.

Why did men break the Law? In other words, Why did they
sin? When the act of sin came to be analyzed it was found to
contain three elements. Proximately it was due to the wicked
impulses of human nature. The Law condemned illicit desires, but
men had such desires and they succumbed to them (Rom. vii.
7 ff.). The reason of this was partly a certain corruption of
human nature inherited from Adam. The corruption alone would
not have been enough apart from the consentient will; neither
would the will have been so acted upon if it had not been for
the inherited corruption (Rom. v. 12–14). But there was yet a third
element, independent of both these. They operated through the
man himself; but there was another influence which operated without him. It is remarkable how St. Paul throughout these chapters,
Rom. v, vi, vii, constantly personifies Sin as a pernicious and deadly
force at work in the world, not dissimilar in kind to the other great
counteracting forces, the Incarnation of Christ and the Gospel.
Now personifications are not like dogmatic definitions, and the
personification in this instance does not always bear exactly the
same meaning. In ch. v, when it is said that 'Sin entered into the
world,' the general term 'Sin' includes, and is made up of, the sins
of individuals. But in chaps. vi and vii the personified Sin is set
over against the individual, and expressly distinguished from him.
Sin is not to be permitted to reign within the body (vi. 12); the
members are not to be placed at the disposal of Sin (vi. 13); to
Sin the man is enslaved (vi. 6, 17, 20; vii. 14), and from Sin he is
emancipated (vi. 18, 22), or in other words, it is to Sin that he dies
(vi. 9, 11); Sin takes up its abode within his heart (vii. 17, 20):
it works upon him, using the commandment as its instrument, and
so is fatal to him (vii. 8, 11).

In all this the usage is consistent: a clear distinction is drawn
at once between the will and the bodily impulses which act upon
the will and a sort of external Power which makes both the will and
the impulses subservient to it. What is the nature of this Power?
Is it personal or impersonal? We could not tell from this particular
context. No doubt personal attributes and functions are assigned
to it, but perhaps only figuratively as part of the personification.
To answer our questions we shall have to consider the teaching of
the Apostle elsewhere. It is clear enough that, like the rest of his
countrymen (see Charles, *Book of Enoch*, p. 52 f.), St. Paul did
believe in a personal agency of Evil. He repeatedly uses the personal name Satan; he ascribes to him not only mischief-making in
the Church (1 Thess. ii. 18; 2 Cor. ii. 11), but the direct temptation of individual Christians (1 Cor. vii. 5); he has his followers on
whom he is sometimes invited to wreak his will (1 Cor. v. 5;

1 Tim. i. 20); supernatural powers of deceiving or perverting men
are attributed to him (2 Thess. ii. 9 κατ' ἐνέργειαν τοῦ Σατανᾶ ἐν πάσῃ
δυνάμει καὶ σημείοις καὶ τέρασι ψεύδους: cf. 2 Cor. xi. 14). The
Power of Evil does not stand alone but has at its disposal a whole
army of subordinate agents (ἀρχαί, ἐξουσίαι, κοσμοκράτορες τοῦ σκότους
τούτου Eph. vi. 12; cf. Col. ii. 15). There is indeed a whole
hierarchy of evil spirits as there is a hierarchy of good (Eph. i. 21),
and Satan has a court and a kingdom just as God has. He is 'the
god of the existing age' (ὁ θεὸς τοῦ αἰῶνος τούτου 2 Cor. iv. 4), and
exercises his rule till the final triumph of the Messiah (2 Thess. ii.
8 f.; 1 Cor. xv. 24 f.).

We see therefore that just as in the other books of the N.T.
the Gospels, the Apocalypse, and the other Apostolic Epistles, evil
is referred to a personal cause. And although it is doubtless true
that in chaps. vi, vii, where St. Paul speaks most directly of the
baleful activity of Sin, he does not intend to lay special stress on
this; his language is of the nature of personification and does not
necessarily imply a person; yet, when we take it in connexion with
other language elsewhere, we see that in the last resort he would
have said that there was a personal agency at work. It is at least
clear that he is speaking of an influence external to man, and
acting upon him in the way in which spiritual forces act.

St. Paul regards the beginnings of sin as traceable to the Fall of Adam.
In this he is simply following the account in Gen. iii; and the question
naturally arises, What becomes of that account and of the inferences which
St. Paul draws from it, if we accept the view which is pressed upon us by
the comparative study of religions and largely adopted by modern criticism,
that it is not to be taken as a literal record of historical fact, but as the
Hebrew form of a story common to a number of Oriental peoples and going
back to a common root? When we speak of a ' Hebrew form ' of this story
we mean a form shaped and moulded by those principles of revelation of
which the Hebrew race was chosen to be the special recipient. From this
point of view it becomes the typical and summary representation of a series
of facts which no discovery of flint implements and half-calcined bones can
ever reproduce for us. In some way or other as far back as history goes,
and we may believe much further, there has been implanted in the human
race this mysterious seed of sin, which like other characteristics of the race
is capable of transmission. The tendency to sin is present in every man who
is born into the world. But the tendency does not become actual sin until
it takes effect in defiance of an express command, in deliberate disregard of
a known distinction between right and wrong. How men came to be
possessed of such a command, by what process they arrived at the conscious
distinction of right and wrong, we can but vaguely speculate. Whatever it
was we may be sure that it could not have been presented to the imagination
of primitive peoples otherwise than in such simple forms as the narrative
assumes in the Book of Genesis. The really essential truths all come out in
that narrative—the recognition of the Divine Will, the act of disobedience
to the Will so recognized, the perpetuation of the tendency to such disobedience; and we may add perhaps, though here we get into a region of
surmises, the connexion between moral evil and physical decay, for the surest
pledge of immortality is the relation of the highest part of us, the soul,

through righteousness to God. These salient principles, which may have been due in fact to a process of gradual accretion through long periods, are naturally and inevitably summed up as a group of single incidents. Their essential character is not altered, and in the interpretation of primitive beliefs we may safely remember that 'a thousand years in the sight of God are but as one day.' We who believe in Providence and who believe in the active influence of the Spirit of God upon man, may well also believe that the tentative gropings of the primaeval savage were assisted and guided and so led up to definite issues, to which he himself perhaps at the time could hardly give a name but which he learnt to call ' sin ' and ' disobedience,' and the tendency to which later ages also saw to have been handed on from generation to generation in a way which we now describe as 'heredity.' It would be absurd to expect the language of modern science in the prophet who first incorporated the traditions of his race in the Sacred Books of the Hebrews. He uses the only kind of language available to his own intelligence and that of his contemporaries. But if the language which he does use is from that point of view abundantly justified, then the application which St. Paul makes of it is equally justified. He too expresses truth through symbols, and in the days when men can dispense with symbols his teaching may be obsolete, but not before.

The need for an Incarnation and the need for an Atonement are not dependent upon any particular presentation, which may be liable to correction with increasing knowledge, of the origin of sin. They rest, not on theory or on anything which can be clothed in the forms of theory, but on the great outstanding facts of the actual sin of mankind and its ravages. We take these facts as we see them, and to us they furnish an abundant explanation of all that God has done to counteract them. How they are in their turn to be explained may well form a legitimate subject for curiosity, but the historical side of it at least has but a very slight bearing on the interpretation of the N.T.

History of the Interpretation of the Pauline doctrine of δικαίωσις.

In order to complete our commentary on the earlier portion of the Epistle, it will be convenient to sum up, as shortly as is possible, the history of the doctrine of Justification, so far as it is definitely connected with exegesis. To pursue the subject further than that would be beside our purpose; but so much is necessary since the exposition of the preceding chapters has been almost entirely from one point of view. We shall of course be obliged to confine ourselves to certain typical names.

Just at the close of the Apostolic period the earliest speculation on the subject of Justification meets us. Clement of Rome, in his Epistle to the Corinthians, writes clearly guarding against any practical abuses which may arise from St. Paul's teaching. He has before him the three writers of the N.T. who deal most definitely with 'faith' and 'righteousness,' and from them constructs a system of life and action. He takes the typical example, that of Abraham, and asks, ' Wherefore was our father Abraham blessed ! ' The answer combines that of St. Paul and St. James. ' Was it not because he wrought righteousness and truth through faith ?' (§ 31 οὐχὶ δικαιοσύνην καὶ ἀλήθειαν διὰ πίστεως ποιήσας ;). And throughout there is the same co-ordination of different types of doctrine. ' We are justified by works and not by words ' (§ 30 ἔργοις δικαιούμενοι καὶ μὴ λόγοις). But again (§ 32) : ' And so we, having been called through His will in Christ Jesus, are not justified through ourselves or through our own wisdom or understanding or piety or works which we wrought in holiness of heart, but through faith whereby the Almighty God justified all men that have been from the beginning.' But

Clemens Romanus.

dangerous theories as to conduct, which arise from holding such beliefs in too crude a manner, are at once guarded against (§ 33): 'What then must we do, brethren? Must we idly abstain from doing good, and forsake love? May the Master never allow this to befall us at least . . . We have seen that all the righteous were adorned in good works . . . Seeing then that we have this pattern, let us conform ourselves with all diligence to His will; let us with all our strength work the work of righteousness.' Clement writes as a Christian of the second generation who inherits the teaching and phraseology of the Apostolic period. 'Faith,' 'Works,' 'Righteousness,' are ideas which have become part of the Christian life; the need of definition has not arisen. The system of conduct which should be exhibited as the result of the different elements of this life is clearly realized. What St. Paul and St. James each in his different way arrived at is accomplished. For the exact meaning of St. Paul, however, and the understanding of his teaching, we get no aid. Bishop Lightfoot, while showing how Clement 'has caught the spirit of the Pauline teaching,' yet dwells, and dwells rightly, on 'the defect in the dogmatic statement.' (See Lightfoot, *Clement*, i. 96, 397.)

The question of Justification never became a subject of controversy in the early church, and consequently the Fathers contented themselves as Clement had done with a clear practical solution. We cannot find in them either an answer to the more subtle questions which later theologians have asked or much assistance as to the exact exegesis of St. Paul's language.

Origen.

How little Origen had grasped some points in St. Paul's thought may be seen by his comment on Rom. iii. 20 *Ex operibus igitur legis quod non iustificabitur omnis caro in conspectu eius, hoc modo intelligendum puto: quia omnis qui caro est et secundum carnem vivit, non potest iustificari ex lege Dei, sicut et alibi dicit idem Apostolus, quia* qui in carne sunt Deo placere non possunt (*in Rom.* iii. 6; *Opp.* tom. vi. 194, ed. Lommatzsch). But in many points his teaching is clear and strong. All Justification is by faith alone (iii. 9, p. 217 *et dicit sufficere solius fidei iustificationem, ita ut credens quis tantummodo iustificetur, etiamsi nihil ab eo operis fuerit expletum*). It is the beginning of the Christian life, and is represented as the bringing to an end of a state of enmity. We who were followers of the devil, our tyrant and enemy, can if we will by laying down his arms and taking up the banner of Christ have peace with God, a peace which has been purchased for us by the blood of Christ (iv. 8, p. 285, on Rom. v. 1). The process of justification is clearly one of 'imputation' (*fides ad iustitiam reputetur* iv. 1, p. 240, on Rom. iv. 1-8), and is identified with the Gospel teaching of the forgiveness of sins; the two instances of it which are quoted being the penitent thief and the woman with the alabaster box of ointment (Luke vii. 37-42). But the need for good works is not excluded: *sed fortassis haec aliquis audiens resolvatur et bene agendi negligentiam capiat, si quidem ad iustificandum fides sola sufficiat. ad quem dicemus, quia post iustificationem si iniuste quis agat, sine dubio iustificationis gratiam sprevit . . . indulgentia namque non futurorum sed praeteritorum criminum datur* (iii. 9, p. 219, on Rom. iii. 27, 28). Faith without works is impossible (iv. 1, p. 234): rather faith is the root from which they spring: *non ergo ex operibus radix iustitiae, sed ex radice iustitiae fructus operum crescit, illa scilicet radice iustitiae, qua Deus accepto fert iustitiam sine operibus* (iv. 1, p. 241; see also the comment on Rom. ii. 5, 6 in ii. 4, p. 81). We may further note that in the comment on Rom. i. 17 and iii. 24 the *iustitia Dei* is clearly interpreted as the Divine attribute.

Chrysostom.

The same criticism which was passed on Origen applies in an equal or even greater degree to Chrysostom. Theologically and practically the teaching is vigorous and well balanced, but so far as exegesis is concerned St. Paul's conception and point of view are not understood. The circumstances which had created these conceptions no longer existed

For example, commenting on Rom. ii. 10 he writes: 'it is upon works
that punishment and reward depend, not upon circumcision or uncircumcision'; making a distinction which the Apostle does not between the
moral and ceremonial law. The historical situation is clearly grasped and
is brought out very well at the beginning of *Hom.* vii: 'He has accused
the Gentiles, he has accused the Jews; what follows to mention next is the
righteousness which is by faith. For if the law of nature availed not, and
the written Law was of no advantage, but both weighed down those that
used them not aright, and made it plain that they were worthy of greater
punishment, then the salvation which is by grace was henceforth necessary.'
The meaning of δικαιοσύνη Θεοῦ is well brought out. 'The declaring of
His righteousness is not only that He is Himself righteous, but that He
doth also make them that are filled with the putrefying scars of sin suddenly
righteous' (*Hom.* vii. on iii. 24, 25). It may be interesting to quote the
exposition of the passage which follows. He explains διὰ τὴν πάρεσιν τῶν
προγεγονότων ἁμαρτημάτων thus: διὰ τὴν πάρεσιν, τουτέστι τὴν νέκρωσιν.
οὐκέτι γὰρ ὑγείας ἐλπὶς ἦν, ἀλλ' ὥσπερ σῶμα παραλυθὲν τῆς ἄνωθεν ἐδεῖτο
χειρός, οὕτω καὶ ἡ ψυχὴ νεκρωθεῖσα, giving πάρεσις the meaning of 'paralysis,' the paralysis of spiritual life which has resulted from sin. Generally
δικαιόω seems clearly to be taken as 'make righteous,' even in passages
where it will least bear such an interpretation; for instance on iv. 5 (*Hom.*
viii.) δύναται ὁ θεὸς τὸν ἐν ἀσεβείᾳ βεβιωκότα τοῦτον ἐξαίφνης οὐχὶ κολάσεως
ἐλευθερῶσαι μόνον, ἀλλὰ καὶ δίκαιον ποιῆσαι, ... εἰ γὰρ μακάριος οὕτως
ὁ λαβὼν ἄφεσιν ἀπὸ χάριτος πολλῷ μᾶλλον ὁ δικαιωθείς, and on iv. 25 (*Hom.*
ix) ἐπὶ τούτῳ γὰρ καὶ ἀπέθανε καὶ ἀνέστη ἵνα δικαίους ἐργάσηται. Yet his
usage is not consistent, for on Rom. viii. 33 he writes: 'He does not say,
it is God that forgave our sins, but what is much greater :—" It is God that
justifieth." For when the Judge's sentence declares us just (δικαίους ἀπο-
φαίνει), and such a judge too, what signifieth the accuser?'

No purpose would be served by entering further into the views of the Theodoret
Greek commentators; but one passage of Theodoret may be quoted as
an instance of the way in which all the fathers connect Justification and
Baptism. On Rom. v. 1, 2 (vid. p. 53) he writes: ἡ πίστις μὲν ὑμῖν ἐδωρή-
σατο τῶν ἁμαρτημάτων τὴν ἄφεσιν καὶ ἀμώμους καὶ δικαίους διὰ τῆς τοῦ λουτροῦ
παλλιγγενεσίας ἀπέφηνε· προσήκει δὲ ὑμᾶς τὴν πρὸς τὸν θεὸν γεγενημένην
φυλάττειν εἰρήνην.

To sum up the teaching of the Greek Fathers. They put in the very front of
everything, the Atonement through the death of Christ, without as a rule
elaborating any theory concerning it: this characteristic we find from
the very beginning: it is as strong in Ignatius as in any later Father:
they all think that it is by faith we are justified, and at the same time lay
immense stress on the value, but not the merits, of good works: they seem
all very definitely to connect Justification with Baptism and the beginning
of the Christian life, so much so indeed that as is well known even the
possibility of pardon for post-baptismal sin was doubted by some : but they
have no theory of Justification as later times demand it; they are never close
and exact in the exegesis of St. Paul; and they are without the historical
conditions which would enable them to understand his great antithesis of
'Law' and 'Gospel,' 'Faith' and 'Works,' 'Merit' and 'Grace.'

The opinions of St. Augustine are of much greater importance. Although St. Augus-
he does not approach the question from the same point of view as the tine.
Reformation theologians, he represents the source from which came the
mediaeval tendency which created that theology. His most important
expositions are those contained in *De Spiritu et Litera* and *In Psalmum
XXXI Enarratio II*: this Psalm he describes as *Psalmus gratiae Dei
et iustificationis nostrae nullis praecedentibus meritis nostris, sed prae-
veniente nos misericordia Domini Dei nostri* ... His purpose is to prove

as against any form of Pelagianism that our salvation comes from no merits of our own but only from the Divine grace which is given us. This leads to three main characteristics in his exposition of the Romans. (1) For, first, good works done by those who are not in a state of grace are valueless : *nemo computet bona opera sua ante fidem : ubi fides non erat bonum opus non erat* (*Enarratio* § 4). Hence he explains Rom. ii. 5, 13 ff. of works done not in a state of nature but of grace. In ii. 13 the Apostle is referring to the Gentiles who have accepted the Gospel ; and the 'Law written in their hearts' is the law not of the O.T. but of the N.T. : he naturally compares 2 Cor. iii. 3 and Rom. ii. 26 (*De Sp. et Lit.* §§ 44- 49). (2) Then, secondly, St. Augustine's exposition goes on somewhat different lines from those of the Apostle's argument. He makes the whole aim of the early portion of the Romans to be the proof of the necessity of *grace.* Men have failed without grace, and it is only by means of it that they can do any works which are acceptable to God. This from one point of view really represents St. Paul's argument, from another it is very much removed from it. It had the tendency indeed to transfer the central point in connexion with human salvation from the atoning death of Christ accepted by Faith to the gift of the Divine Grace received from God. Although in this relation, as often, St. Augustine's exposition is deeper than that of the Greek fathers, it leads to a much less correct interpretation. (3) For, thirdly, there can be no doubt that it leads directly to the doctrine of 'infused' grace. It is quite true that Chrysostom has perhaps even more definitely interpreted δικαιοῦσθαι of 'making just,' and that Augustine in one place admits the possibility of interpreting it either as 'making just' or 'reckoning just' (*De Sp. et Lit.* § 45). But although he admits the two interpretations so far as concerns the words, practically his whole theory is that of an infusion of the grace of faith by which men are made just. So in his comment on i. 17 he writes : *haec est iustitia Dei, quae in Testamento Veteri velata, in Novo revelatur : quae ideo iustitia Dei dicitur, quod* impertiendo eam iustos facit (*De Sp. et Lit.* § 18) : and again : *credenti inquit in eum qui iustificat impium deputatur fides eius ad iustitiam. si iustificatur impius* ex impio fit iustus (*Enarratio* § 6) : so *non tibi Deus reddit debitam poenam, sed donat indebitam gratiam*: so *De Sp. et Lit.* § 56 : *haec est iustitia Dei, quam non solum docet per legis praeceptum, verum etiam dat per Spiritus donum.*

St. Augustine's theory is in fact this ; faith is a gift of grace which in- fused into men, enables them to produce works good and acceptable to God. The point of view is clearly not that of St. Paul, and it is the source of the mediaeval theory of grace with all its developments.

Aquinas. This theory as we find it elaborated in the *Summa Theologiae*, has so far as it concerns us three main characteristics. (1) In the first place it elaborates the Augustinian theory of Grace instead of the Pauline theory of Justification. It is quite clear that in St. Paul χάρις is the favour of God to man, and not a gift given by God to man ; but *gratia* in St. Thomas has evidently this latter signification : *cum gratia omnem naturae creatae facultatem excedat, eo quod nihil aliud sit quam participatio quaedam divinae naturae quae omnem aliam naturam excedit* (*Summa Theologiae*, Prima Secundae Qu. cxii. 1). So also : *donum gratiae . . . gratiae infusio . . . infundit donum gratiae iustifi- cantis* (cxiii. 3). (2) Secondly, it interprets *iustificare* to 'make just,' and in consequence looks upon justification as not only *remissio peccatorum*, but also an infusion of grace. This question is discussed fully in Qu. cxiii. Art. 2. The conclusion arrived at is : *quum iustitiae Dei repugnet poenam dimittere vigente culpa, nullius autem hominis qualis modo nascitur, reatus poenae absque gratia tolli queat ; ad culpae quoque hominis qualis modo nascitur, remissionem, gratiae infusionem requiri manifestum est.* The primary text on which this conclusion is based is Rom. iii. 24 *iustificati gratis per gratiam* *ipsius*, which is therefore clearly interpreted to mean 'made just by an infusion of grace'; and it is argued that the effect of the Divine love on us is grace by which a man is made worthy of eternal life, and that therefore remission of guilt cannot be understood unless it be accompanied by the infusion of grace. (3) The words quoted above, 'by which a man is made worthy of eternal life' (*dignus vita aeterna*) introduce us to a third point in the mediaeval theory of justification: indirectly by its theory of merit *de congruo* and *de condigno* it introduced just that doctrine of merit against which St. Paul had directed his whole system. This subject is worked out in Qu. cxiv, where it is argued (Art. 1) that in a sense we can deserve something from God. Although (Art. 2) a man cannot deserve life eternal in a state of nature, yet (Art. 3) after justification he can: *Homo meretur uitam aeternam ex condigno.* This is supported by Rom. viii. 17 *si filii et haeredes*, it being argued that we are sons to whom is owed the inheritance *ex ipso iure adoptionis*.

However defensible as a complete whole the system of the *Summa* may be, there is no doubt that nothing so complicated can be grasped by the popular mind, and that the teaching it represents led to a wide system of religious corruption which presented a very definite analogy with the errors which St. Paul combated; it is equally clear that it is not the system of Justification put forward by St. Paul. It will be convenient to pass on directly to the teaching of Luther, and to put it in direct contrast with the teaching of Aquinas. Although it arose primarily against the teaching of the later Schoolmen, whose teaching, especially on the subject of merit *de congruo* and *de condigno*, was very much developed, substantially it represents a revolt against the whole mediaeval theory.

Luther's main doctrines were the following. Through the law man learns **Luther** his sinfulness: he learns to say with the prophet, 'there is none that doeth good, no not one.' He learns his own weakness. And then arises the cry: 'Who can give me any help?' Then in its due season comes the saving word of the Gospel, 'Be of good cheer, my son, thy sins are forgiven. Believe in Jesus Christ who was crucified for thy sins.' This is the beginning of salvation; in this way we are freed from sin, we are justified and there is given unto us life eternal, not on account of our own merits and works, but on account of faith by which we approached Christ. (Luther on Galatians ii. 16; *Opp.* ed. 1554, p. 308.)

As against the mediaeval teaching the following points are noticeable, (1) In the first place Justification is quite clearly a doctrine of '*iustitia imputata*': *Deus acceptat seu reputat nos iustos solum propter fidem in Christum.* It is especially stated that we are not free from sin. As long as we live we are subject to the stain of sin: only our sins are not imputed to us. (2) Secondly, Luther inherits from the Schoolmen the distinction of *fides informis* and *fides formata cum charitate*; but whereas they had considered that it was *fides formata* which justifies, with him it is *fides informis*. He argued that if it were necessary that faith should be united with charity to enable it to justify, then it is no longer faith alone that justifies, but charity: faith becomes useless and good works are brought in. (3) Thirdly, it is needless to point out that he attacks, and that with great vigour, all theories of merit *de congruo* and *de condigno*. He describes them thus: *talia monstra portenta et horribiles blasphemiae debebant proponi Turcis et Iudaeis, non ecclesiae Christi.*

The teaching of the Reformation worked a complete change in the exegesis **Calvin** of St. Paul. A condition of practical error had arisen, clearly in many ways resembling that which St. Paul combated, and hence St. Paul's conceptions are understood better. The ablest of the Reformation commentaries is certainly that of Calvin; and the change produced may be seen most clearly in one point. The attempt that had been made to evade the meaning of St. Paul's words as to Law, by applying them only to the ceremonial

Law, he entirely brushes away (on iii. 20); again, he interprets *iustificare* as 'to reckon just,' in accordance with the meaning of the Greek word and the context of iv. 5. The scheme of Justification as laid down by Luther is applied to the interpretation of the Epistle, but his extravagant language is avoided. The distinction of *fides informis* and *formata* is condemned as unreal; and it is seen that what St. Paul means by works being unable to justify is not that they cannot do so in themselves, but that no one can fulfil them so completely as to be 'just.' We may notice that on ii. 6 he points out that the words can be taken in quite a natural sense, for reward does not imply merit, and on ii. 13 that he applies the passage to Gentiles not in a state of grace, but says that the words mean that although Gentiles had knowledge and opportunity they had sinned, and therefore would be necessarily condemned.

The Reformation theology made St. Paul's point of view comprehensible, but introduced errors of exegesis of its own. It added to St. Paul's teaching of 'imputation' a theory of the imputation of Christ's merits, which became the basis of much unreal systematization, and was an incorrect interpretation of St. Paul's meaning. The unreal distinction of *fides informis* and *formata*, added to Luther's own extravagant language, produced a strong antinomian tendency. 'Faith' almost comes to be looked upon as a meritorious cause of justification; an unreal faith is substituted for dead works; and faith becomes identified with 'personal assurance' or 'self-assurance.' Moreover, for the ordinary expression of St. Paul, 'we are justified by faith,' was substituted 'we are saved by faith,' a phrase which, although once used by St. Paul, was only so used in the somewhat vague sense of σώζειν, that at one time applies to our final salvation, at another to our present life within the fold of the Church; and the whole Christian scheme of sanctification, rightly separated in idea from justification, became divorced in fact from the Christian life.

The Reformation teaching created definitely the distinction between *iustitia imputata* and *iustitia infusa*, and the Council of Trent defined Justification thus: *iustificatio non est sola peccatorum remissio, sed etiam sanctificatio et renovatio interioris hominis per voluntariam susceptionem gratiae et donorum* (Sess. VI. cap. vii).

Cornelius a Lapide.

A typical commentary on the Romans from this point of view is that of Cornelius a Lapide. On i. 17 he makes a very just distinction between our justification which comes by faith and our salvation which comes through the Gospel, namely, all that is preached in the Gospel, the death and merits of Christ, the sacraments, the precepts, the promises. He argues from ii. 13 that works have a place in justification; and that our justification consists in the gift to us of the Divine justice, that is, of grace and charity and other virtues.

This summary has been made sufficiently comprehensive to bring out the main points on which interpretation has varied. It is clear from St. Paul's language that he makes a definite distinction in thought between three several stages which may be named Justification, Sanctification, Salvation. Our Christian life begins with the act of faith by which we turn to Christ; that is sealed in baptism through which we receive remission of sins and are incorporated into the Christian community, being made partakers of all the spiritual blessings which that implies: then if our life is consistent with these conditions we may hope for life eternal not for our own merits but for Christ's sake. The first step, that of Remission of sins, is Justification: the life that follows in the Christian community is the life of Sanctification. These two ideas are connected in time in so far as the moment in which our sins are forgiven begins the new life; but they are separated in thought, and it is necessary for us that this should be so, in order that we may realize that unless we come to Christ in the self-surrender of faith nothing can profit us. There is a close connexion again between Justification and Salvation ; the one represents the beginning of the process of which the other is the conclusion, and in so far as the first step is the essential one the life of the justified on earth can be and is spoken of as the life of the saved ; but the two are separated both in thought and in time, and this is so that we may realize that our life, as we are accepted by faith, endowed with the gift of God's Holy Spirit, and incorporated into the Christian community, must be holy. By our life we shall be judged (see the notes on ii. 6, 13) : we must strive to make our character such as befits us for the life in which we hope to share : but we are saved by Christ's death ; and the initial act of faith has been the hand which we stretched out to receive the divine mercy.

Our historical review has largely been a history of the confusion of these three separate aspects of the Gospel scheme.

THE MYSTICAL UNION OF THE CHRISTIAN
WITH CHRIST.

VI. 1–14. *If more sin only means more grace, shall we go on sinning ? Impossible. The baptized Christian cannot sin. Sin is a direct contradiction of the state of things which baptism assumes. Baptism has a double function. (1) It brings the Christian into personal contact with Christ, so close that it may be fitly described as union with Him. (2) It expresses symbolically a series of acts corresponding to the redeeming acts of Christ.*

Immersion = Death.

Submersion = Burial (the ratification of Death).

Emergence = Resurrection.

All these the Christian has to undergo in a moral and spiritual sense, and by means of his union with Christ. As Christ by His death on the Cross ceased from all contact with sin, so the Christian, united with Christ in his baptism, has done once for all with sin, and lives henceforth a reformed life dedicated to God. [This at least is the ideal, whatever may be the reality.] (vv. 1–11.) Act then as men who have thrown off the dominion of Sin. Dedicate all your powers to God. Be not afraid ; Law, Sin's ally, is superseded in its hold over you by Grace (vv. 12–14).

[1] OBJECTOR. Is not this dangerous doctrine ? If more sin means more grace, are we not encouraged to go on sinning ?

[2]ST. PAUL. A horrible thought ! When we took the decisive step and became Christians we may be said to have died to sin, in such a way as would make it flat contradiction to live any longer in it.

[3]Surely you do not need reminding that all of us who were immersed or baptized, as our Christian phrase runs, ' *into* Christ,' i. e. into the closest allegiance and adhesion to Him, were so immersed or baptized into a special relation to His *Death*. I mean that the Christian, at his baptism, not only professes obedience to Christ but enters into a relation to Him so intimate that it may be described as actual union. Now this union, taken in connexion with the peculiar symbolism of Baptism, implies a great deal more. That symbolism recalls to us with great vividness the redeeming acts of Christ—His Death, Burial, and Resurrection. And our union with Christ involves that we shall repeat those acts, in such sense as we may, i. e. in a moral and spiritual sense, in our own persons.

[4]When we descended into the baptismal water, that meant that we died with Christ—to sin. When the water closed over our heads, that meant that we lay buried with Him, in proof that our death to sin, like His death, was real. But this carries with it the third step in the process. As Christ was raised from among the dead by a majestic exercise of Divine power, so we also must from henceforth conduct ourselves as men in whom has been implanted a new principle of life.

[5]For it is not to be supposed that we can join with Christ in one thing and not join with Him in another. If, in undergoing a death like His, we are become one with Christ as the graft becomes one with the tree into which it grows, we must also be one with Him by undergoing a resurrection like His, i. e. at once a moral, spiritual, and physical resurrection. [6]For it is matter of experience that our Old Self—what we were before we became Christians—was nailed to the Cross with Christ in our baptism : it was killed by a process so like the Death of Christ and so wrought in conjunction with Him that it too may share in the name and associations of His Crucifixion. And the object of this crucifixion of our Old Self was that the bodily sensual part of us, prolific home and haunt of sin, might be so paralyzed and

disabled as henceforth to set us free from the service of Sin. [7] For just as no legal claim can be made upon the dead, so one who is (ethically) dead is certified 'Not Guilty' and exempt from all the claims that Sin could make upon him.

[8] But is this all? Are we to stop at the death to sin? No; there is another side to the process. If, when we became Christians, we died with Christ (morally and spiritually), we believe that we shall also live with Him (physically, as well as ethically and spiritually): [9] because we know for a fact that Christ Himself, now that He has been once raised from the dead, will not have the process of death to undergo again. Death has lost its hold over Him for ever. [10] For He has done with Death, now that He has done once for all with Sin, by bringing to an end that earthly state which alone brought Him in contact with it. Henceforth He lives in uninterrupted communion with God.

[11] In like manner do you Christians regard yourselves as dead, inert and motionless as a corpse, in all that relates to sin, but instinct with life and responding in every nerve to those Divine claims and Divine influences under which you have been brought by your union with Jesus Messiah.

[12] I exhort you therefore not to let Sin exercise its tyranny over this frail body of yours by giving way to its evil passions. [13] Do not, as you are wont, place hand, eye, and tongue, as weapons stained with unrighteousness, at the service of Sin; but dedicate yourselves once for all, like men who have left the ranks of the dead and breathe a new spiritual life, to God; let hand, eye, and tongue be weapons of righteous temper for Him to wield. [14] You may rest assured that in so doing Sin will have no claims or power over you, for you have left the *régime* of Law (which, as we shall shortly see, is a stronghold of Sin) for that of Grace.

1. The fact that he has just been insisting on the function of sin to act as a provocative of Divine grace recalls to the mind of the Apostle the accusation brought against himself of saying 'Let us do evil, that good may come' (iii. 8). He is conscious that his own teaching, if pressed to its logical conclusion, is open to this charge; and he states it in terms which are not exactly those which would be used by his adversaries but such as might seem to express the one-sided development of his own thought. Of course he does not allow the consequence for a moment; he repudiates

it however not by proving a *non sequitur*, but by showing how this
train of thought is crossed by another, even more fundamental.
He is thus led to bring up the second of his great pivot-doctrines,
the Mystical Union of the Christian with Christ dating from his
Baptism. Here we have another of those great elemental forces in
the Christian Life which effectually prevents any antinomian conclusion such as might seem to be drawn from different premises.
St. Paul now proceeds to explain the nature of this force and the
way in which the Christian is related to it.

The various readings in this chapter are unimportant. There can be no
question that we should read ἐπιμένωμεν for ἐπιμενοῦμεν in ver. 1; ζήσομεν
and not ζήσωμεν in ver. 2; and that τῷ Κυρίῳ ἡμῶν should be omitted at the
end of ver. 11. In that verse the true position of εἶναι is after ἑαυτούς
(א* B C, Cyr.-Alex. Jo.-Damasc.): some inferior authorities place it after
νεκρούς μέν: the Western text (A D E F G, Tert.; cf. also Pesh. Boh. Arm.
Aeth.) omits it altogether.

2. οἵτινες ἀπεθάνομεν. Naturally the relative of quality : ' we,
being what we are, men who died (in our baptism) to sin,' &c.

3. ἢ ἀγνοεῖτε: ' Can you deny this, or is it possible that you are
not aware of all that your baptism involves?' St. Paul does not
like to assume that his readers are ignorant of that which is to him
so fundamental. The deep significance of Baptism was universally
recognized ; though it is hardly likely that any other teacher would
have expressed that significance in the profound and original
argument which follows.

ἐβαπτίσθημεν εἰς Χριστὸν Ἰησοῦν: ' were baptized unto union
with' (not merely ' obedience to') 'Christ.' The act of baptism
was an act of *incorporation* into Christ. Comp. esp. Gal. iii. 27
ὅσοι γὰρ εἰς Χριστὸν ἐβαπτίσθητε, Χριστὸν ἐνεδύσασθε.

This conception lies at the root of the whole passage. All the
consequences which St. Paul draws follow from this union, incorporation, identification of the Christian with Christ. On the origin
of the conception, see below.

εἰς τὸν θάνατον αὐτοῦ ἐβαπτίσθημεν. This points back to ἀπεθάνομεν
above. The central point in the passage is *death*. The Christian
dies because Christ died, and he is enabled to realize His death
through his union with Christ.

But why is baptism said to be specially 'into Christ's *death*'?
The reason is because it is owing primarily to the Death of Christ
that the condition into which the Christian enters at his baptism
is such a changed condition. We have seen that St. Paul does
ascribe to that Death a true objective efficacy in removing the
barrier which sin has placed between God and man. Hence, as
it is Baptism which makes a man a Christian, so is it the Death
of Christ which wins for the Christian his special immunities
and privileges, The sprinkling of the Blood of Christ seals that

covenant with His People to which Baptism admits them. But this
is only the first step : the Apostle goes on to show how the Death
of Christ has a subjective as well as an objective side for the
believer.

4. συνετάφημεν . . . θάνατον. A strong majority of the best
scholars (Mey.-W. Gif. Lips. Oltr. Go.) would connect εἰς τὸν
θάνατον with διὰ τοῦ βαπτίσματος and not with συνετάφημεν, because of
(i) ἐβαπτ. εἰς τ. θαν. αὐτ. just before; (ii) a certain incongruity in
the connexion of συνετάφ. with εἰς τὸν θάνατον : death precedes burial
and is not a result or object of it. We are not sure that this
reasoning is decisive. (i) St. Paul does not avoid these ambiguous
constructions, as may be seen by iii. 25 ὃν προέθετο . . . διὰ τῆς πίστεως
ἐν τῷ αὐτοῦ αἵματι, where ἐν τῷ αὐτοῦ αἵματι goes with προέθετο and
not with διὰ τῆς πίστεως. (ii) The ideas of 'burial' and 'death' are
so closely associated that they may be treated as correlative to each
other—burial is only death sealed and made certain. ' Our baptism
was a sort of funeral ; a solemn act of consigning us to that death
of Christ in which we are made one with Him,' Va. (iii) There is
a special reason for saying here not ' we were buried into burial,'
but ' we were buried into death,' because ' death ' is the keynote of
the whole passage, and the word would come in appropriately to
mark the transition from Christ to the Christian. Still these arguments do not amount to proof that the second connexion is right,
and it is perhaps best to yield to the weight of authority. For the
idea compare esp. Col. ii. 12 συνταφέντες αὐτῷ ἐν τῷ βαπτίσματι ἐν ᾧ
καὶ συνηγέρθητε.

εἰς τὸν θάνατον is best taken as = 'into that death (of His),' the
death just mentioned : so Oltr. Gif. Va. Mou., but not Mey.-W.
Go., who prefer the sense ' into death ' (in the abstract). In any
case there is a stress on the idea of death ; but the clause and the
verse which follow will show that St. Paul does not yet detach the
death of the Christian from the death of Christ.

διὰ τῆς δόξης τοῦ πατρός : δόξης here practically = 'power'; but
it is power viewed externally rather than internally ; the stress is
laid not so much on the inward energy as on the signal and
glorious manifestation. Va. compares Jo. xi. 40, 23, where 'thou
shalt see the glory of God' = 'thy brother shall rise again.' See
note on iii. 23.

5. σύμφυτοι : 'united by growth'; the word exactly expresses
the process by which a graft becomes united with the life of a tree.
So the Christian becomes ' grafted into ' Christ. For the metaphor
we may compare xi. 17 σὺ δὲ ἀγριέλαιος ὢν ἐνεκεντρίσθης ἐν αὐτοῖς, καὶ
συγκοινωνὸς τῆς ῥίζης καὶ τῆς πιότητος τῆς ἐλαίας ἐγένου, and Tennyson's
'*grow incorporate* into thee.'

It is a question whether we are to take σύμφ. γεγόν. directly with
τῷ ὁμοιώμ. κ.τ.λ. or whether we are to supply τῷ Χριστῷ and make

τῷ ὁμοιώμ. dat. of respect. Probably the former, as being simpler and more natural, so far at least as construction is concerned, though no doubt there is an ellipse in meaning which would be more exactly represented by the fuller phrase. Such condensed and strictly speaking inaccurate expressions are common in language of a quasi-colloquial kind. St. Paul uses these freer modes of speech and is not tied down by the rules of formal literary composition.

6. γινώσκοντες : see *Sp. Comm.* on 1 Cor. viii. 1 (p. 299), where γινώσκω as contrasted with οἶδα is explained as signifying 'appreciative or experimental acquaintance.' A slightly different explanation is given by Gif. *ad loc.*, '*noting* this,' as of the idea involved in the fact, a knowledge which results from the exercise of understanding (νοῦς).

ὁ παλαιὸς ἡμῶν ἄνθρωπος : 'our old self'; cp. esp. Suicer, *Thes.* i. 352, where the patristic interpretations are collected (ἡ προτέρα πολιτεία Theodrt.; ὁ κατεγνωσμένος βίος Euthym.-Zig., &c.).

This phrase, with its correlative ὁ καινὸς ἄνθρωπος, is a marked link of connexion between the acknowledged and disputed Epp. (cf. Eph. ii. 15; iv. 22, 24; Col. iii. 9). The coincidence is the more remarkable as the phrase would hardly come into use until great stress began to be laid upon the necessity for a change of life, and may be a coinage of St. Paul's. It should be noted however that ὁ ἐντὸς ἄνθρωπος goes back to Plato (Grm.-Thay. s. v. ἄνθρωπος, 1. e.).

συνεσταυρώθη : cf. Gal. ii. 20 Χριστῷ συνεσταύρωμαι. There is a difference between the thought here and in *Imit. Xti.* II. xii. 3 'Behold! in the cross all doth consist, and all lieth in our dying thereon; for there is no other way unto life, and unto true inward peace, but the way of the holy cross, and of daily mortification.' This is rather the 'taking up the cross' of the Gospels, which is a daily process. St. Paul no doubt leaves room for such a process (Col. iii. 5, &c.); but here he is going back to that which is its root, the one decisive ideal act which he regards as taking place in baptism : in this the more gradual lifelong process is anticipated.

καταργηθῇ. For καταργεῖν see on iii. 3. The word is appropriately used in this connexion : 'that the body of sin may be paralyzed,' reduced to a condition of absolute impotence and inaction, as if it were dead.

τὸ σῶμα τῆς ἁμαρτίας : the body of which sin has taken possession. Parallel phrases are vii. 24 τοῦ σώματος τοῦ θανάτου τούτου: Phil. iii. 21 τὸ σῶμα τῆς ταπεινώσεως ἡμῶν : Col. ii. 11 [ἐν τῇ ἀπεκδύσει] τοῦ σώματος τῆς σαρκός. The gen. has the general sense of ' belonging to,' but acquires a special shade of meaning in each case from the context; ' the body which is given over to death,' ' the body in its present state of degradation,' ' the body which is so apt to be the instrument of its own carnal impulses.'

Here τὸ σῶμα τῆς ἁμαρτίας must be taken closely together, because it is not the body, *simply as such*, which is to be killed, but the body *as the seat of sin*. This is to be killed, so that Sin may lose its slave.

τοῦ μηκέτι δουλεύειν. On τοῦ with inf. as expressing purpose see esp. Westcott, *Hebrews*, p. 342.

τῇ ἁμαρτίᾳ : ἁμαρτία, as throughout this passage, is personified as a hard taskmaster: see the longer note at the end of the last chapter.

7. ὁ γὰρ ἀποθανὼν . . . ἁμαρτίας. The argument is thrown into the form of a general proposition, so that ὁ ἀποθανών must be taken in the widest sense, 'he who has undergone death in any sense of the term'—physical or ethical. The primary sense is however clearly physical: 'a dead man has his quittance from any claim that Sin can make against him': what is obviously true of the physically dead is inferentially true of the ethically dead. Comp. 1 Pet. iv. 1 ὅτι ὁ παθὼν σαρκὶ πέπαυται ἁμαρτίας : also the Rabbinical parallel quoted by Delitzsch *ad loc.* ' when a man is dead he is free from the law and the commandments.'

Delitzsch goes so far as to describe the idea as an 'acknowledged *locus communis*,' which would considerably weaken the force of the literary coincidence between the two Apostles.

δεδικαίωται ἀπὸ τῆς ἁμαρτίας. The sense of δεδικαίωται is still forensic : 'is declared righteous, acquitted from guilt.' The idea is that of a master claiming legal possession of a slave : proof being put in that the slave is dead, the verdict must needs be that the claims of law are satisfied and that he is no longer answerable ; Sin loses its suit.

8. συζήσομεν. The different senses of 'life' and 'death' always lie near together with St. Paul, and his thought glides backwards and forwards from one to another almost imperceptibly ; now he lays a little more stress on the physical sense, now on the ethical ; at one moment on the present state and at another on the future. Here and in ver. 9 the future eternal life is most prominent ; but ver. 10 is transitional, and in ver. 11 we are back again at the stand-point of the present.

9. If the Resurrection opened up eternity to Christ it will do so also to the Christian.

κυριεύει. Still the idea of master and slave or vassal. Death loses its *dominium* over Christ altogether. That which gave Death its hold upon Him was sin, the human sin with which He was brought in contact by His Incarnation. The connexion was severed once for all by Death, which set Him free for ever.

10. ὁ γὰρ ἀπέθανε. The whole clause forms a kind of cognate accus. after the second ἀπέθανεν (Win. § xxiv. 4, p. 209 E. T.); Euthym.-Zig. paraphrases τὸν θάνατον ὃν ἀπέθανε διὰ τὴν ἁμαρτίαν ἀπέθανε τὴν ἡμετέραν, where however τῇ ἁμαρτίᾳ is not rightly represented by διὰ τὴν ἁμαρτίαν.

τῇ ἁμαρτίᾳ ἀπέθανεν. In what sense did Christ die to sin? The phrase seems to point back to ver. 7 above: Sin ceased to have any claim upon Him. But how could Sin have a claim upon Him 'who had no acquaintance with sin' (2 Cor. v. 21)? The same verse which tells us this supplies the answer: τὸν μὴ γνόντα ἁμαρτίαν ὑπὲρ ἡμῶν ἁμαρτίαν ἐποίησεν, 'the Sinless One for our sake was treated as if He were sinful.' The sin which hung about Him and wreaked its effects upon Him was not His but ours (cp. 1 Pet. ii. 22, 24). It was in His Death that this pressure of human sin culminated; but it was also in His Death that it came to an end, decisively and for ever.

ἐφάπαξ. The decisiveness of the Death of Christ is specially insisted upon in Ep. to Hebrews. This is the great point of contrast with the Levitical sacrifices: they did and it did not need to be repeated (cf. Heb. vii. 27; ix. 12, 26, 28; x. 10; also 1 Pet. iii. 18).

ζῇ τῷ Θεῷ. Christ died for (in relation to) Sin, and lives henceforth for God. The old chain which by binding Him to sin made Him also liable to death, is broken. No other power κυριεύει αὐτοῦ but God.

This phrase ζῇ τῷ Θεῷ naturally suggests 'the moral' application to the believer.

11. λογίζεσθε ἑαυτούς. The man and his 'self' are distinguished. The 'self' is not the 'whole self,' but only that part of the man which lay under the dominion of sin. [It will help us to bear this in mind in the interpretation of the next chapter.] This part of the man is dead, so that sin has lost its slave and is balked of its prey; but his true self is alive, and alive *for God*, through its union with the risen Christ, who also lives only for God.

λογίζεσθε: not indic. (as Beng. Lips.) but imper., preparing the way, after St. Paul's manner, for the direct exhortation of the next paragraph.

ἐν Χριστῷ Ἰησοῦ. This phrase is the summary expression of the doctrine which underlies the whole of this section and forms, as we have seen, one of the main pillars of St. Paul's theology. The chief points seem to be these. (1) The relation is conceived as a local relation. The Christian has his being 'in' Christ, as living creatures 'in' the air, as fish 'in' the water, as plants 'in' the earth (Deissmann, p. 84; see below). (2) The order of the words is invariably ἐν Χριστῷ Ἰησοῦ, not ἐν Ἰησοῦ Χριστῷ (Deissmann, p. 88; cp. also Haussleiter, as referred to on p. 86 *sup.*). We find however ἐν τῷ Ἰησοῦ in Eph. iv. 21, but not in the same strict application. (3) In agreement with the regular usage of the words in this order ἐν Χρ. Ἰ. always relates to the glorified Christ regarded as πνεῦμα, not to the historical Christ. (4) The corresponding expression Χριστὸς ἔν τινι is best explained by the same analogy of 'the air.' Man lives and breathes 'in the air,' and the air is also 'in the man' (Deissmann, p. 92).

Deissmann's monograph is entitled *Die neutestamentliche Formel in Christo Jesu*, Marburg, 1892. It is a careful and methodical investigation of the subject, somewhat too rigorous in pressing all examples of the use into the same mould, and rather inclined to realistic modes of conception. A very interesting question arises as to the origin of the phrase. Herr Deissmann regards it as a creation—and naturally as one of the most original creations—of St. Paul. And it is true that it is not found in the Synoptic Gospels. Approximations however are found more or less sporadically, in 1 St. Peter (iii. 16; v. 10, 14; always in the correct text ἐν Χριστῷ), in the Acts (iv. 2 ἐν τῷ Ἰησοῦ: 9, 10 ἐν τῷ ὀνόματι Ἰησοῦ Χριστοῦ: 12; xiii. 39 ἐν τούτῳ πᾶς ὁ πιστεύων δικαιοῦται), and in full volume in the Fourth Gospel (ἐν ἐμοί, μένειν ἐν ἐμοί Jo. vi. 56; xiv. 20, 30; xv. 2–7; xvi. 33; xvii. 21), in the First Epistle of St. John (ἐν αὐτῷ, ἐν τῷ υἱῷ εἶναι, μένειν ii. 5, 6, 8, 24, 27, 28; iii. 6, 24; v. 11, 20; ἔχειν τὸν υἱόν v. 12), and also in the Apocalypse (ἐν Ἰησοῦ i. 9; ἐν Κυρίῳ xiv. 13). Besides the N. T. there are the Apostolic Fathers, whose usage should be investigated with reference to the extent to which it is directly traceable to St. Paul*. The phrase ἐν Χριστῷ Ἰησοῦ occurs in 1 Clem. xxxii. 4; xxxviii. 1; Ign. *Eph.* i. 1; *Trall.* ix. 2; *Rom.* i. 1; ii. 2. The commoner phrases are ἐν Χριστῷ in Clem. Rom. and ἐν Ἰησοῦ Χριστῷ which is frequent in Ignat. The distinction between ἐν Ἰησοῦ Χριστῷ and ἐν Χριστῷ Ἰησοῦ is by this time obliterated. In view of these phenomena and the usage of N. T. it is natural to ask whether all can be accounted for on the assumption that the phrase originates entirely with St. Paul. In spite of the silence of Evv. Synopt. it seems more probable that the suggestion came in some way ultimately from our Lord Himself. This would not be the only instance of an idea which caught the attention of but few of the first disciples but was destined afterwards to wider acceptance and expansion.

12. βασιλευέτω: cf. v. 21 of Sin; v. 14, 17 of Death.

With this verse comp. Philo, *De Gigant.* 7 (Mang. i. 266) Αἴτιον δὲ τῆς ἀνεπιστημοσύνης μέγιστον ἡ σάρξ καὶ ἡ πρὸς σάρκα οἰκείωσις.

13. Observe the change of tense: παριστάνετε, 'go on yielding,' by the weakness which succumbs to temptation whenever it presses; παραστήσατε, 'dedicate by one decisive act, one resolute effort.'

ὅπλα: 'weapons' (cf. esp. Rom. xiii. 12; 2 Cor. vi. 7; x. 4). ἀδικίας and δικαιοσύνης are *gen. qualitatis*. For a like military metaphor more fully worked out comp. Eph. vi. 11–17.

14. ἁμαρτία γάρ. You are not, as you used to be, constantly harassed by the assaults of sin, aggravated to your consciences by the prohibitions of Law. The fuller explanation of this aggravating effect of Law is coming in what follows, esp. in ch. vii; and it is just like St. Paul to 'set up a finger-post,' pointing to the course his argument is to take, in the last clause of a paragraph. It is like

---

* It is rather strange that this question does not appear to be touched either by Bp. Lightfoot or by Gebhardt and Harnack. There is more to the point in the excellent monograph on Ignatius by Von der Goltz in *Texte u. Unters.* xii. 3, but the particular group of phrases is not directly treated.

him too to go off at the word νόμον into a digression, returning to
the subject with which the chapter opened, and looking at it from
another side.

The Doctrine of Mystical Union with Christ.

How did St. Paul arrive at this doctrine of the Mystical Union?
Doubtless by the guiding of the Holy Spirit. But that guiding, as
it usually does, operated through natural and human channels.
The channel in this instance would seem to be psychological. The
basis of the doctrine is the Apostle's own experience. His conversion was an intellectual change, but it was also something much
more. It was an intense personal apprehension of Christ, as
Master, Redeemer and Lord. But that apprehension was so
persistent and so absorbing; it was such a dominant element in
the life of the Apostle that by degrees it came to mean little less
than an actual *identification of will*. In the case of ordinary friendship and affection it is no very exceptional thing for unity of purpose
and aim so to spread itself over the character, and so to permeate
thought and feeling, that those who are joined together by this
invisible and spiritual bond seem to act and think almost as if they
were a single person and not two. But we can understand that in
St. Paul's case with an object for his affections so exalted as Christ,
and with influences from above meeting so powerfully the upward
motions of his own spirit, the process of identification had a more
than common strength and completeness. It was accomplished in
that sphere of spiritual emotion for which the Apostle possessed
such remarkable gifts—gifts which caused him to be singled out as
the recipient of special Divine communications. Hence it was that
there grew up within him a state of feeling which he struggles to
express and succeeds in expressing through language which is
practically the language of *union*. Nothing short of this seemed to
do justice to the degree of that identification of will which the
Apostle attained to. He spoke of himself as *one* with Christ. And
then his thoughts were so concentrated upon the culminating acts
in the Life of Christ—the acts which were in a special sense associated with man's redemption—His Death, Burial and Resurrection
—that when he came to analyze his own feelings, and to dissect
this idea of *oneness*, it was natural to him to see in it certain stages,
corresponding to those great acts of Christ, to see in it something
corresponding to death, something corresponding to burial (which
was only the emphasizing of death), and something corresponding
to resurrection.

Here there came in to help the peculiar symbolism of Baptism. An
imagination as lively as St. Paul's soon found in it analogies to the
same process. That plunge beneath the running waters was like

a death; the moment's pause while they swept on overhead was like a burial; the standing erect once more in air and sunlight was a species of resurrection. Nor did the likeness reside only in the outward rite, it extended to its inner significance. To what was it that the Christian died? He died to his *old self*, to all that he had been, whether as Jew or Gentile, before he became a Christian. To what did he rise again? Clearly to that *new life* to which the Christian was bound over. And in this spiritual death and resurrection the great moving factor was that one fundamental principle of union with Christ, identification of will with His. It was this which enabled the Christian to make his parting with the past and embracing of new obligations real.

There is then, it will be seen, a meeting and coalescence of a number of diverse trains of thought in this most pregnant doctrine. On the side of Christ there is first the loyal acceptance of Him as Messiah and Lord, that acceptance giving rise to an impulse of strong adhesion, and the adhesion growing into an identification of will and purpose which is not wrongly described as union. Further, there is the distributing of this sense of union over the cardinal acts of Christ's Death, Burial and Resurrection. Then on the side of the man there is his formal ratification of the process by the undergoing of Baptism, the symbolism of which all converges to the same end; and there is his practical assumption of the duties and obligations to which baptism and the embracing of Christianity commit him—the breaking with his tainted past, the entering upon a new and regenerate career for the future.

The vocabulary and working out of the thought in St. Paul are his own, but the fundamental conception has close parallels in the writings of St. John and St. Peter, the New Birth through water and Spirit (John iii. 5), the being begotten again of incorruptible seed (1 Pet. i. 23), the comparison of baptism to the ark of Noah (1 Pet. iii. 20, 21) in St. Peter; and there is a certain partial coincidence even in the ἀπεκύησεν of St. James (Jas. i. 18).

It is the great merit of Matthew Arnold's *St. Paul and Protestantism*, whatever its defects and whatever its one-sidedness, that it did seize with remarkable force and freshness on this part of St. Paul's teaching. And the merit is all the greater when we consider how really high and difficult that teaching is, and how apt it is to shoot over the head of reader or hearer. Matthew Arnold saw, and expressed with all his own lucidity, the foundation of simple psychological fact on which the Apostle's mystical language is based. He gives to it the name of 'faith,' and it is indeed the only kind of faith which he recognizes. Nor is he wrong in giving the process this name, though, as it happens, St. Paul has not as yet spoken of 'faith' in this connexion, and does not so speak of it until he comes to Eph. iii. 17. It was really faith, the living apprehension of Christ, which lies at the bottom of all the language of identification and union.

'If ever there was a case in which the wonder-working power of attachment, in a man for whom the moral sympathies and the desire for righteousness were all-powerful, might employ itself and work its wonders, it was here. Paul felt this power penetrate him; and he felt, also, how by perfectly identifying himself through it with Christ, and in no other way, could he ever get the confidence and force to do as Christ did. He thus found a point in which the mighty world outside man, and the weak world inside him, seemed to combine for his salvation. The struggling stream of duty, which had not volume enough to bear him to his goal, was suddenly reinforced by the immense tidal wave of sympathy and emotion. To this new and potent influence Paul gave the name of *faith*' (*St. Paul and Protestantism*, p. 69 f.).

'It is impossible to be in presence of this Pauline conception of faith without remarking on the incomparable power of edification which it contains. It is indeed a crowning evidence of that piercing practical religious sense which we have attributed to Paul. ... The elemental power of sympathy and emotion in us, a power which extends beyond the limits of our own will and conscious activity, which we cannot measure and control, and which in each of us differs immensely in force, volume, and mode of manifestation, he calls into full play, and sets it to work with all its strength and in all its variety. But one unalterable object is assigned by him to this power: *to die with Christ to the law of the flesh, to live with Christ to the law of the mind.* This is the doctrine of the *necrosis* (2 Cor. iv. 10), Paul's central doctrine, and the doctrine which makes his profoundness and originality. ... Those multitudinous motions of appetite and self-will which reason and conscience disapproved, reason and conscience could yet not govern, and had to yield to them. This, as we have seen, is what drove Paul almost to despair. Well, then, how did Paul's faith, working through love, help him here? It enabled him to reinforce duty by affection. In the central need of his nature, the desire to govern these motions of unrighteousness, it enabled him to say: *Die to them! Christ did.* If any man be in Christ, said Paul,—that is, if any man identifies himself with Christ by attachment so that he enters into his feelings and lives with his life,—he is a new creature; he can do, and does, what Christ did. First, he suffers with him. Christ, throughout His life and in His death, presented His body a living sacrifice to God; every self-willed impulse, blindly trying to assert itself without respect of the universal order, he died to. You, says Paul to his disciple, are to do the same. ... If you cannot, your attachment, your faith, must be one that goes but a very little way. In an ordinary human attachment, out of love to a woman, out of love to a friend, out of love to a child, you can suppress quite easily, because by sympathy you become one with them and their feelings, this or that impulse of selfishness which happens to conflict with them, and which hitherto you have obeyed. *All* impulses of selfishness conflict with Christ's feelings, He showed it by dying to them all; if you are one with Him by faith and sympathy, you can die to them also. Then, secondly, if you thus die with Him, you become transformed by the renewing of your mind, and rise with Him. ... You rise with Him to that harmonious conformity with the real and eternal order, that sense of pleasing God who trieth the hearts, which is life and peace, and which grows more and more till it becomes glory' (*ibid.* pp. 75–78).

Another striking presentation of the thought of this passage will be found in a lay sermon, *The Witness of God*, by the philosopher, T. H. Green (London, 1883; also in *Works*). Mr. Green was as far removed as Matthew Arnold from conventional theology, and there are traces of Hegelianism in what follows for which allowance should be made, but his mind had a natural affinity for this side of St. Paul's teaching, and he has expressed it with great force and moral intensity. To this the brief extracts given will do but imperfect justice, and the sermon is well worth reading in its entirety.

'The death and rising again of the Christ, as [St. Paul] conceived them, were not separate and independent events. They were two sides of the same act—an act which relatively to sin, to the flesh, to the old man, to all which separates from God, is death; but which, just for that reason, is the birth of a new life relatively to God, ... God was in [Christ], so that what He did, God did. A death unto life, a life out of death, must then be in some way the essence of the divine nature—must be an act which, though exhibited once for all in the crucifixion and resurrection of Christ, was yet eternal— the act of God Himself. For that very reason, however, it was one perpetually re-enacted, and to be re-enacted, by man. If Christ died for all, all died in Him: all were buried in His grave to be all made alive in His resurrection ... In other words, He constitutes in us a new intellectual consciousness, which transforms the will and is the source of a new moral life.' There is special value in the way in which the difference is brought out between the state of things to which the individual can attain by his own effort and one in which the change is wrought from without. The first ' would be a self-renunciation which would be really the acme of self-seeking. On the other hand, presented as the continuous act of God Himself, as the eternal self-surrender of the Divine Son to the Father, it is for us and may be in us, but is not of us. Nay, it is just because not of us, that it may be in us. Because it is the mind of Christ, and Christ is God's, in the contemplation of it we are taken out of ourselves, we slip the natural man and appropriate that mind which we behold. Constrained by God's manifested love, we cease to be our own that Christ may become ours' (*The Witness of God*, pp. 7–10).

We may quote lastly an estimate of the Pauline conception in the history of Religion. ' It is in Christendom that, according to the providence of God, this power has been exhibited; not indeed either adequately or exclusively, but most fully. In the religions of the East, the idea of a death to the fleshly self as the end of the merely human, and the beginning of a divine life, has not been wanting; nor, as a mere idea, has it been very different from that which is the ground of Christianity. But there it has never been realized in action, either intellectually or morally. The idea of the withdrawal from sense has remained abstract. It has not issued in such a struggle with the superficial view of things, as has gradually constituted the science of Christendom. In like manner that of self-renunciation has never emerged from the esoteric state. It has had no outlet into the life of charity, but a back-way always open into the life of sensual licence, and has been finally mechanized in the artificial vacancy of the dervish or fakir' (*ibid.* p. 21).

One of the services which Mr. Green's lay sermon may do us is in helping us to understand—not the whole but part of the remarkable conception of 'The Way' in Dr. Hort's posthumous *The Way, the Truth, and the Life* (Cambridge and London, 1893). When it is contended, 'first that the whole seeming maze of history in nature and man, the tumultuous movement of the world in progress, has running through it one supreme dominating Way; and second, that He who on earth was called Jesus the Nazarene *is* that Way' (*The Way*, &c. p. 20 f.), we can hardly be wrong, though the point might have been brought out more clearly, in seeking a scriptural illustration in St. Paul's teaching as to the Death, Burial, and Resurrection of Christ. These to him are not merely isolated historical events which took place once for all in the past. They did so take place, and their historical reality, as well as their direct significance in the Redemption wrought out by Christ, must be insisted upon. But they are more than this: they constitute a law, a predisposed pattern or plan, which other human lives have to follow. ' Death unto life,' ' life growing out of death,' is the inner principle or secret, applied in an indefinite variety of ways, but running through the history of most, perhaps all, religious aspiration and attainment. Everywhere there must be the death of an old self and the birth of a new. It must be admitted that the group of conceptions united by St. Paul, and, as it would seem, yet more widely extended by St. John, is difficult to grasp intellectually, and has doubtless been acted upon in many a simple unspeculative life in which there was never any attempt to formulate it exactly in words.   But the conception belongs to the length and depth and height of the Gospel : here, as we see it in St. Paul, it bears all the impress of his intense and prophet-like penetration : and there can be little doubt that it is capable of exercising a stronger and more dominating influence on the Christian consciousness than it has done.   This must be our excuse for expanding the doctrine at rather considerable length, and for invoking the assistance of those who, just by their detachment from ordinary and traditional Christianity, have brought to bear a freshness of insight in certain directions which has led them, if not exactly to discoveries, yet to new and vivid realization of truths which to indolent minds are obscured by their very familiarity.

THE TRANSITION FROM LAW TO GRACE.
ANALOGY OF SLAVERY.

VI. 15-23. *Take an illustration from common life—the condition of slavery.   The Christian was a slave of sin; his business was uncleanness; his wages, death.   But he has been emancipated from this service, only to enter upon another—that of Righteousness.*

[15] Am I told that we should take advantage of our liberty as subjects of Grace and not of Law, to sin? Impossible! [16] Are you not aware that to render service and obedience to any one is to be the slave of that person or power to which obedience is rendered? And so it is here. You are either slaves of Sin, and the end before you death; or you are true to your rightful Master, and the end before you righteousness. [17] But, thank God, the time is past when you were slaves of Sin ; and at your baptism you gave cordial assent to that standard of life and conduct in which you were first instructed and to the guidance of which you were then handed over by your teachers. [18] Thus you were emancipated from the service of Sin, and were transferred to the service of Righteousness.

[19] I am using a figure of speech taken from every-day human relations. If 'servitude' seems a poor and harsh metaphor, it is one which the remains of the natural man that still cling about you will at least permit you to understand. Yours must be an *undivided* service. Devote the members of your body as unreservedly

to the service of righteousness for progressive consecration to God, as you once devoted them to Pagan uncleanness and daily increasing licence. ²⁰ I exhort you to this. Why? Because while you were slaves to Sin, you were freemen in regard to Righteousness. ²¹ What good then did you get from conduct which you now blush to think of? Much indeed! For the goal to which it leads is death. ²² But now that, as Christians, you are emancipated from Sin and enslaved to God, you have something to show for your service—closer and fuller consecration, and your goal, eternal Life! ²³ For the wages which Sin pays its votaries is Death; while you receive—no wages, but the bountiful gift of God, the eternal Life, which is ours through our union with Jesus Messiah, our Lord.

15-23. The next two sections (vi. 15-23; vii. 1-6) might be described summarily as a description of the Christian's release, what it is and what it is not. The receiving of Christian Baptism was a great dividing-line across a man's career. In it he entered into a wholly new relation of self-identification with Christ which was fraught with momentous consequences looking both backwards and forwards. From his sin-stained past he was cut off as it were by death: towards the future he turned radiant with the quickening influence of a new life. St. Paul now more fully expounds the nature of the change. He does so by the help of two illustrations, one from the state of slavery, the other from the state of wedlock. Each state implied certain ties, like those by which the convert to Christianity was bound before his conversion. But the cessation of these ties does not carry with it the cessation of all ties; it only means the substitution of new ties for the old. So is it with the slave, who is emancipated from one service only to enter upon another. So is it with the wife who, when released by the death of one husband, is free to marry again. In the remaining verses of this chapter St. Paul deals with the case of Slavery. Emancipation from Sin is but the prelude to a new service of Righteousness.

15. The Apostle once more reverts to the point raised at the beginning of the chapter, but with the variation that the incentive to sin is no longer the seeming good which Sin works by calling down grace, but the freedom of the state of grace as opposed to the strictness of the Law. St. Paul's reply in effect is that Christian freedom consists not in freedom to sin but in freedom from sin.

ἀμαρτήσωμεν : from a late aor. ἡμάρτησα, found in LXX (Veitch, *Irreg. Verbs*, p. 49). Chrys. *codd.* Theodrt. and others, with minuscules, read ἀμαρτήσομεν.

16. A general proposition to which our Lord Himself had

appealed in 'No man can serve two masters' (Matt. vi. 24). There
are still nearer parallels in John viii. 34; 2 Pet. ii. 19 : passages
however which do not so much prove direct dependence on St. Paul
as that the thought was 'in the air' and might occur to more
writers than one.

ἤτοι... ἤ : these disjunctives state a dilemma in a lively and emphatic
way, implying that one limb or the other must be chosen (Bäumlein, *Par-
tikellehre*, p. 244; Kühner, *Gram.* § 540. 5).

17. εἰς ὅν . . . διδαχῆς : stands for [ὑπηκούσατε] τύπῳ διδαχῆς εἰς
ὅν παρεδόθητε. We expect rather ὅς ὑμῖν παρεδόθη : it seems more
natural to say that the teaching is handed over to the persons
taught than that the persons taught are handed over to the teaching. The form of phrase which St. Paul uses however expresses
well the experience of Christian converts. Before baptism they
underwent a course of simple instruction, like that in the ' Two
Ways' or first part of the *Didaché* (see the reff. in Hatch, *Hibbert
Lectures*, p. 314). With baptism this course of instruction ceased,
and they were left with its results impressed upon their minds.
This was to be henceforth their standard of living.

τύπον διδαχῆς. For τύπος see the note on ch. **v. 14.** The third
of the senses there given (' pattern,' ' exemplar,' ' standard') is by
far the most usual with St. Paul, and there can be little doubt that
that is the meaning here. So among the ancients Chrys. (τίς δὲ ὁ
τύπος τῆς διδαχῆς; ὀρθῶς ζῆν καὶ μετὰ πολιτείας ἀρίστης) Euthym.-Zig.
(εἰς τύπον, ἤγουν τὸν κανόνα καὶ ὅρον τῆς εὐσεβοῦς πολιτείας), and
among moderns all the English commentators with Oltr. and Lips.
To suppose, as some leading Continental scholars (De W. Mey.-W.
Go.) have done, that some special ' type of doctrine,' whether
Jewish-Christian or Pauline, is meant, is to look with the eyes of
the nineteenth century and not with those of the first (cf. Hort,
Rom. and Eph. p. 32 'Nothing like this notion of a plurality of
Christian τύποι διδαχῆς occurs anywhere else in the N. T., and it is
quite out of harmony with all the context').

19. ἀνθρώπινον λέγω. St. Paul uses this form of phrase (cf.
Gal. iii. 15 κατὰ ἄνθρωπον λέγω) where he wishes to apologize for
having recourse to some common (or as he would have called it
' carnal') illustration to express spiritual truths. So Chrys. (first
explanation) ὡσανεὶ ἔλεγεν, ἀπὸ ἀνθρωπίνων λογισμῶν, ἀπὸ τῶν ἐν
συνηθείᾳ γινομένων.

διὰ τὴν ἀσθένειαν τῆς σαρκός. Two explanations are possible :
(1) ' because of the moral hindrances which prevent the practice of
Christianity' (Chrys. Theodrt. Weiss and others); (2) 'because
of the difficulties of apprehension, from defective spiritual experience, which prevent the understanding of its deeper truths' (most
moderns). Clearly this is more in keeping with the context. In

any case the clause refers to what has gone before, not (as Orig. Chrys., &c.) to what follows.

σάρξ = human nature in its weakness, primarily physical and moral, but secondarily intellectual. It is intellectual weakness in so far as this is determined by moral, by the limitations of character: cf. φρονεῖν τὰ τῆς σαρκός, φρόνημα τῆς σαρκός Rom. viii. 5 f.; σοφοὶ κατὰ σάρκα 1 Cor. i. 26. The idea of this passage is similar to that of 1 Cor. iii. 2 γάλα ὑμᾶς ἐπότισα, οὐ βρῶμα· οὔπω γὰρ ἠδύνασθε.

τῇ ἀκαθαρσίᾳ. ἀκαθαρσία and ἀνομία fitly describe the characteristic features of Pagan life (cf. i. 24 ff.). As throughout the context these forms of sin are personified; they obtain a mastery over the man; and εἰς τὴν ἀνομίαν describes the effect of that mastery—'to the practice of iniquity.' With these verses (19-21) compare especially 1 Pet. iv. 1-5.

εἰς ἁγιασμόν. Mey. (but not Weiss) Lips. Oltr. Go. would make ἁγιασμός here practically = ἁγιωσύνη, i. e. not so much the process of consecration as the result of the process. There is certainly this tendency in language; and in some of the places in which the word is used it seems to have the sense of the resulting state (e. g. 1 Thess. iv. 4, where it is joined with τιμή; 1 Tim. ii. 15, where it is joined with πίστις and ἀγάπη). But in the present passage the word may well retain its proper meaning : the members are to be handed over to Righteousness to be (gradually) made fit for God's service, not to become fit all at once. So Weiss Gif. Va. Mou. ('course of purification'). For the radical meaning see the note on ἅγιος ch. i. 7, and Dr. A. B. Davidson, *Hebrews*, p. 206: ἁγιασμός = 'the process of fitting for acceptable worship,' a sense which comes out clearly in Heb. xii. 14 διώκετε . . . τὸν ἁγιασμὸν οὗ χωρὶς οὐδεὶς ὄψεται τὸν Κύριον. The word occurs some ten times (two vv. ll.) in LXX and in *Ps. Sol.* xvii. 33, but is not classical.

21. τίνα οὖν . . . ἐπαισχύνεσθε ; Where does the question end and the answer begin? (1) Most English commentators and critics (Treg. WH. RV. as well as Gif. Va.) carry on the question to ἐπαισχύνεσθε. In that case ἐκείνων must be supplied before ἐφ' οἷς, and its omission might be due to the reflex effect of ἐκείνων in the sentence following (comp. ἀποθανόντες ἐν ᾧ κατειχόμεθα vii. 6 below). There would then be a common enough ellipse before τὸ γὰρ τέλος, 'What fruit had ye . . .? [None:] for the end,' &c. (2) On the other hand several leading Germans (Tisch. Weiss Lips., though not Mey.) put the question at τότε, and make ἐφ' οἷς ἐπαισχύνεσθε part of the answer. 'What fruit had ye then? Things [pleasures, gratifications of sense] of which you are now ashamed: for their end is death.' So, too, Theod.-Mops. (in Cramer) expressly: κατ' ἐρώτησιν ἀναγνωστέον τὸ τίνα οὖν κάρπον εἴχετε τότε, εἶτα κατὰ ἀπόκρισιν ἐφ' οἷς νῦν ἐπαισχύνεσθε. Both interpretations are possible, but the former, as it would seem, is more simple and natural

(Gif.). When two phrases link together so easily as ἐφ᾽ οἷς ἔπασχ.
with what precedes, it is a mistake to separate them except for
strong reasons; nor does there appear to be sufficient ground for
distinguishing between near consequences and remote.

τὸ γάρ : τὸ μὲν γάρ Ν° B D* E F G. There is the usual ambiguity of
readings in which B alone joins the Western authorities. The probability is
that the reading belongs to the Western element in B, and that μέν was
introduced through erroneous antithesis to νυνὶ δέ.

23. ὀψώνια. From a root πεπ- we get ἕψω, ὄψον, 'cooked' meat, fish, &c.
as contrasted with bread. Hence the compound ὀψώνιον (ὠνέομαι, 'to buy') =
(1) provision-money, ration-money, or the rations in kind given to troops;
(2) in a more general sense, 'wages.' The word is said to have come in
with Menander : it is proscribed by the Atticists, but found freely in Polybius,
1 Macc. &c. (Sturz, *Dial. Maced.* p. 187).

χάρισμα. Tertullian, with his usual picturesque boldness, translates this by
donativum (*De Res. Carn.* c. 47 *Stipendia enim delinquentiae mors, donativum
autem dei vita aeterna*). It is not probable that St. Paul had this particular
antithesis in his mind, though no doubt he intends to contrast ὀψώνια and
χάρισμα.

THE TRANSITION FROM LAW TO GRACE.
ANALOGY OF MARRIAGE.

VII. 1-6. *Take another illustration from the Law of
Marriage. The Marriage Law only binds a woman while
her husband lives. So with the Christian. He was wedded,
as it were, to his old sinful state ; and all that time he was
subject to the law applicable to that state. But this old life
of his was killed through his identification with the death of
Christ; so as to set him free to contract a new marriage—
with Christ, no longer dead but risen : and the fruit of that
marriage should be a new life quickened by the Spirit.*

¹ I say that you are free from the Law of Moses and from Sin.
You will see how : unless you need to be reminded of a fact which
your acquaintance with the nature of Law will readily suggest to
you, that Law, for the man who comes under it, is only in force
during his lifetime. ² Thus for instance a woman in wedlock is
forbidden by law to desert her living husband. But if her husband
should die, she is absolved from the provisions of the statute 'Of
the Husband.' ³ Hence while her husband is alive, she will be
styled 'an adulteress' if she marry another man : but if her

husband die, she is free from that statute, so that no one can call her an adulteress, though she be married to another man.

⁴ We may apply this in an allegory, in which the wife is the Christian's 'self' or 'ego'; the first husband, his old unregenerate state, burdened with all the penalties attaching to it.

You then, my brethren in Christ, had this old state killed in you —brought to an abrupt and violent end—by your identification with the crucified Christ, whose death you reproduce spiritually. And this death of your old self left you free to enter upon a new marriage with the same Christ, who triumphed over death— a triumph in which you too share—that in union with Him you, and indeed all of us Christians, may be fruitful in good works, to the glory and praise of God. ⁵ Our new marriage must be fruitful, as our old marriage was. When we had nothing better to guide us than this frail humanity of ours, so liable to temptation, at that time too a process of generation was going on. The impressions of sense, suggestive of sin, stimulated into perverse activity by their legal prohibition, kept plying this bodily organism of ours in such a way as to engender acts that only went to swell the garners of Death. ⁶ But now all that has been brought to an end. Law and the state of sin are so inextricably linked together, that in dying, at our baptism, a moral death, to that old state of sin we were absolved or discharged from the Law, which used to hold us prisoners under the penalties to which sin laid us open. And through this discharge we are enabled to serve God in a new state, the ruling principle of which is Spirit, in place of that old state, presided over by Written Law.

1-6. The text of this section—and indeed of the whole chapter —is still, ' Ye are not under Law, but under Grace'; and the Apostle brings forward another illustration to show how the transition from Law to Grace has been effected, and what should be its consequences.

In the working out of this illustration there is a certain amount of intricacy, due to an apparent shifting of the stand-point in the middle of the paragraph. The Apostle begins by showing how with the death of her husband the law which binds a married woman becomes a dead letter. He goes on to say in the application, not 'The Law is dead to you,' but 'You are dead to the Law'—which looks like a change of position, though a legitimate one.

Gif. however may be right in explaining the transition rather differently, viz. by means of the παλαιὸς ἄνθρωπος of ch. vi. 6. The 'self' of the man is double; there is an 'old self' and a 'new self'; or rather the 'self' remains the same throughout, but it passes through different states, or phases. Bearing this in mind we shall find the metaphor work out consistently.

The Wife = the true self, or ego, which is permanent through all change.

The (first) Husband = the old state before conversion to Christianity.

The 'law of the husband' = the law which condemned that old state.

The new Marriage = the union upon which the convert enters with Christ.

The crucial phrase is ὑμεῖς ἐθανατώθητε in ver. 4. According to the way in which we explain this will be our explanation of the whole passage. See the note *ad loc.*

There is yet another train of thought which comes in with vv. 4–6. The idea of marriage naturally suggests the offspring of marriage. In the case of the Christian the fruit of his union with Christ is a holy life.

1. Ἢ ἀγνοεῖτε: ['surely you know this—that the régime of Law has come to an end, and that Grace has superseded it.] Or do you require to be told that death closes all accounts, and therefore that the state of things to which Law belongs ceased through the death of the Christian with Christ—that mystical death spoken of in the last chapter?'

γινώσκουσι γὰρ νόμον λαλῶ: 'I speak' (lit. 'am talking') 'to men acquainted with Law.' At once the absence of the article and the nature of the case go to show that what is meant here is not Roman Law (Weiss), of which there is no reason to suppose that St. Paul would possess any detailed knowledge, nor yet the Law of Moses more particularly considered (Lips.), but a general principle of all Law; an obvious axiom of political justice—that death clears all scores, and that a dead man can no longer be prosecuted or punished (cf. Hort, *Rom. and Eph.* p. 24).

2. ἡ γὰρ ὕπανδρος γυνή: ['the truth of this may be proved by a case in point.] For a woman in the state of wedlock is bound by law to her living husband.' ὕπανδρος: a classical word, found in LXX.

κατήργηται: 'is completely (perf.) absolved or discharged' (lit. 'nullified' or 'annulled,' her status as a wife is abolished). The two correlative phrases are treated by St. Paul as practically convertible: 'the woman is annulled from the law,' and 'the law is annulled to the woman.' For καταργεῖν see on iii. 3.

ἀπὸ τοῦ νόμου τοῦ ἀνδρός: from that section of the statute-book which is headed 'The Husband,' the section which lays down his rights and duties. Gif. compares 'the law of the leper' Lev. xiv. 2; 'the law of the Nazirite' Num. vi. 13.

3. χρηματίσει. The meanings of χρηματίζειν ramify in two directions. The fundamental idea is that of 'transacting business' or 'managing affairs.' Hence we get on the one hand, from the notion of doing business under a certain name, from Polybius onwards (1) 'to bear a name or title' (χρηματίζει βασιλεύς Polyb. V. lvii. 2); and so simply, as here, 'to be called or styled' (Acts xi. 26 ἐγένετο . . . χρηματίσαι πρῶτον ἐν Ἀντιοχείᾳ τοὺς μαθητὰς Χριστιανούς) ; and on the other hand (2) from the notion of 'having dealings with,' 'giving audience to' a person, in a special sense, of the 'answers, communications, revelations,' given by an oracle or by God. So six times in LXX of Jerem., Joseph. *Antiq.*, Plutarch, &c. From this sense we get pass. 'to be warned or admonished' by God (Matt. ii. 12, 22; Acts x. 22; Heb. viii. 5; xi. 7). Hence also subst. χρηματισμός, 'a Divine or oracular response,' 2 Macc. ii. 4; Rom. xi. 4. Burton (*M. and T.* § 69) calls the fut. here a 'gnomic future' as stating 'what will customarily happen when occasion offers.'

τοῦ μὴ εἶναι = ὥστε μὴ εἶναι: the stress is thrown back upon ἐλευθέρα, 'so as not to be,' 'causing her not to be,'—not 'so that she is.' According to Burton τοῦ μή here denotes 'conceived result'; but see the note on ὥστε δουλεύειν in ver. 6 below.

4. ὥστε with indic. introduces a consequence which follows as a matter of fact.

καὶ ὑμεῖς ἐθανατώθητε. We have said that the exact interpretation of the whole passage turns upon this phrase. It is commonly explained as another way of saying 'You had the Law killed to you.' So Chrys. ἀκόλουθον ἦν εἰπεῖν, τοῦ νόμου τελευτήσαντος οὐ κρίνεσθε μοιχείας, ἀνδρὶ γενόμενοι ἑτέρῳ. Ἀλλ᾽ οὐκ εἶπεν οὕτως, ἀλλὰ πῶς; Ἐθανατώθητε τῷ νόμῳ (cf. Euthym.-Zig.). In favour of this is the parallel κατήργηται ἀπὸ τοῦ νόμου τοῦ ἀνδρός in ver. 2, and κατηργήθημεν ἀπὸ τοῦ νόμου in ver. 6. But on the other hand it is strange to speak of the same persons at one moment as 'killed' and the next as 'married again.' There is therefore a strong attraction in the explanation of Gif., who makes ὑμεῖς = not the whole self but the old self, *i.e.* the old state of the self which was really 'crucified with Christ' (ch. vi. 6), and the death of which really leaves the man (= the wife in the allegory) free to contract a new union. This moral death of the Christian to his past also does away with the Law. The Law had its hold upon him only through sin; but in discarding his sins he discards also the pains and penalties which attached to them. Nothing can touch him further. His old heathen or Jewish antecedents have passed away; he is under obligation only to Christ.

καὶ ὑμεῖς. The force of καί here is, 'You, my readers, as well as the wife in the allegory.'

διὰ τοῦ σώματος τοῦ Χριστοῦ. The way in which the death of the 'old man' is brought about is through the identification of the

Christian with the Death of Christ. The Christian takes his place, as it were, with Christ upon the Cross, and there has his old self crucified. The 'body' of Christ here meant is the 'crucified body': the Christian shares in that crucifixion, and so gets rid of his sinful past. We are thus taken back to the symbolism of the last chapter (vi. 6), to which St. Paul also throws in an allusion in τῷ ἐκ νεκρῶν ἐγερθέντι. The two lines of symbolism really run parallel to each other and it is easy to connect them.

ὁ παλαιὸς ἄνθρωπος = The Husband:
Crucifixion of the παλ. ἄνθ. = Death of the Husband:
Resurrection = Re-Marriage:
ζῆν, δουλεύειν τῷ Θεῷ = καρποφορεῖν τῷ Θεῷ.

εἰς τὸ γενέσθαι ὑμᾶς ἑτέρῳ. Lips. takes this not of 'being married to another husband,' but of 'joining another *master*,' on the ground that there is no marriage to the *Law*. This however (1) is unnecessary, because marriage to the 'old man' carries with it subjection to the Law, so that the dissolution of the marriage involves release from the Law by a step which is close and inevitable; (2) it is wrong, because of καρποφορῆσαι, which it is clearly forced and against the context to refer, as Lips. does, to anything but the offspring of marriage.

καρποφορήσωμεν τῷ Θεῷ. The natural sequel to the metaphor of 'Marriage.' The 'fruit' which the Christian, wedded to Christ, is to bear is of course that of a reformed life.

5. ὅτε γὰρ ἦμεν ἐν τῇ σαρκί. This verse develops the idea contained in καρποφορήσωμεν: the new marriage ought to be fruitful, because the old one was. εἶναι ἐν τῇ σαρκί is the opposite of εἶναι ἐν τῷ πνεύματι: the one is a life which has no higher object than the gratification of the senses, the other is a life permeated by the Spirit. Although σάρξ is human nature especially on the side of its frailty, it does not follow that there is any dualism in St. Paul's conception or that he regards the body as inherently sinful. Indeed this very passage proves the contrary. It implies that it is possible to be 'in the body' without being 'in the flesh.' The body, as such, is plastic to influences of either kind: it may be worked upon by Sin through the senses, or it may be worked upon by the Spirit. In either case the motive-force comes from without. The body itself is neutral. See esp. the excellent discussion in Gifford, pp. 48–52.

τὰ παθήματα τῶν ἁμαρτιῶν: πάθημα has the same sort of ambiguity as our word 'passion.' It means (1) an 'impression,' esp. a 'painful impression' or suffering; (2) the reaction which follows upon some strong impression of sense (cf. Gal. v. 24). The gen. τῶν ἁμαρτιῶν = 'connected with sins,' 'leading to sins.'

τὰ διὰ τοῦ νόμου. Here St. Paul, as his manner is, 'throws up a finger-post' which points to the coming section of his argument. The phrase διὰ τοῦ νόμου is explained at length in the next paragraph : it refers to the effect of Law in calling forth and aggravating sin.

ἐνηργεῖτο. The pricks and stings of passion were active in our members (cf. 1 Thess. ii. 13 ; 2 Thess. ii. 7 ; 2 Cor. i. 6, iv. 12 ; Gal. v. 6, &c.).

τῷ θανάτῳ : *dat. commodi,* contrasted with καρποφ. τῷ Θεῷ above.

6. νυνὶ δὲ κατηργήθημεν ἀπὸ τοῦ νόμου. 'But as it is we' (in our peccant part, the old man) 'were discharged or annulled from the Law' (*i.e.* we had an end put to our relations with the Law; by the death of our old man there was nothing left on which the Law could wreak its vengeance; we were 'struck with atrophy' in respect to it : see on ver. 2). πῶς ἡμεῖς κατηργήθημεν ; τοῦ κατεχομένου παρὰ τῆς ἁμαρτίας ἀνθρώπου παλαιοῦ ἀποθανόντος καὶ ταφέντος Chrys. We observe how Chrys. here practically comes round to the same side as Gif.

The renderings of κατηργήθημεν are rather interesting, and show the difficulty of finding an exact equivalent in other languages : *evacuati sumus* Tert.; *soluti sumus* Codd. Clarom. Sangerm. Vulg. (= 'we were unbounden' Wic. ; 'we are loosed' Rhem.) ; 'we are delivered' Tyn. Cran. Genev. AV. ; 'we are discharged' RV.; *nous avons été dégagés* Oltr. (*Le Nouveau Test.,* Geneva, 1874) ; *nun aber sind wir für das Gesetz nicht mehr da* Weizsäcker (*Das Neue Test.,* Freiburg i. B. 1882, ed. 2).

ἀποθανόντες. AV. apparently read ἀποθανόντος, for which there is no MS. authority, but which seems to be derived by a mistake of Beza following Erasmus from a comment of Chrysostom's (see Tisch. *ad loc.*). The Western text (D E F G, *codd. ap.* Orig.-lat. and most Latins) boldly corrects to τοῦ θανάτου, which would go with τοῦ νόμου, and which gives an easier construction, though not a better sense. After ἀποθανόντες we must supply ἐκείνῳ, just as in vi. 21 we had to supply ἐκείνων.

ἐν ᾧ κατειχόμεθα. The antecedent of ἐν ᾧ is taken by nearly all commentators as equivalent to τῷ νόμῳ (whether ἐκείνῳ or τούτῳ is regarded as masc. or better neutr.). Gif. argues against referring it to the 'old state,' 'the old man,' that this is not sufficiently suggested by the context. But wherever 'death' is spoken of it is primarily this 'old state,' or 'old man' which dies, so that the use of the term ἀποθανόντες alone seems enough to suggest it. It was this old sinful state which brought man under the grip of the Law; when the sinful life ceased the Law lost its hold.

ὥστε δουλεύειν : not 'so that we serve' (RV. and most commentators), but 'so *as to* serve,' i. e. 'enabling us to serve.' The stress is thrown back upon κατηργήθημεν,—we were so completely discharged as to set us free to serve.

The true distinction between ὥστε with infin. and ὥστε with indic., which is not always observed in RV., is well stated by Goodwin, *Moods and Tenses,* ed. 1889, § 584 (with the quotation from Shilleto, *De Fals. Leg.* App. in the note), and for N. T. by the late Canon T. S. Evans in the *Expos.* for 1882, i. 3 ff. : ὥστε with indic. states the definite result which as a matter of fact *does* follow ; ὥστε with infin. states the contemplated result which in the natural course *ought to* follow. ὥστε with indic. lays stress on the effect; ὥστε with infin. on the cause. Thus in 1 Cor. i. 7 ὥστε ὑστερεῖσθαι = 'causing or inspiring you to feel behindhand' (see *Sp. Comm. ad loc.*); in Matt. xiii. 32 γίνεται δένδρον, ὥστε ἐλθεῖν τὰ πετεινὰ καὶ κατασκηνοῦν = 'becomes a tree *big enough for* the birds to come,' &c. It will be seen that the distinction corresponds to the difference in the general character of the two moods.

ἐν καινότητι πνεύματος . . . παλαιότητι γράμματος. In each case the gen. is what is called of 'apposition': it denotes that in which the newness, or oldness, consists. The essential feature of the new state is that it is one of 'Spirit'; of the old state, that it is regulated by 'written Law.' The period of the Paraclete has succeeded to the period which took its character from the Sinaitic legislation. The Christian life turns on an inspiration from above, not on an elaborate code of commands and prohibitions. A fuller explanation of the καινότης πνεύματος is given in ch. viii.

It is perhaps well to remind the reader who is not careful to check the study of the English versions by the Greek that the opposition between γράμμα and πνεῦμα is not exactly identical with that which we are in the habit of drawing between 'the letter' and 'the spirit' as the 'literal' and 'spiritual sense' of a writing. In this antithesis γράμμα is with St. Paul always the Law of Moses, as a written code, while πνεῦμα is the operation of the Holy Spirit characteristic of Christianity (cf. Rom. ii. 29; 2 Cor. iii. 6).

LAW AND SIN.

VII. 7-25. *If release from Sin means release from Law, must we then identify Law with Sin? No. Law reveals the sinfulness of Sin, and by this very revelation stirs up the dormant Sin to action. But this is not because the Law itself is evil—on the contrary it is good—but that Sin may be exposed and its guilt aggravated* (vv. 7-13).

This is what takes place. I have a double self. But my better self is impotent to prevent me from doing wrong (vv. 14-17). *It is equally impotent to make me do right* (vv. 18-21). *There is thus a constant conflict going on, from which, unaided, I can hope for no deliverance. But, God be thanked, through Christ deliverance comes!* (vv. 21-25).

⁷ I spoke a moment ago of sinful passions working through Law, and of the death to Sin as carrying with it a release from the Law. Does it follow that the Law itself is actually a form of Sin? An

intolerable thought! On the contrary it was the Law and nothing else through which I learnt the true nature of Sin. For instance, I knew the sinfulness of covetous or illicit desire only by the Law saying 'Thou shalt not covet.' ⁸ But the lurking Sin within me started into activity, and by the help of that express command, provoking to that which it prohibited, led me into all kinds of conscious and sinful covetousness. For without Law to bring it out Sin lies dead—inert and passive. ⁹ And while sin was dead, I—my inner self—was alive, in happy unconsciousness, following my bent with no pangs of conscience excited by Law. But then came this Tenth Commandment; and with its coming Sin awoke to life, while I—sad and tragic contrast—died the living death of sin, precursor of eternal death. ¹⁰ And the commandment which was given to point men the way to life, this very commandment was found in my case to lead to death. ¹¹ For Sin took advantage of it, and by the help of the commandment—at once confronting me with the knowledge of right and provoking me to do that which was wrong—it betrayed me, so that I fell; and the commandment was the weapon with which it slew me. ¹² The result is that the Law, as a whole, is holy, inasmuch as it proceeds from God: and each single commandment has the like character of holiness, justice, and beneficence. ¹³ Am I then to say that a thing so excellent in itself to me proved fatal? Not for a moment. It was rather the demon Sin which wrought the mischief. And the reason why it was permitted to do so was that it might be shown in its true colours, convicted of being the pernicious thing that it is, by the fact that it made use of a good instrument, Law, to work out upon me the doom of death. For this reason Sin was permitted to have its way, in order that through its perverted use of the Divine commandment it might be seen in all its utter hideousness.

¹⁴ The blame cannot attach to the Law. For we all know that the Law has its origin from the Spirit of God and derives its character from that Spirit, while I, poor mortal, am made of frail human flesh and blood, sold like any slave in the market into the servitude of Sin. ¹⁵ It is not the Law, and not my own deliberate self, which is the cause of the evil; because my actions are executed blindly with no proper concurrence of the will. I purpose one

way, I act another.   I hate a thing, but do it.   [16] And by this very fact that I hate the thing that I do, my conscience bears testimony to the Law, and recognizes its excellence.   [17] So that the state of the case is this.   It is not I, my true self, who put into act what is repugnant to me, but Sin which has possession of me.   [18] For I am aware that in me as I appear to the outer world—in this ' body that does me grievous wrong,' there dwells (in any permanent and predominating shape) nothing that is good.   The will indeed to do good is mine, and I can command it; but the performance I cannot command.   [19] For the actual thing that I do is not the good that I wish to do; but my moral agency appears in the evil that I wish to avoid.   [20] But if I thus do what I do not wish to do, then the active force in me, the agent that carries out the act, is not my true self (which is rather seen in the wish to do right), but the tyrant Sin which holds possession of me.   [21] I find therefore this law— if so it may be called—this stern necessity laid upon me from without, that much as I wish to do what is good, the evil lies at my door.   [22] For I am a divided being.   In my innermost self, the thinking and reasoning part of me, I respond joyfully to the Law of God.   [23] But then I see a different Law dominating this bodily organism of mine, and making me do its behests.   This other Law takes the field in arms against the Law of Reason and Conscience, and drags me away captive in the fetters of Sin, the Power which has such a fatal grip upon my body.   [24] Unhappy man that I am— torn with a conflict from which there seems to be no issue!   This body from which proceed so many sinful impulses; this body which makes itself the instrument of so many acts of sin; this body which is thus dragging me down to death.—How shall I ever get free from it?   What Deliverer will come and rescue me from its oppression?

[25] A Deliverer has come.   And I can only thank God, approach-ing His Presence in humble gratitude, through Him to whom the deliverance is due—Jesus Messiah, our Lord.

Without His intervention—so long as I am left to my own unaided self—the state that I have been describing may be briefly summarized.   In this twofold capacity of mine I serve two masters: with my conscience I serve the Law of God; with my bodily organism the Law of Sin.

7. So far Sin and Law have been seen in such close connexion that it becomes necessary to define more exactly the relation between them. In discussing this the Apostle is led to consider the action of both upon the character and the struggle to which they give rise in the soul.

It is evident that Marcion had this section, as Tertullian turns against him St. Paul's refusal to listen to any attack upon the Law, which Marcion ascribed to the Demiurge: *Abominatur apostolus criminationem legis . . . Quid deo imputas legis quod legi eius apostolus imputare non audet? Atquin et accumulat*: Lex sancta, et praeceptum eius iustum et bonum. *Si taliter veneratur legem creatoris, quomodo ipsum destruat nescio.*

ὁ νόμος ἁμαρτία. It had just been shown (ver. 5) that Sin *makes use of* the Law to effect the destruction of the sinner. Does it follow that Sin is to be *identified* with the Law? Do the two so overlap each other that the Law itself comes under the description of Sin? St. Paul, like every pious Jew, repels this conclusion with horror.

ἀλλά contradicts emphatically the notion that the Law is Sin. On the contrary the Law first told me what Sin was.

οὐκ ἔγνων. It is not quite certain whether this is to be taken hypothetically (for οὐκ ἂν ἔγνων, ἄν omitted to give a greater sense of actuality, Kühner, *Gr. Gramm.* ii. 176 f.) or whether it is simply temporal. Lips. Oltr. and others adopt the hypothetical sense both here and with οὐκ ᾔδειν below. Gif. Va. make both οὐκ ἔγνων and οὐκ ᾔδειν plain statement of fact. Mey.-W. Go. take οὐκ ἔγνων temporally, οὐκ ᾔδειν hypothetically. As the context is a sort of historical retrospect the simple statement seems most in place.

τήν τε γὰρ ἐπιθυμίαν. τε γάρ is best explained as = 'for also,' ' for indeed ' (Gif. Win. § liii. p. 561 E. T.; otherwise Va.). The general proposition is proved by a concrete example.

ἔγνων . . . ᾔδειν retain their proper meanings: ἔγνων, 'I learnt,' implies more intimate experimental acquaintance; ᾔδειν is simple knowledge that there was such a thing as lust.

ἐπιθυμήσεις. The Greek word has a wider sense than our ' covet '; it includes every kind of illicit desire.

8. ἀφορμὴν λαβοῦσα: ' getting a start,' finding a *point d'appui*, or, as we should say, ' something to take hold of.' In a military sense ἀφορμή = 'a base of operations' (Thuc. i. 90. 2, &c.). In a literary sense ἀφορμὴν λαβεῖν = ' to take a hint,' ' adopt a suggestion'; cf. Eus. *Ep. ad Carpianum* ἐκ τοῦ πονήματος τοῦ προειρημένου ἀνδρὸς εἰληφὼς ἀφορμάς. And so here in a moral sense: Sin exists, but apart from Law it has nothing to work upon, no means of producing guilt. Law gives it just the opportunity it wants.

ἡ ἁμαρτία: see p. 145, *sup.*

διὰ τῆς ἐντολῆς. The prep. διά and the position of the word

show that it is better taken with κατειργάσατο than with ἀφορμ.
λαβ. ἐντολή is the single commandment; νόμος the code as a
whole.

χωρὶς γὰρ . . . νεκρά. A standing thought which we have had
before, iv. 15; v. 13: cf. iii. 20.

9. ἔζων (ἔζην B; ἔζουν 17). St. Paul uses a vivid figurative
expression, not of course with the full richness of meaning which
he sometimes gives to it (i. 17; viii. 13, &c.). He is describing
the state prior to Law primarily in himself as a child before the
consciousness of law has taken hold upon him; but he uses this
experience as typical of that both of individuals and nations before
they are restrained by express command. The 'natural man'
flourishes; he does freely and without hesitation all that he has
a mind to do; he puts forth all his vitality, unembarrassed by
the checks and thwartings of conscience. It is the kind of life
which is seen at its best in some of the productions of Greek art.
Greek life had no doubt its deeper and more serious side; but
this comes out more in its poetry and philosophy: the frieze of
the Parthenon is the consummate expression of a life that does
not look beyond the morrow and has no inward perplexities to
trouble its enjoyment of to-day. See the general discussion below.

ἀνέζησεν: 'sprang into life' (T. K. Abbott). Sin at first is
there, but dormant; not until it has the help of the Law does it
become an active power of mischief.

11. ἐξηπάτησέ με. The language is suggested by the description of the Fall (Gen. iii. 13 LXX; cf. 2 Cor. xi. 3; 1 Tim. ii.
14). Sin here takes the place of the Tempter there. In both
cases the 'commandment'—acknowledged only to be broken—
is the instrument which is made use of to bring about the disastrous and fatal end.

12. ὁ μὲν νόμος. The μέν expects a following δέ. St. Paul had
probably intended to write ἡ δὲ ἁμαρτία κατηργάσατο ἐν ἐμοὶ τὸν
θάνατον, or something of the kind; but he digresses to explain how
a good Law can have evil consequences, and so he fails to complete the sentence on the same plan on which he had begun it. On
St. Paul's view of the nature and functions of the Law see below.

It is hardly safe to argue with Zahn (Gesch. d. K. ii. 517) from the language of Tertullian (given above on ver. 7) that that writer had before him
a corrupt Marcionitic text—not, Zahn thinks, actually due to Marcion, but
corrupted since his time—ἡ ἐντολὴ αὐτοῦ δικαία for ἡ ἐντ. ἁγία καὶ δικαία.
It is more probable that Tert. is reproducing his text rather freely: in De
Pudic. 6 he leaves out καὶ δικαία, lex quidem sancta est et praeceptum
sanctum et optimum (the use of superlative for positive is fairly common in
Latin versions and writers).

13. Why was this strange perversion of so excellent a thing as
the Law permitted? This very perversion served to aggravate the

horror of Sin: not content with the evil which it is in itself it must needs turn to evil that which was at once Divine in its origin and beneficent in its purpose. To say this was to pronounce its condemnation: it was like giving it full scope, so that the whole world might see (φανῇ) of what extremities (καθ᾽ ὑπερβολήν) Sin was capable.

14. The section which follows explains more fully by a psychological analysis *how* it is that the Law is broken and that Sin works such havoc. There is a germ of good in human nature, a genuine desire to do what is right, but this is overborne by the force of temptation acting through the bodily appetites and passions.

πνευματικός. The Law is 'spiritual,' as the Manna and the Water from the Rock were 'spiritual' (1 Cor. x. 3, 4) in the sense of being 'Spirit-caused' or 'Spirit-given,' but with the further connotation that the character of the Law is such as corresponds to its origin.

σάρκινος (σαρκικός אᶜ L P *al.*) denotes simply the *material* of which human nature is composed, 'made of flesh and blood' (1 Cor. iii. 1; 2 Cor. iii. 3), and as such exposed to all the temptations which act through the body.

There has been considerable controversy as to the bearing of the antithesis in St. Paul between the σάρξ and πνεῦμα. It has been maintained that this antithesis amounts to dualism, that St. Paul regards the σάρξ as inherently evil and the cause of evil, and that this dualistic conception is Greek or Hellenistic and not Jewish in its origin. So, but with differences among themselves, Holsten (1855, 1868), Rich. Schmidt (1870), Lüdemann (1872), and to some extent Pfleiderer (1873). [In the second edition of his *Paulinismus* (1890), Pfleiderer refers so much of St. Paul's teaching on this head as seems to go beyond the O. T. not to Hellenism, but to the later Jewish doctrine of the Fall, much as it has been expounded above, p. 136 ff. In this we need not greatly differ from him.] The most elaborate reply was that of H. H. Wendt, *Die Begriffe Fleisch und Geist* (Gotha, 1878), which was made the basis of an excellent treatise in English by Dr. W. P. Dickson, *St. Paul's Use of the Terms Flesh and Spirit*, Glasgow, 1883. Reference may also be made to the well-considered statement of Dr. Gifford (*Romans*, pp. 48–52). The controversy may now be regarded as practically closed. Its result is summed up by Lipsius in these decisive words: 'The Pauline anthropology rests entirely on an Old Testament base; the elements in it which are supposed to be derived from Hellenistic dualism must simply be denied (*sind einfach zu bestreiten*).' The points peculiar to St. Paul, according to Lipsius, are the sharper contrast between the Divine πνεῦμα and the human ψυχή, and the reading of a more ethical sense into σάρξ, which was originally physical, so that in Gal. v. 19 ff., Rom. viii. 4 ff. the σάρξ becomes a principle directly at war with the πνεῦμα. In the present passage (Rom. vii. 14–25) the opposing principle is ἁμαρτία, and the σάρξ is only the material medium (*Substrat*) of sensual impulses and desires. We may add that this is St. Paul's essential view, of which all else is but the variant expression.

15. κατεργάζομαι = *perficio, perpetro*, 'to carry into effect,' 'put into execution'; πράσσω = *ago*, to act as a moral and responsible being: ποιῶ = *facio,* to produce a certain result without reference to its moral character, and simply as it might be produced by inanimate mechanism (see also the notes on ch. i. 32 : ii. 9). Of course the specific sense may not be always marked by the context, but here it is well borne out throughout. For a fuller account of the distinction see Schmidt, *Lat. u. Gr. Synonymik*, p. 294 ff.

οὐ γινώσκω appears to describe the harmonious and conscious working of will and motive, the former deliberately accepting and carrying out the promptings of the latter. The man acts, so to speak, blindly : he is not a fully conscious agent : a force which he cannot resist takes the decision out of his hands.

ὃ θέλω. The exact distinction between θέλω and βούλομαι has been much disputed, and is difficult to mark. On the whole it seems that, especially in N. T. usage, βούλομαι lays the greater stress on the idea of purpose, deliberation, θέλω on the more emotional aspect of will : in this context it is evidently something short of the final act of volition, and practically = 'wish,' 'desire.' See especially the full and excellent note in Grm.-Thay.

17. νυνὶ δέ : 'as it is,' 'as the case really lies' ; the contrast is logical, not temporal.

ἡ οἰκοῦσα ἐν ἐμοὶ ἁμαρτία. [Read ἐνοικοῦσα with ℵ B, Method. (*ap.* Phot. *cod.*, *non autem ap.* Epiph.)] This indwelling Sin corresponds to the indwelling Spirit of the next chapter : a further proof that the Power which exerts so baneful an influence is not merely an attribute of the man himself but has an objective existence.

18. ἐν ἐμοί, τοῦτ' ἔστιν, κ.τ.λ. The part of the man in which Sin thus establishes itself is not his higher self, his conscience, but his lower self, the 'flesh,' which, if not itself evil, is too easily made the instrument of evil.

παράκειταί μοι : 'lies to my hand,' 'within my reach.'

οὐ ℵ A B C 47 67** *al.*, Edd. : οὐχ εὑρίσκω D E F G K L P &c.
20. ὃ οὐ θέλω B C D E F G *al.*, WH. RV. : ὃ οὐ θέλω ἐγω ℵ A K L P &c., Tisch. WH. *marg.*

21. εὑρίσκω ἄρα τὸν νόμον : 'I find then this rule,' 'this constraining principle,' hardly 'this constantly recurring experience,' which would be too modern. The νόμος here mentioned is akin to the ἕτερον νόμον of ver. 23. It is not merely the observed fact that the will to do good is forestalled by evil, but the coercion of the will that is thus exercised. Lips. seems to be nearest to the mark, *das Gesetz d. h. die objectiv mir auferlegte Nothwendigkeit.*

Many commentators, from Chrysostom onwards, have tried to make τὸν νόμον = the Mosaic Law : but either (i) they read into the passage more than the context will allow ; or (ii) they give to the sentence a construction which is linguistically intolerable. The best attempt in this direction is prob. that of Va. who translates, 'I find then with regard to the Law, that to me who would fain do that which is good, to me (I say) that which is evil is present.' He supposes a double break in the construction : (1) τὸν νόμον put as if the sentence had been intended to run 'I find then the

Law—when I wish to do good—powerless to help me'; and (2) ἐμοί repeated for the sake of clearness. It is apparently in a similar sense that Dr. T. K. Abbott proposes as an alternative rendering (the first being as above), 'With respect to the law, I find,' &c. But the anacoluthon after τὸν νόμον seems too great even for dictation to an amanuensis. Other expedients like those of Mey. (not Mey.-W.) Fri. Ew. are still more impossible. See esp. Gif. Additional Note, p. 145.

22. συνήδομαι τῷ νόμῳ τοῦ Θεοῦ: what it approves, I gladly and cordially approve.

κατὰ τὸν ἔσω ἄνθρωπον. St. Paul, as we have seen (on vi. 6), makes great use of this phrase ἄνθρωπος, which goes back as far as Plato. Now he contrasts the 'old' with the 'new man' (or, as we should say, the 'old' with the 'new *self*'); now he contrasts the 'outer man,' or the body (ὁ ἔξω ἄνθρωπος 2 Cor. iv. 16), with the 'inner man,' the conscience or reason (2 Cor. iv. 16; Eph. iii. 16).

23. ἕτερον νόμον: 'a different law' (for the distinction between ἕτερος, 'different,' and ἄλλος, 'another,' 'a second,' see the commentators on Gal. i. 6, 7).

There are two Imperatives (νόμοι) within the man: one, that of conscience; the other, that proceeding from the action of Sin upon the body. One of these Imperatives is the moral law, 'Thou shalt' and 'Thou shalt not'; the other is the violent impulse of passion.

τῷ νόμῳ τοῦ νοός μου. For νοῦς see on i. 28: it is the rational part of conscience, the faculty which decides between right and wrong: strictly speaking it belongs to the region of morals rather than to that of intercourse with God, or religion; but it may be associated with and brought under the influence of the πνεῦμα (Eph. iv. 23 ἀνανεοῦσθαι τῷ πνεύματι τοῦ νοός: cf. Rom. xii. 2), just as on the other hand it may be corrupted by the flesh (Rom. i. 28).

24. ταλαίπωρος ἐγὼ ἄνθρωπος. A heart-rending cry, from the depths of despair. It is difficult to think of this as exactly St. Paul's own experience: as a Christian he seems above it, as a Pharisee below it—self-satisfaction was too ingrained in the Pharisaic temper, the performance of Pharisaic righteousness was too well within the compass of an average will. But St. Paul was not an ordinary Pharisee. He dealt too honestly with himself, so that sooner or later the self-satisfaction natural to the Pharisee must give way: and his experience as a Christian would throw back a lurid light on those old days 'of which he was now ashamed.' So that, what with his knowledge of himself, and what with his sympathetic penetration into the hearts of others, he had doubtless materials enough for the picture which he has drawn here with such extraordinary power. He has sat for his own likeness; but there are ideal traits in the picture as well.

ἐκ τοῦ σώματος τοῦ θανάτου τούτου. In construction τούτου might go with σώματος ('from this body of death') : but it is far better to take it in the more natural connexion with θανάτου; 'the body of this death' which already has me in its clutches. Sin and death are inseparable : as the body involves me in sin it also involves me in mortality; physical death to be followed by eternal, the death of the body by the death of the soul.

25. ἄρα οὖν κ.τ.λ. A terse compressed summary of the previous paragraph, vv. 7–24, describing in two strokes the state of things prior to the intervention of Christ. The expression is that which comes from deep feeling. The particular phrases hardly seem to need further explanation.

εὐχαριστῶ τῷ Θεῷ. The true reading is probably χάρις τῷ Θεῷ. The evidence stands thus.

χάρις τῷ Θεῷ B, Sah., Orig. semel Hieron. semel.

χάρις δὲ τῷ Θεῷ ℵᵃ C² (de C* non liquet) minusc. aliq., Boh. Arm., Cyr.-Alex. Jo.-Damasc.

ἡ χάρις τοῦ Θεοῦ D E 38, d e Vulg., Orig.-lat. bis Hieron. semel Ambrstr.

ἡ χάρις τοῦ Κυρίου F G, f g, cf. Iren.-lat.

εὐχαριστῶ τῷ Θεῷ ℵ* A K L P &c., Syrr. Goth., Orig. bis Chrys. Theodrt. al. [εὐχαριστῶ Θεῷ Method. ap. Epiph. cod., sed χάρις τῷ Θεῷ vel χάρις δὲ τῷ Θεῷ Epiph. edd. pr.; vid. Bonwetsch, Methodius von Olympus, i. 204.]

It is easy to see how the reading of B would explain all the rest. The reading of the mass of MSS. would be derived from it (not at once but by successive steps) by the doubling of two pairs of letters,

τογτογ[εγ]χαριc[τω]τωθεω.

The descent of the other readings may be best represented by a table.

The other possibility would be that εὐχαριστῶ τῷ Θεῷ had got reduced to χάρις τῷ Θεῷ by successive dropping of letters. But this must have taken place very early. It is also conceivable that χάρις δέ preceded χάρις only.

The Inward Conflict.

Two subjects for discussion are raised, or are commonly treated as if they were raised, by this section. (1) Is the experience described that of the regenerate or unregenerate man? (2) Is it, or is it not, the experience of St. Paul himself?

1 (a). Origen and the mass of Greek Fathers held that the passage refers to the unregenerate man. (i) Appeal is made to such expressions as πεπραμένος ὑπὸ τὴν ἁμαρτίαν ver. 14, κατεργάζομαι

[τὸ κακόν] vv. 19, 20, ταλαίπωρος ἐγὼ ἄνθρωπος ver. 24. It is argued that language like this is nowhere found of the regenerate state. (ii) When other expressions are adduced which seem to make for the opposite conclusion, it is urged that parallels to them may be quoted from Pagan literature, e.g. the *video meliora* of Ovid and many other like sayings in Euripides, Xenophon, Seneca, Epictetus (see Dr. T. K. Abbott on ver. 15 of this chapter). (iii) The use of the present tense is explained as dramatic. The Apostle throws himself back into the time which he is describing.

(β) Another group of writers, Methodius (ob. 310 A.D.), Augustine and the Latin Fathers generally, the Reformers especially on the Calvinistic side, refer the passage rather to the regenerate. (i) An opposite set of expressions is quoted, μισῶ [τὸ κακόν] ver. 15, θέλω ποιεῖν τὸ καλόν ver. 21, συνήδομαι τῷ νόμῳ ver. 22. It is said that these are inconsistent with the ἀπηλλοτριωμένοι καὶ ἐχθροί of Col. i. 21 and with descriptions like that of Rom. viii. 7, 8. (ii) Stress is laid on the present tenses : and in proof that these imply a present experience, reference is made to passages like 1 Cor. ix. 27 ὑπωπιάζω μου τὸ σῶμα καὶ δουλαγωγῶ. That even the regenerate may have this mixed experience is thought to be proved, e.g. by Gal. v. 17.

Clearly there is a double strain of language. The state of things described is certainly a conflict in which opposite forces are struggling for the mastery.

Whether such a state belongs to the regenerate or the unregenerate man seems to push us back upon the further question, What we mean by ' regenerate.' The word is used in a higher and a lower sense. In the lower sense it is applied to all baptized Christians. In that sense there can be little doubt that the experience described may fairly come within it.

But on the other hand, the higher stages of the spiritual life seem to be really excluded. The sigh of relief in ver. 25 marks a dividing line between a period of conflict and a period where conflict is practically ended. This shows that the present tenses are in any case not to be taken too literally. Three steps appear to be distinguished, (i) the life of unconscious morality (ver. 9), happy, but only from ignorance and thoughtlessness ; (ii) then the sharp collision between law and the sinful appetites waking to activity ; (iii) the end which is at last put to the stress and strain of this collision by the intervention of Christ and of the Spirit of Christ, of which more will be said in the next chapter. The state there described is that of the truly and fully regenerate ; the prolonged struggle which precedes seems to be more rightly defined as *inter regenerandum* (Gif. after Dean Jackson).

Or perhaps we should do better still to refuse to introduce so technical a term as ' regeneration ' into a context from which it is wholly absent. St. Paul, it is true, regarded Christianity as operating a change in man. But here, whether the moment described is before or after the embracing of Christianity, in any case abstraction is made of all that is Christian. Law and the soul are brought face to face with each other, and there is nothing between them. Not until we come to ver. 25 is there a single expression used which belongs to Christianity. And the use of it marks that the conflict is ended.

(2) As to the further question whether St. Paul is speaking of himself or of 'some other man' we observe that the crisis which is described here is not at least the same as that which is commonly known as his 'Conversion.' Here the crisis is moral; there it was in the first instance intellectual, turning upon the acceptance of the proposition that Jesus was truly the Messiah. The decisive point in the conflict may be indeed the appropriation of Christ through His Spirit, but it is at least not an intellectual conviction, such as might exist along with a severe moral struggle. On the other hand, the whole description is so vivid and so sincere, so evidently wrung from the anguish of direct personal experience, that it is difficult to think of it as purely imaginary. It is really not so much imaginary as imaginative. It is not a literal photograph of any one stage in the Apostle's career, but it is a constructive picture drawn by him in bold lines from elements supplied to him by self-introspection. We may well believe that the regretful reminiscence of bright unconscious innocence goes back to the days of his own childhood before he had begun to feel the conviction of Sin. The incubus of the Law he had felt most keenly when he was a 'Pharisee of the Pharisees.' Without putting an exact date to the struggle which follows we shall probably not be wrong in referring the main features of it especially to the period before his Conversion. It was then that the powerlessness of the Law to do anything but aggravate sin was brought home to him. And all his experience, at whatever date, of the struggle of the natural man with temptation is here gathered together and concentrated in a single portraiture. It would obviously be a mistake to apply a generalized experience like this too rigidly. The process described comes to different men at different times and in different degrees; to one early, to another later; in one man it would lead up to Christianity, in another it might follow it; in one it would be quick and sudden, in another the slow growth of years. We cannot lay down any rule. In any case it is the mark of a genuine faith to be able to say with the Apostle, 'Thanks be to God through Jesus Christ our Lord.' It is just in his manner to sum up thus in a sentence what he is about to expand into a chapter. The break occurs at a very suitable place : ch. viii is the true conclusion to ch. vii.

St. Paul's View of the Law.

It was in his view of the Mosaic Law that St. Paul must have seemed most revolutionary to his countrymen. And yet it would be a mistake to suppose that he ever lost that reverence for the Law as a Divine institution in which every Jew was born and bred and to which he himself was still more completely committed by his early education as a Pharisee (Gal. i. 14; Phil. iii. 5 f.). This old feeling of his comes out in emotional passages like Rom. ix. 4 (cf. iii. 2; ii. 25, &c.). And even where, as in the section before us, he is bringing out most forcibly the ineffectiveness of the Law to restrain human passion the Apostle still lays down expressly that the Law itself is ' holy and righteous and good'; and a little lower down (ver. 14) he gives it the epithet ' spiritual,' which is equivalent to ascribing to it a direct Divine origin.

It was only because of his intense sincerity and honesty in facing facts that St. Paul ever brought himself to give up his belief in the sufficiency of the Law; and there is no greater proof of his power and penetration of mind than the way in which, when once his thoughts were turned into this channel, he followed out the whole subject into its inmost recesses. We can hardly doubt that his criticism of the Law as a principle of religion dates back to a time before his definite conversion to Christianity. The process described in this chapter clearly belongs to a period when the Law of Moses was the one authority which the Apostle recognized. It represents just the kind of difficulties and struggles which would be endured long before they led to a complete shifting of belief, and which would only lead to it then because a new and a better solution had been found. The apparent suddenness of St. Paul's conversion was due to the tenacity with which he held on to his Jewish faith and his reluctance to yield to conclusions which were merely negative. It was not till a whole group of positive convictions grew up within him and showed their power of supplying the vacant place that the Apostle withdrew his allegiance, and when he had done so came by degrees to see the true place of the Law in the Divine economy.

From the time that he came to write the Epistle to the Romans the process is mapped out before us pretty clearly.

The doubts began, as we have seen, in psychological experience. With the best will in the world St. Paul had found that really to keep the Law was a matter of infinite difficulty. However much it drew him one way there were counter influences which drew him another. And these counter influences proved the stronger of the two. The Law itself was cold, inert, passive. It pointed severely to the path of right and duty, but there its function ended; it gave no help towards the performance of that which it required. Nay, by a certain strange perversity in human nature, it seemed actually to provoke to disobedience. The very fact that a thing was forbidden seemed to make its attractions all the greater (Rom. vii. 8). And so the last state was worse than the first. The one sentence in which St. Paul sums up his experience of Law is διὰ νόμου ἐπίγνωσις ἁμαρτίας (Rom. iii. 20). Its effect therefore was only to increase the condemnation : it multiplied sin (Rom. v. 20); it worked wrath (Rom. iv. 15); it brought mankind under a curse (Gal. iii. 10).

And this was equally true of the individual and of the race ; the better and fuller the law the more glaring was the contrast to the practice of those who lived under it. The Jews were at the head of all mankind in their privileges, but morally they were not much better than the Gentiles. In the course of his travels St. Paul was led to visit a number of the scattered colonies of Jews, and when he compares them with the Gentiles he can only turn upon them a biting irony (Rom. ii. 17-29).

The truth must be acknowledged ; as a system, Law of whatever kind had failed. The breakdown of the Jewish Law was most complete just because that law was the best. It stood out in history as a monument, revealing the right and condemning the wrong, heaping up the pile of human guilt, and nothing more. On a large scale for the race, as on a small scale for the individual, the same verdict held, διὰ νόμου ἐπίγνωσις ἁμαρτίας.

Clearly the fault of all this was not with the Law. The fault lay in the miserable weakness of human nature (Rom. viii. 3). The Law, as a code of commandments, did all that it was intended to do. But it needed to be supplemented. And it was just this supplementing which Christianity brought, and by bringing it set the Law in its true light and in its right place in the evolution of the Divine plan. St. Paul sees spread before him the whole expanse of history. The dividing line across it is the Coming of the Messiah. All previous to that is a period of Law—first of imperfect law, such law as was supplied by natural religion and conscience ; and then of relatively perfect law, the law given by God from Sinai. It was not to be supposed that this gift of law increased the sum of human happiness. Rather the contrary. In the infancy of the world, as in the infancy of the individual, there was a blithe unconsciousness of right and wrong ; impulse was followed wherever it led ; the primrose path of enjoyment had no dark shadow cast over it. Law was this dark shadow. In proportion as it became stricter, it deepened the gloom. If law had been kept, or where law was kept, it brought with it a new kind of happiness; but to a serious spirit like St. Paul's it seemed as if the law was never kept—never satisfactorily

kept—at all. There was a Rabbinical commonplace, a stern
rule of self-judgement, which was fatal to peace of mind: 'Whosoever shall keep the whole law and yet stumble in one point,
he is become guilty of all' (Jas. ii. 10; cf. Gal. iii. 16; Rom.
x. 5). Any true happiness therefore, any true relief, must be
sought elsewhere. And it was this happiness and relief which
St. Paul sought and found in Christ. The last verse of ch. vii
marks the point at which the great burden which lay upon the
conscience rolls away; and the next chapter begins with an
uplifting of the heart in recovered peace and serenity; 'There is
therefore now no condemnation to them that are in Christ Jesus.'

Taken thus in connexion with that new order of things into
which it was to pass and empty itself, the old order of Law had at
last its difficulties cleared away. It remained as a stage of
salutary and necessary discipline. All God's ways are not bright
upon the surface. But the very clouds which He draws over the
heavens will break in blessings; and break just at that moment
when their darkness is felt to be most oppressive. St. Paul himself saw the gloomy period of law through to its end (τέλος γὰρ
νόμου Χριστὸς εἰς δικαιοσύνην παντὶ τῷ πιστεύοντι Rom. x. 4); and
his own pages reflect, better than any other, the new hopes and
energies by which it was succeeded.

LIFE IN THE SPIRIT.
THE FRUITS OF THE INCARNATION.

VIII. 1–4. *The result of Christ's interposition is to
dethrone Sin from its tyranny in the human heart, and to
instal in its stead the Spirit of Christ. Thus what the
Law of Moses tried to do but failed, the Incarnation has
accomplished.*

[1] This being so, no verdict of 'Guilty' goes forth any longer
against the Christian. He lives in closest union with Christ.
[2] The Spirit of Christ, the medium of that union, with all its life-
giving energies, enters and issues its laws from his heart, dis-
possessing the old usurper Sin, putting an end to its authority and
to the fatal results which it brought with it. [3] For where the old
system failed, the new system has succeeded. The Law of Moses
could not get rid of Sin. The weak place in its action was that
our poor human nature was constantly tempted and fell. But now
God Himself has interposed by sending the Son of His love to

take upon Him that same human nature with all its attributes
except sin: in that nature He died to free us from sin: and this
Death of His carried with it a verdict of condemnation against Sin
and of acquittal for its victims; ⁴ so that from henceforth what the
Law lays down as right might be fulfilled by us who regulate our
lives not according to the appetites and passions of sense, but at
the dictates of the Spirit.

1 ff. This chapter is, as we have seen, an expansion of χάρις τῷ
Θεῷ διὰ Ἰησοῦ Χριστοῦ τοῦ Κυρίου ἡμῶν in the last verse of ch. vii.   It
describes the innermost circle of the Christian Life from its beginning to its end—that life of which the Apostle speaks elsewhere
(Col. iii. 3) as 'hid with Christ in God.'   It works gradually up
through the calm exposition and pastoral entreaty of vv. 1–17 to
the more impassioned outlook and deeper introspection of vv. 18–30,
and thence to the magnificent climax of vv. 31–39.

There is evidence that Marcion retained vv. 1–11 of this chapter, probably
with no very noticeable variation from the text which has come down to us
(we do not know which of the two competing readings he had in ver. 10).
Tertullian leaps from viii. 11 to x. 2, implying that much was cut out, but
we cannot determine how much.

1. κατάκριμα.   One of the formulae of Justification: κατάκρισις
and κατάκριμα are correlative to δικαίωσις, δικαίωμα; both sets of
phrases being properly forensic.   Here, however, the phrase τοῖς
ἐν X. Ἰ. which follows shows that the initial stage in the Christian
career, which is in the strictest sense the stage of Justification, has
been left behind and the further stage of union with Christ has
succeeded to it.   In this stage too there is the same freedom from
condemnation, secured by a process which is explained more fully
in ver. 3 (cf. vi. 7–10).   The κατάκρισις which used to fall upon the
sinner now falls upon his oppressor Sin.

μὴ κατὰ σάρκα περιπατοῦσιν, ἀλλὰ κατὰ πνεῦμα.   An interpolation
introduced (from ver. 4) at two steps: the first clause μὴ κατὰ σάρκα περιπατοῦσιν in A Dᵇ 137, f m Vulg. Pesh. Goth. Arm., Bas. Chrys.; the second
clause ἀλλὰ κατὰ πνεῦμα in the mass of later authorities Nᶜ Dᶜ E K L P &c.;
the older uncials with the Egyptian and Ethiopic Versions, the Latin Version
of Origen and perhaps Origen himself with a fourth-century dialogue attributed to him, Athanasius and others omit both.

2. ὁ νόμος τοῦ Πνεύματος = the authority exercised by the Spirit.
We have had the same somewhat free use of νόμος in the last
chapter, esp. in ver. 23 ὁ νόμος τοῦ νοός, ὁ νόμος τῆς ἁμαρτίας : it is no
longer a 'code' but an authority producing regulated action such
as would be produced by a code.

τοῦ Πνεύματος τῆς ζωῆς.   The gen. expresses the 'effect wrought'
(Gif.), but it also expresses more : the Spirit brings life because it
essentially *is* life.

ἐν Χριστῷ Ἰησοῦ goes with ἠλευθέρωσε: the authority of the Spirit operating through the union with Christ, freed me, &c.　For the phrase itself see on ch. vi. 11

ἠλευθέρωσέ με. A small group of important authorities (‎א B F G, m Pesh., Tert. 1/2 *vel potius* 2/2 Chrys. *codd.*) has ἠλευθέρωσέν σε. The combination of ‎א B with Latin and Syriac authorities shows that this reading must be extremely early, going back to the time before the Western text diverged from the main body. Still it can hardly be right, as the second person is nowhere suggested in the context, and it is more probable that σε is only a mechanical repetition of the last syllable of ἠλευθέρωσε (ϲε). Dr. Hort suggests the omission of both pronouns (ἡμᾶς also being found), and although the evidence for this is confined to some MSS. of Arm. (to which Dr. Hort would add 'perhaps' the commentary of Origen as represented by Rufinus, but this is not certain), it was a very general tendency among scribes to supply an object to verbs originally without one. We do not expect a return to first pers. sing. after τοῖς ἐν X. Ἰ., and the scanty evidence for omission may be to some extent paralleled, e. g. by that for the omission of εὑρηκέναι in iv. 1, for εἴ γε in v. 6, or for χάρις τῷ Θεῷ in vii. 25. But we should hardly be justified in doing more than placing με in brackets.

ἀπὸ τοῦ νόμου τῆς ἁμαρτίας καὶ τοῦ θανάτου = the authority exercised by Sin and ending in Death: see on vii. 23, and on ὁ νόμ. τ. πνεύμ. above.

3. τὸ γὰρ ἀδύνατον τοῦ νόμου. Two questions arise as to these words. (1) What is their construction?　The common view, adopted also by Gif. (who compares Eur. *Troad.* 489), is that they form a sort of nom. absolute in apposition to the sentence. Gif. translates, 'the impotence (see below) of the Law being this that,' &c.　It seems, however, somewhat better to regard the words in apposition not as nom. but as accus.

A most accomplished scholar, the late Mr. James Riddell, in his ' Digest of Platonic Idioms' (*The Apology of Plato*, Oxford, 1877, p. 122), lays down two propositions about constructions like this: ' (i) These Noun-Phrases and Neuter-Pronouns are *Accusatives*. The prevalence of the Neuter Gender makes this difficult to prove; but such instances as are decisive afford an analogy for the rest: Theaet. 153 C ἐπὶ τούτοις τὸν κολοφῶνα, ἀναγκάζω προσβιβάζων κ.τ.λ. Cf. Soph. *O. T.* 603 καὶ τῶνδ' ἔλεγχον ... πεύθου, and the Adverbs ἀρχήν, ἀκμήν, τὴν πρώτην, &c. (ii) They represent, by Apposition or Substitution, *the sentence itself.* To say, that they are Cognate Accusatives, or in Apposition with the (unexpressed) Cognate Accus., would be inadequate to the facts. For (1) in most of the instances the sense points out that the Noun-Phrase or Pronoun stands over against the sentence, or portion of a sentence, as a whole; (2) in many of them, not the internal force but merely the rhetorical or logical form of the sentence is in view. It might be said that they are Predicates, while the sentence itself is the Subject.' [Examples follow, but that from *Theaet.* given above is as clear as any.] This seems to criticize by anticipation the view of Va., who regards τὸ ἀδύν. as accus. but practically explains it as in apposition to a cognate accus. which is not expressed: ' The impossible thing of the Law ... God [effected; that is He] condemned sin in the flesh.' It is true that an apt parallel is quoted from 2 Cor. vi. 13 τὴν δὲ αὐτὴν ἀντιμισθίαν πλατύνθητε καὶ ὑμεῖς: but this would seem to come under the same rule. The argument that if τὸ ἀδύν. had been accus. it would probably have stood at the end of

the sentence, like τὴν λογικὴν λατρείαν ὑμῶν in Rom. xii. 1, appears to be
refuted by τὸν κολοφῶνα in *Theaet.* above. Win. *Gr.* § xxxii. 7, p. 290 E. T.
while recognizing the accus. use (§ lix. 9, p. 669 E. T.), seems to prefer to
take τὸ ἀδύν. as nom. So too Mey. Lips. &c.

(2) Is τὸ ἀδύν. active or passive? Gif., after Fri. (cf. also Win.
ut sup.) contends for the former, on the ground that if ἀδύν. were
passive it should be followed by τῷ νόμῳ not τοῦ νόμου. Tertullian
(*De Res. Carn.* 46) gives the phrase an active sense and retains the
gen., *quod invalidum erat legis.* But on the other hand if not Origen
himself, at least Rufinus the translator of Origen has a passive
rendering, and treats τοῦ νόμου as practically equivalent to τῷ νόμῳ:
quod impossibile erat legi*. Yet Rufinus himself clearly uses
impossibilis in an active sense in his comment; and the Greek of
Origen, as given in Cramer's *Catena*, p. 125, appears to make τὸ
ἀδύν. active: ὥσπερ γὰρ ἡ ἀρετὴ ἰδίᾳ φύσει ἰσχυρά, οὕτω καὶ ἡ κακία καὶ
τὰ ἀπ' αὐτῆς ἀσθενῆ καὶ ἀδύνατα . . . τοῦ τοιούτου νόμου ἡ φύσις ἀδύνατός
ἐστι. Similarly Cyr.-Alex. (who finds fault with the structure of the
sentence): τὸ ἀδύνατον, τουτέστι τὸ ἀσθενοῦν. Vulg. and Cod. Clarom.
are slightly more literal: *quod impossibile erat legis.* The gen. might
mean that there was a spot within the range or domain of Law
marked 'impossible,' a portion of the field which it could not
control. On the whole the passive sense appears to us to be more
in accordance with the Biblical use of ἀδύν. and also to give a somewhat easier construction: if τὸ ἀδύν. is active it is not quite a simple
case of apposition to the sentence, but must be explained as a sort
of nom. absolute ('The impotence of the Law being this that,' &c.,
Gif.), which seems rather strained. But it must be confessed that
the balance of ancient authority is strongly in favour of this way of
taking the words, and that on a point—the natural interpretation of
language—where ancient authority is especially valuable.

An induction from the use of LXX and N. T. would seem to show that
ἀδύνατος masc. and fem. was always active (so twice in N. T., twenty-two
times [3 vv. ll.] in LXX, Wisd. xvii. 14 τὴν ἀδύνατον ὄντως νύκτα καὶ ἐξ
ἀδυνάτου ᾅδου μυχῶν ἐπελθοῦσαν, being alone somewhat ambiguous and
peculiar), while ἀδύν. neut. was always passive (so five times in LXX, seven
in N. T.). It is true that the exact phrase τὸ ἀδύνατον does not occur, but
in Luke xviii. 27 we have τὰ ἀδύνατα παρὰ ἀνθρώποις δυνατά ἐστι παρὰ τῷ Θεῷ.

ἐν ᾧ: not 'because' (Fri. Win. Mey. Alf.), but 'in which' or
'wherein,' defining the point in which the impossibility (inability)
of the Law consisted. For ἠσθένει διὰ τῆς σαρκός comp. vii. 22, 23.
The Law points the way to what is right, but frail humanity is
tempted and falls, and so the Law's good counsels come to nothing.

τὸν ἑαυτοῦ υἱόν. The emphatic ἑαυτοῦ brings out the community
of nature between the Father and the Son: cf. τοῦ ἰδίου υἱοῦ ver. 32;
τοῦ υἱοῦ τῆς ἀγάπης αὐτοῦ Col. i. 13.

* The text is not free from suspicion.

ἐν ὁμοιώματι σαρκὸς ἁμαρτίας : the flesh of Christ is 'like' ours inasmuch as it is flesh; 'like,' and only 'like,' because it is not sinful: *ostendit nos quidem habere carnem peccati, Filium vero Dei similitudinem habuisse carnis peccati, non carnem peccati* (Orig.-lat.).

Pfleiderer and Holsten contend that even the flesh of Christ was 'sinful flesh,' i.e. capable of sinning ; but they are decisively refuted by Gif. p. 165. Neither the Greek nor the argument requires that the flesh of Christ shall be regarded as *sinful flesh*, though it is His Flesh—His Incarnation—which brought Him into contact with Sin.

καὶ περὶ ἁμαρτίας. This phrase is constantly used in the O.T. for the 'sin-offering'; so 'more than fifty times in the Book of Leviticus alone' (Va.); and it is taken in this sense here by Orig.-lat. *Quod hostia pro peccato factus est Christus, et oblatus sit pro purgatione peccatorum, omnes Scripturae testantur* ... *Per hanc ergo hostiam carnis suae, quae dicitur* pro peccato, *damnavit peccatum in carne*, &c. The ritual of the sin-offering is fully set forth in Lev. iv. The most characteristic feature in it is the sprinkling with blood of the horns of the altar of incense. Its object was to make atonement especially for sins of ignorance. It was no doubt typical of the Sacrifice of Christ. Still we need not suppose the phrase περὶ ἁμαρτ. here specially limited to the sense of 'sin-offering.' It includes every sense in which the Incarnation and Death of Christ had relation to, and had it for their object to remove, human sin.

κατέκρινε τὴν ἁμαρτίαν ἐν τῇ σαρκί. The key to this difficult clause is supplied by ch. vi. 7–10. By the Death of Christ upon the Cross, a death endured in His human nature, He once and for ever broke off all contact with Sin, which could only touch Him through that nature. Henceforth Sin can lay no claim against Him. Neither can it lay any claim against the believer; for the believer also has died with Christ. Henceforth when Sin comes to prosecute its claim, it is cast in its suit and its former victim is acquitted. The one culminating and decisive act by which this state of things was brought about is the Death of Christ, to which all the subsequent immunity of Christians is to be referred.

The parallel passage, vi. 6–11, shows that this summary condemnation of Sin takes place in the Death of Christ, and not in His Life; so that κατέκρινε cannot be adequately explained either by the proof which Christ's Incarnation gave that human nature *might* be sinless, or by the contrast of His sinlessness with man's sin. In Matt. xii. 41, 42 ('the men of Nineveh shall rise up in the judgement with this generation, and shall condemn it,' &c.) κατακρίνειν has this sense of 'condemn by contrast,' but there is a greater fulness of meaning here.

The ancients rather miss the mark in their comments on this passage. Thus Orig.-lat. *damnavit peccatum, hoc est, fugavit peccatum et abstulit* (comp. T. K. Abbott, 'effectually condemned so as to expel'): but it does not appear how this was done. The commoner view is based on Chrys., who claims for the incarnate Christ a threefold victory over Sin, as not yielding to it, as overcoming it (in a forensic sense), and convicting it of injustice in handing over to death His own sinless body as if it were sinful. Similarly Euthym.-Zig. and others in part. Cyr.-Alex. explains the victory of Christ over Sin as passing over to the Christian through the indwelling of the Holy Ghost and the Eucharist (διὰ τῆς μυστικῆς εὐλογίας). This is at least right in so far as it lays stress on the identification of the Christian with Christ. But the victory over sin does not rest on the mere fact of sinlessness, but on the absolute severance from sin involved in the Death upon the Cross and the Resurrection.

ἐν τῇ σαρκί goes with κατέκρινε. The Death of Christ has the efficacy which it has because it is the death of His Flesh: by means of death He broke for ever the power of Sin upon Him (vi. 10; Heb. vii. 16; x. 10; 1 Pet. iii. 18); but through the mystical union with Him the death of His Flesh means the death of ours (Lips.).

4. τὸ δικαίωμα: 'the justifying,' Wic., 'the justification,' Rhem. after Vulg. *iustificatio*; Tyn. is better, 'the rightewesnes requyred of (i. e. by) the lawe.' We have already seen that the proper sense of δικαίωμα is 'that which is laid down as right,' 'that which has the force of right': hence it = here the statutes of the Law, as righteous statutes. Comp. on i. 32; ii. 26.

It is not clear how Chrys. (= Euthym.-Zig.) gets for δικαίωμα the sense τὸ τέλος, ὁ σκοπός, τὸ κατόρθωμα.

τοῖς μὴ κατὰ σάρκα περιπατοῦσιν: 'those who walk by the rule of the flesh,' whose guiding principle is the flesh (and its gratification). The antithesis of Flesh and Spirit is the subject of the next section.

THE LIFE OF THE FLESH AND THE LIFE OF THE SPIRIT.

VIII. 5-11. *Compare the two states. The life of self-indulgence involves the breach of God's law, hostility to Him, and death. Submission to the Spirit brings with it true life and the sense of reconciliation. You therefore, if you are sincere Christians, have in the presence of the Spirit a sure pledge of immortality.*

⁵ These two modes of life are directly opposed to one another. If any man gives way to the gratifications of sense, then these and nothing else occupy his thoughts and determine the bent of his character. And on the other hand, those who let the Holy Spirit

guide them fix their thoughts and affections on things spiritual.
⁶ They are opposed in their nature; they are opposed also in their
consequences. For the consequence of having one's bent towards
the things of the flesh is death—both of soul and body, both here
and hereafter. Just as to surrender one's thoughts and motives to
the Spirit brings with it a quickened vitality through the whole man,
and a tranquillizing sense of reconciliation with God.

⁷ The gratifying of the flesh can lead only to death, because it
implies hostility to God. It is impossible for one who indulges the
flesh at the same time to obey the law of God. ⁸ And those who
are under the influence of the flesh cannot please God. ⁹ But you,
as Christians, are no longer under the influence of the flesh. You
are rather under that of the Spirit, if the Spirit of God (which, be it
remembered, is the medium of personal contact with God and
Christ) is really in abiding communion with you. ¹⁰ But if Christ,
through His Spirit, thus keeps touch with your souls, then mark
how glorious is your condition. Your body it is true is doomed to
death, because it is tainted with sin; but your spirit—the highest
part of you—has life infused into it because of its new state of
righteousness to which life is so nearly allied. ¹¹ In possessing the
Spirit you have a guarantee of future resurrection. It links you to
Him whom God raised from the dead. And so even these perishable human bodies of yours, though they die first, God will restore
to life, through the operation of (or, having regard to) that Holy
Spirit by whom they are animated.

5. φρονοῦσιν: 'set their minds, or their hearts upon.' φρονεῖν
denotes the whole action of the φρήν, i.e. of the affections and will
as well as of the reason; cf. Matt. xvi. 23 οὐ φρονεῖς τὰ τοῦ Θεοῦ,
ἀλλὰ τὰ τῶν ἀνθρώπων: Rom. xii. 16; Phil. iii. 19; Col. iii. 2, &c.

6. φρόνημα: the content of φρονεῖν, the general bent of thought
and motive. Here, as elsewhere in these chapters, σάρξ is that side
of human nature on which it is morally weak, the side on which
man's physical organism leads him into sin.

θάνατος. Not merely is the φρόνημα τῆς σαρκός death in *effect*,
inasmuch as it has death for its goal, but it is also a present death,
inasmuch as its present condition contains the seeds which by
their own inherent force will develop into the death both of body
and soul.

ζωή. In contrast with the state of things just described, where
the whole bent of the mind is towards the things of the Spirit, not

only is there 'life' in the sense that a career so ordered will issue in life; it has already in itself the germs of life. As the Spirit itself is in Its essence living, so does It impart that which must live.

For a striking presentation of the Biblical doctrine of Life see Hort, *Hulsean Lectures*, pp. 98 ff., 189 ff. The following may be quoted: 'The sense of life which Israel enjoyed was, however, best expressed in the choice of the name "life" as a designation of that higher communion with God which grew forth in due time as the fruit of obedience and faith. The psalmist or wise man or prophet, whose heart had sought the face of the Lord, was conscious of a second or divine life, of which the first or natural life was at once the image and the foundation; a life not imprisoned in some secret recess of his soul, but filling his whole self, and overflowing upon the earth around him' (p. 98). Add St. Paul's doctrine of the indwelling Spirit, and the intensity of his language becomes intelligible.

εἰρήνη = as we have seen not only (i) the state of reconciliation with God, but (ii) the sense of that reconciliation which diffuses a feeling of harmony and tranquillity over the whole man.

7. This verse assigns the reason why the 'mind of the flesh is death,' at the same time bringing out the further contrast between the mind of the flesh and that of the Spirit suggested by the description of the latter as not only 'life' but 'peace.' The mind of the flesh is the opposite of peace; it involves hostility to God, declared by disobedience to His Law. This disobedience is the natural and inevitable consequence of giving way to the flesh.

8. οἱ δέ: not as AV. 'so then,' as if it marked a consequence or conclusion from ver. 7, but 'And': ver. 8 merely repeats the substance of ver. 7 in a slightly different form, no longer abstract but personal. The way is thus paved for a more direct application to the readers.

9. ἐν σαρκί, ... ἐν πνεύματι. Observe how the thought mounts gradually upwards. εἶναι ἐν σαρκί = 'to be under the domination of [the] flesh'; corresponding to this εἶναι ἐν πνεύματι = 'to be under the domination of [the] spirit,' i.e. in the first instance, the human spirit. Just as in the one case the man takes his whole bent and bias from the lower part of his nature, so in the other case he takes it from the highest part of his nature. But that highest part, the πνεῦμα, is what it is by virtue of its affinity to God. It is essentially that part of the man which holds communion with God: so that the Apostle is naturally led to think of the Divine influences which act upon the πνεῦμα. He rises almost imperceptibly through the πνεῦμα of man to the Πνεῦμα of God. From thinking of the way in which the πνεῦμα in its best moods acts upon the character he passes on to that influence from without which keeps it in its best moods. This is what he means when he says εἴπερ Πνεῦμα Θεοῦ οἰκεῖ ἐν ὑμῖν. οἰκεῖν ἐν denotes a settled permanent penetrative influence. Such an influence, from the Spirit of God, St. Paul assumes to be inseparable from the higher life of the Christian.

The way in which ἐν σαρκί is opposed to ἐν πνεύματι, and further the way in which ἐν πνεύματι passes from the spirit of man to the Spirit of God, shows that we must not press the local significance of the preposition too closely. We must not interpret any of the varied expressions which the Apostle uses in such a sense as to infringe upon the distinctness of the human and Divine personalities. The one thing which is characteristic of personality is distinctness from all other personalities; and this must hold good even of the relation of man to God. The very ease with which St. Paul changes and inverts his metaphors shows that the Divine immanence with him nowhere means Buddhistic or Pantheistic absorption. We must be careful to keep clear of this, but short of it we may use the language of closest intimacy. All that friend can possibly receive from friend we may believe that man is capable of receiving from God. See the note on ἐν Χριστῷ Ἰησοῦ in vi. 11; and for the antithesis of σάρξ and πνεῦμα the small print note on vii. 14.

εἰ δέ τις. A characteristic delicacy of expression: when he is speaking on the positive side St. Paul assumes that his readers have the Spirit, but when he is speaking on the negative side he will not say bluntly 'if *you* have not the Spirit,' but he at once throws his sentence into a vague and general force, 'if any one has not,' &c.

There are some good remarks on the grammar of the conditional clauses in this verse and in vv. 10, 25, in Burton, *M. and T.* §§ 469, 242, 261.

οὐκ ἔστιν αὐτοῦ: he is no true Christian. This amounts to saying that all Christians 'have the Spirit' in greater or less degree.

10. εἰ δὲ Χριστός. It will be observed that St. Paul uses the phrases Πνεῦμα Θεοῦ, Πνεῦμα Χριστοῦ, and Χριστός in these two verses as practically interchangeable. On the significance of this in its bearing upon the relation of the Divine Persons see below.

τὸ μὲν σῶμα νεκρὸν δι' ἁμαρτίαν. St. Paul is putting forward first the negative and then the positive consequences of the indwelling of Christ, or the Spirit of Christ, in the soul. But what is the meaning of 'the body is dead because of sin?' Of many ways of taking the words, the most important seem to be these: (i) 'the body is dead *imputative*, in baptism (vi. 2 ff.), as a consequence of sin which made this implication of the body in the Death of Christ necessary' (Lips.). But in the next verse, to which this clearly points forward, the stress lies not on death imputed but on physical death. (ii) 'The body is dead *mystice*, as no longer the instrument of sin (*sans énergie productrice des actes charnels*), because of sin— to which it led' (Oltr.). This is open to the same objection as the last, with the addition that it does not give a satisfactory explanation of δι' ἁμαρτίαν. (iii) It remains to take νεκρόν in the plain sense of 'physical death,' and to go back for δι' ἁμαρτίαν not to vi. 2 ff. but to v. 12 ff., so that it would be the sin of Adam and his descendants (Aug. Gif. Go.) perpetuated to the end of time. Oltr. objects that νεκρόν in this case ought to be θνητόν, but the use of νεκρόν gives a more vivid and pointed contrast to ζωή—'a dead thing.'

τὸ δὲ πνεῦμα ζωὴ διὰ δικαιοσύνην. Clearly the πνεῦμα here meant is the human πνεῦμα which has the properties of life infused into it by the presence of the Divine πνεῦμα. ζωή is to be taken in a wide sense, but with especial stress on the future eternal life. διὰ δικαιοσύνην is also to be taken in a wide sense: it includes all the senses in which righteousness is brought home to man, first imputed, then imparted, then practised.

11. St. Paul is fond of arguing from the Resurrection of Christ to the resurrection of the Christian (see p. 117 *sup.*). Christ is the ἀπαρχή (1 Cor. xv. 20, 23: the same power which raised Him will raise us (1 Cor. vi. 14; 2 Cor. iv. 14); Phil. iii. 21; 1 Thess. iv. 14). But nowhere is the argument given in so full and complete a form as here. The link which connects the believer with Christ, and makes him participate in Christ's resurrection, is the possession of His Spirit (cp. 1 Thess. iv. 14 τοὺς κοιμηθέντας διὰ τοῦ Ἰησοῦ ἄξει σὺν αὐτῷ).

διὰ τοῦ ἐνοικοῦντος αὐτοῦ Πνεύματος. The authorities for the two readings, the gen. as above and the acc. διὰ τὸ ἐνοικοῦν αὐτοῦ Πνεῦμα, seem at first sight very evenly divided. For gen. we have a long line of authorities headed by ℵ A C, Clem.-Alex. For acc. we have a still longer line headed by B D, Orig. Iren.-lat.

In fuller detail the evidence is as follows:

διὰ τοῦ ἐνοικοῦντος κ.τ.λ. ℵ A C P² *al.*, *codd. ap.* Ps.-Ath. *Dial. c. Macedcn.*, Boh. Sah. Harcl. Arm. Aeth., Clem.-Alex. Method. (*codd. Graec. locorum ab* Epiphanio *citatorum*) Cyr.-Hieros *codd. plur. et ed.* Did. 4/5 Bas 4/4 Chrys. *ad* 1 Cor. xv. 45, Cyr.-Alex. *ter, al. plur.*

διὰ τὸ ἐνοικοῦν κ.τ.λ. B D E F G K L P &c., *codd. ap.* Ps.-Ath. *Dial. c. Macedon.*; Vulg. Pesh. (Sah. *codd.*); Iren.-lat. Orig. *pluries*; Method. *vers. slav. et codd.* Epiphanii 1/3 *et ex parte* 2/3, Cyr.-Hieros. *cod.* Did.-lat. *semel* (*interp.* Hieron.) Chrys. *ad loc.* Tert. Hil. *al. plur.*

When these lists are examined, it will be seen at once that the authorities for the gen. are predominantly Alexandrian, and those for the acc. predominantly Western. The question is how far in each case this main body is reinforced by more independent evidence. From this point of view a somewhat increased importance attaches to Harcl. Arm. Hippol. Cyr.-Hieros. Bas. on the side of the gen. and to B, Orig. on the side of the acc. The testimony of Method. is not quite clear. The first place in which the passage occurs is a quotation from Origen: here the true reading is probably διὰ τὸ ἐνοικοῦν, as elsewhere in that writer. The other two places belong to Methodius himself. Here too the Slavonic version has in both cases acc.; the Greek preserved in Epiphanius has in one instance acc., in the other gen. It is perhaps on the whole probable that Method. himself read acc. and that gen. is due to Epiphanius, who undoubtedly was in the habit of using gen. In balancing the opposed evidence we remember that there is a distinct Western infusion in both B and Orig. in St. Paul's Epistles, so that the acc.

may rest not on the authority of two families of text, but only of one. On the other hand, to Alexandria we must add Palestine, which would count for something, though not very much, as being within the sphere of Alexandrian influence, and Cappadocia, which would count for rather more; but what is of most importance is the attesting of the Alexandrian reading so far West as Hippolytus. Too much importance must not be attached to the assertion of the orthodox controversialist in the *Dial. c. Macedonios*, that gen. is found in 'all the ancient copies'; the author of the dialogue allows that the reading is questionable.

On the whole the preponderance seems to be slightly on the side of the gen., but neither reading can be ignored. Intrinsically the one reading is not clearly preferable to the other. St. Paul might have used equally well either form of expression. It is however hardly adequate to say with Dr. Vaughan that if we read the acc. the reference is 'to the ennobling and consecrating effect of the indwelling of the Holy Spirit in the human body.' The prominent idea is rather that the Holy Spirit is Itself essentially a Spirit *of Life*, and therefore it is natural that where It is life should be. The gen. brings out rather more the direct and personal agency of the Holy Spirit, which of course commended the reading to the supporters of orthodox doctrine in the Macedonian controversy.

The Person and Work of the Holy Spirit.

The doctrine of the Spirit of God or the Holy Spirit is taken over from the O.T., where we have it conspicuously in relation to Creation (Gen. i. 2), in relation to Prophecy (1 Sam. x. 10; xi. 6; xix. 20, 23, &c.), and in relation to the religious life of the individual (Ps. li. 11) and of the nation (Is. lxiii. 10 f.). It was understood that the Messiah had a plenary endowment of this Spirit (Is. xi. 2). And accordingly in the N.T. the Gospels unanimously record the visible, if symbolical, manifestation of this endowment (Mark i. 10; Jo. i. 32). And it is an expression of the same truth when in this passage and elsewhere St. Paul speaks of the Spirit of Christ convertibly with Christ Himself. Just as there are many passages in which he uses precisely the same language of the Spirit of God and of God Himself, so also there are many others in which he uses the same language of the Spirit of Christ and of Christ Himself. Thus the 'demonstration of the Spirit' is a demonstration also of the 'power of God' (1 Cor. ii. 4, 5); the working of the Spirit is a working of God Himself (1 Cor. xii. 11 compared with ver. 6) and of Christ (Eph. iv. 11 compared with 1 Cor. xii. 28, 4). To be 'Christ's' is the same thing as to 'live in the Spirit' (Gal. v. 22 ff.). Nay, in one place Christ is expressly identified with 'the Spirit': 'the Lord is the Spirit' (2 Cor. iii. 17): a passage which has a seemingly remarkable parallel in Ignat. *Ad Magn.* xv ἔρρωσθε ἐν ὁμονοίᾳ Θεοῦ, κεκτημένοι ἀδιάκριτον πνεῦμα, ὅς ἐστιν Ἰησοῦς

Χριστός (where however Bp. Lightfoot makes the antecedent to ὅς
not πνεῦμα but the whole sentence ; his note should be read).   The
key to these expressions is really supplied by the passage before us,
from which it appears that the communication of Christ to the soul
is really the communication of His Spirit.   And, strange to say, we
find this language, which seems so individual, echoed not only possibly
by Ignatius but certainly by St. John.   As Mr. Gore puts it (*Bampton
Lectures*, p. 132), 'In the coming of the Spirit the Son too was to
come ; in the coming of the Son, also the Father.   " He will come
unto you," " I will come unto you," " We will come unto you " are
interchangeable phrases ' (cf. St. John xiv. 16–23).

This is the first point which must be borne clearly in mind : in
their relation to the human soul the Father and the Son act through
and are represented by the Holy Spirit.   And yet the Spirit is not
merged either in the Father or in the Son.   This is the complementary truth.   Along with the language of identity there is other
language which implies distinction.

It is not only that the Spirit of God is related to God in the
same sort of way in which the spirit of man is related to the man.
In this very chapter the Holy Spirit is represented as standing over
against the Father and pleading with Him (Rom. viii. 26 f.), and
a number of other actions which we should call ' personal ' are
ascribed to Him—'dwelling' (vv. 9, 11), 'leading' (ver. 14),
'witnessing' (ver. 16), 'assisting' (ver. 26).   In the last verse of
2 Corinthians St. Paul distinctly co-ordinates the Holy Spirit with
the Father and the Son.   And even where St. John speaks of the
Son as coming again in the Spirit, it is not as the same but as
'other'; 'another Paraclete will He give you' (St. John xiv. 16).
The language of identity is only partial, and is confined within
strict limits.   Nowhere does St. Paul give the name of ' Spirit ' to
Him who died upon the Cross, and rose again, and will return
once more to judgement.   There is a method running through the
language of both Apostles.

The doctrine of the Holy Trinity is really an extension,
a natural if not necessary consequence, of the doctrine of the
Incarnation.   As soon as it came to be clearly realized that the
Son of God had walked the earth as an individual man among
men it was inevitable that there should be recognized a distinction, and such a distinction as in human language could only
be described as 'personal' in the Godhead.   But if there was
a twofold distinction, then it was wholly in accordance with the
body of ideas derived from the O. T. to say also a threefold
distinction.

It is interesting to observe that in the presentation of this last
step in the doctrine there is a difference between St. Paul and
St. John corresponding to a difference in the experience of the

two Apostles. In both cases it is this actual experience which
gives the standpoint from which they write. St. John, who had
heard and seen and handled the Word of Life, who had stood
beneath the cross and looked into the empty tomb, when he
thinks of the coming of the Paraclete naturally thinks of Him
as ' another Paraclete.' St. Paul, who had not had the same
privileges, but who was conscious that from the moment of his
vision upon the road to Damascus a new force had entered into
his soul, as naturally connects the force and the vision, and sees in
what he feels to be the work of the Spirit the work also of the
exalted Son. To St. John the first visible Paraclete and the
second invisible could not but be different; to St. Paul the invisible influence which wrought so powerfully in him seemed to
stream directly from the presence of Him whom he had heard
from heaven call him by his name.

SONSHIP AND HEIRSHIP.

VIII. 12-17. *Live then as men bound for such a destiny,
ascetics as to your worldly life, heirs of immortality. The
Spirit implanted and confirms in you the consciousness of
your inheritance. It tells you that you are in a special sense
sons of God, and that you must some day share the glory to
which Christ, your Elder Brother, has gone.*

[12] Such a destiny has its obligations. To the flesh you owe
nothing. [13] If you live as it would have you, you must inevitably
die. But if by the help of the Spirit you sternly put an end to
the licence of the flesh, then in the fullest sense you will live.

[14] Why so? Why that necessary consequence? The link is
here. All who follow the leading of God's Spirit are certainly by
that very fact special objects of His favour. They do indeed enjoy
the highest title and the highest privileges. They are His *sons*.

[15] When you were first baptized, and the communication of the
Holy Spirit sealed your admission into the Christian fold, the
energies which He imparted were surely not those of a slave.
You had not once more to tremble under the lash of the Law.
No: He gave you rather the proud inspiring consciousness of
men admitted into His family, adopted as His sons. And the
consciousness of that relation unlocks our lips in tender filial
appeal to God as our Father. [16] Two voices are distinctly heard:

one we know to be that of the Holy Spirit; the other is the voice
of our own consciousness. And both bear witness to the same
fact that we are children of God. ¹⁷But to be a child implies
something more. The child will one day inherit his father's
possessions. So the Christian will one day enter upon that
glorious inheritance which his Heavenly Father has in store for
him and on which Christ as his Elder Brother has already entered.
Only, be it remembered, that in order to share in the glory, it is
necessary first to share in the sufferings which lead to it.

12. Lipsius would unite vv. 12, 13 closely with the foregoing;
and no doubt it is true that these verses only contain the
conclusion of the previous paragraph thrown into a hortatory
form. Still it is usual to mark this transition to exhortation by
a new paragraph (as at vi. 12); and although a new idea (that
of heirship) is introduced at ver. 14, that idea is only subordinate to the main argument, the assurance which the Spirit gives
of future life. See also the note on οὖν in x. 14.

13. πνεύματι. The antithesis to σάρξ seems to show that this
is still, as in vv. 4, 5, 9, the human πνεῦμα, but it is the human
πνεῦμα in direct contact with the Divine.

τὰς πράξεις : of wicked doings, as in Luke xxiii. 51.

14. The phrases which occur in this section, Πνεύματι Θεοῦ
ἄγονται, τὸ Πνεῦμα συμμαρτυρεῖ τῷ πνεύματι ἡμῶν, are clear proof that
the other group of phrases ἐν πνεύματι εἶναι, or τὸ Πνεῦμα οἰκεῖ (ἐνοικεῖ)
ἐν ἡμῖν are not intended in any way to impair the essential distinctness and independence of the human personality. There is no
such Divine 'immanence' as would obliterate this. The analogy
to be kept in view is the personal influence of one human being
upon another. We know to what heights this may rise. The
Divine influence may be still more subtle and penetrative, but it is
not different in kind.

υἱοὶ Θεοῦ. The difference between υἱός and τέκνον appears to be
that whereas τέκνον denotes the natural relationship of child to
parent, υἱός implies, in addition to this, the recognized *status* and
legal privileges reserved for sons. Cf. Westcott on St. John i. 12
and the parallels there noted.

15. πνεῦμα δουλείας. This is another subtle variation in the
use of πνεῦμα. From meaning the human spirit under the influence of the Divine Spirit πνεῦμα comes to mean a particular
state, habit, or temper of the human spirit, sometimes in itself
(πνεῦμα ζηλώσεως Num. v. 14, 30; πν. ἀκηδίας Is. lxi. 3; πν. πορνείας
Hos. iv. 12), but more often as due to supernatural influence, good
or evil (πν. σοφίας κ.τ.λ. Is. xi. 2; πν. πλανήσεως Is. xix. 14; πν.
κρίσεως Is. xxviii. 6; πν. κατανύξεως Is. xxix. 10 (= Rom. xi. 8);

πν. χάριτος καὶ οἰκτιρμοῦ Zech. xii. 10 ; πν. ἀσθενείας Luke xiii. 11 ;
πν. δειλίας 2 Tim. i. 7 ; τὸ πν. τῆς πλάνης 1 Jo. iv. 6). So here
πν. δουλείας = such a spirit as accompanies a state of slavery, such
a servile habit as the human πνεῦμα assumes among slaves. This
was not the temper which you had imparted to you at your baptism (ἐλάβετε). The slavery is that of the Law : cf. Gal. iv. 6, 7,
24, v. 1.

πάλιν εἰς φόβον: 'so as to relapse into a state of fear.' The
candidate for baptism did not emerge from the terrors of the
Law only to be thrown back into them again.

υἱοθεσίας : a word coined, but rightly coined, from the classical
phrase υἱὸς τίθεσθαι (θετὸς υἱός). It seems however too much to
say with Gif. that the coinage was probably due to St. Paul himself. 'No word is more common in Greek inscriptions of the
Hellenistic time : the idea, like the word, is native Greek' (E. L.
Hicks in *Studia Biblica*, iv. 8). This doubtless points to the
quarter from which St. Paul derived the word, as the Jews had
not the practice of adoption.

'Αββᾶ, ὁ πατήρ. The repetition of this word, first in Aramaic
and then in Greek, is remarkable and brings home to us the fact
that Christianity had its birth in a bilingual people. The same
repetition occurs in Mark xiv. 36 ('Abba, Father, all things are
possible to Thee') and in Gal. iv. 6 : it gives a greater intensity of
expression, but would only be natural where the speaker was
using in both cases his familiar tongue. Lightfoot (*Hor. Heb.* on
Mark xiv. 36) thinks that in the Gospel the word 'Αββᾶ only was
used by our Lord and ὁ Πατήρ added as an interpretation by
St. Mark, and that in like manner St. Paul is interpreting for the
benefit of his readers. The three passages are however all too
emotional for this explanation: interpretation is out of place in
a prayer. It seems better to suppose that our Lord Himself,
using familiarly both languages, and concentrating into this word
of all words such a depth of meaning, found Himself impelled
spontaneously to repeat the word, and that some among His
disciples caught and transmitted the same habit. It is significant
however of the limited extent of strictly Jewish Christianity that
we find no other original examples of the use than these three.

16. αὐτὸ τὸ Πνεῦμα : see on ver. 14 above.

συμμαρτυρεῖ: cf. ii. 15; ix. 2. There the 'joint-witness' was
the subjective testimony of conscience, confirming the objective
testimony of a man's works or actions ; here consciousness is
analyzed, and its *data* are referred partly to the man himself, partly
to the Spirit of God moving and prompting him.

17. κληρονόμοι. The idea of a κληρονομία is taken up and
developed in N. T. from O. T. and Apocr. (Ecclus, *Ps. Sol.*,
4 Ezr.). It is also prominent in Philo, who devotes a whole

treatise to the question *Quis rerum divinarum heres sit?* (Mang. i.
473 ff.). Meaning originally (i) the simple possession of the Holy
Land, it came to mean (ii) its permanent and assured possession
(Ps. xxv [xxiv]. 13; xxxvi [xxxvii]. 9, 11 &c.); hence (iii)
specially the secure possession won by the Messiah (Is. lx. 21;
lxi. 7; and so it became (iv) a symbol of all Messianic blessings
(Matt. v. 5; xix. 29; xxv. 34, &c.). Philo, after his manner,
makes the word denote the bliss of the soul when freed from the
body.

It is an instance of the unaccountable inequalities of usage that whereas
κληρονομεῖν, κληρονομία occur almost innumerable times in LXX, κληρονόμος
occurs only five times (once in Symmachus); in N. T. there is much greater
equality (κληρονομεῖν eighteen, κληρονομία fourteen, κληρονόμος fifteen).

συγκληρονόμοι. Our Lord had described Himself as 'the Heir'
in the parable of the Wicked Husbandmen (Matt. xxi. 38). This
would show that the idea of κληρονομία received its full Christian
adaptation directly from Him (cf. also Matt. xxv. 34).

εἴπερ συμπάσχομεν. St. Paul seems here to be reminding his
hearers of a current Christian saying: cf. 2 Tim. ii. 11 πιστὸς ὁ
λόγος, Εἰ γὰρ συναπεθάνομεν καὶ συζήσομεν· εἰ ὑπομένομεν καὶ συμβασι-
λεύσομεν. This is another instance of the Biblical conception of
Christ as the Way (His Life not merely an example for ours, but
in its main lines presenting a fixed type or law to which the lives
of Christians must conform); cf. p. 196 above, and Dr. Hort's
The Way, the Truth, and the Life there referred to. For εἴπερ see
on iii. 30.

SUFFERING THE PATH TO GLORY.

VIII. 18–25. *What though the path to that glory lies
through suffering? The suffering and the glory alike are
parts of a great cosmical movement, in which the irrational
creation joins with man. As it shared the results of his
fall, so also will it share in his redemption. Its pangs are
pangs of a new birth (vv. 18–22).*

*Like the mute creation, we Christians too wait painfully
for our deliverance. Our attitude is one of hope and not of
possession (vv. 23–25).*

[18] What of that? For the sufferings which we have to undergo
in this phase of our career I count not worth a thought in view
of that dazzling splendour which will one day break through
the clouds and dawn upon us. [19] For the sons of God will stand
forth revealed in the glories of their bright inheritance. And for

that consummation not they alone but the whole irrational creation, both animate and inanimate, waits with eager longing; like spectators straining forward over the ropes to catch the first glimpse of some triumphal pageant.

[20] The future and not the present must satisfy its aspirations. For ages ago Creation was condemned to have its energies marred and frustrated. And that by no act of its own : it was God who fixed this doom upon it, but with the hope [21] that as it had been enthralled to death and decay by the Fall of Man so too the Creation shall share in the free and glorious existence of God's emancipated children. [22] It is like the pangs of a woman in child-birth. This universal frame feels up to this moment the throes of travail—feels them in every part and cries out in its pain. But where there is travail, there must needs also be a birth.

[23] Our own experience points to the same conclusion. True that in those workings of the Spirit, the *charismata* with which we are endowed, we Christians already possess a foretaste of good things to come. But that very foretaste makes us long—anxiously and painfully long—for the final recognition of our Sonship. We desire to see these bodies of ours delivered from the evils that beset them and transfigured into glory.

[24] Hope is the Christian's proper attitude. We were saved indeed, the groundwork of our salvation was laid, when we became Christians. But was that salvation in possession or in prospect? Certainly in prospect. Otherwise there would be no room for hope. For what a man *sees* already in his hand he does not hope for as if it were future. [25] But in our case we do not see, and we do hope; therefore we also wait for our object with steadfast fortitude.

18. λογίζομαι γάρ. At the end of the last paragraph St. Paul has been led to speak of the exalted privileges of Christians involved in the fact that they are *sons* of God. The thought of these privileges suddenly recalls to him the contrast of the sufferings through which they are passing. And after his manner he does not let go this idea of 'suffering' but works it into his main argument. He first dismisses the thought that the present suffering can be any real counter-weight to the future glory; and then he shows that not only is it not this, but that on the contrary it actually points forward to that glory. It does this on the grandest

scale. In fact it is nothing short of an universal law that suffering marks the road to glory. All the suffering, all the imperfection, all the unsatisfied aspiration and longing of which the traces are so abundant in external nature as well as in man, do but point forward to a time when the suffering shall cease, the imperfection be removed and the frustrated aspirations at last crowned and satisfied; and this time coincides with the glorious consummation which awaits the Christian.

True it is that there goes up as it were an universal groan, from creation, from ourselves, from the Holy Spirit who sympathizes with us; but this groaning is but the travail-pangs of the new birth, the entrance upon their glorified condition of the risen sons of God.

λογίζομαι : here in its strict sense, 'I calculate,' 'weigh mentally,' 'count up on the one side and on the other.'

ἄξια... πρός. In Plato, *Gorg.* p. 471 E, we have οὐδενὸς ἄξιός ἐστι πρὸς τὴν ἀλήθειαν : so that with a slight ellipse οὐκ ἄξια ... πρὸς τὴν δόξαν will = 'not worth (considering) in comparison with the glory.' Or we may regard this as a mixture of two constructions, (1) οὐκ ἄξια τῆς δόξης, i. e. 'not an equivalent for the glory'; comp. Prov. viii. 11 πᾶν δὲ τίμιον οὐκ ἄξιον αὐτῆς (sc. τῆς σοφίας) ἐστίν, and (2) οὐδενὸς λόγου ἄξια πρὸς τὴν δόξαν : comp. Jer. xxiii. 28 τί τὸ ἄχυρον πρὸς τὸν σῖτον;

The thought has a near parallel in 4 Ezra vii. 3 ff. Compare (*e.g.*) the following (vv. 12–17): *Et facti sunt introitus huius saeculi angusti et dolentes et laboriosi, pauci autem et mali et periculorum pleni et labore magno opere fulti ; nam maioris saeculi introitus spatiosi et securi et facientes immortalitatis fructum. Si ergo non ingredientes ingressi fuerintque vivunt angusta et vana haec, non poterunt recipere quae sunt reposita ... iusti autem ferent angusta sperantes spatiosa.* Compare also the quotations from the Talmud in Delitzsch *ad loc.* The question is asked, What is the way to the world to come? And the answer is, Through suffering.

μέλλουσαν: emphatic, 'is destined to,' 'is certain to.' The position of the word is the same as in Gal. iii. 23, and serves to point the contrast to τοῦ νῦν καιροῦ.

δόξαν : the heavenly brightness of Christ's appearing : see on iii. 23.

εἰς ἡμᾶς : to reach and include us in its radiance.

19. ἀποκαραδοκία : cf. Phil. i. 20 κατὰ τὴν ἀποκαραδοκίαν καὶ ἐλπίδα μου : the verb ἀποκαραδοκεῖν occurs in Aquila's version of Ps. xxxvii [xxxvi]. 7, and the subst. frequently in Polyb. and Plutarch (see Grm.-Thay. s. v., and Ell. Lft. on Phil. i. 20). A highly expressive word ' to strain forward,' lit. 'await with outstretched head.' This sense is still further strengthened by the compound, ἀπο- denoting diversion from other things and concentration on a single object.

This passage (especially vv. 17, 22) played a considerable part in the system of Basilides, as described in Hippol. *Ref. Omn. Haer.* vii. 25-27.

τῆς κτίσεως: see on i. 20. Here the sense is given by the context ; ἡ κτίσις is set in contrast with the 'sons of God,' and from the allusion to the Fall which follows evidently refers to Gen. iii. 17, 18 'Cursed is the ground for thy sake . . . thorns also and thistles shall it bring forth to thee.' The commentators however are not wrong in making the word include here the whole irrational creation. The poetic and penetrating imagination of St. Paul sees in the marks of imperfection on the face of nature, in the signs at once of high capacities and poor achievement, the visible and audible expression of a sense of something wanting which will one day be supplied.

Oltr. and some others argue strenuously, but in vain, for giving to κτίσις, throughout the whole of this passage, the sense not of the world of nature, but of the world of man (similarly Orig.). He tries to get rid of the poetic personification of nature and to dissociate St. Paul from Jewish doctrine as to the origin of death and decay in nature, and as to its removal at the coming of the Messiah. But (i) there is no sufficient warrant for limiting κτίσις to humanity ; (ii) it is necessary to deny the sufficiently obvious reference to Gen. iii. 17–19 (where, though the 'ground' or 'soil' only is mentioned, it is the earth's surface as the seed-plot of life); (iii) the Apostle is rather taken out of the mental surroundings in which he moved than placed in them : see below on 'The Renovation of Nature.'

The ancients generally take the passage as above (ἡ κτίσις ἡ ἄλογος expressly Euthym.-Zig). Orig.-lat., as expressly, has *creaturam utpote rationabilem* ; but he is quite at fault, making τῇ ματαιότητι = 'the body.' Chrys. and Euthym.-Zig. call attention to the personification of Nature, which they compare to that in the Psalms and Prophets, while Diodorus of Tarsus refers the expressions implying life rather to the Powers (δυνάμεις) which preside over inanimate nature and from which it takes its forms. The sense commonly given to ματαιότητι is = φθορά.

τὴν ἀποκάλυψιν τῶν υἱῶν τοῦ Θεοῦ. The same word ἀποκάλυψις is applied to the Second Coming of the Messiah (which is also an ἐπιφανεία 2 Thess. ii. 8) and to that of the redeemed who accompany Him : their new existence will not be like the present, but will be in 'glory' (δόξα) both reflected and imparted. This revealing of the sons of God will be the signal for the great transformation.

The Jewish writings use similar language. To them also the appearing of the Messiah is an ἀποκάλυψις : 4 Ezra xiii. 32 *et erit cum fient haec, et contingent signa quae ante ostendi tibi et tunc revelabitur filius meus quem vidisti ut virum ascendentem* ; *Apoc. Bar.* xxxix. 7 *et erit, cum appropinquaverit tempus finis eius ut cadat, tunc revelabitur principatus Messiae mei qui similis est fonti et viti, et cum revelatus fuerit eradicabit multitudinem congregationis eius* (the Latin of this book, it will be remembered, is Ceriani's version from the Syriac, and not ancient like that of 4 Ezra). The object of the Messiah's appearing is the same as with St. Paul, to deliver creation from its ills : 4 Ezra xiii. 26, 29 *ipse est quem conservat Altissimus multis*

*temporibus qui per semetipsum liberabit creaturam suam et ipse disponet
qui derelicti sunt . . . ecce dies veniunt, quando incipiet Altissimus liberare
eos qui super terram sunt*: Apoc. Bar. xxxii. 6 *quando futurum est ut Fortis
innovet creaturam suam* (= 4 Ezra vii. 75 [Bensly] *donec veniant tempora
illa, in quibus incipies creaturam renovare*). The Messiah does not come
alone : 4 Ezra xiii. 51 *non poterit quisque super terram videre filium meum
vel eos qui cum eo sunt nisi in tempore diei.* He collects round Him
a double multitude, consisting partly of the ten tribes who had been carried
away into captivity, and partly of those who were left in the Holy Land
(*ibid.* vv. 12, 39 ff., 48 f.).

ἀπεκδέχεται : another strong compound, where ἀπο- contains the
same idea of '*concentrated* waiting' as in ἀποκαραδοκία above.

20. τῇ . . . ματαιότητι : ματαιότης ματαιοτήτων is the refrain of the
Book of Ecclesiastes (Eccl. i. 2, &c.; cf. Ps. xxxix. 5, 11 [xxxviii. 6,
12] cxliv [cxliii]. 4) : that is μάταιον which is 'without result' (μάτην),
'ineffective,' 'which does not reach its end'—the opposite of
τέλειος : the word is therefore appropriately used of the *disappointing*
character of present existence, which nowhere reaches the perfection
of which it is capable.

ὑπετάγη : by the Divine sentence which followed the Fall (Gen.
iii. 17-19).

οὐχ ἑκοῦσα : not through its own fault, but through the fault of
man, i. e. the Fall.

διὰ τὸν ὑποτάξαντα : 'by reason of Him who subjected it,' i.e. not
man in general (Lips.) ; nor Adam (Chrys. *al.*); nor the Devil
(Go.), but (with most commentators, ancient as well as modern)
God, by the sentence pronounced after the Fall. It is no argument
against this reference that the use of διά with acc. in such a connexion is rather unusual (so Lips.).

ἐπ' ἐλπίδι qualifies ὑπετάγη. Creation was made subject to
vanity—not simply and absolutely and there an end, but 'in hope
that,' &c. Whatever the defects and degradation of nature, it was
at least left with the hope of rising to the ideal intended for it.

21. ὅτι. The majority of recent commentators make ὅτι (= 'that')
define the substance of the hope just mentioned, and not (= ' because ') give a reason for it. The meaning in any case is much
the same, but this is the simpler way to arrive at it.

καὶ αὐτὴ ἡ κτίσις : not only Christians but even the mute creation
with them.

ἀπὸ τῆς δουλείας τῆς φθορᾶς. δουλείας corresponds to ὑπετάγη, the
state of subjection or thraldom to dissolution and decay. The
opposite to this is the full and free development of all the powers
which attends the state of δόξα. 'Glorious liberty' is a poor
translation and does not express the idea : δόξα, 'the glorified state,'
is the leading fact, not a subordinate fact, and ἐλευθερία is its
characteristic, ' the liberty of the glory of the children of God.'

22. οἴδαμεν γάρ introduces a fact of common knowledge (though

the apprehension of it may not have been so common as he assumes) to which the Apostle appeals.

συστενάζει καὶ συνωδίνει. It seems on the whole best to take the συν- in both instances as = 'together,' i.e. in all the parts of which creation is made up (so. Theod.-Mops. expressly: βούλεται δὲ εἰπεῖν ὅτι συμφώνως ἐπιδείκνυται τοῦτο πᾶσα ἡ κτίσις· ἵνα τὸ παρὰ πάσης τὸ αὐτὸ γένεσθαι ὁμοίως, παιδεύσῃ τούτους τὴν πρὸς ἅπαντας κοινωνίαν αἱρεῖσθαι τῇ τῶν λυπηρῶν καρτερίᾳ). Oltr. gets out of it the sense of 'inwardly' (= ἐν ἑαυτοῖς), which it will not bear: Fri. Lips. and others, after Euthym.-Zig. make it = 'with men' or 'with the children of God'; but if these had been pointed to, there would not be so clear an opposition as there is at the beginning of the next verse (οὐ μόνον δέ, ἀλλὰ καὶ αὐτοί). The two verses must be kept apart.

23. οὐ μόνον δέ. Not only does nature groan, but we Christians also groan: our very privileges make us long for something more.

τὴν ἀπαρχὴν τοῦ Πνεύματος: 'the first-fruits, or first instalment of the gift of the Spirit.' St. Paul evidently means all the phenomena of that great outpouring which was specially characteristic of the Apostolic Age from the Day of Pentecost onwards, the varied charismata bestowed upon the first Christians (1 Cor. xii. &c.), but including also the moral and spiritual gifts which were more permanent (Gal. v. 22 f.). The possession of these gifts served to quicken the sense of the yet greater gifts that were to come. Foremost among them was to be the transforming of the earthly or 'psychical' body into a spiritual body (1 Cor. xv. 44 ff.). St. Paul calls this a 'deliverance,' i. e. a deliverance from the 'ills that flesh is heir to': for ἀπολύτρωσις see on iii. 24.

ἔχοντες ἡμεῖς: ἡμεῖς is placed here by אAC 5. 47. 80, also by Tisch. RV. and (in brackets) by WH.

υἱοθεσίαν: see on ver. 15 above. Here υἱοθ. = the manifested, realized, act of adoption—its public promulgation.

24. τῇ γὰρ ἐλπίδι ἐσώθημεν. The older commentators for the most part (not however Luther Beng. Fri.) took the dat. here as dative of the instrument, 'by hope were we saved.' Most moderns (including Gif. Go. Oltr. Mou. Lid.) take it as dat. modi, 'in hope were we saved;' the main ground being that it is more in accordance with the teaching of St. Paul to say that we were saved by faith, or from another point of view—looking at salvation from the side of God—by grace (both terms are found in Eph. ii. 8) than by hope. This seems preferable. Some have held that Hope is here only an aspect of Faith: and it is quite true that the definition of Faith in Heb. xi. 1 (ἔστι δὲ πίστις ἐλπιζομένων ὑπόστασις, πραγμάτων ἔλεγχος οὐ βλεπομένων), makes it practically equivalent to Hope. But that is just one of the points of distinction between Ep. to Heb.

P

and St. Paul. In Heb. Faith is used somewhat vaguely of belief in God and in the fulfilment of His promises. In St. Paul it is far more often Faith *in Christ*, the first act of accepting Christianity (see p. 33 above). This belongs essentially to the past, and to the present as growing directly out of the past; but when St. Paul comes to speak of the future he uses another term, ἐλπίς. No doubt when we come to trace this to its origin it has its root in the strong conviction of the Messiahship of Jesus and its consequences; but the two terms are not therefore identical, and it is best to keep them distinct.

Some recent Germans (Holsten, Weiss, Lips.) take the dat. as *dativus commodi*, '*for* hope were we saved.' But this is less natural. To obtain this sense we should have to personify Hope more strongly than the context will bear. Besides Hope is an attribute or characteristic of the Christian life, but not its end.

ἐλπὶς δὲ βλεπομένη : ἐλπίς here = 'the thing hoped for,' just as κτίσις = 'the thing created'; a very common usage.

ὃ γὰρ βλέπει, τίς ἐλπίζει; This terse reading is found only in B 47 *marg.*, which adds τὸ παλαιὸν οὕτως ἔχει : it is adopted by RV. *text*, WH. *text*. Text. Recept. has [ὃ γὰρ βλέπει τις] τί καὶ [ἐλπίζει], of which τί alone is found in Western authorities (D F G, Vulg. Pesh. *al.*), and καί alone in א* 47*. Both RV. and WH. give a place in the margin to τί καὶ ἐλπίζει and τίς καὶ ὑπομένει [ὑπομένει with א* A 47 *marg.*].

25. The point of these two verses is that the attitude of hope, so distinctive of the Christian, implies that there is more in store for him than anything that is his already.

δι᾽ ὑπομονῆς: constancy and fortitude under persecution, &c., pointing back to the 'sufferings' of ver. 18 (cf. on ii. 7; v. 4; and for the use of διά ii. 27).

The Renovation of Nature.

We have already quoted illustrations of St. Paul's language from some of the Jewish writings which are nearest to his own in point of time. They are only samples of the great mass of Jewish literature. To all of it this idea of a renovation of Nature, the creation of new heavens and a new earth is common, as part of the Messianic expectation which was fulfilled unawares to many of those by whom it was entertained. The days of the Messiah were to be the 'seasons of refreshing,' the 'times of restoration of all things,' which were to come from the face of the Lord (Acts iii. 19, 21). The expectation had its roots in the O. T., especially in those chapters of the Second Part of Isaiah in which the approaching Return from Captivity opens up to the prophet such splendid visions for the future. The one section Is. lxv. 17-25 might well be held to warrant most of the statements in the Apocrypha and Talmud.

The idea of the 'new heavens and new earth' is based directly upon Is. lxv. 17, and is found clearly stated in the Book of *Enoch*, xlv. 4 f. 'I will transform the heaven and make it an eternal blessing and light. And I will transform the earth and make it a blessing and cause Mine elect ones to dwell upon it' (where see Charles' note). There is also an application of Ps. cxiv. 4, with an added feature which illustrates exactly St. Paul's ἀποκάλυψις τῶν υἱῶν τοῦ Θεοῦ: 'In those days will the mountains leap like rams and the hills will skip like lambs satisfied with milk, and they will all become angels in heaven. Their faces will be lighted up with joy, because in those days the Elect One has appeared, and the earth will rejoice and the righteous will dwell upon it, and the elect will go to and fro upon it' (*Enoch* li. 4 f.). We have given parallels enough from 4 Ezra and the *Apocalypse of Baruch*, and there is much in the Talmud to the same effect (cf. Weber, *Altsyn. Theol.* p. 380 ff.; Schürer, *Neutest. Zeitgesch.* ii. 453 ff., 458 f.; Edersheim, *Life and Times*, &c. ii. 438).

It is not surprising to find the poetry of the prophetic writings hardened into fact by Jewish literalism; but it is strange when the products of this mode of interpretation are attributed to our Lord Himself on authority no less ancient than that of Papias of Hierapolis, professedly drawing from the tradition of St. John. Yet Irenaeus (*Adv. Haer.* V. xxxiii. 3) quotes in such terms the following: 'The days will come, in which vines shall grow, each having ten thousand shoots and on each shoot ten thousand branches, and on each branch again ten thousand twigs, and on each twig ten thousand clusters, and on each cluster ten thousand grapes, and each grape when pressed shall yield five and twenty measures of wine . . . Likewise also a grain of wheat shall produce ten thousand heads, and every head shall have ten thousand grains, and every grain ten pounds of fine flour, bright and clean; and the other fruits, seeds and the grass shall produce in similar proportions, and all the animals using these fruits which are products of the soil, shall become in their turn peaceable and harmonious.' It happens that this saying, or at least part of it, is actually extant in *Apoc. Bar.* xxix. 5 (cf. *Orac. Sibyll.* iii. 620–623, 744 ff.), so that it clearly comes from some Jewish source. In view of an instance like this it seems possible that even in the N. T. our Lord's words may have been defined in a sense which was not exactly that originally intended owing to the current expectation which the disciples largely shared.

And yet on the whole, even if this expectation was by the Jews to some extent literalized and materialized, some of its essential features were preserved. Corresponding to the new abode pre-

pared for it there was to be a renewed humanity: and that not
only in a physical sense based on Is. xxxv. 5 f. ('Then the eyes of
the blind shall be opened, and the ears of the deaf shall be un-
stopped,' &c.), but also in a moral sense; the root of evil was to be
plucked out of the hearts of men and a new heart was to be implanted in them: the Spirit of God was to rest upon them (Weber,
Altsyn. Theol. p. 382). There was to be no unrighteousness in
their midst, for they were all to be holy (*Ps. Sol.* xvii. 28 f., 36,
&c.). The Messiah was to rule over the nations, but not merely by
force; Israel was to be a true light to the Gentiles (Schürer, *op. cit.*
p. 456).

If we compare these Jewish beliefs with what we find here in the
Epistle to the Romans there are two ways in which the superiority
of the Apostle is most striking. (1) There runs through his words
an intense sympathy with nature in and for itself. He is one of
those (like St. Francis of Assisi) to whom it is given to read as it
were the thoughts of plants and animals. He seems to lay his ear
to the earth and the confused murmur which he hears has a meaning
for him: it is creation's yearning for that happier state intended for
it and of which it has been defrauded. (2) The main idea is not,
as it is so apt to be with the Rabbinical writers, the mere glorifica-
tion of Israel. By them the Gentiles are differently treated.
Sometimes it is their boast that the Holy Land will be reserved
exclusively for Israel: 'the sojourner and the stranger shall dwell
with them no more' (*Ps. Sol.* xvii. 31). The only place for the
Gentiles is 'to serve him beneath the yoke' (*ibid.* ver. 32). The
vision of the Gentiles streaming to Jerusalem as a centre of religion
is exceptional, as it must be confessed that it is also in O. T.
Prophecy. On the other hand, with St. Paul the movement is
truly cosmic. The 'sons of God' are not selected for their own
sakes alone, but their redemption means the redemption of a world
of being besides themselves.

THE ASSISTANCE OF THE SPIRIT.

VIII. 26, 27. *Meanwhile the Holy Spirit itself assists in
our prayers.*

[26] Nor are we alone in our struggles. The Holy Spirit supports our helplessness. Left to ourselves we do not know what
prayers to offer or how to offer them. But in those inarticulate
groans which rise from the depths of our being, we recognize the
voice of none other than the Holy Spirit. He makes intercession;

and His intercession is sure to be answered. ²⁷ For God Who
searches the inmost recesses of the heart can interpret His own
Spirit's meaning. He knows that His own Will regulates Its
petitions, and that they are offered for men dedicated to His service.

26. ὡσαύτως. As we groan, so also does the Holy Spirit groan
with us, putting a meaning into our aspirations which they would
not have of themselves. All alike converges upon that 'Divine
event, to which the whole creation moves.' This view of the
connexion (Go., Weiss, Lips.), which weaves in this verse with
the broad course of the Apostle's argument, seems on the whole
better than that which attaches it more closely to the words immediately preceding, ' as hope sustains us so also does the Spirit
sustain us' (Mey. Oltr. Gif. Va. Mou.).

συναντιλαμβάνεται : ἀντιλαμβάνεσθαι = 'to take hold of at the
side (ἀντί), so as to support'; and this sense is further strengthened by the idea of association contained in συν-. The same
compound occurs in LXX of Ps. lxxxviii [lxxxix]. 22, and in
Luke x. 40.

τῇ ἀσθενείᾳ : decisively attested for ταῖς ἀσθενείαις. On the way in
which we are taking the verse the reference will be to the vague-
ness and defectiveness of our prayers; on the other view to our
weakness under suffering implied in δι' ὑπομονῆς. But as ὑπομονή
suggests rather a certain amount of victorious resistance, this application of ἀσθένεια seems less appropriate.

τὸ γὰρ τί προσευξώμεθα. The art. makes the whole clause object
of οἴδαμεν. Gif. notes that this construction is characteristic of
St. Paul and St. Luke (in the latter ten times; in the former Rom.
xiii. 9; Gal. v. 14; Eph. iv. 9; 1 Thess. iv. 1). τί προσευξ. is
strictly rather, 'What we ought to pray' than 'what we ought to
pray for,' i. e. 'how we are to word our prayers,' not ' what we are
to choose as the objects of prayer.' But as the object determines
the nature of the prayer, in the end the meaning is much the
same.

καθὸ δεῖ. It is perhaps a refinement to take this as = 'according to, in proportion to, our need' (Mey.-W. Gif.); which brings out
the proper force of καθό (cf. Baruch i. 6 v. l.) at the cost of putting
a sense upon δεῖ which is not found elsewhere in the N. T., where
it always denotes obligation or objective necessity. Those of the
Fathers who show how they took it make καθὸ δεῖ = τίνα τρόπον
δεῖ προσευξ., which also answers well to κατὰ Θεόν in the next
verse.

ὑπερεντυγχάνει : ἐντυγχάνω means originally 'to fall in with,' and
hence 'to accost with entreaty,' and so simply 'to entreat'; in this
sense it is not uncommon and occurs twice in this Epistle (viii. 34;
xi. 2). The verse contains a statement which the unready of

speech may well lay to heart, that all prayer need not be formulated, but that the most inarticulate desires (springing from a right
motive) may have a shape and a value given to them beyond
anything that is present and definable to the consciousness.   This
verse and the next go to show that St. Paul regarded the action of
the Holy Spirit as personal, and as distinct from the action of the
Father.   The language of the Creeds aims at taking account of
these expressions, which agree fully with the triple formula of
2 Cor. xiii. 14; Matt. xxviii. 19.   Oltr. however makes τὸ πνεῦμα in
both verses = 'the human spirit,' against the natural sense of
ὑπερεντυγχάνει and ὑπὲρ ἁγίων, which place the object of intercession
outside the Spirit itself, and against κατὰ Θεόν, which would be by
no means always true of the human spirit.

ὑπερεντυγχάνει is decisively attested (א*ABDFG &c.).   Text. Recept.
has the easier ἐντυγχάνει ὑπὲρ ἡμῶν.

27. ὅτι.   Are we to translate this 'because' (Weiss Go. Gif. Va.)
or 'that' (Mey. Oltr. Lips. Mou.)?   Probably the latter; for if we
take ὅτι as assigning a reason for οἶδε τί τὸ φρόνημα, the reason would
not be adequate: God would still 'know' the mind, or intention,
of the Spirit even if we could conceive it as not κατὰ Θεόν and
not ὑπὲρ ἁγίων.   It seems best therefore to make ὅτι describe the
nature of the Spirit's intercession.

κατὰ Θεόν = κατὰ τὸ θέλημα τοῦ Θεοῦ: cf. 2 Cor. vii. 9–11.

The Jews had a strong belief in the value of the intercessory prayer of
their great saints, such as Moses (*Ass. Moys.* xi. 11, 17; xii. 6), Jeremiah
(*Apoc. Bar.* ii. 2): cf. Weber, p. 287 ff.   But they have nothing like the
teaching of these verses.

THE ASCENDING PROCESS OF SALVATION.

VIII. 28-30. *With what a chain of Providential care
does God accompany the course of His chosen!   In eternity,
the plan laid and their part in it foreseen; in time, first
their call, then their acquittal, and finally their reception
into glory.*

[28] Yet another ground of confidence.   The Christian knows that
all things (including his sufferings) can have but one result, and
that a good one, for those who love God and respond to the call
which in the pursuance of His purpose He addresses to them.
[29] Think what a long perspective of Divine care and protection lies
before them!   First, in eternity, God marked them for His own,
as special objects of His care and instruments of His purpose.

Then, in the same eternity, He planned that they should share in the glorified celestial being of the Incarnate Son—in order that He, as Eldest Born, might gather round Him a whole family of the redeemed. [30] Then in due course, to those for whom He had in store this destiny He addressed the call to leave their worldly lives and devote themselves to His service. And when they obeyed that call He treated them as righteous men, with their past no longer reckoned against them. And so accounted righteous He let them participate (partially now as they will do more completely hereafter) in His Divine perfection.

28. οἴδαμεν δέ passes on to another ground for looking confidently to the future. The Christian's career *must* have a good ending, because at every step in it he is in the hands of God and is carrying out the Divine purpose.

πάντα συνεργεῖ: a small but important group of authorities, A B, Orig. 2/6 or 2/7 (cf. Boh. Sah. Aeth.), adds ὁ Θεός; and the insertion lay so much less near at hand than the omission that it must be allowed to have the greater appearance of originality. With this reading συνεργεῖ must be taken transitively, 'causes all things to work.'

The Bohairic Version, translated literally and preserving the idioms, is 'But we know that those who love God, He habitually works with them in every good thing, those whom He has called according to His purpose.' The Sahidic Version (as edited by Amélineau in *Zeitschrift für Aegypt. Sprache*, 1887) is in part defective but certainly repeats Θεός: 'But we know that those who love God, God . . . them in every good thing,' &c. From this we gather that the Version of Upper Egypt inserted ὁ Θεός, and that the Version of Lower Egypt omitted it but interpreted συνεργεῖ transitively as if it were present. It would almost seem as if there was an exegetical tradition which took the word in this way. It is true that the extract from Origen's Commentary in the *Philocalia* (ed. Robinson, p. 226 ff.) not only distinctly and repeatedly presents the common reading but also in one place (p. 229) clearly has the common interpretation. But Chrysostom (*ad loc.*) argues at some length as if he were taking συνεργεῖ transitively with ὁ Θεός for subject. Similarly Gennadius (in Cramer's *Catena*), also Theodoret and Theodorus Monachus (preserved in the *Catena*). It would perhaps be too much to claim all these writers as witnesses to the reading συνεργεῖ ὁ Θεός, but they may point to a tradition which had its origin in that reading and survived it. On the other hand it is possible that the reading may have grown out of the interpretation.

For the use of συνεργεῖ there are two rather close parallels in *Test. XII Patr.*: Issach. 3 ὁ Θεὸς συνεργεῖ τῇ ἁπλότητί μου, and Gad 4 τὸ γὰρ πνεῦμα τοῦ μίσους . . . συνεργεῖ τῷ Σατανᾷ ἐν πᾶσιν εἰς θάνατον τῶν ἀνθρώπων· τὸ δὲ πνεῦμα τῆς ἀγάπης ἐν μακροθυμίᾳ συνεργεῖ τῷ νόμῳ τοῦ Θεοῦ εἰς σωτηρίαν ἀνθρώπων.

τοῖς κατὰ πρόθεσιν κλητοῖς οὖσιν. With this clause St. Paul introduces a string of what may be called the technical terms of his

theology, marking the succession of stages into which he divides
the normal course of a Christian life—all being considered not
from the side of human choice and volition, but from the side of
Divine care and ordering.   This is summed up at the outset in the
phrase κατὰ πρόθεσιν, the comprehensive plan or design in accordance with which God directs the destinies of men.   There can be
no question that St. Paul fully recognizes the freedom of the human
will.   The large part which exhortation plays in his letters is conclusive proof of this.   But whatever the extent of human freedom
there must be behind it the Divine Sovereignty.   It is the practice
of St. Paul to state alternately the one and the other without
attempting an exact delimitation between them.   And what he has
not done we are not likely to succeed in doing.   In the passage
before us the Divine Sovereignty is in view, not on its terrible but
on its gracious side.   It is the proof how ' God worketh all things
for good to those who love Him.'   We cannot insist too strongly
upon this; but when we leave the plain declarations of the Apostle
and begin to draw speculative inferences on the right hand or on
the left we may easily fall into cross currents which will render any
such inferences invalid.   See further the note on Free-Will and
Predestination at the end of ch. xi.

In further characterizing ' those who love God ' St. Paul naturally strikes the point at which their love became manifest by the
acceptance of the Divine Call.   This call is one link in the chain
of Providential care which attends them :   and it suggests the other
links which stretch far back into the past and far forward into the
future.   By enumerating these the Apostle completes his proof
that the love of God never quits His chosen ones.

The enumeration follows the order of succession in time.

For πρόθεσις see on ch. ix. 11 ἡ κατ᾽ ἐκλογὴν πρόθεσις τοῦ Θεοῦ,
which would prove, if proof were needed, that the purpose is that
of God and not of man (κατ᾽ οἰκείαν προαίρεσιν Theoph. and the
Greek Fathers generally): comp. also Eph. i. 11; iii. 11; 2 Tim.
i. 9.

It was one of the misfortunes of Greek theology that it received a bias in
the Free-Will controversy from opposition to the Gnostics (cf. p. 269 *inf.*)
which it never afterwards lost, and which seriously prejudiced its exegesis
wherever this question was concerned. Thus in the present instance, the great
mass of the Greek commentators take κατὰ πρόθεσιν to mean ' in accordance
with the man's own προαίρεσις or free act of choice' (see the extracts in
Cramer's *Catena* 'e cod. Monac.'; and add Theoph. Oecum. Euthym.-Zig.).
The two partial exceptions are, as we might expect, Origen and Cyril of
Alexandria, who however both show traces of the influences current in the
Eastern Church. Origen also seems inclined to take it of the *propositum
bonum et bonam voluntatem quam circa Dei cultum gerunt*; but he admits
the alternative that it may refer to the purpose of God. If so, it refers to
this purpose as determined by His foreknowledge of the characters and
conduct of men. Cyril of Alexandria asks the question, Whose purpose is
intended? and decides that it would not be wrong to answer τὴν τε τοῦ

κεκληκότος καὶ τὴν ἑαυτῶν. He comes to this decision however rather on dogmatic than on exegetical grounds.

It is equally a straining of the text when Augustine distinguishes two kinds of call, one *secundum propositum*, the call of the elect, and the other of those who are not elect. *Non enim omnes vocati* secundum propositum *sunt vocati: quoniam multi vocati, pauci electi. Ipsi ergo secundum propositum vocati qui electi ante constitutionem mundi* (*Cont. duas Epist. Pelag.* ii. 10. § 22, cf. *Cont. Julian.* v. 6, § 14). In the idea of a double call, Augustine seems to have been anticipated by Origen, who however, as we have seen, gives a different sense to κατὰ πρόθεσιν: *omnes quidem vocati sunt, non tamen omnes* secundum propositum *vocati sunt* (ed. Lomm. vii. 128).

κλητοῖς: 'called,' implying that the call has been obeyed. The κλῆσις is not *au salut* (Oltr.), at least in the sense of final salvation, but simply to become Christians: see on i. 1.

29. ὅτι: certainly here 'because,' assigning a reason for πάντα συνεργεῖ ὁ Θεὸς εἰς ἀγαθόν, not 'that' (= *c'est que* Oltr.).

οὓς προέγνω. The meaning of this phrase must be determined by the Biblical use of the word ' know,' which is very marked and clear: e.g. Ps. i. 6 'The Lord knoweth (γιγνώσκει) the way of the righteous'; cxliv [cxliii]. 3 'Lord, what is man that Thou takest knowledge of him (ὅτι ἐγνώσθης αὐτῷ LXX)? Or the son of man that Thou makest account of him?' Hos. xiii. 5 'I did know (ἐποίμαινον) thee in the wilderness.' Am. iii. 2 'You only have I known (ἔγνων) of all the families of the earth.' Matt. vii. 23 'Then will I profess unto them I never knew (ἔγνων) you,' &c. In all these places the word means 'to take note of,' 'to fix the regard upon,' as a preliminary to selection for some especial purpose. The compound προέγνω only throws back this 'taking note' from the historic act in time to the eternal counsel which it expresses and executes.

This interpretation (which is very similar to that of Godet and which approaches, though it is not exactly identical with, that of a number of older commentators, who make προέγνω = *praediligere, approbare*) has the double advantage of being strictly conformed to Biblical usage and of reading nothing into the word which we are not sure is there. This latter objection applies to most other ways of taking the passage: e.g. to Origen's, when he makes the foreknowledge a foreknowledge of character and fitness, προανατενίσας οὖν ὁ Θεὸς τῷ εἱρμῷ τῶν ἐσομένων, καὶ κατανοήσας ῥοπὴν τοῦ ἐφ' ἡμῖν τῶνδέ τινων ἐπὶ εὐσέβειαν καὶ ὁρμὴν ἐπὶ ταύτην μετὰ τὴν ῥοπὴν κ.τ.λ. (*Philocal.* xxv. 2. p. 227, ed. Robinson; the comment *ad loc.* is rather nearer the mark, *cognovisse suos dicitur, hoc est in dilectione habuisse sibique sociasse*, but there too is added *sciens quales essent*). Cyril of Alexandria (and after him Meyer) supplies from what follows προεγνώσθησαν ὡς ἔσονται σύμμορφοι τῆς εἰκόνος τοῦ Υἱοῦ αὐτοῦ, but this belongs properly only to προώρισε. Widest from the mark are those who, like Calvin, look beyond the immediate choice to final salvation: *Dei autem praecognitio, cuius hic Paulus meminit, non nuda est praescientia . . . sed adoptio qua filios suos a reprobis semper discrevit.* On the other hand, Gif. keeps closely to the context in explaining, '"Foreknew" as the individual objects of His purpose (πρόθεσις) and therefore foreknew as "them that love God."' The only defect in this seems to be that it does not sufficiently take account of the O. T. and N. T. use of γιγνώσκω.

καὶ προώρισε. The Apostle overleaps for the moment intermediate steps and carries the believer onward to the final consummation of God's purpose in respect to him. This is exactly
defined as ' conformity to the image of His Son.'

συμμόρφους denotes inward and thorough and not merely superficial likeness.

τῆς εἰκόνος. As the Son is the image of the Father (2 Cor. iv.
4; Col. i. 15), so the Christian is to reflect the image of His
Lord, passing through a gradual assimilation of mind and character
to an ultimate assimilation of His δόξα, the absorption of the
splendour of His presence.

εἰς τὸ εἶναι αὐτὸν πρωτότοκον ἐν πολλοῖς ἀδελφοῖς. As the final
cause of all things is the glory of God, so the final cause of the
Incarnation and of the effect of the Incarnation upon man is that
the Son may be surrounded by a multitude of the redeemed.
These He vouchsafes to call His ' brethren.' They are a ' family,'
the entrance into which is through the Resurrection. As Christ
was the first to rise, He is the ' Eldest-born ' (πρωτοτοκος ἐκ τῶν
νεκρῶν, ἵνα γένηται ἐν πᾶσιν αὐτὸς πρωτεύων Col. i. 18). This is
different from the ' first-born of all creation ' (Col. i. 15). πρωτότοκος is a metaphorical expression ; the sense of which is determined
by the context ; in Col. i. 15 it is relative to creation, here it is
relative to the state to which entrance is through the Resurrection
(see Lightfoot's note on the passage in Col.).

30. οὓς δὲ προώρισε κ.τ.λ. Having taken his readers to the end
of the scale, the δόξα in which the career of the Christian cul-
minates, the Apostle now goes back and resolves the latter part of
the process into its subdivisions, of which the landmarks are
ἐκάλεσεν, ἐδικαίωσεν, ἐδόξασε. These are not quite exhaustive :
ἡγίασεν might have been inserted after ἐδικαίωσεν ; but it is sufficiently implied as a consequence of ἐδικαίωσεν and a necessary
condition of ἐδόξασε : in pursuance of the Divine purpose that
Christians should be conformed to Christ, the first step is the call ;
this brings with it, when it is obeyed, the wiping out of past sins,
or justification ; and from that there is a straight course to the
crowning with Divine glory. ἐκάλεσεν and ἐδικαίωσεν are both
naturally in the aorist tense as pointing to something finished
and therefore past : ἐδόξασεν is not strictly either finished or past,
but it is attracted into the same tense as the preceding verbs ; an
attraction which is further justified by the fact that, though not
complete in its historical working out, the step implied in ἐδόξασεν
is both complete and certain in the Divine counsels. To God
there is neither ' before nor after.'

THE PROOFS AND ASSURANCE OF DIVINE LOVE.

VIII. 31-39. *With the proofs of God's love before him, the Christian has nothing to fear. God, the Judge, is on his side, and the ascended Christ intercedes for him* (vv. 31-34).

The love of God in Christ is so strong that earthly sufferings and persecutions—nay, all forms and phases of being—are powerless to intercept it, or to bar the Christian's triumph (vv. 35-39).

[31] What conclusion are we to draw from this? Surely the strongest possible comfort and encouragement. With God on our side what enemy can we fear? [32] As Abraham spared not Isaac, so He spared not the Son who shared His Godhead, but suffered Him to die for all believers. Is not this a sure proof that along with that one transcendent gift His bounty will provide all that is necessary for our salvation? [33] Where shall accusers be found against those whom God has chosen? When God pronounces righteous, [34] who shall condemn? For us Christ has died; I should say rather rose again; and not only rose but sits enthroned at His Father's side, and there pleads continually for us. [35] His love is our security. And that love is so strong that nothing on earth can come between us and it. The sea of troubles that a Christian has to face, hardship and persecution of every kind, are powerless against it; [36] though the words of the Psalmist might well be applied to us, in which, speaking of the faithful few in his own generation, he described them as 'for God's sake butchered all day long, treated like sheep in the shambles.' [37] We too are no better than they. And yet, crushed and routed as we may seem, the love of Christ crowns us with surpassing victory. [38] For I am convinced that no form or phase of being, whether abstract or personal; not life or its negation; not any hierarchy of spirits; no dimension of time; no supernatural powers; [39] no dimension of space; no world of being invisible to us now,—will ever come between us and the love which God has brought so near to us in Jesus Messiah our Lord.

32. ὅς γε τοῦ ἰδίου υἱοῦ οὐκ ἐφείσατο. A number of emphatic expressions are crowded together in this sentence : ὅς γε, 'the same God who'; τοῦ ἰδίου υἱοῦ, 'His own Son,' partaker of His own nature; οὐκ ἐφείσατο, the word which is used of the offering of Isaac in Gen. xxii. 16, and so directly recalls that offering—the greatest sacrifice on record. For the argument comp. v. 6–10.

33–35. The best punctuation of these verses is that which is adopted in RV. *text* (so also Orig. Chrys. Theodrt. Mey. Ell. Gif. Va. Lid.). There should not be more than a colon between the clauses Θεὸς ὁ δικαιῶν· τίς ὁ κατακρινῶν; God is conceived of as Judge : where He acquits, who can condemn ? Ver. 34 is then immediately taken up by ver. 35 : Christ proved His love by dying for us ; who then shall part us from that love ? The Apostle clearly has in his mind Is. l. 8, 9 'He is near that justifieth men ; who will contend with me ? . . . Behold, the Lord God will help me ; who is he that shall condemn me ? ' This distinctly favours the view that each affirmation is followed by a question relating to that affirmation. The phrases ὁ κατακρινῶν and ὁ δικαιῶν form a natural antithesis, which it is wrong to break up by putting a full stop between them and taking one with what precedes, the other with what follows.

On the view taken above, Θεὸς ὁ δικαιῶν and Χριστὸς Ἰησοῦς ὁ ἀποθανών are both answers to τίς ἐγκαλέσει; and τίς ὁ κατακρινῶν; τίς ἡμᾶς χωρίσει; are subordinate questions, suggested in the one case by δικαιῶν, in the other by ἐντ. ὑπὲρ ἡμῶν. We observe also that on this view ver. 35 is closely linked to ver. 34. The rapid succession of thought which is thus obtained, each step leading on to the next, is in full accordance with the spirit of the passage.

Another way of taking it is to put a full stop at δικαιῶν, and to make τίς ἐγκαλέσει; τίς ὁ κατακρινῶν; two distinct questions with wholly distinct answers. So Fri. Lips. Weiss Oltr. Go. Others again (RV. *marg.* Beng. De W. Mou.) make all the clauses questions (Θεὸς ὁ δικαιῶν; ἐντυγχ. ὑπὲρ ἡμῶν;) But these repeated challenges do not give such a nervous concatenation of reasoning.

33. τίς ἐγκαλέσει; another of the forensic terms which are so common in this Epistle ; 'Who shall impeach such as are elect of God ? '

ἐκλεκτῶν. We have already seen (note on i. 1) that with St. Paul κλητοί and ἐκλεκτοί are not opposed to each other (as they are in Matt. xxii. 14) but are rather to be identified. By reading into κλητοί the implication that the call is accepted, St. Paul shows that the persons of whom this is true are also objects of God's choice. By both terms St. Paul designates not those who are destined for final salvation, but those who are 'summoned' or 'selected' for the privilege of serving God and carrying out His will. If their career runs its normal course it must issue in salvation, the 'glory' reserved for them; this lies as it were at the end of the avenue; but ἐκλεκτῶν only shows that they are in the right way to reach it. At least no external power can bar them from it; if they lose it, they will do so by their own fault.

κατακρίνων: κατακρινῶν RV. *text* Mou. This is quite possible, but δικαιῶν suggests the present.

34. Χριστὸς Ἰησοῦς ℵ A C F G L, Vulg. Boh. Arm. Aeth., Orig.-lat. Did. Aug.: Χριστός (om. Ἰησοῦς) B D E K &c., Syrr., Cyr.-Jerus. Chrys. *al.* Another instance of B in alliance with authorities otherwise Western and Syrian. WH. bracket Ἰησ.

ἐγερθεὶς ἐκ νεκρῶν ℵ* A C *al. plur.*, RV. WH[1]: *om. ἐκ νεκρῶν* ℵ° B D E F G K L &c., Ti. WH[2]. The group which inserts ἐκ νεκρῶν is practically the same as that which inserts Ἰησοῦς above.

ὃς καί. Stroke follows stroke, each driving home the last. ' It is Christ who died—nay rather (*immo vero*) rose from the dead—who (καί should be omitted here) is at the right hand of God—who also intercedes for us.' It is not a dead Christ on whom we depend, but a living. It is not only a living Christ, but a Christ enthroned, a Christ in power. It is not only a Christ in power, but a Christ of ever-active sympathy, constantly (if we may so speak) at the Father's ear, and constantly pouring in intercessions for His struggling people on earth. A great text for the value and significance of the Ascension (cf. Swete, *Apost. Creed*, p. 67 f.).

35. ἀπὸ τῆς ἀγάπης τοῦ Χριστοῦ. There is an alternative reading τοῦ Θεοῦ for which the authorities are ℵ B, Orig. (1/3 doubtfully in the Greek, but 6/7 in Rufinus' Latin translation); Eus. 4/6; Bas. 2/6; Hil. 1/2 and some others. RV. WH. note this reading in marg. But of the authorities B Orig.-lat. 2/7 read in full ἀπὸ τῆς ἀγάπης τοῦ Θεοῦ τῆς ἐν Χριστῷ Ἰησοῦ, which is obviously taken from ver. 39. Even in its simpler form the reading is open to suspicion of being conformed to that verse: to which however it may be replied that Χριστοῦ may also be a correction from the same source. On the whole Χριστοῦ seems more probable, and falls in better with the view maintained above of the close connexion of vv. 34, 35.

'The love of Christ' is unquestionably 'the love of Christ for us,' not our love for Christ: cf. v. 5.

θλῖψις κ.τ.λ. We have here a splendid example of καύχησις ἐν ταῖς θλίψεσιν of which St. Paul wrote in ch. v. 3 ff. The passage shows how he soared away in spirit above those 'sufferings of this present time' which men might inflict, but after that had nothing more that they could do. On θλῖψις ἢ στενοχωρία see ii. 9; for διωγμός cf. 2 Cor. xi. 23 ff., 32 f.; xii. 10, &c.; for λιμὸς ἢ γυμνότης, 1 Cor. iv. 11; 2 Cor. xi. 27; for κίνδυνος 2 Cor. xi. 26; 1 Cor xv. 30.

36. ὅτι ἕνεκά σου. The quotation is exact from LXX of Ps. xliv [xliii]. 23: ὅτι belongs to it.

ἕνεκεν is decisively attested here: in the Psalm B has ἕνεκα, ℵ A T ἕνεκεν, where there is a presumption against the reading of B.

θανατούμεθα ὅλην τὴν ἡμέραν: cf. 1 Cor. xv. 31 καθ' ἡμέραν ἀποθνήσκω : 'tota die, hoc est, omni vitae meae tempore' Orig. πρόβατα σφαγῆς : sheep destined for slaughter; cf. Zech. xi. 4 τὰ πρόβατα τῆς σφαγῆς (cf. Jer. xii. 3 πρόβατα εἰς σφαγήν Cod. Marchal. marg.).

The Latin texts of this verse are marked and characteristic. Tertullian, *Scorp.* 13 *Tua causa mortificamur tota die, deputati sumus ut pecora iugulationis.* Cyprian, *Test.* iii. 18 (the true text; cf. *Epist.* xxxi. 4) *Causa tui occidimur tota die, deputati sumus ut oves victimae.* Hilary of Poitiers, *Tract. in Ps.* cxviii. (ed. Zingerle, p. 429) *Propter te mortificamur tota die, deputati sumus sicut oves occisionis.* Irenaeus, *Adv. Haer.* II. xxii. 2 (*Latine* ; cf. IV. xvi. 2) *Propter te morte afficimur tota die, aestimati sumus ut oves occisionis.* (Similarly Cod. Clarom. *Speculum Augustini,* codd. ML) Vulgate (Cod. Amiat.) *Propter te mortificamur tota die, aestimati sumus ut oves occisionis.* Here two types of text stand out clearly: that of Cyprian at one end of the scale, and that of the Vulgate (with which we may group Iren.-lat. Cod. Clarom. and the *Speculum*) at the other. Hilary stands between, having *deputati* in common with Cyprian, but on the whole leaning rather to the later group. The most difficult problem is presented by Tertullian, who approaches Cyprian in *Tua causa* and *deputati*, and the Vulgate group in *mortificamur* : in *pecora iugulationis* he stands alone. This passage might seem to favour the view that in Tertullian we had the primitive text from which all the rest were derived. That hypothesis however would be difficult to maintain systematically; and in any case there must be a large element in Tertullian's text which is simply individual. The text before us may be said to give a glimpse of the average position of a problem which is still some way from solution.

37. ὑπερνικῶμεν. Tertullian and Cyprian represent this by the coinage *supervincimus* (Vulg. Cod. Clarom. Hil. *superamus*) ; 'overcome strongly' Tyn.; 'are more than conquerors' Genev., happily adopted in AV.

διὰ τοῦ ἀγαπήσαντος ἡμᾶς points back to τῆς ἀγάπης τοῦ Χριστοῦ in ver. 35.

38. οὔτε ἄγγελοι οὔτε ἀρχαί. 'And He will call on all the host of the heavens and all the holy ones above, and the host of God, the Cherubim, Seraphim, and Ophanim, and all the angels of power, and all the angels of principalities, and the Elect One, and the other powers on the earth, over the water, on that day' Enoch lxi. 10. St. Paul from time to time makes use of similar Jewish designations for the hierarchy of angels: so in 1 Cor. xv. 24; Eph. i. 21 ἀρχή, ἐξουσία, δύναμις, κυριότης, πᾶν ὄνομα ὀνομαζόμενον : iii. 10; vi. 12; Col. i. 16 (θρόνοι, κυριότητες, ἀρχαί, ἐξουσίαι) ; ii. 10, 15. The whole world of spirits is summed up in Phil. ii. 10 as ἐπουράνιοι, ἐπιγεῖοι, καταχθόνιοι. It is somewhat noticeable that whereas the terms used are generally abstract, in several places they are made still more abstract by the use of the sing. instead of plur., ὅταν καταργήσῃ πᾶσαν ἀρχὴν καὶ πᾶσαν ἐξουσίαν καὶ δύναμιν 1 Cor. xv. 24 ; ὑπεράνω πάσης ἀρχῆς καὶ ἐξουσίας κ.τ.λ. Eph. i. 21 ; ἡ κεφαλὴ πάσης ἀρχῆς καὶ ἐξουσίας Col. ii. 10.

It is also true (as pointed out by Weiss, *Bibl. Theol.* § 104;
Anm. 1. 2) that the leading passages in which St. Paul speaks of
angels are those in which his language aims at embracing the
whole κόσμος. He is very far from a θρησκεία τῶν ἀγγέλων such as he
protests against in the Church at Colossae (Col. ii. 18). At the
same time the parallels which have been given (see also below
under δυνάμεις) are enough to show that the Apostle must not be
separated from the common beliefs of his countrymen. He held
that there was a world of spirits brought into being like the rest of
creation by Christ (Col. i. 16). These spirits are ranged in
a certain hierarchy to which the current names are given. They
seem to be neither wholly good nor wholly bad, for to them too
the Atonement of the Cross extends (Col. i. 20 ἀποκαταλλάξαι τὰ
πάντα εἰς αὐτόν . . . εἴτε τὰ ἐπὶ τῆς γῆς εἴτε τὰ ἐν τοῖς οὐρανοῖς). There
is a sense in which the Death on the Cross is a triumph over them
(Col. ii. 15). They too must acknowledge the universal sovereignty
of Christ (1 Cor. xv. 24; cf. Eph. i. 10); and they form part of
that kingdom which He hands over to the Father, that ' God may
be all in all' (1 Cor. xv. 28). On the whole subject see Everling,
Die paulinische Angelologie u. Dämonologie, Göttingen, 1888.

For ἄγγελοι the Western text (D E F G, Ambrstr. Aug. Amb.) has
ἄγγελος. There is also a tendency in the Western and later authorities to
insert οὔτε ἐξουσίαι before or after ἀρχαί, obviously from the parallel passages
in which the words occur together.

οὔτε δυνάμεις. There is overwhelming authority (אּ A B C D &c.)
for placing these words after οὔτε μέλλοντα. We naturally expect
them to be associated with ἀρχαί, as in 1 Cor. xv. 24; Eph. i. 21.
It is possible that in one of the earliest copies the word may have
been accidentally omitted, and then added in the margin and re-
inserted at the wrong place. We seem to have a like primitive
corruption in ch. iv. 12 (τοῖς στοιχοῦσιν). But it is perhaps more
probable that in the rush of impassioned thought St. Paul inserts
the words as they come, and that thus οὔτε δυνάμεις may be slightly
belated. It has been suggested that St. Paul takes alternately
animate existences and inanimate. When not critically controlled,
the order of association is a very subtle thing.

For the word compare 'the angels of power' and 'the other powers on
the earth' in the passage from the Book of Enoch quoted above; also *Test.
XII Patr.* Levi 3 ἐν τῷ τρίτῳ (sc. οὐρανῷ) εἰσὶν αἱ δυνάμεις τῶν παρεμβολῶν,
οἱ ταχθέντες εἰς ἡμέραν κρίσεως, ποιῆσαι ἐκδίκησιν ἐν τοῖς πνεύμασι τῆς πλάνης
καὶ τοῦ Βελίαρ.

39. οὔτε ὕψωμα οὔτε βάθος. Lips. would give to the whole
context a somewhat more limited application than is usually
assigned to it. He makes οὔτε ἐνεστ. . . βάθος all refer to angelic
powers: 'neither now nor at the end of life (when such spirits
were thought to be most active) shall the spirits either of the

height or from the depth bar our entrance into the next world,
where the love of Christ will be still nearer to us.' This is also
the view of Origen (see below). But it is quite in the manner of
St. Paul to personify abstractions, and the sense attached to them
cannot well be too large: cf. esp. Eph. iii. 18 τί τὸ πλάτος καὶ μῆκος
καὶ ὕψος καὶ βάθος, and 2 Cor. x. 5 πᾶν ὕψωμα ἐπαιρόμενον κατὰ τῆς
γνώσεως τοῦ Θεοῦ.

The common patristic explanation of ὕψωμα is 'things above the heavens,'
and of βάθος, 'things beneath the earth.' Theod. Monach. ὕψωμα μὲν τὰ
ἄγαν ἐπίδοξα, βάθος δὲ τὰ ἄγαν ἄδοξα. Theodoret βάθος δὲ τὴν γέενναν,
ὕψωμα τὴν βασιλείαν. Origen (in Cramer's Catena) explains ὕψωμα of the
'spiritual hosts of wickedness in the heavenly places' (Eph. vi. 12), and
βάθος of τὰ καταχθόνια. The expanded version of Rufinus approaches still
more nearly to the theory of Lipsius: Similiter et altitudo et profundum
impugnant nos, sicut et David dicit multi qui debellant me de alto: sine
dubio cum a spiritibus nequitiae de caelestibus urgeretur: et sicut iterum
dicit: de profundis clamavi ad te, Domine: cum ab his qui in inferno
deputati sunt et gehennae spiritibus impugnaretur.

οὔτε τις κτίσις ἑτέρα. The use of ἑτέρα and not ἄλλη seems to
favour the view that this means not exactly 'any other created
thing' but 'any other kind of creation,' 'any other mode of being,'
besides those just enumerated and differing from the familiar world
as we see it.

Origen (in Cramer) would like to take the passage in this way. He asks
if there may not be another creation besides this visible one, 'in its nature
visible though not as yet seen'—a description which might seem to anticipate
the discoveries of the microscope and telescope. Comp. Balfour, *Foundations
of Belief*, p. 71 f. 'It is impossible therefore to resist the conviction that
there must be an indefinite number of aspects of Nature respecting which
science never can give us any information, even in our dreams. We must
conceive ourselves as feeling our way about this dim corner of the illimit-
able world, like children in a darkened room, encompassed by we know
not what; a little better endowed with the machinery of sensation than the
protozoon, yet poorly provided indeed as compared with a being, if such
a one could be conceived, whose senses were adequate to the infinite variety
of material Nature.'

ἀπὸ τῆς ἀγάπης τοῦ Θεοῦ τῆς ἐν Χριστῷ Ἰησοῦ. This is the full
Christian idea. The love of Christ is no doubt capable of being
isolated and described separately (2 Cor. v. 14; Eph. iii. 19), but
the love of Christ is really a manifestation of the love of God.
A striking instance of the way in which the whole Godhead
co-operates in this manifestation is ch. v. 5-8: the love of *God*
is poured out in our hearts through *the Holy Spirit*, because *Christ*
died for us; and *God* commends His love because *Christ* died.
The same essential significance runs through this section (note
esp. vv. 31-35, 39).

THE APOSTLE'S SORROW OVER ISRAEL'S UNBELIEF.

IX. 1–5. *The thought of this magnificent prospect fills me with sorrow for those who seem to be excluded from it— my own countrymen for whom I would willingly sacrifice my dearest hopes—excluded too in spite of all their special privileges and their high destiny.*

[1] How glorious the prospect of the life in Christ! How mournful the thought of those who are cut off from it! There is no shadow of falsehood in the statement I am about to make. As one who has his life in Christ I affirm a solemn truth; and my conscience, speaking under the direct influence of God's Holy Spirit, bears witness to my sincerity. [2] There is one grief that I cannot shake off, one distressing weight that lies for ever at my heart. [3] Like Moses when he came down from the mount, the prayer has been in my mind: Could I by the personal sacrifice of my own salvation for them, even by being cut off from all communion with Christ, in any way save my own countrymen? Are they not my own brethren, my kinsmen as far as earthly relationship is concerned? [4] Are they not God's own privileged people? They bear the sacred name of Israel with all that it implies; it is they whom He declared to be His 'son,' His 'firstborn' (Exod. iv. 22); their temple has been illuminated by the glory of the Divine presence; they are bound to Him by a series of covenants repeatedly renewed; to them He gave a system of law on Mount Sinai; year after year they have offered up the solemn worship of the temple; they have been the depositories of the Divine promises; [5] their ancestors are the patriarchs, who were accounted righteous before God; from them in these last days has come the Messiah as regards his natural descent—that Messiah who although sprung from a human parent is supreme over all things, none other than God, the eternal object of human praise!

IX–XI. St. Paul has now finished his main argument. He has expounded his conception of the Gospel. But there still remains a difficulty which could not help suggesting itself to every thoughtful reader, and which was continually being raised by one class of Christians at the time when he wrote. How is this new scheme of righteousness and salvation apart from law

consistent with the privileged position of the Jews? They had
been the chosen race (we find St. Paul enumerating their privileges),
through them the Messiah had come, and yet it appeared they
would be rejected if they would not accept this new righteousness
by faith. How is this consistent with the justice of God?

The question has been continually in the Apostle's mind. It
has led him to emphasize more than once the fact that the new
εὐαγγέλιον if for both Jew and Greek, is yet for the Jew first (i. 16;
ii. 9). It has led him to lay great stress on the fact that the Jews
especially had sinned (ii. 17). Once indeed he has begun to
discuss it directly (iii. 1); 'What advantage then is there in being
a Jew?' but he postponed it for a time, feeling that it was necessary
first to complete his main argument. He has dwelt on the fact
that the new way of salvation can be proved from the Old Testament (chap. iv). Now he is at liberty to discuss in full the question:
How is this conception of Christ's work consistent with the fact of
the rejection of the Jews which it seems to imply?

The answer to this question occupies the remainder of the
dogmatic portion of the Epistle, chaps. ix–xi, generally considered
to be the third of its principal divisions. The whole section may
be subdivided as follows: in ix. 6–29 the faithfulness and justice of
God are vindicated; in ix. 30–x. 21 the guilt of Israel is proved;
in chap. xi St. Paul shows the divine purpose which is being fulfilled
and looks forward prophetically to a future time when Israel will
be restored, concluding the section with a description of the Wisdom
of God as far exceeding all human speculation.

Marcion seems to have omitted the whole of this chapter with the possible
exception of vv. 1-3. Tert. who passes from viii. 11 to x. 2 says *salio et
hic amplissimum abruptum intercisae scripturae* (*Adv. Marc.* v. 14). See
Zahn, *Gesch. des N. T. Kanons* p. 518.

1. We notice that there is no grammatical connexion with the
preceding chapter. A new point is introduced and the sequence
of thought is gradually made apparent as the argument proceeds.
Perhaps there has been a pause in writing the Epistle, the amanuensis has for a time suspended his labours. We notice also that
St. Paul does not here follow his general habit of stating the
subject he is going to discuss (as he does for example at the
beginning of chap. iii), but allows it gradually to become evident.
He naturally shrinks from mentioning too definitely a fact which is
to him so full of sadness. It will be only too apparent to what he
refers; and tact and delicacy both forbid him to define it more
exactly.

ἀλήθειαν λέγω ἐν Χριστῷ: 'I speak the truth in Christ, as one
united with Christ'; cf. 2 Cor. ii. 17 ἀλλ' ὡς ἐξ εἰλικρινείας, ἀλλ' ὡς
ἐκ Θεοῦ, κατέναντι Θεοῦ ἐν Χριστῷ λαλοῦμεν: xii. 19. St. Paul has just

described that union with Christ which will make any form of sin impossible; cf. viii. 1, 10; and the reference to this union gives solemnity to an assertion for which it will be difficult to obtain full credence.

οὐ ψεύδομαι. A Pauline expression. 1 Tim. ii. 7 ἀλήθειαν λέγω, οὐ ψεύδομαι: 2 Cor. xi. 31; Gal. i. 20.

συμμαρτυρούσης: cf. ii. 15; viii. 16. The conscience is personified so as to give the idea of a second and a separate witness. Cf. Oecumenius *ad loc.* μέγα θέλει εἰπεῖν, διὸ προοδοποιεῖ τῷ πιστευθῆναι, τρεῖς ἐπιφερόμενος μάρτυρας, τὸν Χριστόν, τὸ Ἅγιον Πνεῦμα, καὶ τὴν ἑαυτοῦ συνείδησιν.

ἐν Πνεύματι Ἁγίῳ with συμμαρτυρούσης. St. Paul adds further solemnity to his assertion by referring to that union of his spirit with the Divine Spirit of which he had spoken in the previous chapter. Cf. viii. 16 αὐτὸ τὸ Πνεῦμα συμμαρτυρεῖ τῷ πνεύματι ἡμῶν.

St. Paul begins with a strong assertion of the truth of his statement as a man does who is about to say something of the truth of which he is firmly convinced himself, although facts and the public opinion of his countrymen might seem to be against him. Cf. Chrys. *ad loc.* πρότερον δὲ διαβεβαιοῦται περὶ ὧν μέλλει λέγειν· ὅπερ πολλοῖς ἔθος ποιεῖν ὅταν μέλλωσί τι λέγειν παρὰ τοῖς πολλοῖς ἀπιστούμενον καὶ ὑπὲρ οὗ σφόδρα ἑαυτούς εἰσι πεπεικότες.

2. ὅτι: 'that,' introducing the subordinate sentence dependent on the idea of assertion in the previous sentence. St. Paul does not mention directly the cause of his grief, but leaves it to be inferred from the next verse.

λύπη (which is opposed to χαρά Jn. xvi. 20) appears to mean grief as a state of mind; it is rational or emotional: ὀδύνη on the other hand never quite loses its physical associations; it implies the anguish or smart of the heart (hence it is closely connected with τῇ καρδίᾳ) which is the result of λύπη.

With the grief of St. Paul for his countrymen, we may compare the grief of a Jew writing after the fall of Jerusalem, who feels both the misfortune and the sin of his people, and who like St. Paul emphasizes his sorrow by enumerating their close relationship to God and their ancestral pride: 4 Ezra viii. 15-18 *et nunc dicens dicam, de omni homine tu magis scis, de populo autem tuo, ob quem doleo, et de haereditate tua, propter quam lugeo, et propter Israël, propter quem tristis sum, et de semine Iacob, propter quod conturbor. Ibid.* x. 6-8 *non vides luctum nostrum et quae nobis contigerunt? quoniam Sion mater nostra omnium in tristitia contristatur, et humilitate humiliata est, et luget validissime . . .* 21-22 *vides enim quoniam sanctificatio nostra deserta effecta est, et altare nostrum demolitum est, et templum nostrum destructum est, et psalterium nostrum humiliatum est, et hymnus noster conticuit, et exsultatio nostra dissoluta est, et lumen candelabri nostri extinctum est, et arca testamenti nostri direpta est. Apoc. Baruch.* xxxv. 3 *quomodo enim ingemiscam super Sione, et quomodo lugebo super Ierusalem? quia in loco isto ubi prostratus sum nunc, olim summus sacerdos offerebat oblationes sanctas.*

3. This verse which is introduced by γάρ does not give the reason of his grief but the proof of his sincerity.

ηὐχόμην: 'the wish was in my mind' or perhaps 'the prayer was in my heart.' St. Paul merely states the fact of the wish without regard to the conditions which made it impossible. Cf. Lft. on Gal. iv. 20 'The thing is spoken of in itself, prior to and independently of any conditions which might affect its possibility.' See also Acts xxv. 22, and Burton, *M. and T.* § 33.

ἀνάθεμα: 'accursed,' 'devoted to destruction.' The word was originally used with the same meaning as ἀνάθημα (of which it was a dialectic variation, see below), 'that which is offered or consecrated to God.' But the translators of the Old Testament required an expression to denote that which is devoted to God for destruction, and adopted ἀνάθεμα as a translation of the Hebrew חֵרֶם: see Levit. xxvii. 28, 29 πᾶν δὲ ἀνάθεμα ὃ ἐὰν ἀναθῇ ἄνθρωπος τῷ Κυρίῳ ... οὐκ ἀποδώσεται οὐδὲ λυτρώσεται ... καὶ πᾶν ὃ ἐὰν ἀνατεθῇ ἀπὸ τῶν ἀνθρώπων οὐ λυτρωθήσεται, ἀλλὰ θανάτῳ θανατωθήσεται: Deut. vii. 26; Josh. vi. 17 καὶ ἔσται ἡ πόλις ἀνάθεμα, αὐτὴ καὶ πάντα ὅσα ἐστὶν ἐν αὐτῇ, Κυρίῳ σαβαώθ. And with this meaning it is always used in the New Testament: Gal. i. 8, 9; 1 Cor. xvi. 22. The attempt to explain the word to mean 'excommunication' from the society—a later use of the Hebrew in Rabbinical writers and the Greek in ecclesiastical—arose from a desire to take away the apparent profanity of the wish.

There is some doubt and has been a good deal of discussion as to the distinction in meaning between ἀνάθεμα and ἀνάθημα. It was originally dialectic, ἀνάθημα being the Attic form (ἀνάθημα ἀττικῶς, ἀνάθεμα ἑλληνικῶς Moeris, p. 28) and ἀνάθεμα being found as a substitute in non-Attic works (*Anth. P.* 6. 162, *C. I. G.* 2693 d and other instances are quoted by the Dictionaries). The Hellenistic form was the one naturally used by the writers of the LXX, and it gradually became confined to the new meaning attached to the word, but the distinction seems never to have become certain and MSS. and later writers often confuse the two words. In the LXX (although Hatch and Redpath make no distinction) our present texts seem to preserve the difference of the two words. The only doubtful passage is 2 Macc. ii. 13; here A reads ἀνάθεμα where we should expect ἀνάθημα, but V (the only other MS. quoted by Swete) and the authorities in Holmes and Parsons have ἀνάθημα. In the N.T. ἀνάθημα occurs once, Luke xxi. 5, and then correctly (but the MSS. vary, ἀνάθημα B L, ἀνάθεμα ℵ A D). The Fathers often miss the distinction and explain the two words as identical: so Ps.-Just. *Quaest. et Resp.* 121; Theod. on Rom. ix. 3, and Suidas; they are distinguished in Chrys. on Rom. ix. 3 as quoted by Suidas, but not in Field's ed. No certain instance is quoted of ἀνάθημα for ἀνάθεμα, but ἀνάθεμα could be and was used dialectically for ἀνάθημα. On the word generally see esp. Trench *Syn.* i. § 5; Lft. Gal. i. 8; Fri. on Rom. ix. 3.

αὐτὸς ἐγώ. The emphasis and position of these words emphasizes the willingness for personal sacrifice; and they have still more force when we remember that St. Paul has just declared that nothing in heaven or earth can separate him from the love of Christ. Chrys. *ad loc.* τί λέγεις, ὦ Παῦλε; ἀπὸ τοῦ Χριστοῦ τοῦ ποθουμένου, οὗ μήτε βασιλεία σε, μήτε γέεννα ἐχώριζε, μήτε τὰ νοούμενα, μήτε ἄλλα τοσαῦτα, ἀπὸ τούτου νῦν εὔχη ἀνάθεμα εἶναι;

ἀπὸ τοῦ Χριστοῦ : 'separated from the Christ,' a pregnant use of the preposition. The translation of the words as if they were ὑπὸ τ. Χ. arises from a desire to soften the expression.

κατὰ σάρκα : cf. iv. 1 'as far as earthly relations are concerned'; spiritually St. Paul was a member of the spiritual Israel, and his kinsmen were the ἀδελφοί of the Christian society.

The prayer of St. Paul is similar to that of Moses : Exod. xxxii. 32 'Yet now, if thou wilt forgive their sin— ; and if not, blot me, I pray thee, out of thy book which thou hast written.' On this Clem. Rom. liii. 5 comments as follows : ὦ μεγάλης ἀγάπης, ὦ τελειότητος ἀνυπερβλήτου, παρρησιάζεται θεράπων πρὸς Κύριον, αἰτεῖται ἄφεσιν τῷ πλήθει ἢ καὶ ἑαυτὸν ἐξαλειφθῆναι μετ' αὐτῶν ἀξιοῖ. In answer to those who have found difficulties in the passage it is enough to say with Prof. Jowett that they arise from 'the error of explaining the language of feeling as though it were that of reasoning and reflection.'

There are one or two slight variations of reading in ver. 3, αὐτὸς ἐγώ was placed before ἀνάθ. εἶν. by C K L, Vulg., and later authorities with T R, and ὑπό (D E G) substituted for ἀπό (א A B C &c.). Both variations arise from a desire to modify the passage.

4. οἵτινές εἰσιν : 'inasmuch as they are.' St. Paul's grief for Israel arises not only from his personal relationship and affection, but also from his remembrance of their privileged position in the Divine economy.

Ἰσραηλῖται : used of the chosen people in special reference to the fact that, as descendants of him who received from God the name of Israel, they are partakers of those promises of which it was a sign. The name therefore implies the privileges of the race; cf. Eph. ii. 12 ἀπηλλοτριωμένοι τῆς πολιτείας τοῦ Ἰσραὴλ καὶ ξένοι τῶν διαθηκῶν τῆς ἐπαγγελίας : and as such it could be used metaphorically of the Christians (ὁ Ἰσραὴλ τοῦ Θεοῦ Gal. vi. 16 ; cf. ver. 6 inf.) ; a use which would of course be impossible for the merely national designation Ἰουδαῖοι.

'Israel' is the title used in contemporary literature to express the special relations of the chosen people to God. Ps. Sol. xiv. 3 ὅτι ἡ μερὶς καὶ ἡ κληρονομία τοῦ Θεοῦ ἐστιν ὁ Ἰσραήλ : Ecclus. xvii. 15 μερὶς Κυρίου Ἰσραήλ ἐστίν : Jubilees xxxiii. 18 'For Israel is a nation holy unto God, and a nation of inheritance for its God, and a nation of priesthood and royalty and a possession.' Thus the word seems to have been especially connected with the Messianic hope. The Messianic times are 'the day of gladness of Israel' (Ps. Sol. x. 7), the blessing of Israel, the day of God's mercy towards Israel (ib. xvii. 50, 51 μακάριοι οἱ γινόμενοι ἐν ταῖς ἡμέραις ἐκείναις ἰδεῖν τὰ

ἀγαθὰ Ἰσραὴλ ἐν συναγωγῇ φυλῶν, ἃ ποιήσει ὁ Θεός. ταχύναι ὁ Θεὸς ἐπὶ
Ἰσραὴλ τὸ ἔλεος αὐτοῦ). When therefore St. Paul uses this name he
reminds his readers that it is just those for whose salvation above
all, according to every current idea, the Messiah was to come, who
when he has come are apparently cut off from all share in the
privileges of his kingdom.

υἱοθεσία : 'the adoption,' 'status of an adopted son' : on the
origin of the word and its use in relation to Christian privileges see
above, Rom. viii. 15. Here it implies that relationship of Israel to
God described in Exod. iv. 22 τάδε λέγει Κύριος Υἱὸς πρωτότοκός μου
Ἰσραήλ : Deut. xiv. 1; xxxii. 6; Jer. xxxi. 9; Hos. xi. 1. So Jubilees
i. 21 'I will be a Father unto them, and they shall be My children,
and they shall all be called children of the living God. And every
angel and every spirit will know, yea they will know that these are
My children, and that I am their Father in uprightness and
in righteousness and that I love them.'

ἡ δόξα : 'the visible presence of God among His people' (see
on iii. 23). δόξα is in the LXX the translation of the Hebrew
כְּבוֹד יְהוָה, called by the Rabbis the Shekinah (שְׁכִינָה), the
bright cloud by which God made His presence known on earth;
cf. Exod. xvi. 10, &c. Hence τὸ κάλλος τῆς δόξης αὐτοῦ Ps. Sol. ii. 5,
ἀπὸ θρόνου δόξης ib. ver. 20, Wisd. ix. 10, imply more than the mere
beauty of the temple, and when St. Stephen, Acts vii. 2, speaks of
ὁ Θεὸς τῆς δόξης his words would remind his hearers of the visible
presence of God which they claimed had sanctified Jerusalem and the
temple. On late Rabbinical speculations concerning the Shekinah
see Weber Altsyn. Theol. p. 179.

αἱ διαθῆκαι : 'the covenants,' see Hatch Essays on Biblical
Greek, p. 47. The plural is used not with reference to the two
covenants the Jewish and the Christian, but because the original
covenant of God with Israel was again and again renewed
(Gen. vi. 18; ix. 9; xv. 18; xvii. 2, 7, 9; Ex. ii. 24). Comp. Ecclus.
xliv. 11 μετὰ τοῦ σπέρματος αὐτῶν διαμενεῖ ἀγαθὴ κληρονομία, ἔκγονα αὐτῶν
ἐν ταῖς διαθήκαις ; Wisdom xviii. 22 λόγῳ τὸν κολάζοντα ὑπέταξεν, ὅρκους
πατέρων καὶ διαθήκας ὑπομνήσας. According to Irenaeus, III. xi. 11
(ed. Harvey) there were four covenants : καὶ διὰ τοῦτο τέσσαρες ἐδό-
θησαν καθολικαὶ διαθῆκαι τῇ ἀνθρωπότητι· μία μὲν τοῦ κατακλυσμοῦ τοῦ
Νῶε, ἐπὶ τοῦ τόξου· δευτέρα δὲ τοῦ Ἀβραάμ, ἐπὶ τοῦ σημείου τῆς περιτομῆς·
τρίτη δὲ ἡ νομοθεσία ἐπὶ τοῦ Μωϋσέως· τετάρτη δὲ ἡ τοῦ Εὐαγγελίου, διὰ
τοῦ Κυρίου ἡμῶν Ἰησοῦ Χριστοῦ *.

The Jews believed that they were bound to God and that God
was bound to them by a covenant which would guarantee to them
His protection in the future. According to St. Paul it was just
those who were not bound to Him by a covenant who would
receive the Divine protection. On the idea of the Covenant and

---

* In the Latin version the four covenants are Adam, Noah, Moses, Christ.

its practical bearing on Jewish life see Schürer *Geschichte*, ii. p. 388.

ἡ νομοθεσία: a classical word, occurring also in Philo. 'The giving of the law.' 'The dignity and glory of having a law communicated by express revelation, and amidst circumstances so full of awe and splendour.' Vaughan.

The current Jewish estimation of the Law (ὁ νόμος ὁ ὑπάρχων εἰς τὸν αἰῶνα Baruch iv. 1) it is unnecessary to illustrate, but the point in the mention of it here is brought out more clearly if we remember that all the Messianic hopes were looked upon as the reward of those who kept the Law. So *Ps. Sol.* xiv. 1 πιστὸς Κύριος τοῖς ἀγαπῶσιν αὐτὸν ἐν ἀληθείᾳ . . . τοῖς πορευομένοις ἐν δικαιοσύνῃ προσταγμάτων αὐτοῦ, ἐν νόμῳ ὡς ἐνετείλατο ἡμῖν εἰς ζωὴν ἡμῶν. It was one of the paradoxes of the situation that it was just those who neglected the Law who would, according to St. Paul's teaching, inherit the promises.

ἡ λατρεία: 'the temple service.' Heb. ix. 1, 6; 1 Macc. ii. 19, 22. As an illustration of Jewish opinion on the temple service may be quoted *Pirqe Aboth*, i. 2 (Taylor, p. 26) 'Shimeon ha-Çaddiq was of the remnants of the great synagogue. He used to say, On three things the world is stayed; on the Thorah, and on the Worship, and on the bestowal of kindnesses.' According to the Rabbis one of the characteristics of the Messianic age will be a revival of the temple services. (Weber *Altsyn. Theol.* p. 359.)

αἱ ἐπαγγελίαι: 'the promises made in the O. T. with special reference to the coming of the Messiah.' These promises were of course made to the Jews, and were always held to apply particularly to them. While sinners were to be destroyed before the face of the Lord, the saints of the Lord were to inherit the promises (cf. *Ps. Sol.* xii. 8); and in Jewish estimation sinners were the gentiles and saints the chosen people. Again therefore the choice of terms emphasizes the character of the problem to be discussed. See note on i. 2, and the note of Ryle and James on *Ps. Sol. loc. cit.*; cf. also Heb. vi. 12; xi. 13; Gal. iii. 19; 1 Clem. x. 2.

αἱ διαθῆκαι ℵ C L, Vulg. *codd.* Boh. &c. has been corrected into ἡ διαθήκη B D F G, Vulg. *codd. pauc.*; also ἐπαγγελίαι into ἐπαγγελία D E F G, Boh. Both variations are probably due to fancied difficulties.

5. οἱ πατέρες: 'the patriarchs.' Acts iii. 13, vii. 32. On the 'merits' of the patriarchs and their importance in Jewish theology see the note on p. 330.

ἐξ ὧν ὁ Χριστὸς τὸ κατὰ σάρκα. Cf. 1 Clem. xxxii. 2 ἐξ αὐτοῦ ὁ Κύριος Ἰησοῦς τὸ κατὰ σάρκα. ὁ Χρ. is not a personal name, but must be translated 'the Messiah.' Not only have the Jews been united to God by so many ties, but the purpose for which they have been selected has been fulfilled. The Messiah has come forth from them, and yet they have been rejected.

ὁ ὢν ἐπὶ πάντων Θεός, κ.τ.λ.: with Χριστός (see below), 'who is
over all, God blessed for ever.' πάντων is probably neuter, cf. xi. 36.
This description of the supreme dignity of Him who was on His
human side of Jewish stock serves to intensify the conception of
the privileged character of the Jewish race.

The Privileges of Israel.

By this enumeration of the privileges of Israel St. Paul fulfils two
purposes in his argument. He gives firstly the facts which
intensify his sorrow. Like the writer of 4 Ezra his grief is
heightened by the remembrance of the position which his countrymen have held in the Divine economy. Every word in the long
list calls to mind some link which had united them, the Chosen
People, with God; every word reminds us of the glory of their past
history; and it is because of the great contrast suggested between
the destiny of Israel and their actual condition that his grief is so
profound.

But the Apostle has another and more important thought to
emphasize. He has to show the reality and the magnitude of the
problem before him, and this list of the privileges of Israel just emphasizes it. It was so great as almost to be paradoxical. It was this.
Israel was a chosen people, and was chosen for a certain purpose.
According to the teaching of the Apostle it had attained this end:
the Messiah, whose coming represented in a sense the consummation of its history, had appeared, and yet from any share in the
glories of this epoch the Chosen People themselves were cut off.
All the families of the earth were to be blessed in Israel: Israel
itself was not to be blessed. They were in an especial sense the
sons of God: but they were cut off from the inheritance. They
were bound by special covenants to God: the covenant had been
broken, and those outside shared in the advantages. The glories of
the Messianic period might be looked upon as a recompense for
the long years of suffering which a faithful adhesion to the Law and
a loyal preservation of the temple service had entailed: the blessings were to come for those who had never kept the Law. The
promises were given to and for Israel: Israel alone would not
inherit them.

Such was the problem. The pious Jew, remembering the
sufferings of his nation, pictured the Messianic time as one when
these should all pass away; when all Israel—pure and without stain
—should be once more united; when the ten tribes should be
collected from among the nations; when Israel which had suffered
much from the Gentiles should be at last triumphant over them.
All this he expected. The Messiah had come: and Israel, the

Messiah's own people, seemed to be cut off and rejected from the blessings which it had itself prepared for the world.　How was this problem to be solved?　(Cf. 4 Ezra xiii; Schürer, *Geschichte*, ii. 452 sq.)

The Punctuation of Rom. ix. 5.

καὶ ἐξ ὧν ὁ Χριστὸς τὸ κατὰ σάρκα, ὁ ὢν ἐπὶ πάντων, Θεὸς εὐλογητὸς εἰς τοὺς αἰῶνας· ἀμήν.

The interpretation of Rom. ix. 5 has probably been discussed at greater length than that of any other verse of the N.T.　Besides long notes in various commentaries, the following special papers may be mentioned: Schultz, in *Jahrbücher für deutsche Theologie*, 1868, vol. xiii. pp. 462–506; Grimm, *Zwth.*, 1869, pp. 311–322; Harmsen, ib. 1872, pp. 510, 521 : but England and America have provided the fullest discussions—by Prof. Kennedy and Dr. Gifford, namely, *The Divinity of Christ, a sermon preached on Christmas Day*, 1882, *before the University of Cambridge, with an appendix on* Rom. ix. 5 *and* Titus ii. 13, by Benjamin Hall Kennedy, D.D., Cambridge, 1883; *Caesarem Appello, a letter to Dr. Kennedy*, by Edwin Hamilton Gifford, D.D., Cambridge, 1883; and *Pauline Christology, I. Examination of* Rom. ix. 5, *being a rejoinder to the Rev. Dr. Gifford's reply*, by Benjamin Hall Kennedy, D.D., Cambridge, 1883 : by Prof. Dwight and Dr. Ezra Abbot, in *J. B. Exeg.* June and December, 1881, pp. 22–55, 87–154; and 1883, pp. 90–112.　Of these the paper of Dr. Abbot is much the most exhaustive, while that of Dr. Gifford seems to us on the whole to show the most exegetical power.

Special literature.

Dismissing minor variations, there are four main interpretations (all of them referred to in the RV.) which have been suggested :

Alternative interpretations.

(*a*) Placing a comma after σάρκα and referring the whole passage to Christ. So RV.

(*b*) Placing a full stop after σάρκα and translating ' He who is God over all be blessed for ever,' or ' is blessed for ever.'　So RV. *marg.*

(*c*) With the same punctuation translating ' He who is over all is God blessed for ever.'　RV. *marg.*

(*d*) Placing a comma after σάρκα and a full stop at πάντων, ' who is over all.　God be (or is) blessed for ever.'　RV. *marg.*

It may be convenient to point out at once that the question is one of interpretation and not of criticism.　The original MSS. of the Epistles were almost certainly destitute of any sort of punctuation.　Of MSS. of the first century we have one containing a portion of Isocrates in which a few dots are used, but only to divide words, never to indicate pauses in the sense; in the MS. of the Πολιτεία of Aristotle, which dates from the end of the first or beginning of the second century, there is no punctuation whatever except that a slight space is left before a quotation : this latter probably is as close a representation as we can obtain in the present day of the original form of the books of the N.T.　In carefully written MSS., the work of professional scribes, both before and during the first century, the more important pauses in the sense were often indicated but lesser pauses rarely or never; and, so far as our knowledge enables us to speak, in roughly written MSS. such as were no doubt those of the N.T., there is no punctuation at all until about the third century.　Our present MSS. (which begin in the fourth century) do not therefore represent an early tradition.　If there were any traditional punctuation we should have to seek it rather in early versions or in second and third century Fathers : the punctuation of the MSS. is interesting in the history of interpretation, but has no other value.

The original MSS. were ginal MSS. without punctuation.

History of the interpretation.

(1) The Versions.

(2) The Fathers.

The history of the interpretation must be passed over somewhat cursorily. For our earliest evidence we should naturally turn to the older versions, but these seem to labour under the same obscurity as the original. It is however probably true that the traditional interpretation of all of them is to apply the doxology to Christ.

About most of the Fathers however there is no doubt. An immense preponderance of the Christian writers of the first eight centuries refer the word to Christ. This is certainly the case with Irenaeus, *Haer.* III. xvii. 2, ed. Harvey; Tertullian, *Adv. Prax.* 13, 15; Hippolytus, *Cont. Noct.* 6 (cf. Gifford, *op. cit.* p. 60); Novatian, *Trin.* 13; Cyprian, *Test.* ii. 6, ed. Hartel; *Syn. Ant. adv. Paul. Sam.* in Routh, *Rel. Sacrae,* iii. 291, 292; Athanasius, *Cont. Arian.* I. iii. 10; Epiphanius, *Haer.* lvii. 2, 9, ed. Oehler; Basil, *Adv. Eunom.* iv. p. 282; Gregory of Nyssa, *Adv. Eunom.* 11; Chrysostom, *Hom. ad Rom.* xvi. 3, &c.; Theodoret, *Ad Rom.* iv. p. 100; Augustine, *De Trinitate,* ii. 13; Hilarius, *De Trinitate,* viii. 37, 38; Ambrosius, *De Spiritu Sancto,* i. 3. 46; Hieronymus, *Ep. CXXI. ad Algas.* Qu. ix; Cyril Al., *Cont. Iul.* x. pp. 327, 328. It is true also of Origen (*in Rom.* vii. 13) if we may trust Rufinus' Latin translation (the subject has been discussed at length by Gifford, *op. cit.* p. 31; Abbot, *J. B. Exeg.* 1883, p. 103; WH. *ad loc.*). Moreover there is no evidence that this conclusion was arrived at on dogmatic grounds. The passage is rarely cited in controversy, and the word Θεός was given to our Lord by many sects who refused to ascribe to him full divine honours, as the Gnostics of the second century and the Arians of the fourth. On the other hand this was a useful text to one set of heretics, the Sabellians; and it is significant that Hippolytus, who has to explain that the words do not favour Sabellianism, never appears to think of taking them in any other way.

(3) The older MSS.

The strongest evidence against the reference to Christ is that of the leading uncial MSS. Of these ℵ has no punctuation, A undoubtedly puts a point after σάρκα, and also leaves a slight space. The punctuation of this chapter is careful, and certainly by the original hand; but as there is a similar point and space between Χριστοῦ and ὑπέρ in ver. 3, a point between σάρκα and οἵτινες, and another between Ἰσραηλῖται and ὧν, there is no reason as far as punctuation is concerned why ὁ ὤν should not refer to Χριστός as much as οἵτινες does to ἀδελφῶν.* B has a colon after σάρκα, but leaves no space, while there is a space left at the end of the verse. The present colon is however certainly not by the first hand, and whether it covers an earlier stop or not cannot be ascertained. C has a stop after σάρκα. The difference between the MSS. and the Fathers has not been accounted for and is certainly curious.

Against ascribing these words to Christ some patristic evidence has been found. Origen (Rufinus) *ad loc.* tells us there were certain persons who thought the ascription of the word Θεός to Christ difficult, for St. Paul had already called him υἱὸς Θεοῦ. The long series of extracts made by Wetstein *ad loc.* stating that the words ὁ ἐπὶ πάντων Θεός cannot be used of the Son are not to the point, for the Son here is called not ὁ ἐπὶ πάντων Θεός, but ἐπὶ πάντων Θεός, and some of the writers he quotes expressly interpret the passage of the Christ elsewhere. Again, Cyril of Alexandria (*Cont. Iul.* x. p. 327) quotes the Emperor Julian to the effect that St. Paul never calls Christ Θεός, but although this is certainly an interesting statement, this passage, which Cyril quotes against him, might easily have been overlooked. Two writers, and two only, Photius (*Cont. Man.* iii. 14) and Diodorus (Cramer's *Catena,* p. 162), definitely ascribe the words to the Father.

(4) Modern criticism.

The modern criticism of the passage began with Erasmus, who pointed

---

* For information on this point and also on the punctuation of the older papyri, we are much indebted to Mr. F. G. Kenyon, of the British Museum.

out that there were certainly three alternative interpretations possible, and that as there was so much doubt about the verse it should never be used against heretics. He himself wavers in his opinion. In the Commentary he seems to refer the words to the Father, in the Paraphrase (a later but popular work) he certainly refers them to the Son. Socinus, it is interesting to note, was convinced by the position of εὐλογητός (see below) that the sentence must refer to Christ. From Erasmus' time onwards opinions have varied, and have been influenced, as was natural, largely by the dogmatic opinions of the writer; and it seems hardly worth while to quote long lists of names on either side, when the question is one which must be decided not by authority or theological opinion but by considerations of language.

The discussion which follows will be divided into three heads:— (1) Grammar; (2) Sequence of thought; (3) Pauline usage.

The first words that attract our attention are τὸ κατὰ σάρκα, and a parallel naturally suggests itself with Rom. i. 3, 4. As there St. Paul describes the human descent from David, but expressly limits it κατὰ σάρκα, and then in contrast describes his Divine descent κατὰ πνεῦμα ἁγιωσύνης; so here the course of the argument having led him to lay stress on the human birth of Christ as a Jew, he would naturally correct a one-sided statement by limiting that descent to the earthly relationship and then describe the true nature of Him who was the Messiah of the Jews. He would thus enhance the privileges of his fellow-countrymen, and put a culminating point to his argument. τὸ κατὰ σάρκα leads us to expect an antithesis, and we find just what we should have expected in ὁ ὢν ἐπὶ πάντων Θεός.

The gram-matical passage. (1) τὸ κατὰ σάρκα.

Is this legitimate? It has been argued first of all that the proper antithesis to σάρξ is πνεῦμα. But this objection is invalid. Θεός is in a considerable number of cases used in contrast to σάρξ (Luke iii. 6; 1 Cor. i. 29; Col iii. 22; Philemon 16; 2 Chron. xxxii. 8; Ps. lv [lvi]. 5; Jer. xvii. 5; Dan. ii. 11; cf. Gifford, p. 40, to whom we owe these instances).

Again it is argued that the expression τὸ κατὰ σάρκα as opposed to κατὰ σάρκα precludes the possibility of such a contrast in words. While κατὰ σάρκα allows the expression of a contrast, τὸ κατὰ σάρκα would limit the idea of a sentence but would not allow the limitation to be expressed. This statement again is incorrect. Instances are found in which there is an expressed contrast to such limitations introduced with the article (see Gifford, p. 39; he quotes Isocrates, p. 32 e; Demosth. cont. Eubul. p. 1299, l. 14).

But although neither of these objections is valid, it is perfectly true that neither κατὰ σάρκα nor τὸ κατὰ σάρκα demands an expressed antithesis (Rom. iv. 1; Clem. Rom. i. 32). The expression τὸ κατὰ σάρκα cannot therefore be quoted as decisive; but probably any one reading the passage for the first time would be led by these words to expect some contrast and would naturally take the words that follow as a contrast.

The next words concerning which there has been much discussion are ὁ ὤν. It is argued on the one hand that ὁ ὤν is naturally relatival in character and equivalent to ὅς ἐστι, and in support of this statement 2 Cor. xi. 31 is quoted: ὁ Θεὸς καὶ πατὴρ τοῦ Κυρίου Ἰησοῦ οἶδεν, ὁ ὢν εὐλογητὸς εἰς τοὺς αἰῶνας, ὅτι οὐ ψεύδομαι—a passage which is in some respects an exact parallel. On the other hand passages are quoted in which the words do not refer to anything preceding, such as Jn. iii. 31 ὁ ἄνωθεν ἐρχόμενος ἐπάνω πάντων ἐστίν· ὁ ὢν ἐκ τῆς γῆς ἐκ τῆς γῆς ἐστι, καὶ ἐκ τῆς γῆς λαλεῖ: and οἱ ὄντες in Rom. viii. 5, 8. The question is a nice one. It is perfectly true that ὁ ὤν can be used in both ways; but it must be noticed that in the last instances the form of the sentence is such as to take away all ambiguity, and to compel a change of subject. In this case, as there is a noun immediately preceding to which the words would naturally refer, as there is no sign of a change of subject, and as there is no finite verb in the sentence following, an ordinary reader would consider that the words ὁ ὢν ἐπὶ πάντων Θεός refer to what precedes unless

(2) ὁ ὤν.

they suggest so great an antithesis to his mind that he could not refer them to Christ.

But further than this: no instance seems to occur, at any rate in the N.T., of the participle ὤν being used with a prepositional phrase and the noun which the prepositional phrase qualifies. If the noun is mentioned the substantive verb becomes unnecessary. Here ὁ ἐπὶ πάντων Θεός would be the correct expression, if Θεός is the subject of the sentence; if ὤν is added Θεός must become predicate. This excludes the translation (*b*.) 'He who is God over all be (or is) blessed for ever.' It still leaves it possible to translate as (*c*.) 'He who is over all is God blessed for ever,' but the reference to Χριστός remains the most natural interpretation, unless, as stated above, the word Θεός suggests in itself too great a contrast.

(3) The position of εὐλογητός.

It has thirdly been pointed out that if this passage be an ascription of blessing to the Father, the word εὐλογητός would naturally come first, just as the word 'Blessed' would in English. An examination of LXX usage shows that except in cases in which the verb is expressed and thrown forward (as Ps. cxii [cxiii]. 2 εἴη τὸ ὄνομα Κυρίου εὐλογημένον) this is almost invariably its position. But the rule is clearly only an empirical one, and in cases in which stress has to be laid on some special word, it may be and is broken (cf. *Ps. Sol.* viii. 40, 41). As ὁ ὤν ἐπὶ πάντων Θεός if it does not refer to ὁ Χριστός must be in very marked contrast with it, there would be a special emphasis on the words, and the perversion of the natural order becomes possible. These considerations prevent the argument from the position of εὐλογητός being as decisive as some have thought it, but do not prevent the balance of evidence being against the interpretation as a doxology referring to the Father.

The result of an examination of the grammar of the passage makes it clear that if St. Paul had intended to insert an ascription of praise to the Father we should have expected him to write εὐλογητὸς εἰς τοὺς αἰῶνας ὁ ἐπὶ πάντων Θεός. If the translation (*d*.) suggested above, which leaves the stop at πάντων, be accepted, two difficulties which have been urged are avoided, but the awkwardness and abruptness of the sudden Θεὸς εὐλογητὸς εἰς τοὺς αἰῶνας make this interpretation impossible. We have seen that the position of εὐλογητός makes a doxology (*b*.) improbable, and the insertion of the participle makes it very unnatural. The grammatical evidence is in favour of (*a*.), i.e. the reference of the words to ὁ Χριστός, unless the words ὁ ὤν ἐπὶ πάντων Θεός contain in themselves so marked a contrast that they could not possibly be so referred.

The connexion of thought.

We pass next to the connexion of thought. Probably not many will doubt that the interpretation which refers the passage to Christ (*a*.) admirably suits the context. St. Paul is enumerating the privileges of Israel, and as the highest and last privilege he reminds his readers that it was from this Jewish stock after all that Christ in His human nature had come, and then in order to emphasize this he dwells on the exalted character of Him who came according to the flesh as the Jewish Messiah. This gives a perfectly clear and intelligible interpretation of the passage. Can we say the same of any interpretation which applies the words to the Father?

Those who adopt this latter interpretation have generally taken the words as a doxology, 'He that is over all God be blessed for ever,' or 'He that is God over all be blessed for ever.' A natural criticism that at once arises is, how awkward the sudden introduction of a doxology! how inconsistent with the tone of sadness which pervades the passage! Nor do the reasons alleged in support of this interpretation really avoid the difficulty. It is quite true of course that St. Paul was full of gratitude for the privileges of his race and especially for the coming of the Messiah, but that is not the thought in his mind. His feeling is one of sadness and of failure: it is necessary for him to argue that the promise of God has not failed. Nor again does a reference to Rom. i. 25 support the interpretation. It is quite true that there we have a doxology in the midst of a passage of great sadness; but like 2 Cor. xi. 31 that is an instance of the ordinary Rabbinic and oriental usage of adding an ascription of praise when the name of God has been introduced.   That would not apply in the present case where there is no previous mention of the name of God.   It is impossible to say that a doxology could not stand here; it is certainly true that it would be unnatural and out of place.

So strongly does Dr. Kennedy feel the difficulties both exegetical and Prof. grammatical of taking these words as a blessing addressed to the Father, Kennedy's that being unable to adopt the reference to Christ, he considers that they interpreta occur here as a strong assertion of the Divine unity introduced at this tion. place in order to conciliate the Jews: ' He who is over all is God blessed for ever.'   It is difficult to find anything in the context to support this opinion, St. Paul's object is hardly to conciliate unbelieving Jews, but to solve the difficulties of believers, nor does anything occur in either the previous or the following verses which might be supposed to make an assertion of the unity of God either necessary or apposite.   The inter- pretation fails by ascribing too great subtlety to the Apostle.

Unless then Pauline usage makes it absolutely impossible to refer the Pauline expressions Θεός and ἐπὶ πάντων to Christ, or to address to Him such usage. a doxology and make use in this connexion of the decidedly strong word (1) Θεός. εὐλογητός, the balance of probability is in favour of referring the passage to Him.   What then is the usage of St. Paul?   The question has been somewhat obscured on both sides by the attempt to prove that St. Paul could or could not have used these terms of Christ, i. e. by making the difficulty theological and not linguistic.   St. Paul always looks upon Christ as being although subordinate to the Father at the head of all creation (1 Cor. xi. 3; xv. 28; Phil. ii. 5-11; Col. i. 13-20), and this would quite justify the use of the expression ἐπὶ πάντων of Him.   So also if St. Paul can speak of Christ as εἰκὼν τοῦ Θεοῦ (2 Cor. iv. 4; Col. i. 15), as ἐν μορφῇ Θεοῦ ὑπάρχων, and ἴσα Θεῷ (Phil. ii. 6), he ascribes to Him no lesser dignity than would be implied by Θεός as predicate.   The question rather is this: was Θεός so definitely used of the 'Father' as a proper name that it could not be used of the Son, and that its use in this passage as definitely points to the Father as would the word πατήρ if it were substituted?   The most significant passage referred to is 1 Cor. xii. 4-6, where it is asserted that Θεός is as much a proper name as κύριος or πνεῦμα and is used in marked distinc- tion to κύριος.   But this passage surely suggests the answer.   Κύριος is clearly used as a proper name of the Son, but that does not prevent St. Paul elsewhere speaking of the Father as Κύριος, certainly in quotations from the O. T. and probably elsewhere (1 Cor. iii. 5), nor of Χριστός as πνεῦμα (2 Cor. iii. 16).   The history of the word appears to be this.   To one brought up as a Jew it would be natural to use it of the Father alone, and hence complete divine prerogatives would be ascribed to the Son somewhat earlier than the word itself was used.   But where the honour was given the word used predicatively would soon follow.   It was habitual at the beginning of the second century as in the Ignatian letters, it is undoubted in St. John where the Evangelist is writing in his own name, it probably occurs Acts xx. 28 and perhaps Titus ii. 14.   It must be admitted that we should not expect it in so early an Epistle as the Romans; but there is no impossibility either in the word or the ideas expressed by the word occurring so early.

So again with regard to doxologies and the use of the term εὐλογητός. (2) Doxo- The distinction between εὐλογητός and εὐλογημένος which it is attempted to logies ad- make cannot be sustained: and to ascribe a doxology to the Son would be dressed to a practical result of His admittedly divine nature which would gradually Christ. show itself in language.   At first the early Jewish usage would be adhered to; gradually as the dignity of the Messiah became realized, a change would take place in the use of words.   Hence we find doxologies appearing definitely in later books of the N. T., probably in 2 Tim. iv. 18, certainly in

Rev. v. 13 and 2 Pet. iii. 18. Again we can assert that we should not expect it in so early an Epistle as the Romans, but, as Dr. Liddon points out, 2 Thess. i. 12 implies it as does also Phil. ii. 5-8; and there is no reason why language should not at this time be beginning to adapt itself to theological ideas already formed.

Conclusion.   Throughout there has been no argument which we have felt to be quite conclusive, but the result of our investigations into the grammar of the sentence and the drift of the argument is to incline us to the belief that the words would naturally refer to Christ, unless Θεός is so definitely a proper name that it would imply a contrast in itself. We have seen that that is not so. Even if St. Paul did not elsewhere use the word of the Christ, yet it certainly was so used at a not much later period. St. Paul's phraseology is never fixed; he had no dogmatic reason against so using it. In these circumstances with some slight, but only slight, hesitation we adopt the first alternative and translate 'Of whom is the Christ as concerning the flesh, who is over all, God blessed for ever. Amen.'

THE REJECTION OF ISRAEL NOT INCONSISTENT WITH THE DIVINE PROMISES.

IX. 6-13. *For it is indeed true. With all these privileges Israel is yet excluded from the Messianic promises.*

Now in the first place does this imply, as has been urged, that the promises of God have been broken? By no means. The Scriptures show clearly that physical descent is not enough. The children of Ishmael and the children of Esau, both alike descendants of Abraham to whom the promise was given, have been rejected. There is then no breach of the Divine promise, if God rejects some Israelites as He has rejected them.

[6] Yet in spite of these privileges Israel is rejected. Now it has been argued: ' If this be so, then the Divine word has failed. God made a definite promise to Israel. If Israel is rejected, that promise is broken.' An examination of the conditions of the promise show that this is not so. It was never intended that all the descendants of Jacob should be included in the Israel of privilege, [7] no more in fact than that all were to share the full rights of sons of Abraham because they were his offspring. Two instances will prove that this was not the Divine intention. Take first the words used to Abraham in Gen. xxi. 12 when he cast forth Hagar and her child: ' In Isaac shall thy seed be called.' These words show that although there were then two sons of Abraham, one only, Isaac, was selected to be the heir, through

whom the promise was to be inherited.   ⁸ And the general conclusion follows: the right of being 'sons of God,' i. e. of sharing that
adoption of which we spoke above as one of the privileges of Israel,
does not depend on the mere accident of human birth, but those
born to inherit the promise are reckoned by God as the descendants
to whom His words apply.   ⁹ The salient feature is in fact the promise, and not the birth; as is shown by the words used when the
promise was given at the oak of Mamre (Gen. xviii. 10) 'At this
time next year will I come and Sarah shall have a son.'   The
promise was given before the child was born or even conceived,
and the child was born because of the promise, not the promise
given because the child was born.

¹⁰ A second instance shows this still more clearly.   It might be
argued in the last case that the two were not of equal parentage:
Ishmael was the son of a female slave, and not of a lawful wife:
in the second case there is no such defect.   The two sons of
Isaac and Rebecca had the same father and the same mother:
moreover they were twins, born at the same time.   ¹¹ The object
was to exhibit the perfectly free character of the Divine action,
that purpose of God in the world which works on a principle of
selection not dependent on any form of human merit or any con-
vention of human birth, but simply on the Divine will as revealed
in the Divine call; and so before they were born, before they had
done anything good or evil, a selection was made between the two
sons.   ¹² From Gen. xxv. 23 we learn that it was foretold to
Rebecca that two nations, two peoples were in her womb, and that
the elder should serve the younger.   God's action is independent
of human birth; it is not the elder but the younger that is selected.
¹³ And the prophecy has been fulfilled.   Subsequent history may
be summed up in the words of Malachi (i. 2, 3) 'Jacob have
I loved, and Esau have I hated.'

6. The Apostle, after conciliating his readers by a short preface,
now passes to the discussion of his theme.   He has never definitely
stated it, but it can be inferred from what he has said.   The connexion in thought implied by the word δέ is rather that of passing
to a new stage in the argument, than of sharply defined opposition
to what has preceded.   Yet there is some contrast: he sighs over
the fall, yet that fall is not so absolute as to imply a break in God's
purpose.

οὐχ οἷον δὲ ὅτι : 'the case is not as though.' 'This grief of mine for my fellow countrymen is not to be understood as meaning.' Lipsius. The phrase is unique: it must clearly not be interpreted as if it were οὐχ οἷόν τε, 'it is not possible that': for the τε is very rarely omitted, and the construction in this case is always with the infinitive, nor does St. Paul want to state what it is impossible should have happened, but what has not happened. The common ellipse οὐχ ὅτι affords the best analogy, and the phrase may be supposed to represent οὐ τοιοῦτον δέ ἐστι οἷον ὅτι. (Win. § lxiv. 1. 6; E. T. p. 746.)

ἐκπέπτωκεν : 'fallen from its place,' i.e. perished and become of no effect. So 1 Cor. xiii. 8 ἡ ἀγάπη οὐδέποτε ἐκπίπτει (TR); James i. 11.

ὁ λόγος τοῦ Θεοῦ : 'the Word of God,' in the sense of 'the declared purpose of God,' whether a promise or a threat or a decree looked at from the point of view of the Divine consistency. This is the only place in the N. T. where the phrase occurs in this sense ; elsewhere it is used by St. Paul (2 Cor. ii. 17; iv. 2; 2 Tim. ii. 9; Tit. ii. 5), in Heb. xiii. 7, in Apoc. i. 9; vi. 9; xx. 4, and especially by St. Luke in the Acts (twelve times) to mean 'the Gospel' as preached ; once (in Mark vii. 13), it seems to mean the O. T. Scriptures ; here it represents the O. T. phrase ὁ λόγος τοῦ Κυρίου: cf. Is. xxxi. 2 καὶ ὁ λόγος αὐτοῦ (i. e. τοῦ Κυρίου) οὐ μὴ ἀθετηθῇ.

οἱ ἐξ Ἰσραήλ : the offspring of Israel according to the flesh, the υἱοὶ Ἰσραήλ of ver. 27.

οὗτοι Ἰσραήλ. Israel in the spiritual sense (cf. ver. 4 on Ἰσραηλῖται which is read here also by D E F G, Vulg., being a gloss to bring out the meaning), the Ἰσραὴλ τοῦ Θεοῦ of Gal. vi. 16, intended for the reception of the Divine promise. But St. Paul does not mean here to distinguish a spiritual Israel (i. e. the Christian Church) from the fleshly Israel, but to state that the promises made to Israel might be fulfilled even if some of his descendants were shut out from them. What he states is that not all the physical descendants of Jacob are necessarily inheritors of the Divine promises implied in the sacred name Israel. This statement, which is the ground on which he contests the idea that God's word has failed, he has now to prove.

7. οὐδ' ὅτι. The grammatical connexion of this passage with the preceding is that of an additional argument ; the logical connexion is that of a proof of the statement just made. St. Paul could give scriptural proof, in the case of descent from Abraham, of what he had asserted in the case of descent from Jacob, and thus establish his fundamental principle—that inheritance of the promises is not the necessary result of Israelitish descent.

σπέρμα Ἀβραάμ. The word σπέρμα is used in this verse, first of natural seed or descent, then of seed according to the promise.

Both senses occur together in Gen. xxi. 12, 13; and both are found elsewhere in the N. T., Gal. iii. 29 εἰ δὲ ὑμεῖς Χριστοῦ, ἄρα τοῦ Ἀβραὰμ σπέρμα ἐστέ: Rom. xi. 1 ἐγὼ ... ἐκ σπέρματος Ἀβραάμ. The nominative to the whole sentence is πάντες οἱ ἐξ Ἰσραήλ. 'The descendants of Israel have not all of them the legal rights of inheritance from Abraham because they are his offspring by natural descent.'

ἀλλ'. Instead of the sentence being continued in the same form as it began in the first clause, a quotation is introduced which completes it in sense but not in grammar: cf. Gal. iii. 11, 12; 1 Cor. xv. 27.

ἐν Ἰσαὰκ κληθήσεταί σοι σπέρμα: 'in (i. e. through) Isaac will those who are to be your true descendants and representatives be reckoned.' ἐν (as in Col. i. 16 ἐν αὐτῷ ἐκτίσθη τὰ πάντα) implies that Isaac is the starting-point, place of origin of the descendants, and therefore the agent through whom the descent takes place; so Matt. ix. 34 ἐν τῷ ἄρχοντι τῶν δαιμονίων: 1 Cor. vi. 2. σπέρμα (cf. Gen. xii. 7 τῷ σπέρματί σου δώσω τὴν γῆν: Gen. xv. 5 οὕτως ἔσται τὸ σπέρμα σου) is used collectively to express the whole number of descendants, not merely the single son Isaac. The passage means that the sons of Israel did not inherit the promise made to Abraham because they were his offspring—there were some who were his offspring who had not inherited them; but they did so because they were descendants of that one among his sons through whom it had been specially said that his true descendants should be counted.

The quotation is taken from the LXX of Gen. xxi. 12, which it reproduces exactly. It also correctly reproduces both the language and meaning of the original Hebrew. The same passage is quoted in Heb. xi. 18.

The opinion expressed in this verse is of course exactly opposite to the current opinion—that their descent bound Israel to God by an indissoluble bond. See the discussion at the end of this section.

κληθήσεται: 'reckoned,' 'considered,' 'counted as the true σπέρμα'; not as in ver. 11, and as it is sometimes taken here, 'called,' 'summoned' (see below).

The uses of the word καλέω are derived from two main significations, (1) to 'call,' 'summon,' (2) to 'summon by name,' hence 'to name.' It may mean (1) to 'call aloud' Heb. iii. 13, to 'summon,' to 'summon to a banquet' (in these senses also in the LXX), so 1 Cor. x. 27; Matt. xxii. 3; from these is derived the technical sense of 'calling to the kingdom.' This exact usage is hardly found in the LXX, but Is. xlii. 6 (ἐγὼ Κύριος ὁ Θεὸς ἐκάλεσά σε ἐν δικαιοσύνῃ), Is. li. 2 (ὅτι εἷς ἦν καὶ ἐκάλεσα αὐτόν, καὶ εὐλόγησα αὐτὸν καὶ ἠγάπησα αὐτὸν καὶ ἐπλήθυνα αὐτόν) approach it. In this sense it is confined to the epistles of St. Paul with Hebrews and St. Peter, the word hardly occurring at all in St. John and not in this sense elsewhere

R

(although κλητός is so used Matt. xxii. 14). The full construction is καλεῖν τινα εἴς τι, I Thess. ii. 12 τοῦ καλοῦντος ὑμᾶς εἰς τὴν ἑαυτοῦ βασιλείαν καὶ δόξαν: but the word was early used absolutely, and so ὁ καλῶν of God (so Rom. iv. 17: viii. 30; ix. 11, 24). The technical use of the term comes out most strongly in I Cor. vii and in the derived words (see on κλητός Rom. i. 1, 7). (2) In the second group of meanings the ordinary construction is with a double accusative, Acts xiv. 12 ἐκάλουν τε τὸν Βαρνάβαν Δία (so Rom. ix. 25, and constantly in LXX), or with ὀνόματι, ἐπὶ τῷ ὀνόματι as Luke i. 59, 61, although the Hebraism καλέσουσι τὸ ὄνομα αὐτοῦ Ἐμμανουήλ (Matt. i. 23) occurs. But to 'call by name' has associations derived on the one side from the idea of calling over, reckoning, accounting; hence such phrases as Rom. ix. 7 (from Gen. xxi. 12 LXX), and on the other from the idea of affection suggested by the idea of calling by name, so Rom. ix. 26 (from LXX Hos. ii. 1[i. 10]). These derivative uses of the word occur independently both in Greek, where κέκλημαι may be used to mean little more than 'to be,' and in Hebrew. The two main meanings can always be distinguished, but probably in the use of the word each has influenced the other; when God is said to be 'He that calls us' the primary idea is clearly that of invitation, but the secondary idea of 'calling by name,' i.e. of expressing affection, gives a warmer colouring to the idea suggested.

8. τοῦτ' ἔστιν. From this instance we may deduce a general principle.

τὰ τέκνα τῆς σαρκός: *liberi quos corporis vis genuerit.* Fri.

τέκνα τοῦ Θεοῦ: bound to God by all those ties which have been the privilege and characteristic of the chosen race.

τὰ τέκνα τῆς ἐπαγγελίας: *liberi quos Dei promissum procreavit.* Fri. Cf. Gal. iv. 23 ἀλλ' ὁ μὲν ἐκ τῆς παιδίσκης κατὰ σάρκα γεγέννηται, ὁ δὲ ἐκ τῆς ἐλευθέρας δι' ἐπαγγελίας: 28 ἡμεῖς δέ, ἀδελφοί, κατὰ Ἰσαὰκ ἐπαγγελίας τέκνα ἐσμέν.

All these expressions (τέκνα τοῦ Θεοῦ, τέκνα τῆς ἐπαγγελίας) are used elsewhere of Christians, but that is not their meaning in this passage. St. Paul is concerned in this place to prove not that any besides those of Jewish descent might inherit the promises, but merely that not all of Jewish descent necessarily and for that very reason must enjoy all the privileges of that descent. Physical connexion with the Jewish stock was not in itself a ground for inheriting the promise. That was the privilege of those intended when the promise was first spoken, and who might be considered to be born of the promise. This principle is capable of a far more universal application, an application which is made in the Epistle to the Galatians (iii. 29; iv. 28, &c.), but is not made here.

9. ἐπαγγελίας must be the predicate of the sentence thrown forward in order to give emphasis and to show where the point of the argument lies. 'This word is one of promise,' i.e. if you refer to the passage of Scripture you will see that Isaac was the child of promise, and not born κατὰ σάρκα; his birth therefore depends upon the promise which was in fact the efficient cause of it, and not the promise upon his birth. And hence is deduced a general law: a mere connexion with the Jewish race κατὰ σάρκα does not necessarily imply a share in the ἐπαγγελία, for it did not according to the original conditions.

κατὰ τὸν καιρὸν τοῦτον ἐλεύσομαι, καὶ ἔσται τῇ Σάρρᾳ υἱός. St. Paul combines Gen. xviii. 10 (LXX) ἐπαναστρέφων ἥξω πρὸς σὲ κατὰ τὸν καιρὸν τοῦτον εἰς ὥρας, καὶ ἕξει υἱὸν Σάρρα ἡ γυνή σου: and 14 (LXX) εἰς τὸν καιρὸν τοῦτον ἀναστρέψω πρὸς σὲ εἰς ὥρας, καὶ ἔσται τῇ Σάρρᾳ υἱός. The Greek text is a somewhat free translation of the Hebrew, but St. Paul's deductions from the passage are quite in harmony with both its words and its spirit.

κατὰ τὸν καιρὸν τοῦτον is shown clearly by the passage in Genesis to mean 'at this time in the following year,' i. e. when a year is accomplished; but the words have little significance for St. Paul: they are merely a reminiscence of the passage he is quoting, and in the shortened form in which he gives them, the meaning, without reference to the original passage, is hardly clear.

10. οὐ μόνον δέ: see on v. 3, introducing an additional or even stronger proof or example. 'You may find some flaw in the previous argument; after all Ishmael was not a fully legitimate child like Isaac, and it was for this reason (you may say) that the sons of Ishmael were not received within the covenant; the instance that I am now going to quote has no defect of this sort, and it will prove the principle that has been laid down still more clearly.'

ἀλλὰ καὶ Ῥεβέκκα, κ.τ.λ.: the sentence beginning with these words is never finished grammatically; it is interrupted by the parenthesis in ver. 11 μήπω γὰρ γεννηθέντων . . . καλοῦντος, and then continued with the construction changed; cf. v. 12, 18; 1 Tim. i. 3.

ἐξ ἑνός are added to emphasize the exactly similar birth of the two sons. The mother's name proves that they have one mother, these words show that the father too was the same. There are none of the defective conditions which might be found in the case of Isaac and Ishmael. Cf. Chrys. ad loc. (Hom. in Rom. xvi. p. 610) ἡ γὰρ Ῥεβέκκα καὶ μόνη τῷ Ἰσαὰκ γέγονε γυνή, καὶ δύο τεκοῦσα παῖδας, ἐκ τοῦ Ἰσαὰκ ἔτεκεν ἀμφοτέρους· ἀλλ' ὅμως οἱ τεχθέντες τοῦ αὐτοῦ πατρὸς ὄντες, τῆς αὐτῆς μητρός, τὰς αὐτὰς λύσαντες ὠδῖνας, καὶ ὁμοπάτριοι ὄντες καὶ ὁμομήτριοι, καὶ πρὸς τούτοις καὶ δίδυμοι, οὐ τῶν αὐτῶν ἀπήλαυσαν.

κοίτην ἔχουσα: 'having conceived'; cf. Fri. ad loc.

τοῦ πατρὸς ἡμῶν: 'the ancestor of the Jewish race.' St. Paul is here identifying himself with the Jews, 'his kinsmen according to the flesh.' The passage has no reference to the composition of the Roman community.

11. μήπω γάρ, κ.τ.λ. In this verse a new thought is introduced, connected with but not absolutely necessary for the subject under discussion. The argument would be quite complete without it. St. Paul has only to prove that to be of Jewish descent did not in itself imply a right to inherit the promise. That Esau was re-

jected and Jacob chosen is quite sufficient to establish this. But the instance suggests another point which was in the Apostle's mind, and the change in construction shows that a new difficulty, or rather another side of the question—the relation of these events to the Divine purpose—has come forward. It is because he desires to bring in this point that he breaks off the previous sentence. The γάρ then, as so often, refers to something latent in the Apostle's mind, which leads him to introduce his new point, and is explained by the sentence ἵνα ... μένῃ, 'and this incident shows also the absolute freedom of the Divine election and purpose, for it was before the children were born that the choice was made and declared.'

μήπω ... μηδέ: 'although they were not yet born nor had done anything good or evil.' The subjective negative shows that the note of time is introduced not merely as an historical fact but as one of the conditions which must be presumed in estimating the significance of the event. The story is so well known that the Apostle is able to put first without explanation the facts which show the point as he conceives it.

ἵνα ... μένῃ. What is really the underlying principle of the action is expressed as if it were its logical purpose; for St. Paul represents the events as taking place in the way they did in order to illustrate the perfect freedom of the Divine purpose.

ἡ κατ' ἐκλογὴν πρόθεσις τοῦ Θεοῦ: 'the Divine purpose which has worked on the principle of selection.' These words are the key to chaps. ix–xi and suggest the solution of the problem before St. Paul. πρόθεσις is a technical Pauline term occurring although not frequently in the three later groups of Epistles: Rom. viii. 28; ix. 11; Eph. i. 10, 11 ἐν αὐτῷ, ἐν ᾧ καὶ ἐκληρώθημεν, προορισθέντες κατὰ πρόθεσιν τοῦ τὰ πάντα ἐνεργοῦντος κατὰ τὴν βουλὴν τοῦ θελήματος αὐτοῦ: iii. 11 κατὰ πρόθεσιν τῶν αἰώνων ἣν ἐποίησεν ἐν τῷ Χ. Ἰ. τῷ Κυρίῳ ἡμῶν: 2 Tim. i. 9 τοῦ σώσαντος ἡμᾶς καὶ καλέσαντος κλήσει ἁγίᾳ, οὐ κατὰ τὰ ἔργα ἡμῶν, ἀλλὰ κατ' ἰδίαν πρόθεσιν καὶ χάριν: the verb also is found once in the same sense, Eph. i. 9 κατὰ τὴν εὐδοκίαν αὐτοῦ, ἣν προέθετο ἐν αὐτῷ. From Aristotle onwards πρόθεσις had been used to express purpose; with St. Paul it is the 'Divine purpose of God for the salvation of mankind,' the 'purpose of the ages' determined in the Divine mind before the creation of the world. The idea is apparently expressed elsewhere in the N. T. by βουλή (Luke vii. 30; Acts ii. 23; iv. 28; xx. 27) which occurs once in St. Paul (Eph. i. 11), but no previous instance of the word πρόθεσις in this sense seems to be quoted. The conception is worked out by the Apostle with greater force and originality than by any previous writer, and hence he needs a new word to express it. See further the longer note on St. Paul's Philosophy of History, p. 342. ἐκλογή expresses an essentially O. T. idea (see below) but was itself a new

word, the only instances quoted in Jewish literature earlier than
this Epistle being from the *Psalms of Solomon*, which often show
an approach to Christian theological language.   It means (1)
'the process of choice,' 'election.' *Ps. Sol.* xviii. 6 καθαρίσαι ὁ Θεὸς
Ἰσραὴλ εἰς ἡμέραν ἐλέου ἐν εὐλογίᾳ, εἰς ἡμέραν ἐκλογῆς ἐν ἀνάξει Χριστοῦ
αὐτοῦ; ix. 7; Jos. *B. J.* II. viii. 14; Acts ix. 15; Rom. xi. 5, 28;
1 Thess. i. 4; 2 Pet. i. 10.   In this sense it may be used of man's
election of his own lot (as in Josephus and perhaps in *Ps. Sol.*
ix. 7), but in the N. T. it is always used of God's election.   (2) As
abstract for concrete it means ἐκλεκτοί, those who are chosen,
Rom. xi. 7.   (3) In Aquila Is. xxii. 7 ; Symmachus and Theodotion, Is. xxxvii. 24, it means 'the choicest,' being apparently employed to represent the Hebrew idiom.

μένῃ : the opposite to ἐκπέπτωκεν (ver. 6) : the subjunctive shows
that the principles which acted then are still in force.

οὐκ ἐξ ἔργων ἀλλ' ἐκ τοῦ καλοῦντος.   These words qualify the
whole sentence and are added to make more clear the absolute
character of God's free choice.

We must notice (1) that St. Paul never here says anything about
the principle on which the call is made; all he says is that it is not
the result of ἔργα.   We have no right either with Chrysostom
(ἵνα φανῇ φησὶ τοῦ Θεοῦ ἡ ἐκλογὴ ἡ κατὰ πρόθεσιν καὶ πρόγνωσιν γενομένη)
to read into the passage foreknowledge or to deduce from the
passage an argument against Divine foreknowledge.   The words
are simply directed against the assumption of human merit.   And
(2) nothing is said in this passage about anything except 'election'
or 'calling' to the kingdom.   The gloss of Calvin *dum alios ad
salutem praedestinat, alios ad aeternam damnationem* is nowhere
implied in the text.

So Gore (*Studia Biblica*, iii. p. 44) 'The absolute election of
Jacob,—the "loving" of Jacob and the "hating" of Esau,—has
reference simply to the election of one to higher privileges as head
of the chosen race, than the other.   It has nothing to do with their
eternal salvation.   In the original to which St. Paul is referring
Esau is simply a synonym for Edom.'

φαῦλον is the reading of the RV. and modern editors with ℵ A B, a few
minuscules, and Orig. κακόν which occurs in TR. with D F G K L etc. and
Fathers after Chrysostom was early substituted for the less usual word.
A similar change has been made in 2 Cor. v. 10.
For the πρόθεσις τοῦ Θεοῦ of the RV. the TR. reads τοῦ Θεοῦ πρόθεσις with
the support of only a few minuscules.

12. ὁ μείζων κ.τ.λ.   The quotation is made accurately from the
LXX of Gen. xxv. 23 καὶ εἶπε Κύριος αὐτῇ Δύο ἔθνη ἐν τῇ γαστρί σου
εἰσιν, καὶ δύο λαοὶ ἐκ τῆς κοιλίας σου διασταλήσονται· καὶ λαὸς λαοῦ ὑπερέξει,
καὶ ὁ μείζων δουλεύσει τῷ ἐλάσσονι (cf. Hatch, *Essays in Biblical Greek*,
p. 163).   God's election or rejection of the founder of the race is

part of the process by which He elects or rejects the race. In either case the choice has been made independently of merits either of work or of ancestry. Both were of exactly the same descent, and the choice was made before either was born.

ὁ μείζων ... τῷ ἐλάσσονι: 'the elder,' 'the younger.' This use of the words seems to be a Hebraism; see Gen. x. 21 καὶ τῷ Σὴμ ἐγενήθη ... ἀδελφῷ Ἰάφεθ τοῦ μείζονος : ib. xxix. 16 ὄνομα τῇ μείζονι Λεία, καὶ ὄνομα τῇ νεωτέρᾳ Ῥαχήλ. But the dictionaries quote in support of the use Σκιπίων ὁ μέγας Pol. XVIII. xviii. 9. The instances quoted of μικρός (Mk. xv. 40; Mt. xviii. 6, 10, 14, &c.) are all equally capable of being explained of stature.

13. τὸν Ἰακὼβ ἠγάπησα, τὸν δὲ Ἡσαῦ ἐμίσησα. St. Paul concludes his argument by a second quotation taken freely from the LXX of Mal. i. 2, 3 οὐκ ἀδελφὸς ἦν Ἡσαῦ τοῦ Ἰακώβ ; λέγει Κύριος· καὶ ἠγάπησα τὸν Ἰακώβ, τὸν δὲ Ἡσαῦ ἐμίσησα.

What is the exact object with which these words are introduced? (1) The greater number of commentators (so Fri. Weiss Lipsius), consider that they simply give the explanation of God's conduct. 'God chose the younger brother and rejected the elder not from any merit on the part of the one or the other, but simply because He loved the one and hated the other.' The aorists then refer to the time before the birth of the two sons; there is no reference to the peoples descended from either of them, and St. Paul is represented as vindicating the independence of the Divine choice in relation to the two sons of Isaac.

(2) This explanation has the merit of simplicity, but it is probably too simple. (i) In the first place, it is quite clear that St. Paul throughout has in his mind in each case the descendants as well as the ancestors, the people who are chosen and rejected as well as the fathers through whom the choice is made (cf. ver. 7). In fact this is necessary for his argument. He has to justify God's dealing, not with individuals, but with the great mass of Jews who have been rejected. (ii) Again, if we turn to the original contexts of the two quotations in vv. 12, 13 there can be no doubt that in both cases there is reference not merely to the children but to their descendants. Gen. xxv. 23 'Two nations are in thy womb, and two peoples shall be separated even from thy bowels;' Mal. i. 3 'But Esau I hated, and made his mountains a desolation, and gave his heritage to the jackals of the wilderness. Whereas *Edom* saith,' &c. There is nothing in St. Paul's method of quotation which could prevent him from using the words in a sense somewhat different from the original; but when the original passage in both cases is really more in accordance with his method and argument, it is more reasonable to believe that he is not narrowing the sense. (iii) As will become more apparent later, St. Paul's argument is to show that throughout God's action there is running a 'purpose

according to election.' He does not therefore wish to say that it
is merely God's love or hate that has guided Him.

Hence it is better to refer the words, either directly or indirectly, to the choice of the nation as well as the choice of the
founder (so Go. Gif. Liddon). But a further question still remains
as to the use of the aorist. We may with most commentators
still refer it to the original time when the choice was made:
when the founders of the nations were in the womb, God chose
one nation and rejected another because of his love and hatred.
But it is really better to take the whole passage as corroborating the
previous verse by an appeal to history. 'God said the elder shall
serve the younger, and, as the Prophet has shown, the whole of subsequent history has been an illustration of this. Jacob God has
selected for His love; Esau He has hated: He has given his mountains for a desolation and his heritage to the jackals.'

ἠγάπησα ... ἐμίσησα. There is no need to soften these words
as some have attempted, translating 'loved more' and 'loved less.'
They simply express what had been as a matter of fact and was
always looked upon by the Jews as God's attitude towards the two
nations. So *Thanchuma*, p. 32. 2 (quoted by Wetstein, ii. 438) *Tu
inveni es omnes transgressiones, quas odit Deus S. B. fuisse in Esavo.*

How very telling would be the reference to Esau and Edom an acquaintance with Jewish contemporary literature will show. Although in Deut. xxiii. 7
it was said 'Thou shalt not abhor an Edomite, for he is thy brother,' later
events had obliterated this feeling of kinship; or perhaps rather the feeling of
relationship had exasperated the bitterness which the hostility of the two
nations had aroused. At any rate the history is one of continuous hatred on
both sides. So in Ps. cxxxvii. 7 and in the Greek Esdras the burning of the
temple is ascribed to the Edomites (see also Obadiah and Jer. xlix. 7-22).
Two extracts from Apocryphal works will exhibit this hatred most clearly.
In *Enoch* lxxxix. 11-12 (p. 233, ed. Charles) the patriarchal history is
symbolized by different animals : 'But that white bull (Abraham) which was
born amongst them begat a wild ass (Ishmael) and a white bull with it
(Isaac), and the wild ass multiplied. But that bull which was born from
him begat a black wild boar (Esau) and a white sheep (Jacob); and that
wild boar begat many boars, but that sheep begat twelve sheep.' Here
Esau is represented by the most detested of animals, the pig. So in
Jubilees xxxvii. 22 sq. (trans. Charles) the following speech is characteristically put into the mouth of Esau : 'And thou too (Jacob) dost hate me and
my children for ever, and there is no observing the tie of brotherhood with
thee. Hear these words which I declare unto thee : if the boar can change
its skin and make its bristles as soft as wool : or if it can cause horns to
sprout forth on its head like the horns of a stag or of a sheep, then I will
observe the tie of brotherhood with thee, for since the twin male offspring
were separated from their mother, thou hast not shown thyself a brother to
me. And if the wolves make peace with the lambs so as not to devour or
rob them, and if their hearts turn towards them to do good, then there will
be peace in my heart towards thee. And if the lion becomes the friend of
the ox, and if he is bound under one yoke with him and ploughs with him
and makes peace with him, then I will make peace with thee. And when
the raven becomes white as the raza (a large white bird), then I know that

I shall love thee and make peace with thee. Thou shalt be rooted out and thy son shall be rooted out and there shall be no peace for thee.' (See also Jos. *Bell. Jud.* IV. iv. 1, 2; Hausrath, *New Testament Times*, vol. i. pp. 67, 68, *Eng. Trans.*)

The Divine Election.

St. Paul has set himself to prove that there was nothing in the promise made to Abraham, by which God had 'pledged Himself to Israel' (Gore, *Studia Biblica*, iii. 40), and bound Himself to allow all those who were Abraham's descendants to inherit these promises. He proves this by showing that in two cases, as was recognized by the Jews themselves, actual descendants from Abraham had been excluded. Hence he deduces the general principle, 'There was from the first an element of inscrutable selectiveness in God's dealings within the race of Abraham' (Gore, *ib.*). The inheritance of the promise is for those whom God chooses, and is not a necessary privilege of natural descent. The second point which he raises, that this choice is independent of human merit, he works out further in the following verses.

On the main argument it is sufficient at present to notice that it was primarily an *argumentum ad hominem* and as such was absolutely conclusive against those to whom it was addressed. The Jews prided themselves on being a chosen race; they prided themselves especially on having been chosen while the Ishmaelites and the Edomites (whom they hated) had been rejected. St. Paul analyzes the principle on which the one race was chosen and the other rejected, and shows that the very same principles would perfectly justify God's action in further dealing with it. God might choose some of them and reject others, just as he had originally chosen them and not the other descendants of Abraham.

That this idea of the Divine *Election* was one of the most fundamental in the O. T. needs no illustration. We find it in the Pentateuch, as Deut. vii. 6 'For thou art an holy people unto the Lord, thy God: the Lord, thy God, hath chosen thee to be a peculiar people unto himself above all peoples that are on the face of the earth:' in the Psalms, as Ps. cxxxv. 4 'For the Lord hath chosen Jacob unto himself, and Israel for his peculiar treasure': in the Prophets, as Is. xli. 8, 9 'But thou Israel, my servant, Jacob whom I have chosen, the seed of Abraham my friend; thou whom I have taken hold of from the ends of the earth and called thee from the corners thereof, and said unto thee, Thou art my servant, I have chosen thee and not cast thee away.' And this idea of Israel being the elect people of God is one of those which were seized and grasped most tenaciously by contemporary Jewish thought. But between the conception as held by St. Paul's con-

temporaries and the O. T. there were striking differences. In the
O. T. it is always looked upon as an act of condescension and love
of God for Israel, it is for this reason that He redeemed them from
bondage, and purified them from sin (Deut. vii. 8; x. 15; Is. xliv.
21, 22); although the Covenant is specified it is one which involves
obligations on Israel (Deut. vii. 9, &c.): and the thought again and
again recurs that Israel has thus been chosen not merely for their
own sake but as an instrument in the hand of God, and not merely
to exhibit the Divine power, but also for the benefit of other nations
(Gen. xii. 3; Is. lxvi. 18, &c.). But among the Rabbis the idea of
Election has lost all its higher side. It is looked on as a covenant
by which God is bound and over which He seems to have no control.
Israel and God are bound in an indissoluble marriage (*Shemoth
rabba* l. 51): the holiness of Israel can never be done away with,
even although Israel sin, it still remains Israel (*Sanhedrin* 55): the
worst Israelite is not profane like the heathen (*Bammidbar rabba* 17):
no Israelite can go into Gehenna (*Pesikta* 38 a): all Israelites have
their portion in the world to come (*Sanhedrin* 1), and much more
to the same effect. (See Weber *Altsyn. Theol.* p. 51, &c., to whom
are due most of the above references.)

And this belief was shared by St. Paul's contemporaries. 'The
planting of them is rooted for ever: they shall not be plucked out
all the days of the heaven: for the portion of the Lord and the
inheritance of God is Israel' (*Ps. Sol.* xiv. 3); 'Blessed art thou of
the Lord, O Israel, for evermore' (*ib.* viii. 41); 'Thou didst choose
the seed of Abraham before all the nations, and didst set thy name
before us, O Lord: and thou wilt abide among us for ever' (*ib.* ix.
17, 18). While Israel is always to enjoy the Divine mercy, sinners,
i.e. Gentiles, are to be destroyed before the face of the Lord
(*ib.* xii. 7, 8). So again in 4 Ezra, they have been selected while
Esau has been rejected (iii. 16). And this has not been done as part
of any larger Divine purpose; Israel is the end of the Divine action;
for Israel the world was created (vi. 55); it does not in any way
exist for the benefit of other nations, who are of no account; they
are as spittle, as the dropping from a vessel (vi. 55, 56). More
instances might be quoted (*Jubilees* xix. 16; xxii. 9; *Apoc. Baruch*
xlviii. 20, 23; lxxvii. 3), but the above are enough to illustrate the
position St. Paul is combating. The Jew believed that his race
was joined to God by a covenant which nothing could dissolve,
and that he and his people alone were the centre of all God's
action in the creation and government of the world.

This idea St. Paul combats. But it is important to notice how
the whole of the O. T. conception is retained by him, but
broadened and illuminated. Educated as a Pharisee, he had
held the doctrine of election with the utmost tenacity. He had
believed that his own nation had been chosen from among all the

kingdoms of the earth. He still holds the doctrine, but the Christian revelation has given a meaning to what had been a narrow privilege, and might seem an arbitrary choice. His view is now widened. The world, not Israel, is the final end of God's action. This is the key to the explanation of the great difficulty the rejection of Israel. Already in the words that he has used above ἡ κατ᾽ ἐκλογὴν πρόθεσις he has shown the principle which he is working out. The mystery which had been hidden from the foundation of the world has been revealed (Rom. xvi. 26). There is still a Divine ἐκλογή, but it is now realized that this is the result of a πρόθεσις, a universal Divine purpose which had worked through the ages on the principle of election, which was now beginning to be revealed and understood, and which St. Paul will explain and vindicate in the chapters that follow (cf. Eph. i. 4, 11 ; iii. 11).

We shall follow St. Paul in his argument as he gradually works it out. Meanwhile it is convenient to remember the exact point he has reached. He has shown that God has not been untrue to any promise in making a selection from among the Israel of his own day ; He is only acting on the principle He followed in selecting the Israelites and rejecting the Edomites and Ishmaelites. By the introduction of the phrase ἡ κατ᾽ ἐκλογὴν πρόθεσις St. Paul has also suggested the lines on which his argument will proceed.

THE REJECTION OF ISRAEL NOT INCONSISTENT WITH THE DIVINE JUSTICE.

IX. 14-29. *But secondly it may be urged: ' Surely then God is unjust.' No, if you turn to the Scriptures you will see that He has the right to confer His favours on whom He will (as He did on Moses) or to withhold them (as He did from Pharaoh) (vv. 14-18).*

If it is further urged, Why blame me if I like Pharaoh reject God's offer, and thus fulfil His will? I reply, It is your part not to cavil but to submit. The creature may not complain against the Creator, any more than the vessel against the potter (vv. 19-21). Still less when God's purpose has been so beneficent, and that to a body so mixed as this Christian Church of ours, chosen not only from the Jews but also from the Gentiles (vv. 22-24) ;—as indeed was foretold (vv. 25-29).

[14] But there is a second objection which may be raised. 'If what you say is true that God rejects one and accepts another apart from either privilege of birth or human merit, is not His conduct arbitrary and unjust?' What answer shall we make to this? Surely there is no injustice with God. Heaven forbid that I should say so. I am only laying down clearly the absolute character of the Divine sovereignty. [15] The Scripture has shown us clearly the principles of Divine action in two typical and opposed incidents: that of Moses exhibiting the Divine grace, that of Pharaoh exhibiting the Divine severity. Take the case of Moses. When he demanded a sign of the Divine favour, the Lord said (Ex. xxxiii. 17-19) 'Thou hast found grace in my sight, and I know thee by name ... I will make all my goodness pass before thee ; I will be gracious to whom I will be gracious, and will show mercy on whom I will show mercy.' [16] These words imply that grace comes to man not because he is determined to attain it, not because he exerts himself for it as an athlete in the races, but because he has found favour in God's sight, and God shows mercy towards him : they prove in fact the perfect spontaneousness of God's action. [17] So in the case of Pharaoh. The Scripture (in Ex. ix. 16) tells us that at the time of the plagues of Egypt these words were addressed to him : 'I have given thee thy position and place, that I may show forth in thee my power, and that my name might be declared in all the earth.' [18] Those very Scriptures then to which you Jews so often and so confidently appeal, show the absolute character of God's dealings with men. Both the bestowal of mercy or favour and the hardening of the human heart depend alike upon the Divine will.

[19] But this leads to a third objection. If man's destiny be simply the result of God's purpose, if his hardness of heart is a state which God Himself causes, why does God find fault? His will is being accomplished. There is no resistance being offered. Obedience or disobedience is equally the result of His purpose. [20] Such questions should never be asked. Consider what is involved in your position as man. A man's relation to God is such that whatever God does the man has no right to complain or object or reply. The Scriptures have again and again represented the relation of God to man under the image of a potter and the

vessels that he makes. Can you conceive (to use the words of the prophet Isaiah) the vessel saying to its maker: 'Why did you make me thus?' [21] The potter has complete control over the lump of clay with which he works, he can make of it one vessel for an honourable purpose, another for a dishonourable purpose. This exactly expresses the relation of man to his Maker. God has made man, made him from the dust of the earth. He has as absolute control over His creature as the potter has. No man before Him has any right, or can complain of injustice. He is absolutely in God's hands. [22] This is God's sovereignty; even if He had been arbitrary we could not complain. But what becomes of your talk of injustice when you consider how He has acted? Although a righteous God would desire to exhibit the Divine power and wrath in a world of sin; even though He were dealing with those who were fit objects of His wrath and had become fitted for destruction; yet He bore with them, full of long-suffering for them, [23] and with the purpose of showing all the wealth of His glory on those who are vessels deserving His mercy, whom as we have already shown He has prepared even from the beginning, [24] a mercy all the greater when it is remembered that we whom He has called for these privileges are chosen not only from the Jews, but also from the Gentiles, Gentiles who were bound to Him by no covenant. Surely then there has been no injustice but only mercy.

[25] And remember finally that this Divine plan of which you complain is just what the prophets foretold. They prophesied the calling of the Gentiles. Hosea (i. 10, and ii. 23) described how those who were not within the covenant should be brought into it and called by the very name of the Jews under the old Covenant, 'the people of God,' 'the beloved of the Lord,' 'the sons of the living God.' [26] And this wherever throughout the whole world they had been placed in the contemptuous position of being, as he expressed it, 'no people.' [27] Equally do we find the rejection of Israel—all but a remnant of it—foretold. Isaiah (x. 22) stated, 'Even though the number of the children of Israel be as the sand of the seashore, yet it is only a remnant that shall be saved, [28] for a sharp and decisive sentence will the Lord execute upon the earth.' [29] And similarly in an earlier chapter (i. 9) he had foretold the com-

plete destruction of Israel with the exception of a small remnant: 'Unless the Lord of Sabaoth had left us a seed, we should have been as Sodom, and we should have been like unto Gomorrah.'

14-29. St. Paul now states for the purpose of refutation a possible objection. He has just shown that God chooses men independently of their works according to His own free determination, and the deduction is implied that He is free to choose or reject members of the chosen race. The objection which may be raised is, 'if what you say is true, God is unjust,' and the argument would probably be continued, 'we know God is not unjust, therefore the principles laid down are not true.' In answer, St. Paul shows that they cannot be unjust or inconsistent with God's action, for they are exactly those which God has declared to be His in those very Scriptures on which the Jews with whom St. Paul is arguing would especially rely.

14. τί οὖν ἐροῦμεν; see on iii. 5, a very similar passage: εἰ δὲ ἡ ἀδικία ἡμῶν Θεοῦ δικαιοσύνην συνίστησι, τί ἐροῦμεν; μὴ ἄδικος ὁ Θεὸς ὁ ἐπιφέρων τὴν ὀργήν; . . . μὴ γένοιτο. The expression is used as always to introduce an objection which is stated only to be refuted.

μή : implying that a negative answer may be expected, as in the instance just quoted.

παρὰ τῷ Θεῷ. Cf. ii. 11 οὐ γάρ ἐστι προσωποληψία παρὰ τῷ Θεῷ : Eph. vi. 9; Prov. viii. 30, of Wisdom dwelling with God, ἤμην παρ' αὐτῷ ἁρμόζουσα.

μὴ γένοιτο. Cf. iii. 4. The expression is generally used as here to express St. Paul's horror at an objection 'which he has stated for the purpose of refutation and which is blasphemous in itself or one that his opponent would think to be such.'

15-19. According to Origen, followed by many Fathers and some few modern commentators, the section vv. 15-19 contains not St. Paul's own words, but a continuation of the objection put into the mouth of his opponent, finally to be refuted by the indignant disclaimer of ver. 20. Such a construction which was adopted in the interest of free-will is quite contrary to the structure of the sentence and of the argument. In every case in which μὴ γένοιτο occurs it is followed by an answer to the objection direct or indirect. Moreover if this had been the construction the interrogative sentence would not have been introduced by the particle μή expecting a negative answer, but would have been in a form which would suggest an affirmative reply.

15. τῷ γὰρ Μωσῇ λέγει. The γάρ explains and justifies the strong denial contained in μὴ γένοιτο. Too much stress must not be laid on the emphasis given to the name by its position; yet it is obvious that the instance chosen adds considerably to the strength of the argument. Moses, if any one, might be considered to have deserved God's mercy, and the name of Moses would be that most respected by St. Paul's opponents. λέγει without a nominative for Θεὸς λέγει is a common idiom in quotations (cf. Rom. xv. 10; Gal. iii. 16; Eph. iv. 8; v. 14).

ἐλεήσω ὃν ἂν ἐλεῶ, κ.τ.λ: 'I will have mercy on whomsoever I have mercy.' The emphasis is on the ὃν ἄν, and the words are quoted to mean that as it is God who has made the offer of salvation to men, it is for Him to choose who are to be the recipients of His grace, and not for man to dictate to Him. The quotation is from the LXX of Ex. xxxiii. 19 which is accurately reproduced. It is a fairly accurate translation of the original, there being only a slight change in the tenses. The Hebrew is 'I am gracious to whom I will be gracious,' the LXX 'I will be gracious to whomsoever I am gracious.' But St. Paul uses the words with a somewhat different emphasis. Moses had said, 'Show me, I pray thee, thy glory.' And He said, 'I will make all my goodness pass before thee, and will proclaim the name of the Lord before thee: and I will be gracious to whom I will be gracious, and will show mercy on whom I will show mercy.' The point of the words in the original context is rather the certainty of the Divine grace for those whom God has selected; the point which St. Paul wishes to prove is the independence and freedom of the Divine choice.

ἐλεήσω . . . οἰκτειρήσω. The difference between these words seems to be something the same as that between λύπη and ὀδύνη in ver. 2. The first meaning 'compassion,' the second 'distress' or 'pain,' such as expresses itself in outward manifestation. (Cf. Godet, ad loc.)

16. ἄρα οὖν introduces as an inference from the special instance given the general principle of God's method of action. Cf. ver. 8 τοῦτ' ἔστιν, ver. 11 ἵνα, where the logical method in each case is the same although the form of expression is different.

τοῦ θέλοντος, κ.τ.λ. 'God's mercy is in the power not of human desire or human effort, but of the Divine compassion itself.' The genitives are dependent on the idea of mercy deduced from the previous verse. With θέλοντος may be compared Jo. i. 12, 13 ἔδωκεν αὐτοῖς ἐξουσίαν τέκνα Θεοῦ γενέσθαι . . . οἳ οὐκ ἐξ αἱμάτων, οὐδὲ ἐκ θελήματος σαρκός, οὐδὲ ἐκ θελήματος ἀνδρός, ἀλλ' ἐκ Θεοῦ ἐγεννήθησαν. The metaphor of τοῦ τρέχοντος is a favourite one with St. Paul (1 Cor. ix. 24, 26; Phil. ii. 16; Gal. ii. 2; v. 7).

In vv. 7-13 St. Paul might seem to be dealing with families or groups of people; here however he is distinctly dealing with individuals and lays down the principle that God's grace does not necessarily depend upon anything but God's will. 'Not that I have not reasons to do it, but that I need not, in distributing of mercies which have no foundation in the merits of men, render

any other reason or motive but mine own will, whereby I may do
what I will with mine own.' Hammond.

The MSS. vary curiously in the orthography of ἐλεέω, ἐλεάω. In ver. 16
‍אABDEFG support ἐλεάω (ἐλεῶντος), B³K &c. ἐλεέω (ἐλεοῦντος); in
ver. 18 the position is reversed, ἐλεάω (ἐλεᾷ) having only DFG in its
favour; in Jude 22 ἐλεάω (ἐλεᾶτε) is supported by ‍אB alone. See WH.
Introd. ii. App. p. 166.

17. λέγει γὰρ ἡ γραφή : 'and as an additional proof showing
that the principle just enunciated (in ver. 16) is true not merely in
an instance of God's mercy, but also of His severity, take the
language which the Scripture tells us was addressed to Pharaoh.'
On the form of quotation cf. Gal. iii. 8, 22 ; there was probably no
reason for the change of expression from ver. 15; both were well-
known forms used in quoting the O. T. and both could be used
indifferently.

τῷ Φαραώ. The selection of Moses suggested as a natural
contrast that of his antagonist Pharaoh. In God's dealings with
these two individuals, St. Paul finds examples of His dealings with
the two main classes of mankind.

εἰς αὐτὸ τοῦτο, κ.τ.λ. : taken with considerable variations, which in
some cases seem to approach the Hebrew, from the LXX of Ex. ix.
16 (see below). The quotation is taken from the words which Moses
was directed to address to Pharaoh after the sixth plague, that of
boils. 'For now I had put forth my hand and smitten thee and
thy people with pestilence, and thou hadst been cut off from the
earth; but in very deed for this cause have I made thee to stand,
for to show thee my power, and that my name may be declared
throughout all the earth.' The words in the original mean that
God has prevented Pharaoh from being slain by the boils in order
that He might more completely exhibit His power; St. Paul by
slightly changing the language generalizes the statement and
applies the words to the whole appearance of Pharaoh in the field
of history. Just as the career of Moses exhibits the Divine mercy,
so the career of Pharaoh exhibits the Divine severity, and in both
cases the absolute sovereignty of God is vindicated.

ἐξήγειρα : 'I have raised thee up, placed thee in the field of
history.' There are two main interpretations of this word possible. (1) It has been taken to mean, 'I have raised thee up
from sickness,' so Gif. and others, 'I have preserved thee and not
taken thy life as I might have done.' This is in all probability the
meaning of the original Hebrew, 'I made thee to stand,' and
certainly that of the LXX, which paraphrases the words διετηρήθης.
It is supported also by a reading in the Hexapla διετήρησά σε, by the
Targum of Onkelos *Sustinui te ut ostenderem tibi*, and the Arabic
Te reservavi ut ostenderem tibi. Although ἐξεγείρειν does not seem
to occur in this sense, it is used 1 Cor. vi. 14 of resurrection from

the dead, and the simple verb ἐγείρειν in James v. 15 means 'raising from sickness.' The words may possibly therefore have this sense, but the passage as quoted by St. Paul could not be so interpreted. Setting aside the fact that he probably altered the reading of the LXX purposely, as the words occur here without any allusion to the previous sickness, the passage would be meaningless unless reference were made to the original, and would not justify the deduction drawn from it ὃν δὲ θέλει σκληρύνει.

(2) The correct interpretation (so Calv. Beng. Beyschlag Go. Mey. Weiss. Lips. Gore) is therefore one which makes St. Paul generalize the idea of the previous passage, and this is in accordance with the almost technical meaning of the verb ἐξεγείρειν in the LXX. It is used of God calling up the actors on the stage of history. So of the Chaldaeans Hab. i. 6 διότι ἰδοὺ ἐγὼ ἐξεγείρω τοὺς Χαλδαίους : of a shepherd for the people Zech. xi. 16 διότι ἰδοὺ ἐγὼ ἐξεγείρω ποιμένα ἐπὶ τὴν γῆν: of a great nation and kings Jer. xxvii. 41 ἰδοὺ λαὸς ἔρχεται ἀπὸ βορρᾶ, καὶ ἔθνος μέγα καὶ βασιλεῖς πολλοὶ ἐξεγερθήσονται ἀπ' ἐσχάτου τῆς γῆς. This interpretation seems to be supported by the Samaritan Version, subsistere te feci, and certainly by the Syriac, ob id te constitui ut ostenderem ; and it expresses just the idea which the context demands, that God had declared that Pharaoh's position was owing to His sovereign will and pleasure—in order to carry out His Divine purpose and plan.

The interpretation which makes ἐξεγείρειν mean 'call into being,' 'create,' has no support in the usage of the word, although not inconsistent with the context; and 'to rouse to anger' (Aug. de W. Fri. &c.) would require some object such as θυμόν, as in 2 Macc. xiii. 4.

The readings of the Latin Versions are as follows : Quia in hoc ipsum excitavi te, d e f, Vulg.; quia ad hoc ipsum te suscitavi, Orig.-lat. ; quia in hoc ipsum excitavi te suscitavi te, g; quia in hoc ipsum te servavi, Ambrstr., who adds alii codices sic habent, ad hoc te suscitavi. Sive servavi sive suscitavi unus est sensus.

The reading of the LXX is καὶ ἕνεκεν τούτου διετηρήθης ἵνα ἐνδείξωμαι ἐν σοὶ τὴν ἰσχύν μου, καὶ ὅπως διαγγελῇ τὸ ὄνομά μου ἐν πάσῃ τῇ γῇ. St. Paul's variations are interesting.

(1) εἰς αὐτὸ τοῦτο is certainly a better and more emphatic representation of the Hebrew than the somewhat weak τούτου ἕνεκεν. The expression is characteristically Pauline (Rom. xiii. 6; 2 Cor. v. 5; Eph. vi. 18, 22; Col. iv. 8).

(2) ἐξήγειρά σε represents better than the LXX the grammar of the Hebrew, 'I made thee to stand,' but not the sense. The variants of the Hexapla (διετήρησα) and other versions suggest that a more literal translation was in existence, but the word was very probably St. Paul's own choice, selected to bring out more emphatically the meaning of the passage as he understood it.

(3) ἐνδείξωμαι ἐν σοί. St. Paul here follows the incorrect translation of the LXX. The Hebrew gives as the purpose of God's action that Pharaoh may know God's power, and as a further consequence that God's name may be known in the world. The LXX assimilates the first clause to the second and gives it a similar meaning.

(4) ὅπως . . . ὅπως. Here St. Paul obliterates the distinction which the
LXX (following the Hebrew) had made of ἵνα . . . ὅπως. But this alteration
was only a natural result of the change in the LXX itself, by which the two
clauses had become coordinate in thought.

(5) For δύναμιν the LXX reads ἰσχύν. The reading of St. Paul appears
as a variant in the Hexapla.

18. ἄρα οὖν. Just as ver. 16 sums up the argument of the first part
of this paragraph, so this verse sums up the argument as it has
been amplified and expounded by the additional example.

σκληρύνει: 'hardens'; the word is suggested by the narrative of
Exodus from which the former quotation is taken (Ex. iv. 21; vii.
3; ix. 12; x. 20, 27; xi. 10; xiv. 4, 8, 17) and it must be translated in
accordance with the O. T. usage, without any attempt at softening
or evading its natural meaning.

The Divine Sovereignty in the Old Testament.

A second objection is answered and a second step in the argument laid down. God is not unjust if He select one man or one
nation for a high purpose and another for a low purpose, one man
for His mercy and another for His anger. As is shown by the
Scriptures, He has absolute freedom in the exercise of His Divine
sovereignty. St. Paul is arguing against a definite opponent,
a typical Jew, and he argues from premises the validity of which
that Jew must admit, namely, the conception of God contained in
the O. T. There this is clearly laid down—the absolute sovereignty of God, that is to say, His power and His right to dispose
the course of human actions as He will. He might select Israel
for a high office, and Edom for a degraded part: He might
select Moses as an example of His mercy, Pharaoh as an example
of His anger. If this be granted He may (on grounds which the
Jew must admit), if He will, select some Jews and some Gentiles
for the high purpose of being members of His Messianic kingdom,
while He rejects to an inferior part the mass of the chosen people.

This is St. Paul's argument. Hence there is no necessity for
softening (as some have attempted to do) the apparently harsh
expression of ver. 18, 'whom He will He hardeneth.' St. Paul
says no more than he had said in i. 20–28, where he described the
final wickedness of the world as in a sense the result of the Divine
action. In both passages he is isolating one side of the Divine
action; and in making theological deductions from his language
these passages must be balanced by others which imply the Divine
love and human freedom. It will be necessary to do this at the
close of the discussion. At present we must be content with
St. Paul's conclusion, that God as sovereign has the absolute right
and power of disposing of men's lives as He will.

s

We must not soften the passage. On the other hand, we must not read into it more than it contains : as, for example, Calvin does. He imports various extraneous ideas, that St. Paul speaks of election to salvation and of reprobation to death, that men were created that they might perish, that God's action not only might be but was arbitrary : *Hoc enim vult efficere apud nos, ut in ea quae apparet inter electos et reprobos diversitate, mens nostra contenta sit quod ita visum fuerit Deo, alios illuminare in salutem, alios in mortem excaecare . . . Corruit ergo frivolum illud effugium quod de praescientia Scholastici habent. Neque enim praevideri ruinam impiorum a Domino Paulus tradit, sed eius consilio et voluntate ordinari, quemadmodum et Solomo docet, non modo praecognitum fuisse impiorum interitum, sed impios ipsos fuisse destinato creatos ut perirent.*

The Apostle says nothing about eternal life or death. He says nothing about the principles upon which God does act ; he never says that His action is arbitrary (he will prove eventually that it is not so), but only that if it be no Jew who accepts the Scripture has any right to complain. He never says or implies that God has created man for the purpose of his damnation. What he does say is that in His government of the world God reserves to Himself perfect freedom of dealing with man on His own conditions and not on man's. So Gore, *op. cit.* p. 40, sums up the argument : ' God always revealed Himself as retaining His liberty of choice, as refusing to tie Himself, as selecting the historic examples of His hardening judgement and His compassionate good will, so as to baffle all attempts on our part to create His vocations by our own efforts, or anticipate the persons whom He will use for His purposes of mercy or of judgement.'

19. ἐρεῖς μοι οὖν. Hardly are the last words ὃν δὲ θέλει σκλη-ρύνει out of St. Paul's mouth than he imagines his opponent in controversy catching at an objection, and he at once takes it up and forestalls him. By substituting this phrase for the more usual τί οὖν ἐροῦμεν, St. Paul seems to identify himself less with his opponent's objection.

μοι οὖν is the reading of א^c A B P, Orig. 1/3 Jo.-Damasc.; οὖν μοι of the TR. is supported by D E F G K L &c., Vulg. Boh., Orig. 2/3 and Orig.-lat. Chrys. Thdrt. It is the substitution of the more usual order.

τί ἔτι μέμφεται : ' why considering that it is God who hardens me does He still find fault?' Why does he first produce a position of disobedience to His will, and then blame me for falling into it ? The ἔτι implies that a changed condition has been produced which makes the continuation of the previous results surprising. So Rom. iii. 7 εἰ δὲ ἡ ἀλήθεια τοῦ Θεοῦ ἐν τῷ ἐμῷ ψεύσματι ἐπερίσσευσεν εἰς τὴν δόξαν αὐτοῦ, τί ἔτι κἀγὼ ὡς ἁμαρτωλὸς κρίνομαι ; Rom. vi. 2 οἵτινες ἀπεθάνομεν τῇ ἁμαρτίᾳ, πῶς ἔτι ζήσομεν ἐν αὐτῇ ;

τί ἔτι μέμφεται is read by TR. and RV. with ℵ A K L P &c., Vulg. Syrr. Boh., and many Fathers. B D E F G, Orig.-lat. Hieron. insert οὖν after τί.

βουλήματι, which occurs in only two other passages in the N. T. (Acts xxvii. 43; 1 Pet. iv. 3) seems to be substituted for the ordinary word θέλημα as implying more definitely the deliberate purpose of God.

ἀνθέστηκε. Perfect with present sense; cf. Rom. xiii. 2 ὥστε ὁ ἀντιτασσόμενος τῇ ἐξουσίᾳ τῇ τοῦ Θεοῦ διαταγῇ ἀνθέστηκεν, Winer, § xl. 4, p. 342, E. T. The meaning is not: 'who is able to resist,' but 'what man is there who is resisting God's will?' There is no resistance being offered by the man who disobeys; he is only doing what God has willed that he should do.

20. ὦ ἄνθρωπε. The form in which St. Paul answers this question is rhetorical, but it is incorrect to say that he refuses to argue. The answer he gives, while administering a severe rebuke to his opponent, contains also a logical refutation. He reminds him that the real relation of every man to God (hence ὦ ἄνθρωπε) is that of created to Creator, and hence not only has he no right to complain, but also God has the Creator's right to do what He will with those whom He has Himself moulded and fashioned.

μενοῦνγε : 'nay rather,' a strong correction. The word seems to belong almost exclusively to N. T. Greek, and would be impossible at the beginning of a sentence in classical Greek. Cf. Rom. x. 18; Phil. iii. 8; but probably not Luke xi. 28.

ὦ ἄνθρωπε μενοῦνγε is read by ℵ A B (but B om. γε as in Phil. iii. 8), Orig. 1/4 Jo.-Damasc.; μενοῦνγε is omitted by D F G, d e f g Vulg., Orig.-lat., and inserted before ὦ ἄνθρωπε by ℵ° Dᵒ K L P and later MSS., Orig. 3/4, Chrys. Theod.-mops Thdrt. &c. The same MSS. (F G d f g) and Orig.-lat. omit the word again in x. 18, and in Phil. iii. 8 B D E F G K L and other authorities read μὲν οὖν alone. The expression was omitted as unusual by many copyists, and when restored in the margin crept into a different position in the verse.

μὴ ἐρεῖ τὸ πλάσμα, κ.τ.λ. The conception of the absolute power of the Creator over His creatures as represented by the power of the potter over his clay was a well-known O. T. idea which St. Paul shared with his opponent and to which therefore he could appeal with confidence. Both the idea and the language are borrowed from Is. xlv. 8–10 ἐγώ εἰμι Κύριος ὁ κτίσας σε· ποῖον βέλτιον κατεσκεύασα ὡς πηλὸν κεραμέως ... μὴ ἐρεῖ ὁ πηλὸς τῷ κεραμεῖ Τί ποιεῖς, ὅτι οὐκ ἐργάζῃ οὐδὲ ἔχεις χεῖρας; μὴ ἀποκριθήσεται τὸ πλάσμα πρὸς τὸν πλάσαντα αὐτό· and Is. xxix. 16 οὐχ ὡς ὁ πηλὸς τοῦ κεραμέως λογισθήσεσθε; μὴ ἐρεῖ τὸ πλάσμα τῷ πλάσαντι αὐτὸ Οὐ σύ με ἔπλασας; ἢ τὸ ποίημα τῷ ποιήσαντι Οὐ συνετῶς με ἐποίησας; Cf. also Is. lxiv. 8; Jer. xviii. 6; Eccles. xxxvi. [xxxiii.] 13.

21. ἢ οὐκ ἔχει ἐξουσίαν: 'if you do not accept this you will be compelled to confess that the potter has not complete control over his clay—an absurd idea.' The unusual position of τοῦ πηλοῦ, which

should of course be taken with ἐξουσίαν, is intended to emphasize
the contrast between κεραμεύς and πηλός, as suggesting the true
relations of man and God.

φυράματος : 'the lump of clay.' Cf. Rom. xi. 16; 1 Cor. v. 6, 7 ;
Gal. v. 9. The exact point to which this metaphor is to be pressed
may be doubtful, and it must always be balanced by language used
elsewhere in St. Paul's Epistles ; but it is impossible to argue that
there is no idea of creation implied : the potter is represented not
merely as adapting for this or that purpose a vessel already made,
but as making out of a mass of shapeless material one to which he
gives a character and form adapted for different uses, some
honourable, some dishonourable.

ὁ μὲν εἰς τιμὴν σκεῦος, κ.τ.λ.: cf. Wisd. xv. 7 (see below):
2 Tim. ii. 20 ἐν μεγάλῃ δὲ οἰκίᾳ οὐκ ἔστι μόνον σκεύη χρυσᾶ καὶ
ἀργυρᾶ, ἀλλὰ καὶ ξύλινα καὶ ὀστράκινα, καὶ ἃ μὲν εἰς τιμήν, ἃ δὲ εἰς ἀτιμίαν.
But there the side of human responsibility is emphasized, ἐὰν οὖν τις
ἐκκαθάρῃ ἑαυτὸν ἀπὸ τούτων, ἔσται σκεῦος εἰς τιμήν, κ.τ.λ.

The point of the argument is clear. Is there any injustice if
God has first hardened Pharaoh's heart and then condemned him,
if Israel is rejected and then blamed for being rejected? The answer
is twofold. In vv. 19-21 God's conduct is shown to be right under
all circumstances. In vv. 22 sq. it is explained or perhaps rather
hinted that He has a beneficent purpose in view. In vv. 19-21
St. Paul shows that for God to be unjust is impossible. As He has
made man, man is absolutely in His power. Just as we do not
consider the potter blameable if he makes a vessel for a dishonourable purpose, so we must not consider God unjust if He chooses to
make a man like Pharaoh for a dishonourable part in history. *Post-
quam demonstratum est, Deum ita egisse, demonstratum etiam est omnibus, qui Mosi credunt, eum convenienter suae iustitiae egisse.* Wetstein.

As in iii. 5 St. Paul brings the argument back to the absolute
fact of God's justice, so here he ends with the absolute fact of
God's power and right. God had not (as the Apostle will show)
acted arbitrarily, but if He had done so what was man that he
should complain?

22. εἰ δὲ θέλων ὁ Θεός, κ.τ.λ.: 'but if God, &c., what will you say
then?' like our English idiom 'What and if.' There is no apodosis to the sentence, but the construction, although grammatically
incomplete, is by no means unusual : cf. Jo. vi. 61, 62 τοῦτο ὑμᾶς
σκανδαλίζει ; ἐὰν οὖν θεωρῆτε τὸν υἱὸν τοῦ ἀνθρώπου ἀναβαίνοντα ὅπου
ἦν τὸ πρότερον; Acts xxiii. 9 οὐδὲν κακὸν εὑρίσκομεν ἐν τῷ ἀνθρώπῳ
τούτῳ· εἰ δὲ πνεῦμα ἐλάλησεν αὐτῷ ἢ ἄγγελος ; Luke xix. 41, 42 καὶ ὡς
ἤγγισεν, ἰδὼν τὴν πόλιν ἔκλαυσεν ἐπ᾽ αὐτῇ λέγων ὅτι Εἰ ἔγνως ἐν τῇ ἡμέρᾳ
ταύτῃ καὶ σὺ τὰ πρὸς εἰρήνην. There is no difficulty (as Oltramare
seems to think) in the length of the sentence. All other constructions, such as an attempt to find an apodosis in καὶ ἵνα

γνωρίσῃ, in οὓς καὶ ἐκάλεσεν, or even in ver. 31 τί οὖν ἐροῦμεν, are needlessly harsh and unreal. The δέ (which differs from οὖν : cf. Jo. vi. 62 ; Acts xxiii. 9), although not introducing a strong opposition to the previous sentence, implies a change of thought. Enough has been said to preserve the independence of the Divine will, and St. Paul suggests another aspect of the question, which will be expounded more fully later;—one not in any way opposed to the freedom of the Divine action, but showing as a matter of fact how this freedom has been exhibited. 'But if God, notwithstanding His Divine sovereignty, has in His actual dealings with mankind shown such unexpected mercy, what becomes of your complaints of injustice?'

θέλων. There has been much discussion as to whether this should be translated 'because God wishes,' or 'although God wishes.' (1) In the former case (so de W. and most commentators) the words mean, 'God because He wishes to show the terrible character of His wrath restrains His hands, until, as in the case of Pharaoh, He exhibits His power by a terrible overthrow. He hardened Pharaoh's heart in order that the judgement might be more terrible.' (2) In the latter case (Mey.-W. Go. Lips. Gif.), ' God, although His righteous anger might naturally lead to His making His power known, has through His kindness delayed and borne with those who had become objects that deserved His wrath.' That this is correct is shown by the words ἐν πολλῇ μακρο-θυμίᾳ, which are quite inconsistent with the former interpretation, and by the similar passage Rom. ii. 4, where it is distinctly stated τὸ χρηστὸν τοῦ Θεοῦ εἰς μετάνοιάν σε ἄγει. Even if St. Paul occasionally contradicts himself, that is no reason for making him do so unnecessarily. As Liddon says the three points added in this sentence, the natural wrath of God against sin and the violation of His law, the fact that the objects of His compassion were σκεύη ὀργῆς, and that they were fitted for destruction, all intensify the difficulty of the Divine restraint.

ἐνδείξασθαι τὴν ὀργὴν καὶ γνωρίσαι τὸ δυνατὸν αὐτοῦ are reminiscences of the language used in the case of Pharaoh, ἐνδείξωμαι ἐν σοὶ τὴν δύναμίν μου.

σκεύη ὀργῆς : ' vessels which deserve God's anger '; the image of the previous verse is continued. The translation 'destined for God's anger' would require σκεύη εἰς ὀργήν : and the change of construction from the previous verse must be intentional.

κατηρτισμένα εἰς ἀπώλειαν : ' prepared for destruction.' The construction is purposely different from that of the corresponding words ἃ προητοίμασεν. St. Paul does not say ' whom God prepared for destruction' (Mey.), although in a sense at any rate he could have done so (ver. 18 and i. 24, &c.), for that would conflict with the argument of the sentence; nor does he say that they had fitted themselves for destruction (Chrys. Theoph. Oecum. Grotius Beng.), although, as the argument in chap. x shows, he could have done so, for this would have been to impair the conception of God's freedom of action which at present he wishes to emphasize; but he says just what is necessary for his immediate purpose—they were fitted for eternal destruction (ἀπώλεια opp. to σωτηρία). That is the point to which he wishes to attract our attention.

23. καὶ ἵνα γνωρίσῃ. These words further develop and explain God's action so as to silence any objection. St. Paul states that God has not only shown great long-suffering in bearing with those fitted for destruction, but has done so in order to be able to show mercy to those whom He has called: the καί therefore couples ἵνα γνωρίσῃ in thought with ἐν πολλῇ μακροθυμίᾳ. St. Paul is no longer (see ver. 24) confining himself to the special case of Pharaoh, although he still remembers it, as his language shows, but he is considering the whole of God's dealings with the unbelieving Jews, and is laying down the principles which will afterwards be worked out in full—that the Jews had deserved God's wrath, but that He had borne with them with great long-suffering both for their own sakes and for the ultimate good of His Church. In these verses, as in the expression ἡ κατ' ἐκλογὴν πρόθεσις, St. Paul is in fact hinting at the course of the future argument, and in that connexion they must be understood.

On the exact construction of these words there has been great variety of opinion, and it may be convenient to mention some divergent views. (1) WH. on the authority of B, several minuscules, Vulg. Boh. Sah., Orig.-lat. 3/3 omit καί. This makes the construction simpler, but probably for that very reason should be rejected. A reviser or person quoting would naturally omit καί : it is difficult to understand why it should be inserted : moreover on such a point as this the authority of versions is slighter, since to omit a pleonastic καί would come within the ordinary latitude of interpretation necessary for their purpose. There is some resemblance to xvi. 27. In both cases we find the same MS. supporting a reading which we should like to accept, but which has much the appearance of being an obvious correction. (2) Calv. Grot. de W. Alf. and others make καί couple θέλων and ἵνα γνωρίσῃ. But this obliges us to take θέλων . . . ἐνδείξασθαι as expressing the purpose of the sentence which is both impossible Greek and gives a meaning inconsistent with μακροθυμίᾳ. (3) Fri. Beyschlag and others couple ἵνα γνωρίσῃ and εἰς ἀπώλειαν; but this is to read an idea of purpose into κατηρτισμένα which it does not here possess. (4) To make καὶ ἵνα give the apodosis of the sentence εἰ δὲ ἤνεγκεν (Ols. Ewald, &c.), or to create a second sentence repeating εἰ, καὶ εἰ ἵνα . . . (supposing a second ellipse), or to find a verb hidden in ἐκάλεσεν, supposing that St. Paul meant to write καὶ εἰ ἵνα γνωρίσῃ . . . ἐκάλεσεν but changed the construction and put the verb into a relative sentence (Go. Oltramare); all these are quite impossible and quite unnecessary constructions.

τὸν πλοῦτον, κ.τ.λ. : cf. ii. 4: Eph. iii. 16 κατὰ τὸ πλοῦτος τῆς δόξης αὐτοῦ.

ἃ προητοίμασεν εἰς δόξαν : the best commentary on these words is Rom. viii. 28–30.

We may note the very striking use made of this metaphor of the potter's wheel and the cup by Browning, *Rabbi ben Ezra*, xxvi-xxxii. We may especially illustrate the words ἃ προητοίμασεν εἰς δόξαν.

> But I need now as then,
> Thee, God, who mouldest men;
> . . . . . .
> So take and use thy work!
> Amend what flaws may lurk,
> What strain o' the stuff, what warpings past the aim!
> My times be in Thy hand!
> Perfect the cup as planned!
> Let age approve of youth, and death complete the same!

24. οὓς καὶ ἐκάλεσεν ἡμᾶς : ' even us whom He has called.' The οὓς is attracted into the gender of ἡμᾶς. The relative clause gives an additional fact in a manner not unusual with St. Paul. Rom. i. 6 ἐν οἷς ἐστε καὶ ὑμεῖς: 2 Tim. i. 10 φωτίσαντος δὲ ζωὴν καὶ ἀφθαρσίαν διὰ τοῦ εὐαγγελίου, εἰς ὃ ἐτέθην ἐγὼ κήρυξ. The calling of the Gentiles is introduced not because it was a difficulty St. Paul was discussing, but because, as he shows afterwards, the calling of the Gentiles had come through the rejection of the Jews.

There have been two main lines of interpretation of the above three verses. (1) According to the one taken above they modify and soften the apparent harshness of the preceding passage (19-21). That this is the right view is shown by the exegetical considerations given above, and by the drift of the argument which culminating as it does in a reference to the elect clearly implies some mitigation in the severity of the Divine power as it has been described. (2) The second view would make the words of ver. 22 continue and emphasize this severity of tone : ' And even if God has borne with the reprobate for a time only in order to exhibit more clearly the terror of His wrath, and in order to reveal His mercy to the elect, even then what right have you—man that you are—to complain ?' Cf. Calvin : *Ea si dominus ad aliquod tempus patienter sustinet . . . ad demonstranda suae severitatis iudicia . . . ad virtutem suam illustrandam, . . . praeterea quo inde notior fiat et clarius elucescat suae in electos misericordiae amplitudo : quid in hac dispensatione misericordiae dignum ?*

25. ὡς καί : ' and this point, the rejection of the Jews and the calling of the Gentiles, is foretold by the prophet.' St. Paul now proceeds to give additional force to his argument by a series of quotations from the O. T., which are added as a sort of appendix to the first main section of his argument

καλέσω . . . ἠγαπημένην—quoted from the LXX of Hosea ii. 23 with some alterations. In the original passage the words refer to the ten tribes. A son and daughter of Hosea are named Lo-

ammi, ' not a people' and Lo-ruhamah, 'without mercy,' to signify
the fallen condition of the ten tribes; and Hosea prophesies their
restoration (cf. Hosea i. 6, 8, 9). St. Paul applies the principle
which underlies these words, that God can take into His covenant
those who were previously cut off from it, to the calling of the
Gentiles. A similar interpretation of the verse was held by the
Rabbis. *Pesachim* viii. f. *Dixit R. Eliezer: Non alia de causa in
exilium et captivitatem misit Deus S. B. Israelem inter nationes, nisi
ut facerent multos proselytos S. D. Oseae* ii. 25 (23) *et seram eam
mihi in terram. Numquid homo seminat satum nisi ut colligat
multos coros tritici?* Wetstein.

The LXX reads ἐλεήσω τὴν οὐκ ἠλεημένην, καὶ ἐρῶ τῷ οὐ λαῷ μου Λαός μου
εἶ σύ, but for the first clause which agrees with the Hebrew the Vatican
substitutes ἀγαπήσω τὴν οὐκ ἠγαπημένην. St. Paul inverts the order of the
clauses, so that the reference to τὸν οὐ λαόν μου, which seems particularly to
suit the Gentiles, comes first, and for ἐρῶ substitutes καλέσω which naturally
crept in from the ἐκάλεσεν of the previous verse, and changes the construction of the clause to suit the new word. In the second clause St. Paul seems
to have used a text containing the reading of the Vatican MS., for the latter
can hardly have been altered to harmonize with him. St. Peter makes use of
the passage with the reading of the majority of MSS.: οἱ ποτὲ οὐ λαός, νῦν δὲ
λαὸς Θεοῦ, οἱ οὐκ ἠλεημένοι, νῦν δὲ ἐλεηθέντες (1 Pet. ii. 10).

καλέσω with a double accusative can only mean ' I will name,'
although the word has been suggested by its previous occurrence
in another sense.

26. καὶ ἔσται, ἐν τῷ τόπῳ . . . ἐκεῖ κ.τ.λ. St. Paul adds a passage
with a similar purport from another part of Hosea (i. 10). The
meaning is the same and the application to the present purpose
based on exactly the same principles. The habit had probably
arisen of quoting passages to prove the calling of the Gentiles; and
these would become commonplaces, which at a not much later date
might be collected together in writing, see Hatch, *Essays in Biblical
Greek*, p. 103, and cf. Rom. iii. 10. The only difference between
St. Paul's quotation and the LXX is that he inserts ἐκεῖ: this insertion
seems to emphasize the idea of the place, and it is somewhat difficult
to understand what place is intended. (1) In the original the place
referred to is clearly Palestine: and if that be St. Paul's meaning
he must be supposed to refer to the gathering of the nations at
Jerusalem and the foundation of a Messianic kingdom there
(cf. xi. 26). St. Paul is often strongly influenced by the language and
even the ideas of Jewish eschatology, although in his more spiritual
passages he seems to be quite freed from it. (2) If we neglect
the meaning of the original, we may interpret ἐκεῖ of the whole
world. ' Wheresoever on earth there may be Gentiles, who have
had to endure there the reproach of being not God's people, in
that place they shall be called God's people, for they will become
members of His Church and it will be universal.'

27, 28. St. Paul has supported one side of his statement from the O. T., namely, that Gentiles should be called; he now passes on to justify the second, namely, that only a remnant of the Jews should be saved.

27. ἐὰν ᾖ ὁ ἀριθμός ... ἐπὶ τῆς γῆς : quoted from the LXX of Is. x. 22, but considerably shortened. The LXX differs considerably from the Hebrew, which the translators clearly did not understand. But the variations in the form do not affect the meaning in any case. St. Paul reproduces accurately the idea of the original passage. The context shows that the words must be translated 'only a remnant shall be saved,' and that it is the cutting off of Israel by the righteous judgement of God that is foretold. Prof. Cheyne in 1884 translated the Hebrew : 'For though thy people, O Israel, were as the sand of the sea, only a remnant of them shall return : a final work and a decisive, overflowing with righteousness! For a final work and a decisive doth the Lord, Jehovah Sabaoth, execute within all the land.'

28. λόγον γὰρ συντελῶν καὶ συντέμνων ποιήσει Κύριος ἐπὶ τῆς γῆς : συντελῶν, 'accomplishing,' συντέμνων, 'abridging.' Cf. Is. xxviii. 22 διότι συντετελεσμένα καὶ συντετμημένα πράγματα ἤκουσα παρὰ Κυρίου Σαβαώθ, ἃ ποιήσει ἐπὶ πᾶσαν τὴν γῆν. 'For a word, accomplishing and abridging it, that is, a sentence conclusive and concise, will the Lord do upon the earth.'

Three critical points are of some interest:

(1) The variations in the MSS. of the Gr. Test. For ὑπόλειμμα (ὑπόλιμμα WH.) of the older MSS. (א A B, Eus.), later authorities read κατάλειμμα to agree with the LXX. In ver. 28 λόγον γὰρ συντελῶν καὶ συντέμνων ποιήσει Κύριος ἐπὶ τῆς γῆς is the reading of א A B a few minusc., Pesh. Boh. Aeth., Eus. 2/3; Western and Syrian authorities add after συντέμνων, ἐν δικαιοσύνῃ· ὅτι λόγον συντετμημένον to suit the LXX. Alford defends the TR. on the plea of homoeoteleuton (συντέμνων and συντετμημένον), but the insertion of γάρ after λόγον which is preserved in the TR. (where it is ungrammatical) and does not occur in the text of the LXX, shows that the shortened form was what St. Paul wrote.

(2) The variations from the LXX. The LXX reads καὶ ἐὰν γένηται ὁ λαὸς Ἰσραὴλ ὡς ἡ ἄμμος τῆς θαλάσσης, τὸ κατάλειμμα αὐτῶν σωθήσεται. λόγον συντελῶν καὶ συντέμνων ἐν δικαιοσύνῃ ὅτι λόγον συντετμημένον Κύριος ποιήσει ἐν τῇ οἰκουμένῃ ὅλῃ. St. Paul substitutes ἀριθμὸς τῶν υἱῶν Ἰσραήλ, a reminiscence from Hosea i. 10, the words immediately preceding those quoted by him above. The later part of the quotation he considerably shortens.

(3) The variations of the LXX from the Hebrew. These appear to arise from an inability to translate. For 'a final work and a decisive, overflowing with righteousness,' they wrote 'a word, accomplishing and abridging it in righteousness,' and for 'a final work and a decisive,' 'a word abridged will the Lord do,' &c.

29. προείρηκεν : 'has foretold.' A second passage is quoted in corroboration of the preceding.

εἰ μὴ Κύριος κ.τ.λ.; quoted from the LXX of Is. i. 9, which

again seems adequately to represent the Hebrew. 'Even in the
O. T., that book from which you draw your hopes, it is stated that
Israel would be completely annihilated and forgotten but for
a small remnant which would preserve their seed and name.'

The Power and Rights of God as Creator.

St. Paul in this section (vv. 19-29) expands and strengthens
the previous argument. He had proved in vv. 14-18 the absolute
character of the Divine sovereignty from the O. T.; he now
proves the same from the fundamental relations of God to man
implied in that fact which all his antagonists must admit—that
God had created man. This he applies in an image which was
common in the O. T. and the Apocryphal writings, that of the
potter and the clay. God has created man, and, as far as the
question of 'right' and 'justice' goes, man cannot complain of
his lot. He would not exist but for the will of God, and whether
his lot be honourable or dishonourable, whether he be destined for
eternal glory or eternal destruction, he has no ground for speaking of injustice. The application to the case in point is very
clear. If the Jews are to be deprived of the Messianic salvation,
they have, looking at the question on purely abstract grounds,
no right or ground of complaint. Whether or no God be
arbitrary in His dealings with them does not matter: they must
submit, and that without murmuring.

This is clearly the argument. We cannot on the one hand
minimize the force of the words by limiting them to a purely
earthly destination: as Beyschlag, 'out of the material of the
human race which is at His disposal as it continues to come into
existence to stamp individuals with this or that historical destination,' implying that St. Paul is making no reference either to the
original creation of man or to his final destination, in both points
erroneously. St. Paul's argument cannot be thus limited. It is
entirely based on the assumption that God has created man, and
the use of the words εἰς δόξαν, εἰς ἀπώλειαν prove conclusively that
he is looking as much as he ever does to the final end and
destination of man. To limit them thus entirely deprives the
passage of any adequate meaning.

But on the other side it is equally necessary to see exactly how
much St. Paul does say, and how much he does not. He never
says, he carefully avoids saying, that God has created men for
reprobation. What his argument would bear is that, supposing
we isolate this point, the 'rights' of man against God or of God
against man, then, even if God had created man for reprobation,
man could have no grounds for complaint.

We must in fact remember—and it is quite impossible to under‐
stand St. Paul if we do not—that the three chapters ix-xi form
one very closely reasoned whole. Here more than anywhere else
in his writings, more clearly even than in i. 16—iii. 26, does St. Paul
show signs of a definite method. He raises each point separately,
argues it and then sets it aside. He deliberately isolates for a time
the aspect under discussion. So Mr. Gore (*op. cit.* p. 37): 'His
method may be called abstract or ideal : that is to say, he makes
abstraction of the particular aspect of a subject with which he is
immediately dealing, and—apparently indifferent to being misun‐
derstood—treats it in isolation; giving, perhaps, another aspect of
the same subject in equal abstraction in a different place.' He
isolates one side of his argument in one place, one in another,
and just for that very reason we must never use isolated texts.
We must not make deductions from one passage in his writings
separated from its contexts and without modifying it by other
passages presenting other aspects of the same questions. The
doctrinal deductions must be made at the end of chap. xi and not
of chap. ix.

St. Paul is gradually working out a sustained argument. He
has laid down the principle that God may choose and reject whom
He wills, that He may make men for one purpose or another just
as He wills, and if He will in quite an arbitrary manner. But it is
already pointed out that this is not His method. He has shown
long-suffering and forbearance. Some there were whom He had
created, that had become fitted for destruction—as will be shown
eventually, by their own act. These He has borne with—both
for their own sakes, to give them room for repentance, and be‐
cause they have been the means of exhibiting His mercy on those
whom He has prepared for His glory. The Apostle lays down
the lines of the argument he will follow in chap. xi.

The section concludes with a number of quotations from the
O. T., introduced somewhat irregularly so far as method and
arrangement go, to recall the fact that this Divine plan, which we
shall find eventually worked out more fully, had been foretold by
the O. T. Prophets.

(The argument of Rom. ix-xi is put for English readers in the
most accessible and clearest form by Mr. Gore in the paper often
quoted above in *Studia Biblica*, iii. 37, 'The argument of Romans
ix-xi.')

The Relation of St. Paul's Argument in chap. ix to the Book of Wisdom.

In a note at the end of the first chapter of the Romans the very marked
resemblance that exists between St. Paul's language there and certain

passages in the Book of Wisdom has been pointed out. Again in the ninth chapter the same resemblance meets us, and demands some slight treatment in this place. The passages referred to occur mostly in Wisdom xi, xii.

There is first of all similarity of subject. Wisdom x-xix form like Rom. ix-xi a sort of Philosophy of History. The writer devotes himself to exhibiting Wisdom as a power in the world, and throughout (influenced perhaps by associations connected with the place of his residence) contrasts the fortunes of the Israelites and Egyptians, just as St. Paul makes Moses and Pharaoh his two typical instances.

And this resemblance is continued in details.

The impossibility of resisting the Divine power is more than once dwelt on, and in language which has a very close resemblance with passages in the Romans.

Rom. ix. 19, 20 ἐρεῖς μοι οὖν, Τί ἔτι μέμφεται ; τῷ γὰρ βουλήματι αὐτοῦ τίς ἀνθέστηκε ; . . . μὴ ἐρεῖ τὸ πλάσμα τῷ πλάσαντι, Τί με ἐποίησας οὕτως ;	Wisd. xi. 21 καὶ κράτει βραχίονός σου τίς ἀντιστήσεται ; xii. 12 τίς γὰρ ἐρεῖ, Τί ἐποίησας ; ἢ τίς ἀντιστήσεται τῷ κρίματί σου ; τίς δὲ ἐγκαλέσει σοι κατὰ ἐθνῶν ἀπολωλότων, ἃ σὺ ἐποίησας ; ἢ τίς εἰς κατάστασίν σοι ἐλεύσεται ἔκδικος κατὰ ἀδίκων ἀνθρώπων ;

Both writers again lay great stress on the forbearance of God.

Rom. ix. 22, 23 εἰ δὲ θέλων ὁ Θεὸς ἐνδείξασθαι τὴν ὀργὴν καὶ γνωρίσαι τὸ δυνατὸν αὐτοῦ ἤνεγκεν ἐν πολλῇ μακροθυμίᾳ σκεύη ὀργῆς κατηρτισμένα εἰς ἀπώλειαν, καὶ ἵνα γνωρίσῃ τὸν πλοῦτον τῆς δόξης αὐτοῦ ἐπὶ σκεύη ἐλέους κ.τ.λ.	Wisd. xii. 10 κρίνων δὲ κατὰ βραχὺ ἐδίδους τόπον μετανοίας. xii. 20 εἰ γὰρ ἐχθροὺς παίδων σου καὶ ὀφειλομένους θανάτῳ μετὰ τοσαύτης ἐτιμώρησας προσοχῆς καὶ δεήσεως, δοὺς χρόνους καὶ τόπον δι' ὧν ἀπαλλαγῶσι τῆς κακίας, μετὰ πόσης ἀκριβείας ἔκρινας τοὺς υἱούς σου ;

So again we have the image of the potter used by both, although neither the context nor the purpose is quite similar.

Rom. ix. 21 ἢ οὐκ ἔχει ἐξουσίαν ὁ κεραμεὺς τοῦ πηλοῦ, ἐκ τοῦ αὐτοῦ φυράματος ποιῆσαι ὃ μὲν εἰς τιμὴν σκεῦος, ὃ δὲ εἰς ἀτιμίαν ;	Wisd. xv. 7 καὶ γὰρ κεραμεὺς ἁπαλὴν γῆν θλίβων ἐπίμοχθον πλάσσει πρὸς ὑπηρεσίαν ἡμῶν ἕκαστον· ἀλλ' ἐκ τοῦ αὐτοῦ πηλοῦ ἀνεπλάσατο τά τε τῶν καθαρῶν ἔργων δοῦλα σκεύη, τά τε ἐναντία, πάνθ' ὁμοίως· τούτων δὲ ἑτέρου τίς ἑκάστου ἐστὶν ἡ χρῆσις, κριτὴς ὁ πηλουργός.

The particular resemblance of special passages and of the general drift of the argument combined with similar evidence from other parts of the Epistle seems to suggest some definite literary obligation. But here the indebtedness ceases. The contrast is equally instructive. The writer of the Book of Wisdom uses broad principles without understanding their meaning, is often self-contradictory, and combines with ideas drawn from his Hellenic culture crude and inconsistent views. The problem is the distinction between the positions of Jews and Gentiles in the Divine economy. Occasionally we find wide universalist sentiments, but he always comes back to a strong nationalism. At one time he says (xi. 23-26) : ' But Thou hast mercy upon all . . . Thou lovest all the things that are, and abhorrest nothing which Thou hast made . . . Thou sparest all : for they are Thine, O Lord, Thou Lover of souls.' But shortly after we read (xii. 10) : ' Thou gavest them place for repentance, not being ignorant that their cogitation would never be changed.' We soon find in fact that the philosophy of the Book of Wisdom is strictly limited by the nationalist sympathies of the writer. The

Gentiles are to be punished by God for being enemies of His people and for their idolatry. Any forbearance has been only for a time and that largely for the moral instruction thus indirectly to be given to the Jews. The Jews have been punished,—but only slightly, and with the purpose of teaching them : the Gentiles for their idolatry deserve ' extreme damnation.'

If St. Paul learnt from the Book of Wisdom some expressions illustrating the Divine power, and a general aspect of the question : he obtained nothing further. His broad views and deep insight are his own. And it is interesting to contrast a Jew who has learnt many maxims which conflict with his nationalism but yet retains all his narrow sympathies, with the Christian Apostle full of broad sympathy and deep insight, who sees in human affairs a purpose of God for the benefit of the whole world being worked out.

A History of the Interpretation of Rom. ix. 6-29.

The difficulties of the ninth chapter of the Romans are so great that few will ever be satisfied that they have really understood it : at any rate an acquaintance with the history of exegesis upon it will make us hesitate to be too dogmatic about our own conclusions A survey of some of the more typical lines of comment (nothing more can be attempted) will be a fitting supplement to the general discussion given above on its meaning.

The earliest theologians who attempted to construct a system out of Gnostics St. Paul's writings were the Gnostics. They found the Epistle to the Romans, or to speak more correctly certain texts and ideas selected from the Epistle (such as Rom. v. 14 and viii. 19; cf. Hip. *Ref.* vii. 25) and generally misinterpreted, very congenial. And, as might naturally be expected, the doctrine of election rigidly interpreted harmonized with their own exclusive religious pretensions, and with the key-word of their system φύσις. We are not surprised therefore to learn that Rom. ix, especially ver. 14 sq., was one of their strongholds, nor do we require to be told how they interpreted it (see Origen *De Princ.* III. ii. 8, vol. xxi. p. 267, ed. Lomm. = *Philoc.* xxi. vol. xxv. p. 170; *Comm. in Rom. Praef.* vol. vi. p. 1 ; and Tert. *Adv. Marcion.* ii. 14).

The interest of the Gnostic system of interpretation is that it determined Origen the direction and purpose of Origen, who discusses the passage not only in his *Commentary*, written after 244 (vii. 15-18, vol. vii. pp. 160-180), but also in the third book of the *De Principiis*, written before 231 (*De Prin.* III. ii. 7-22, vol. xxi. pp. 265-303 = *Philoc.* xxi. vol. xxv. pp. 164-190), besides some few other passages. His exegesis is throughout a strenuous defence of freewill. Exegetically the most marked feature is that he puts vv. 14-19 into the mouth of an opponent of St. Paul, an interpretation which influenced subsequent patristic commentators. Throughout he states that God calls men because they are worthy, not that they are worthy because they are called ; and that they are worthy because they have made themselves so. Cf. *ad Rom.* vii. 17 (Lomm. vii. 175) *Ut enim Iacob esset vas ad honorem sanctificatum, et utile Domino, ad omne opus bonum paratum,* ANIMA EIUS EMENDAVERAT SEMET IPSAM : *et videns Deus puritatem eius, et potestatem habens ex eadem massa facere aliud vas ad honorem, aliud ad contumeliam, Iacob quidem, qui ut diximus emundaverat semet ipsum, fecit vas ad honorem, Esau* VERO, CUIUS ANIMAM NON ITA PURAM NEC ITA SIMPLICEM VIDIT, *ex eadem massa fecit vas ad contumeliam.* To the question that may be asked, how or when did they make themselves such, the answer is, ' In a state of pre-existence.' *De Princ.* II. ix. 7, Lomm. xxi. 225 *igitur sicut de Esau et Iacob diligentius perscrutatis scripturis invenitur, quia non est iniustitia apud Deum* . . . SI EX PRAECEDENTIS VIDELICET VITAE MERITIS *digne eum electum esse sentiamus a Deo, ita ut fratri praeponi mereretur.*

See also III. i. 21. Lomm. xxi. 300. The hardening of Pharaoh's heart he explains by the simile of rain. The rain is the same for all, but under its influence well-cultivated fields send forth good crops, ill-cultivated fields thistles, &c. (cf. Heb. vi. 7, 8). So it is a man's own soul which hardens itself by refusing to yield to the Divine grace. The simile of the potter he explains by comparing 2 Tim. ii. 20, 21. 'A soul which has not cleansed itself nor purged itself of its sins by penitence, becomes thereby a vessel for dishonour.' And God knowing the character of the souls He has to deal with, although He does not foreknow their future, makes use of them—as for example Pharaoh—to fulfil that part in history which is necessary for His purpose.

Influence of Origen.

Origen's interpretation of this passage, with the exception of his doctrine of pre-existence, had a very wide influence both in the East and West. In the West his interpretation is followed in the main by Jerome (*Epist.* 120 *ad Hedibiam de quaestionibus* 12, cap. 10, Migne xxii. 997), by Pelagius (Migne xxx. 687–691), and Sedulius Scotus (Migne ciii. 83–93). In the East, after its influence had prevailed for a century and a half, it became the starting-point of the Antiochene exegesis. Of this school Diodore is unfortunately represented to us only in isolated fragments; Theodore is strongly influenced by Origen; Chrysostom therefore may be taken as its best and most distinguished representative. His comment is contained in the XVIth homily on the Romans, written probably before his departure from Antioch, that is before the year 398.

Chrysostom.

Chrysostom is like Origen a strong defender of Freewill. As might be expected in a member of the Antiochene school, he interprets the passage in accordance with the purpose of St. Paul, i.e. to explain how it was the Jews had been rejected. He refers ver. 9 to those who have become true sons of God by Baptism. 'You see then that it is not the children of the flesh that are the children of God, but that even in nature itself the generation by means of Baptism from above was sketched out beforehand. And if you tell me of the womb, I have in return to tell you of the water.' On ver. 16 he explains that Jacob was called because he was worthy, and was known to be such by the Divine foreknowledge: ἡ κατ᾿ ἐκλογὴν πρόθεσις τοῦ Θεοῦ is explained as ἡ ἐκλογὴ ἡ κατὰ πρόθεσιν καὶ πρόγνωσιν γενομένη. On vv. 14–20 Chrysostom does not follow Origen, nor yet does he interpret the verses as expressing St. Paul's own mind; but he represents him in answer to the objection that in this case God would be unjust, as putting a number of hard cases and texts which his antagonist cannot answer and thus proving that man has no right to object to God's action, or accuse Him of injustice, since he cannot understand or follow Him. 'What the blessed Paul aimed at was to show by all that he said that only God knoweth who are worthy.' Verses 20, 21 are not introduced to take away Freewill, but to show up to what point we ought to obey God. For if he were here speaking of the will, God would be Himself the creator of good or evil, and men would be free from all responsibility in these matters, and St. Paul would be inconsistent with himself. What he does teach is that 'man should not contravene God, but yield to His incomprehensible wisdom.' On vv. 22–24 he says that Pharaoh has been fitted for destruction by his own act; that God has left undone nothing which should save him, while he himself had left undone nothing which would lead to his own destruction. Yet God had borne with him with great long-suffering, wishing to lead him to repentance. 'Whence comes it then that some are vessels of wrath, and some of mercy? Of their own free choice. God however being very good shows the same kindness to both.'

The commentaries of Chrysostom became supreme in the East, and very largely influenced all later Greek commentators, Theodoret (sec. v), Photius (sec. ix), Oecumenius (sec. x), Theophylact (sec. xi), Euthymius Zigabenus (sec. xii), &c.

The tradition of the Greek commentators is preserved in the Russian Church. Russian Modern Sclavonic theology presents an interesting subject for study, as it is comment derived directly from Chrysostom and John of Damascus, and has hardly aries. been illuminated or obscured by the strong, although often one-sided, influence of Augustine and Western Scholasticism. In the Commentary of Bishop Theophanes [*] on the Romans (he died in 1894) published at Moscow in 1890, we find these characteristics very clearly. Just as in Chrysostom we find the passage interpreted in accordance not with *à priori* theories as to Grace and Predestination, but with what was clearly St. Paul's purpose, the problem of the 'Unbelief of the Jews in the presence of Christianity.' And also as in Chrysostom we find vv. 11, 12 explained on the grounds of Foreknowledge, and Pharaoh's destruction ascribed to his own act. On ver. 18: 'The word "he hardeneth" must not be understood to mean that God by His power effected a hardening in the heart of the disobedient like Pharaoh, but that the disobedient in character, under the working of God's mercies, themselves, according to their evil character do not soften themselves, but more and more harden themselves in their obstinacy and disobedience.' So again on vv. 22, 23: 'God prepared the one to be vessels of mercy, the others fashioned themselves into vessels of wrath.' And the commentary on these verses concludes thus: 'Do not be troubled and do not admit of the thought that there is any injustice, or that the promise has failed; but on the contrary believe, that God in all his works is good and right, and rest yourselves in devotion to His wise and for us unsearchable destinations and divisions.' There is, in fact, a clear conception of the drift and purpose of St. Paul's argument, but a fear of one-sided predestination teaching makes a complete grasp of the whole of the Apostle's meaning impossible.

The commentary generally quoted under the name of Ambrosiaster has an Augustine interest as containing probably the earliest correct exposition of vv. 14-19. But it is more convenient to pass at once to St. Augustine. His exposition of this passage was to all appearance quite independent of that of any of his predecessors.

The most complete exposition of the ninth chapter of Romans is found in the treatise *Ad Simplicianum*, i. qu. 2, written about the year 397, and all the leading points in this exposition are repeated in his last work, the *Opus imperfectum contra Iulianum*, i. 141. The main characteristics of the commentary are that (1) he ascribes vv. 14-19 to St. Paul himself, and considers that they represent his own opinions, thus correcting the false exegesis of Origen and Chrysostom, and (2) that he takes a view of the passage exactly opposite to that of the latter. The purpose of St. Paul is to prove that works do not precede grace but follow it, and that Election is not based on foreknowledge, for if it were based on foreknowledge then it would imply merit. *Ad Simplic.* i. qu. 2, § 2 *Ut scilicet non se quisque arbitretur ideo percepisse gratiam, quia bene operatus est; sed bene operari non posse, nisi per fidem perceperit gratiam* ... § 3 *Prima est igitur gratia, secunda opera bona.* The instance of Jacob and Esau proves that the gift of the Divine grace is quite gratuitous and independent of human merit—that grace in fact precedes faith. § 7 *Nemo enim credit qui non vocatur* ... *Ergo ante omne meritum est gratia.* Even the will to be saved must come from God. *Nisi eius vocatione non volumus.* And again: § 10 *Noluit ergo Esau et non cucurrit : sed et si voluisset et cucurrisset, Dei adiutorio pervenisset, qui ei etiam velle et currere vocando praestaret, nisi vocationis contemptu reprobus fieret.* It is then shown that God can call whom He will, if He only wills to make His grace congruous. Why then does He not do so? The answer lies in the incomprehensibility of the Divine justice. The question whom He will pity and whom He will not

* For a translation of portions of this Commentary, we are indebted to the kindness of Mr. W. J. Birkbeck, of Magdalen College, Oxford.

depends upon the hidden justice of God which no human standard can measure.
§ 16 *Sit igitur hoc fixum atque immobile in mente sobria pietate atque stabili
in fide, quod nulla est iniquitas apud Deum: atque ita tenacissime firmissi-
meque credatur, id ipsum quod Deus cuius vult miseretur et quem vult obdurat,
hoc est, cuius vult miseretur, et cuius non vult non miseretur, esse alicuius
occultae atque ab humano modulo investigabilis aequitatis*: and so again, *aequi-
tate occultissima et ab humanis sensibus remotissima iudicat.* God is always
just. His mercy cannot be understood. Those whom He calls, He calls out of
pity; those whom He does not, He refuses to call out of justice. It is not merit
or necessity or fortune, but the depths of the wisdom and knowledge of God
which distinguishes vessels of wrath from vessels of mercy. And so it is for
the sake of the vessels of mercy that He postpones the punishment of the
vessels of anger. They are the instruments of the safety of others whom
God pities.

Enough has been said to show the lines of St. Augustine's interpretation.
Although from time to time there might be controversies about his views on
Grace, and there might be a tendency to modify some of the harder sides of
his system, yet his exegesis of this passage, as compared with that of Origen
or Chrysostom, became supreme in the West. It influenced first the exegesis
and doctrine of the Schoolmen, and then that of the Reformation and of Calvin.

For the middle ages it may be sufficient to take Abelard (1079-1142) and
Thomas Aquinas (1227-1274). Both were largely influenced by Augustine;
but whereas in the case of Abelard the influence was only indirect, in
Aquinas we have the clearest and most perfect example of the Augustinian
exposition.

Abelard.

Abelard (Migne clxxviii. 911) makes a somewhat strange division of the
Epistle, attaching the exposition of ix. 1-5 to the end of chap. viii. He
begins his fourth book with ix. 6. In vv. 6-13 he sees a vindication of the
freedom of the Divine will in conferring grace, but only in relation to Jacob.
'That the election of Jacob,' he says, 'that is the predestination, may remain
unmoved.' The choice depends solely on the Divine grace. Verses 14-19 he
explains as the objection of an opponent, to which St. Paul gives an answer,
ver. 20, 'Who art thou?' The answer is a rebuke to the man who would
accuse God of iniquity. God may do what He will with those whom He has
created: *imo multo potius Deo licere quocunque modo voluerit creaturam suam
tractare atque disponere, qui obnoxius nullo tenetur debito, antequam quid-
quam illa promereatur.* Men have no more right to complain than the
animals of their position. There is no injustice with God. He does more
for mankind by the impiety of Judas than by the piety of Peter. *Quis enim
fidelium nesciat, quam optime usus sit summa illa impietate Iudae, cuius
exsecrabili perditione totius humani generis redemptionem est operatus.*
Then he argues at some length the question why man should not complain,
if he is not called as others are called to glory; and somewhat inconsistently
he finds the solution in perseverance. God calls all, He gives grace to all,
but some have the energy to follow the calling, while others are slothful
and negligent. *Sic et Deo nobis quotidie regnum coelorum offerente, alius
regni ipsius desiderio accensus in bonis perseverat operibus, alius in sua
torpescit ignavia.* On vv. 22, 23 he says God bore with the wickedness of
Pharaoh both to give him an opportunity to repent, and that He might use
his crimes for the common good of mankind.

Aquinas.

In contrast with the somewhat hesitating and inconsistent character of
Abelard's exposition, Aquinas stands out as one of the best and clearest commentaries written from the Augustinian standpoint. The modern reader must
learn to accustom himself to the thoroughness with which each point is
discussed, and the minuteness of the sub-divisions, but from few exponents will
he gain so much insight into the philosophical questions discussed, or the
logical difficulties the solution of which is attempted.

The purpose of the section is, he says, to discuss the origin of Grace, to do which the Apostle makes use of the opportunity afforded by the difficulties implied in the rejection of the Jews. *Apostolus supra necessitatem et virtutem gratiae demonstravit* : *hic incipit agere de origine gratiae, utrum ex sola Dei electione detur, aut detur ex meritis praecedentium operum, occasione accepta ex eo, quod Iudaei qui videbantur divinis obsequiis mancipati, exciderant a gratia.* In vv. 6–13 the errors of the Jews, of the Manichaeans (who believed that human actions were controlled by the stars which appeared at the time of their birth), of the Pelagians, of Origen (the pre-existence of souls) are condemned, and it is shown that God chose men, not because they were holy, but that they might be holy: *unum alteri praeeligit, non quia sanctus erat, sed ut sanctus esset.* In vv. 14–18 St. Paul shows from Scripture that there is no injustice either in Predestination or in Reprobation. God has predestined the just to life for merits which He has Himself conferred on them, the wicked to destruction for sins which come from themselves. *Deus proposuit se puniturum malos propter peccata, quae a se ipsis habent non a Deo. Iustos autem proposuit se praemiaturum propter merita quae a se ipsis non habent.* All lies in the will of God ; we notice indeed that among other erroneous opinions one, that of *merita consequentia gratiam,*—the view apparently of Abelard—is refuted. There is no injustice. ' Distributive justice has a place in cases of debt, but not in cases of pity.' If a man relieves one beggar, but not another, he is not unjust ; he is kind-hearted towards one. Similarly if a man forgives only one of two offenders, he is not unjust ; he is merciful towards one, just towards the other.

In the instance of Pharaoh two readings are discussed, *servavi* and *excitavi.* If the first be taken it shows that, as the wicked are worthy of immediate destruction, if they are saved it is owing to the clemency of God ; if the second, God does not cause wickedness, except by permitting it ; He allows the wicked by His good judgement to fall into sin on account of the iniquity they have committed. *Quod quidem non est intelligendum hoc modo quod Deus in homine causat malitiam, sed est intelligendum permissive, quia scilicet in iusto suo iudicio permittit aliquos ruere in peccatum propter praecedentes iniquitates. Deus malitiam ordinat non causat.* In vv. 19–24 he says there are two questions. (1) Why, speaking generally, should He choose some men and not choose others ? (2) Why should He choose this or that man and not someone else ? The second of these is treated in vv. 19–21 ; to it there is no answer but the righteous will of God. No man can complain of being unjustly treated, for all are deserving of punishment. The answer to the first is contained in vv. 22–24. In order to exhibit both His justice and His mercy, there must be some towards whom He shows His justice, some towards whom He can show His mercy. The former are those who are naturally fitted for eternal damnation : God has done nothing but allow them to do what they wish. *Vasa apta in interitum* he defines as *in se habentia aptitudinem ad aeternam damnationem* ; and adds *Hoc autem solus Deus circa eos agit, quod eos permittit agere quae concupiscunt.* He has in fact borne with them both for their own sakes, and for the sake of those whom He uses to exhibit the abundance of His goodness—a goodness which could not be apparent unless it could be contrasted with the fate of the condemned. *Signanter autem dicit [ut ostenderet divitias gloriae suae] quia ipsa condernatio et reprobatio malorum quae est secundum Dei iustitiam, manifestat et commendat sanctorum gloriam qui ab ipsa tali miseria liberantur.*

The antithesis which was represented among patristic commentators by Augustine and Chrysostom was exaggerated at the Reformation by Calvin and Arminius. Each saw only his own side. Calvin followed Augustine, and exaggerated his harshest teaching : Arminius showed a subtle power of finding Freewill even in the most unlikely places.

The object of St. Paul, according to Calvin, is to maintain the freedom of

Calvin. the Divine election. This is absolutely gratuitous on God's part, and quite independent of man. In the salvation of the just there is nothing above God's goodness, in the punishment of the wicked there is nothing above His severity: the one He predestinates to salvation, the other to eternal damnation. This determination is quite independent of foreknowledge, for there can be nothing in man's fallen nature which can make God show kindness to him. The predestination of Pharaoh to destruction is dependent on a just but secret counsel of God: the word 'to harden' must be taken not only *permissive*, but as signifying the action of the Divine wrath. The ruin of the wicked is described not as foreseen, but as ordained by His will and counsel. It was not merely foreknown, but, as Solomon says, the wicked were created that they might perish. There is no means of telling the principle by which one is taken and another rejected; it lies in the secret counsels of God. None deserve to be accepted. The wrath of God against Pharaoh was postponed that others might be terrified by the horrible judgement, that God's power might be displayed, and His mercy towards the elect made more clear. As God is especially said to prepare the vessels of glory for glory, it follows that the preparation of the vessels of wrath equally comes from Him; otherwise the Apostle would have said that they had prepared themselves for destruction. Before they were created their fate was assigned to them. They were created for destruction.

Arminius. Arminius represents absolute antagonism on every point to these views. The purpose of the chapter is, he says, the same as that of the Epistle, looked at from a special point of view. While the aim of the Epistle is to prove 'Justification by Faith,' in this chapter St. Paul defends his argument against Jews who had urged: 'It overthrows the promises of God, therefore it is not true.' By the words addressed to Rebecca He signified that He had from eternity resolved not to admit to His privileges all the children of Abraham, but those only whom He should select in accordance with the plan He had laid down. This plan was to extend His mercy to those who had faith in Him when He called and who believed on Christ, not to those who sought salvation by works. The passage that follows (ver. 14 ff.) shows that God has decided to give His mercy in His own way and on His own plan, that is to give it not to him who runs, to him that is who strives after it by works, but to him who seeks it in the way that He has appointed. And this is perfectly just, because He has Himself announced this as His method. Then the image of the potter and the clay is introduced to prove, not the absolute sovereignty of God, but His right to do what He will, that is to name His own conditions. He has created man to become something better than he was made. God has made man a vessel: man it is who makes himself a bad vessel. God decrees on certain conditions to make men vessels of glory or vessels of wrath according as they do or do not fulfil these conditions. The condition is Justification by Faith.

The systems of Arminius and Calvin were for the most part supreme during the seventeenth and eighteenth centuries in the exegesis of this chapter, although there were from time to time signs of historical methods of interpretation. Hammond for example, the English divine of the seventeenth century, in his paraphrase adopts methods very much beyond those of his time. But gradually at the beginning of the present century the defects or inadequacy of both views became apparent. It was quite clear that as against Arminius Calvin's interpretation of chap. ix was correct, that St. Paul's object in it was not to prove or defend justification by faith, but to discuss the question behind it, why it was that some had obtained justification by faith and others had not. But equally clear was it that Calvin's interpretation, or rather much of what he had read into his interpretation, was inconsistent with chap. x, and the language which St. Paul habitually uses elsewhere. This apparent inconsistency then must be recognized. How must it be treated? Various answers have been given. Fritzsche asserts *Fritzsche* that St. Paul is carried away by his argument and unconsciously contradicts himself. 'It is evident that what St. Paul writes is not only inconsistent with itself but absolutely contradictory.' If the Jews, it is asserted in chap. ix, were first chosen and then rejected, it was the malignity of God and not their own perversity which caused their fall. If God had decreed their fall for a time (chap. xi), they could not be blamed if they had fallen; and yet in chap. x they are blamed. *Multis saepe accidit ut amicum fortunae fulmine percussum erecturi studio consolandi argumentis cupide uterentur neque ab omni parte firmis et quorum unum cum altero parum consisteret. Et melius sibi Paulus consensisset, si Aristotelis non Gamalielis alumnus fuisset.*

Meyer admits the discrepancy but explains it differently. 'As often as we *Meyer.* treat only one of the two truths, *God is absolutely free and all-sufficient,* and *man has moral freedom and is in virtue of his proper self-determination and responsibility a liberum agens, the author of his salvation or perdition,* and carry it out in a consistent theory and therefore in a one-sided method, we are compelled to speak in such a manner that the other truth appears to be annulled.' ... 'The Apostle has here wholly taken his position on the absolute standpoint of the theory of our dependence upon God, and that with all the boldness of clear consistency.' ... 'He allows the claims of both modes of consideration to stand side by side, just as they exist side by side within the limits of human thought.' According to Meyer in fact the two points of view are irreconcileable in thought, and St. Paul recognizing this does not attempt to reconcile them.

It would be impossible to enumerate all the different varieties of opinion in the views of modern scholars. One more specimen will be sufficient. The solution offered by Beyschlag. He maintains that all interpretations are *Beyschlag* wrong which consider that St. Paul is concerned with anything either before or after this life. It is no eternal decree of God, nor is it the future destiny of mankind that he is dealing with. It is merely their position in history and in the world. Why has he chosen one race (the Jews) for one purpose, another race (the Egyptians) for another? He is dealing with nations not individuals, with temporal not spiritual privileges.

The above sketch will present the main lines of interpretation of these verses, and will serve as a supplement to the explanation which has been given above. We must express our obligations in compiling it to Weber (Dr. Valentin), *Kritische Geschichte der Exegese des 9. Kapitels resp. der Verse 14–23 des Römerbriefes, bis auf Chrysostomus und Augustinus einschiesslich,* and to Beyschlag (Dr. Willibald), *Die paulinische Theodicee, Römer IX–XI,* who have materially lightened the labour incurred.

ISRAEL ITSELF TO BLAME FOR ITS REJECTION.

IX. 30–X. 13. *The reason that God has rejected Israel is that, though they sought righteousness, they sought it in their own way by means of works, not in God's way through faith. Hence when the Messiah came they stumbled as had been foretold* (vv. 30–33). *They refused to give up their own method, that of Law, although Law had come to an end in Christ* (x. 1–4), *and this in spite of the fact that the old* *system was difficult if not impossible* (ver. 5), *while the new system was easy and within the reach of all* (vv. 6–10), *indeed universal in its scope* (vv. 11–13).

IX. [30] What then is the position of the argument so far? One fact is clear. A number of Gentiles who did not profess to be in pursuit of righteousness have unexpectedly come upon it; a righteousness however of which the characteristic is that it is not earned by their own efforts but is the product of faith in a power outside them. [31] Israel on the other hand, the chosen people of God, although making strenuous efforts after a rule of moral and religious life that would win for them righteousness, have not succeeded in attaining to the accomplishment of such a rule. [32] How has this come about? Because they sought it in their own way, not in God's way. They did not seek it by faith, but their aim was to pursue it by a rigid performance of works. [33] And hence that happened to them which the Prophet Isaiah foretold. He spoke (xxviii. 16) of a rock which the Lord would lay in Zion and foretold that if a man put his trust in it, he would never have cause to be ashamed. But elsewhere (viii. 14) he calls it 'a stone of stumbling and a rock of offence,' implying that those who have not this faith will consider it a stumbling-block in their way. This rock is, as you have always been told, the Messiah. The Messiah has come; and the Jews through want of faith have regarded as a cause of offence that which is the corner stone of the whole building.

X. [1] Let me pause for a moment, brethren. It is a serious accusation that I am bringing against my fellow-countrymen. But I repeat that I do it from no feeling of resentment. How great is my heart's good will for them! How earnest my prayer to God for their salvation! [2] For indeed as a fellow-countryman, as one who was once as they are, I can testify that they are full of zeal for God. That is not the point in which they have failed; it is that they have not guided their zeal by that true knowledge which is the result of genuine spiritual insight. [3] Righteousness they strove after, but there were two ways of attaining to it. The one was God's method: of that they remained ignorant. The other was their own method: to this they clung blindly and wilfully. They refused to submit to God's plan of salvation.

⁴Their own method was based on a rigid performance of legal enactments. But that has been ended in Christ. Now there is a new and a better way, one which has two characteristics; it is based on the principle of faith, and it is universal and for all men alike. ⁵(1) It is based on the principle of faith. Hence it is that while the old method was difficult, if not impossible, the new is easy and open to all. The old method righteousness by law, that is by the exact performance of legal rules, is aptly described by Moses when he says (Lev. xviii. 5), 'the man who does these things shall live,' i. e. Life in all its fulness here and hereafter was to be gained by undeviating strictness of conduct; and that condition we have seen (i. 18–iii. 20) was impossible of fulfilment. ⁶But listen to the proclamation which righteousness by faith makes to mankind. It speaks in well-known words which have become through it more real. ' There is no need for you to say, Who will go up into heaven ? Heaven has come to you; Christ has come down and lived among men. ⁷There is no need to search the hidden places of the deep. Christ has risen. There is no need therefore to seek the living among the dead. You are offered something which does not require hard striving or painful labour. ⁸The word of God is very nigh thee, in thy heart and in thy mouth.' And that word of God is the message of faith, the Gospel which proclaims 'believe and thou shalt be saved'; and this Gospel we preach throughout the world. ⁹All it says to you is : ' With thy mouth thou must confess Jesus as sovereign Lord, with thy heart thou must believe that God raised Him from the dead.' ¹⁰For that change of heart which we call faith, brings righteousness, and the path of salvation is entered by the confession of belief in Christ which a man makes at his baptism.

¹¹(2) This is corroborated by what the Prophet Isaiah said (xxviii. 16) in words quoted above (ix. 33), the full meaning of which we now understand : 'Everyone that believeth in Him (i. e. the Messiah) shall not be ashamed.' Moreover this word of his, ' everyone,' introduces the second characteristic of the new method. It is universal. ¹²And that means that it applies equally to Jew and to Greek. We have shown that the new covenant is open for Greeks as well as Jews; it is also true to say that the conditions demanded are the same for Jew as for Greek. The Jew cannot

keep to his old methods; he must accept the new. And this must be so, because there is for all men alike one Redeemer, who gives the wealth of His salvation to all those whoever they may be who call on His name. [13] And so the prophet Joel, foretelling the times of the foundation of the Messianic kingdom, says (ii. 32) 'Everyone that shall call on the name of the Lord (i. e. of the Messiah) shall be saved.' When the last days come, in the times of storm and anguish, it is the worshippers of the Messiah, those who are enrolled as His servants and call on His Name, who will find a strong salvation.

IX. 30-X. 21. St. Paul now passes to another aspect of the subject he is discussing. He has considered the rejection of Israel from the point of view of the Divine justice and power, he is now to approach it from the side of human responsibility. The concluding verses of the ninth chapter and the whole of the tenth are devoted to proving the guilt of Israel. It is first sketched out in ix. 30–33. Israel have sought righteousness in the wrong way, in that they have rejected the Messiah. Then St. Paul, overwhelmed with the sadness of the subject, pauses for a moment (x. 1, 2) to emphasize his grief. He returns to the discussion by pointing out that they have adhered to their own method instead of accepting God's method (vv. 2, 3). And this in spite of several circumstances; (1) that the old method has been done away with in Christ (ver. 4); (2) that while the old method was hard and difficult the new is easy and within the reach of all (vv. 5–10); (3) that the new method is clearly universal and intended for all alike (vv. 11–13). At ver. 14 he passes to another aspect of the question: it might still be asked: Had they full opportunities of knowing? In vv. 14–21 it is shown that both through the full and universal preaching of the Gospel, and through their own Prophets, they have had every opportunity given them.

30. τί οὖν ἐροῦμεν; The οὖν, as is almost always the case in St. Paul, sums up the results of the previous paragraph. What then is the conclusion of this discussion? 'It is not that God's promise has failed, but that while Gentiles have obtained "righteousness," the Jews, though they strove for it, have failed.' This summary of the result so far arrived at leads to the question being asked; Why is it so? And that introduces the second point in St. Paul's discussion—the guilt of the Jews.

ὅτι ἔθνη κ.τ.λ. There are two constructions possible for these words. 1. The sentence ὅτι ... τὴν ἐκ πίστεως may contain the answer to the question asked in τί οὖν ἐροῦμεν; This interpretation is probably right. The difficulty, however, is that nowhere else in this Epistle, where St. Paul uses the expression τί οὖν ἐροῦμεν, does he give it an immediate answer. He follows it by a second question (as in ix. 14); and this is not a mere accident. It is a result of the sense of deliberation contained in the previous words with which a second question rather than a definite statement seems to harmonize. 2. The alternative rendering would be to take the words ὅτι . . . ἔφθασεν, as such a second question. 'What shall we say then? Shall we say that, while Gentiles who did not seek righteousness have obtained it, Israel has not attained to it?' The answer to this question then would be a positive one, not given directly but implied in the further one διατί; 'Yes, but why?'—The difficulty in this construction, which must tell against it, is the awkwardness of the appended sentence δικαιοσύνην δὲ τὴν ἐκ πίστεως. Lipsius' suggestion that ὅτι = 'because' is quite impossible.

ἔθνη: 'heathen,' not 'the heathen'; some, not all: *nam nonnulli pagani fidem tum Christo adiunxerant, τὸ πλήρωμα τῶν ἐθνῶν ad Christi sacra nondum accesserat.* Fri.

διώκοντα . . . κατέλαβε: 'correlative terms for pursuing and overtaking' (Field, *Otium Norvicense,* iii. p. 96). The metaphor as in τρέχοντος (ver. 16) is taken from the racecourse, and probably the words were used without the original meaning being lost sight of: cf. 1 Cor. ix. 24. The two words are coupled together Exod. xv. 9, Ecclus. xi. 10; xxvii. 8; Phil. iii. 12; Herod. ii. 30; Lucian, *Hermot.* 77. διώκειν is a characteristic Pauline word occurring in letters of all periods: 1 Thess. (1), 1 Cor. (1), Rom. (4), Phil. (2), 1 Tim. (1), 2 Tim. (1).

δικαιοσύνην δέ limits and explains the previous use of the word. 'But remember, (and this will explain any difficulty that you may have), that it was ἐκ πίστεως': cf. iii. 22 δικαιοσύνη δὲ Θεοῦ: 1 Cor. ii. 6 σοφίαν δὲ λαλοῦμεν ἐν τοῖς τελείοις· σοφίαν δὲ οὐ τοῦ αἰῶνος τούτου.

Some small variations of reading may be just noticed. In ver. 31 the second δικαιοσύνης after εἰς νόμον of the TR. is omitted by decisive authority, as also is νόμου (after ἔργων) in ver. 32, and γάρ after προσέκοψαν. In ver. 33 πᾶς read by the TR. has crept in from x. 11, and Western MSS. read οὐ μὴ καταισχυνθῇ to harmonize with the LXX.

31. Ἰσραὴλ δὲ κ.τ.λ. These words contain the real difficulty of the statement, of which alone an explanation is necessary, and is given. 'In spite of the fact that some Gentiles even without seeking it have attained righteousness, Israel has failed.'

νόμον δικαιοσύνης: 'a rule of life which would produce righteousness': cf. iii. 27 νόμος πίστεως: vii. 21.

οὐκ ἔφθασε: 'did not attain it'; they are represented as continually pursuing after something, the accomplishment of which as continually escapes them. All idea of anticipation has been lost in φθάνω in later Greek, cf. Phil. iii. 16; Dan. iv. 19 (Theod.) ἔφθασεν εἰς τὸν οὐρανόν.

32. ὅτι οὐκ ἐκ πίστεως . . . προσέκοψαν. Two constructions are possible for these words. (1) We may put a comma at ἔργων and supply διώκοντες. Then the passage will run: ' Why did they not attain it? because pursuing after it not by faith but by works they stumbled,' &c. ; or (2) we may put a full stop at ἔργων and supply ἐδίωξαν. ' Why did they not attain it? because they pursued after it not by faith but by works, they stumbled,' &c. The sentence has more emphasis if taken in this way, and the grammatical construction is on the whole easier.

ἀλλ' ὡς ἐξ ἔργων. The ὡς introduces a subjective idea. St. Paul wishes to guard himself from asserting definitely that ἐξ ἔργων was a method by which νόμον δικαιοσύνης might be pursued. He therefore represents it as an idea of the Jews, as a way by which they thought they could gain it. So in 2 Cor. ii. 17 ἀλλ' ὡς ἐξ εἰλικρινείας represents the purpose and aim of the Apostle; 2 Cor. xi. 17 ὃ λαλῶ, οὐ κατὰ Κύριον λαλῶ, ἀλλ' ὡς ἐν ἀφροσύνῃ represents an aspect from which his words may be regarded; Philem. 14 ἵνα μὴ ὡς κατὰ ἀνάγκην τὸ ἀγαθόν σου ᾖ ἀλλὰ κατὰ ἑκούσιον: ' even the appearance of constraint must be avoided' (cf. Lightfoot, ad loc.). The ὡς gives a subjective idea to the phrase with which it is placed, but the exact force must be determined by the context.

προσέκοψαν: προσκόπτειν τινί means not 'to stumble over by inadvertence,' but ' to be annoyed with,' ' show irritation at.' The Jews, in that the cross was to them a σκάνδαλον, had stumbled over Christ, shown themselves irritated and annoyed, and expressed their indignation, see Grm. Thayer, sub voc.

τῷ λίθῳ τοῦ προσκόμματος : ' a stone which causes men to stumble.' Taken from the LXX of Is. viii. 14. The stone at which the Jewish nation has stumbled, which has been to them a cause of offence, is the Christ, who has come in a way, which, owing to their want of faith, has prevented them from recognizing or accepting Him, cf. 1 Pet. ii. 8.

33. ἰδού, τίθημι ἐν Σιὼν κ.τ.λ. The quotation is taken from the LXX of Is. xxviii. 16, fused with words from Is. viii. 14. The latter part of the verse is quoted again x. 11, and the whole in 1 Pet. ii. 6.

A comparison of the different variations is interesting. (1) The LXX reads ἰδοὺ ἐγὼ ἐμβάλλω εἰς τὰ θεμέλια Σιών. In both the passages in the N.T. the words are ἰδοὺ τίθημι ἐν Σιών. (2) For the LXX λίθον πολυτελῆ ἐκλεκτὸν ἀκρογωνιαῖον ἔντιμον, St. Peter reads ἀκρογωνιαῖον ἐκλεκτὸν ἔντιμον: while St. Paul substitutes λίθον προσκόμματος καὶ πέτραν σκανδάλου taken from Is. viii. 14 καὶ οὐχ ὡς λίθου προσκόμματι συναντήσεσθε οὐδὲ ὡς πέτρας πτώματι. Here St. Peter ii. 8 agrees with St. Paul in writing πέτρα σκανδάλου ‍οι πέτρας πτώματι. (3) The LXX proceeds εἰς τὰ θεμέλια αὐτῆς, which both

St. Peter and St. Paul omit. (4) The LXX proceeds καὶ ὁ πιστεύων οὐ μὴ
καταισχυνθῇ. Both St. Peter and St. Paul bring out the personal reference
by inserting ἐπ' αὐτῷ, while St. Paul reads καταισχυνθήσεται and in x. 11
adds πᾶς.

ἐπ' αὐτῷ. Personal, of the Messiah, 'He that believeth on Him
shall not be ashamed.' St. Paul inserts the words, both here and in
x. 11, to emphasize the personal reference. If the reference were
impersonal, the feminine would be required to agree with the
nearest word πέτρα.

καταισχυνθήσεται. Either an incorrect translation of the Hebrew,
or based on a different reading. The RV. of Isaiah reads ' shall
not make haste.'

In the O. T. neither of these passages has any direct Messianic
reference. In both Jehovah is the rock founded on Zion. In
Is. viii. 14 He is represented as a ' stumbling-block' to the
unbeliever ; in Is. xxviii. 16 He is the strength of those that believe
in Him. But from the very beginning the word λίθος was applied
to Christ, primarily with reference to Ps. cxviii. 22 'the Stone
which the builders rejected' (Matt. xxi. 42 ; Mark xii. 10 ; Luke
xx. 17; Acts iv. 11 by St. Peter). The other passages in which
the word λίθος was used in the LXX came to be applied as here,
and in Eph. ii. 20 ἀκρογωνιαίου is used almost as a proper name.
By the time of Justin Martyr λίθος is used almost as a name of the
Christ : ἔστω καὶ ταῦτα οὕτως ἔχοντα ὡς λέγεις, καὶ ὅτι παθητὸς Χριστὸς
προεφητεύθη μέλλειν εἶναι καὶ λίθος κέκληται (Dial. 36. p. 122 C. ed.
Otto) : ὁ γὰρ Χριστὸς βασιλεὺς καὶ ἱερεὺς καὶ θεὸς καὶ κύριος καὶ ἄγγελος
καὶ ἄνθρωπος καὶ ἀρχιστράτηγος καὶ λίθος (ib. 34. p. 112 D.) These
quotations seem to imply that λίθος was a name for the Messiah
among the Jews, and that Justin wishes to prove that Christ fulfils
that title, and this seems to be corroborated by quotations from
Jewish writings, not only in later books but even earlier. In Is.
viii. 14, Sanhedrin 38. 1 Filius Davidis non venit donec duae
domus patrum ex Israele deficiant, quae sunt Aechmalotarcha Baby-
lonicus et princeps terrae Israeliticae q. d. Et erit in Sanctuarium
et in lapidem percussionis et petram offensionis duabus domibus
Israel. Is. xxviii. 16 is paraphrased by the Targum Jonathan,
Ecce ego constituam in Sion regem, regem fortem, potentem et
terribilem ; corroborabo eum et confortabo eum dicit Propheta.
Iusti autem qui crediderint haec cum venerit tribulatio non com-
movebuntur, and some apparently read regem Messias regem
potentem. Ps. cxviii. 22 is paraphrased by the same Targum,
Puerum despexerunt aedificatores, qui fuit inter filios Israel et
meruit constitui rex et dominator. For these and other reff. see
Schoettgen, ii. 160, 606.

A comparison of Romans and 1 Peter shows that both Apostles
agree in quoting the same passages together, and both have

a number of common variants from the normal text of the LXX. This may have arisen from St. Peter's acquaintance with the Romans; but another hypothesis may be suggested, which will perhaps account for the facts more naturally. We know that to prove from the Scriptures that Jesus was the Christ, was the constant practice of the early Christians. Is it not possible that even as early as this there may have been collections of O. T. texts used for controversial purposes arranged according to their subjects, as were the later *Testimonia* of Cyprian, where one of the chapters is headed: *Quod idem et lapis dictus sit (Test.* ii. 16)? See on ix. 25, 26 *supra.*

X. 1. There is no break in the argument between this chapter and vv. 30–33 of chap. ix; but before expanding this part of the subject, the Apostle pauses for a moment, impelled by his own strong feelings and the deep tragedy of his countryman's rejection, to express his sorrow and affection.

Marcion admitted into his text ver. 2–4, which he was able to use as a proof text of his fundamental doctrine that the Jews had been ignorant of the 'higher God.' The whole or almost the whole passage which follows x. 5–xi. 32, he appears to have omitted, Zahn, p. 518. Tert. *Adv. Marc.* v. 13.

ἀδελφοί. The position increases the emphasis of a word always used by the Apostle when he wishes to be specially emphatic. The thought of the Christian brotherhood intensifies the contrast with the Israelites who are excluded.

μέν: without a corresponding δέ. The logical antithesis is given in ver. 3.

εὐδοκία: 'good will,' 'good pleasure,' not 'desire,' which the word never means.

The word εὐδοκία means 'good pleasure' either (1) in relation to oneself when it comes to mean 'contentment,' Ecclus. xxix. 23 ἐπὶ μικρῷ καὶ μεγάλῳ εὐδοκίαν ἔχε: ib. xxxv (xxxii). 14 οἱ ὀρθρίζοντες εὑρήσουσι εὐδοκίαν: 2 Thess. i. 11 καὶ πληρώσῃ πᾶσαν εὐδοκίαν ἀγαθωσύνης καὶ ἔργον πίστεως ἐν δυνάμει: *Ps. Sol.* xvi. 12: or (2) in relation to others, 'good will,' ' benevolence,' Ecclus. ix. 12 μὴ εὐδοκήσῃς ἐν εὐδοκίᾳ ἀσεβῶν: Phil. i. 15 τινὲς μὲν διὰ φθόνον καὶ ἔριν, τινὲς δὲ καὶ δι' εὐδοκίαν τὸν Χριστὸν κηρύσσουσιν: (3) in this sense it came to be used almost technically of the good will of God to man, Eph. i. 5 κατὰ τὴν εὐδοκίαν τοῦ θελήματος αὐτοῦ: i. 9 κατὰ τὴν εὐδοκίαν αὐτοῦ: *Ps. Sol.* viii. 39.

The above interpretation of the word is different from that taken by Fritzsche (*ad loc.*), Lft. (ad Phil. i. 15), Grm. Thayer, *Lex.* (s. v.), Philippi and Tholuck (*ad loc.*). The word seems never to be used unqualified to mean ' desire '; the instance quoted by Lft. does not support it.

ἡ δέησις: *non orasset Paulus si absolute reprobati essent.* Beng. εἰς σωτηρίαν = ἵνα σωθῶσι; cf. ver. 4 εἰς δικαιοσύνην and i. 5 εἰς ὑπακοὴν πίστεως.

The additions ἡ before πρὸς τὸν Θεόν and ἐστιν before εἰς σωτηρίαν in the TR. are grammatical explanations. The reading τοῦ Ἰσραήλ for αὐτῶν may have been merely an explanatory gloss, or may have arisen through the verse being the beginning of a lesson in church services.

2. μαρτυρῶ γάρ. This gives the reason for St. Paul's grief.
He had been a Jew περισσοτέρως ζηλωτὴς ὑπάρχων (Gal. i. 14; cf.
Acts xxii. 3) and hence he knew only too well the extent both of
their zeal and of their ignorance.

ζῆλον Θεοῦ. Obj. genitive : ' zeal for God ' (not as in 2 Cor.
xi. 2). An O. T. expression : Judith. ix. 4 ἐζήλωσαν τὸν ζῆλόν σου :
Ps. lxviii [lxix]; cxviii [cxix]. 139 ὁ ζῆλος τοῦ οἴκου σου : 1 Macc.
ii. 58 ζῆλος νόμου. Jowett quotes Philo, *Leg. ad Caium*, § 16 (Mang.
ii. 562) ' Ready to endure death like immortality rather than suffer
the neglect of the least of their national customs.' St. Paul selects
the very word which the Jew himself would have chosen to express
just that zeal on which more than anything else he would have
prided himself.

κατ᾽ ἐπίγνωσιν. The Jews were destitute, not of γνῶσις, but of
the higher disciplined knowledge, of the true moral discernment
by which they might learn the right way. ἐπίγνωσις (see Lft. on
Col. i. 9, to whose note there is nothing to add) means a higher
and more perfect knowledge, and hence it is used especially and
almost technically for knowledge of God, as being the highest
and most perfect form : see on i. 28 and cf. iii. 20.

3. ἀγνοοῦντες γάρ. This verse gives the reason for οὐ κατ᾽
ἐπίγνωσιν, and the antithesis to ἡ μὲν εὐδοκία. ἀγνοοῦντες means ' not
knowing,' ' being ignorant of,' not ' misunderstanding.' St. Paul
here states simply the fact of the ignorance of his fellow-countrymen ; he does not yet consider how far this ignorance is culpable :
that point he makes evident later (vv. 14 sq.).

τὴν τοῦ Θεοῦ δικαιοσύνην . . . τὴν ἰδίαν. St. Paul contrasts two
methods of righteousness. On the one side there was the righteousness which came from God, and was to be sought in the manner
He had prescribed, on the other was a righteousness which they
hoped to win by their own methods, and by their own merit.
Their zeal had been blind and misdirected. In their eagerness to
pursue after the latter, they had remained ignorant of and had not
submitted to the method (as will be shown, a much easier one)
which God Himself had revealed.

ὑπετάγησαν. Middle, ' submit themselves,' cf. Jas. iv. 7 ; 1 Pet.
ii. 13 ; v. 5 ; Winer, § xxxix, 2. p. 327 E.T.

The second δικαιοσύνην after ἰδίαν of the TR. is supported by ℵ only
among good authorities, and by Tisch. only among recent editors; it is
omitted by A B D E P, Vulg. Boh. Arm., and many Fathers.

4. τέλος γὰρ νόμου κ.τ.λ. St. Paul has in the preceding verse
been contrasting two methods of obtaining δικαιοσύνη ; one, that
ordained by God, as ix. 32 shows, a method ἐκ πίστεως ; the other
that pursued by the Jews, a method διὰ νόμου. The latter has ceased
to be possible, as St. Paul now proves by showing that, by the coming
of Christ Law as a means of obtaining righteousness had been

brought to an end. The γάρ therefore introduces the reason, not
for the actual statement of ver. 3, that the Jews had not submitted
to the Divine method, but for what was implied—that they were
wrong in so doing.

τέλος : ‘ end,’ ‘ termination.’ Law as a method or principle of
righteousness had been done away with in Christ. ‘ Christ is the
end of law as death is the end of life.’ Gif. Cf. Dem. *C. Eubuliden*,
1306, 25 καίτοι πᾶσίν ἐστιν ἀνθρώποις τέλος τοῦ βίου θάνατος (quoted
by Fri. and by many writers after him).

The theological idea of this verse is much expanded in later
Epistles, and is connected definitely with the death of Christ : Eph.
ii. 15 ‘He abolished in His flesh the enmity, even the law of
commandments contained in ordinances’; Col. ii. 14 ‘Having
blotted out the bond written in ordinances that was against us,
which was contrary to us : and He hath taken it out of the way,
nailing it to the cross.’ This last passage is paraphrased by Lft. :
‘ Then and there [Christ] cancelled the bond which stood valid
against us (for it bore our own signature), the bond which engaged
us to fulfil all the law of ordinances, which was our stern pitiless
tyrant. Ay, this very bond hath Christ put out of sight for ever,
nailing it to His cross, and rending it with His body, and killing
it in His death.’ And as he points out, a wider reference must
be given to the expression; it cannot be confined to the Jews.
The ordinances, although primarily referring to the Mosaic law,
‘ will include all forms of positive decrees in which moral or social
principles are embodied or religious duties defined ; and the “ bond ”
is the moral assent of the conscience which (as it were) signs and
seals the obligation.’

‘ Although the moral law is eternal, yet under the Gospel it loses
its form of external law, and becomes an internal principle of life.’
Lid.

νόμου : ‘ Law ’ as a principle (so Weiss, Oltramare, Gif.), not
the Law, the Mosaic Law (so the mass of commentators). It is
not possible indeed to lay stress on the absence of the article here,
because the article being dropped before τέλος it is naturally also
dropped before νόμου (see on ii. 13), and although St. Paul might
have written τὸ γὰρ τέλος τοῦ νόμου, yet this would not exactly have
suited his purpose, for τέλος is the predicate of the sentence thrown
forward for emphasis. But that the application of the term must
be general is shown by the whole drift of the argument (see below),
by the words παντὶ τῷ πιστεύοντι proving that the passage cannot be
confined to the Jews, and consequently not to the Mosaic law, and
by the correct reading in ver. 5 τὴν ἐκ νόμου (see critical note).

The interpretation of this verse has been much confused owing
to incorrect translations of τέλος (fulfilment, aim), the confusion of
νόμος and ὁ νόμος, and a misapprehension of the drift of the passage.

That the version given above is correct is shown (1) by the meaning of τέλος. It is quite true that Christ is the τελείωσις of the Law, that in Him what was typical has its fulfilment; but τέλος never means τελείωσις (as it is taken here by Orig. Erasmus, &c.). Again, it is equally true that the Law is the παιδαγωγός that brings men to Christ, and that Christ can be described as the object or goal of the Law (as the passage is taken by Chrys., other fathers, and Va. amongst English commentators): but τέλος is only used once in this sense in St. Paul's Epistles (1 Tim. i. 5), Χριστός would become the predicate, τέλος would then require the article, and νόμος would have to be interpreted of the Jewish Law. The normal meaning of the word, and the correct one here, is that of 'termination' (so Aug. De W. Mey. Fri. Weiss, Oltramare); (2) by the meaning of νόμος (see above). This is interpreted incorrectly of the Jewish Law only by almost all commentators (Orig. Chrys. and all the Fathers, Erasmus, Calv. De W. Mey. Va.); (3) by the context. This verse is introduced to explain ver. 3, which asserts that of two methods of obtaining righteousness one is right, the other wrong. St. Paul here confirms this by showing that the one has come to an end so as to introduce the other. It is his object to mark the contrast between the two methods of righteousness and not their resemblance.

But the misinterpretation is not confined to this verse, it colours the interpretation of the whole passage. It is not St. Paul's aim to show that the Jews ought to have realized their mistake because the O. T. dispensation pointed to Christ, but to contrast the two methods. It is only later (vv. 14 f.) that he shows that the Jews had had full opportunities and warnings.

εἰς δικαιοσύνην παντὶ τῷ πιστεύοντι : 'so that δικαιοσύνη may come to everyone that believes,' 'so that everyone by believing may obtain δικαιοσύνη.'

Omni credenti, tractatur τὸ credenti v. 5 sq., τὸ omni v. 11 sq. παντι, omni ex iudaeis et gentibus. Beng.

5-10. St. Paul proceeds to describe the two modes of obtaining δικαιοσύνη in language drawn from the O. T., which had become proverbial.

5. Μωσῆς γὰρ γράφει κ.τ.λ. Taken from Lev. xviii. 5, which is quoted also in Gal. iii. 12. The original (ἃ ποιήσας ἄνθρωπος ζήσεται ἐν αὐτοῖς) is slightly modified to suit the grammar of this passage, τὴν δικαιοσύνην τὴν ἐκ νόμου being made the object of ποιήσας. St. Paul quotes the words to mean that the condition of obtaining life by law is that of fulfilment, a condition which in contrast to the other method described immediately afterwards is hard, if not impossible. On this difficulty of obeying the law he has laid stress again and again in the first part of the Epistle, and it is this

that he means by τὸν νόμον τῶν ἐντολῶν in Eph. ii. 15 (quoted above).

ζήσεται : shall obtain life in its deepest sense both here and hereafter (see pp. 180, 196).

There are a number of small variations in the text of this verse. (1) ὅτι is placed before τὴν δικαιοσύνην by א* A D*, Vulg. Boh., Orig.-lat., after νόμου by א° B D° E F G K L P &c., Syrr., Chrys. Thdrt. &c. (2) ἐκ νόμου is read by א B, ἐκ τοῦ νόμου by the mass of later authorities. (3) ὁ ποιήσας is read without any addition by א* A D E, Vulg., Orig.-lat., αὐτά is added by B F G K L P &c., Syrr., Chrys. Thdrt. &c., eam by d**e†. (4) ἄνθρωπος is om. by F G, Chrys. (5) ἐν αὐτῇ is read by א A B minusc. pauc., Vulg. Boh. Orig.-lat., ἐν αὐτοῖς D E F G K L P &c. Syrr., Chrys. Thdrt. &c.

The original text was ὅτι τὴν δικαιοσύνην τὴν ἐκ νόμου ὁ ποιήσας ἄνθρωπος ζήσεται ἐν αὐτῇ. The alteration of αὐτά . . . αὐτοῖς came from a desire to make the passage correspond with the LXX, or Gal. iii. 12 (hence the omission of ἄνθρωπος), and this necessitated a change in the position of ὅτι. τοῦ νόμου arose from an early misinterpretation. The mixed text of B γράφει τὴν δικαιοσύνην τὴν ἐκ νόμου ὅτι ὁ ποιήσας αὐτὰ ἄνθρωπος ζήσεται ἐν αὐτῇ and of D γράφει ὅτι τὴν δικαιοσύνην τὴν ἐκ τοῦ νομοῦ ὁ ποιήσας ἄνθρωπος ζήσεται ἐν αὐτοῖς are curious, but help to support א A Vulg. Boh.

6-8. The language of St. Paul in these verses is based upon the LXX of Deut. xxx. 11-14. Moses is enumerating the blessings of Israel if they keep his law : 'if thou shalt obey the voice of the Lord thy God, to keep His commandments and His statutes which are written in this book of the law; if thou turn unto the Lord thy God with all thine heart, and with all thy soul'; he then goes on (the RV. translation is here modified to suit the LXX): ' 11 [For this commandment which I command thee this day, it is not too hard for thee, nor is it far from thee. 12 Not in heaven above] *saying, Who shall go up for us into heaven* [and receive it for us, and having heard of it we shall do it? 13 Nor is it beyond the sea], *saying, Who will go over to the further side of the sea for us,* [and receive it for us, and make it heard by us, and we shall do it?] 14 *But the word is very nigh thee, in thy mouth, and in thy heart,* [and in thy hands, that thou mayest do it].' The Apostle selects certain words out of this passage and uses them to describe the characteristics of the new righteousness by faith as he conceives it.

It is important to notice the very numerous variations between the quotation and the LXX. In the first place only a few phrases are selected : the portions not quoted are enclosed in brackets in the translation given above. Then in those sentences that are quoted there are very considerable changes : (1) for the λέγων of the LXX, which is an ungrammatical translation of the Hebrew, and is without construction, is substituted μὴ εἴπῃς ἐν τῇ καρδίᾳ σου from Deut. viii. 17, ix. 4 : (2) for τίς διαπεράσει ἡμῖν εἰς τὸ πέραν τῆς θαλάσσης is substituted τίς καταβήσεται εἰς τὴν ἄβυσσον in order to make the passage better suit the purpose for which it is quoted : (3) in

† The Bohairic Version is quoted incorrectly in support of this reading. The *eam* read there does not imply a variant, but was demanded by the idiom of the language.

ver. 8 the words σφόδρα ... ἐν ταῖς χερσί σου are omitted (this agrees with the Hebrew), as also ποιεῖν αὐτό.

6. ἡ δὲ ἐκ πίστεως δικαιοσύνη οὕτω λέγει. It is noticeable that St. Paul does not introduce these words on the authority of Scripture (as ver. 11), nor on the authority of Moses (as ver. 5), but merely as a declaration of righteousness in its own nature. On the personification compare that of Wisdom in Prov. i. 20; Lk. xi. 49; of παράκλησις Heb. xii. 5.

τίς ἀναβήσεται εἰς τὸν οὐρανόν; In the original passage these words mean : The law which I command you is not far off, it is not in heaven, so that you will have to ask, Who will go up to bring it down for us? it is very near and not hard to attain. St. Paul uses the same words to express exactly the same idea, but with a completely different application. ' The Gospel as opposed to the Law is not difficult or hard to attain to.'

τοῦτ' ἔστι, Χριστὸν καταγαγεῖν : ' that is to say, to bring Christ down.' Just as Moses had said that there was no need for anyone to go up into heaven to bring down the law, so it is true—far more true indeed—to say that there is no need to go into heaven to bring down the object of faith and source of righteousness—Christ. Christ has become man and dwelt among us. Faith is not a difficult matter since Christ has come.

The interpretations suggested of this and the following verses have been very numerous. τοῦτ' ἔστιν occurs three times in this passage, and we must give it the same force in each place. In the third instance (ver. 8) it is used to give a meaning or explanation to the word τὸ ῥῆμα, which occurs in the quotation ; it introduces in fact what would be technically known as a ' Midrash' on the text quoted (so Mey. Lid. Lips. and apparently Va. Gif.). That is the meaning with which the phrase has been used in ix. 8, and is also the meaning which it must have here. The infinitive cannot be dependent on τοῦτ' ἔστι (for in all the passages where the phrase is used the words that follow it are in the same construction as the words that precede), but is dependent on ἀναβήσεται which it explains: so Xen. *Mem.* I. v. 2 (Goodwin, *Greek Moods and Tenses*, § 97) εἰ βουλοίμεθα τῷ ἐπιτρέψαι ἢ παῖδας παιδεῦσαι, ἢ χρήματα διασῶσαι. In this and similar cases it is not necessary to emphasize strongly the idea of purpose as do Fri. (*nempe ut Christum in orbem terrarum deducat*) and Lips. (*nämlich um Christum herabzuholen*), the infinitive is rather epexegetical (so apparently Va. Gif.). The LXX here reads τίς ἀναβήσεται ... καὶ λήψεται ; the construction is changed because τοῦτ' ἔστιν καὶ κατάξει would hardly have been clear.

Of other interpretations, some do not suit the grammar. ' That would be the same thing as to say Who will bring Christ down?' would require τίς κατάξει τὸν Χριστόν. Weiss translates ' that would be the same thing as to bring Christ down,' apparently making the infinitive dependent on τοῦτ' ἔστιν. Other translations or paraphrases do not suit the context: 'Do not attempt great things, only believe': or, 'Do not waver and ask, Is Christ really come? only believe.' The object of the passage is not to exhort to faith or to show the necessity of faith—that has been done in the early part of the Epistle; but to prove that the method of faith was one which, for several reasons, should not have been ignored and left on one side by the Jews.

7. ἤ, Τίς καταβήσεται . . . ἀναγαγεῖν: 'nor is it necessary to search the depth, since Christ is risen from the dead.' St. Paul substitutes τίς καταβήσεται εἰς τὴν ἄβυσσον for the more ordinary τίς διαπεράσει ἡμῖν εἰς τὸ πέραν τῆς θαλάσσης, both because it makes a more suitable contrast to the first part of the sentence, and because it harmonizes better with the figurative meaning he wishes to draw from it. ἄβυσσος in the O. T. meant originally the 'deep sea,' 'the great deep' or 'the depths of the sea,' Ps. cvi (cvii). 26 ἀναβαίνουσιν ἕως τῶν οὐρανῶν, καὶ καταβαίνουσιν ἕως τῶν ἀβύσσων, and the deep places of the earth, Ps. lxx (lxxi). 20 καὶ ἐκ τῶν ἀβύσσων τῆς γῆς πάλιν ἀνήγαγές με, and so had come to mean Tartarus or the Lower World; τὸν δὲ τάρταρον τῆς ἀβύσσου Job. xli. 23, where the reference to τάρταρος is due to the LXX; cf. Eur. Phoen. 1632 (1605) ταρτάρου ἄβυσσα χάσματα. Elsewhere in the N. T. it is so used of the abode of demons (Luke viii. 31) and the place of torment (Rev. ix. 1). This double association of the word made it suitable for St. Paul's purpose; it kept up the antithesis of the original, and it also enabled him to apply the passage figuratively to the Resurrection of Christ after His human soul had gone down into Hades.

On the *descensus ad inferos*, which is here referred to in indefinite and untechnical language, cf. Acts ii. 27; 1 Peter iii. 19; iv. 6; and Lft. on Ign. *Magn.* ix; see also Swete, *Apost.-creed*, p. 57 ff.

8. τὸ ῥῆμα τῆς πίστεως. 'The message, the subject of which is faith'; πίστις does not mean 'the faith,' i. e. 'the Gospel message' (Oltramare), but, as elsewhere in this chapter, faith as the principle of righteousness. Nor does the phrase mean the Gospel message which appeals to faith in man (Lid.), but the Gospel which preaches faith, cf. x. 17. On ῥῆμα cf. 1 Peter i. 25 τὸ δὲ ῥῆμα Κυρίου μένει εἰς τὸν αἰῶνα. τοῦτο δέ ἐστι τὸ ῥῆμα τὸ εὐαγγελισθὲν εἰς ὑμᾶς.

ὃ κηρύσσομεν. This gives the reason why the new way of righteousness is easy to attain, being as it is brought home to every one, and suggests a thought which is worked out more fully in ver. 14 f.

In what sense does St. Paul use the O. T. in vv. 6-8? The difficulty is this. In the O. T. the words are used by Moses of the Law: how can St. Paul use them of the Gospel as against the Law?

The following considerations will suggest the answer to be given :

(1) The context of the passage shows that there is no stress laid on the fact that the O. T. is being quoted. The object of the argument is to describe the characteristics of δικαιοσύνη ἐκ πίστεως, not to show how it can be proved from the O. T.

(2) The Apostle carefully and pointedly avoids appealing to Scripture, altering his mode of citation from that employed in the previous verse. *Mosen non citat, quia sensum Mosis non sequitur, sed tantum ab illo verba mutuatur,* Vatablus, *ap. Crit. Sacr. ad loc.*

(3) The quotation is singularly inexact. An ordinary reader fairly well acquainted with the O. T. would feel that the language had a familiar ring, but could not count it as a quotation.

(4) The words had certainly become proverbial, and many instances of them so used have been quoted. Philo, *Quod omn. prob. lib.* § 10 (quoted by Gifford), 'And yet what need is there either of long journeys over the land, or of long voyages for the sake of investigating and seeking out virtue, the roots of which the Creator has laid not at any great distance, but so near, as the wise law-giver of the Jews says, "They are in thy mouth, and in thy heart, and in thy hands," intimating by these figurative expressions the words and actions and designs of men ?' *Bava Mezia,* f. 94. 1 (quoted by Wetstein) *Si quis dixerit mulieri, Si adscenderis in firmamentum, aut descenderis in abyssum, eris mihi desponsata, haec conditio frustranea est*; 4 Ezra iv. 8 *dicebas mihi fortassis : In abyssum non descendi, neque in infernum adhuc, neque in coelis unquam ascendi*; Baruch iii. 29, 30 τίς ἀνέβη εἰς τὸν οὐρανὸν καὶ ἔλαβεν αὐτήν, καὶ κατεβίβασεν αὐτὴν ἐκ τῶν νεφελῶν; τίς διέβη πέραν τῆς θαλάσσης καὶ εὗρεν αὐτήν (of Wisdom); *Jubilees* xxiv. 32 'For even if he had ascended to heaven, they would bring him down from there . . . and even if he descends into Sheôl, there too shall his judgement be great' ; cp. also Amos ix. 2.

(5) St. Paul certainly elsewhere uses the words of Scripture in order to express his meaning in familiar language, cf. ver. 18 ; xi. 1.

For these reasons it seems probable that here the Apostle does not intend to base any argument on the quotation from the O. T., but only selects the language as being familiar, suitable, and proverbial, in order to express what he wishes to say.

It is not necessary therefore to consider that St. Paul is interpreting the passage of Christ by Rabbinical methods (with Mey. Lid. and others), nor to see in the passage in Deuteronomy a prophecy of the Gospel (Fri.) or a reference to the Messiah, which is certainly not the primary meaning. But when we have once realized that no argument is based on the use of the O. T., it does not follow that the use of its language is without motive. Not only has it a great rhetorical value, as Chrysostom sees with an orator's instinct : 'he uses the words which are found in the O. T., being always at

U

pains to keep quite clear of the charges of love of novelties and of opposition to it'; but also there is to St. Paul a correspondence between the O. T. and N. T.: the true creed is simple whether Law on its spiritual side or Gospel (cf. Aug. *De Natura et Gratia*, § 83).

9. ὅτι ἐὰν ὁμολογήσῃς κ.τ.λ. This verse corresponds to and applies the preceding verse. The subject of the ῥῆμα which is preached by the Apostles is the person of Christ and the truth of His Resurrection. Κύριος refers to ver. 6, the Resurrection (ὅτι ὁ Θεὸς αὐτὸν ἤγειρεν ἐκ νεκρῶν) to ver. 7. The power of Christ lies in these two facts, namely His Incarnation and His Resurrection, His Divine nature and His triumph over death. What is demanded of a Christian is the outward confession and the inward belief in Him, and these sum up the conditions necessary for salvation.

The ordinary reading in this verse is ἐὰν ὁμολογήσῃς ἐν τῷ στόματί σου Κύριον Ἰησοῦν, for which WH. substitute τὸ ῥῆμα ἐν τῷ στόματί σου ὅτι Κύριος Ἰησοῦς. τὸ ῥῆμα has the authority of B 71, Clem.-Alex. and perhaps Cyril, ὅτι K. Ἰ. of B, Boh., Clem.-Alex. and Cyril 2/3. The agreement in the one case of B and Boh., in the other of B and Clem.-Alex. against nearly all the other authorities is noticeable.

10. καρδίᾳ γὰρ πιστεύεται κ.τ.λ. St. Paul explains and brings out more fully the application of the words he has last quoted. The beginning of the Christian life has two sides : internally it is the change of heart which faith implies; this leads to righteousness, the position of acceptance before God: externally it implies the 'confession of Christ crucified' which is made in baptism, and this puts a man into the path by which in the end he attains salvation; he becomes σωζόμενος.

11. λέγει γὰρ ἡ γραφή κ.τ.λ. Quoted from Is. xxviii. 16 (see above, ix. 33) with the addition of πᾶς to bring out the point on which emphasis is to be laid. St. Paul introduces a proof from Scripture of the statement made in the previous verse that faith is the condition of salvation, and at the same time makes it the occasion of introducing the second point in the argument, namely, the universal character of this new method of obtaining righteousness.

In ver. 4 he has explained that the old system of δικαιοσύνη ἐκ νόμου has been done away with in Christ to make way for a new one which has two characteristics : (1) that it is ἐκ πίστεως: this has been treated in vv. 5–10; (2) that it is universal: this he now proceeds to develope.

12. οὐ γάρ ἐστι διαστολὴ Ἰουδαίου τε καὶ Ἕλληνος. St. Paul first explains the meaning of this statement, namely, the universal character of the Gospel, by making it clear that it is the sole method for Jews as well as for Gentiles. This was both a warning and a consolation for the Jews. A warning if they thought that, in spite of the preaching of the Gospel, they might seek salvation in their own way; a consolation if once they realized the burden of the law and that they might be freed from it. The Jews have in this relation no special privileges (cf. i. 16; ii. 9, 10; iii. 9; 1 Cor. i. 24; xii. 13; Gal. iii. 28; Col. iii. 11); they must obtain δικαιοσύνη by the same methods and on the same conditions as the Gentiles. This St. Paul has already proved on the ground that they equally with the Gentiles have sinned (iii. 23). He now deduces it from the nature and the work of the Lord.

ὁ γὰρ αὐτὸς Κύριος πάντων, cf. 1 Cor. xii. 5. This gives the reason for the similarity of method for all alike : 'it is the same Lord who redeemed all mankind alike, and conferred upon all alike such wealth of spiritual blessings.' It is better to take Κύριος πάντων as predicate for it contains the point of the sentence, 'The same Lord is Lord of all' (so the RV.).

Κύριος must clearly refer to Christ, cf. vv. 9, 11. He is called Κύριος πάντων Acts x. 36, and cf. ix. 5, and Phil. ii. 10, 11.

πλουτῶν: 'abounding in spiritual wealth,' cf. esp. Eph. iii. 8 τοῖς ἔθνεσιν εὐαγγελίσασθαι τὸ ἀνεξιχνίαστον πλοῦτος τοῦ Χριστοῦ.

τοὺς ἐπικαλουμένους αὐτόν. ἐπικαλεῖσθαι τὸν Κύριον, or more correctly ἐπικαλεῖσθαι τὸ ὄνομα τοῦ Κυρίου, is the habitual LXX translation of a common Hebrew formula. From the habit of beginning addresses to a deity by mentioning his name, it became a technical expression for the suppliant to a god, and a designation of his worshippers. Hence the Israelites were οἱ ἐπικαλούμενοι τὸν Κύριον or τὸ ὄνομα Κυρίου. They were in fact specially distinguished as the worshippers of Jehovah. It becomes therefore very significant when we find just this expression used of the Christians as the worshippers of Christ, ὁ Κύριος, in order to designate them as apart from all others, cf. 1 Cor. i. 2 σὺν πᾶσι τοῖς ἐπικαλουμένοις τὸ ὄνομα τοῦ Κυρίου ἡμῶν Ἰησοῦ Χριστοῦ. There is a treatise on the subject by A. Seeberg, *Die Anbetung des Herrn bei Paulus*, Riga, 1891, see especially pp. 38, 43–46.

13. πᾶς γὰρ ὃς ἂν ἐπικαλέσηται. St. Paul sums up and clenches his argument by the quotation of a well-known passage of Scripture, Joel ii. 32 (the quotation agrees with both the LXX and the Hebrew texts). The original passage refers to the prophetic conception of the 'day of the Lord.' 'The sun shall be turned into darkness, and the moon into blood, before the great and terrible day of the Lord come.' At that time 'whosoever shall call on the name of the Lord' shall be saved. This salvation (σωθήσεται, cf. ver. 9 σωθήσῃ, 10 σωτηρίαν), the Jewish expectation of safety in the Messianic kingdom when the end comes, is used of that Christian salvation which is the spiritual fulfilment of Jewish prophecy.

Κυρίου. The term Κύριος is applied to Christ by St. Paul in

quotations from the O. T. in 2 Thess. i. 9; 1 Cor. ii. 16; x. 21, 26; 2 Cor. iii. 16, and probably in other passages.

This quotation, besides concluding the argument of vv. 1-13, suggests the thought which is the transition to the next point discussed—the opportunities offered to all of hearing this message.

ISRAEL'S UNBELIEF NOT EXCUSED BY WANT OF OPPORTUNITY.

X. 14-21. *This unbelief on the part of Israel was not owing to want of knowledge. Fully accredited messengers— such a body as is necessary for preaching and for faith— have announced the Gospel. There is no land but has heard the voices of the Evangelical preachers (vv. 14-18). Nor was it owing to want of understanding. Their own Prophets warned them that it was through disobedience that they would reject God's message (vv. 19-21).*

[14] All then that is required for salvation is sincerely and genuinely to call on the Lord. But there are conditions preliminary to this which are necessary; perhaps it may be urged, that these have not been fulfilled. Let us consider what these conditions are. If a man is to call on Jesus he must have faith in Him; to obtain faith it is necessary that he must hear the call; that again implies that heralds must have been sent forth to proclaim this call. [15] And heralds imply a commission. Have these conditions been fulfilled? Yes. Duly authorized messengers have preached the Gospel. The fact may be stated in the words of the Prophet Isaiah (lii. 7) describing the welcome approach of the messengers who bring news of the return from captivity—that great type of the other, Messianic, Deliverance: 'How beautiful are the feet of them that preach good tidings.'

[16] But it may be urged, in spite of this, all did not give it a patient and submissive hearing. This does not imply that the message has not been given. In fact Isaiah in the same passage in which he foretold the Apostolic message, spoke also of the incredulity with which the message is received (liii. 1) 'Lord, who hath believed our message?' [17] Which incidentally confirms what we were saying a moment ago: Faith can only come from the

message heard, and the message heard implies the message sent—
the message, that is, about Christ.

[18] But it may be alleged : We grant it was preached, but that
does not prove that Israel heard it. Is that possible, when in the
words of Psalm xix 'the voices of God's messengers went forth
into all lands, and their words to the limits of the known world?'

[19] Or another excuse : 'Israel heard but did not understand.'
Can you say that of Israel? From the very beginning of its history
a long succession of its Prophets foretold the Divine scheme.
Moses, to begin with, wrote (Deut. xxxii. 21) 'I will excite you
to jealousy at a nation outside the pale, that does not count as a
nation at all. I will rouse your anger at seeing yourselves out-
stripped by a nation whom you regard as possessing no intelligence
for the things of religion.' [20] Isaiah too was full of boldness. In
the face of his fellow-countrymen he asserted (lxv. 1) that God's
mercies should be gained by those who had not striven after them
(the Gentiles). [21] And then he turns round to Israel and says that
although God had never ceased stretching out His arms to them
with all the tenderness of a mother, they had received His call with
disobedience, and His message with criticism and contradiction.
The Jews have fallen, not because of God's unfaithfulness or injustice, not because of want of opportunity, but because they are a
rebellious people—a people who refuse to be taught, who choose
their own way, who cleave to that way in spite of every warning
and of every message.

14-21. This section seems to be arranged on the plan of suggesting a series of difficulties, and giving short decisive answers to
each : (1) 'But how can men believe the Gospel unless it has been
fully preached?'(v. 14). *Answer.* 'It has been preached as Isaiah
foretold' (ver. 15). (2) 'Yet, all have not accepted it' (ver. 16).
Answer. 'That does not prove that it was not preached. Isaiah
foretold also this neglect of the message' (vv. 16, 17). (3) 'But
perhaps the Jews did not hear' (v. 18). *Answer.* 'Impossible.
The Gospel has been preached everywhere.' (4) 'But perhaps
they did not understand' (ver. 19). *Answer.* 'That again is impossible. The Gentiles, a people without any real knowledge,
have understood. The real fact is they were a disobedient, self-
willed people.' The object is to fix the guilt of the Jews by removing every defence which might be made on the ground of want
of opportunities.

'The passage which follows (14–21) is in style one of the most obscure portions of the Epistle.' This statement of Jowett's is hardly exaggerated. 'The obscurity arises,' as he proceeds to point out, 'from the argument being founded on passages of the Old Testament.' These are quoted without explanation, and without their relation to the argument being clearly brought out. The first difficulty is to know where to make a division in the chapter. Some put it after ver. 11 (so Go.) making vv. 11–21 a proof of the extension of the Gospel to the Gentiles; some after ver. 13 (Chrys. Weiss, Oltr. Gif.); some after ver. 15 (Lid. WH. Lips.). The decision of the question will always depend on the opinion formed of the drift of the passage, but we are not without structural assistance. It may be noticed throughout these chapters that each succeeding paragraph is introduced by a question with the particle οὖν: so ix. 14 τί οὖν ἐροῦμεν; 30; xi. 1, 11. And this seems to arise from the meaning of the particle: it sums up the conclusion of the preceding paragraph as an introduction to a further step in the argument. This meaning will exactly suit the passage under consideration. 'The condition of salvation is to call on the Lord'—that is the conclusion of the last section: then the Apostle goes on, 'if this be so, what then (οὖν) are the conditions necessary for attaining it, and have they been fulfilled?' the words forming a suitable introduction to the next stage in the argument. This use of οὖν to introduce a new paragraph is very common in St. Paul. See especially Rom. v. 1, vi. 1, xii. 1; Eph. iv. 1; 1 Tim. ii. 1; 2 Tim. ii. 1, besides other less striking instances. It may be noticed that it is not easy to understand the principle on which WH. have divided the text of these chapters, making no break at all at ix. 29, beginning a new paragraph at chap. x, making a break here at ver. 15, making only a slight break at chap. xi, and starting a new paragraph at ver. 13 of that chapter at what is really only a parenthetical remark.

X. 14, 15. The main difficulty of these verses centres round two points: With what object are they introduced? And what is the quotation from Isaiah intended to prove?

1. One main line of interpretation, following Calvin, considers that the words are introduced to justify the preaching of the Gospel to the Gentiles; in fact to support the πᾶς of the previous verse. God must have intended His Gospel to go to the heathen, for a duly commissioned ministry (and St. Paul is thinking of himself) has been sent out to preach it. The quotation then follows as a justification from prophecy of the ministry to the Gentiles. The possibility of adopting such an interpretation must depend partly on the view taken of the argument of the whole chapter (see the General Discussion at the end), but in any case the logical connexion is wrong. If that were what St. Paul had intended to say, he must have written, 'Salvation is intended for Gentile as well as Jew, for God has commissioned His ministers to preach to them: a commission implies preaching, preaching implies faith, faith implies worship, and worship salvation. The conversion of the Gentiles is the necessary result of the existence of an apostolate of the Gentiles.' It will be seen that St. Paul puts the argument exactly in the opposite way, in a manner in fact in which he could never prove this conclusion.

2. Roman Catholic commentators, followed by Liddon and

Gore, consider that the words are introduced in order to justify an apostolic or authorized ministry. But this is to introduce into the passage an idea which is quite alien to it, and which is unnecessary for the argument.

3. The right interpretation of the whole of this paragraph seems to be that of Chrysostom. The Jews, it has been shown, have neglected God's method of obtaining righteousness; but in order, as he desires, to convict them of guilt in this neglect, St. Paul must show that they have had the opportunity of knowing about it, that their ignorance (ἀγνοοῦντες ver. 3) is culpable. He therefore begins by asking what are the conditions necessary for 'calling upon the Lord?' and then shows that these conditions have been fulfilled. There may still be some question as to the meaning of the quotation. (1) It may be introduced merely as corroborative of the last chain in the argument (so most commentators). This need of a commissioned ministry corresponds to the joy and delight experienced when they arrive. Or better, (2) it may be looked upon as stating the fulfilment of the conditions. 'Yes, and they have come, a fact that no one can fail to recognize, and which was foretold by the Prophet Isaiah.' So Chrysostom, who sums up the passage thus: 'If the being saved, then, came of calling upon Him, and calling upon Him from believing, and believing from hearing, and hearing from preaching, and preaching from being sent, and if they were sent, and did preach, and the prophet went round with them to point them out, and proclaim them, and say that these were they whom they showed of so many ages ago, whose feet even they praised because of the matter of their preaching; then it is quite clear that the not believing was their own fault only. And that because God's part had been fulfilled completely.'

14. πῶς οὖν ἐπικαλέσωνται. The word οὖν, as often in St. Paul, marks a stage in the argument. 'We have discovered the new system of salvation: what conditions are necessary for its acceptance?' The question is not the objection of an adversary, nor merely rhetorical, but rather deliberative (see Burton, *M. and T.* § 169): hence the subjunctive (see below) is more suitable than the future which we find in ix. 30. The subject of ἐπικαλέσωνται is implied in vv. 12, 13, 'those who would seek this new method of salvation by calling on the name of the Lord.'

In this series of questions in vv. 14, 15 the MSS. vary between the subjunctive and the future. Generally the authority for the subjunctive strongly preponderates: ἐπικαλέσωνται ℵ A B D E F G, πιστεύσωσιν ℵ B D E F G P, κηρύξωσιν ℵ A B D E K L P. In the case of ἀκούσωσιν there is a double variation. ℵᵒ A² (A *latet*) B and some minuscules read ἀκούσωσιν; ℵ D E F G K P and some minuscules read ἀκούσονται; L etc., Clem.-Alex. Ath. Chrys. *edd.* Theodrt. and the TR. read ἀκούσουσι. Here however the double variant makes the subjunctive almost certain. Although the form ἀκούσουσι is possible in N.T. Greek, it is most improbable that it should have arisen as a corruption from ἀκούσονται, and it is too weakly supported to be the correct reading. ἀκούσωσιν, which will explain both variants and harmonizes with the other subjunctives, is therefore correct. B here alone among the leading MSS. is correct throughout.

οὗ οὐκ ἤκουσαν: 'how can they believe on Him whom they have not heard preaching?' οὗ is for εἰς τοῦτον οὗ: and as ἀκούειν τινος means not 'to hear of some one,' but 'to hear some one preaching or speaking,' it must be so translated, and what follows must be interpreted by assuming that the preaching of Christ's messengers is identical with the preaching of Christ Himself. This interpretation (that of Mey. and Gif.), although not without difficulties, is probably better than either of the other solutions proposed. It is suggested that οὗ may be for ὅν, and the passage is translated 'of whom they have not heard'; but only a few instances of this usage are quoted, and they seem to be all early and poetical. The interpretation of Weiss, οὗ = where, completely breaks the continuity of the sentences.

15. κηρύξωσιν. The nominative is οἱ κηρύσσοντες, which is implied in κηρύσσοντος.

By means of this series of questions St. Paul works out the conditions necessary for salvation back to their starting-point. Salvation is gained by calling on the Lord; this implies faith. Faith is only possible with knowledge. Knowledge implies an instructor or preacher. A preacher implies a commission. If therefore salvation is to be made possible for everyone, there must have been men sent out with a commission to preach it.

καθὼς γέγραπται, Ὡς ὡραῖοι οἱ πόδες τῶν εὐαγγελιζομένων ἀγαθά. By introducing this quotation St. Paul implies that the commissioned messengers have been sent, and the conditions therefore necessary for salvation have been fulfilled. 'Yes, and they have been sent: the prophet's words are true describing the glorious character of the Evangelical preachers.'

The quotation is taken from Isaiah lii. 7, and resembles the Hebrew more closely than our present LXX text. In the original it describes the messengers who carry abroad the glad tidings of the restoration from captivity. But the whole of this section of Isaiah was felt by the Christians to be full of Messianic import, and this verse was used by the Rabbis of the coming of the Messiah (see the references given by Schoettgen, Hor. Heb. ii. 179). St. Paul quotes it because he wishes to describe in O. T. language the fact which will be recognized as true when stated, and to show that these facts are in accordance with the Divine method. 'St. Paul applies the exclamation to the appearance of the Apostles of Christ upon the scene of history. Their feet are ὡραῖοι in his eyes, as they announce the end of the captivity of sin, and publish εἰρήνη (Eph. vi. 15 τὸ εὐαγγέλιον τῆς εἰρήνης) made by Christ, through the blood of His Cross, between God and man, between earth and heaven (2 Cor. v. 18–20; Eph. ii. 17; Col. i. 20); and all the blessings of goodness (τὰ ἀγαθά) which God in Christ bestows on the Redeemed, especially δικαιοσύνη.' Liddon.

There are two critical questions in connexion with this quotation: the reading of the Greek text and its relation to the Hebrew and to the LXX.

(1) The RV. reads ὡς ὡραῖοι οἱ πόδες τῶν εὐαγγελιζομένων ἀγαθά: the TR. inserts τῶν εὐαγγ. εἰρήνην after οἱ πόδες. The balance of authority is strongly in favour of the RV. The clause is omitted by ℵ A B C *minusc. pauc.* Aegyptt. (Boh. Sah.) Aeth., Clem.-Alex. Orig. and Orig.-lat.: it is inserted by D E F G K L P &c., Vulg. Syrr. (Pesh. Harcl.) Arm. Goth., Chrys. Iren.-lat. Hil. *al.* The natural explanation is that the insertion has been made that the citation may correspond more accurately to the LXX. This end is not indeed altogether attained, for the LXX reads ἀκοὴν εἰρήνης, and the omission might have arisen from Homoeoteleuton; but these considerations can hardly outweigh the clear preponderance of authority.

There is a somewhat similar difficulty about a second minor variation. The RV. reads ἀγαθά with A B C D E F G P, Orig. Eus. Jo.-Damasc., the TR. has τὰ ἀγαθά with ℵ etc. Clem.-Alex. Chrys. and most later authorities. Here the LXX omits the article, and it is difficult quite to see why it should have been inserted by a corrector; whereas if it had formed part of the original text he could quite naturally have omitted it.

(2) The LXX translation is here very inexact. πάρειμι ὡς ὥρα ἐπὶ τῶν ὀρέων, ὡς πόδες εὐαγγελιζομένου ἀκοὴν εἰρήνης, ὡς εὐαγγελιζόμενος ἀγαθά. St. Paul's words approach much more nearly to the Hebrew (RV.) 'How beautiful upon the mountains are the feet of him that bringeth good tidings, that publisheth peace, that bringeth good tidings of good, that publisheth salvation.' He shortens the quotation, makes it plural instead of singular to suit his purpose, and omits the words 'upon the mountains,' which have only a local significance.

16. ἀλλ' οὐ πάντες. An objection suggested. 'Yet, in spite of the fact that this message was sent, all did not obey the Gospel.' οὐ πάντες is a *meiosis*; cf. τί γὰρ εἰ ἠπίστησάν τινες; (iii. 3).

ὑπήκουσαν, like ὑπετάγησαν (ver. 3), seems to imply the idea of voluntary submission: cf. vi. 16, 17 δοῦλοί ἐστε ᾧ ὑπακούετε ... ὑπηκούσατε δὲ ἐκ καρδίας εἰς ὃν παρεδόθητε.

τῷ εὐαγγελίῳ. The word is of course suggested by the quotation of the previous verse.

Ἡσαΐας γὰρ λέγει κ.τ.λ. 'But this fact does not prove that no message had been sent; it is indeed equally in accordance with prophecy, for Isaiah, in a passage immediately following that in which he describes the messengers, describes also the failure of the people to receive the message.' With γάρ cf. Matt. i. 20 ff. The quotation is from the LXX of Is. liii. 1. Κύριε, as Origen pointed out, does not occur in the Hebrew.

ἀκοῇ: means (1) 'hearing,' 'the faculty by which a thing is heard'; (2) 'the substance of what is heard,' 'a report, message.' In this verse it is used in the second meaning, 'who hath believed our report?' In ver. 17, it shades off into the first, 'faith comes by hearing.' It is quite possible of course to translate 'report' or 'message' there also, but then the connexion of idea with ver. 18 μὴ οὐκ ἤκουσαν is obscured.

It has been questioned to whom St. Paul is referring in this and the preceding verses—the Gentiles or the Jews. The language is quite general and equally applicable to either, but the whole drift of the argument shows that it is of the Jews the Apostle is thinking. Grotius makes vv. 14 and 15 the objection of an opponent to which St. Paul replies in ver. 16 ff.

17. ἄρα ἡ πίστις. 'Hence may be inferred (in corroboration of what was said above) that the preliminary condition necessary for faith is to have heard, and to have heard implies a message.' This sentence is to a certain extent parenthetical, merely emphasizing a fact already stated; yet the language leads us on to the excuse for unbelief suggested in the next verse.

διὰ ῥήματος Χριστοῦ: 'a message about Christ.' Cf. ver. 8 τὸ ῥῆμα τῆς πίστεως ὃ κηρύσσομεν. St. Paul comes back to the phrase he has used before, and the use of it will remind his readers that this message has been actually sent.

Χριστοῦ is the reading of ℵ B C D E *minusc. pauc.*, Vulg. Sah. Boh. Arm. Aeth. Orig.-lat. 2/2, Ambrst. Aug.—Θεοῦ of ℵᶜ A Dᵇᵒ K L P *al. pler.*, Syrr., Clem.-Alex. Chrys. Theodrt.

St. Paul has laid down the conditions which make faith possible, a Gospel and messengers of the Gospel; the language he has used reminds his readers that both these have come. Yet, in spite of this, the Jews have not obeyed. He now suggests two possible excuses.

18. ἀλλὰ λέγω: 'but it may be said in excuse: It is possible that those whom you accuse of not obeying the Gospel message have never heard of it?' On μὴ οὐ see Burton, *M. and T.* § 468.

μενοῦνγε: an emphatic corrective, 'with a slight touch of irony' (Lid.); cf. ix. 20.

εἰς πᾶσαν τὴν γῆν κ.τ.λ. St. Paul expresses his meaning in words borrowed from Psalm xix. (xviii.) 5, which he cites word for word according to the LXX, but without any mark of quotation. What stress does he intend to lay on the words? Does he use them for purely literary purposes to express a well-known fact? or does he also mean to prove the fact by the authority of the O. T. which foretold it?

1. Primarily at any rate St. Paul wishes to express a well-known fact in suitable language. 'What do you say? They have not heard! Why the whole world and the ends of the earth have heard. And have you, amongst whom the heralds abode such a long time, and of whose land they were, not heard?' Chrys.

2. But the language of Scripture is not used without a point. In the original Psalm these words describe how universally the

works of nature glorify God. By using them St. Paul 'compares
the universality of the preaching of the Gospel with the universality
with which the works of nature proclaim God.' Gif.

A second difficulty is raised by older commentators. As a matter
of fact the Gospel had not been preached everywhere; and some
writers have inverted this argument, and used this text as a proof
that even as early as this Christianity had been universally preached.
But all that St. Paul means to imply is that it is universal in its
character. Some there were who might not have heard it; some
Jews even might be among them. He is not dealing with individuals. The fact remained true that, owing to the universal
character of its preaching, those whose rejection of it he is considering had at any rate as a body had the opportunities of hearing
of it.

19. ἀλλὰ λέγω, μὴ Ἰσραὴλ οὐκ ἔγνω; a second excuse is suggested:
'surely it cannot be that it was from ignorance that Israel failed?'

(1) What is the meaning of the somewhat emphatic introduction
of Ἰσραήλ? It has been suggested that it means a change of
subject. That while the former passage refers to Gentiles, or
to Gentiles as well as Jews, here the writer at last turns to Israel in
particular. But there has been no hint that the former passage
was dealing with the Gentiles, and if such a contrast had been
implied Ἰσραήλ would have had to be put in a much more prominent place, περὶ δὲ τοῦ Ἰσραὴλ λέγω, μὴ οὐκ ἔγνω; The real reason
for the introduction of the word is that it gives an answer to
the question, and shows the untenable character of the excuse.
Has Israel, Israel with its long line of Prophets, and its religious
privileges and its Divine teaching, acted in ignorance? When
once 'Israel' has been used there can be no doubt of the answer.

(2) But, again, what is it suggested that Israel has not known?
As the clause is parallel with μὴ οὐκ ἤκουσαν, and as no hint is given
of any change, the object must be the same, namely ῥῆμα Χριστοῦ,
the message concerning the Messiah. All such interpretations as
the 'calling of the Gentiles' or 'the universal preaching of the
Gospel' are outside the line of argument.

(3) But how is this consistent with ἀγνοοῦντες ver. 3? The
contradiction is rather formal than real. It is true Israel's zeal
was not guided by deep religious insight, and that they clung
blindly and ignorantly to a method which had been condemned;
but this ignorance was culpable: if they did not know, they might
have known. From the very beginning of their history their
whole line of Prophets had warned them of the Divine plan.

(4) The answer to this question is given in three quotations
from the O. T. Israel has been warned that their Messiah
would be rejected by themselves and accepted by the Gentiles.
They cannot plead that the message was difficult to understand;

even a foolish people (it was foretold) would accept it, and thus
stir up Israel to jealousy. Nor again can they plead that it was
difficult to find; for Isaiah with great boldness has stated that men
who never sought or asked for it would find it. The real reason
was that the Israelites are a disobedient and a stubborn people,
and, although God has all day long stretched forth His hands to
them, they will not hear Him.

πρῶτος Μωσῆς. εὐθὺς Μωσῆς. 'Even as early in Israel's history as
Moses.'

ἐγὼ παραζηλώσω ὑμᾶς κ.τ.λ.: taken from Deut. xxxii. 21 substantially according to the LXX (ὑμᾶς is substituted for αὐτούς). In
the original the words mean that as Israel has roused God's jealousy
by going after no-gods, so He will rouse Israel's jealousy by
showing His mercy to those who are no-people.

20. Ἡσαΐας δὲ ἀποτολμᾷ. St. Paul's position in opposing the
prejudices of his countrymen made him feel the boldness of Isaiah
in standing up against the men of his own time. The citation is
from Isaiah lxv. 1 according to the LXX, the clauses of the
original being inverted. The words in the original refer to the
apostate Jews. St. Paul applies them to the Gentiles; see on
ix. 25, 26.

B D* F G with perhaps Sah. and Goth. add ἐν twice before τοῖς, a Western
reading which has found its way into B (cf. xi. 6). It does not occur in
א A C Dᵇᶜ E L P etc., and many Fathers.

21. πρὸς δὲ τὸν Ἰσραὴλ λέγει κ.τ.λ. This citation (Is. lxv. 2)
follows almost immediately that quoted in ver. 20, and like it
is taken from the LXX, with only a slight change in the order.
In the original both this verse and the preceding are addressed
to apostate Israel; St. Paul applies the first part to the Gentiles,
the latter part definitely to Israel.

The Argument of ix. 30–x. 21: Human Responsibility.

We have reached a new stage in our argument. The first step
was the vindication of God's faithfulness and justice: the second
step has been definitely to fix guilt on man. It is clearly laid
down that the Jews have been rejected through their own fault.
They chose the wrong method. When the Messiah came, instead
of accepting Him, they were offended. They did not allow their
zeal for God to be controlled by a true spiritual knowledge. And
the responsibility for this is brought home to them. All possible
excuses, such as want of opportunity, insufficient knowledge,
inadequate warning, are suggested, but rejected. The Jews are
a disobedient people and they have been rejected for their disobedience.

Now it has been argued that such an interpretation is inconsistent with Chap. ix. That proves clearly, it is asserted, that grace comes to man, not in answer to man's efforts, but in accordance with God's will. How then can St. Paul go on to prove that the Jews are to blame? In order to avoid this assumed inconsistency, the whole section, or at any rate the final portion, has been interpreted differently: vv. 11–21 are taken to defend the Apostolic ministry to the Gentiles and to justify from the O. T. the calling of the Gentiles and the rejection of the Jews: vv. 14, 15 are used by St. Augustine to prove that there can be no faith without the Divine calling; by Calvin, that as there is faith among the Gentiles, there must have been a Divine call, and so the preaching to them is justified. Then the quotations in vv. 18–21 are considered to refer to the Gentiles mainly; they are merely prophecies of the facts stated in ix. 30, 31 and do not imply and are not intended to imply human responsibility.

An apparent argument in favour of this interpretation is suggested by the introductory words ix. 30, 31. It is maintained that two propositions are laid down there; one the calling of the Gentiles, the other the rejection of the Jews, and both these have to be justified in the paragraph that follows. But, as a matter of fact, this reference to the Gentiles is clearly introduced not as a main point to be discussed, but as a contrast to the rejection of Israel. It increases the strangeness of that fact, and with that fact the paragraph is concerned. This is brought out at once by the question asked διὰ τί; which refers, as the answer shows, entirely to the rejection of Israel. If the Apostle were not condemning the Jews there would be no reason for his sorrow (x. 1) and the palliation for their conduct which he suggests (x. 2); and when we come to examine the structure of the latter part we find that all the leading sentences are concerned not with the defence of any ' calling,' but with fixing the guilt of those rejected : for example ἀλλ' οὐ πάντες ὑπήκουσαν (v. 16), ἀλλὰ λέγω, μὴ οὐκ ἤκουσαν; (v. 18), μὴ Ἰσραὴλ οὐκ ἔγνω; (v. 19). As there is nowhere any reference to Gentiles rejecting the message, the reference must be to the Jews; and the object of the section must be to show the reason why (although Gentiles have been accepted) the Jews have been rejected. The answer is given in the concluding quotation, which sums up the whole argument. It is because the Jews have been a disobedient and gainsaying people. Chrysostom, who brings out the whole point of this section admirably, sums up its conclusion as follows: ' Then to prevent them saying, But why was He not made manifest to us also? he sets down what is more than this, that I not only was made manifest, but I even continued with My hands stretched out, inviting them, and displaying all the concern of an affectionate father, and a fond mother that is set on

her child. See how he has brought us a most lucid answer
to all the difficulties before raised, by showing that it was from
their own temper that ruin had befallen them, and that they are
wholly undeserving of pardon.'

We must accept the interpretation then which sees in this
chapter a proof of the guilt of the Jews. St. Paul is in fact
looking at the question from a point of view different from that
which he adopted in Chap. ix. There he assumes Divine Sovereignty,
and assuming it shows that God's dealings with the Jews are
justified. Now he assumes human responsibility, and shows that
assuming it the Jews are guilty. Two great steps are passed in
the Divine Theodicy. We need not anticipate the argument, but
must allow it to work itself out. The conclusion may suggest
a point of view from which these two apparently inconsistent
attitudes can be reconciled.

St. Paul's Use of the Old Testament.

In Chaps. ix–xi St. Paul, as carrying on a long and sustained
argument, which, if not directed against Jewish opponents, discusses
a question full of interest to Jews from a Jewish point of view,
makes continued use of the O. T., and gives an opportunity for
investigating his methods of quotation and interpretation.

The text of his quotations is primarily that of the LXX. According to Kautzsch (*De Veteris Testamenti locis a Paulo Apostolo
allegatis*), out of eighty-four passages in which St. Paul cites the
O. T. about seventy are taken directly from the LXX or do not
vary from it appreciably, twelve vary considerably, but still show
signs of affinity, and two only, both from the book of Job (Rom.
xi. 35 = Job xli. 3 (11); 1 Cor. iii. 19 = Job v. 13) are definitely independent and derived either from the Hebrew text or some quite
distinct version. Of those derived from the LXX a certain number,
such for example as Rom. x. 15, show in some points a resemblance
to the Hebrew text as against the LXX. We have probably not
sufficient evidence to say whether this arises from a reminiscence
of the Hebrew text (conscious or unconscious), or from an Aramaic Targum, or from the use of an earlier form of a LXX text.
It may be noticed that St. Paul's quotations sometimes agree with
late MSS. of the LXX as against the great uncials (cf. iii. 4, 15 ff.).
As to the further question whether he cites from memory or by
reference, it may be safely said that the majority of the quotations
are from memory; for many of them are somewhat inexact, and
those which are correct are for the most part short and from well-
known books. There is a very marked distinction between these
and the long literary quotations of the Epistle to the Hebrews.

In his formulae of quotation St. Paul adopts all the various forms which seem to have been in use in the Rabbinical schools, and are found in Rabbinical writings. Even his less usual expressions may be paralleled from them (cf. xi. 2). Another point of resemblance may be found in the series of passages which he strings together from different books (cf. iii. 10) after the manner of a Rabbinical discourse. St. Paul was in fact educated as a Rabbi in Rabbinical schools and consequently his method of using the O. T. is such as might have been learnt in these schools.

But how far is his interpretation Rabbinical? It is not quite easy to answer this question directly. It is perhaps better to point out first of all some characteristics which it possesses.

In the first place it is quite clearly not 'historical' in the modern sense of the word. The passages are quoted without regard to their context or to the circumstances under which they were written. The most striking instances of this are those cases in which the words of the O. T. are used in an exactly opposite sense to that which they originally possessed. For instance in ix. 25, 26 words used in the O. T. of the ten tribes are used of the Gentiles, in x. 6–8 words used of the Law are applied to the Gospel as against the Law. On the other hand Rabbinical interpretations in the sense in which they have become proverbial are very rare. St. Paul almost invariably takes the literal and direct meaning of the words (although without regard to their context), he does not allegorize or play upon their meaning, or find hidden and mysterious principles. There are some obvious exceptions, such as Gal. iv. 22 ff., but for the most part St. Paul's interpretation is not allegorical, nor in this sense of the term Rabbinical.

Speaking broadly, St. Paul's use of the O. T. may be described as literal, and we may distinguish three classes of texts. There are firstly those, and they are the largest number, in which the texts are used in a sense corresponding to their O. T. meaning. All texts quoted in favour of moral principles, or spiritual ideas, or the methods of Divine government may be grouped under this head. The argument in ix. 20, 21 is correctly deduced from O. T. principles; the quotation in ix. 17 is not quite so exactly correct, but the principle evolved is thoroughly in accordance with O. T. ideas. So again the method of Divine Election is deduced correctly from the instances quoted in ix. 6–13. Controversially these arguments were quite sound; actually they represent the principles and ideas of the O. T.

A second class of passages consists of those in which, without definitely citing the O. T., the Apostle uses its language in order to express adequately and impressively the ideas he has to convey. A typical instance is that in x. 18, where the words of the Psalm are used in quite a different sense from that which they have in

the original, and without any definite formula of citation. So in
x. 6–8 (see the note) the O. T. language is used rather than a text
from it cited. The same is true in a number of other passages
where, as the text of Westcott and Hort exhibits clearly, ideas
borrowed from the O. T. are expressed in language which is
borrowed, but without any definite sign of quotation. That this is
the natural and normal use of a religious book must clearly be
recognized. 'For [the writers of the N. T. the Scripture], was
the one thesaurus of truth. They had almost no other books.
The words of the O. T. had become a part of their mental furni-
ture, and they used them to a certain extent with the freedom with
which they used their own ideas' (Toy, *Quotations*, &c. p. xx). It
is a use which is constantly being made of the Bible at the present
day, and when we attempt to analyze the exact force it is intended
to convey, it is neither easy nor desirable to be precise. Between
the purely rhetorical use on the one side and the logical proof on
the other there are infinite gradations of ideas, and it is never quite
possible to say how far in any definite passage the use is purely
rhetorical and how far it is intended to suggest a definite argument.

But there is a third class of instances in which the words are
used in a sense which the original context will not bear, and yet the
object is to give a logical proof. This happens mainly in a certain
class of passages; in those in which the Law is used to condemn
the Law, in those in which passages not Messianic are used with
a Messianic bearing, and in those (a class connected with the last)
in which passages are applied to the calling of the Gentiles which
do not refer to that event in the original. Here controversially the
method is justified. Some of the passages used Messianically by the
Christians had probably been so used by the Rabbis before them.
In all cases the methods they adopted were those of their contemporaries, however incorrect they may have been. But what of the
method in relation to our own times? Are we justified in using it?
The answer to that must be sought in a comparison of their teaching
with that of the Rabbis. We have said that controversially it was
justified. The method was the same as, and as good as, that of
their own time; but it was no better. As far as method goes the
Rabbis were equally justified in their conclusions. There is in
fact no standard of right and wrong, when once it is permitted to
take words in a sense which their original context will not bear.
Anything can be proved from anything.

Where then does the superiority of the N. T. writers lie? In
their correct interpretation of the spirit of the O. T. 'As ex-
pounders of religion, they belong to the whole world and to all
time; as logicians, they belong to the first century. The essence
of their writing is the Divine spirit of love and righteousness that
filled their souls, the outer shell is the intellectual form in which

the spirit found expression in words. Their comprehension of the deeper spirit of the O. T. thought is one thing: the logical method by which they sought formally to extend it is quite another' (Toy, *Quotations, &c.* p. xxi). This is just one of those points in which we must trace the superiority of the N. T. writers to its root and take from them that, and not their faulty exegesis.

An illustration may be drawn from Church History. The Church inherited equally from the Jewish schools, the Greek Philosophers, and the N. T. writers an unhistorical method of interpretation; and in the Arian controversy (to take an example) it constantly makes use of this method. We are learning to realize more and more how much of our modern theology is based on the writings of St. Athanasius; but that does not impose upon us the necessity of adopting his exegesis. If the methods that he applies to the O. T. are to be admitted it is almost as easy to deduce Arianism from it. Athanasius did not triumph because of those exegetical methods, but because he rightly interpreted (and men felt that he had rightly interpreted) the spirit of the N. T. His creed, his religious insight, to a certain extent his philosophy, we accept: but not his exegetical methods.

So with the O. T. St. Paul triumphed, and the Christian Church triumphed, over Judaism, because they both rightly interpreted the spirit of the O. T. We must accept that interpretation, although we shall find that we arrive at it on other grounds. This may be illustrated in two main points.

It is the paradox of ch. x that it condemns the Law out of the Law; that it convicts the Jews by applying to them passages, which in the original accuse them of breaking the Law, in order to condemn them for keeping it. But the paradox is only apparent. Running through the O. T., in the books of the Law as well as in those of the Prophets, is the prophetic spirit, always bringing out the spiritual truths and lessons concealed in or guarded by the Law in opposition to the formal adherence to its precepts. This spirit the Gospel inherits. 'The Gospel itself is a reawakening of the spirit of prophecy. There are many points in which the teaching of St. Paul bears a striking resemblance to that of the old Prophets. It is not by chance that so many quotations from them occur in his writings. Separated from Joel, Amos, Hosea, Micah, and Isaiah by an interval of about 800 years, he felt a kind of sympathy with them; they expressed his inmost feelings; like them he was at war with the evil of the world around. When they spoke of forgiveness of sins, of non-imputation of sins, of a sudden turning to God, what did this mean but righteousness by faith? When they said, "I will have mercy and not sacrifice," here also was imaged the great truth, that salvation was not of the Law ... Like the elder Prophets, he came not "to build up a temple made with

x

hands," but to teach a moral truth : like them he went forth alone, and not in connexion with the church at Jerusalem : like them he was looking for and hastening to the day of the Lord' (Jowett). This represents the truth, as the historical study of the O. T. will prove ; or rather one side of the truth. The Gospel is not merely the reawakening of the spirit of prophecy ; it is also the fulfilment of the spiritual teaching of Law. It was necessary for a later writer—the author of the Epistle to the Hebrews—when controversy was less bitter to bring this out more fully. Christ not only revived all the teaching of the Prophets, righteousness, mercy, peace ; He also exhibited by His death the teaching of the Law, the heinousness of sin, the duty of sacrifice, the spiritual union of God and man.

The same lines of argument will justify the Messianic use of the O. T. If we study it historically the reality of the Messianic interpretation remains just as clear as it was to St. Paul. Allegorical and incorrect exegesis could never create an idea. They only illustrate one which has been suggested in other ways. The Messianic interpretation, and with it the further idea of the universality of the Messianic kingdom, arose because they are contained in the O. T. Any incorrectness of exegesis that there may be lies not in the ideas themselves but in finding them in passages which have probably a different meaning. We are not bound, and it would be wrong to bind ourselves, by the incorrect exegesis of particular passages ; but the reality and truth of the Messianic idea and the universal character of the Messianic kingdom, as prophesied in the O. T. and fulfilled in the N. T., remain one of the most real and impressive facts in religious history. Historical criticism does not disprove this ; it only places it on a stronger foundation and enables us to trace the origin and growth of the idea more accurately (cf. Sanday, *Bampton Lectures*, pp. 404, 405).

The value of St. Paul's exegesis therefore lies not in his true interpretation of individual passages, but in his insight into the spiritual meaning of the O. T. ; we need not use his methods, but the books of the Bible will have little value for us if we are not able to see in them the spiritual teaching which he saw. In the cause of truth, as a guide to right religious ideas, as a fatal enemy to many a false and erroneous and harmful doctrine, historical criticism and interpretation are of immense value ; but if they be divorced from a spiritual insight, such as can be learnt only by the spiritual teaching of the N. T., which interprets the O. T. from the standpoint of its highest and truest fulfilment, they will become as barren and unproductive as the strangest conceits of the Rabbis or the most unreal fancies of the Schoolmen.

[See, besides other works : Jowett, *Contrasts of Prophecy*, in his edition of the Romans ; Toy, *Quotations in the New Testament,*

New York, 1884; Kautzsch, *De Veteris Testamenti locis a Paulo Apostolo allegatis*, Lipsiae, 1869; Clemen (Dr. August), *Ueber den Gebrauch des Alten Testaments im Neuen Testamente, und speciell in den Reden Jesu* (Einladungsschrift, &c., Leipzig, 1891); Turpie (David McCalman), *The Old Testament in the New*, London, 1868.]

THE REJECTION OF ISRAEL NOT COMPLETE.

XI. 1-10. Israel then has refused to accept the salvation offered it; is it therefore rejected? No. At any rate the rejection is not complete. Now as always in the history of Israel, although the mass of the people may be condemned to disbelief, there is a remnant that shall be saved.

[1] The conclusion of the preceding argument is this. It is through their own fault that Israel has rejected a salvation which was fully and freely offered. Now what does this imply? Does it mean that God has rejected His chosen people? Heaven forbid that I should say this! I who like them am an Israelite, an Israelite by birth and not a proselyte, a lineal descendant of Abraham, a member of the tribe that with Judah formed the restored Israel after the exile. [2] No, God has not rejected His people. He chose them for His own before all time and nothing can make Him change His purpose. If you say He has rejected them, it only shows that you have not clearly grasped the teaching of Scripture concerning the Remnant. Elijah on Mt. Horeb brought just such an accusation against his countrymen. [3] He complained that they had forsaken the covenant, that they had overthrown God's altars, that they had slain His Prophets; just as the Jews at the present day have slain the Messiah and persecuted His messengers. Elijah only was left, and his life they sought. The whole people, God's chosen people, had been rejected. [4] So he thought; but the Divine response came to him, that there were seven thousand men left in Israel who had not bowed the knee to Baal. There was a kernel of the nation that remained loyal. [5] Exactly the same circumstances exist now as then. Now as then the mass of the people are unfaithful, but there is a remnant of loyal ad-

herents to the Divine message:—a remnant, be it remembered, chosen by God by an act of free favour: ⁶that is to say those whom God has in His good pleasure selected for that position, who have in no way earned it by any works they have done, or any merit of their own.　If that were possible Grace would lose all its meaning: there would be no occasion for God to show free favour to mankind.

⁷It is necessary then at any rate to modify the broad statement that has been made.　Israel, it is true, has failed to obtain the righteousness which it sought; but, although this is true of the nation as a whole, there is a Remnant of which it is not true. Those whom God selected have attained it.　But what of the rest? Their hearts have been hardened.　Here again we find the same conditions prevailing throughout Israel's history.　⁸Isaiah declared (xxix. 10; vi. 9, 10) how God had thrown the people into a state of spiritual torpor.　He had given them eyes which could not see, and ears which could not hear.　All through their history the mass of the people has been destitute of spiritual insight.　⁹And again in the book of Psalms, David (lxix. 23, 24) declares the Divine wrath against the unfaithful of the nation: 'May their table be their snare.'　It is just their position as God's chosen people, it is the Law and the Scriptures, which are their boast, that are to be the cause of their ruin.　They are to be punished by being allowed to cleave fast to that to which they have perversely adhered.　¹⁰'Let their eyes be blinded, so that they cannot see light when it shines upon them: let their back be ever bent under the burden to which they have so obstinately clung.'　This was God's judgement then on Israel for their faithlessness, and it is God's judgement on them now.

1–36.　St. Paul has now shown (1) (ix. 6–29) that God was perfectly free, whether as regards promise or His right as Creator, to reject Israel; (2) (ix. 30–x. 21) that Israel on their side by neglecting the Divine method of salvation offered them have deserved this rejection.　He now comes to the original question from which he started, but which he never expressed, and asks, Has God, as might be thought from the drift of the argument so far, really cast away His people?　To this he gives a negative answer, which he proceeds to justify by showing (1) that this rejection is only partial (xi. 1–10), (2) only temporary (xi. 11–25), and (3) that in all this Divine action there has been a purpose deeper and wiser than man can altogether understand (xi. 26–36).

1. λέγω οὖν. This somewhat emphatic phrase occurring here
and in ver. 11 seems to mark a stage in the argument, the οὖν as
so often summing up the result so far arrived at. The change of
particle shows that we have not here a third question parallel to
the ἀλλὰ λέγω of x. 18, 19.

μὴ ἀπώσατο ὁ Θεὸς τὸν λαὸν αὐτοῦ; 'Is it possible that God has
cast away His people?' The form of the question implies necessarily a negative answer and suggests an argument against it. (1)
By the juxtaposition of ὁ Θεός and τὸν λαὸν αὐτοῦ. Israel is God's
people and so He cannot reject them. *Ipsa* populi eius *appellatio
rationem negandi continet.* Beng. (2) By the use made of the
language of the O. T. Three times in the O. T. (1 Sam. xii. 22;
Ps. xciii [xciv]. 14; xciv [xcv]. 4) the promise οὐκ ἀπώσεται Κύριος
τὸν λαὸν αὐτοῦ occurs. By using words which must be so well
known St. Paul reminds his readers of the promise, and thus again
implies an answer to the question.

This very clear instance of the merely literary use of the language
of the O. T. makes it more probable that St. Paul should have
adopted a similar method elsewhere, as in x. 6 ff., 18.

μὴ γένοιτο. St. Paul repudiates the thought with horror. All
his feelings as an Israelite make it disloyal in him to hold it.

καὶ γὰρ κ.τ.λ. These words have been taken in two ways. (1)
As a proof of the incorrectness of the suggestion. St. Paul was an
Israelite, and he had been saved; therefore the people as a whole
could not have been rejected. So the majority of commentators
(Go. Va. Oltr. Weiss). But the answer to the question does not
occur until St. Paul gives it in a solemn form at the beginning of
the next verse; he would not therefore have previously given
a reason for its incorrectness. Moreover it would be inconsistent
with St. Paul's tact and character to put himself forward so prominently.

(2) It is therefore better to take it as giving 'the motive for his
deprecation, not a proof of his denial' (Mey. Gif. Lips.). Throughout this passage, St. Paul partly influenced by the reality of his
own sympathy, partly by a desire to put his argument in a form as
little offensive as possible, has more than once emphasized his own
kinship with Israel (ix. 1–3; x. 1). Here for the first time, just
when he is going to disprove it, he makes the statement which has
really been the subject of the two previous passages, and at once,
in order if possible to disarm criticism, reminds his readers that he
is an Israelite, and that therefore to him, as much as to them, the
supposition seems almost blasphemous.

Ἰσραηλίτης κ.τ.λ. Cf. 2 Cor. xi. 22; Phil. iii. 5.

ὃν προέγνω, which is added by Lachmann after τὸν λαὸν αὐτοῦ, has the
support of A D Chrys. and other authorities, but clearly came in from ver. 2.

2. οὐκ ἀπώσατο. St. Paul gives expressly and formally a negative answer to the question he has just asked, adding emphasis by repeating the very words he has used.

ὃν προέγνω. The addition of these words gives a reason for the emphatic denial of which they form a part. Israel was the race which God in His Divine foreknowledge had elected and chosen, and therefore He could not cast it off. The reference in this chapter is throughout to the election of the nation as a whole, and therefore the words cannot have a limiting sense (Orig. Chrys. Aug.), 'that people whom He foreknew,' i. e. those of His people whom He foreknew; nor again can they possibly refer to the spiritual Israel, as that would oblige a meaning to be given to λαός different from that in ver. 1. The word προέγνω may be taken, (1) as used in the Hebrew sense, to mean 'whom He has known or chosen beforehand.' So γινώσκειν in the LXX. Amos iii. 2 ὑμᾶς ἔγνων ἐκ πασῶν τῶν φυλῶν τῆς γῆς. And in St. Paul 1 Cor. viii. 3 εἰ δέ τις ἀγαπᾷ τὸν Θεόν, οὗτος ἔγνωσται ὑπ' αὐτοῦ. Gal. iv. 9 νῦν δὲ γνόντες Θεόν, μᾶλλον δὲ γνωσθέντες ὑπὸ Θεοῦ. 2 Tim. ii. 19 ἔγνω Κύριος τοὺς ὄντας αὐτοῦ. Although there is no evidence for this use of προγινώσκειν it represents probably the idea which St. Paul had in his mind (see on viii. 29). (2) But an alternative interpretation taking the word in its natural meaning of foreknowledge, must not be lost sight of, ' that people of whose history and future destiny God had full foreknowledge.' This seems to be the meaning with which the word is generally used (Wisd. vi. 13; viii. 8; xviii. 6; Just. Mart. Apol. i. 28; Dial. 42. p. 261 B.); so too πρόγνωσις is used definitely and almost technically of the Divine foreknowledge (Acts ii. 23); and in this chapter St. Paul ends with vindicating the Divine wisdom which had prepared for Israel and the world a destiny which exceeds human comprehension.

ἢ οὐκ οἴδατε: cf. ii. 4; vi. 3; vii. 1; ix. 21. 'You must admit this or be ignorant of what the Scripture says.' The point of the quotation lies not in the words which immediately follow, but in the contrast between the two passages; a contrast which represented the distinction between the apparent and the real situation at the time when the Apostle wrote.

ἐν Ἠλίᾳ: 'in the section of Scripture which narrates the story of Elijah.' The O. T. Scriptures were divided into paragraphs to which were given titles derived from their subject-matter; and these came to be very commonly used in quotations as references. Many instances are quoted from the Talmud and from Hebrew commentators: Berachoth, fol. 2. col. 1, fol. 4. col. 2 id quod scriptum est apud Michäel, referring to Is. vi. 6. So Taanijoth, ii. 1; Aboth de-Rabbi Nathan, c. 9; Shir hashirim rabba i. 6, where a phrase similar to that used here, 'In Elijah,' occurs, and the same passage is quoted, 'I have been very jealous for the Lord, the God of Hosts.' So also Philo, De Agricultura, p. 203 (i. 317 Mang.) λέγει γὰρ ἐν ταῖς ἀραῖς, referring to Gen. iii. 15. The phrase ἐπὶ τῆς βάτου Mark xii. 26; Luke xx. 37; Clem. *Hom.* xvi. 14; *Apost. Const.* v. 20, is often explained in a similar manner, but very probably incorrectly, the ἐπί being perhaps purely local. The usage exactly corresponds to the method used in quoting the Homeric poems. As the Rabbis divided the O. T. into sections so the Rhapsodists divided Homer, and these sections were quoted by their subjects, ἐν Ἕκτορος ἀναιρέσει, ἐν νεκυίᾳ. (See Fri. Delitzsch *ad loc.*, Surenhusius, Βίβλος καταλλαγῆς, p. 31.)

ἐντυγχάνει: 'he accuses Israel before God.' The verb ἐν-τυγχάνειν means, (1) 'to meet with,' (2) 'to meet with for the purposes of conversation,' 'have an interview with,' Acts xxv. 24; hence (3) 'to converse with,' 'plead with,' Wisdom viii. 21, either on behalf of some one (ὑπέρ τινος) Rom. viii. 27, 34; Heb. vii. 25; or against some one (κατά τινος), and so (4) definitely 'to accuse' as here and 1 Macc. xi. 25 καὶ ἐνετύγχανον κατ' αὐτοῦ τινες ἄνομοι τῶν ἐκ τοῦ ἔθνους: viii. 32; x. 61, 63.

The TR. adds λέγων at the end of this verse with ℵ* L *al. pler.*, it is omitted by ℵᶜABCDEFGP *min. pauc.*, Vulg. Sah. Boh., and most Fathers.

3. Κύριε, τοὺς προφήτας κ.τ.λ. The two quotations come from 1 Kings xix. 10, 14, 18; the first being repeated twice. Elijah has fled to Mt. Horeb from Jezebel, and accuses his countrymen before God of complete apostasy; he alone is faithful. God answers that even although the nation as a whole has deserted Him, yet there is a faithful remnant, 7,000 men who have not bowed the knee to Baal. There is an analogy, St. Paul argues, between this situation and that of his own day. The spiritual condition is the same. The nation as a whole has rejected God's message, now as then; but now as then also there is a faithful remnant left, and if that be so God cannot be said to have cast away His people.

The quotation is somewhat shortened from the LXX, and the order of the clauses is inverted, perhaps to put in a prominent position the words τοὺς προφήτας σου ἀπέκτειναν to which there was most analogy during St. Paul's time (cf. Acts vii. 52; 1 Thess. ii. 14). The καί between the clauses of the TR. is read by D E L and later MSS. Justin Martyr, *Dial.* 39. p. 257 D, quotes the words as in St. Paul and not as in the LXX: Καὶ γὰρ Ἡλίας περὶ ὑμῶν πρὸς τὸν Θεὸν ἐντυγχάνων οὕτως λέγει· Κύριε, τοὺς προφήτας σου ἀπέκτειναν καὶ τὰ θυσιαστήριά σου κατέσκαψαν κἀγὼ ὑπελείφθην μόνος καὶ ζητοῦσι τὴν ψυχήν μου. καὶ ἀποκρίνεται αὐτῷ, Ἔτι εἰσί μοι ἑπτακισχίλιοι ἄνδρες, οἳ οὐκ ἔκαμψαν γόνυ τῇ Βάαλ.

4. ὁ χρηματισμός: 'the oracle.' An unusual sense for the word, which occurs here only in the N. T., but is found in 2 Macc. ii. 4; Clem. Rom. xvii. 5; and occasionally elsewhere. The verb χρηματίζειν meant (1) originally 'to transact business'; then (2) 'to consult,' 'deliberate'; hence (3) 'to give audience,' 'answer after deliberation'; and so finally (4) of an oracle 'to give a response, taking the place of the older χράω; and so it is used in the N. T. of the Divine warning Mat. ii. 12, 22 χρηματισθέντες κατ' ὄναρ: Luke ii. 26; Acts x. 22; Heb. viii. 5; xi. 7: cf. Jos. *Antt.* V. i. 14; X. i. 3; XI. iii. 4. From this usage of the verb χρηματίζω was derived χρηματισμός, as the more usual χρησμός from χράω. See also p. 173.

τῇ Βάαλ: substituted by St. Paul (as also by Justin Martyr, *loc. cit.*) for the LXX τῷ Βάαλ, according to a usage common in other passages in the Greek Version.

The word Baal, which means 'Lord,' appears to have been originally used as one of the names of the God of Israel, and as such became a part of many Jewish names, as for example Jerubbaal (Jud. vi. 32; vii. 1), Eshbaal (1 Chron. ix. 39), Meribbaal (1 Chron. ix. 40), &c. But gradually the special association of the name with the idolatrous worship of the Phoenician god caused the use of it to be forbidden. Hosea ii. 16, 17 'and it shall be at that day, saith the Lord, that thou shalt call me Ishi; and shalt call me no more Baali. For I will take away the names of the Baalim out of her mouth, and they shall no more be mentioned by their name.' Owing to this motive a tendency arose to obliterate the name of Baal from the Scriptures: just as owing to a feeling of reverence 'Elohim' was substituted for 'Jehovah' in the second and third books of the Psalms. This usage took the form of substituting *Bosheth*, 'abomination,' for Baal. So Eshbaal (1 Chr. viii. 33, ix. 39) became Ishbosheth (2 Sam. ii. 8; iii. 8); Meribbaal (1 Chr. ix. 40) Mephibosheth (2 Sam. ix. 6 ff.); Jerubbaal Jerubbesheth (2 Sam. xi. 21). See also Hosea ix. 10; Jer. iii. 24; xi. 13. Similarly in the LXX αἰσχύνη represents in one passage Baal of the Hebrew text, 3 Kings xviii. 19, 25. But it seems to have been more usual to substitute αἰσχύνη in reading for the written Βάαλ, and as a sign of this *Qeri* the feminine article was written; just as the name Jehovah was written with the pointing of Adonai. This usage is most common in Jeremiah, but occurs also in the books of Kings, Chronicles, and other Prophets. It appears not to occur in the Pentateuch. The plural ταῖς occurs 2 Chr. xxiv. 7; xxxiii. 3. This, the only satisfactory explanation of the feminine article with the masculine name, is given by Dillmann, *Monatsberichte der Akademie der Wissenschaft zu Berlin*, 1881, p. 601 ff. and has superseded all others.

The LXX version is again shortened in the quotation, and for καταλείψω is substituted κατέλιπον ἐμαυτῷ, which is an alternative and perhaps more exact translation of the Hebrew.

5. οὕτως οὖν. The application of the preceding instance to the circumstances of the Apostle's own time. The facts were the same. St. Paul would assume that his readers, some of whom were Jewish Christians, and all of whom were aware of the existence of such a class, would recognize this. And if this were so the same deduction might be made. As then the Jewish people were not rejected, because the remnant was saved; so now there is a remnant, and this implies that God has not cast away His people as such.

λεῖμμα (on the orthography cf. WH. ii. *App.* p. 154, who read λίμμα), 'a remnant.' The word does not occur elsewhere in the N. T., and in the O. T. only twice, and then not in the technical sense of the 'remnant.' The usual word for that is τὸ καταλειφθέν.

κατ᾽ ἐκλογὴν χάριτος. Predicate with γέγονεν. 'There has come to be through the principle of selection which is dependent on the Divine grace or favour.' This addition to the thought, which is further explained in ver. 6, reminds the reader of the result of the previous discussion: that 'election' on which the Jews had always laid so much stress had operated, but it was a selection on the part of God of those to whom He willed to give His grace, and not an election of those who had earned it by their works.

6. εἰ δὲ χάριτι κ.τ.λ. A further explanation of the principles of election. If the election had been on the basis of works, then the Jews might have demanded that God's promise could only be fulfilled if all who had earned it had received it: St. Paul, by reminding them of the principles of election already laid down, implies that the promise is fulfilled if the remnant is saved. God's people are those whom He has chosen; it is not that the Jews are chosen because they are His people.

ἐπεὶ ἡ χάρις οὐκέτι γίνεται χάρις: 'this follows from the very meaning of the idea of grace.' *Gratia nisi gratis sit gratia non est.* St. Augustine.

The TR. after γίνεται χάρις adds εἰ δὲ ἐξ ἔργων, οὐκέτι ἐστὶ χάρις· ἐπεὶ τὸ ἔργον οὐκέτι ἐστὶν ἔργον with אᶜ(B) L and later MSS., Syrr., Chrys. and Thdrt. (in the text, but they do not refer to the words in their commentary). B reads εἰ δὲ ἐξ ἔργων, οὐκέτι χάρις· ἐπεὶ τὸ ἔργον οὐκέτι ἐστὶ χάρις. The clause is omitted by א* A C D E F G P, Vulg. Aegyptt. (Boh. Sah.) Arm., Orig.-lat. Jo.-Damasc. Ambrst. *Patr.-latt.* There need be no doubt that it is a gloss, nor is the authority of B of any weight in support of a Western addition such as this against such preponderating authority. This is considered by WH. to be the solitary or almost the solitary case in which B possibly has a Syrian reading (Introd. ii. 150).

7. τί οὖν; This verse sums up the result of the discussion in vv. 2-6. 'What then is the result? In what way can we modify the harsh statement made in ver. 1? It is indeed still true that Israel as a nation has failed to obtain what is its aim, namely righteousness: but at the same time there is one portion of it, the elect, who have attained it.'

ἡ δὲ ἐκλογή: i.e. οἱ ἐκλεκτοί. The abstract for the concrete suggests the reason for their success by laying stress on the idea rather than on the individuals.

οἱ δὲ λοιποὶ ἐπωρώθησαν: 'while the elect have attained what they sought, those who have failed to attain it have been hardened.' They have not failed because they have been hardened, but they have been hardened because they have failed; cf. i. 24 ff., where sin is represented as God's punishment inflicted on man for their rebellion. Here St. Paul does not definitely say by whom, for that is not the point it interests him to discuss at present: he has represented the condition of Israel both as the result of God's action (ch. ix) and of their own (ch. x). Here as in κατηρτισμένα

ix. 22, he uses the colourless passive without laying stress on the cause: the quotation in ver. 8 represents God as the author, ἔπταισαν in ver. 11 suggests that they are free agents.

The verb πωρόω (derived from πῶρος a callus or stone formed in the bladder) is a medical term used in Hippocrates and elsewhere of a bone or hard substance growing when bones are fractured, or of a stone forming in the bladder. Hence metaphorically it is used in the N. T., and apparently there only of the heart becoming hardened or callous: so Mark vi. 52; Jo. xii. 40; Rom. xi. 7; 2 Cor. iii. 14: while the noun πώρωσις occurs in the same sense, Mark iii. 5; Rom. xi. 25; Eph. iv. 18. The idea is in all these places the same, that a covering has grown over the heart, making men incapable of receiving any new teaching however good, and making them oblivious of the wrong they are doing. In Job xvii. 7 (πεπώρωνται γὰρ ἀπὸ ὀργῆς οἱ ὀφθαλμοί μου) the word is used of blindness, but again only of moral blindness; anger has caused as it were a covering to grow over the eyes. There is therefore no need to take the word to mean 'blind,' as do the grammarians (Suidas, πωρός, ὁ τυφλός: πεπώρωται, τετύφλωται: Hesychius, πεπωρωμένοι, τετυφλωμένοι) and the Latin Versions (excaecati, obcaecati). It is possible that this translation arose from a confusion with πηρός (see on κατανύξεως below) which was perhaps occasionally used of blindness (see Prof. Armitage Robinson in Academy, 1892, p. 305), although probably then as a specialized usage for the more general 'maimed.' Although the form πηρόω occurs in some MSS. of the N. T., yet the evidence against it is in every case absolutely conclusive, as it is also in the O. T. in the one passage where the word occurs.

8. καθὼς γέγραπται. St. Paul supports and explains his last statement οἱ δὲ λοιποὶ ἐπωρώθησαν by quotations from the O. T. The first which in form resembles Deut. xxix. 4, modified by Is. xxix. 10; vi. 9, 10, describes the spiritual dulness or torpor of which the prophet accuses the Israelites. This he says had been given them by God as a punishment for their faithlessness. These words will equally well apply to the spiritual condition of the Apostle's own time, showing that it is not inconsistent with the position of Israel as God's people, and suggesting a general law of God's dealing with them.

The following extracts, in which the words that St. Paul has made use of are printed in spaced type, will give the source of the quotation. Deut. xxix. 4 καὶ οὐκ ἔδωκεν Κύριος ὁ Θεὸς ὑμῖν καρδίαν εἰδέναι καὶ ὀφθαλμοὺς βλέπειν καὶ ὦτα ἀκούειν ἕως τῆς ἡμέρας ταύτης. Is. xxix. 10 ὅτι πεπότικεν ὑμᾶς Κύριος πνεύματι κατανύξεως: cf. Is. vi. 9, 10 ἀκοῇ ἀκούσετε καὶ οὐ μὴ συνῆτε καὶ βλέποντες βλέψετε καὶ οὐ μὴ ἴδητε. ... καὶ εἶπα Ἕως πότε, Κύριε; While the form resembles the words in Deut., the historical situation and meaning of the quotation are represented by the passages in Isaiah to which St. Paul is clearly referring.

πνεῦμα κατανύξεως: 'a spirit of torpor,' a state of dull insensibility to everything spiritual, such as would be produced by drunkenness, or stupor. Is. xxix. 10 (RV.) 'For the Lord hath poured out upon you the spirit of deep sleep, and hath closed your eyes, the prophets; and your heads, the seers, hath He covered.'

The word κατάνυξις is derived from κατανύσσομαι. The simple verb νύσσω is used to mean to 'prick' or 'strike' or 'dint.' The compound verb would mean, (1) to 'strike' or 'prick violently,' and hence (2) to 'stun'; no instance is quoted of it in its primary sense, but it is common (3) especially in the LXX of strong emotions, of the prickings of lust Susan. 10 (Theod.); of strong grief Gen. xxxiv. 7; Ecclus. xiv. 1; and so Acts ii. 37 κατενύγησαν τῇ καρδίᾳ of being strongly moved by speaking. Then (4) it is used of the stunning effect of such emotion which results in speechlessness : Is. vi. 5 ὢ τάλας ἐγὼ ὅτι κατανένυγμαι : Dan. x. 15 ἔδωκα τὸ πρόσωπόν μου ἐπὶ τὴν γῆν καὶ κατενύγην, and so the general idea of torpor would be derived. The noun κατάνυξις appears to occur only twice, Is. xxix. 10 πνεῦμα κατανύξεως, Ps. lix [lx]. 4 οἶνον κατανύξεως. In the former case it clearly means 'torpor' or 'deep sleep,' as both the context and the Hebrew show, in the latter case probably so. It may be noticed that this definite meaning of 'torpor' or 'deep sleep' which is found in the noun cannot be exactly paralleled in the verb; and it may be suggested that a certain confusion existed with the verb νυστάζω, which means 'to nod in sleep,' 'be drowsy,' just as the meaning of ἐριθεία was influenced by its resemblance to ἔρις (cf. ii. 8). On the word generally see Fri. ii. p. 558 ff.

ἕως τῆς σήμερον ἡμέρας: cf. Acts vii. 51 'Ye stiffnecked and uncircumcised in heart and ears, ye do always resist the Holy Ghost: as your fathers did so do ye.' St. Stephen's speech illustrates more in detail the logical assumptions which underlie St. Paul's quotations. The chosen people have from the beginning shown the same obstinate adherence to their own views and a power of resisting the Holy Ghost; and God has throughout punished them for their obstinacy by giving them over to spiritual blindness.

9. καὶ Δαβὶδ λέγει κ.τ.λ.: quoted from the LXX of Ps. lxviii [lxix]. 23, 24 γενηθήτω ἡ τράπεζα αὐτῶν ἐνώπιον αὐτῶν εἰς παγίδα, καὶ εἰς ἀνταπόδοσιν καὶ σκάνδαλον· σκοτισθήτωσαν κ.τ.λ. (which is ascribed in the title to David) with reminiscences of Ps. xxxiv [xxxv]. 8, and xxvii [xxviii]. 4. The Psalmist is represented as declaring the Divine wrath against those who have made themselves enemies of the Divine will. Those who in his days were the enemies of the spiritual life of the people are represented in the Apostle's days by the Jews who have shut their ears to the Gospel message.

ἡ τράπεζα αὐτῶν: 'their feast.' The image is that of men feasting in careless security, and overtaken by their enemies, owing to the very prosperity which ought to be their strength. So to the Jews that Law and those Scriptures wherein they trusted are to become the very cause of their fall and the snare or hunting-net in which they are caught.

σκάνδαλον: 'that over which they fall,' 'a cause of their destruction.'

ἀνταπόδομα: Ps. xxvii [xxviii]. 4. 'A requital,' 'recompense.' The Jews are to be punished for their want of spiritual insight by being given over to blind trust in their own law; in fact being given up entirely to their own wishes.

10. σκοτισθήτωσαν κ.τ.λ. 'May their eyes become blind, so that they have no insight, and their backs bent like men who are continually groping about in the dark!' They are to be like those described by Plato as fast bound in the cave: even if they are brought to the light they will only be blinded by it, and will be unable to see. The judgement upon them is that they are to be ever bent down with the weight of the burden which they have wilfully taken on their backs.

It may be worth noticing that Lipsius, who does not elsewhere accept the theory of interpolations in the text, suggests that vv. 9, 10 are a gloss added by some reader in the margin after the fall of Jerusalem (cf. Holsten, *Z.f. w. T.* 1872, p. 455; Michelsen, *Th. T.* 1887, p. 163; *Protestanten-bibel*, 1872, p. 589; *E. T.* ii. 154). It is suggested that διαπαντὸς is inconsistent with ver. 11 ff. But it has not been noticed that in ver. 11 we have a change of metaphor, ἔπταισαν, which would be singularly out of place if it came immediately after ver. 8. As it is, this word is suggested and accounted for by the metaphors employed in the quotation introduced in ver. 9. If we omit vv. 9, 10 we must also omit ver. 11. There is throughout the whole Epistle a continuous succession of thought running from verse to verse which makes any theory of interpolation impossible. (See Introduction, § 9.)

The Doctrine of the Remnant.

The idea of the 'Remnant' is one of the most typical and significant in the prophetic portions of the O. T. We meet it first apparently in the prophetic narrative which forms the basis of the account of Elijah in the book of Kings, the passage which St. Paul is quoting. Here a new idea is introduced into Israel's history, and it is introduced in one of the most solemn and impressive narratives of that history. The Prophet is taken into the desert to commune with God; he is taken to Sinai, the mountain of God, which played such a large part in the traditions of His people, and he receives the Divine message in that form which has ever marked off this as unique amongst theophanies, the 'still small voice,' contrasted with the thunder, and the storm, and the earthquake. And the idea that was thus introduced marks a stage in the religious history of the world, for it was the first revelation of the idea of personal as opposed to national consecration. Up to that time it was the nation as a whole that was bound to God, the nation as a whole for which sacrifices were offered, the nation as a whole for which kings had fought and judges legislated. But the nation as a whole had deserted Jehovah, and the Prophet records that it is the loyalty of the individual Israelites who had remained true to Him that must henceforth be reckoned. The nation will be chastised, but the remnant shall be saved.

The idea is a new one, but it is one which we find continuously from this time onwards; spiritualized with the more spiritual ideas of the later prophets. We find it in Amos (ix. 8-10), in Micah (ii.

12, v. 3), in Zephaniah (iii. 12, 13), in Jeremiah (xxiii. 3), in Ezekiel (xiv. 14–20, 22), but most pointedly and markedly in Isaiah. The two great and prominent ideas of Isaiah's prophecy are typified in the names given to his two sons,—the reality of the Divine vengeance (Maher-shalal-hash-baz) and the salvation of the Remnant (Shear-Jashub) and, through the Holy and Righteous Remnant, of the theocratic nation itself (vii. 3 ; viii. 2, 18; ix. 12; x. 21, 24); and both these ideas are prominent in the narrative of the call (vi. 9–13) 'Hear ye indeed, but understand not, and see ye indeed, but perceive not. Make the heart of this people fat, and make their ears heavy, and shut their eyes ... Then said I, Lord, how long ? And He answered, Until cities be waste without inhabitant and homes without men, and the land become utterly waste.' But this is only one side. There is a true stock left. 'Like the terebinth and the oak, whose stock remains when they are cut down and sends forth new saplings, so the holy seed remains as a living stock and a new and better Israel shall spring from the ruin of the ancient state' (Robertson Smith, *Prophets of Israel*, p. 234). This doctrine of a Remnant implied that it was the individual who was true to his God, and not the nation, that was the object of the Divine solicitude; that it was in this small body of individuals that the true life of the chosen nation dwelt, and that from them would spring that internal reformation, which, coming as the result of the Divine chastisement, would produce a whole people, pure and undefiled, to be offered to God (Is. lxv. 8, 9).

The idea appealed with great force to the early Christians. It appealed to St. Stephen, in whose speech one of the main currents of thought seems to be the marvellous analogy which runs through all the history of Israel. The mass of the people has ever been unfaithful; it is the individual or the small body that has remained true to God in all the changes of Israel's history, and these the people have always persecuted as they crucified the Messiah. And so St. Paul, musing over the sad problem of Israel's unbelief, finds its explanation and justification in this consistent trait of the nation's history. As in Elijah's time, as in Isaiah's time, so now the mass of the people have rejected the Divine call; but there always has been and still is the true Remnant, the Remnant whom God has selected, who have preserved the true life and ideal of the people and thus contain the elements of new and prolonged life.

And this doctrine of the 'Remnant' is as true to human nature as it is to Israel's history. No church or nation is saved *en masse*, it is those members of it who are righteous. It is not the mass of the nation or church that has done its work, but the select few who have preserved the consciousness of its high calling. It is by the selection of individuals, even in the nation that has been chosen, that God has worked equally in religion and in all the different lines along which the path of human development has progressed.

[On the Remnant see especially Jowett, *Contrasts of Prophecy*, in *Romans* ii. p. 290; and Robertson Smith, *The Prophets of Israel*, pp. 106, 209, 234, 258. The references are collected in Oehler, *Theologie des alten Testaments*, p. 809.]

THE REJECTION OF ISRAEL NOT FINAL.

XI. 11-24. *The Rejection of Israel is not complete, nor will it be final. Its result has been the extension of the Church to the Gentiles. The salvation of these will stir the Jews to jealousy; they will return to the Kingdom, and this will mean the final consummation* (vv. 10–15).

Of all this the guarantee is the holiness of the stock from which Israel comes. God has grafted you Gentiles into that stock against the natural order; far more easily can He restore them to a position which by nature and descent is theirs (vv. 16–24).

[11] The Rejection of Israel then is only partial. Yet still there is the great mass of the nation on whom God's judgement has come: what of these? Is there no further hope for them? Is this stumbling of theirs such as will lead to a final and complete fall? By no means. It is only temporary, a working out of the Divine purpose. This purpose is partly fulfilled. It has resulted in the extension of the Messianic salvation to the Gentiles. It is partly in the future; that the inclusion of these in the Kingdom may rouse the Jews to emulation and bring them back to the place which should be theirs and from which so far they have been excluded. [12] And consider what this means. Even the transgression of Israel has brought to the world a great wealth of spiritual blessings; their repulse has enriched the nations, how much greater then will be the result when the chosen people with their numbers completed have accepted the Messiah? [13] In these speculations about my countrymen, I am not disregarding my proper mission to you Gentiles. It is with you in my mind that I am speaking. I will put it more strongly. I do all I can to glorify my ministry as Apostle to the Gentiles, [14] and this in hopes that I may succeed

in bringing salvation to some at any rate of my countrymen by thus moving them to emulation.   [15] And my reason for this is what I have implied just above, that by the return of the Jews the whole world will receive what it longs for.   The rejection of them has been the means of reconciling the world to God by the preaching to the Gentiles; their reception into the Kingdom, the gathering together of the elect from the four winds of heaven, will inaugurate the final consummation, the resurrection of the dead, and the eternal life that follows.

[16] But what ground is there for thus believing in the return of the chosen people to the Kingdom?   It is the holiness of the race. When you take from the kneading trough a piece of dough and offer it to the Lord as a heave-offering, do you not consecrate the whole mass?   Do not the branches of a tree receive life and nourishment from the roots?   So it is with Israel.   Their fore-fathers the Patriarchs have been consecrated to the Lord, and in them the whole race; from that stock they obtain their spiritual life, a life which must be holy as its source is holy.   [17] For the Church of God is like a 'green olive tree, fair with goodly fruit,' as the Prophet Jeremiah described it.   Its roots are the Patriarchs; its branches the people of the Lord.   Some of these branches have been broken off; Israelites who by birth and descent were members of the Church.   Into their place you Gentiles, by a process quite strange and unnatural, have been grafted, shoots from a wild olive, into a cultivated stock.   Equally with the old branches which still remain on the tree you share in the rich sap which flows from its root.   [18] Do not for this reason think that you may insolently boast of the position of superiority which you occupy.   If you are inclined to do so, remember that you have done nothing, that all the spiritual privileges that you possess simply belong to the stock on which you by no merit of your own have been grafted. [19] But perhaps you say: 'That I am the favoured one is shown by this that others were cut off that I might be grafted in.'   [20] I grant what you say; but consider the reason.   It was owing to their want of faith that they were broken off: you on the other hand owe your firm position to your faith, not to any natural superiority. [21] It is an incentive therefore not to pride, as you seem to think, but to fear.   For if God did not spare the holders of the birthright,

no grafted branches but the natural growth of the tree, He certainly will be no more ready to spare you, who have no such privileges to plead. [22] Learn the Divine goodness, but learn and understand the Divine severity as well. Those who have fallen have experienced the severity, you the goodness; a goodness which will be continued if you cease to be self-confident and simply trust: otherwise you too may be cut off as they were. [23] Nor again is the rejection of the Jews irrevocable. They can be grafted again into the stock on which they grew, if only they will give up their unbelief. For they are in God's hands; and God's power is not limited. He is able to restore them to the position from which they have fallen. [24] For consider. You are the slip cut from the olive that grew wild, and yet, by a process which you must admit to be entirely unnatural, you were grafted into the cultivated stock. If God could do this, much more can He graft the natural branches of the cultivated olive on to their own stock from which they were cut. You Gentiles have no grounds for boasting, nor have the Jews for despair. Your position is less secure than was theirs, and if they only trust in God, their salvation will be easier than was yours.

11. St. Paul has modified the question of ver. 1 so far: the rejection of Israel is only partial. But yet it is true that the rest, that is the majority, of the nation are spiritually blind. They have stumbled and sinned. Does this imply their final exclusion from the Messianic salvation? St. Paul shows that it is not so. It is only temporary and it has a Divine purpose.

λέγω οὖν. A new stage in the argument. ‘I ask then as to this majority whose state the prophets have thus described.’ The question arises immediately out of the preceding verses, but is a stage in the argument running through the whole chapter, and raised by the discussion of Israel's guilt in ix. 30–x. 21.

μὴ ἔπταισαν, ἵνα πέσωσι; ‘have they (i. e. those who have been hardened, ver. 8) stumbled so as to fall?’ *Numquid sic offenderunt, ut caderent?* Is their failure of such a character that they will be finally lost, and cut off from the Messianic salvation? ἵνα expresses the contemplated result. The metaphor in ἔπταισαν (which is often used elsewhere in a moral sense, Deut. vii. 25; James ii. 10; iii. 2; 2 Pet. i. 10) seems to be suggested by σκάνδαλον of ver. 9. The meaning of the passage is given by the contrast between πταίειν and πεσεῖν; a man who stumbles may recover himself, or he may fall completely. Hence πέσωσιν is here used of a complete and irrevocable fall. Cf. Is. xxiv. 20 κατίσχυσε γὰρ ἐπ᾽ αὐτῆς ἡ ἀνομία, καὶ πεσεῖται καὶ οὐ μὴ δύνηται ἀναστῆναι: *Ps. Sol.* iii. 13 ἔπεσεν ὅτι πονηρὸν τὸ πτῶμα αὐτοῦ, καὶ οὐκ ἀναστήσεται: Heb. iv. 11. It is no argument against this that the same word is used in vv. 22, 23 of a fall which is not irrevocable: the ethical meaning must be in each case determined by the context, and here the contrast with ἔπταισαν suggests a fall that is irrevocable.

There is a good deal of controversy among grammarians as to the admission of a laxer use of ἵνα, a controversy which has a tendency to divide scholars by nations; the German grammarians with Winer at their head (§ liii. 10. 6, p. 573 E. T.) maintain that it always preserves, even in N. T. Greek, its classical meaning of purpose; on the other hand, English commentators such as Lightfoot (on Gal. v. 17), Ellicott (on 1 Thess. v. 4), and Evans (on 1 Cor. vii. 29) admit the laxer use. Evans says ' that ἵνα, like our "that," has three uses: (1) *final* (in order that he may go), (2) *definitive* (I advise that he go), (3) *subjectively ecbatic* (have they stumbled that they should fall)'; and it is quite clear that it is only by reading into passages a great deal which is not expressed that commentators can make ἵνα in all cases mean 'in order that.' In 1 Thess. v. 4 ὑμεῖς δέ, ἀδελφοί, οὐκ ἐστὲ ἐν σκότει, ἵνα ἡ ἡμέρα ὑμᾶς ὡς κλέπτης καταλάβῃ, where Winer states that there is 'a Divine purpose of God,' this is not expressed either in the words or the context. In 1 Cor. vii. 29 ὁ καιρὸς συνεσταλμένος ἐστί, τὸ λοιπὸν ἵνα καὶ οἱ ἔχοντες γυναῖκας ὡς μὴ ἔχοντες ὦσι, 'is it probable that a state of sitting loose to worldly interests should be described as the aim or purpose of God in curtailing the season of the great tribulation?' (Evans.) Yet Winer asserts that the words ἵνα καὶ οἱ ἔχοντες κ.τ.λ. express the (Divine) purpose for which ὁ καιρὸς συνεσταλμένος ἐστί. So again in the present passage it is only a confusion of ideas that can see any purpose. If St. Paul had used a passive verb such as ἐπωρώθησαν then we might translate, 'have they been hardened in order that they may fall?' and there would be no objection in logic or grammar, but as St. Paul has written ἔπταισαν, if there is a purpose in the passage it ascribes stumbling as a deliberate act undertaken with the purpose of falling. We cannot here any more than elsewhere read in a Divine purpose where it is neither implied nor expressed, merely for the sake of defending an arbitrary grammatical rule.

μὴ γένοιτο. St. Paul indignantly denies that the final fall of Israel was the contemplated result of their transgression. The result of it has already been the calling of the Gentiles, and the final purpose is the restoration of the Jews also.

τῷ αὐτῶν παραπτώματι: 'by their false step,' continuing the metaphor of ἔπταισαν.

ἡ σωτηρία τοῖς ἔθνεσιν. St. Paul is here stating an historical fact. His own preaching to the Gentiles had been caused definitely by the rejection of his message on the part of the Jews. Acts xiii. 45–48; cf. viii. 4; xi. 19; xxviii. 28.

εἰς τὸ παραζηλῶσαι αὐτούς: 'to provoke them (the Jews) to jealousy.' This idea had already been suggested (x. 19) by the quotation from Deuteronomy Ἐγὼ παραζηλώσω ὑμᾶς ἐπ᾽ οὐκ ἔθνει.

St. Paul in these two statements sketches the lines on which the Divine action is explained and justified. God's purpose has been to use the disobedience of the Jews in order to promote the calling of the Gentiles, and He will eventually arouse the Jews to give up their unbelief by emulation of the Gentiles. Εἶτα κατασκευάζει, ὅτι τὸ πταῖσμα αὐτῶν διπλὴν οἰκονομίαν ἐργάζεται· τά τε γὰρ ἔθνη ἀντεισάγει καὶ αὐτοὺς δὲ παρακνίζον καὶ ἐρεθίζον ἐπιστρέφει, μὴ φέροντας τὴν τοσαύτην τῶν ἐθνῶν τιμήν. Euthym.-Zig.

12. St. Paul strengthens his statement by an argument drawn from the spiritual character of the Jewish people. If an event which has been so disastrous to the nation has had such a beneficial result, how much more beneficial will be the result of the entrance of the full complement of the nation into the Messianic kingdom?

πλοῦτος κόσμου: the enriching of the world by the throwing open to it of the kingdom of the Messiah: cf. x. 12 ὁ γὰρ αὐτὸς Κύριος πάντων, πλουτῶν εἰς πάντας τοὺς ἐπικαλουμένους αὐτόν.

τὸ ἥττημα αὐτῶν: 'their defeat.' From one point of view the unbelief of the Jews was a transgression (παράπτωμα), from another it was a defeat, for they were repulsed from the Messianic kingdom, since they had failed to obtain what they sought.

ἥττημα occurs only twice elsewhere: in Is. xxxi. 8 οἱ δὲ νεανίσκοι ἔσονται εἰς ἥττημα, πέτρᾳ γὰρ περιληφθήσονται ὡς χάρακι καὶ ἡττηθήσονται: and in 1 Cor. vi. 7 ἤδη μὲν οὖν ὅλως ἥττημα ὑμῖν ἐστιν, ὅτι κρίματα ἔχετε μεθ' ἑαυτῶν. The correct interpretation of the word as derived from the verb would be a 'defeat,' and this is clearly the meaning in Isaiah. It can equally well apply in 1 Cor., whether it be translated a 'defeat' in that it lowers the Church in the opinion of the world, or a 'moral defeat,' hence a 'defect.' The same meaning suits this passage. The majority of commentators however translate it here 'diminution' (see especially Gif. *Sp. Comm.* pp. 194, 203), in order to make the antithesis to πλήρωμα exact. But as Field points out (*Otium Norv.* iii. 97) there is no reason why the sentence should not be rhetorically faulty, and it is not much improved by giving ἥττημα the meaning of 'impoverishment' as opposed to 'replenishment.'

τὸ πλήρωμα αὐτῶν: 'their complement,' 'their full and completed number.' See on xi. 25.

The exact meaning of πλήρωμα has still to be ascertained. 1. There is a long and elaborate note on the word in Lft. *Col.* p. 323 ff. He starts with asserting that 'substantives in -μα formed from the perfect passive, appear always to have a passive sense. They may denote an abstract notion or a concrete thing; they may signify the action itself regarded as complete, or the product of the action: but in any case they give the result of the agency involved in the corresponding verb.' He then takes the verb πληροῦν and shows that it has two senses, (i) 'to fill,' (ii) 'to fulfil' or 'complete'; and deriving the fundamental meaning of the word πλήρωμα from the latter usage makes it mean in the N. T. always 'that which is completed.' 2. A somewhat different view of the termination -μα is given by the late T. S. Evans in a note on 1 Cor. v. 6 in the *Sp. Comm.* (part of which is quoted above on Rom. iv. 2.) This would favour the active sense *id quod implet* or *adimplet*, which appears to be the proper sense of the English word 'complement' (see the Philological Society's *Eng. Dict.* s.v.). Perhaps the term 'concrete' would most adequately express the normal meaning of the termination.

13, 14. These two verses present a good deal of difficulty, of rather a subtle kind.

1. What is the place occupied by the words ὑμῖν δὲ λέγω κ.τ.λ. in the argument? (i) Some (Hort, WH, Lips.) place here the beginning of a new paragraph, so Dr. Hort writes: 'after a passage on the rejection of unbelieving Israel, and on God's ultimate purpose involved in it, St. Paul turns swiftly round.' But an examination of the context will show that there is really no break in the ideas. The thought raised by the question in ver. 11 runs through the whole paragraph to ver. 24, in fact really to ver. 32, and the reference to the Gentiles in ver. 17 ff. is clearly incidental. Again ver. 15 returns directly to ver. 12, repeating the same idea, but in a way to justify also ver. 13. (ii) These verses in their appeal to the Gentiles are therefore incidental, almost parenthetic, and are introduced to show that this argument has an application to Gentiles as well as Jews.

2. But what is the meaning of μὲν οὖν (that this is the correct reading see below)? It is usual to take οὖν in its ordinary sense of therefore, and then to explain μέν by supposing an anacoluthon, or by finding the contrast in some words that follow. So Gif. 'St. Paul, with his usual delicate courtesy and perfect mastery of Greek, implies that this is but one part (μέν) of his ministry, chosen as he was to bear Christ's name "before Gentiles and kings and the children of Israel." Winer and others find the antithesis in εἴ πως παραζηλώσω. But against these views may be urged two reasons, (i) the meaning of μὲν οὖν. The usage at any rate in the N. T. is clearly laid down by Evans on 1 Cor. vi. 3 (*Speaker's Comm.* p. 285), 'the οὖν may signify then or therefore only when the μέν falls back upon the preceding word, because it is expectant of a coming δέ or ἀτάρ,' otherwise, as is pointed out, the μέν must coalesce with the οὖν, and the idea is either 'corrective and substi- tutive of a new thought, or confirmative of what has been stated and addititious.' Now if there is this second use of μὲν οὖν possible, unless the δέ is clearly expressed the mind naturally would suggest it, especially in St. Paul's writings where μὲν οὖν is generally so used: and as a matter of fact no instance is quoted in the N. T. where οὖν in μὲν οὖν has its natural force in a case where it is not followed by δέ (Heb. ix. 1 quoted by Winer does not apply, see Westcott *ad loc.*). But (ii) further οὖν is not the particle required here. What St. Paul requires is not an apology for referring to the Gentiles, but an apology to the Gentiles for devoting so much attention to the Jews.

If these two points are admitted the argument becomes much clearer. St. Paul remembers that the majority of his readers are Gentiles; he has come to a point where what he has to say touches them nearly; he therefore shows parenthetically how his love for his countrymen, and his zeal in carrying out his mission to the Gentiles, combine towards producing the same end. 'Do not think that what I am saying has nothing to do with you Gentiles. It makes me even more zealous in my work for you. That ministry of mine to the Gentiles I do honour to and exalt, seeking in this way if perchance I may be able to move my countrymen to jealousy.' Then in ver. 15 he shows how this again reacts upon the general scheme of his ministry. 'And this I do, because their return to the Church will bring on that final consummation for which we all look forward.'

13. ὑμῖν δὲ λέγω κ.τ.λ. The δέ expresses a slight contrast in thought, and the ὑμῖν is emphatic: 'But it is to you Gentiles I am speaking. Nay more, so far as I am an Apostle of Gentiles, I glorify my ministry: if thus by any means,' &c.

ἐθνῶν ἀπόστολος: comp. Acts xxii. 21; Gal. ii. 7, 9; 1 Tim. ii. 7.

τὴν διακονίαν μου δοξάζω. He may glorify his ministry, either (i) by his words and speech; if he teaches everywhere the duty of preaching to the Gentiles he exalts that ministry: or (ii), perhaps better, by doing all in his power to make it successful: comp. 1 Cor. xii. 26 εἴτε δοξάζεται μέλος.

This verse and the references to the Gentiles that follow seem to show conclusively that St. Paul expected the majority of his readers to be Gentiles. Comp. Hort, *Rom. and Eph.* p. 22 'Though the Greek is ambiguous the context appears to me decisive for taking ὑμῖν as the Church itself, and not as a part of it. In all the long previous discussion bearing on the Jews, occupying nearly two and a half chapters, the Jews are invariably spoken of in the third person. In the half chapter that follows the Gentiles are constantly spoken of in the second person. Exposition has here passed into exhortation and warning, and the warning is exclusively addressed to Gentiles: to Christians who had once been Jews not a word is addressed.'

The variations in reading in the particles which occur in this verse suggest that considerable difficulties were felt in its interpretation. For ὑμῖν δέ ℵ A B P *minusc. pauc.*, Syrr. Boh. Arm., Theodrt. *cod.* Jo.-Damasc.; we find in C ὑμῖν οὖν; while the TR with D E F G L &c. Orig.-lat. Chrys. &c. has ὑμῖν γάρ. Again μὲν οὖν is read by ℵ A B C P, Boh., Cyr.-Al. Jo.-Damasc.; μέν only by TR with L &c., Orig.-lat. Chrys. &c. (so Meyer); while the Western group D E F G and some minuscules omit both.

It may be noticed in the Epp. of St. Paul that wherever μὲν οὖν or μενοῦν γε occur there is considerable variation in the reading.

Rom. ix. 20: μενοῦνγε ℵ A K L P &c., Syrr. Boh.; μὲν οὖν B; omit altogether D F G.

x. 18: μενοῦνγε om. F G d, Orig.-lat.

1 Cor. vi. 4: μὲν οὖν most authorities; F G γοῦν.

vi. 7: μὲν οὖν A B C &c.; μέν ℵ D Boh.

Phil. iii. 8: μὲν οὖν B D E F G K L &c.; μενοῦνγε ℵ A P Boh.

The Western MSS. as a rule avoid the expression, while B is consistent in preferring it.

14. εἴ πως παραζηλώσω. εἴ πως is used here interrogatively with the aorist subjunctive (cp. Phil. iii. 10, 11). The grammarians explain the expression by saying that we are to understand with it σκοπῶν. εἴ πως occurs Acts xxvii. 12 with the optative, Rom. i. 10 with the future.

15. The two previous verses have been to a certain extent parenthetical; in this verse the Apostle continues the argument of ver. 12, repeating in a stronger form what he has there said, but in such a way as to explain the statement made in vv. 13, 14, that by thus caring for his fellow-countrymen he is fulfilling his mission to the Gentile world. The casting away of the Jews has meant the reconciliation of the world to Christ. Henceforth there is no more a great wall of partition separating God's people from the rest of the world. This is the first step in the founding of the Messianic kingdom; but when all the people of Israel shall have come in there will be the final consummation of all things, and this means the realization of the hope which the reconciliation of the world has made possible.

ἀποβολή: the rejection of the Jews for their faithlessness. The meaning of the word is defined by the contrasted πρόσληψις.

καταλλαγὴ κόσμου: cf. vv. 10, 11. The reconciliation was the immediate result of St. Paul's ministry, which he describes elsewhere (2 Cor. v. 18, 19) as a ministry of reconciliation; its final result, the hope to which it looks forward, is salvation (καταλλαγέντες σωθησόμεθα): the realization of this hope is what every Gentile must long for, and therefore whatever will lead to its fulfilment must be part of St. Paul's ministry.

πρόσληψις: the reception of the Jews into the kingdom of the Messiah. The noun is not used elsewhere in the N.T., but the meaning is shown by the parallel use of the verb (cf. xiv. 3; xv. 7).

ζωὴ ἐκ νεκρῶν. The meaning of this phrase must be determined by that of καταλλαγὴ κόσμου. The argument demands something much stronger than that, which may be a climax to the section. It may either be (1) used in a figurative sense, cf. Ezek. xxxvii. 3 ff.; Luke xv. 24, 32 ὁ ἀδελφός σου οὗτος νεκρὸς ἦν, καὶ ἔζησε· καὶ ἀπολωλώς, καὶ εὑρέθη. In this sense it would mean the universal diffusion of the Gospel message and a great awakening of spiritual life as the result of it. Or (2), it may mean the 'general Resurrection' as a sign of the inauguration of the Messianic Kingdom. In this sense it would make a suitable antithesis to καταλλαγή. The reconciliation of the heathen and their reception into the Church on earth was the first step in a process which led ultimately to their σωτηρία. It gave them grounds for hoping for that which they should enjoy in the final consummation. And this consummation would come when the kingdom was completed. In all contemporary Jewish literature the Resurrection (whether partial or general)

is a sign of the inauguration of the new era.   Schürer, *Geschichte*, &c.
ii. p. 460; *Jubilees* xxiii. 29 'And at that time the Lord will heal
his servants, and they will arise and will see great peace and will
cast out their enemies; and the just shall see it and be thankful
and rejoice in joy to all eternity.'   *Enoch* li. 1 (p. 139 ed. Charles)
'And in those days will the earth also give back those who are
treasured up within it, and Sheôl also will give back that which it
has received, and hell will give back that which it owes.   And he
will choose the righteous and holy from among them : for the day
of their redemption has drawn nigh.'   As in the latter part of this
chapter St. Paul seems to be largely influenced by the language
and forms of the current eschatology, it is very probable that the
second interpretation is the more correct; cf. Origen viii. 9, p. 257
*Tunc enim erit assumtio Israel, quando iam et mortui vitam recipient
et mundus ex corruptibili incorruptibilis fiet, et mortales immortalitate
donabuntur*; and see below ver. 26.

16. St. Paul gives in this verse the grounds of his confidence in
the future of Israel.   This is based upon the holiness of the Patriarchs
from whom they are descended and the consecration to God which
has been the result of this holiness.   His argument is expressed in
two different metaphors, both of which however have the same
purpose.

ἀπαρχὴ . . . φύραμα.   The metaphor in the first part of the
verse is taken from Num. xv. 19, 20 'It shall be, that when ye
eat of the bread of the land, ye shall offer up an heave offering
unto the Lord.   Of the first of your dough (ἀπαρχὴν φυράματος LXX)
ye shall offer up a cake for an heave offering : as ye do the heave
offering of the threshing floor, so shall ye heave it.'   By the offering
of the first-fruits, the whole mass was considered to be consecrated ;
and so the holiness of the Patriarchs consecrated the whole people
from whom they came.   That the meaning of the ἀπαρχή is the
Patriarchs (and not Christ or the select remnant) is shown by the
parallelism with the second half of the verse, and by the explanation
of St. Paul's argument given in ver. 28 ἀγαπητοὶ διὰ τοὺς πατέρας.

ἁγία : 'consecrated to God as the holy nation' in the technical
sense of ἅγιος, cf. i. 7.

ῥίζα . . . κλάδοι.   The same idea expressed under a different
image.   Israel the Divine nation is looked upon as a tree; its
roots are the Patriarchs; individual Israelites are the branches.
As then the Patriarchs are holy, so are the Israelites who belong
to the stock of the tree, and are nourished by the sap which
flows up to them from those roots.

17-24. The metaphor used in the second part of ver. 16 suggests
an image which the Apostle developes somewhat elaborately.   The
image of an olive tree to describe Israel is taken from the Prophets ;
Jeremiah xi. 16 'The Lord called thy name, A green olive tree,

fair with goodly fruit: with the noise of a great tumult He hath
kindled fire upon it, and the branches of it are broken'; Hosea
xiv. 6 'His branches shall spread, and his beauty shall be as the
olive tree, and his smell as Lebanon.'   Similar is the image of the
vine in Is. v. 7; Ps. lxxx. 8; and (of the Christian Church) in John
xv. 1 ff.

The main points in this simile are the following:—

> The olive = the Church of God, looked at as one continuous
> body; the Christian Church being the inheritor of the
> privileges of the Jewish Church.

> The root or stock (ῥίζα) = that stock from which Jews and
> Christians both alike receive their nourishment and strength,
> viz. the Patriarchs, for whose faith originally Israel was
> chosen (cf. vv. 28, 29).

> The branches (οἱ κλάδοι) are the individual members of the
> Church who derive their nourishment and virtue from the
> stock or body to which they belong.   These are of two
> kinds:

> The original branches; these represent the Jews.   Some have
> been cut off from their want of faith, and no longer derive
> any nourishment from the stock.

> The branches of the wild olive which have been grafted in.
> These are the Gentile Christians, who, by being so grafted
> in, have come to partake of the richness and virtue of the
> olive stem.

From this simile St. Paul draws two lessons. (1) The first is
to a certain extent incidental.   It is a warning to the heathen
against undue exaltation and arrogance.   By an entirely unnatural
process they have been grafted into the tree.   Any virtue that
they may have comes by no merit of their own, but by the virtue
of the stock to which they belong; and moreover at any moment
they may be cut off.   It will be a less violent process to cut off
branches not in any way belonging to the tree, than it was to cut
off the original branches.   But (2)—and this is the more important result to be gained from the simile, as it is summed up in
ver. 24—if God has had the power against all nature to graft in
branches from a wild olive and enable them to bear fruit, how much
more easily will He be able to restore to their original place the
branches which have been cut off.

St. Paul thus deduces from his simile consolation for Israel, but
incidentally also a warning to the Gentile members of the Church—
a warning made necessary by the great importance ascribed to
them in ver. 11 f.   Israel had been rejected for their sake.

17. τινές: a meiosis.   Cf. iii. 3 τί γὰρ εἰ ἠπίστησάν τινες; Τινὲς δὲ
εἶπε, παραμυθούμενος αὐτούς, ὡς πολλάκις εἰρήκαμεν, ἐπεὶ πολλῷ πλείους οἱ
ἀπιστήσαντες.   Euthym.-Zig.

ἐξεκλάσθησαν. The same simile is used, with a different application, *Enoch* xxvi. 1 καὶ ἐκεῖθεν ἐφώδευσα εἰς τὸ μέσον τῆς γῆς, καὶ ἴδον τόπον ηὐλογημένον, ἐν ᾧ δένδρα ἔχοντα παραφυάδας μενούσας καὶ βλαστούσας τοῦ δένδρου ἐκκοπέντος.

ἀγριέλαιος : 'the wild olive.' The olive, like the apple and most other fruit trees, requires to have a graft from a cultivated tree, otherwise the fruit of the seedling or sucker will be small and valueless. The ungrafted tree is the natural or wild olive. It is often confused with the oleaster (*Eleagnus angustifolius*), but quite incorrectly, this being a plant of a different natural order, which however like the olive yields oil, although of an inferior character. See Tristram, *Natural Hist. of the Bible*, pp. 371–377.

ἐνεκεντρίσθης ἐν αὐτοῖς : 'wert grafted in amongst the branches of the cultivated olive.' St. Paul is here describing a wholly unnatural process. Grafts must necessarily be of branches from a cultivated olive inserted into a wild stock, the reverse process being one which would be valueless and is never performed. But the whole strength of St. Paul's argument depends upon the process being an unnatural one (cf. ver. 24 καὶ παρὰ φύσιν ἐνεκεντρίσθης); it is beside the point therefore to quote passages from classical writers, which, even if they seem to support St. Paul's language, describe a process which can never be actually used. They could only show the ignorance of others, they would not justify him. Cf. Origen viii. 10, p. 265 *Sed ne hoc quidem lateat nos in hoc loco, quod non eo ordine Apostolus olivae et oleastri similitudinem posuit, quo apud agricolas habetur. Illi enim magis olivam oleastro inserere, et non olivae oleastrum solent : Paulus vero Apostolica auctoritate ordine commutato res magis causis, quam causas rebus aptavit.*

συγκοινωνός : 1 Cor. ix. 23 ; Phil. i. 7 ; and cf. Eph. iii. 6 εἶναι τὰ ἔθνη συγκληρονόμα καὶ σύσσωμα καὶ συμμέτοχα τῆς ἐπαγγελίας ἐν Χριστῷ Ἰησοῦ διὰ τοῦ εὐαγγελίου.

τῆς ῥίζης τῆς πιότητος τῆς ἐλαίας : comp. Jud. ix. 9 καὶ εἶπεν αὐτοῖς ἡ ἐλαία, Μὴ ἀπολείψασα τὴν πιότητά μου . . . πορεύσομαι ; *Test. XII. Pat.* Levi, 8 ὁ πέμπτος κλάδον μοι ἐλαίας ἔδωκε πιότητος. The genitive τῆς πιότητος is taken by Weiss as a genitive of quality, as in the quotation above, and so the phrase comes to mean 'the fat root of the olive.' Lips. explains 'the root from which the fatness of the olive springs.'

The genitive τῆς πιότητος seemed clumsy and unnatural to later revisers, and so was modified either by the insertion of καί after ῥίζης, as in א A and later MSS. with Vulg. Syrr. Arm. Aeth., Orig.-lat. Chrys., or by the omission of τῆς ῥίζης in Western authorities D F G Iren.-lat.

18. μὴ κατακαυχῶ τῶν κλάδων. St. Paul seems to be thinking of Gentile Christians who despised the Jews, both such as had become believers and such as had not. The Church of Corinth could furnish many instances of new converts who were carried

away by a feeling of excessive confidence, and who, partly on
grounds of race, partly because they had understood or thought
they had understood the Pauline teaching of ἐλευθερία, were full of
contempt for the Jewish Christians and the Jewish race. Incidentally St. Paul takes the opportunity of rebuking such as them.

οὐ σὺ τὴν ῥίζαν κ.τ.λ. 'All your spiritual strength comes from
the stock on which you have been grafted.' In the ordinary process
it may be when a graft of the cultivated olive is set on a wild stock
the goodness of the fruit comes from the graft, but in this case it is
the reverse; any merit, any virtue, any hope of salvation that the
Gentiles may have arises entirely from the fact that they are grafted
on a stock whose roots are the Patriarchs and to which the Jews,
by virtue of their birth, belong.

19. ἐρεῖς οὖν. The Gentile Christian justifies his feeling of
confidence by reminding St. Paul that branches (κλάδοι, not οἱ
κλάδοι) had been cut off to let him in: therefore, he might argue,
I am of more value than they, and have grounds for my self-
confidence and contempt.

20. καλῶς. St. Paul admits the statement, but suggests that the
Gentile Christian should remember what were the conditions on
which he was admitted. The Jews were cast off for want of faith, he
was admitted for faith. There was no merit of his own, therefore
he has no grounds for over-confidence: 'Be not high-minded;
rather fear, for if you trust in your merit instead of showing faith
in Christ, you will suffer as the Jews did for their self-confidence
and want of faith.'

21. εἰ γὰρ ὁ Θεὸς κ.τ.λ. This explains the reason which made
it right that they should fear. ' The Jews—the natural branches—
disbelieved and were not spared; is it in any way likely that you,
if you disbelieve, will be spared when they were not—you who have
not any natural right or claim to the position you now occupy?'

οὐδέ σου φείσεται is the correct reading (with ℵ A B C P *min. pauc.*, Boh.,
Orig.-lat., &c.); either because the direct future seemed too strong or under
the influence of the Latin (*ne forte nec tibi parcat* Vulg. and Iren.-lat.) μήπως
οὐδέ σου was read by D F G L &c., Syrr. Chrys. &c., then φείσεται was changed
into φείσηται (*min. pauc.* and Chrys.) for the sake of the grammar, and found
its way into the TR.

22. The Apostle sums up this part of his argument by deducing
from this instance the two sides of the Divine character. God is full
of goodness (χρηστότης, cf. ii. 4) and loving-kindness towards mankind, and that has been shown by His conduct towards those
Gentiles who have been received into the Christian society. That
goodness will always be shown towards them if they repose their
confidence on it, and do not trust in their own merits or the
privileged position they enjoy. On the other hand the treatment
of the Jews shows the severity which also belongs to the character

of God; a severity exercised against them just because they trusted
in themselves. God can show the same severity against the Gentiles
and cut them off as well as the Jew.

ἀποτομία and χρηστότης should be read in the second part of the verse,
with אABC Orig. Jo.-Damasc. against the accusative of the Western and
Syrian text. D has a mixed reading, ἀποτομίαν and χρηστότης: the assimilation was easier in the first word than in the second. The Θεοῦ after
χρηστότης is omitted by later MSS. with Clem.-Alex., Orig. from a desire
for uniformity.

ἐὰν ἐπιμείνῃς. The condition of their enjoying this goodness is
that they trust in it, and not in their position.

καὶ σύ: emphatic like the ἐγώ of ver. 19 'You too as well as the
Jews.'

23. St. Paul now turns from the warning to the Gentile Christians,
which was to a certain extent incidental, to the main subject of the
paragraph, the possibility of the return of the Jews to the Divine
Kingdom; their grafting into the Divine stock.

καὶ ἐκεῖνοι δέ : ' yes, and they too.'

24. This verse sums up the main argument. If God is so
powerful that by a purely unnatural process (παρὰ φύσιν) He can
graft a branch of wild olive into a stock of the cultivated plant, so
that it should receive nourishment from it ; can He not equally well,
nay far more easily, reingraft branches which have been cut off
the cultivated olive into their own stock ? The restoration of
Israel is an easier process than the call of the Gentiles.

The Merits of the Fathers.

In what sense does St. Paul say that Israelites are holy because
the stock from which they come is holy (ver. 16), that they are
ἀγαπητοὶ διὰ τοὺς πατέρας (ver. 28)? He might almost seem to be
taking up himself the argument he has so often condemned, that
the descent of the Jews from Abraham is sufficient ground for
their salvation.

The greatness of the Patriarchs had become one of the commonplaces of Jewish Theology. For them the world was created (*Apoc.
Baruch*, xxi. 24). They had been surrounded by a halo of myth
and romance in popular tradition and fancy (see the note on iv. 3),
and very early the idea seems to have prevailed that their virtues
had a power for others as well as for themselves. Certainly Ezekiel
in the interests of personal religion has to protest against some
such view : ' Though these three men, Noah, Daniel, and Job, were
in it, they should deliver but their own souls by their righteousness,
saith the Lord God' (Ezek. xiv. 14). We know how this had
developed by the time of our Lord, and the cry had arisen: 'We

have Abraham for our father' (see note on ii. 3). At a later date
the doctrine of the merits of the Fathers had been developed
into a system. As Israel was an organic body, the several
members of which were closely bound together, the superfluous
merits of the one part might be transferred to another. Of
Solomon before he sinned it was said that he earned all by his
own merit, after he sinned by the merit of the Fathers (*Kohel
rabba* 60ᶜ). A comment on the words of Cant. i. 5 'I am black,
but comely,' closely resembles the dictum of St. Paul in ver. 18
'The congregation of Israel speaks : I am black through mine
own works, but *lovely through the works of my fathers*' (*Shemoth
rabba*, c. 23). So again : 'Israel lives and endures, because it
supports itself on the fathers' (*ib.* c. 44). A very close parallel to
the metaphor of ver. 17 f. is given by *Wajjikra rabba*, c. 36 'As
this vine supports itself on a trunk which is dry, while it is itself
fresh and green, so Israel supports itself on the merit of the fathers,
although they already sleep.' So the merit of the fathers is a general
possession of the whole people of Israel, and the protection of the
whole people in the day of Redemption (*Shemoth rabba*, c. 44 ;
Beresch rabba, c. 70). So *Pesikta* 153ᵇ 'The Holy One spake to
Israel: My sons, if ye will be justified by Me in the judgement,
make mention to Me of the merits of your fathers, so shall ye be
justified before Me in the judgement' (see Weber, *Altsyn. Theol.*
p. 280 f.).

Now, although St. Paul lays great stress on the merits of the
Fathers, it becomes quite clear that he had no such idea as this in
his mind ; and it is convenient to put the developed Rabbinical
idea side by side with his teaching in order to show at once the
resemblance and the divergence of the two views. It is quite clear
in the first place that the Jews will not be restored to the Kingdom
on any ground but that of Faith ; so ver. 23 ἐὰν μὴ ἐπιμείνωσι τῇ
ἀπιστίᾳ. And in the second place St. Paul is dealing (as becomes
quite clear below) not with the salvation of individuals, but with
the restoration of the nation as a whole. The merits of the Fathers
are not then looked upon as the cause of Israel's salvation, but as
a guarantee that Israel will attain that Faith which is a necessary
condition of their being saved. It is a guarantee from either of
two points of view. So far as our Faith is God's gift, and so far
as we can ascribe to Him feelings of preference or affection for one
race as opposed to another (and we can do so just as much as
Scripture does), it is evidence that Israel has those qualities
which will attract to it the Divine Love. Those qualities of the
founders of the race, those national qualities which Israel inherits,
and which caused it to be selected as the Chosen People, these it
still possesses. And on the other side so far as Faith comes by
human effort or character, so far that Faith of Abraham, for which

he was accounted righteous before God, is a guarantee that the same Faith can be developed in his descendants.   After all it is because they are a religious race, clinging too blindly to their own views, that they are rejected, and not because they are irreligious. They have a zeal for God, if not according to knowledge.   When the day comes that that zeal is enlisted in the cause of the Messiah, the world will be won for Christ; and that it will be so enlisted the sanctity and the deep religious instinct of the Jewish stock as exhibited by the Patriarchs is, if not certain proof, at any rate evidence which appeals with strong moral force.

MERCY TO ALL THE ULTIMATE PURPOSE OF GOD.

XI. 25-36. All this is the unfolding of a mystery. The whole world, both Jew and Gentile, shall enter the Kingdom; but a passing phase of disobedience has been allowed to the Jews now, as to the Gentiles in the past, that both alike, Jew as well as Gentile, may need and receive the Divine mercy (vv. 25-32).   What a stupendous exhibition of the Divine mercy and wisdom (vv. 33-36)!

[25] But I must declare to you, my brethren, the purpose hitherto concealed, but now revealed in these dealings of God with His people. I must not leave you ignorant. I must guard you against self-conceit on this momentous subject.   That hardening of heart which has come upon Israel is only partial and temporary. It is to last only until the full complement of the Gentiles has entered into Christ's kingdom. [26] When this has come about then the whole people of Israel shall be saved.   So Isaiah (lix. 20) described the expected Redeemer as one who should come forth from the Holy city and should remove impieties from the descendants of Jacob, and purify Israel: [27] he would in fact fulfil God's covenant with His people, and that would imply, as Isaiah elsewhere explains (xxvii. 9), a time when God would forgive Israel's sins.   This is our ground for believing that the Messiah who has come will bring salvation to Israel, and that He will do it by exercising the Divine prerogative of forgiveness; if Israel now needs forgiveness this only makes us more confident of the truth of the prophecy.   [28] In the Divine plan, according to which the message of salvation has been preached, the Jews are treated as enemies of God, that room may

be found for you Gentiles in the kingdom; but this does not alter
the fact that by the Divine principle of selection, they are still the
beloved of the Lord, chosen for the sake of their ancestors, the
Patriarchs. [29] God has showered upon them His blessings and
called them to His privileges, and He never revokes the choice
He has made. [30] There is thus a parallelism between your case
and theirs. You Gentiles were once disobedient to God. Now it
has been Israel's turn to be disobedient; and that disobedience has
brought to you mercy. [31] In like manner their present disobedience
will have this result: that they too will be recipients of the same
mercy that you have received. [32] And the reason for the disobedience may be understood in both cases, if we look to the final
purpose. God has, as it were, locked up all mankind, first Gentiles
and then Jews, in the prison-house of unbelief, that He may be able
at last to show His mercy on all alike.

[33] When we contemplate a scheme like this spread out before us
in vast panorama, how forcibly does it bring home to us the inexhaustible profundity of that Divine mind by which it was planned!
The decisions which issue from that mind and the methods by which
it works are alike inscrutable to man. [34] Into the secrets of the
Almighty none can penetrate. No counsellor stands at His ear to
whisper words of suggestion. [35] Nothing in Him is derived from
without so as to be claimed back again by its owner. [36] He is the
source of all things. Through Him all things flow. He is the
final cause to which all things tend. Praised for ever be His
name! Amen.

25-36. St. Paul's argument is now drawing to a close. He has
treated all the points that are necessary. He has proved that
the rejection of Israel is not contrary to Divine justice or Divine
promises. He has convicted Israel of its own responsibility. He
has shown how historically the rejection of Israel had been the
cause of preaching the Gospel to the heathen, and this has led to
far-reaching speculation on the future of Israel and its ultimate
restoration; a future which may be hoped for in view of the spiritual
character of the Jewish race and the mercy and power of God.
And now he seems to see all the mystery of the Divine purpose
unfolded before him, and he breaks away from the restrained and
formal method of argument he has hitherto imposed upon himself.
Just as when treating of the Resurrection, his argument passes into
revelation, 'Behold, I tell you a mystery' (1 Cor. xv. 51): so here

he declares not merely as the result of his argument, but as an authoritative revelation, the mystery of the Divine purpose.

25. οὐ γὰρ θέλω ὑμᾶς ἀγνοεῖν: cf. i. 13; 1 Cor. x. 1; xii. 1; 2 Cor. i. 8; 1 Thess. iv. 13 : a phrase used by St. Paul to emphasize something of especial importance which he wishes to bring home to his readers. It always has the impressive addition of 'brethren.' The γάρ connects the verse immediately with what precedes, but also with the general argument. St. Paul's argument is like a ladder; each step follows from what precedes; but from time to time there are, as it were, resting-places which mark a definite point gained towards the end he has in view.

τὸ μυστήριον τοῦτο. On the meaning of 'mystery' in St. Paul see Lightfoot, *Colossians*, i. 26; Hatch, *Ess. in Bibl. Gk.* p. 57 ff. Just at the time when Christianity was spreading, the mysteries as professing to reveal something more than was generally known, especially about the future state, represented the most popular form of religion, and from them St. Paul borrows much of his phraseology. So in Col. i. 28, 1 Cor. ii. 6 we have τέλειον, in Phil. iv. 12 μεμύημαι, in Eph. i. 13 σφραγίζεσθαι; so in Ign. *Ephes.* 12 Παύλου σύμμυσται. But whereas among the heathen μυστήριον was always used of a mystery concealed, with St. Paul it is a mystery revealed. It is his mission to make known the Word of God, the mystery which has been kept silent from eternal ages, but has now been revealed to mankind (1 Cor. ii. 7; Eph. iii. 3, 4; Rom. xvi. 25). This mystery, which has been declared in Christianity, is the eternal purpose of God to redeem mankind in Christ, and all that is implied in that. Hence it is used of the Incarnation (1 Tim. iii. 16), of the crucifixion of Christ (1 Cor. ii. 1, 7), of the Divine purpose to sum up all things in Him (Eph. i. 9), and especially of the inclusion of the Gentiles in the kingdom (Eph. iii. 3, 4; Col. i. 26, 27; Rom. xvi. 25). Here it is used in a wide sense of the whole plan or scheme of redemption as revealed to St. Paul, by which Jews and Gentiles alike are to be included in the Divine Kingdom, and all things are working up, although in ways unseen and unknown, to that end.

ἵνα μὴ ἦτε παρ' ἑαυτοῖς φρόνιμοι : 'that you may not be wise in your own conceits,' i. e. by imagining that it is in any way through your own merit that you have accepted what others have refused: it has been part of the eternal purpose of God.

ἐν ἑαυτοῖς ought probably to be read with A B, Jo.-Damasc. instead of παρ' ἑαυτοῖς ℵ C D L &c., Chrys. &c., as the latter would probably be introduced from xii. 16. Both expressions occur in the LXX. Is. v. 21 οἱ συνετοὶ ἐν ἑαυτοῖς, Prov. iii. 7 μὴ ἴσθι φρόνιμος παρὰ σεαυτῷ.

πώρωσις κ.τ.λ.: 'a hardening in part' (cf. ἐκ μέρους 1 Cor. xii. 27). St. Paul asserts once more what he has constantly insisted on throughout this chapter, that this fall of the Jews is only partial (cf. vv. 5, 7, 17), but here he definitely adds a point to which he has been working up in the previous section, that it is only temporary and that the limitation in time is 'until all nations of the earth come into the kingdom'; cf. Luke xxi. 24 'and Jerusalem shall be trodden down of the Gentiles, until the times of the Gentiles be fulfilled.'

τὸ πλήρωμα τῶν ἐθνῶν: the full completed number, the complement of the Gentiles, i. e. the Gentile world as a whole, just as in ver. 12 τὸ πλήρωμα is the Jewish nation as a whole.

There was a Jewish basis to these speculations on the completed number. *Apoc. Baruch* xxiii. 4 *quia quando peccavit Adam et decreta fuit mors contra eos qui gignerentur,* tunc numerata est multitudo eorum *qui gignerentur, et numero illi praeparatus est locus ubi habitarent viventes et ubi custodirentur mortui,* nisi ergo compleatur numerus praedictus *non vivet creatura* ... 4 (5) Ezra ii. 40, 41 (where Jewish ideas underlie a Christian work) *recipe, Sion,* numerum tuum *et conclude candidatos tuos, qui legem Domini compleverunt: filiorum tuorum, quos optabas,* plenus est numerus: *roga imperium Domini ut sanctificetur populus tuus qui vocatus est ab initio.*

εἰσέλθῃ was used almost technically of entering into the Kingdom or the Divine glory or life (cf. Matt. vii. 21; xviii. 8; Mark ix. 43–47.), and so came to be used absolutely in the same sense (Matt. vii. 13; xxiii. 13; Luke xiii. 24).

26. καὶ οὕτω: 'and so,' i. e. by the whole Gentile world coming into the kingdom and thus rousing the Jews to jealousy, cf. ver. 11 f. These words ought to form a new sentence and not be joined with the preceding, for the following reasons: (1) the reference of οὕτω is to the sentence ἄχρις οὗ κ.τ.λ. We must not therefore make οὕτω ... σωθήσεται coordinate with πώρωσις ... γέγονεν and subordinate to ὅτι, for if we did so οὕτω would be explained by the sentence with which it is coordinated, and this is clearly not St. Paul's meaning. He does not mean that Israel will be saved *because* it is hardened. (2) The sentence, by being made independent, acquires much greater emphasis and force.

πᾶς Ἰσραήλ. In what sense are these words used? (1) The whole context shows clearly that it is the actual Israel of history that is referred to. This is quite clear from the contrast with τὸ πλήρωμα τῶν ἐθνῶν in ver. 25, the use of the term Israel in the same verse, and the drift of the argument in vv. 17–24. It cannot be interpreted either of the spiritual Israel, as by Calvin, or the remnant according to the election of grace, or such Jews as believe, or all who to the end of the world shall turn unto the Lord.

(2) πᾶς must be taken in the proper meaning of the word: 'Israel as a whole, Israel as a nation,' and not as necessarily including every individual Israelite. Cf. 1 Kings xii. 1 καὶ εἶπε Σαμουὴλ πρὸς πάντα Ἰσραήλ: 2 Chron. xii. 1 ἐγκατέλιπε τὰς ἐντολὰς Κυρίου καὶ πᾶς Ἰσραὴλ μετ' αὐτοῦ: Dan. ix. 11 καὶ πᾶς Ἰσραὴλ παρέβησαν τον νόμον σου καὶ ἐξέκλιναν τοῦ μὴ ἀκοῦσαι τῆς φωνῆς σου.

σωθήσεται: 'shall attain the σωτηρία of the Messianic age by being received into the Christian Church': the Jewish conception of the Messianic σωτηρία being fulfilled by the spiritual σωτηρία of Christianity. Cf. x. 13.

So the words of St. Paul mean simply this. The people of Israel as a nation, and no longer ἀπὸ μέρους, shall be united with the Christian Church. They do not mean that every Israelite shall finally be saved. Of final salvation St. Paul is not now thinking, nor of God's dealings with individuals, nor does he ask about those who are already dead, or who will die before this salvation of Israel is attained. He is simply considering God's dealings with the nation as a whole. As elsewhere throughout these chapters, St. Paul is dealing with peoples and classes of men. He looks forward in prophetic vision to a time when the whole earth, including the kingdoms of the Gentiles (τὸ πλήρωμα τῶν ἐθνῶν) and the people of Israel (πᾶς Ἰσραήλ), shall be united in the Church of God.

26, 27. καθὼς γέγραπται. The quotation is taken from the LXX of Is. lix. 20, the concluding words being added from Is. xxvii. 9. The quotation is free: the only important change, however, is the substitution of ἐκ Σιών for the ἕνεκεν Σιών of the LXX. The Hebrew reads 'and a Redeemer shall come to Zion, and unto them that turn from transgression in Jacob.' The variation apparently comes from Ps. xiii. 7, lii. 7 (LXX) τίς δώσει ἐκ Σιὼν τὸ σωτήριον τοῦ Ἰσραήλ;

The passage occurs in the later portion of Isaiah, just where the Prophet dwells most fully on the high spiritual destinies of Israel; and its application to the Messianic kingdom is in accordance with the spirit of the original and with Rabbinic interpretation. St. Paul uses the words to imply that the Redeemer, who is represented by the Prophets as coming from Zion, and is therefore conceived by him as realized in Christ, will in the end redeem the whole of Israel. The passage, as quoted, implies the complete purification of Israel from their iniquity by the Redeemer and the forgiveness of their sins by God.

In these speculations St. Paul was probably strongly influenced, at any rate as to their form, by Jewish thought. The Rabbis connected these passages with the Messiah: cf. *Tract. Sanhedrin*, f. 98. 1 'R. Jochanan said: When thou shalt see the time in which many troubles shall come like a river upon Israel, then expect the Messiah himself as says Is. lix. 19.' Moreover a universal restoration of Israel was part of the current Jewish expectation. All Israel should be collected together. There was to be a kingdom in Palestine, and in order that Israel as a whole might share in this there was to be a general resurrection. Nor was the belief in the coming in of the fulness of the Gentiles without parallel.

Although later Judaism entirely denied all hope to the Gentiles, much of the Judaism of St. Paul's day still maintained the O. T. belief (Is. xiv. 2; lxvi. 12, 19-21; Dan. ii. 44; vii. 14, 27). So *Enoch* xc. 33 'And all that had been destroyed and dispersed and all the beasts of the field and all the birds of the heaven assembled in that house, and the Lord of the sheep rejoiced with great joy because they were all good and had returned to his house.' *Orac. Sibyll.* iii. 710 f. καὶ τότε δὴ νῆσοι πᾶσαι πόλιες τ᾽ ἐρέουσιν . . . δεῦτε, πεσόντες ἄπαντες ἐπὶ χθονὶ λισσώμεσθα ἀθάνατον βασιλῆα, θεὸν μέγαν ἀέναόν τε. *Ps. Sol.* xvii. 33–35 'And he shall purge Jerusalem and make it holy, even as it was in the days of old, so that the nations may come from the ends of the earth to see his glory, bringing as gifts her sons that had fainted, and may see the glory of the Lord, wherewith God hath glorified her.' The centre of this kingdom will be Jerusalem (compare the extract given above), and it is perhaps influenced by these conceptions that St. Paul in ix. 26 inserts the word 'there' and here reads ἐκ Σιών. If this be so, it shows how, although using so much of the forms and language of current conceptions, he has spiritualized just as he has broadened them. Gal. iv. 26 shows that he is thinking of a Jerusalem which is above, very different from the purified earthly Jerusalem of the Rabbis; and this enables us to see how here also a spiritual conception underlies much of his language.

ὁ ῥυόμενος: Jesus as the Messiah. Cf. 1 Thess. i. 10.

27. καὶ αὕτη κ.τ.λ.: 'and whensoever I forgive their sins then shall my side of the covenant I have made with them be fulfilled.'

28. κατὰ μὲν τὸ εὐαγγέλιον: 'as regards the Gospel order, the principles by which God sends the Gospel into the world.' This verse sums up the argument of vv. 11–24.

ἐχθροί: treated by God as enemies and therefore shut off from Him.

δι᾽ ὑμᾶς: 'for your sake, in order that you by their exclusion may be brought into the Messianic Kingdom.'

κατὰ δὲ τὴν ἐκλογήν: 'as regards the principle of election:' 'because they are the chosen race.' That this is the meaning is shown by the fact that the word is parallel to εὐαγγέλιον. It cannot mean here, as in vv. 5, 6, 'as regards the elect,' i. e. the select remnant. It gives the grounds upon which the chosen people were beloved. With ἀγαπητοί, cf. ix. 25; the quotation there probably suggested the word.

διὰ τοὺς πατέρας: cf. ix. 4; xi. 16 f.: 'for the sake of the Patriarchs' from whom the Israelites have sprung and who were well-pleasing to God.

29. St. Paul gives the reason for believing that God will not desert the people whom He has called, and chosen, and on whom He has showered His Divine blessings. It lies in the unchangeable

nature of God: He does not repent Him of the choice that He has
made.

ἀμεταμέλητα: 2 Cor. vii. 10. The Divine gifts, such as have
been enumerated in ix. 4, 5, and such as God has showered upon
the Jews, bear the impress of the Giver. As He is not one who
will ever do that for which He will afterwards feel compunction,
His feelings of mercy towards the Jews will never change.

ἡ κλῆσις: the calling to the Kingdom.

30. The grounds for believing that God does not repent for the
gifts that He has given may be gathered from the parallelism
between the two cases of the Jews and the Gentiles, in one of which
His purpose has been completed, in the other not so. The Gentile
converts were disobedient once, as St. Paul has described at length
in the first chapter, but yet God has now shown pity on them, and
to accomplish this He has taken occasion from the disobedience of
the Jews: the same purpose and the same plan of providence may
be seen also in the case of the Jews. God's plan is to make disobedience an opportunity of showing mercy. The disobedience
of the Jews, like that of the Gentiles, had for its result the manifestation of the mercy of God.

The ὑμεῖς shows that this verse is written, as is all this chapter,
with the thought of Gentile readers prominently before the writer's
mind.

31. τῷ ὑμετέρῳ ἐλέει: 'by that same mercy which was shown to
you.' If the Jews had remained true to their covenant God would
have been able on His side merely to exhibit fidelity to the
covenant. As they have however been disobedient, they equally
with the Gentiles are recipients of the Divine mercy. These words
τῷ ὑμετέρῳ ἐλέει go with ἐλεηθῶσι, cf. Gal. ii. 10; 2 Cor. xii. 7, as is
shown by the parallelism of the two clauses

νῦν δὲ ἠλεήθητε   τῇ τούτων ἀπειθείᾳ

τῷ ὑμετέρῳ ἐλέει   ἵνα καὶ αὐτοὶ νῦν ἐλεηθῶσι.

This parallelism of the clauses may account for the presence of
the second νῦν with ἐλεηθῶσι, which should be read with א B D, Boh.,
Jo. Damasc. It was omitted by Syrian and some Western authorities
(A E F G, &c. Vulg. Syrr. Arm. Aeth., Orig.-lat. rell.) because it
seemed hardly to harmonize with facts. The authorities for it
are too varied for it to be an accidental insertion arising from a
repetition of the previous νῦν.

32. St. Paul now generalizes from these instances the character
of God's plan, and concludes his argument with a maxim which
solves the riddle of the Divine action. There is a Divine purpose
in the sin of mankind described in i. 18-iii. 20; there is a Divine

purpose in the faithlessness of the Jews. The object of both alike is to give occasion for the exhibition of the Divine mercy. If God has shut men up in sin it is only that He may have an opportunity of showing His compassion. So in Gal. iii. 22 ἀλλὰ συνέκλεισεν ἡ γραφὴ τὰ πάντα ὑπὸ ἁμαρτίαν, ἵνα ἡ ἐπαγγελία ἐκ πίστεως Ἰησοῦ Χριστοῦ δοθῇ τοῖς πιστεύουσι, the result of sin is represented as being to give the occasion for the fulfilment of the promise and the mission of the Messiah. All God's dealings with the race are in accordance with His final purpose. However harsh they may seem, when we contemplate the final end we can only burst forth into thankfulness to God.

συνέκλεισε γὰρ ὁ Θεός: cf. i. 24 f., and see below, p. 347.

συνέκλεισε: Ps. lxxviii [lxxvii]. 62 'He gave his people over unto the sword (συνέκλεισεν εἰς ῥομφαίαν).' Used with the pregnant sense of giving over so that there can be no escape.

τοὺς πάντας. Not necessarily every single individual, but all looked at collectively, as the πλήρωμα τῶν ἐθνῶν and πᾶς Ἰσραήλ. All the classes into which the world may be divided, Jew and Gentile alike, will be admitted into the Messianic Kingdom or God's Church. The reference is not here any more than elsewhere to the final salvation of every individual.

33. St. Paul has concluded his argument. He has vindicated the Divine justice and mercy. He has shown how even the reign of sin leads to a beneficent result. And now, carried away by the contrast between the apparent injustice and the real justice of God, having demonstrated that it is our knowledge and not His goodness that is at fault when we criticize Him, he bursts forth in a great ascription of praise to Him, declaring the unfathomable character of His wisdom.

We may notice that this description of the Divine wisdom represents not so much the conclusion of the argument as the assumption that underlies it. It is because we believe in the infinite character of the Divine power and love that we are able to argue that if in one case unexpectedly and wonderfully His action has been justified, therefore in other cases we may await the result, resting in confidence on His wisdom.

Marcion's text, which had omitted everything between x. 5 and xi. 34 (see on ch. x) here resumes. Tert. quotes vv. 32, 33 as follows: *o profundum divitiarum et sapientiae Dei, et ininvestigabiles viae eius*, omitting καὶ γνώσεως and ὡς ἀνεξερεύνητα τὰ κρίματα αὐτοῦ. Then follow vv. 34, 35 without any variation. On ver. 36 we know nothing. See Zahn, p. 518.

βάθος: 'inexhaustible wealth.' Cf. Prov. xviii. 3 βάθος κακῶν, troubles to which there is no bottom. The three genitives that follow are probably coordinate; πλούτου means the wealth of the Divine grace, cf. x. 12; σοφίας and γνώσεως are to be distinguished as meaning the former, a broad and comprehensive survey of things in their special relations, what we call Philosophy; the latter an intuitive penetrating perception of particular truths (see Lft. on Col. i. 9).

ἀνεξερεύνητα: Prov. xxv. 3, Sym.; and perhaps Jer. xvii. 9, Sym. (Field, *Hexapla*, ii. 617), 'unsearchable'; κρίματα, not judicial decisions, but judgements on the ways and plans of life. Cf. Ecclus. xvii. 12 διαθήκην αἰῶνος ἔστησεν μετ᾽ αὐτῶν, καὶ τὰ κρίματα αὐτοῦ ὑπέδειξεν αὐτοῖς.

ἀνεξιχνίαστοι: 'that cannot be traced out,' Eph. iii. 8; Job v. 9; ix. 10; xxxiv. 24. This passage seems to have influenced 1 Clem. Rom. xx. 5 ἀβύσσων τε ἀνεξιχνίαστα .... συνέχεται προστάγμασιν.

34. τίς γὰρ ἔγνω κ.τ.λ. This is taken from Is. xl. 13, varying only very slightly from the LXX. It is quoted also 1 Cor. ii. 16.

35. ἢ τίς προέδωκεν αὐτῷ, καὶ ἀνταποδοθήσεται αὐτῷ; taken from Job xli. 11, but not the LXX, which reads (ver. 2) τίς ἀντιστήσεταί μοι καὶ ὑπομενεῖ; The Hebrew (RV.) reads, 'Who hath first given unto me that I should repay him?' It is interesting to notice that the only other quotation in St. Paul which varies very considerably from the LXX is also taken from the book of Job (1 Cor. iii. 19, cf. Job v. 13), see p. 302. This verse corresponds to ὦ βάθος πλούτου. 'So rich are the spiritual gifts of God, that none can make any return, and He needs no recompense for what He gives.'

36. God needs no recompense, for all things that are exist in Him, all things come to man through Him, and to Him all return. He is the source, the agent, and the final goal of all created things and all spiritual life.

Many commentators have attempted to find in these words a reference to the work of the different persons of the Trinity (see esp. Liddon, who restates the argument in the most successful form). But (1) the prepositions do not suit this interpretation: δι᾽ αὐτοῦ indeed expresses the attributes of the Son, but εἰς αὐτόν can not naturally or even possibly be used of the Spirit. (2) The whole argument refers to a different line of thought. It is the relation of the Godhead as a whole to the universe and to created things. God (not necessarily the Father) is the source and inspirer and goal of all things.

This fundamental assumption of the infinite character of the Divine wisdom was one which St. Paul would necessarily inherit from Judaism. It is expressed most clearly and definitely in writings produced immediately after the fall of Jerusalem, when the pious Jew who still preserved a belief in the Divine favour towards Israel could find no hope or solution of the problem but in a tenacious adherence to what he could hold only by faith. God's ways are deeper and more wonderful than man could ever understand or fathom: only this was certain—that there was a Divine purpose of love towards Israel which would be shown in God's own time. There are many resemblances to St. Paul, not only in thought but in expression. *Apoc. Baruch* xiv. 8, 9 *Sed quis, Dominator Domine, assequetur iudicium tuum? aut quis investigabit profundum viae tuae? aut quis supputabit gravitatem*

semitae tuae? aut quis poterit cogitare consilium tuum incomprehensibile!
aut quis unquam ex natis inveniet principium aut finem sapientiae tuae?...
xx. 4 *et tunc ostendam tibi iudicium virtutis meae, et vias* [*in*]*investigabiles*
... xxi. 10 *tu enim solus es vivens immortalis et* [*in*]*investigabilis et*
numerum hominum nosti ... liv. 12, 13 *ecquis enim assimilabitur in mira-*
bilibus tuis, Deus, aut quis comprehendet cogitationem tuam profundam
vitae? Quia tu consilio tuo gubernas omnes creaturas quas creavit dextera
tua, et tu omnem fontem lucis apud te constituisti, et thesaurum sapientiae
subtus thronum tuum praeparasti ... lxxv *quis assimilabitur, Domine, boni-*
tati tuae? est enim incomprehensibilis. Aut quis scrutabitur miserationes
tuas, quae sunt infinitae? aut quis comprehendet intelligentiam tuam? aut
quis poterit consonare cogitationes mentis tuae? 4 Ezra v. 34 *torquent me*
renes mei per omnem horam quaerentem apprehendere semitam Altissimi et
investigare partem iudicii eius. et dixit ad me Non potes ... 40 *et dixit ad*
me Quomodo non potes facere unum de his quae dicta sunt, sic non poteris
invenire iudicium meum aut finem caritatis quam populo promisi.

The Argument of Romans IX–XI.

In the summary that has been given (pp. 269–275) of the various
opinions which have been held concerning the theology of this
section, and especially of ch. ix, it will have been noticed that
almost all commentators, although they differed to an extraordinary
degree in the teaching which they thought they had derived from
the passage, agreed in this, that they assumed that St. Paul was
primarily concerned with the questions that were exercising their
own minds, as to the conditions under which grace is given to man,
and the relation of the human life to the Divine will. Throughout
the seventeenth and eighteenth centuries a small number of commentators are distinguished from the general tendency by laying
stress on the fact that both in the ninth and in the eleventh chapter,
it is not the lot of the individual that is being considered, nor
eternal salvation, but that the object of the Apostle is to explain
the rejection of the Jews as a nation; that he is therefore dealing
with nations, not individuals, and with admission to the Christian
Church as representing the Messianic σωτηρία and not directly with
the future state of mankind. This view is very ably represented by
the English philosopher Locke; it is put forward in a treatise which
has been already referred to by Beyschlag (p. 275) and forms the
basis of the exposition of the Swiss commentator Oltramare, who
puts the position very shortly when he says that St. Paul is speaking
not of the scheme of election or of election in itself, but 'of God's
plan for the salvation of mankind, a plan which proceeded on the
principle of election.'

It is true that commentators who have adopted this view (in
particular Beyschlag) have pressed it too far, and have used it to
explain or explain away passages to which it will not apply; but it
undoubtedly represents the main lines of the Apostle's argument
and his purpose throughout these chapters. In order to estimate

his point of view our starting-point must be the conclusion he arrives at. This, as expressed at the end of ch. xi, is that God wishes to show His mercy upon all alike; that the world as a whole, the fulness of the Gentiles and all Israel, will come into the Messianic Kingdom and be saved; that the realization of this end is a mystery which has now been revealed, and that all this shows the greatness of the Divine wisdom; a wisdom which is guiding all things to their final consummation by methods and in ways which we can only partially follow.

The question at issue which leads St. Paul to assert the Divine purpose is the fact which at this time had become apparent; Israel as a nation was rejected from the Christian Church. If faith in the Messiah was to be the condition of salvation, then the mass of the Jews were clearly excluded. The earlier stages of the argument have been sufficiently explained. St. Paul first proves (ix. 6-29) that in this rejection God had been neither untrue to His promise nor unjust. He then proves (ix. 30-x. 13) that the Israelites were themselves guilty, for they had rejected the Messiah, although they had had full and complete knowledge of His message, and full warning. But yet there is a third aspect from which the rejection of Israel may be regarded—that of the Divine purpose. What has been the result of this rejection of Israel? It has led to the calling of the Gentiles,—this is an historical fact, and guided by it we can see somewhat further into the future. Here is a case where St. Paul can remember how different had been the result of his own failure from what he had expected. He can appeal to his own experience. There was a day, still vividly before his mind, when in the Pisidian Antioch, full of bitterness and a sense of defeat, he had uttered those memorable words ' from henceforth we will go to the Gentiles.' This had seemed at the moment a confession that his work was not being accomplished. Now he can see the Divine purpose fulfilled in the creation of the great Gentile churches, and arguing from his own experience in this one case, where God's purpose has been signally vindicated, he looks forward into the future and believes that, by ways other than we can follow, God is working out that eternal purpose which is part of the revelation he has to announce, the reconciliation of the world to Himself in Christ. He concludes therefore with this ascription of praise to God for His wisdom and mercy, emphasizing the belief which is at once the conclusion and the logical basis of his argument.

St. Paul's Philosophy of History.

The argument then of this section of the Epistle is not a discussion of the principles on which grace is given to mankind, but a philosophy of History. In the short concluding doxology to the Epistle—a conclusion which sums up the thought which underlies so much of the previous argument—St. Paul speaks of the mystery which has been kept silent in eternal times, but is now revealed, 'the Counsel,' as Dr. Hort (in Lft. *Biblical Essays*, p. 325) expresses it, 'of the far-seeing God, the Ruler of ages or periods, by which the mystery kept secret from ancient times is laid open in the Gospel for the knowledge and faith of all nations.' So again in Eph. i. 4–11 he speaks of the foreknowledge and plan which God had before the foundation of the world; a plan which has now been revealed: the manifestation of His goodness to all the nations of the world. St. Paul therefore sees a plan or purpose in history; in fact he has a philosophy of History. The characteristics of this theory we propose shortly to sum up.

(1) From Rom. v. 12 ff. we gather that St. Paul divides history into three periods represented typically by Adam, Moses, Christ, excluding the period before the Fall, which may be taken to typify an ideal rather than to describe an actual historical period. Of these the first period represents a state not of innocence but of ignorance. 'Until the Law, i. e. from Adam to Moses, sin was in the world; but sin is not imputed when there is no law.' It is a period which might be represented to us by the most degraded savage tribes. If sin represents failure to attain an ideal, they are sinful; but if sin represents guilt, they cannot be condemned, or at any rate only to a very slight degree and extent. Now if God deals with men in such a condition, how does He do so? The answer is, by the Revelation of Law; in the case of the Jewish people, by the Revelation of the Mosaic Law. Now this revelation of Law, with the accompanying and implied idea of judgement, has fulfilled certain functions. It has in the first place convicted man of sin; it has shown him the inadequacy of his life and conduct. 'For I had not known lust, except the law had said, Thou shalt not lust.' It has taught him the difference between right and wrong, and made him feel the desire for a higher life. And so, secondly, it has been the schoolmaster leading men to Christ. It has been the method by which mankind has been disciplined, by which they have been gradually prepared and educated. And thirdly, Law has taught men their weakness. The ideal is there; the desire to attain it is there; a struggle to attain it begins, and that struggle convinces us of our own weakness and of the power of sin over us. We not only learn a need for higher ideals; we learn also the need we have for a more powerful helper. This is the discipline of Law, and it prepares the way for the higher and fuller revelation of the Gospel.

These three stages are represented for us typically, and most clearly in the history of the Jewish dispensation. Even here of course there is an element of inexactness in them. There was a knowledge of right and wrong before Moses, there was an increase in knowledge after him; but yet the stages do definitely exist. And they may be found also running through the whole of history; they are not confined to the Jewish people. The stage of primitive ignorance is one through which presumably every race of men has passed; some in fact have not yet passed beyond it: but there has been progress upwards, and the great principle which has accompanied and made possible that progress is Law. The idea of Law in St. Paul is clearly not exhausted in the Jewish law, although that of course is the highest example of it. All peoples have been under law in some form. It is a great holy beneficent principle, but yet it is one which may become a burden. It is represented by the law of the conscience; it is witnessed by the moral judgements which men have in all ages passed on one another; it is embodied in codes and ordinances and bodies of law; it is that in fact which distinguishes for men the difference between right and wrong. The principle has worked, or is working, among mankind everywhere, and is meant to be the preparation of, as it creates the need for, the highest revelation, that of the Gospel.

(2) These three stages represent the first point in St. Paul's scheme of history. A second point is the idea of Election or Selection, or rather that of the ' Purpose of God which worketh by Selection.' God did not will to redeem mankind ' by a nod as He might have done, for that, as Athanasius puts it, would be to undo the work of creation; but He accepts the human conditions which He has created and uses them that the world may work out its own salvation. So, as St. Paul feels, He has selected Israel to be His chosen people; they have become the depositary of Divine truth and revelation, that through them, when the fulness of time has come, the world may receive Divine knowledge. This is clearly the conception underlying St. Paul's teaching, and looking back from the vantage ground of History we can see how true it is. To use modern phraseology, an 'ethical monotheism' has been taught the world through the Jewish race and through it alone. And St. Paul's principle may be extended further. He himself speaks of the ' fulness of time,' and it is no unreal philosophy to believe that the purpose of God has shown itself in selecting other nations also for excellence in other directions, in art, in commerce, in science, in statesmanship; that the Roman Empire was built up in order to create a sphere in which the message of the Incarnation might work; that the same purpose has guided the Church in the centuries which have followed. An historian like Renan would tell us that the freer development of the Christian Church was only made possible by the fall of Jerusalem and the divorce from Judaism. History tells us how the Arian persecutions occasioned the conversion of the Goths, and how the division of the Church

at the schism of East and West, or at the time of the Reformation, occasioned new victories for Christianity. Again and again an event which to contemporaries must have seemed disastrous has worked out beneficially; and so, guided by St. Paul's example, we learn to trust in that Divine wisdom and mercy which in some cases where we can follow its track has been so deeply and unexpectedly vindicated, and which is by hypothesis infinite in power and wisdom and knowledge.

(3) These then are two main points in St. Paul's teaching; first, the idea of gradual progress upwards implied in the stages of Adam, Moses, Christ; secondly, the idea of a purpose running through history, a purpose working by means of Selection. But to what end? The end is looked at under a twofold aspect; it is the completion of the Messianic Kingdom, and the exhibition of the Divine mercy. In describing the completion of the Messianic Kingdom, St. Paul uses, as in all his eschatological passages, the forms and phrases of the Apocalyptic literature of his time, but reasons have been given for thinking that he interpreted them, at any rate to a certain extent, in a spiritual manner. There is perhaps a further difficulty, or at any rate it may be argued that St. Paul is mistaken as regards the Jews, in that he clearly expected that at some time not very remote they would return to the Messianic Kingdom; yet nothing has yet happened which makes this expectation any more probable. We may argue in reply that so far as there was any mistaken expectation, it was of the nearness of the last times, and that the definite limit fixed by St. Paul, 'until the fulness of the Gentiles come in,' has not yet been reached. But it is better to go deeper, and to ask whether it is not the case that the rejection of the Jews now as then fulfils a purpose in the Divine plan? The well-known answer to the question, 'What is the chief argument for Christianity?'—'the Jews'—reminds us of the continued existence of that strange race, living as sojourners among men, the ever-present witnesses to a remote past which is connected by our beliefs intimately with the present. By their traditions to which they cling, by the O. T. Scriptures which they preserve by an independent chain of evidence, by their hopes, and by their highest aspirations, they are a living witness to the truth of that which they reject. They have their purpose still to fulfil in the Divine plan.

St. Paul's final explanation of the purpose of God—the exhibition of the Divine mercy—suggests the solution of another class of questions. In all such speculations there is indeed a difficulty, —the constant sense of the limitations of human language as applied to what is Divine; and St. Paul wishes us to feel these limitations, for again and again he uses such expressions as 'I speak as a man.' But yet granting this, the thought does

supply a solution of many problems. Why does God allow sin?
Why does He shut up men under sin? It is that ultimately He
may exhibit the depths of His Divine mercy. We may feel that
some such scheme of the course of history as was sketched out
above explains for us much that is difficult, but yet we always
come back to an initial question, Why does God allow such a state
of affairs to exist? We may grant that it comes from the free-will
of man ; but if God be almighty He must have created man with
that free-will. We may speak of His limitation of His own powers,
and of His Redemption of man without violating the conditions of
human life and nature; but if He be almighty, it is quite clear
that He could have prevented all sin and misery by a single act.
What answer can we make? We can only say, as St. Paul does,
that it is that He may reveal the Divine mercy; if man had not been
created so as to need this mercy, we should never have known the
Love of God as revealed in His Son. That is the farthest that
our speculations may legitimately go.

(4) But one final question. What evidence does St. Paul give
for a belief in the Divine purpose in history? It is twofold. On
the one hand, within the limited circle of our own knowledge or
experience, we can see that things have unexpectedly and wonderfully worked out so as to indicate a purpose. That was St. Paul's
experience in the preaching to the Gentiles. Where we have more
perfect knowledge and can see the end, there we see God's purpose
working. And on the other hand our hypothesis is a God of
infinite power and wisdom. If we have faith in this intellectual
conception, we believe that, where we cannot understand, our failure
arises from the limitations not of God's power and will, but of our
own intelligence.

An illustration may serve to bring this home. We can read
in such Jewish books as 4 Ezra or the *Apocalypse of Baruch* the
bewilderment and confusion of mind of a pious Jew at the fall
of Jerusalem. Every hope and aspiration that he had seems
shattered. But looked at from the point of view of Christianity,
and the wider development of Christianity, that was an inevitable
and a necessary step in the progress of the Church. If we believe
in a Divine purpose in history, we can see it working here quite
clearly. Yet to many a contemporary the event must have been
inexplicable. We can apply the argument to our time. In the
past, where we can trace the course of events, we have evidence of
the working of a Divine purpose, and so in the present, where so
much is obscure and dark, we can believe that there is still a Divine
purpose working, and that all the failures and misfortunes and
rebuffs of the time are yet steps towards a higher end. *Et dixit
ad me : Initio terreni orbis et antequam starent exitus saeculi . . ., et
antequam investigarentur praesentes anni, et antequam abalienarentur*

eorum qui nunc peccant adinventiones et consignati essent qui fide thesaurizaverunt: tunc cogitavi et facta sunt per me solum et non per alium, ut et finis per me et non per alium (4 Ezra vi. 1–6).

The Salvation of the Individual. Free-will and Predestination.

While the 'Nationalist' interpretation of these chapters has been adopted, it has at the same time been pointed out that, although it correctly represents St. Paul's line of argument, it cannot be legitimately used as it has been to evade certain difficulties which have been always felt as to his language. St. Paul's main line of argument applies to nations and peoples, but it is quite clear that the language of ix. 19–23 applies and is intended to apply equally to individuals. Further it is impossible to say, as Beyschlag does, that there is no idea in the Apostle's mind of a purpose before time. It is God's purpose 'before the foundation of the world' which is being expounded. And again, it is quite true to say that the election is primarily an election to privilege; yet there is a very intimate connexion between privilege and eternal salvation, and the language of ix. 22, 23 'fitted unto destruction,' 'prepared unto glory,' cannot be limited to a merely earthly destiny. Two questions then still remain to be answered. What theory is implied in St. Paul's language concerning the hope and future of individuals whether Christian or unbelievers, and what theory is implied as to the relation between Divine foreknowledge and human free-will?

We have deliberately used the expression 'what theory is implied?'; for St. Paul never formally discusses either of these questions; he never gives a definite answer to either, and on both he makes statements which appear inconsistent. Future salvation is definitely connected with privilege, and the two are often looked at as effect and cause. 'If while we were enemies we were reconciled to God through the death of His Son, much more being reconciled shall we be saved by His life' (v. 10). 'Whom He called, them He also justified: and whom He justified, them He also glorified' (viii. 30). But, although the assurance of hope is given by the Divine call, it is not irrevocable. 'By their unbelief they were broken off, and thou standest by thy faith. Be not highminded, but fear: for if God spared not the natural branches, neither will He spare thee' (xi. 20, 21). Nor again is future salvation to be confined to those who possess external privileges. The statement is laid down, in quite an unqualified way, that 'glory and honour and peace' come 'to everyone that worketh good, to the Jew first, and also to the Greek' (ii. 10). Again, there is no definite and unqualified statement either in

support of or against universalism; on the one side we have
statements such as those in a later Epistle (1 Tim. ii. 4) 'God our
Saviour, who willeth that all men should be saved and come to the
knowledge of the truth'; or again, 'He has shut all up to disobedience,
but that He might have mercy upon all' (Rom. xi. 32). On the
other side there is a strong assertion of 'wrath in the day of wrath
and revelation of the righteous judgement of God, who will render
to every man according to his works; ... unto them that are factious and obey not the truth, but obey unrighteousness, wrath and
indignation, tribulation and anguish, upon every soul of man that
worketh evil' (ii. 5–9). St. Paul asserts both the goodness and the
severity of God. He does not attempt to reconcile them, nor need
we. He lays down very clearly and definitely the fact of the Divine
judgement, and he brings out prominently three characteristics of it:
that it is in accordance with works, or perhaps more correctly on
the basis of works, that is of a man's whole life and career; that it
will be exercised by a Judge of absolute impartiality,—there is no
respect of persons; and that it is in accordance with the opportunities which a man has enjoyed. For the rest we must leave the
solution, as he would have done, to that wisdom and knowledge
and mercy of God of which he speaks at the close of the eleventh
chapter.

There is an equal inconsistency in St. Paul's language regarding
Divine sovereignty and human responsibility. Ch. ix implies arguments which take away Free-will; ch. x is meaningless without the
presupposition of Free-will. And such apparent inconsistency of
language and ideas pervades all St. Paul's Epistles. 'Work out your
own salvation, for it is God that worketh in you both to will and to do
of His good pleasure' (Phil. ii. 12, 13). Contrast again 'God gave
them up unto a reprobate mind,' and 'wherefore thou art without
excuse' (Rom. i. 18; ii. 1). Now two explanations of this language
are possible. It may be held (as does Fritzsche, see p. 275) that
St. Paul is unconscious of the inconsistency, and that it arises
from his inferiority in logic and philosophy, or (as Meyer) that he
is in the habit of isolating one point of view, and looking at the
question from that point of view alone. This latter view is correct;
or rather, for reasons which will be given below, it can be held and
stated more strongly. The antinomy, if we may call it so, of
chaps. ix and x is one which is and must be the characteristic
of all religious thought and experience.

(1) That St. Paul recognized the contradiction, and held it
consciously, may be taken as proved by the fact that his view
was shared by that sect of the Jews among whom he had been
brought up, and was taught in those schools in which he had
been instructed. Josephus tells us that the Pharisees attributed
everything to Fate and God, but that yet the choice of right and

wrong lay with men (Φαρισαῖοι ... εἱμαρμένῃ τε καὶ θεῷ προσάπτουσι πάντα καὶ τὸ μὲν πράττειν τὰ δίκαια, καὶ μή, κατὰ τὸ πλεῖστον ἐπὶ τοῖς ἀνθρώποις κεῖσθαι, βοηθεῖν δὲ εἰς ἕκαστον καὶ τὴν εἱμαρμένην B. J. II. viii. 14; comp. *Ant.* XIII. v. 9 ; XVIII. i. 3): and so in *Pirqê Aboth*, iii. 24 (p. 73 ed. Taylor) 'Everything is foreseen ; and free-will is given: and the world is judged by grace ; and everything is according to work.' (See also *Ps. Sol.* ix. 7 and the note on Free-will in Ryle and James' edition, p. 96, to which all the above references are due.) St. Paul then was only expanding and giving greater meaning to the doctrine in which he had been brought up. He had inherited it but he deepened it. He was more deeply conscious of the mercy of God in calling him ; he felt more deeply the certainty of the Divine protection and guidance. And yet the sense of personal responsibility was in an equal degree intensified. 'But I press forward, if so be I may apprehend, seeing that also I was apprehended by Christ' (Phil. iii. 12).

(2) Nor again is any other solution consistent with the reality of religious belief. Religion, at any rate a religion based on morality, demands two things. To satisfy our intellectual belief the God whom we believe in must be Almighty, i. e. omnipotent and omniscient ; in order that our moral life may be real our Will must be free. But these beliefs are not in themselves consistent. If God be Almighty He must have created us with full knowledge of what we should become, and the responsibility therefore for what we are can hardly rest with ourselves. If, on the other hand, our Will is free, there is a department where God (if we judge the Divine mind on the analogy of human minds) cannot have created us with full knowledge. We are reduced therefore to an apparently irreconcilable contradiction, and that remains the language of all deeply religious minds. We are free, we are responsible for what we do, but yet it is God that worketh all things. This antithesis is brought out very plainly by Thomas Aquinas. God he asserts is the cause of everything (*Deus causa est omnibus operantibus ut operentur, Cont. Gent.* III. lxvii), but the Divine providence does not exclude Free-will. The argument is interesting : *Adhuc providentia est multiplicativa bonorum in rebus gubernatis. Illud ergo per quod multa bona subtraherentur a rebus, non pertinet ad providentiam. Si autem libertas voluntatis tolleretur, multa bona subtraherentur. Tolleretur enim laus virtutis humanae, quae nulla est si homo libere non agit, tolleretur enim iustitia praemiantis et punientis, si non libere homo ageret bonum et malum, cessaret etiam circumspectio in consiliis, quae de his quae in necessitate aguntur, frustra tractarentur, esset igitur contra providentiae rationem si subtraheretur voluntatis libertas* (*ib.* lxxiii). And he sums up the whole relation of God to natural causes, elsewhere showing how this same principle applies to the human will : *patet etiam quod non sic idem*

*effectus causae naturali et divinae virtuti attribuitur, quasi partim
a Deo, partim a naturali agenti fiat, sed totus ab utroque secundum
alium modum, sicut idem effectus totus attribuitur instrumento, et
principali agenti etiam totus (ib.* lxx). See also *Summa Theologiae,
Pars Prima,* cv. art. 5 ; *Prima Secundae,* cxiii).

> This is substantially also the view taken by Mozley, *On the Augustinian
> Doctrine of Predestination.* The result of his argument is summed up as
> follows, pp. 326, 327 : 'Upon this abstract idea, then, of the Divine Power, as
> an unlimited power, rose up the Augustinian doctrine of Predestination and
> good ; while upon the abstract idea of Free-will, as an unlimited faculty,
> rose up the Pelagian theory. Had men perceived, indeed, more clearly and
> really than they have done, their ignorance as human creatures, and the
> relation in which the human reason stands to the great truths involved in
> this question, they might have saved themselves the trouble of this whole
> controversy. They would have seen that this question cannot be determined
> absolutely, one way or another; that it lies between two great contradictory
> truths, neither of which can be set aside, or made to give way to the other ;
> two opposing tendencies of thought, inherent in the human mind, which go
> on side by side, and are able to be held and maintained together, although
> thus opposite to each other, because they are only incipient, and not final
> and complete truths ;—the great truths, I mean, of the Divine Power on the
> one side, and man's Free-will, or his originality as an agent, on the other.
> And this is in fact, the mode in which this question is settled by the practical
> common-sense of mankind. . . . The plain natural reason of mankind is thus
> always large and comprehensive ; not afraid of inconsistency, but admitting
> all truth which presents itself to its notice. It is only when minds begin to
> philosophize that they grow narrow,—that there begins to be felt the appeal
> to consistency, and with it the temptation to exclude truths.'

(3) We can but state the two sides ; we cannot solve the problem.
But yet there is one conception in which the solution lies. It is in
a complete realization of what we mean by asserting that God is
Almighty. The two ideas of Free-will and the Divine sovereignty
cannot be reconciled in our own mind, but that does not prevent
them from being reconcilable in God's mind. We are really
measuring Him by our own intellectual standard if we think
otherwise. And so our solution of the problem of Free-will, and
of the problems of history and of individual salvation, must finally
lie in the full acceptance and realization of what is implied by the
infinity and the omniscience of God.

THE NEW LIFE.

XII. 1, 2. *With this wonderful programme of salvation
before you offer to God a sacrifice, not of slaughtered beasts,
but of your living selves, your own bodies, pure and free
from blemish, your spiritual service. Do not take pattern*

*by the age in which you live, but undergo complete moral
reformation with the will of God for your standard.*

XII–XV. 12. We now reach the concluding portion of the
Epistle, that devoted to the practical application of the previous
discussion. An equally marked division between the theoretical
and the practical portion is found in the Epistle to the Ephesians
(chap. iv); and one similar, although not so strongly marked, in
Galatians (v. 1 or 2); Colossians (iii. 1); 1 Thessalonians (iv. 1);
2 Thessalonians (iii. 6). A comparison with the Epistles of St.
Peter and St. John will show how special a characteristic of St.
Paul is this method of construction. The main idea running
through the whole section seems to be that of peace and unity for
the Church in all relations both internal and external. As St. Paul
in the earlier portion of the Epistle, looking back on the controversies
through which he has passed, solves the problems which had been
presented in the interests no longer of victory, but of peace, so in
his practical exhortation he lays the foundation of unity and
harmony on deep and broad principles. A definite division may
be made between chaps. xii, xiii, in which the exhortations are
general in character, and xiv–xv. 12, in which they arise directly
out of the controversies which are disturbing the Church. Yet
even these are treated from a general point of view, and not in
relation to any special circumstances. In the first section, the
Apostle does not appear to follow any definite logical order, but
touches on each subject as it suggests itself or is suggested by the
previous ideas; it may be roughly divided as follows: (1) a general
introduction on the character of the Christian life (xii. 1, 2); (ii)
the right use of spiritual gifts especially in relation to Church
order (3–8); (iii) a series of maxims mainly illustrating the great
principle of ἀγάπη (9–21); (iv) duties towards rulers and those in
authority (xiii. 1–7); (v) a special exhortation to ἀγάπη, as including
all other commandments (8–10); (vi) an exhortation to a spiritual
life on the ground of the near approach of the παρουσία (11–14).

Tertullian quotes the following verses of this chapter from Marcion: 9, 10a,
12, 14b, 16b, 17a, 18, 19. There is no evidence that any portion was
omitted, but ver. 18 may have stood after ver. 19, and in the latter γέγραπται
is naturally cut off and a γάρ inserted. The other variations noted by Zahn
seem less certain (Zahn, *Geschichte des N. T. Kanons*, p. 518; Tert. *adv.
Marc.* v. 14).

1. παρακαλῶ οὖν. A regular formula in St. Paul: Eph. iv. 1;
1 Tim. ii. 1; 1 Cor. iv. 16. As in the passage in the Ephesians,
the οὖν refers not so much to what immediately precedes as to the
result of the whole previous argument. 'As you are justified by
Christ, and put in a new relation to God, I exhort you to live in
accordance with that relation.' But although St. Paul is giving the

practical results of his whole previous argument, yet (as often with him, cf. xi. 11) the words are directly led up to by the conclusion of the previous chapter and the narration of the wisdom and mercy of God.

διὰ τῶν οἰκτιρμῶν τοῦ Θεοῦ. Cf. 2 Cor. i. 3 ὁ πατὴρ τῶν οἰκτιρμῶν. Οἰκτιρμός in the singular only occurs once (Col. iii. 12); the plural is a Hebraism directly derived from the LXX (Ps. cxviii. 156 οἱ οἰκτιρμοί σου πολλοί, κύριε, σφόδρα). There is a reference to the preceding chapter, 'As God has been so abundantly merciful to both Jews and Greeks, offer a sacrifice to Him, and let that sacrifice be one that befits His holiness.'

παραστῆσαι: a tech. term (although not in the O.T.) for presenting a sacrifice: cf. Jos. *Ant.* IV. vi. 4 βωμούς τε ἐκέλευσεν ἑπτὰ δείμασθαι τὸν βασιλέα, καὶ τοσούτους ταύρους καὶ κριοὺς παραστῆναι. The word means to 'place beside,' 'present' for any purpose, and so is used of the presentation of Christ in the temple (Luke ii. 22), of St. Paul presenting his converts (Col. i. 28), or Christ presenting His Church (Eph. v. 27), or of the Christian himself (cf. Rom. vi. 13 ff.). In all these instances the idea of 'offering' (which is one part of sacrifice) is present.

τὰ σώματα ὑμῶν. To be taken literally, like τὰ μέλη ὑμῶν in vi. 13, as is shown by the contrast with τοῦ νοός in ver. 2. 'Just as the sacrifice in all ancient religions must be clean and without blemish, so we must offer bodies to God which are holy and free from the stains of passion.' Christianity does not condemn the body, but demands that the body shall be purified and be united with Christ. Our members are to be ὅπλα δικαιοσύνης τῷ Θεῷ (vi. 13); our bodies (τὰ σώματα) are to be μέλη Χριστοῦ (1 Cor. vi. 15); they are the temple of the Holy Spirit (*ib.* ver. 19); we are to be pure both in body and in spirit (*ib.* vii. 34).

There is some doubt as to the order of the words εὐάρεστον τῷ Θεῷ. They occur in this order in Nᶜ B D E F G L and later MSS., Syrr. Boh. Sah., and Fathers; τῷ Θεῷ εὐ. in ℵ A P, Vulg. The former is the more usual expression, but St. Paul may have written τῷ Θεῷ εὐ. to prevent ambiguity, for if τῷ Θεῷ comes at the end of the sentence there is some doubt as to whether it should not be taken with παραστῆσαι.

θυσίαν ζῶσαν: cf. vi. 13 παραστήσατε ἑαυτοὺς τῷ Θεῷ, ὡσεὶ ἐκ νεκρῶν ζῶντας. The bodies presented will be those of men to whom newness of life has been given by union with the risen Christ. The relation to the Jewish rite is partly one of distinction, partly of analogy. The Jewish sacrifice implies slaughter, the Christian continued activity and life; but as in the Jewish rite all ritual requirements must be fulfilled to make the sacrifice acceptable to God, so in the Christian sacrifice our bodies must be holy, without spot or blemish.

ἁγίαν, 'pure,' 'holy,' 'free from stain,' 1 Pet. i. 16; Lev. xix. 2.

So the offering of the Gentiles (Rom. xv. 16) is ἡγιασμένη ἐν Πν. Ἁγ (See on i. 7.)

εὐάρεστον τῷ Θεῷ: cf. Phil. iv. 18 δεξάμενος παρὰ Ἐπαφροδίτου τὰ παρ᾽ ὑμῶν, ὀσμὴν εὐωδίας, θυσίαν δεκτήν, εὐάρεστον τῷ Θεῷ : Rom. xiv. 18; 'Well-pleasing to God.' The formal sacrifices of the old covenant might not be acceptable to God : cf. Ps. li. 16, 17.

τὴν λογικὴν λατρείαν ὑμῶν. Acc. in apposition to the idea of the sentence. Winer, § lix. 9, p. 669, E. T.: cf. 1 Tim. ii. 6 and the note on viii. 3 above. A service to God such as befits the reason (λόγος), i. e. a spiritual sacrifice and not the offering of an irrational animal : cf. 1 Pet. ii. 5. The writer of Test. XII. Pat. Levi 3 seems to combine a reminiscence of this passage with Phil. iv. 18: speaking of the angels, he says προσφέρουσι δὲ Κυρίῳ ὀσμὴν εὐωδίας λογικὴν καὶ ἀναίμακτον προσφοράν.

We may notice the metaphorical use St. Paul makes of sacrificial language : ἐπὶ τῇ θυσίᾳ καὶ λειτουργίᾳ τῆς πίστεως ὑμῶν Phil. ii. 17; ὀσμὴ εὐωδίας (Lev. i. 9) Phil. iv. 18; ὀσμή 2 Cor. ii. 14, 16; λειτουργός, ἱερουργοῦντα, προσφορά Rom. xv. 16. This language passed gradually and almost imperceptibly into liturgical use, and hence acquired new shades of meaning (see esp. Lightfoot, Clement, i. p. 386 sq.).

2. συσχηματίζεσθε...μεταμορφοῦσθε, ' Do not adopt the external and fleeting fashion of this world, but be ye transformed in your inmost nature.' On the distinction of σχῆμα and μορφή preserved in these compounds see Lightfoot, Journal of Classical and Sacred Philology, vol. iii. 1857, p. 114, Philippians, p. 125. Comp. Chrys. ad loc., 'He says not change the fashion, but be transformed, to show that the world's ways are a fashion, but virtue's not a fashion, but a kind of real form, with a natural beauty of its own, not needing the trickeries and fashions of outward things, which no sooner appear than they go to naught. For all these things, even before they come to light, are dissolving. If then thou throwest the fashion aside, thou wilt speedily come to the form.'

There is a preponderance of evidence in favour of the imperatives (συσχηματίζεσθε, μεταμορφοῦσθε) in this verse, B L P all the versions (Latt. Boh. Syrr.), and most Fathers, against A D F G (ℵ varies). The evidence of the Versions and of the Fathers, some of whom paraphrase, is particularly important, as it removes the suspicion of itacism.

τῷ αἰῶνι τούτῳ, 'this world,' 'this life,' used in a moral sense. When the idea of a future Messianic age became a part of the Jewish Theology, Time, χρόνος, was looked upon as divided into a succession of ages, αἰῶνες, periods or cycles of great but limited duration; and the present age was contrasted with the age to come, or the age of the Messiah (cf. Schürer, § 29. 9), a contrast very common among early Christians: Matt. xii. 32 οὔτε ἐν τούτῳ τῷ αἰῶνι οὔτε ἐν τῷ μέλλοντι : Luc. xx. 34, 35 οἱ υἱοὶ τοῦ αἰῶνος τούτου

... οἱ δὲ καταξιωθέντες τοῦ αἰῶνος ἐκείνου τυχεῖν: Eph. i. 21 οὐ μόνον ἐν τῷ αἰῶνι τούτῳ ἀλλὰ καὶ ἐν τῷ μέλλοντι. So *Enoch* xvi. 1 μέχρις ἡμέρας τελειώσεως τῆς κρίσεως τῆς μεγάλης, ἐν ᾗ ὁ αἰὼν ὁ μέγας τελεσθήσεται. As the distinction between the present period and the future was one between that which is transitory and that which is eternal, between the imperfect and the perfect, between that in which οἱ ἄρχοντες τοῦ αἰῶνος τούτου (1 Cor. ii. 6) have power and that in which ὁ βασιλεὺς τῶν αἰώνων (*Enoch* xii. 3) will rule, αἰών like κόσμος in St. John's writings, came to have a moral significance: Gal. i. 4 ἐκ τοῦ αἰῶνος τοῦ ἐνεστῶτος πονηροῦ: Eph. ii. 2 περιεπατήσατε κατὰ τὸν αἰῶνα τοῦ κόσμου τούτου: and so in this passage.

From the idea of a succession of ages (cf. Eph. ii. 7 ἐν τοῖς αἰῶσι τοῖς ἐπερχομένοις) came the expression εἰς τοὺς αἰῶνας (xi. 36), or αἰῶνας τῶν αἰώνων to express eternity, as an alternative for the older form εἰς τὸν αἰῶνα. The latter, which is the ordinary and original O. T. form, arises (like αἰώνιος) from the older and original meaning of the Hebrew '*ôlam*, 'the hidden time,' 'futurity,' and contains rather the idea of an unending period.

τῇ ἀνακαινώσει τοῦ νοός: our bodies are to be pure and free from all the stains of passion; our 'mind' and 'intellect' are to be no longer enslaved by our fleshly nature, but renewed and purified by the gift of the Holy Spirit. Cf. Tit. iii. 5 διὰ λουτροῦ παλιγγενεσίας καὶ ἀνακαινώσεως Πνεύματος Ἁγίου: 2 Cor. iv. 16: Col. iii. 10. On the relation of ἀνακαίνωσις, 'renewal,' to παλιγγενεσία see Trench, *Syn.* § 18. By this renewal the intellectual or rational principle will no longer be a νοῦς σαρκός (Col. ii. 18), but will be filled with the Spirit and coincident with the highest part of human nature (1 Cor. ii. 15, 16).

δοκιμάζειν: cf. ii. 18; Phil. i. 10. The result of this purification is to make the intellect, which is the seat of moral judgement, true and exact in judging on spiritual and moral questions.

τὸ θέλημα τοῦ Θεοῦ, κ.τ.λ., 'That which is in accordance with God's will.' This is further defined by the three adjectives which follow. It includes all that is implied in moral principle, in the religious aim, and the ideal perfection which is the goal of life.

THE RIGHT USE OF SPIRITUAL GIFTS.

XII. 3–8. *Let every Christian be content with his proper place and functions. The society to which we belong is a single body with many members all related one to another. Hence the prophet should not strain after effects for which his faith is insufficient; the minister, the teacher, the exhorter, should each be intent on his special duty. The* *almsgiver, the person in authority, the doer of kindness, should each cultivate a spirit appropriate to what he does.*

3. St. Paul begins by an instance in which the need of an enlightened mind is most necessary; namely, the proper bearing of a Christian in the community, and the right use of spiritual gifts.

διὰ τῆς χάριτος κ.τ.λ. gives emphasis by an appeal to Apostolic authority (cf. i. 5). It is not merely a question of the spiritual progress of the individual, for when St. Paul is speaking of that he uses exhortation (ver. 1), but of the discipline and order of the community; this is a subject which demands the exercise of authority as well as of admonition.

παντὶ τῷ ὄντι. An emphatic appeal to every member of the Christian community, for every one (ἑκάστῳ) has some spiritual gift.

μὴ ὑπερφρονεῖν, 'not to be high-minded above what one ought to be minded, but to direct one's mind to sobriety.' Notice the play on words ὑπερφρονεῖν ... φρονεῖν ... φρονεῖν ... σωφρονεῖν. The φρονεῖν εἰς τὸ σωφρονεῖν would be the fruit of the enlightened intellect as opposed to the φρόνημα τῆς σαρκός (viii. 6).

ἑκάστῳ is after ἐμέρισε, not in apposition to παντὶ τῷ ὄντι, and its prominent position gives the idea of diversity; for the order, cp. 1 Cor. vii. 17. 'According to the measure of faith which God has given each man.' The wise and prudent man will remember that his position in the community is dependent not on any merit of his own, but on the measure of his faith, and that faith is the gift of God. Faith 'being the sign and measure of the Christian life' is used here for all those gifts which are given to man with or as the result of his faith. Two points are emphasized, the diversity ἑκάστῳ ... μέτρον, and the fact that this diversity depends upon God: cf. 1 Cor. vii. 7 ἀλλ' ἕκαστος ἴδιον ἔχει χάρισμα ἐκ Θεοῦ, ὁ μὲν οὕτως, ὁ δὲ οὕτως.

4, 5. Modesty and sobriety and good judgement are necessary because of the character of the community: it is an organism or corporate body in which each person has his own duty to perform for the well-being of the whole and therefore of himself.

This comparison of a social organism to a body was very common among ancient writers, and is used again and again by St. Paul to illustrate the character of the Christian community: see 1 Cor. xii. 12; Eph. iv. 15; Col. i. 18. The use here is based upon that in 1 Cor. xii. 12–31. In the Epistles of the Captivity it is another side of the idea that is expounded, the unity of the Church in Christ as its head.

5. τὸ δὲ καθ' εἷς. An idiomatic expression found in later Greek. Cf. Mark xiv. 19 εἷς καθ' εἷς: John viii. 9: 3 Macc. v. 34 ὁ καθ' εἷς δὲ τῶν φίλων: Lucian *Soloecista* 9; Eus. *H. E.* X. iv, &c. εἷς καθ' εἷς was probably formed on the model of ἓν καθ' ἕν, and then καθ' εἷς came to be treated adverbially and written as one word : hence it could be used, as here, with a neuter article.

6-13. ἔχοντες δὲ χαρίσματα, κ.τ.λ. These words may be taken grammatically either (1) as agreeing with the subject of ἐσμέν, a comma being put at μέλη, or (2) as the beginning of a new sentence and forming the subject of a series of verbs supplied with the various sentences that follow; this is decidedly preferable, for in the previous sentence the comparison is grammatically finished, and ἔχοντες δέ suggests the beginning of a new sentence.

Two methods of construction are also possible for the words κατὰ τὴν ἀναλογίαν τῆς πίστεως ... ἐν τῇ διακονίᾳ, &c. Either they must be taken as dependent on ἔχοντες, or a verb must be supplied with each and the sentences become exhortations. (1) If the first construction be taken the passage will run, ' So are we all one body in Christ, but individually members one of another, having gifts which are different according to the grace which is given us, whether we have prophecy according to the proportion of faith, or a function of ministry in matters of ministration, or whether a man is a teacher in the exercise of functions of teaching, or one who exhorteth in exhortation, one who giveth with singleness of purpose, one who zealously provides, one who showeth mercy cheerfully.' (2) According to the second interpretation we must translate 'having gifts which vary according to the grace given us,—be it prophecy let us use it in proportion to the faith given us, be it ministry let us use it in ministry,' &c.

That the latter (which is that of Mey. Go. Va. Gif.) is preferable is shown by the difficulty of keeping up the former interpretation to the end; few commentators have the hardihood to carry it on as far as ver. 8; nor is it really easier in ver. 7, where the additions ἐν τῇ διακονίᾳ are very otiose if they merely qualify ἔχοντες understood. In spite therefore of the somewhat harsh ellipse, the second construction must be adopted throughout.

6. κατὰ τὴν ἀναλογίαν τῆς πίστεως (sc. προφητεύωμεν). The meaning of πίστεως here is suggested by that in ver. 3. A man's gifts depend upon the measure of faith allotted to him by God, and so he must use and exercise these gifts in proportion to the faith that is in him. If he be σώφρων and his mind is enlightened by the Holy Spirit, he will judge rightly his capacity and power ; if, on the other hand, his mind be carnal, he will try to distinguish himself vain-gloriously and disturb the peace of the community.

Liddon, with most of the Latin Fathers and many later commentators, takes πίστεως objectively : ' The majestic proportion of the (objective) Faith is before him, and, keeping his eye on it, he avoids private crotchets and wild fanaticisms, which exaggerate the relative importance of particular truths to the neglect of others.'

But this interpretation is inconsistent with the meaning he has himself given to πίστις in ver. 3, and gives a sense to ἀναλογίαν which it will not bear ; the difficulty being concealed by the ambiguity of the word ‘ proportion’ in English.

7. διακονίαν, ‘ if we have the gift of ministry, let us use it in ministering to the community, and not attempt ambitiously to prophesy or exhort.’ διακονία was used either generally of all Christian ministrations (so Rom. xi. 13 ; 1 Cor. xii. 5 ; Eph. iv. 12, &c.) or specially of the administration of alms and attendance to bodily wants (1 Cor. xvi. 15 ; 2 Cor. viii. 4, &c.). Here the opposition to προφητεία, διδασκαλία, παράκλησις seems to demand the more confined sense.

ὁ διδάσκων. St. Paul here substitutes a personal phrase because ἔχειν διδασκαλίαν would mean, not to impart, but to receive instruction.

8. ὁ μεταδιδούς : the man who gives alms of his own substance is to do it in singleness of purpose and not with mixed motives, with the thought of ostentation or reward. With ὁ μεταδιδούς, the man who gives of his own, while ὁ διαδιδούς is the man who distributes other persons' gifts, comp. *Test. XII. Patr.* Iss. 7 παντὶ ἀνθρώπῳ ὀδυνομένῳ συνεστέναξα, καὶ πτωχῷ μετέδωκα τὸν ἄρτον μου.

ἁπλότης. The meaning of this word is illustrated best by *Test. XII. Patr.* Issachar, or περὶ ἁπλότητος. Issachar is represented as the husbandman, who lived simply and honestly on his land. ‘And my father blessed me, seeing that I walk in simplicity (ἁπλότης). And I was not inquisitive in my actions, nor wicked and envious towards my neighbour. I did not speak evil of any one, nor attack a man's life, but I walked with a single eye (ἐν ἁπλότητι ὀφθαλμῶν). . . . To every poor and every afflicted man I provided the good things of the earth, in simplicity (ἁπλότης) of heart. . . . The simple man (ὁ ἁπλοῦς) doth not desire gold, doth not ravish his neighbour, doth not care for all kinds of dainty meats, doth not wish for diversity of clothing, doth not promise himself (οὐχ ὑπογράφει) length of days, he receiveth only the will of God . . . he walketh in uprightness of life, and beholdeth all things in simplicity (ἁπλότητι).’ Issachar is the honourable, hardworking, straightforward farmer ; open-handed and open-hearted, giving out of compassion and in singleness of purpose, not from ambition.

The word is used by St. Paul alone in the N. T., and was specially suited to describe the generous unselfish character of Christian almsgiving ; and hence occurs in one or two places almost with the signification of liberality, 2 Cor. ix. 11, 13 ; just as ‘ liberality’ in English has come to have a secondary meaning, and δικαιοσύνη in Hellenistic Greek (Hatch, *Essays in Biblical Greek*, p. 49). Such specialization is particularly natural in the East, where large-hearted generosity is a popular virtue, and where such words as ‘ good’ may be used simply to mean munificent.

ὁ προϊστάμενος, the man that presides, or governs in any position, whether ecclesiastical or other.   The word is used of ecclesiastical officials, 1 Thess. v. 12 ; 1 Tim. v. 17 ; Just. Mart. *Apol.* i. 67 ; and of a man ruling his family (1 Tim. iii. 4, 5, 12), and need not be any further defined.   Zeal and energy are the natural gifts required of any ruler.

ὁ ἐλεῶν. 'Let any man or woman who performs deeds of mercy in the church, do so brightly and cheerfully.'   The value of brightness in performing acts of kindness has become proverbial, Ecclus. xxxii. (xxxv.) 11 ἐν πάσῃ δόσει ἱλάρωσον τὸ πρόσωπόν σου: Prov. xxii. 8 ἄνδρα ἱλαρὸν καὶ δότην εὐλογεῖ ὁ Θεός (quoted 2 Cor. ix. 7); but just as singleminded sincerity became an eminently Christian virtue, so cheerfulness in all the paths of life, a cheerfulness which springs from a warm heart, and a pure conscience and a serene mind set on something above this world, was a special characteristic of the early Christian (Acts ii. 46; v. 41; Phil. i. 4, 18; ii. 18, &c.; 1 Thess. v. 16).

Spiritual Gifts.

The word χάρισμα (which is almost purely Pauline) is used of those special endowments which come to every Christian as the result of God's free favour (χάρις) to men and of the consequent gift of faith.   In Rom. v. 15, vi. 13, indeed, it has a wider signification, meaning the free gift on the part of God to man of forgiveness of sins and eternal life, but elsewhere it appears always to be used for those personal endowments which are the gifts of the Spirit.   In this connexion it is not confined to special or conspicuous endowments or to special offices.   There are, indeed, τὰ χαρίσματα τὰ μείζονα (1 Cor. xii. 31), which are those apparently most beneficial to the community; but in the same Epistle the word is also used of the individual fitness for the married or the unmarried state (1 Cor. vii. 7); and in Rom. i. 13 it is used of the spiritual advantage which an Apostle might confer on the community.   So again, χαρίσματα include miraculous powers, but no distinction is made between them and non-miraculous gifts.   In the passage before us there is the same combination of very widely differing gifts; the Apostle gives specimens (if we may express it so) of various Christian endowments; it is probable that some of them were generally if not always the function of persons specially set apart for the purpose (although not perhaps necessarily holding ecclesiastical office), others would not be confined to any one office, and many might be possessed by the same person.   St. Paul's meaning is: By natural endowments, strengthened with the gifts of the Spirit, you have various powers and capacities : in the use of these it is above all necessary for the good of the community that you should show a wise and prudent judgement, not attempting offices or work for which you are not fitted, nor marring your gifts by exercising them in a wrong spirit.

This being the meaning of χαρίσματα and St. Paul's purpose in this chapter, interpretations of it, as of the similar passage (chap. xii) in the First Epistle to the Corinthians, which have attempted to connect spiritual gifts more closely with the Christian ministry are unfounded. These are of two characters. One, that of Neander, maintains that in the original Church there were no ecclesiastical officers at all but only χαρίσματα, and that as spiritual gifts died out, regularly appointed officers took the place of those who possessed them. The other finds, or attempts to find, an ecclesiastical office for each gift of the Spirit mentioned in this chapter and the parallel passage of the Corinthians, or at any rate argues that there must have been προφῆται, διδάσκαλοι &c., existing as church officers in the Corinthian and Roman communities. Neither of these is a correct deduction from the passages under consideration. In dealing with the χαρίσματα St. Paul is discussing a series of questions only partially connected with the Christian ministry. Every church officer would, we may presume, be considered to have χαρίσματα which would fit him for the fulfilment of such an office; but most, if not all, Christians would also have χαρίσματα. The two questions therefore are on different planes which partially intersect, and deductions from these chapters made in any direction as to the form of the Christian organization are invalid, although they show the spiritual endowments which those prominent in the community could possess.

A comparison of the two passages, 1 Cor. xii. and Rom. xii. 3–8, is interesting on other grounds. St. Paul in the Corinthian Epistle is dealing with a definite series of difficulties arising from the special endowments and irregularities of that church. He treats the whole subject very fully, and, as was necessary, condemns definite disorders. In the Roman Epistle he is evidently writing with the former Epistle in his mind: he uses the same simile: he concludes equally with a list of forms of χαρίσματα—shorter, indeed, but representative; but there is no sign of that directness which would arise from dealing with special circumstances. The letter is written with the experience of Corinth fresh in the writer's mind, but without any immediate purpose. He is laying down directions based on his experience; but instead of a number of different details, he sums up all that he has to say in one general moral principle: Prudence and self-restraint in proportion to the gift of faith. Just as the doctrinal portions of the Epistle are written with the memory of past controversies still fresh, discussing and laying down in a broad spirit positions which had been gained in the course of those controversies, so we shall find that in the practical portion St. Paul is laying down broad and statesmanlike positions which are the result of past experience and deal with circumstances which may arise in any community.

MAXIMS TO GUIDE THE CHRISTIAN LIFE.

XII. 9-21. *The general principles of your life should be a love which is perfectly sincere, depth of moral feeling, consideration for others, zeal, fervour, devoutness, hopefulness, fortitude under persecutions, prayerfulness, eagerness to help your fellow-Christians by sharing what you possess with them and by the ready exercise of hospitality.*

Bless, do not curse, your persecutors. Sympathize with others. Be united in feeling, not ambitious but modest in your aims. Be not self-opinionated or revengeful. Do nothing to offend the world. Leave vengeance to God. Good for evil is the best requital.

9. ἡ ἀγάπη, cf. xiii. 8. The Apostle comes back from directions which only apply to individuals to the general direction to Christian Charity, which will solve all previous difficulties. Euthym.-Zig. διδάσκων γὰρ πῶς ἂν τὰ εἰρημένα κατορθωθείη, ἐπήγαγε τὴν μητέρα πάντων τούτων, λέγω δὴ τὴν εἰς ἀλλήλους ἀγάπην. The sequence of ideas is exactly similar to that in 1 Cor. xii, xiii, and obviously suggested by it. In the section that follows (9-21), ἀγάπη is the ruling thought, but the Apostle does not allow himself to be confined and pours forth directions as to the moral and spiritual life which crowd into his mind.

ἀνυπόκριτος. Wisd. v. 18; xviii. 16; 2 Cor. vi. 6 (ἀγάπη); 1 Tim. i. 5 and 2 Tim. i. 5 (πίστις); Jas. iii. 17 (ἡ ἄνωθεν σοφία); 1 Pet. i. 22 (φιλαδελφία). It is significant that the word is not used in profane writers except once in the adverbial form, and that by Marcus Aurelius (viii. 5).

ἀποστυγοῦντες: sc. ἔστε as ἔστω above, and cf. 1 Pet. ii. 18; iii. 1. An alternative construction is to suppose an anacoluthon, as if ἀγαπᾶτε ἀνυποκρίτως had been read above; cf. 2 Cor. i. 7. The word expresses a strong feeling of horror; the ἀπο- by farther emphasizing the idea of separation gives an intensive force, which is heightened by contrast with κολλώμενοι.

τὸ πονηρὸν . . . τῷ ἀγαθῷ. The characteristic of true genuine love is to attach oneself to the good in a man, while detesting the evil in him. There cannot be love for what is evil, but whoever has love in him can see the good that there is in all.

10. τῇ φιλαδελφίᾳ, 'love of the brethren'; as contrasted with ἀγάπη, which is universal, φιλαδελφία represents affection for the brethren; that is, for all members of the Christian community, cf. 2 Pet. i. 7. Euthym.-Zig. ἀδελφοί ἐστε κατὰ τὴν αὐτὴν διὰ τοῦ βαπτίσματος ἀναγέννησιν καὶ διὰ τοῦτο ἀνάγκην ἔχετε φιλαδελφίας.

φιλόστοργοι: the proper term for strong family affection. Euthym.-Zig. τουτέστι θερμῶς καὶ διαπύρως φιλοῦντες. ἐπίτασις γὰρ φιλίας ἡ στοργή, καὶ τῆς στοργῆς πάντως αὔξησις ἡ φιλοστοργία.

τῇ τιμῇ κ.τ.λ.: cf. Phil. ii. 3 'in lowliness of mind each accounting other better than himself.' The condition and the result of true affection are that no one seeks his own honour or position, and every one is willing to give honour to others. The word προηγούμενοι is somewhat difficult; naturally it would mean 'going before,' 'preceding,' and so it has been translated, (1) 'in matters of honour preventing one another,' being the first to show honour: so Vulg. *invicem praevenientes*; or (2) 'leading the way in honourable actions': 'Love makes a man lead others by the example of showing respect to worth or saintliness,' Liddon; or (3) 'surpassing one another': 'There is nothing which makes friends so much, as the earnest endeavour to overcome one's neighbour in honouring him,' Chrys.

But all these translations are somewhat forced, and are difficult, because προηγεῖσθαι in this sense never takes the accusative. It is, in fact, as admissible to give the word a meaning which it has not elsewhere, as a construction which is unparalleled. A comparison therefore of 1 Thess. v. 13; Phil. ii. 3 suggests that St. Paul is using the word in the quite possible, although otherwise unknown, sense of ἡγούμενοι ὑπερέχοντας. So apparently RV. (=AV.) 'in honour preferring one another,' and Vaughan.

11. τῇ σπουδῇ μὴ ὀκνηροί, 'in zeal not flagging'; the words being used in a spiritual sense, as is shown by the following clauses. Zeal in all our Christian duties will be the natural result of our Christian love, and will in time foster it. On ὀκνηρός cf. Matt. xxv. 26: it is a word common in the LXX of Proverbs (vi. 6, &c.).

τῷ πνεύματι ζέοντες: cf. Acts xviii. 25, 'fervent in spirit'; that is the human spirit instinct with and inspired by the Divine Spirit. The spiritual life is the source of the Christian's love: 'And all things will be easy from the Spirit and the love, while thou art made to glow from both sides,' Chrys.

τῷ Κυρίῳ δουλεύοντες. The source of Christian zeal is spiritual life, the regulating principle our service to Christ. It is not necessary to find any very subtle connexion of thought between these clauses, they came forth eagerly and irregularly from St. Paul's mind. Κυρίῳ may have been suggested by πνεύματι, just as below διώκειν in one sense suggests the same word in another sense.

There is a very considerable balance of authority in favour of κυρίῳ (אABELP &c., Vulg. Syrr. Boh., Gr. Fathers) as against καιρῷ (D F G, Latin Fathers). Cf. Jer. *Ep.* 27 ad Marcellam : *illi legant* spe gaudentes, tempori *servientes, nos legamus* domino servientes. Orig.-lat. *ad loc. scio autem in nonnullis Latinorum exemplis haberi* tempori servientes : *quod non mihi videtur convenienter insertum.* The corruption may have arisen from κ͞ω κ͞ρ͞ω being confused together, a confusion which would be easier from reminiscences of such expressions as Eph. **v.** 16 ἐξαγοραζόμενοι τὸν καιρόν.

12. τῇ ἐλπίδι χαίροντες. See above on ver. 8. The Christian hope is the cause of that Christian joy and cheerfulness of disposition which is the grace of Christian love : cf. 1 Cor. xiii. 7 'Love . . . hopeth all things.'

τῇ θλίψει ὑπομένοντες. Endurance in persecution is naturally connected with the Christian's hope : cf. 1 Cor. xiii. 7 'Love . . . endureth all things.'

It is interesting to notice how strongly, even thus early, persecution as a characteristic of the Christian's life in the world had impressed itself on St. Paul's phraseology : see 1 Thess. i. 6 ; iii. 3, 7 ; 2 Thess. i. 4, 6 ; 2 Cor. i. 4, &c. ; Rom. v. 3 ; viii. 35.

τῇ προσευχῇ προσκαρτεροῦντες : Acts. i. 14 ; ii. 42 ; Col. iv. **2.** Persecution again naturally suggests prayer, for the strength of prayer is specially needed in times of persecution.

13. ταῖς χρείαις τῶν ἁγίων κοινωνοῦντες. This verse contains two special applications of the principle of love—sharing one's goods with fellow-Christians in need, and exercising that hospitality which was part of the bond which knit together the Christian community. With κοινωνεῖν in this sense cf. Phil. iv. **15**; Rom. xv. 26 ; 2 Cor. ix. 13 ; Heb. xiii. 16.

The variation ταῖς μνείαις (D F G, MSS. known to Theod. Mops., Vulg. *cod.* (am), Eus. *Hist. Mart. Pal.*, ed. Cureton, p. 1, Hil. Ambrstr. Aug.) is interesting. In the translation of Origen we read : Usibus sanctorum communicantes. *Memini in latinis exemplaribus magis haberi:* memoriis sanctorum communicantes: *verum nos nec consuetudinem turbamus, nec veritati praeiudicamus, maxime cum utrumque conveniat aedificationi. Nam usibus sanctorum honeste et decenter, non quasi stipem indigentibus praebere, sed censum nostrorum cum ipsis quodammodo habere communem, et meminisse sanctorum sive in collectis solemnibus, sive pro eo, ut ex recordatione eorum proficiamus, aptum et conveniens videtur.* The variation must have arisen at a time when the 'holy' were no longer the members of the community and fellow-Christians, whose bodily wants required relieving, but the 'saints' of the past, whose lives were commemorated. But this custom arose as early as the middle of the second century : cf. *Mart. Polyc.* xviii ἔνθα ὡς δυνατὸν ἡμῖν συναγομένοις ἐν ἀγαλλιάσει καὶ χαρᾷ παρέξει ὁ Κύριος ἐπιτελεῖν τὴν τοῦ μαρτυρίου αὐτοῦ ἡμέραν γενέθλιον, εἴς τε τὴν τῶν προηθληκότων μνήμην καὶ τῶν μελλόντων ἄσκησίν τε καὶ ἑτοιμασίαν : and the variations may, like other peculiarities of the western text, easily have arisen so soon. We cannot however lay any stress on the passage of Origen, as it is probably due to Rufinus. See Bingham, *Ant.* xiii. 9. 5. WH. suggest that it was a clerical error arising from the confusion of χρ and μν in a badly written papyrus MS.

φιλοξενίαν. From the very beginning hospitality was recognized as one of the most important of Christian duties (Heb. xiii. 2; 1 Tim. iii. 2; Tit. i. 8; 1 Pet. iv. 9; compare also Clem. Rom. § 1 τὸ μεγαλοπρεπὲς τῆς φιλοξενίας ὑμῖν ἦθος: § 10 of Abraham διὰ πίστιν καὶ φιλοξενίαν ἐδόθη αὐτῷ υἱὸς ἐν γήρᾳ: § 11 διὰ φιλοξενίαν καὶ εὐσέβειαν Λὼτ ἐσώθη: § 12 διὰ πίστιν καὶ φιλοξενίαν ἐσώθη ʽΡαὰβ ἡ πόρνη § 35). On its significance in the early Church see Ramsay, *The Church in the Roman Empire*, pp. 288, 368. The Christians looked upon themselves as a body of men scattered throughout the world, living as aliens amongst strange people, and therefore bound together as the members of a body, as the brethren of one family. The practical realization of this idea would demand that whenever a Christian went from one place to another he should find a home among the Christians in each town he visited. We have a picture of this intercommunion in the letters of Ignatius; we can learn it at an earlier period from the Second Epistle to the Corinthians (2 Cor. iii. 1; viii. 18, 23, 24). One necessary part of such intercommunion would be the constant carrying out of the duties of hospitality. It was the unity and strength which this intercourse gave that formed one of the great forces which supported Christianity.

14. εὐλογεῖτε τοὺς διώκοντας. The use of the word διώκειν in one sense seems to have suggested its use in another. The resemblance to Matt. v. 44 is very close: 'But I say unto you, Love your enemies, and pray for them that persecute you.' Emphasis is added by the repetition of the maxim in a negative form. Cf. James iii. 9.

15. χαίρειν μετὰ χαιρόντων κ.τ.λ. On the infinitive cf. Winer, § xliii. 5 d, p. 397, E. T. But it seems more forcible and less awkward to take it, as in Phil. iii. 16, as the infinitive used for the emphatic imperative than to suppose a change of construction. 'But that requires more of a high Christian temper, to rejoice with them that do rejoice, than to weep with them that weep. For this nature itself fulfils perfectly: and there is none so hardhearted as not to weep over him that is in calamity: but the other requires a very noble soul, so as not only to keep from envying, but even to feel pleasure with the person who is in esteem. And this is why we placed it first. For there is nothing that ties love so firmly as sharing both joy and pain one with another,' Chrys. *ad loc.* Cf. Ecclus. vii. 34.

16. τὸ αὐτὸ ... φρονοῦντες, 'being harmonious in your relations towards one another': cf. xv. 5; 2 Cor. xiii. 11; Phil. ii. 2; iv. 2. The great hindrance to this would be having too high an estimation of oneself: hence the Apostle goes on to condemn such pride.

μὴ τὰ ὑψηλὰ φρονοῦντες: cf. xi. 20; 1 Cor. xiii. 5 'Love vaunteth

not itself, is not puffed up,' shows how St. Paul is still carrying out
the leading idea of the passage.

τοῖς ταπεινοῖς: prob. neuter; 'allow yourself to be carried along
with, give yourself over to, humble tasks:' 'consentinge to meke
thingis,' Wic. The verb συναπάγειν means in the active 'to lead
along with one,' hence in the passive, 'to be carried away with,' as
by a flood which sweeps everything along with it (Lightfoot on
Gal. ii. 13; cf. 2 Pet. iii. 17), and hence 'to give oneself up to.'

The neuter seems best to suit the contrast with τὰ ὑψηλά and
the meaning of the verb; but elsewhere in the N. T. ταπεινός is
always masculine, and so many take it here: 'make yourselves
equall to them of the lower sorte,' Tyn. Cov. Genev. 'Consentinge to the humble,' Rhen. So Chrys.: 'That is, bring thyself
down to their humble condition, ride or walk with them; do not be
humbled in mind only, but help them also, and stretch forth thy
hand to them.'

μὴ γίνεσθε φρόνιμοι παρ' ἑαυτοῖς: taken apparently from Prov. iii.
7 μὴ ἴσθι φρόνιμος παρὰ σεαυτῷ. Cf. Origen *non potest veram sapientiam Dei scire, qui suam stultitiam quasi sapientiam colit.*

17. μηδενὶ κακὸν ἀντὶ κακοῦ ἀποδιδόντες. Another result of the
principle of love. Mat. v. 43, 44; 1 Thess. v. 15; 1 Pet. iii. 9;
1 Cor. xiii. 5, 6 'Love ... taketh not account of evil; rejoiceth
not in unrighteousness, but rejoiceth with the truth.'

προνοούμενοι καλὰ ἐνώπιον πάντων ἀνθρώπων: cf. Prov. iii. 4,
2 Cor. iv. 2; viii. 21. 'As nothing causes offence so much as
offending men's prejudices, see that your conduct will commend
itself as honourable to men.' Euthym.-Zig. οὐ πρὸς ἐπίδειξιν ἀλλὰ
πρὸς διδασκαλίαν, καὶ ὥστε μηδενὶ δοῦναι πρόφασιν σκανδάλου. This
seems better than to lay all the emphasis on the πάντων, as some
would do.

18. εἰ δυνατόν, 'if it be possible, live peaceably with all men, at
any rate as far as concerns your part (τὸ ἐξ ὑμῶν).' Over what others
will do you can have no control, and if they break the peace it is
not your fault. 'Love seeketh not its own' (1 Cor. xiii. 5).

19. ἀγαπητοί. Added because of the difficulty of the precept not
to avenge oneself.

δότε τόπον τῇ ὀργῇ, 'give room or place to the wrath of God.'
Let God's wrath punish. Euthym.-Zig. ἀλλὰ παραχωρεῖτε τῆς ἐκδικήσεως τῇ ὀργῇ τοῦ Θεοῦ, τῇ κρίσει τοῦ Κυρίου. The meaning of δότε
τόπον is shown by Eph. iv. 27 μηδὲ δίδοτε τόπον τῷ διαβόλῳ, do not
give scope or place to the devil; ἡ ὀργή means the wrath of God:
cf. Rom. v. 9. That this is the right interpretation of the word is
shown by the quotation which follows.

But other interpretations have been often held: δότε τόπον is
translated by some, 'allow space, interpose delay,' i.e. check and
restrain your wrath; by others, 'yield to the anger of your

opponent': neither of these interpretations suits the context or
the Greek.

γέγραπται γάρ.   The quotation which follows comes from Deut.
xxxii. 35, and resembles the Hebrew 'Vengeance is mine and
recompense,' rather than the LXX ἐν ἡμέρᾳ ἐκδικήσεως ἀνταποδώσω :
and the Targum of Onkelos more than either.   The words are
quoted in the same form in Heb. x. 30.

20. ἀλλὰ 'Εὰν πεινᾷ ὁ ἐχθρός σου κ.τ.λ.   Taken from the LXX; cf.
Prov. xxv. 21, 22, agreeing exactly with the text of B, but varying
somewhat from that of A ℵ.   The term ἄνθρακες πυρός clearly means
'terrible pangs or pains,' cf. Ps. cxxxix (cxl). 11 (LXX) ; 4 (5) Ezra
xvi. 54 *Non dicat peccator se non peccasse, quoniam carbones ignis
comburet super caput eius qui dicit : Non peccavi coram domino et
gloria ipsius.*   But with what purpose are we to 'heap coals of fire
on his head'?   Is it (1) that we may be consoled for our kind act
by knowing that he will be punished for his misdeeds?   This is
impossible, for it attributes a malicious motive, which is quite
inconsistent with the context both here and in the O. T.   In the
latter the passage proceeds, 'And the Lord shall reward thee,' implying that the deed is a good one ; here we are immediately told
that we are not to be 'overcome of evil, but overcome evil with
good,' which clearly implies that we are to do what is for our
enemies' benefit.   (2) Coals of fire must, therefore, mean, as most
commentators since Augustine have said, 'the burning pangs of
shame,' which a man will feel when good is returned for evil, and
which may produce remorse and penitence and contrition.
*Potest enim fieri ut animus ferus ac barbarus inimici, si sentiat
beneficium nostrum, si humanitatem, si affectum, si pietatem videat,
compunctionem cordis capiat, commissi poenitudinem gerat, et ex hoc
ignis in eo quidem succendatur, qui eum pro commissi conscientia
torqueat et adurat : et isti erunt carbones ignis, qui super caput eius
ex nostro misericordiae et pietatis opere congregantur,* Origen.

21. μὴ νικῶ ὑπὸ τοῦ κακοῦ κ.τ.λ., 'do not allow yourself to be
overcome by the evil done to you and be led on to revenge and
injury, but conquer your enemies' evil spirit by your own good
disposition.'   A remark which applies to the passage just concluded and shows St. Paul's object, but is also of more general
application.

ON OBEDIENCE TO RULERS.

XIII. 1-7. *The civil power has Divine sanction.   Its
functions are to promote well-being, to punish not the good
but the wicked.   Hence it must be obeyed.   Obedience to it is
a Christian duty and deprives it of all its terrors.*

So too you pay tribute because the machinery of government is God's ordinance. In this as in all things give to all their due.

XIII. The Apostle now passes from the duties of the individual Christian towards mankind in general to his duties in one definite sphere, namely towards the civil rulers. While we adhere to what has been said about the absence of a clearly-defined system or purpose in these chapters, we may notice that one main thread of thought which runs through them is the promotion of peace in all the relations of life. The idea of the civil power may have been suggested by ver. 19 of the preceding chapter, as being one of the ministers of the Divine wrath and retribution (ver. 4): at any rate the juxtaposition of the two passages would serve to remind St. Paul's readers that the condemnation of individual vengeance and retaliation does not apply to the action of the state in enforcing law; for the state is God's minister, and it is the just wrath of God which is acting through it.

We have evidence of the use of vv. 8-10 by Marcion (Tert. *adv. Marc.* **v.** 14) *Merito itaque totam creatoris disciplinam principali praecepto eius conclusit, Diliges proximum tanquam te. Hoc legis supplementum si ex ipsa lege est, quis sit deus legis iam ignoro.* On the rest of the chapter we have no information.

1. πᾶσα ψυχή: cf. ii. 9. The Hebraism suggests prominently the idea of individuality. These rules apply to all however privileged, and the question is treated from the point of view of individual duty.

ἐξουσίαις: abstract for concrete, 'those in authority'; cf. Luke xii. 11; Tit. iii. 1. ὑπερεχούσαις 'who are in an eminent position,' defining more precisely the idea of ἐξουσίαις: cf. 1 Pet. ii. 13; Wisdom vi. 5.

ὑποτασσέσθω. Notice the repetition of words of similar sound, ὑποτασσέσθω . . . τεταγμέναι . . . ἀντιτασσόμενος . . . διαταγῇ, and cf. xii. 3.

οὐ γὰρ ἔστιν ἐξουσία κ.τ.λ. The Apostle gives the reason for this obedience, stating it first generally and positively, then negatively and distributively. No human authority can exist except as the gift of God and springing from Him, and therefore all constituted powers are ordained by Him. The maxim is common in all Hebrew literature, but is almost always introduced to show how the Divine power is greater than that of all earthly sovereigns, or to declare the obligation of rulers as responsible for all they do to One above them. Wisdom vi. 1, 3 ἀκούσατε οὖν, βασιλεῖς, καὶ σύνετε, μάθετε δικασταὶ περάτων γῆς . . . ὅτι ἐδόθη παρὰ τοῦ Κυρίου ἡ κράτησις ὑμῖν καὶ ἡ δυναστεία παρὰ ὑψίστου: *Enoch* xlvi. 5 'And he will put down the kings from their thrones and kingdoms, because they do not extol and praise him, nor thankfully acknowledge whence the kingdom was bestowed upon them': Jos. *Bell. Jud.* II. viii. 7 τὸ πιστὸν παρέξειν πᾶσι, μάλιστα δὲ τοῖς κρατοῦσιν· οὐ γὰρ δίχα Θεοῦ περιγίνεσθαί τινι τὸ ἄρχειν. St. Paul adopts the maxim for a purpose similar to that in which it is used in the last instance, that it is the duty of subjects to obey their rulers, because they are appointed and ordained by God.

The preponderance of authority (א A B L P and many later MSS., Bas. Chrys.) is decisive for εἰ μὴ ὑπὸ Θεοῦ. The Western reading ἀπὸ Θεοῦ was a correction for the less usual expression (D E F G and many later MSS., Orig. Jo.-Damasc.). The reading of the end of the verse should be αἱ δὲ οὖσαι ὑπὸ Θεοῦ τεταγμέναι εἰσίν א A B D F G.

2. ὥστε ὁ ἀντιτασσόμενος κ.τ.λ. The logical result of this theory as to the origin of human power is that resistance to it is resistance to the ordering of God ; and hence those who resist will receive κρίμα—a judgement or condemnation which is human, for it comes through human instruments, but Divine as having its origin and source in God. There is no reference here to eternal punishment.

3. οἱ γὰρ ἄρχοντες. The plural shows that the Apostle is speaking quite generally. He is arguing out the duty of obeying rulers on general principles, deduced from the fact that ' the state ' exists for a beneficent end ; he is not arguing from the special condition or circumstances of any one state. The social organism, as a modern writer might say, is a power on the side of good.

τῷ ἀγαθῷ ἔργῳ: cf. ii. 7 τοῖς μὲν καθ' ὑπομονὴν ἔργου ἀγαθοῦ. In both passages ἔργον is used collectively ; there it means the sum of a man's actions, here the collective work of the state. For the subject cf. 1 Tim. ii. 1, 2 : we are to pray 'for kings and all in authority that we may lead a quiet and peaceable life in all godliness and honesty.'

The singular τῷ ἀγαθῷ ἔργῳ ἀλλὰ τῷ κακῷ is read by א A B D F G P, Boh. Vulg. (*boni operis sed mali*), Clem.-Alex. Iren.-lat. Tert. Orig.-lat. Jo.-Damasc. Later MSS. with E L, Syrr. Arm., Chrys. Thdrt. read τῶν ἀγαθῶν ἔργων . . . κακῶν. Hort suggests an emendation of Patrick Young, τῷ ἀγαθοεργῷ, which has some support apparently from the Aeth. *ei qui facit bonum*: but the antithesis with κακῷ makes this correction improbable.

θέλεις δὲ . . . ἐξουσίαν; The construction is more pointed if these words are made a question.

As the state exists for a good end, if you lead a peaceable life you will have nothing to fear from the civil power.

4. Θεοῦ γὰρ διάκονός ἐστι. Fem. to agree with ἐξουσία, which throughout is almost personified. σοι, 'for thee,' ethical, for thy advantage. εἰς τὸ ἀγαθόν, ' for the good,' to promote good, existing for a good end.

τὴν μάχαιραν. The sword is the symbol of the executive and criminal jurisdiction of a magistrate, and is therefore used of the power of punishing inherent in the government. So Ulpian, *Digest*, i. 18. 6. § 8; Tac. *Hist.* iii. 68; Dio Cassius, xlii. 27.

ἔκδικος εἰς ὀργήν, 'inflicting punishment or vengeance so as to exhibit wrath,' namely the Divine wrath as administered by the ruler who is God's agent (cf. ver. 2 and xii. 19). The repetition of the phrase Θεοῦ διάκονος with both sides of the sentence emphasizes the double purpose of the state. It exists positively for the well-being of the community, negatively to check evil by the infliction of punishment, and both these functions are derived from God.

5. διό: rulers, because as God's ministers they have a Divine order and purpose, are to be obeyed, not only because they have power over men, but also because it is right, διὰ τὴν συνείδησιν (cf. ii. 15, ix. 1).

6. διὰ τοῦτο γὰρ καί, sc. διὰ τὴν συνείδησιν: 'and it is for this reason also.' St. Paul is appealing to a principle which his readers will recognize. It is apparently an admitted rule of the Christian communities that taxes are to be paid, and he points out that the principle is thus recognized of the moral duty of obeying rulers. That he could thus appeal to a recognized practice seems to imply that the words of our Lord (Luke xx. 20–25) had moulded the habits of the early Church, and this suggestion is corroborated by ver. 7 (see the longer note below).

λειτουργοί, 'God's ministers.' Although the word is used in a purely secular sense of a servant, whether of an individual or of a community (1 Kings x. 5; Ecclus. x. 2), yet the very definite meaning which λειτουργὸς Θεοῦ had acquired (Ecclus vii. 30; Heb. viii. 2; see especially the note on Rom. xv. 16) adds emphasis to St. Paul's expression.

προσκαρτεροῦντες must apparently be taken absolutely (as in Xen. *Hell.* VII. v. 14), 'persevering faithfully in their office,' and εἰς αὐτὸ τοῦτο gives the purpose of the office, the same as that ascribed above to the state. These words cannot be taken immediately with προσκαρτεροῦντες, for that verb, as in xii. 13, seems always to govern the dative.

7. St. Paul concludes this subject and leads on to the next by a general maxim which covers all the different points touched upon : 'Pay each one his due.'

τῷ τὸν φόρον, sc. ἀπαιτοῦντι. φόρος is the tribute paid by a subject nation (Luke xx. 22; 1 Macc. x. 33), while τέλος represents the customs and dues which would in any case be paid for the support of the civil government (Matt. xvii. 25; 1 Macc. x. 31).

φόβος is the respectful awe which is felt for one who has power in his hands; τιμήν honour and reverence paid to a ruler : cf. 1 Pet. ii. 17 τὸν Θεὸν φοβεῖσθε· τὸν βασιλέα τιμᾶτε.

A strange interpretation of this verse may be seen in the Gnostic book entitled Πίστις Σοφία, p. 294, ed. Schwartze.

The Church and the Civil Power.

The motive which impelled St. Paul to write this section of the Epistle has (like so many other questions) been discussed at great length with the object of throwing light on the composition of the Roman Church. If the opinion which has been propounded already in reference to these chapters be correct, it will be obvious that here as elsewhere St. Paul is writing, primarily at any rate, with a view to the state of the Church as a whole, not to the particular circumstances of the Roman community: it being recognized at the same time that questions which agitated the whole Christian world would be likely to be reflected in what was already an important centre of Christianity. Whether this opinion be correct or not must depend partly, of course, on our estimate of the Epistle as a whole; but if it be assumed to be so, the character of this passage will amply support it. There is a complete absence of any reference to particular circumstances: the language is throughout general: there is a studied avoidance of any special terms; direct commands such as might arise from particular circumstances are not given: but general principles applicable to any period or place are laid down. As elsewhere in this Epistle, St. Paul, influenced by his past experiences, or by the questions which were being agitated around him, or by the fear of difficulties which he foresaw as likely to arise, lays down broad general principles, applying to the affairs of life the spirit of Christianity as he has elucidated it.

But what were the questions that were in the air when he wrote? There can be no doubt that primarily they would be those current in the Jewish nation concerning the lawfulness of paying taxes and otherwise recognizing the authority of a foreign ruler. When our Lord was asked, 'Is it lawful to give tribute to Caesar or no?' (Matt. xxii. 18 f.; Luke xx. 22 f.), a burning question was at once raised. Starting from the express command ' thou mayest not put a foreigner over thee, which is not thy brother' (Deut. xvii. 15), and from the idea of a Divine theocracy, a large section of the Jews had refused to recognize or pay taxes to the Roman government. Judas the Gaulonite, who said that 'the census was nothing else but downright slavery' (Jos. *Ant.* XVIII. i. 1), or Theudas (ibid. XX. v. 1), or Eleazar, who is represented as saying that 'we have long since made up our minds not to serve the Romans or any other man, but God alone' (*Bell. Jud.* VII. viii. 6), may all serve as instances of a tendency which was very wide spread. Nor was this spirit confined to the Jews of Palestine; elsewhere, both in Rome and in Alexandria, riots had occurred. Nor again was it unlikely that Christianity would be affected by it. A good deal of the phraseology of the early Christians was derived from the Messianic prophecies of the O. T., and these were always liable to be taken in that purely material sense which our Lord had condemned. The fact that St. Luke records the question of the disciples, 'Lord, dost thou at this time restore the kingdom to Israel?' (Acts i. 6) seems to imply that such ideas were current, and the incident at Thessalonica, where St. Paul himself, because he preached the 'kingdom,' was accused of preaching 'another king, one Jesus,' shows how liable even he was to misinterpretation. These instances are quite sufficient to explain how the question was a real one when St. Paul wrote, and why it had occupied his thoughts. It is not necessary to refer it either to Ebionite dualistic views (so Baur), which would involve an anachronism, or to exaggerated Gentile ideas of Christian liberty; we have no record that these were ever perverted in this direction.

Two considerations may have specially influenced St. Paul to discuss the subject in his Epistle to the Romans. The first was the known fact of the turbulence of the Roman Jews; a fact which would be brought before him by his intercourse with Priscilla and Aquila. This may illustrate just the degree of local reference in the Epistle to the Romans. We have emphasized more than once the fact that we cannot argue anything from such passages as this as to the state of the Roman community; but St. Paul would not write in the air, and the knowledge of the character of the Jewish population in Rome gained from political refugees would be just sufficient to suggest this topic. A second cause which would lead him to introduce it would be the fascination which he felt for the power and position of Rome, a fascination which has been already illustrated (Introduction, § 1).

It must be remembered that when this Epistle was written the Roman Empire had never appeared in the character of a persecutor. Persecution had up to this time always come from the Jews or from popular riots. To St. Paul the magistrates who represented the Roman power had always been associated with order and restraint. The persecution of Stephen had probably taken place in the absence of the Roman governor: it was at the hands of the Jewish king Herod that James the brother of John had perished: at Paphos, at Thessalonica, at Corinth, at Ephesus, St. Paul had found the Roman officials a restraining power and all his experience would support the statements that he makes: 'The rulers are not a terror to the good work, but to the evil:' 'He is a minister of God to thee for good:' 'He is a minister of God, an avenger for wrath to him that doeth evil.' Nor can any rhetorical point be made as has been attempted from the fact that Nero was at this time the ruler of the Empire. It may be doubted how far the vices of a ruler like Nero seriously affected the well-being of the provincials, but at any rate when these words were written the world was enjoying the good government and bright hopes of Nero's *Quinquennium*.

The true relations of Christianity to the civil power had been laid down by our Lord when He had said : ' My kingdom is not of this world,' and again : ' Render unto Caesar the things that be Caesar's and to God the things that be God's.' It is difficult to believe that St. Paul had not these words in his mind when he wrote ver. 7, especially as the coincidences with the moral teaching of our Lord are numerous in these chapters. At any rate, starting from this idea he works out the principles which must lie at the basis of Christian politics, that the State is divinely appointed, or permitted by God ; that its end is beneficent ; and that the spheres of Church and State are not identical.

It has been remarked that, when St. Paul wrote, his experience might have induced him to estimate too highly the merits of the Roman government. But although later the relation of the Church to the State changed, the principles of the Church did not. In 1 Tim. ii. 1, 2 the Apostle gives a very clear command to pray for those in authority : ' I exhort therefore, first of all, that supplications, prayers, intercessions, thanksgivings, be made for all men : for kings and all that are in high place ; that we may lead a tranquil and quiet life in all godliness and gravity ' ; so also in Titus iii. 1 ' Put them in mind to be in subjection to rulers, to authorities.' When these words were written, the writer had to some extent at any rate experienced the Roman power in a very different aspect. Still more important is the evidence of 1 Peter. It was certainly written at a time when persecution, and that of an official character, had begun, yet the commands of St. Paul are repeated and with even greater emphasis (1 Pet. ii. 13–17).

The sub-Apostolic literature will illustrate this. Clement is writing to the Corinthians just after successive periods of persecution, yet he includes a prayer of the character which he would himself deliver, in the as yet unsystematized services of the day, on behalf of secular rulers. ' Give concord and peace to us and to all that dwell on the earth . . . while we render obedience to Thine Almighty and most excellent Name, and to our rulers and governors upon the earth. Thou, Lord and Master, hast given them the power of sovereignty through Thine excellent and unspeakable might, that we, knowing the glory and honour which Thou hast given them, may submit ourselves unto them, in nothing resisting Thy will. Grant unto them therefore, O Lord, health, peace, concord, stability, that they may administer the government which Thou hast given them without failure. For Thou, O heavenly Master, King of the ages, givest to the sons of men glory and honour and power over all things that are upon the earth. Do Thou, Lord, direct their counsel according to that which is good and well-pleasing in Thy sight.' Still more significant is the letter of Polycarp, which was written very shortly after he had met Ignatius on his road to martyrdom ; in it he emphasizes the Christian custom by combining the command to pray for rulers with that to love our enemies. 'Pray also for kings and powers and princes and for them that persecute and hate you and for the enemies of the cross, that your fruit may be manifest among all men that ye may be perfect in Him.' (Clem. Rom. lx, lxi; Polyc. *ad Phil.* xii.)

It is not necessary to give further instances of a custom which prevailed extensively or universally in the early Church. It became a commonplace of apologists (Just. Mart. *Apol.* i. 17; Athenagoras, *Leg.* xxxvii; Theophilus, i. 11; Tertullian, *Apol.* 30, 39, *ad Scap.* 2; Dion. Alex. *ap* Eus. *H. E.* VII. xi; Arnob. iv. 36) and is found in all liturgies (cf. *Const. Ap.* viii. 12).

One particular phase in the interpretation of this chapter demands a passing notice. In the hands of the Jacobean and Caroline divines it was held to support the doctrine of Passive Obedience. This doctrine has taken a variety of forms. Some held that a Monarchy as opposed to a Republic is the only scriptural form of government, others that a legitimate line alone has this divine right. A more modified type of this teaching may be represented by a sermon of Bishop Berkeley (*Passive Obedience or the Christian Doctrine of not resisting the supreme power, proved and vindicated upon the principles of the law of nature in a discourse delivered at the College Chapel,* 1712. *Works,* iii. p. 101). He takes as his text Rom. xiii. 2 'Whosoever resisteth the Power, resisteth the ordinance of God.' He begins 'It is not my design to inquire into the particular nature of the government and constitution of these kingdoms.' He then proceeds by assuming that 'there is in every civil community, somewhere or other, placed a supreme power of making laws, and enforcing the observation of them.' His main purpose is to prove that 'Loyalty is a moral virtue, and thou shalt not resist the supreme power, a rule or law of nature, the least breach whereof hath the inherent stain of moral turpitude.' And he places it on the same level as the commandments which St. Paul quotes in this same chapter.

Bishop Berkeley represents the doctrine of Passive Obedience as expounded in its most philosophical form. But he does not notice the main difficulty. St. Paul gives no directions as to what ought to be done when there is a conflict of authority. In his day there could be no doubt that the rule of Caesar was supreme and had become legitimate: all that he had to condemn was an incorrect view of the 'kingdom of heaven' as a theocracy established on earth, whether it were held by Jewish zealots or by Christians. He does not discuss the question, 'if there were two claimants for the Empire which should be supported?' for it was not a practical difficulty when he wrote. So Bishop Berkeley, by his use of the expression 'somewhere or other,' equally evades the difficulty. Almost always when there is a rebellion or a civil war the question at issue is, Who is the rightful governor? which is the power ordained by God?

But there is a side of the doctrine of Passive Obedience which requires emphasis, and which was illustrated by the Christianity of the first three centuries. The early Christians were subject to a power which required them to do that which was forbidden by their religion. To that extent and within those limits they could not and did not obey it; but they never encouraged in any way resistance or rebellion. In all things indifferent the Christian conformed to existing law; he obeyed the law 'not only because of the wrath, but also for conscience sake.' He only disobeyed when it was necessary to do so for conscience sake. The point of importance is the detachment of the two spheres of activity. The Church and the State are looked upon as different bodies, each with a different work to perform. To designate this or that form of government as 'Christian,' and support it on these grounds, would have been quite alien to the whole spirit of those days. The Church must influence the world by its hold on the hearts and consciences of individuals, and in that way, and not by political power, will the Kingdom of God come.

LOVE THE FULFILMENT OF ALL LAW.

XIII. 8–10. *There is one debt which the Christian must always be paying but never can discharge, that of love. All particular precepts are summed up in that of love, which makes injury to any man impossible.*

8. St. Paul passes from our duties towards superiors to that one principle which must control our relations towards all men, love. In xii. 9 the principle of love is introduced as the true solution of all difficulties which may arise from rivalry in the community; here it is represented as at the root of all regulations as to our relations to others in any of the affairs of life.

μηδενὶ μηδὲν ὀφείλετε must be imperative as the negatives show. It sums up negatively the results of the previous verse and suggests the transition, ' Pay every one their due and owe no man anything.'

εἰ μὴ τὸ ἀγαπᾷν ἀλλήλους : ' Let your only debt that is unpaid be that of love—a debt which you should always be attempting to discharge in full, but will never succeed in discharging.' *Permanere tamen et nunquam cessare a nobis debitum caritatis : hoc enim et quotidie solvere et semper debere expedit nobis.* Orig. By this pregnant expression St. Paul suggests both the obligation of love and the impossibility of fulfilling it. This is more forcible than to suppose a change in the meaning of ὀφείλετε : ' Owe no man anything, only ye ought to love one another.'

ὁ γὰρ ἀγαπῶν κ.τ.λ. gives the reason why ' love ' is so important : if a man truly loves another he has fulfilled towards him the whole law. νόμον is not merely the Jewish law, although it is from it that the illustrations that follow are taken, but law as a principle. Just as in the relations of man and God πίστις has been substituted for νόμος, so between man and man ἀγάπη takes the place of definite legal relations. The perfect πεπλήρωκεν implies that the fulfilment is already accomplished simply in the act of love.

9. St. Paul gives instances of the manner in which ' love ' fulfils law. No man who loves another will injure him by adultery, by murder, by theft, &c. They are all therefore summed up in the one maxim ' thou shalt love thy neighbour as thyself,' as indeed they were also in the Old Covenant.

The AV. adds after οὐ κλέψεις in this verse οὐ ψευδομαρτυρήσεις from the O. T. with א P &c., Boh. &c., as against A B D E F G L &c., Vulg. *codd.* and most Fathers. ἐν τῷ before ἀγαπήσεις is omitted by B F G. For σεαυτόν of the older MSS. (א A B D E), later MSS. read ἑαυτόν, both here and elsewhere. In late Greek ἑαυτόν became habitually used for all persons in the reflexive, and scribes substituted the form most usual to them.

The order of the commandments is different from that in the Hebrew text, both in Exodus xx. 13 and Deut. v. 17, namely, (6) Thou shalt do no murder, (7) Thou shalt not commit adultery, (8) Thou shalt not steal. The MSS. of the LXX vary; in Exodus B reads 7, 8, 6, A F 6, 7, 8; in Deut. B reads 7, 6, 8 (the order here), A F 6, 7, 8. The order of Romans is that also of Luke xviii. 20; James ii. 11; Philo *De Decalogo*; Clem.-Alex. *Strom*. vi. 16.

καὶ εἴ τις ἑτέρα shows that St. Paul in this selection has only taken instances and that he does not mean merely to give a summing up of the Jewish law.

ἀνακεφαλαιοῦται: a rhetorical term used of the summing up of a speech or argument, and hence of including a large number of separate details under one head. As used in Eph. i. 10 of God summing up all things in Christ it became a definite theological term, represented in Latin by *recapitulatio* (Iren. III. xxii. 2).

Ἀγαπήσεις τὸν πλησίον σου ὡς ἑαυτόν. Taken from Leviticus xix. 18 where it sums up a far longer list of commandments. It is quoted Matt. xxii. 39; Mark xii. 31; Luke x. 27; Gal. v. 14; James ii. 8 where it is called βασιλικὸς νόμος.

10. ἡ ἀγάπη ... οὐκ ἐργάζεται. Love fulfils all law, because no one who loves another will do him any ill by word or deed. These words sum up what has been said at greater length in 1 Cor. xiii. 4-6.

πλήρωμα, 'complete fulfilment.' The meaning of πλ. here is given by ver. 9 ' He that loveth his neighbour has fulfilled (πεπλή-ρωκεν) law, therefore love is the fulfilment (πλήρωμα) of law.

The History of the word ἀγάπη.

There are three words in Greek all of which may be translated by the English 'love,' ἐράω, φιλέω, ἀγαπάω. Of these ἐράω with its cognate form ἔραμαι was originally associated with the sexual passion and was thence transferred to any strong passionate affection; φιλέω was used rather of warm domestic affection, and so of the love of master and servant, of parents and children, of husband and wife; in Homer, of the love of the gods for men. ἐρᾶν is combined with ἐπιθυμεῖν and contrasted with φιλεῖν as in Xen. *Hier.* xi. 11 ὥστε οὐ μόνον φιλοῖο ἂν ἀλλὰ καὶ ἐρῷο. One special use of ἔρως and ἐράω must be referred to, namely, the Platonic. The intensity and strength of human passion seemed to Plato to represent most adequately the love of the soul for higher things, and so the philosophic ἔρως was used for the highest human desire, that for true knowledge, true virtue, true immortality.

The distinction of φιλέω and ἀγαπάω much resembled that between *amo* and *diligo*. The one expressed greater affection, the other greater esteem. So Dio Cassius xliv. 48 ἐφιλήσατε αὐτὸν ὡς πατέρα καὶ ἠγαπήσατε ὡς εὐερ-γέτην; and John xxi. 15-17 λέγει αὐτῷ πάλιν δεύτερον, Σίμων Ἰωάνου, ἀγαπᾷς με; λέγει αὐτῷ, Ναί, Κύριε· σὺ οἶδας ὅτι φιλῶ σε κ.τ.λ. (see Trench, *Syn.* § xii). It is significant that no distinction is absolute; but φιλέω occasionally, still more rarely ἀγαπάω, are both used incorrectly of the sexual passion. There is too close a connexion between the different forms of human affection to allow any rigid distinction to be made in the use of words.

When these words were adopted into Hellenistic Greek, a gradual change was made in their use. ἐράω and its cognates are very rarely used, and almost invariably in a bad sense. In the N. T. they do not occur at all, the word ἐπιθυμέω being employed instead. Yet occasionally, even in biblical and ecclesiastical Greek, the higher sense of the Platonic ἔρως finds a place (Prov. iv. 6; Wisdom viii. 2; Justin, *Dial.* 8, p. 225 B; Clem.-Alex. *Coh.* 11, p. 90; see Lightfoot, *Ignatius ad Rom.* vii. 2). Between ἀγαπάω and φιλέω a decided preference was shown for the former. It occurs about 268 times (Hatch and Redpath) in a very large proportion of cases as a translation of the Hebrew אָהֵב; φιλέω about twelve times (Trommius), excluding its use as equivalent to *osculor.* This choice was largely due to the use of the Hebrew word to express the love of God to man, and of man to God (Deut. xxiii. 5; xxx. 6; Hosea iii. 1); it was felt that the greater amount of intellectual desire and the greater severity implied in ἀγαπάω fitted it better than φιλέω for this purpose. But while it was elevated in meaning it was also broadened; it is used not only of the love of father and son, of husband and wife, but also of the love of Samson for Delilah (Jud. xvi. 4) and of Hosea's love for his adulterous wife (Hos. iii. 1). Nor can there be any doubt that to Hebrew writers there was in a pure love of God or of righteousness something of the intensity which is the highest characteristic of human passion (Is. lxii. 5). ἀγαπάω in the LXX corresponds in all its characteristics to the English 'love.'

But not only did the LXX use modify the meaning of ἀγαπάω, it created a new word ἀγάπη. Some method was required of expressing the conception which was gradually growing up. Ἔρως had too sordid associations. Φιλία was tried (Wisdom vii. 14; viii. 18), but was felt to be inadequate. The language of the Song of Solomon created the demand for ἀγάπη. (2 Kings 1 or 2 times; Ecclesiastes 2; Canticles 11; Wisdom 2; Ecclus. 1; Jeremiah 1; Ps. Sol. 1.)

The N.T. reproduces the usage of the LXX, but somewhat modified. While ἀγαπάω is used 138 times, φιλέω is used in this sense 22 times (13 in St. John's Gospel); generally when special emphasis has to be laid on the relations of father and son. But the most marked change is in the use of ἀγάπη. It is never used in the Classical writers, only occasionally in the LXX; in early Christian writers its use becomes habitual and general. Nothing could show more clearly that a new principle has been created than this creation of a new word.

In the Vulgate ἀγάπη is sometimes rendered by *dilectio*, sometimes by *caritas*; to this inconsistency are due the variations in the English Authorized Version. The word *caritas* passed into English in the Middle Ages (for details see Eng. Dict. *sub voc.*) in the form 'charity,' and was for some time used to correspond to most of the meanings of ἀγάπη; but as the English Version was inconsistent and no corresponding verb existed the usage did not remain wide. In spite of its retention in 1 Cor. xiii. 'charity' became confined in all ordinary phraseology to 'benevolence,' and the Revised Version was compelled to make the usage of the New Testament consistent.

Whatever loss there may have been in association and in the rhythm of well-known passages, there is an undoubted gain. The history of the word ἀγαπάω is that of the collection under one head of various conceptions which were at any rate partially separated, and the usage of the N. T. shows that the distinction which has to be made is not between φιλέω, ἀγαπάω and ἐράω, but between ἀγάπη and ἐπιθυμία. The English language makes this distinction between the affection or passion in any form, and a purely animal desire, quite plain; although it may be obliterated at times by a natural euphemism. But setting aside this distinction which must be occasionally present to the mind, but which need not be often spoken of, Christianity does not shrink from declaring that in all forms of human passion and affection which are not purely animal there is present that same love which in its highest and most pure development forms the essence and sum of the Christian religion. This affection, however perverted it may be, Christianity does not condemn, but so far as may be elevates and purifies.

The Christian Teaching on Love.

The somewhat lengthy history just given of the word ἀγάπη is a suitable introduction to the history of an idea which forms a fundamental principle of all Christian thought.

The duty of love in some form or other had been a commonplace of moral teaching in times long before Christianity and in many different places. Isolated maxims have been collected in its favour from very varied authors, and the highest pagan teaching approaches the highest Christian doctrine. But in all previous philosophy such teaching was partial or isolated, it was never elevated to a great principle. Maxims almost or quite on a level with those of Christianity we find both in the O. T. and in Jewish writers. The command 'Thou shalt love thy neighbour as thyself' is of course taken directly from the O. T., and is there used to sum up in one general principle a long series of rules. Sayings of great beauty are quoted from the Jewish fathers. ' Hillel said, Be of the disciples of Aaron, loving peace and pursuing peace, loving mankind and bringing them nigh to the Torah' (*Pirqe Aboth* i. 13); or again, 'What is hateful to thyself do not to thy fellow; this is the whole Torah, and the rest is commentary; go study,' also ascribed to Hillel. It is however true in all cases that these maxims, and all such as these, are only isolated instances, that they do not represent the spirit of earlier institutions, and that they form a very insignificant proportion compared with much of a different character.

In Christianity this principle, which had been only partially understood and imperfectly taught, which was known only in isolated examples, yet testified to a universal instinct, was finally put forward as the paramount principle of moral conduct, uniting our moral instincts with our highest religious principles. A new virtue, or rather one hitherto imperfectly understood, had become recognized as the root of all virtues, and a new name was demanded for what was practically a new idea.

In the first place, the new Christian doctrine of love is universal. 'Ye have heard that it was said, Thou shalt love thy neighbour and hate thine enemy : but I say unto you, Love your enemies, and pray for them that persecute you;' and a very definite reason is given, the universal Fatherhood of God. This universalism which underlies all the teaching of Jesus is put in a definite practical form by St. Paul, 'In Christ Jesus there is neither Jew nor Gentile, bond nor free, male nor female.' As it is summed up in a well-known work : 'The first law, then, of the kingdom of God is that all men, however divided from each other by blood or language, have certain mutual duties arising out of their common relation to God' (*Ecce Homo*, chap. xii).

But secondly, the Christian doctrine of love was the substitution of a universal principle for law. All moral precepts are summed up in the one command of love. What is my duty towards others ? Just that feeling which you have towards the persons to whom you are most attached in the world, just that you must feel for every one. If you have that feeling there will be no need for any further command. Love is a principle and a passion, and as such is the fulfilment of the Law. Christ 'declared an ardent, passionate, or devoted state of mind to be the root of virtue'; and this purifying passion, capable of existing in all men alike, will be able to redeem our nature and make laws superfluous.

And thirdly, how is this new Christian spirit possible? It is possible because it is intimately bound up with that love which is a characteristic of the Godhead. 'God is love.' 'A new commandment I give to you, that ye should love one another as I have loved you.' It is possible also because men have learnt to love mankind in Christ. 'Where the precept of love has been given, an image must be set before the eyes of those who are called on to obey it, an ideal or type of man which may be noble and amiable enough to raise the whole race, and make the meanest member of it sacred with reflected glory.' This is what Christ did for us.

These three points will help to elucidate what St. Paul means by ἀγάπη. It is in fact the correlative in the moral world to what faith is in the religious life. Like faith it is universal; like faith it is a principle not a code; like faith it is centred in the Godhead. Hence St. Paul, as St. John (1 John iii. 23), sums up Christianity in Faith and Love, which are finally, united in that Love of God, which is the end and root of both.

THE DAY IS AT HAND.

XIII. 11–14. *The night of this corrupt age is flying. The Parousia is nearing. Cast off your evil ways. Gird yourselves with the armour of light. Take Christ into your hearts. Shun sin and self-indulgence.*

11. The Apostle adds a motive for the Christian standard of life, the nearness of our final salvation.

καὶ τοῦτο, 'and that too': cp. 1 Cor. vi. 6, 8; Eph. ii. 8, &c.: it resumes the series of exhortations implied in the previous sections; there is no need to supply any special words with it.

τὸν καιρόν: used of a definite, measured, or determined time, and so almost technically of the period before the second coming of Christ: cf. 1 Cor. vii. 29 ὁ καιρὸς συνεσταλμένος; Mark i. 15; and so ὁ καιρὸς ὁ ἐνεστώς (Heb. ix. 9).

ὅτι ὥρα ἤδη κ.τ.λ. ἤδη with ἐγερθῆναι. The time of trial on earth is looked upon as a night of gloom, to be followed by a bright morning. We must arouse ourselves from slumber and prepare ourselves for the light.

νῦν γὰρ ἐγγύτερον κ.τ.λ. 'For our completed salvation, no longer that hope of salvation which sustains us here, is appreciably nearer for us than when we first accepted in faith the Messianic message.' ὅτε ἐπιστεύσαμεν refers to the actual moment of the acceptance of Christianity. The language is that befitting those who expect the actual coming of Christ almost immediately, but it will fit the circumstances of any Christian for whom death brings the day.

In ver. 11 the original ὑμᾶς (א A B C P, Clem.-Alex.) has been corrected for the sake of uniformity into ἡμᾶς (אᶜ D E F G L, &c., Boh. Sah.). In ver. 13 ἐν ἔρισι καὶ ζήλοις is a variant of B, Sah., Clem.-Alex. Amb. In ver. 14 B, and Clem.-Alex. read τὸν Χριστὸν Ἰησοῦν, which may very likely be the correct reading.

12. προέκοψεν, 'has advanced towards dawn.' Cf. Luke ii. 52; Gal. i. 14; Jos. Bell. Jud. IV. iv. 6; Just. Dial. p. 277 d.

The contrast of ὕπνος, νύξ, and σκότος with ἡμέρα and φῶς finds many illustrations in Christian and in all religious literature.

ἀποθώμεθα. The works of darkness, i.e. works such as befit the kingdom of darkness, are represented as being cast off like the uncomely garments of the night, for the bright armour which befits the Christian soldier as a member of the kingdom of light. This metaphor of the Christian armour is a favourite one with St. Paul (1 Thess. v. 8; 2 Cor. vi. 7; Rom. vi. 13; and especially Eph. vi. 13 f.); it may have been originally suggested by the Jewish conception of the last great fight against the armies of Antichrist (Dan. xi; Orac. Sib. iii. 663 f.; 4 Ezra xiii. 33; Enoch xc. 16), but in St. Paul the conception has become completely spiritualized.

13. εὐσχημόνως περιπατήσωμεν. The metaphor περιπατεῖν of conduct is very common in St. Paul's Epistles, where it occurs thirty-three times (never in the Past. Epp.); elsewhere in the N. T. sixteen times.

κώμοις, 'rioting,' 'revelry' (Gal. v. 21; 1 Pet. iv. 3). μέθη the drunkenness which would be the natural result and accompaniment of such revelry.

κοίταις καὶ ἀσελγείαις, 'unlawful intercourse and wanton acts.' Ὅρα δὲ τὴν τάξιν· κωμάζων μὲν γάρ τις μεθύει, μεθύων δὲ κοιτάζεται, κοιταζόμενος δὲ ἀσελγαίνει, τοῦ οἴνου τοῦτον τῇ πλησμονῇ πυρπολοῦντος καὶ διερεθίζοντος. Euthym.-Zig.

14. ἐνδύσασθε τὸν Κύριον Ἰησοῦν Χριστόν. Christ is put on first in baptism (vi. 3; Gal. iii. 27), but we must continually renew that life with which we have been clothed (Eph. iv. 24; Col. iii. 12).

τῆς σαρκός with πρόνοιαν: the word is thrown forward in order to emphasize the contrast between the old nature, the flesh of sin, and the new, the life in Christ.

On this passage most commentators compare St. Aug. *Confess.* viii. 12, 23 *Arripui, aperui et legi in silentio capitulum, quo primum coniecti sunt oculi mei*: Non in conversationibus et ebrietatibus, non in cubilibus et impudicitiis, non in contentione et aemulatione: sed induite Dominum Iesum Christum, et carnis providentiam ne feceritis in concupiscentiis. *Nec ultra volui legere, nec opus erat. Statim quippe cum fine huiusce sententiae quasi luce securitatis infusa cordi meo, omnes dubitationis tenebrae diffugerunt.*

The early Christian belief in the nearness of the παρουσία.

There can hardly be any doubt that in the Apostolic age the prevailing belief was that the Second Coming of the Lord was an event to be expected in any case shortly and probably in the lifetime of many of those then living; it is also probable that this belief was shared by the Apostles themselves. For example, so strongly did such views prevail among the Thessalonian converts that the death of some members of the community had filled them with perplexity, and even when correcting these opinions St. Paul speaks of ' we that are alive, that are left unto the coming of our Lord'; and in the second Epistle, although he corrects the erroneous impression which still prevailed that the coming was immediate and shows that other events must precede it, he still contemplates it as at hand. Similar passages may be quoted from all or most of the Epistles, although there are others that suggest that it is by his own death, not by the coming of Christ, that St. Paul expects to attain the full life in Christ to which he looked forward (1 Cor. vii. 29-31; Rom. xiii. 11, 12; Phil. iv. 5; and on the other side 2 Cor. v. 1-10; Phil. i. 23; iii. 11, 20, 21; see Jowett, *Thessalonians*, &c., i. p. 105, who quotes both classes of passages without distinguishing them).

How far was this derived from our Lord's own teaching? There is, it is true, very clear teaching on the reality and the suddenness of the coming of Christ, and very definite exhortation to all Christians to live as expecting that coming. This teaching is couched largely in the current language of Apocalyptic literature

which was often hardly intended to be taken literally even by
Jewish writers; moreover it is certainly mingled with teaching
which was intended to refer to what was a real manifestation of the
Divine power, and very definitely a 'coming of the Lord' in the
O. T. sense of the term, the destruction of Jerusalem. All this
language again is reported to us by those who took it in a literal
sense. The expressions of our Lord quoted as prophetic of His
speedy return are all to a certain extent ambiguous; for example,
'This generation shall not pass away until all these things be fulfilled,' or again 'There be some of them here who shall not taste of
death until they see the Son of man coming with power.' On the
other side there is a very distinct tradition preserved in documents
of different classes recording that when our Lord was asked definitely on such matters His answers were ambiguous. Acts i. 7
'It is not for you to know times and seasons, which the Father
hath set within His own authority.' John xxi. 23 'This saying
therefore went forth among the brethren, that that disciple should
not die: yet Jesus said not unto him, that he should not die; but,
If I will that he tarry till I come, what is that to thee?' Moreover
he affirmed that He Himself was ignorant of the date Mark xiii. 32;
Matt. xxiv. 36 'But of that day and hour knoweth no one, not
even the angels of heaven, neither the Son, but the Father only.'

In the face of these passages it is reasonable to believe that
this ignorance of the Early Church was permitted and that with
a purpose. If so, we may be allowed to speculate as to the service
it was intended to fulfil.

In the first place, this belief in the nearness of the second coming
quickened the religious and moral earnestness of the early Christian.
Believing as intently as he did 'that the fashion of this world passeth
away,' he 'set his affection on things above'; he lived in the world
and yet not of the world. The constant looking forward to the
coming of the Lord produced a state of intense spiritual zeal which
braced the Church for its earliest and hardest task.

And secondly, it has been pointed out very ably how much the
elasticity and mobility of Christianity were preserved by the fact that
the Apostles never realized that they were building up a Church
which was to last through the ages. It became the fashion of
a later age to ascribe to the Apostles a series of ordinances and
constitutions. Any such theory is quite inconsistent with the real
spirit of their time. They never wrote or legislated except so far
as existing needs demanded. They founded such institutions as
were clearly required by some immediate want, or were part of our
Lord's teaching. But they never administered or planned with
a view to the remote future. Their writings were occasional,
suggested by some pressing difficulty; but they thus incidentally
laid down great broad principles which became the guiding principles

of the Church. The Church therefore is governed by case law, not by code law: by broad principles, not by minute regulations. It may seem a paradox, but yet it is profoundly true, that the Church is adapted to the needs of every age, just because the original preachers of Christianity never attempted to adapt it to the needs of any period but their own.

The relation of Chaps. XII–XIV to the Gospels.

There is a very marked resemblance between the moral teaching of St. Paul contained in the concluding section of the Epistle to the Romans, and our Lord's own words; a resemblance which, in some cases, extends even to language.

Rom. xii. 14.	Matt v. 44.
εὐλογεῖτε τοὺς διώκοντας ὑμᾶς· εὐλογεῖτε, καὶ μὴ καταρᾶσθε.	ἀγαπᾶτε τοὺς ἐχθροὺς ὑμῶν, καὶ προσεύχεσθε ὑπὲρ τῶν διωκόντων ὑμᾶς.
Rom. xiii. 7.	Matt. xxii. 21.
ἀπόδοτε πᾶσι τὰς ὀφειλάς κ.τ.λ.	ἀπόδοτε οὖν τὰ Καίσαρος Καίσαρι, καὶ τὰ τοῦ Θεοῦ τῷ Θεῷ.
Rom. xiii. 9.	Matt. xxii. 39, 40.
καὶ εἴ τις ἑτέρα ἐντολή, ἐν τούτῳ τῷ λόγῳ ἀνακεφαλαιοῦται, ἐν τῷ Ἀγαπήσεις τὸν πλησίον σου ὡς ἑαυτόν.	δευτέρα δὲ ὁμοία αὕτη, Ἀγαπήσεις τὸν πλησίον σου ὡς σεαυτόν. ἐν ταύταις ταῖς δυσὶν ἐντολαῖς ὅλος ὁ νόμος κρέμαται καὶ οἱ προφῆται.

To these verbal resemblances must be added remarkable identity of teaching in these successive chapters. Everything that is said about revenge, or about injuring others, is exactly identical with the spirit of the Sermon on the Mount; our duty towards rulers exactly reproduces the lesson given in St. Matthew's Gospel; the words concerning the relation of 'love' to 'law' might be an extract from the Gospel: the two main lines of argument in ch. xiv, the absolute indifference of all external practices, and the supreme importance of not giving a cause of offence to any one are both directly derived from the teaching of Jesus (Matt. xviii. 6, 7, xv. 11–20). This resemblance is brought out very well by a recent writer (Knowling, *Witness of the Epistles*, p. 312): 'Indeed it is not too much to add that the Apostle's description of the kingdom of God (Rom. xiv. 17) reads like a brief summary of its description in the same Sermon on the Mount; the righteousness, peace, and joy, which formed the contents of the kingdom in the Apostle's conception are found side by side in the Saviour's Beatitudes; nor can we fail to notice how both St. Matthew and St. Luke contrast the anxious care for meat and drink with seeking in the first place for the kingdom of God and His righteousness. Nor must it be forgotten that Paul's fundamental idea of righteousness may be said to be rooted in the teaching of Jesus.'

It is well known that there are definite references by St. Paul to the words of our Lord: so 1 Thes. iv. 15 = Matt. xxiv. 31; 1 Cor. vii. 10 = Mark x. 9; 1 Cor. ix. 14 = Luke x. 7; as also in the case of the institution of the Last Supper, 1 Cor. xi. 24. Reminiscences also of the Sermon on the Mount may be found in other Epistles, e. g. James iv. 9 = Matt. v. 4; James v. 12 = Matt. v. 33; 1 Pet. iii. 9 = Matt. v. 39; 1 Pet. iv. 14 = Matt. v. 11, 12, and elsewhere. The resemblances are not in any case sufficient either to prove the use of any document which we possess in its present form, or to prove the use of a different document (see below); but they do show that the teaching of the Apostles was based on some common source, which was identical both in substance and spirit with those words of our Lord contained in the Gospels.

They suggest further that even in cases where we have no direct evidence that Apostolic teaching is based on the Gospel narrative it does not follow that our Lord Himself did not originate it. For Christianity is older than any of its records. The books of the N. T. reflect, they did not originate, the teaching of early Christianity. Moreover, our Lord originated principles. It was these principles which inspired His followers; some of the words which are the product of and which taught those principles are preserved, some are not; but the result of them is contained in the words of the Apostles, which worked out in practical life the principles they had learnt directly or indirectly from the Christ.

A much more exact and definite conclusion is supported with very great industry by Alfred Resch in a series of investigations, the first of which is *Agrapha, Aussercanonische Evangelien-fragmente* in *Texte und Untersuchungen*, v. 4. He argues (pp. 28, 29) that the acquaintance shown by St. Paul with the words and teaching of Jesus implies the use of an *Urcanonische Quellenschrift*, which was also used by St. Mark, as well as the other N. T. writers. It would be of course beside our purpose to examine this theory, but so far as it concerns the passages we are considering it may be noticed: (1) That so far as they go there would be no reason why all St. Paul's teaching should not have been derived from our present Gospels. He does not profess to be quoting, and the verbal reminiscences might quite well represent the documents we possess. (2) That it is equally impossible to argue against the use of different Gospels. The only legitimate conclusion is that there must have been a common teaching of Jesus behind the Apostle's words which was identical in spirit and substantially in words with that contained in our Synoptic Gospels. Some stress is laid by Resch (pp. 245, 302 ff.) on passages which are identical in Romans and 1 Peter. So Rom. xii. 17 = 1 Pet. iii. 9; Rom. xiii. 1, 3 = 1 Pet. ii. 13, 14. The resemblance is undoubted, but a far more probable explanation is that 1 Peter is directly indebted to the Romans (see Introduction § 8). There is no reason to cite these as 'Words of the Lord'; yet it is very probable that much more of the common teaching and even phraseology of the early Church than we are accustomed to imagine goes back to the teaching of Jesus.

ON FORBEARANCE TOWARDS THOSE WHO ARE SCRUPULOUS.

XIV. 1—XV. 13. Receive a scrupulous Christian cordially. Do not be continually condemning him. Some of you have grasped the full meaning of Christian faith, others whose conscience is too tender lay undue stress on particular practices, on rules as to food or the observance of certain days. Do not you whose faith is more robust despise such scruples; nor should they be censorious (vv. 1–5).

Every one should make up his own mind. These things are indifferent in themselves. Only whatever a man does he must look to Christ. In life and death we are all His, whose death and resurrection have made him Lord of all. To Him as to no one else shall we be called upon to give account (vv. 6–12).

We must avoid censoriousness. But equally must we avoid placing obstacles before a fellow-Christian. I believe firmly that nothing is harmful in itself, but it becomes so to the person who considers it harmful. The obligation of love and charity is paramount. Meats are secondary things. Let us have an eye to peace and mutual help. It is not worth while for the sake of a little meat to undo God's work in a brother's soul. Far better abstain from flesh and wine altogether (vv. 13–21).

Keep the robuster faith with which you are blest to yourself and God. To hesitate and then eat is to incur guilt; for it is not prompted by strong faith (vv. 22, 23).

This rule of forbearance applies to all classes of the community. The strong should bear the scruples of the weak. We should not seek our own good, but that of others; following the example of Christ as expounded to us in the Scriptures; those Scriptures which were written for our encouragement and consolation. May God, from whom this encouragement comes, grant you all—weak and strong, Jew and Gentile—to be of one mind, uniting in the praise of God (xv. 1–7).

For Christ has received you all alike. To both Jew and Gentile He has a special mission. To the Jews to exhibit God's veracity, to the Gentiles to reveal His mercy; that Gentile might unite with Jew, as Psalmist and Prophet foretold, in hymns of praise to the glory of God. May God the giver of hope send it richly upon you (vv. 8–13).

XIV. 1—XV. 13. The Apostle now passes on to a further point; the proper attitude to adopt towards matters in themselves indifferent, but concerning which some members of the community might have scruples. The subject is one which naturally connects itself with what we have seen to be the leading thought which underlies these concluding chapters, and in fact the whole Epistle, namely, the peace and unity of the Church, and may have been immediately suggested by the words just preceding: St. Paul has been condemning excessive indulgence; he now passes to the opposite extreme, excessive scrupulousness, which he deals with in a very different way. As Augustine points out, he condemns and instructs more openly the 'strong' who can bear it, while indirectly showing the error of the 'weak.' The arguments throughout are, as we shall see, perfectly general, and the principles applied those characteristic of the moral teaching of the Epistle—the freedom of Christian faith, the comprehensiveness of Christian charity and that duty of peace and unity on which St. Paul never wearies of insisting.

Tertullian (*Adv. Marc.* v. 15) refers to ver. 10, and Origen (*Comm. in Rom.* x. 43, Lomm. vii. p. 453) to ver. 23. Of Marcion's use of the rest of the chapter we know nothing. On chaps. xv, xvi, see Introduction, § 9.

1. τὸν δὲ ἀσθενοῦντα τῇ πίστει: cf. Rom. iv. 19; 1 Cor. viii. 7, 9, 10, 11; ix. 22. 'Weakness in faith,' means an inadequate grasp of the great principle of salvation by faith in Christ; the consequence of which will be an anxious desire to make this salvation more certain by the scrupulous fulfilment of formal rules.

προσλαμβάνεσθε, 'receive into full Christian intercourse and fellowship.' The word is used (1) of God receiving or helping man: Ps. xxvi (xxvii) 10 ὁ πατήρ μου καὶ ἡ μήτηρ μου ἐγκατέλιπόν με, ὁ δὲ κύριος προσελάβετό με: so in ver. 3 below and in Clem. Rom. xlix. 6 ἐν ἀγάπῃ προσελάβετο ἡμᾶς ὁ δεσπότης. But (2) it is also used of men receiving others into fellowship or companionship: 2 Macc. viii. 1 τοὺς μεμενηκότας ἐν τῷ Ἰουδαισμῷ προσλαβόμενοι συνήγαγον εἰς ἑξακισχιλίους. These two uses are combined in xv. 7 'All whom Christ has willed to receive into the Christian community, whether they be Jews or Greeks, circumcised or uncircumcised, every Christian ought to be willing to receive as brothers.'

μὴ εἰς διακρίσεις διαλογισμῶν, 'but not to pass judgements on their thoughts.' Receive them as members of the Christian community, but do not let them find that they have been merely received into a society in which their somewhat too scrupulous thoughts are perpetually being condemned. διακρίσεις, from διακρίνω to 'judge,' 'decide,' 'distinguish,' means the expression of judgements or opinions, as Heb. v. 14 'judgement of good or evil,' 1 Cor. xii. 10 'judgement or discernment of spirits.' διαλογισμῶν means 'thoughts,' often, but not necessarily, with the idea of doubt, hesitation (Luke xxiv. 38), disputes (Phil. ii. 14; 1 Tim. ii. 8), or generally of perverse self-willed speculations. The above interpretation of διακρίσεις is that of most commentators (Mey.-W. Oltr. Va.) and is most in accordance with usage. An equally good sense could be gained by translating (with Lips.) 'not so as to raise doubts in his mind,' or (with Gif.) 'not unto discussions of doubts'; but neither interpretation can be so well supported.

2. The Apostle proceeds to describe the two classes to which he is referring, and then (ver. 3) he gives his commands to both sides.

ὃς μὲν ... ὁ δὲ ἀσθενῶν. With the variation in construction cf. 1 Cor. xii. 8–10; Mark iv. 4; Luke viii. 5. The second ὁ is not for ὅς, but is to be taken with ἀσθενῶν.

πιστεύει, 'hath faith to eat all things'; his faith, i. e. his grasp and hold of the Christian spirit, is so strong that he recognizes how indifferent all such matters in themselves really are.

λάχανα ἐσθίει, 'abstains from all flesh meat and eats only vegetables.' Most commentators have assumed that St. Paul is describing the practice of some definite party in the Roman community and have discussed, with great divergence of opinion, the motive of such a practice. But St. Paul is writing quite generally, and is merely selecting a typical instance to balance the first. He takes, on the one side, the man of thoroughly strong faith, who has grasped the full meaning of his Christianity; and on the other side, one who is, as would generally be admitted, over-scrupulous, and therefore is suitable as the type of any variety of scrupulousness in food which might occur. To both these classes he gives the command of forbearance, and what he says to them will apply to other less extreme cases (see the Discussion on p. 399).

3. ὁ ἐσθίων ... ὁ δὲ μὴ ἐσθίων. St. Paul uses these expressions to express briefly the two classes with which he is dealing (see ver. 6). Pride and contempt would be the natural failing of the one; a spirit of censoriousness of the other.

ὁ Θεὸς γὰρ αὐτὸν προσελάβετο. See ver. 1. God through Christ has admitted men into His Church without imposing on them minute and formal observances; they are not therefore to be criticized or condemned for neglecting practices which God has not required.

4. σὺ τίς εἶ; St. Paul is still rebuking the 'weak.' The man

c c

whom he is condemning is not a household slave, but the servant of God; to God therefore he is responsible.

τῷ ἰδίῳ κυρίῳ. Dat. of reference: cf. vv. 5–8. 'It is to his own master that he is responsible.' He it is to whom he must show whether he has used or misused his freedom, whether he has had the strength to fulfil his work or whether he has failed. πίπτει (xi. 11, 22) of moral failure; στήκει (1 Cor. xvi. 13; Phil. i. 27) of moral stability. In 1 Cor. x. 12 the two are contrasted, ὥστε ὁ δοκῶν ἑστάναι βλεπέτω μὴ πέσῃ.

σταθήσεται δέ: cf. Matt. xii. 25. In spite of your censoriousness he will be held straight, for the same Lord who called him on conditions of freedom to His kingdom is mighty to hold him upright. The Lord will give grace and strength to those whom He has called.

For δυνατεῖ (א A B C D F G), which is an unusual word, later MSS. substituted δυνατός (P, Bas. Chrys.), or δυνατὸς . . . ἐστιν (T R with L and later MSS.). For ὁ Κύριος (א A B C P, Sah. Boh., &c.) ὁ Θεός was introduced from ver. 3 (D E F G L, &c., Vulg., Orig.-lat. Bas. Chrys., &c.), perhaps because of the confusion with τῷ Κυρίῳ above.

5. The Apostle turns to another instance of similar scrupulousness,—the superstitious observance of days. In Galatia he has already had to rebuke this strongly; later he condemns the Colossians for the same reason. Gal. iv. 10, 11 'Ye observe days, and months, and seasons, and years. I am afraid of you, lest by any means I have bestowed labour upon you in vain.' Col. ii. 16, 17 'Let no man therefore judge you in meat, or in drink, or in respect of a feast day or a new moon or a sabbath day: which are a shadow of the things to come; but the body is Christ's.' St. Paul does not in the Romans condemn any one for adherence to this practice, but simply considers the principles which underlie the question, as illustrating (hence γάρ) the general discussion of the chapter. The fundamental principle is that such things are in themselves indifferent, but that each person must be fully assured in his own conscience that he is doing right.

Various commentators have discussed the relation of these directions to Ecclesiastical ordinances, and have attempted to make a distinction between the Jewish rites which are condemned and Christian rites which are enjoined. (So Jerome, *Contra Iovinian.* ii. 16, quoted by Liddon *ad loc.*: *non inter ieiunia et saturitatem aequalia mente dispensat; sed contra eos loquitur, qui in Christum credentes, adhuc iudaizabant.*) No such distinction is possible. The Apostle is dealing with principles, not with special rites, and he lays down the principle that these things in themselves are indifferent; while the whole tenor of his argument is against scrupulousness in any form. So these same principles would apply equally to the scrupulous observance of Ecclesiastical rules, whether as in some places of Sunday, or as in others of Saints' days or Fast days. Such observances if undertaken in a scrupulous spirit are opposed to the very essence of Christian freedom. When once this principle has been grasped a loyal free adhesion to the rules of the Church becomes possible. The Jew and the scrupulous Christian kept their rules of days and seasons, because they believed that their salvation depended on an exact adherence to formal ordinances. The Christian who has grasped the freedom of the Gospel recognizes the indifference in themselves of all such ordinances; but he voluntarily submits to the rules of his Church out of respect for its authority, and he recognizes the value of an external discipline. The Apostolical Constitutions, which representing an early system of Christian discipline, seem to recognize these principles, for they strongly condemn abstinence from food if influenced by any feeling of abhorrence from it, although not if undertaken for the purpose of discipline.

Tisch. (ed. 8) reads here ὃς μὲν γάρ with ℵ A C P, Vulg. Boh. (which he quotes incorrectly on the other side), Bas. Ambrstr. Jo.-Damasc. The γάρ is omitted by ℵ° B D E F G, Syrr., Orig.-lat. Chrys. Thdrt. TR. RV. and inserted between brackets by WH. Lachmann. The insertion is probably right; the balance of external evidence being in its favour, for B here is clearly Western in character.

κρίνει, 'estimates,' 'approves of': Plat. *Phil.* p. 57 E is quoted. παρά, 'passing by' and so 'in preference to.'

πληροφορείσθω. The difference between the Christian and the Jew or the heathen, between the man whose rule is one of faith and the man subject to law, is, that while for the latter there are definite and often minute regulations he must follow, for the former the only laws are great and broad principles. He has the guidance of the Spirit; he must do what his νοῦς, his highest intellectual faculty, tells him to be right. On the word πληροφορείσθω see on iv. 21 and cf. Clem. Rom. xlii πληροφορηθέντες διὰ τῆς ἀναστάσεως.

6. The reason for indifference in these matters is that both alike, both the man who has grasped the Christian principle and the man who is scrupulous, are aiming at the one essential thing, to render service to God, to live as men who are to give account to Him.

ὁ φρονῶν: 'esteem,' 'estimate,' 'observe.' Κυρίῳ, emphatic, is Dat. of reference as above, ver. 4.

ὁ ἐσθίων ... ὁ μὴ ἐσθίων: see ver. 3. Both alike make their meal an occasion of solemn thanksgiving to God, and it is that which consecrates the feast. Is there any reference in εὐχαριστεῖ to the Christian εὐχαριστία?

After Κυρίῳ φρονεῖ the TR. with later authorities (LP &c., Syrr., Bas. Chrys. Thdrt.) add καὶ ὁ μὴ φρονῶν τὴν ἡμέραν Κυρίῳ οὐ φρονεῖ, a gloss which seemed necessary for completing the sentence on the analogy of the last half of the verse. The addition of this clause caused the omission of καί before ὁ ἐσθίων (TR. with some minuscules). That the words καὶ ὁ μὴ φρονῶν were not parts of the original text omitted by homoeoteleuton is shown by the fact that many authorities which insert them still preserve the superfluous καί (Syrr., Bas. Chrys. Thdrt. and many minuscules). Various instances of homoeoteleuton occur, as might be expected, in these verses, but they are in all cases confined to a single or very slight authority. L omits καὶ ὁ μὴ ἐσθίων . . . εὐχ. τῷ θεῷ : 66 omits ἡμέραν to ἡμέραν; minusc. 3 omit ἐσθίει to ἐσθίει.

7-12. St. Paul proceeds to develop more fully, and as a general rule of life, the thought suggested in ver. 6. To God we are responsible whether we live or die; before His judgement-seat we shall appear; therefore we must live as men who are to give account of our lives to Him and not to one another.

7. οὐδεὶς γὰρ . . . ἀποθνήσκει. In life and in death we are not isolated, or solitary, or responsible only to ourselves. It is not by our own act we were created, nor is our death a matter that concerns us alone.

8. τῷ Κυρίῳ : ' but it is to Christ, as men living in Christ's sight and answerable to Him, that we must live; in Christ's sight we shall die. Death does not free us from our obligations, whether we live or die we are the Lord's.' Wetstein compares *Pirqê Aboth*, iv. 32 ' Let not thine imagination assure thee that the grave is an asylum; for perforce thou wast framed, and perforce thou wast born, and perforce thou livest, and perforce thou diest, and perforce thou art about to give account and reckoning before the King of the kings of kings, the Holy One, blessed is He.'

It may be noticed that in these verses St. Paul describes the Christian life from a point of view other than that which he had adopted in chap. viii. There it was the higher aspects of that life as lived in union with Christ, here it is the life lived as in His sight and responsible to Him.

9. The reason for this relation of all men to Christ as servants to their master is that by His death and resurrection Christ has established His Divine Lordship over all alike, both dead and living. Responsibility to Him therefore no one can ever escape.

εἰς τοῦτο is explained by ἵνα κυριεύσῃ.

ἀπέθανε καὶ ἔζησεν must refer to Christ's death and resurrection. ἔζησεν cannot refer to the life of Christ on earth, (1) because of the order of words which St. Paul has purposely and deliberately varied from the order ζῶμεν καὶ ἀποθνήσκωμεν of the previous verses; (2) because the Lordship of Christ is in the theology of St. Paul always connected with His resurrection, not His life, which was a period of humiliation (Rom. viii. 34; 2 Cor. iv. 10, 11); (3) because of the tense; the aorist ἔζησεν could be used of a single definite act which was the beginning of a new life, it could not be used of the continuous life on earth.

νεκρῶν καὶ ζώντων. The inversion of the usual order is owing to the order of words in the previous part of the sentence, ἀπέθ. καὶ ἔζησ. For the κυριότης of Christ (ἵνα κυριεύσῃ) see Phil. ii. 9, 11.

For Χριστός the TR. with later MSS., Syrr., Iren.-lat. reads καὶ Χριστός. ἀπέθανεν καὶ ἔζησεν, the older and most difficult reading (א A B C, Boh., Arm. Aeth. Orig.-lat. Chrys. 1/2) has been explained in various ways; by ἀπέθ. καὶ ἀνέστη F G, Vulg. Orig. and other Fathers; by ἀπέθ. καὶ ἀνέστ. καὶ ἀνέζησεν TR. with minusc. (perhaps conflate); by ἀπέθ. καὶ ἀνέστ. καὶ ἔζησεν, LP. &c., Harkl. and some Fathers: by ἔζησ. καὶ ἀπέθ. καὶ ἀνέστ. DE. Iren.

10. St. Paul applies the argument pointedly to the questions he is discussing. We are responsible to Christ; we shall appear before Him : there is no place for uncharitable judgements or censorious exclusiveness between man and man.

σὺ δὲ τί κρίνεις refers to ὁ μὴ ἐσθίων, ἢ καὶ σύ to ὁ ἐσθίων.

παραστησόμεθα τῷ βήματι τοῦ Θεοῦ. Cf. Acts xxvii. 24 Καίσαρί σε δεῖ παραστῆναι. For βῆμα, in the sense of a judge's official seat, see Matt. xxvii. 19; Jo. xix. 13, &c. God is here mentioned as Judge because (see ii. 16) He judges the world through Christ. In 2 Cor. v. 10 the expression is τοὺς γὰρ πάντας ἡμᾶς φανερωθῆναι δεῖ ἔμπροσθεν τοῦ βήματος τοῦ Χριστοῦ. It is quite impossible to follow Liddon in taking Θεοῦ of Christ in his Divine nature; that would be contrary to all Pauline usage : but it is important to notice how easily St. Paul passes from Χριστός to Θεός. The Father and the Son were in his mind so united in function that They may often be interchanged. God, or Christ, or God through Christ, will judge the world. Our life is in God, or in Christ, or with Christ in God. The union of man with God depends upon the intimate union of the Father and the Son.

Θεοῦ must be accepted as against Χριστοῦ on decisive authority. The latter reading arose from a desire to assimilate the expression to 2 Cor. v. 10.

11. St. Paul supports his statement of the universal character of God's judgement by quoting Is. xlv. 23 (freely acc. to the LXX). In the O. T. the words describe the expectation of the universal character of Messianic rule, and the Apostle sees their complete fulfilment at the final judgement.

ἐξομολογήσεται τῷ Θεῷ, 'shall give praise to God,' according to the usual LXX meaning; cf. xv. 9, which is quoted from Ps. xvii (xviii). 50.

ζῶ ἐγώ, λέγω Κύριος is substituted for κατ' ἐμαυτοῦ ὀμνύω, cf. Num. xiv. 28 &c.; for πᾶσα γλῶσσα κ.τ.λ. the LXX reads ὀμεῖται π. γ. τὸν Θεόν.

12. The conclusion is : it is to God and not to man that each of us has to give account. If Θεῷ be read (see below), it may again be noted how easily St. Paul passes from Κύριος to Θεός (see on ver. 10 and cf. xiv. 3 with xv. 7).

There are several minor variations of text. οὖν is omitted by B D F G P and perhaps the Latin authorities, which read itaque. For δώσει of the TR.

WH. read ἀποδώσει with B D F G Chrys., the Latin authorities reading *reddit* (but Cyprian *dabit*). τῷ Θεῷ at the end of the sentence is omitted by B F G Cypr. Aug. In all these cases B is noticeable as appearing with a group which is almost entirely Western in character.

13. The Apostle now passes to another aspect of the question. He has laid down very clearly the rule that all such points are in themselves indifferent; he has rebuked censoriousness and shown that a man is responsible to God alone. Now he turns completely round and treats the question from the other side. All this is true, but higher than all is the rule of Christian charity, and this demands, above all, consideration for the feelings and consciences of others.

Μηκέτι οὖν . . . κρίνωμεν marks the transition to the second question by summing up the first.

κρίνατε: for the play on words cf. xii. 3, 14, xiii. 1. 'Do not therefore judge one another, but judge this for yourself, i. e. determine this as your course of conduct': cf. 2 Cor. ii. 1.

τὸ μὴ τιθέναι . . . τῷ ἀδελφῷ . . . σκάνδαλον. τιθέναι is suggested by the literal meaning of σκάνδαλον, a snare or stumbling-block which is laid in the path. St. Paul has probably derived the word σκάνδαλον and the whole thought of the passage from our Lord's words reported in Matt. xviii. 6 f. See also his treatment of the same question in 1 Cor. viii. 9 f.

πρόσκομμα . . . ἤ should perhaps be omitted with B, Arm. Pesh. As Weiss points out, the fact that ἤ is omitted in all authorities which omit πρ. proves that the words cannot have been left out accidentally. πρόσκομμα would come in from 1 Cor. viii. 9 and ver. 20 below.

14. In order to emphasize the real motive which should influence Christians, namely, respect for the feelings of others, the indifference of all such things in themselves is emphatically stated.

ἐν Κυρίῳ Ἰησοῦ. The natural meaning of these words is the same as that of ἐν Χρ. (ix. 1); to St. Paul the indifference of all meats in themselves is a natural deduction from his faith and life in Christ. It may be doubted whether he is here referring expressly to the words of Christ (Mark vii. 15; Matt. xv. 11); when doing so his formula is παρέλαβον ἀπὸ τοῦ Κυρίου.

κοινόν. The technical term to express those customs and habits, which, although 'common' to the world, were forbidden to the pious Jew. Jos. *Ant.* XIII. i. 1 τὸν κοινὸν βίον προῃρημένους: 1 Macc. i. 47, 62; Acts x. 14 ὅτι οὐδέποτε ἔφαγον πᾶν κοινὸν καὶ ἀκάθαρτον.

δι' ἑαυτοῦ, 'in itself,' ' in its own nature.'

That δι' ἑαυτοῦ is the right reading is shown by (1) the authority of ℵ B C also of 2 (Cod. Patiriensis, see Introduction, § 7) supported by many later MSS., the Vulgate, and the two earliest commentators Orig.-lat. *In Domino ergo Iesu nihil commune per semetipsum, hoc est natura sui dicitur*, and Chrys. τῇ φύσει φησὶν οὐδὲν ἀκάθαρτον and (2) by the contrast with τῷ λογιζομένῳ. δι' αὐτοῦ, 'through Christ' (so Theodrt. and later comm.) is a correction.

εἰ μὴ τῷ λογιζομένῳ κ.τ.λ. Only if a man supposes that the breach of a ceremonial law is wrong, and is compelled by public opinion or the custom of the Church to do violence to his belief, he is led to commit sin; for example, if at the common Eucharistic meal a man were compelled to eat food against his conscience it would clearly be wrong.

15. εἰ γάρ. The γάρ (which has conclusive manuscript authority) implies a suppressed link in the argument. 'You must have respect therefore for his scruples, although you may not share them, for if,' &c.

λυπεῖται. His conscience is injured and wounded, for he wilfully and knowingly does what he thinks is wrong, and so he is in danger of perishing (ἀπόλλυε).

ὑπὲρ οὗ Χριστὸς ἀπέθανε. Cf. 1 Cor. viii. 10, 11. Christ died to save this man from his sins, and will you for his sake not give up some favourite food?

16. μὴ βλασφημείσθω κ.τ.λ. Let not that good of yours, i. e. your consciousness of Christian freedom (cf. 1 Cor. x. 29 ἡ ἐλευθερία μου), become a cause of reproach. St. Paul is addressing the strong, as elsewhere in this paragraph, and the context seems clearly to point, at least primarily, to opinions within the community, not to the reputation of the community with the outside world. The above interpretation, therefore (which is that of Gifford and Vaughan), is better than that which would refer the passage to the reputation of the Christian community amongst those not belonging to it (Mey-W. Lips. Liddon).

17. Do not lay such stress on this freedom of yours as to cause a breach in the harmony of the Church; for eating and drinking are not the principle of that kingdom which you hope to inherit.

ἡ βασιλεία τοῦ Θεοῦ. An echo of our Lord's teaching. The phrase is used normally in St. Paul of that Messianic kingdom which is to be the reward and goal of the Christian life; so especially 1 Cor. vi. 9, 10, where it is laid down that certain classes shall have no part in it. Hence it comes to mean the principles or ideas on which that kingdom is founded, and which are already exhibited in this world (cf. 1 Cor. iv. 20). The term is, of course, derived through the words of Christ from the current Jewish conceptions of an actual earthly kingdom; how far exactly such conceptions have been spiritualized in St. Paul it may be difficult to say.

βρῶσις καὶ πόσις. If, as is probable, the weak brethren are conceived of as having Judaizing tendencies, there is a special point in this expression. 'If you lay so much stress on eating and drinking as to make a point of indulging in what you will at all costs, you are in danger of falling into the Judaizing course of interpreting the Messianic prophecies literally, and imagining the Messianic kingdom to be one of material plenty' (Iren. V. xxxiii. 3).

These words are often quoted as condemning any form of scrupulousness concerning eating and drinking; but that is not St. Paul's idea. He means that 'eating and drinking' are in themselves so unimportant that every scruple should be respected, and every form of food willingly given up. They are absolutely insignificant in comparison with 'righteousness' and 'peace' and 'joy.'

δικαιοσύνη κ.τ.λ. This passage describes man's life in the kingdom, and these words denote not the relation of the Christian to God, but his life in relation to others. δικαιοσύνη therefore is not used in its technical sense of the relation between God and man, but means righteousness or just dealing; εἰρήνη is the state of peace with one another which should characterize Christians; χαρά is the joy which comes from the indwelling of the Holy Ghost in the community; cf. Acts ii. 46 μετελάμβανον τροφῆς ἐν ἀγαλλιάσει καὶ ἀφελότητι καρδίας.

18. The same statement is generalized. The man who, on the principle implied by these virtues (ἐν τούτῳ, not ἐν τούτοις), is Christ's servant, i. e. who serves Christ by being righteous and conciliatory and charitable towards others, not by harshly emphasizing his Christian freedom, is not only well-pleasing to God, but will gain the approval of men.

δόκιμος τοῖς ἀνθρώποις. The contrast to βλασφημείσθω of ver. 16. Consideration for others is a mark of the Christian character which will recommend a man to his fellow-men. δόκιμος, able to stand the test of inspection and criticism (cf. 2 Tim. ii. 15).

19. οἰκοδομῆς: cf. 1 Cor. xiv. 26 πάντα πρὸς οἰκοδομὴν γινέσθω, 1 Thess. v. 11 οἰκοδομεῖτε εἰς τὸν ἕνα.

διώκομεν (א A B F G L P ℶ) is really more expressive than the somewhat obvious correction διώκωμεν (C D E, Latt.). D E F G add φυλάξωμεν after ἀλλήλους.

20. κατάλυε . . . ἔργον keeps up the metaphor suggested by οἰκοδομῆς. 'Build up, do not destroy, that Christian community which God has founded in Christ.' Cf. 1 Cor. iii. 9 Θεοῦ γάρ ἐσμεν συνεργοί. Θεοῦ γεώργιον, Θεοῦ οἰκοδομή ἐστε. The words εἰρήνη and οἰκοδομή both point to the community rather than the individual Christian.

πάντα μὲν καθαρά: cf. 1 Cor. x. 23 πάντα ἔξεστιν, ἀλλ' οὐ πάντα συμφέρει. πάντα ἔξεστιν, ἀλλ' οὐ πάντα οἰκοδομεῖ.

ἀλλὰ κακόν: the subject to this must be supplied from πάντα. It is a nice question to decide to whom these words refer.' (1) Are they addressed to the strong, those who by eating are likely to give offence to others (so Va. Oltr., and the majority of commentators)?

or (2) are they addressed to the weak, those who by eating what they
think it wrong to eat injure their own consciences (so Gif. Mey.-W.
and others)? In the former case διὰ προσκόμματος (on the διά cf. ii.
27, iv. 11) means 'so as to cause offence,' in the latter 'so as to
take offence' (Tyndale, 'who eateth with hurt of his conscience').
Perhaps the transition to ver. 21 is slightly better if we take (1).

21. A thing in itself indifferent may be wrong if it injures the
consciences of others; on the other hand, to give up what will injure
others is a noble act.

καλόν: cf. 1 Cor. vii. 1 and for the thought 1 Cor. viii. 13 διόπερ,
εἰ βρῶμα σκανδαλίζει τὸν ἀδελφόν μου, οὐ μὴ φάγω κρέα εἰς τὸν αἰῶνα, ἵνα
μὴ τὸν ἀδελφόν μου σκανδαλίσω. We know the situation implied
in the Corinthian Epistle, and that it did not arise from the existence
of a party who habitually abstained from flesh : St. Paul was
merely taking the strongest instance he could think of. It is
equally incorrect therefore to argue from this verse that there was
a sect of vegetarians and total abstainers in Rome. St. Paul
merely takes extreme forms of self-deprivation, which he uses as
instances. 'I would live like an Essene rather than do anything to
offend my brother.'

The TR. adds after προσκόπτει the gloss ἢ σκανδαλίζεται ἢ ἀσθενεῖ with B
Western and Syrian authorities (Nᶜ B D E F G L P, &c., Vulg. Sah., Bas.
Chrys.). They are omitted by N A C コ, Pesh. Boh., Orig. and Orig.-lat. This
is a very clear instance of a Western reading in B ; cf. xi. 6.

22. σὺ πίστιν ἣν ἔχεις. Your faith is sufficient to see that all
these things are a matter of indifference. Be content with that
knowledge, it is a matter for your own conscience and God. Do
not boast of it, or wound those not so strong as yourself.

The preponderance of authorities (N A B C, Vulg. codd. Boh., Orig.-lat.)
compels us to read ἣν ἔχεις. The omission of ἣν (D E F G L P コ, Vulg.
codd. Syrr. Boh., Chrys. &c.) is a Western correction and an improvement.

μακάριος κ.τ.λ. Blessed (see on iv. 6, 7) because of his strong
faith is the man who can courageously do what his reason tells him
that he may do without any doubt or misgiving κρίνων, to 'judge
censoriously so as to condemn,' cf. ii. 1, 3, 27. δοκιμάζει (i. 28,
ii. 18) to 'approve of after testing and examining.'

23. ὁ δὲ διακρινόμενος: see on iv. 20. If a man doubts or
hesitates and then eats, he is, by the very fact that he doubts,
condemned for his weakness of faith. If his faith were strong he
would have no doubt or hesitation.

πᾶν δὲ ὃ οὐκ ἐκ πίστεως, ἁμαρτία ἐστίν. πίστις is subjective, the
strong conviction of what is right and of the principles of salvation.
'Weakly to comply with other persons' customs without being
convinced of their indifference is itself sin.' This maxim (1) is not
concerned with the usual conduct of unbelievers, (2) must not be

extended to cases different in character from those St. Paul is considering. It is not a general maxim concerning faith.

This verse has had a very important part to play in controversy. How important may be seen from the use made of it in Augustine *Contra Iulianum* iv, one passage of which (§ 32) may be quoted: *Ex quo colligitur, etiam ipsa bona opera quae faciunt infideles, non ipsorum esse, sed illius qui bene utitur malis. Ipsorum autem esse peccata quibus et bona male faciunt; quia ea non fideli, sed infideli, hoc est stulta et noxia faciunt voluntate: qualis voluntas, nullo Christiano dubitante, arbor est mala, quae facere non potest nisi fructus malos, id est, sola peccata.* Omne enim, *velis nolis,* quod non est ex fide, peccatum est. Since this time it has been used to support the two propositions that works done before justification are sin and consequently that the heathen are unable to do good works. Into the merits of these controversies it will be apart from our purpose to enter. It is sufficient to notice that this verse is in such a context completely misquoted. As Chrysostom says, 'When a person does not feel sure, nor believe that a thing is clean, how can he do else than sin? Now all these things have been spoken by Paul of the object in hand, not of everything.' The words do not apply to those who are not Christians, nor to the works of those who are Christians done before they became such, but to the conduct of believing Christians; and faith is used somewhat in the way we should speak of a 'good conscience'; 'everything which is not done with a clear conscience is sin.' So Aquinas, *Summa* i. 2, qu. xix, art. v. *omne quod non est ex fide peccatum est, id est, omne quod est contra conscientiam.*

On the doxology (xvi. 25–27), which in some MSS. finds a place here, see the Introduction, § 8.

XV. 1. The beginning of chap. xv is connected immediately with what precedes, and there is no break in the argument until ver. 13 is reached; but towards the close, especially in vv. 7–13, the language of the Apostle is more general. He passes from the special points at issue to the broad underlying principle of Christian unity, and especially to the relation of the two great sections of the Church—the Jewish and the Gentile Christians.

ὀφείλομεν δέ. Such weakness is, it is true, a sign of absence of faith, but we who are strong in faith ought to bear with scruples weak though they may be. οἱ δύνατοι not, as in 1 Cor. i. 26, the rich or the powerful, but as in 2 Cor. xii. 10, xiii. 9, of the morally strong.

βαστάζειν: cf. Gal. vi. 2 ἀλλήλων τὰ βάρη βαστάζετε. In classical Greek the ordinary word would be φέρειν, but βαστάζειν seems to have gradually come into use in the figurative sense. It is used of bearing the cross both literally (John xix. 17), and figuratively (Luke xiv. 27). We find it in later versions of the O. T. In Aq., Symm. and Theod. in Is. xl. 11, lxvi. 12; in the two latter in Is. lxiii. 9; in Matt. viii. 17 quoting Is. liii. 3: in none of these passages is the word used in the LXX. It became a favourite word in Christian literature, Ign. *Ad Polyc.* 1, *Epist. ad Diog.* § 10 (quoted by Lft.).

μὴ ἑαυτοῖς ἀρέσκειν: cf. 1 Cor. x. 33 καθὼς κἀγὼ πάντα πᾶσιν ἀρέσκω, μὴ ζητῶν τὸ ἐμαυτοῦ συμφέρον, where St. Paul is describing his own conduct in very similar circumstances. He strikes at the root of Christian disunion, which is selfishness.

2. εἰς τὸ ἀγαθὸν πρὸς οἰκοδομήν : cf. xiv. 16 ὑμῶν τὸ ἀγαθόν, 19 τὰ τῆς οἰκοδομῆς τῆς εἰς ἀλλήλους. The end or purpose of pleasing them must be the promotion of what is absolutely to their good, further defined by οἰκοδομή, their edification. These words limit and explain what St. Paul means by 'pleasing men.' In Gal. i. 10 (cf. Eph. vi. 6; 1 Thess. ii. 4) he had condemned it. In 1 Cor. ix. 20–23 he had made it a leading principle of his conduct. The rule is that we are to please men for their own good and not our own.

The γάρ after ἕκαστος of the TR. should be omitted. For ἡμῶν some authorities (F G P ⊐, Vulg., many Fathers) read ὑμῶν.

3. καὶ γὰρ ὁ Χριστὸς κ.τ.λ. The precept just laid down is enforced by the example of Christ (cf. xiv. 15). As Christ bore our reproaches, so must we bear those of others.

καθὼς γέγραπται. St. Paul, instead of continuing the sentence, changes the construction and inserts a verse of the O. T. [Ps. lxviii (lxix). 10, quoted exactly according to the LXX], which he puts into the mouth of Christ. For the construction cf. ix. 7.

The Psalm quoted describes the sufferings at the hands of the ungodly of the typically righteous man, and passages taken from it are often in the N. T. referred to our Lord, to whom they would apply as being emphatically 'the just one.' Ver. 4 is quoted John xv. 25, ver. 9 a in John ii. 17, ver. 9 b in Rom. xv. 3, ver. 12 in Matt. xxvii. 27–30, ver. 21 in Matt. xxvii. 34, and John xix. 29, ver. 22 f. in Rom. xi. 9, ver. 25 a in Acts i. 20. (See Liddon, *ad loc.*)

οἱ ὀνειδισμοί κ.τ.λ. In the original the righteous man is represented as addressing God and saying that the reproaches against God he has to bear. St. Paul transfers the words to Christ, who is represented as addressing a man. Christ declares that in suffering it was the reproaches or sufferings of others that He bore.

4. The quotation is justified by the enduring value of the O. T.

προεγράφη, 'were written before,' in contrast with ἡμετέραν: cf. Eph. iii. 3; Jude 4, but with a reminiscence of the technical meaning of γράφειν for what is written as Scripture.

διδασκαλίαν, 'instruction': cf. 2 Tim. iii. 16 πᾶσα γραφὴ θεόπνευστος καὶ ὠφέλιμος πρὸς διδασκαλίαν.

τὴν ἐλπίδα : the specifically Christian feeling of hope. It is the supreme confidence which arises from trust in Christ that in no circumstances will the Christian be ashamed of that wherein he trusteth (Phil. i. 20); a confidence which tribulation only strengthens, for it makes more certain his power of endurance and his experience of consolation. On the relation of patience to hope cf. v. 3 and 1 Thess. i. 3.

This passage, and that quoted above from 2 Tim. iii. 16, lay down very clearly the belief in the abiding value of the O. T. which underlies St. Paul's use of it. But while emphasizing its value they also limit it. The Scriptures are to be read for our moral instruction, 'for reproof, for correction, for instruction which is in righteousness'; for the perfection of the Christian character, 'that the man of God may be complete, furnished unto every good work'; and because they establish the Christian hope which is in Christ. Two points then St. Paul teaches, the permanent value of the great moral and spiritual truths of the O. T., and the witness of the O. T. to Christ. His words cannot be quoted to prove more than this.

> There are in this verse a few idiosyncrasies of B which may be noted but need not be accepted; ἐγράφη (with Vulg. Orig.-lat.) for προεγράφη; πάντα before εἰς τὴν ἡμ. (with P); τῆς παρακλήσεως repeated after ἔχωμεν (with Clem.-Al.). The TR. with Nᶜ A L P ⊐, &c. substitutes προεγράφη for ἐγράφη in the second place, and with Cᶜᵒʳ D E F G P, &c., Vulg. Boh. Harcl. omits the second διά.

5. After the digression of ver. 4 the Apostle returns to the subject of vv. 1–3, and sums up his teaching by a prayer for the unity of the community.

ὁ δὲ Θεὸς τῆς ὑπομονῆς καὶ τῆς παρακλήσεως: cf. ὁ Θεὸς τῆς εἰρήνης (ver. 33; Phil. iv. 9; 1 Thess. v. 23; Heb. xiii. 20), τῆς ἐλπίδος (ver. 13), πάσης παρακλήσεως (2 Cor. i. 3), πάσης χάριτος (1 Pet. v. 10).

τὸ αὐτὸ φρονεῖν: cf. Phil. ii. 2–5 πληρώσατέ μου τὴν χαράν, ἵνα τὸ αὐτὸ φρονῆτε . . . τοῦτο φρονεῖτε ἐν ὑμῖν ὃ καὶ ἐν Χρ. Ἰ.

κατὰ Χριστὸν Ἰησοῦν: cf. 2 Cor. xi. 17 ὃ λαλῶ, οὐ κατὰ Κύριον λαλῶ: Col. ii. 8 οὐ κατὰ Χρ.: Eph. iv. 24 τὸν καινὸν ἄνθρωπον τὸν κατὰ Θεὸν κτισθέντα (Rom. viii. 27, which is generally quoted, is not in point). These examples seem to show that the expression must mean 'in accordance with the character or example of Christ.'

> δῴη for δοίη, a later form, cf. 2 Thess. iii. 16; 2 Tim. i. 16, 18; ii. 25; Eph. i. 17 (but with variant δῴη in the last two cases). Χρ. Ἰησ. (B D E G L, &c., Boh. Chrys.), not Ἰησ. Χρ. ℵ A C F P ⊐ Vulg., Orig.-lat. Theodrt.

6. Unity and harmony of worship will be the result of unity of life.

ὁμοθυμαδόν, 'with unity of mind.' A common word in the Acts (i. 14, &c.).

τὸν Θεὸν καὶ πατέρα τοῦ Κυρίου ἡμῶν Ἰησοῦ Χριστοῦ. This expression occurs also in 2 Cor. i. 3; xi. 31; Eph. i. 3; 1 Pet. i. 3. In Col. i. 3, which is also quoted, the correct reading is τῷ Θεῷ πατρὶ τοῦ Κυρίου ἡμῶν Ἰ. Χ. Two translations are possible: (1) 'God even the Father of our Lord Jesus Christ' (Mey.-W. Gif. Lid., Lips.). In favour of this it is pointed out that while πατήρ expects some correlative word, Θεός is naturally absolute; and that ὁ Θεὸς καὶ

πατήρ occurs absolutely (as in 1 Cor. xv. 24 ὅταν παραδιδοῖ τὴν βασιλείαν τῷ Θεῷ καὶ πατρί), an argument the point of which does not
seem clear, and which suggests that the first argument has not
much weight. (2) It is better and simpler to take the words in
their natural meaning, 'The God and Father of our Lord Jesus
Christ'; (Va. Oltr. Go. and others), with which cf. Eph. i. 17 ὁ Θεὸς
τοῦ Κυρίου ἡμῶν 'Ι. Χ.: Matt. xxvii. 46; Jn. xx. 17; Heb. i. 9.

7. The principles laid down in this section of the Epistle are
now generalized. All whom Christ has received should, without
any distinction, be accepted into His Church. This is intended
to apply especially to the main division existing at that time in the
community, that between Jewish and Gentile Christians.

διὸ προσλαμβάνεσθε ἀλλήλους κ.τ.λ.: the command is no longer
to the strong to admit the weak, but to all sections of the community alike to receive and admit those who differ from them; so
St. Paul probably said ὑμᾶς, not ἡμᾶς. The latter he uses in ver. 1,
where he is identifying himself with the 'strong,' the former he uses
here, where he is addressing the whole community. On διό cf. Eph.
ii. 11; 1 Thess. v. 11: on προσλαμβάνεσθε see xiv. 1, 3.

ὑμᾶς is read by ℵ A C E F G L, Vulg. Boh. Syrr., Orig.-lat. Chrys.; ἡμᾶς
by B D P⅃. B is again Western, and its authority on the distinction between
ἡμᾶς and ὑμᾶς is less trustworthy than on most other points (see WH. ii.
pp. 218, 310).

εἰς δόξαν Θεοῦ with προσελάβετο: 'in order to promote the
glory of God.' As the following verses show, Christ has summoned both Jews and Greeks into His kingdom in order to
promote the glory of God, to exhibit in the one case His faithfulness, in the other His mercy. So in Phil. ii. 11 the object of
Christ's glory is to promote the glory of God the Father.

8. St. Paul has a double object. He writes to remind the Gentiles that it is through the Jews that they are called, the Jews that
the aim and purpose of their existence is the calling of the Gentiles.
The Gentiles must remember that Christ became a Jew to save
them; the Jew that Christ came among them in order that all the
families of the earth might be blessed: both must realize that the
aim of the whole is to proclaim God's glory.

This passage is connected by undoubted links (διό ver. 7; λέγω
γάρ ver. 8) with what precedes, and forms the conclusion of the
argument after the manner of the concluding verses of ch. viii. and
ch. xi. This connexion makes it probable that 'the relations of
Jew and Gentile were directly or indirectly involved in the relations of the weak and the strong.' (Hort, *Rom. and Eph.* p. 29.)

διάκονον ... περιτομῆς: not 'a minister of the circumcised,' still
less a 'minister of the true circumcision of the spirit,' which would
be introducing an idea quite alien to the context, but 'a minister
of circumcision' (so Gifford, who has an excellent note), i. e. to

carry out the promises implied in that covenant the seal of which was circumcision; so 2 Cor. iii. 6 διακόνους καινῆς διαθήκης. In the Ep. to the Galatians (iv. 4, 5) St. Paul had said that Christ was 'born of a woman, born under the law, that He might redeem them which were under the law, that we might receive the adoption of sons.' On the Promise and Circumcision see Gen. xii. 1-3, xvii. 1-14.

The privileges of the Jews which St. Paul dwells on are as follows: (1) Christ has Himself fulfilled the condition of being circumcised: the circumcised therefore must not be condemned. (2) The primary object of this was to fulfil the promises made to the Jews (cf. Rom. ii. 9, 10). (3) It was only as a secondary result of this Messiahship that the Gentiles glorified God. (4) While the blessing came to the Jews ὑπὲρ ἀληθείας to preserve God's consistency, it came to the Gentiles ὑπὲρ ἐλέους for God's loving-kindness.

γεγενῆσθαι, which should be read with א A E L P ⊐ (γεγεννῆσθε); it was altered into the more usual aorist γενέσθαι (B C D F G), perhaps because it was supposed to be co-ordinated with δοξάσαι.

τὰς ἐπαγγελίας τῶν πατέρων : cf. ix. 4, 5.

9. τὰ δὲ ἔθνη ... δοξάσαι. Two constructions are possible for these words: (1) they may be taken as directly subordinate to λέγω γάρ (Weiss, Oltr. Go.). The only object in this construction would be to contrast ὑπὲρ ἐλέους with ὑπὲρ ἀληθείας. But the real antithesis of the passage is between βεβαιῶσαι τὰς ἐπαγγελίας and τὰ ἔθνη δοξάσαι: and hence (2) τὰ δὲ ... ἔθνη ... δοξάσαι should be taken as subordinate to εἰς τό and co-ordinate with βεβαιῶσαι (Gif. Mey. Lid., Va.). With this construction the point of the passage becomes much greater, the call of the Gentiles is shown to be (as it certainly was), equally with the fulfilment of the promise to the Jews, dependent on the covenant made with Abraham (iv. 11, 12, 16, 17).

καθὼς γέγραπται. The Apostle proceeds, as so often in the Epistle, to support his thesis by a series of passages quoted from the O. T.

διὰ τοῦτο κ.τ.λ. : taken almost exactly from the LXX of Ps. xvii (xviii). 50. In the original David, as the author of the Psalm, is celebrating a victory over the surrounding nations : in the Messianic application Christ is represented as declaring that among the Gentiles, i. e. in the midst of, and therefore together with them, He will praise God. ἐξομολογήσομαι, 'I will praise thee' : cf. xiv. 11.

10. Εὐφράνθητε κ.τ.λ. : from the LXX of Deut. xxxii. 43. The Hebrew, translated literally, appears to mean, ' Rejoice, O ye nations, His people.' Moses is represented as calling on the nations to rejoice over the salvation of Israel. St. Paul takes the words as interpreted by the LXX to imply that the Gentiles and chosen people shall unite in the praise of God.

11. Αἰνεῖτε κ.τ.λ.: Ps. cxvi (cxvii). 1. LXX. An appeal to all nations to praise the Lord.

There are slight variations in the Greek text and in the LXX. For πάντα τὰ ἔθνη τὸν Κύριον C F G L have τὸν Κ. π. τ. ἔ. agreeing with the order of the LXX. ἐπαινεσάτωσαν is read by ℵ A B C D E Chrys. (so LXX A ℵ αἰνεσάτωσαν) ἐπαινέσατε by late MSS. with later LXX MSS.

12. Ἔσται ἡ ῥίζα κ.τ.λ.: from Is. xi. 10, a description of the Messianic kingdom, which is to take the place of that Jewish kingdom which is soon to be destroyed. The quotation follows the LXX, which is only a paraphrase of the Hebrew; the latter runs (RV.) 'And it shall come to pass in that day, that the root of Jesse, which standeth for an ensign of the peoples, unto him shall the Gentiles seek.'

13. The Apostle concludes by invoking on his hearers a blessing—that their faith may give them a life full of joy and peace, that in the power of the Holy Spirit they may abound in hope.

ὁ Θεὸς τῆς ἐλπίδος: cf. ver. 5. The special attribute, as in fact the whole of the benediction, is suggested by the concluding words of the previous quotation.

πάσης χαρᾶς καὶ εἰρήνης. The joy and peace with God which is the result of true faith in the Christian's heart. On εἰρήνη see i. 7.

For πληρῶσαι (most MSS.) B F G have the curious variant πληροφορῆσαι. B reads ἐν πάσῃ χάρᾳ καὶ εἰρήνῃ and omits εἰς τὸ περισσεύειν: the peculiarities of this MS. in the last few verses are noticeable. D E F G omit ἐν τῷ πιστεύειν.

The general question of the genuineness of these last two chapters is discussed in the Introduction (§ 9). It will be convenient to mention in the course of the Commentary some few of the detailed objections that have been made to special passages. In xv. 1-13 the only serious objection is that which was first raised by Baur and has been repeated by others since. The statements in this section are supposed to be of too conciliatory a character; especially is this said to be the case with ver. 8. 'How can we imagine,' writes Baur, 'that the Apostle, in an Epistle of such a nature and after all that had passed on the subject, would make such a concession to the Jewish Christians as to call Jesus Christ a minister of circumcision to confirm the promises of God made to the Fathers?' To this it may be answered that that is exactly the point of view of the Epistle. It is brought out most clearly in xi. 17-25; it is implied in the position of priority always given to the Jew (i. 16; ii. 9, 10); it is emphasized in the stress continually laid on the relations of the new Gospel to the Old Testament (ch. iv, &c.), and the importance of the promises which were fulfilled (i. 2; ix. 4). Baur's difficulty arose from an erroneous conception of the teaching and position of St. Paul. For other arguments see Mangold, *Der Römerbrief*, pp. 81-100.

What sect or party is referred to in Rom. XIV?

There has been great diversity of opinion as to the persons referred to in this section of the Epistle to the Romans, but all commentators seem to agree in assuming that the Apostle is

dealing with certain special circumstances which have arisen in the
Church of Rome, and that the weak and the strong represent two
parties in that Church.

1. The oldest explanation appears to be that which sees in these
disputes a repetition of those which prevailed in the Corinthian
Church, as to the same or some similar form of Judaizing practices
(Orig. Chrys. Aug. Neander, &c.). In favour of this may be
quoted the earlier portion of the fifteenth chapter, where there is
clearly a reference to the distinction between Jewish and Gentile
Christians. But against this opinion it is pointed out that such
Jewish objections to 'things offered to idols,' or to meats killed in
any incorrect manner, or to swine's flesh, have nothing to do with
the typical instances quoted, the abstinence altogether from flesh
meat and from wine (vv. 2, 21).

2. A second suggestion (Eichhorn) is that which sees in these
Roman ascetics the influence of the Pythagorean and other heathen
sects which practised and taught abstinence from meat and wine
and other forms of self-discipline. But these again will not satisfy
all the circumstances. These Roman Christians were, it is said, in
the habit of observing scrupulously certain days: and this custom
did not, as far as we know, prevail among any heathen sect.

3. Baur sees here Ebionite Christians of the character represented by the Clementine literature, and in accordance with his
general theory he regards them as representing the majority of
the Roman Church. That this last addition to the theory is tenable
seems impossible. So far as there is any definiteness in St. Paul's
language he clearly represents the 'strong' as directing the policy
of the community. They are told to receive 'him that is weak in
faith'; they seem to have the power to admit him or reject him.
All that he on his side can do is to indulge in excessive criticism.
Nor is the first part of the theory really more satisfactory. Of
the later Ebionites we have very considerable knowledge derived
from the Clementine literature and from Epiphanius (*Haer.* xxx),
but it is an anachronism to discover these developments in a period
nearly two centuries earlier. Nor again is it conceivable that
St. Paul would have treated a developed Judaism in the lenient
manner in which he writes in this chapter.

4. Less objection perhaps applies to the modification of this
theory, which sees in these sectaries some of the Essene influence
which probably prevailed everywhere throughout the Jewish world
(Ritschl, Mey.-W. Lid. Lft. Gif. Oltr.). This view fulfils the
three conditions of the case. The Essenes were Jewish, they were
ascetic, and they observed certain days. If the theory is put in the
form not that Essenism existed as a sect in Rome, which is highly
improbable, but that there was Essene influence in the Jewish community there, it is possible. Yet if any one compares St. Paul's

language in other Epistles with that which he uses here, he will find it difficult to believe that the Apostle would recommend compliance with customs which arose, not from weak-minded scrupulousness, but from a completely inadequate theory of religion and life. Hort (*Rom. and Eph.*, p. 27 f.) writes: 'The true origin of these abstinences must remain somewhat uncertain: but much the most probable suggestion is that they come from an Essene element in the Roman Church, such as afterwards affected the Colossian Church.' But later he modified his opinion (*Judaistic Christianity*, p. 128): 'There is no tangible evidence for Essenism out of Palestine.'

All these theories have this in common, that they suppose St. Paul to be dealing with a definite sect or body in the Roman Church. But as our examination of the Epistle has proceeded, it has become more and more clear that there is little or no special reference in the arguments. Both in the controversial portion and in the admonitory portion, we find constant reminiscences of earlier situations, but always with the sting of controversy gone. St. Paul writes throughout with the remembrance of his own former experience, and not with a view to special difficulties in the Roman community. He writes on all these vexed questions, not because they have arisen there, but because they may arise. The Church of Rome consists, as he knows, of both Jewish and heathen Christians. These discordant elements may, he fears, unless wise counsels prevail produce the same dissensions as have occurred in Galatia or Corinth.

Hort (*Judaistic Christianity*, p. 126) recognizes this feature in the doctrinal portion of the Epistle: 'It is a remarkable fact,' he writes, 'respecting this Epistle to the Romans . . . that while it discusses the question of the Law with great emphasis and fulness, it does so without the slightest sign that there is a reference to a controversy then actually existing in the Roman Church.' Unfortunately he has not applied the same theory to this practical portion of the Epistle: if he had done so it would have presented just the solution required by all that he notices. 'There is no reference,' he writes, 'to a burning controversy.' 'The matter is dealt with simply as one of individual conscience.' He contrasts the tone with that of the Epistle to the Colossians. All these features find their best explanation in a theory which supposes that St. Paul's object in this portion of the Epistle, is the same as that which has been suggested in the doctrinal portion.

If this theory be correct, then our interpretation of the passage is somewhat different from that which has usually been accepted, and is, we venture to think, more natural. When St. Paul says in ver. 2 'the weak man eateth vegetables,' he does not mean that there is a special sect of vegetarians in Rome; but he takes a typical instance of excessive scrupulousness. When again he says 'one man considers one day better than another,' he does not mean that this sect of vegetarians were also strict sabbatarians, but that the same scrupulousness may prevail in other matters. When he speaks of ὁ φρονῶν τὴν ἡμέραν, ὁ μὴ ἐσθίων he is not thinking of any special body of people but rather of special types. When again in ver. 21 he says: 'It is good not to eat flesh, or drink wine, or do anything in which thy brother is offended,' he does not mean that these vegetarians and sabbatarians are also total abstainers; he merely means 'even the most extreme act of self-denial is better than injuring the conscience of a brother.' He had spoken very similarly in writing to the Corinthians: 'Wherefore, if meat maketh my brother to stumble, I will eat no flesh for ever-more, that I make not my brother to stumble' (1 Cor. viii. 13). It is not considered necessary to argue from these words that absti-nence from flesh was one of the characteristics of the Corinthian sectaries; nor is it necessary to argue in a similar manner here.

St. Paul is arguing then, as always in the Epistle, from past experience. Again and again difficulties had arisen owing to different forms of scrupulousness. There had been the difficulties which had produced the Apostolic decree; there were the difficulties in Galatia, 'Ye observe days, and months, and seasons, and years'; there were the difficulties at Corinth. Probably he had already in his experience come across instances of the various ascetic tenden-cies which are referred to in the Colossian and Pastoral Epistles. We have evidence both in Jewish and in heathen writers of the wide extent to which such practices prevailed. In an age when there is much religious feeling there will always be such ideas. The ferment which the spread of Christianity aroused would create them. Hence just as the difficulties which he had experienced with regard to Judaism and the law made St. Paul work out and systematize his theory of the relation of Christianity to personal righteousness, so here he is working out the proper attitude of the Christian towards over-scrupulousness and over-conscientiousness. He is not dealing with the question controversially, but examining it from all sides.

And he lays down certain great principles. There is, first of all, the fundamental fact, that all these scruples are in matters quite indifferent in themselves. Man is justified by 'faith'; that is sufficient. But then all have not strong, clear-sighted faith: they do not really think such actions indifferent, and if they act against their conscience their conscience is injured. Each man must act as he would do with the full consciousness that he is to appear before God's judgement-seat. But there is another side to the question. By indifference to external observances we may injure another man's conscience. To ourselves it is perfectly indifferent whether we conform to such an observance or not. Then we must conform for the sake of our weak brother. We are the strong. We are conscious of our strength. Therefore we must yield to others: not perhaps always, not in all circumstances, but certainly in many cases. Above all, the salvation of the individual soul and the peace and unity of the community must be preserved. Both alike, weak and strong, must lay aside differences on such unimportant matters for the sake of that church for which Christ died.

APOLOGY FOR ADMONITIONS.

XV. 14–21. *These admonitions of mine do not imply that I am unacquainted with your goodness and deep spiritual knowledge. In writing to you thus boldly I am only fulfilling my duty as Apostle to the Gentiles; the priest who stands before the altar and presents to God the Gentile Churches* (vv. 14–17).

And this is the ground of my boldness. For I can boast of my spiritual labours and gifts, and of my wide activity in preaching the Gospel, and that, not where others had done so before me, but where Christ was not yet named (vv. 18–21).

14. The substance of the Epistle is now finished, and there only remain the concluding sections of greeting and encouragement. St. Paul begins as in i. 8 with a reference to the good report of the church. This he does as a courteous apology for the warmth of feeling he has exhibited, especially in the last section; but a comparison with the Galatian letter, where there is an absence of any such compliment, shows that St. Paul's words must be taken to have a very real and definite meaning.

πέπεισμαι δέ: cf. viii. 38, 'Though I have spoken so strongly it does not mean that I am not aware of the spiritual earnestness of your church.'

καὶ αὐτὸς ἐγὼ περὶ ὑμῶν, ὅτι καὶ αὐτοί: notice the emphasis gained by the position of the words. 'And not I inquire of others to know, but *I myself*, that is, I that rebuke, that accuse you.' Chrys.

μεστοί: cf. Rom. i. 29, where also it is combined with πεπληρωμένοι.

πάσης γνώσεως: 'our Christian knowledge in its entirety.' Cf. 1 Cor. xiii. 2 καὶ ἐὰν ἔχω προφητείαν καὶ εἰδῶ τὰ μυστήρια πάντα καὶ πᾶσαν τὴν γνῶσιν, καὶ ἐὰν ἔχω πᾶσαν τὴν πίστιν κ.τ.λ. γνῶσις is used for the true knowledge which consists in a deep and comprehensive grasp of the real principles of Christianity.

τῆς is read by אBP, Clem.-Alex. Jo.-Damasc. It is omitted by ACDEFGL, &c., Chrys. Theodrt.

ἀγαθωσύνης: cf. 2 Thess. i. 11; Gal. v. 22; Eph. v. 9; used only in the LXX, the N. T. and writings derived from them. Generally it means 'goodness' or 'uprightness' in contrast with κακία, as in Ps. li. (lii.) 5 ἠγάπησας κακίαν ὑπὲρ ἀγαθωσύνην: defined more accurately the idea seems to be that derived from ἀγαθός of active beneficence and goodness of heart. Here it is combined with γνῶσις, because the two words represent exactly the qualities which are demanded by the discussion in chap. xiv. St. Paul demands on the one side a complete grasp of the Christian faith as a whole, and on the other 'goodness of heart,' which may prevent a man from injuring the spiritual life of his brother Christians by disregarding their consciences. Both these were, St. Paul is fully assured, realized in the Roman community.

Forms in -σύνη are almost all late and mostly confined to Hellenistic writers. In the N. T. we have ἐλεημοσύνη, ἀσχημοσύνη, ἁγιωσύνη, ἱερωσύνη, μεγαλωσύνη : see Winer, § xvi. 2 β (p. 118, ed. Moulton).

δυνάμενοι καὶ ἀλλήλους νουθετεῖν. Is it laying too much stress on the language of compliment to suggest that these words give a hint of St. Paul's aim in this Epistle? He has grasped clearly the importance of the central position of the Roman Church and its moral qualities, and he realizes the power that it will be for the instruction of others in the faith. Hence it is to them above all that he writes, not because of their defects but of their merits.

It is difficult to believe that any reader will find an inconsistency between this verse and i. 11 or the exhortations of chap. xiv, whatever view he may hold concerning St. Paul's general attitude towards the Roman Church. It would be perfectly natural in any case that, after rebuking them on certain points on which he felt they needed correction, he should proceed to compliment them for the true knowledge and goodness which their spiritual condition exhibited. He could do so because it would imply a true estimate of the state of the Church, and it would prevent any offence being taken at his freedom of speech. But if the view suggested on chap. xiv. and throughout the Epistle be correct, and these special admonitions arise rather from the condition of the Gentile churches as a whole, the words gain even more point. 'I am not finding fault with you, I am warning you of dangers you may incur, and I warn you especially owing to your prominent and important position.'

15. τολμηρότερον. The boldness of which St. Paul accuses himself is not in sentiment, but in manner. It was ἀπὸ μέρους, 'in part of the Epistle'; vi. 12 ff., 19; viii. 9; xi. 17 ff.; xii. 3; xiii. 3 ff., 13 ff., xiv.; xv. 1, have been suggested as instances.

ἐπαναμιμνήσκων. Wetstein quotes ἕκαστον ὑμῶν, καίπερ ἀκριβῶς εἰδότα, ὅμως ἐπαναμνῆσαι βούλομαι Demosthenes, *Phil.* 74, 7 The ἐπί seems to soften the expression 'suggesting to your memory.' St. Paul is not teaching any new thing, or saying anything which a properly instructed Christian would not know, but putting more clearly and definitely the recognized principles and commands of the Gospel.

διὰ τὴν χάριν τὴν δοθεῖσάν μοι. On St. Paul's Apostolic grace cf. i. 5 δι' οὗ ἐλάβομεν χάριν καὶ ἀποστολήν: xii. 3 λέγω γὰρ διὰ τῆς χάριτος τῆς δοθείσης μοι.

It is probably preferable to read τολμηροτέρως (A B, WH.) for τολμηρό-τερον. The TR. adds ἀδελφοί after ἔγραψα ὑμῖν against the best authorities (ℵ A B C, Boh., Orig. Aug. Chrys.); the position of the word varies even in MSS. in which it does occur. ὑπό is a correction of the TR. for ἀπό (ℵ B F Jo.-Damasc.).

16. λειτουργόν seems to be used definitely and technically as in the LXX of a priest. See esp. 2 Esdras xx. 36 (Neh. x. 37) τοῖς ἱερεῦσι τοῖς λειτουργοῦσιν ἐν οἴκῳ Θεοῦ ἡμῶν. So in Heb. viii. 2 of our Lord, who is ἀρχιερεύς and τῶν ἁγίων λειτουργός: see the note on i. 9. Generally in the LXX the word seems used of the Levites as opposed to the priests as in 2 Esdras xx. 39 (Neh. x. 40) καὶ οἱ ἱερεῖς καὶ οἱ λειτουργοί, but there is no such idea here.

ἱερουργοῦντα, 'being the sacrificing priest of the Gospel of God.' St. Paul is standing at the altar as priest of the Gospel, and the offering which he makes is the Gentile Church.

ἱερουργεῖν means (1) to ' perform a sacred function,' hence (2) especially to 'sacrifice'; and so τὰ ἱερουργήθεντα means ' the slain victims '; and then (3) to be a priest, to be one who performs sacred functions. Its con-struction is two-fold : (1) it may take the accusative of the thing sacrificed ; so Bas. in Ps. cxv καὶ ἱερουργήσω σοι τὴν τῆς αἰνέσεως θυσίαν ; or (2) ἱερουργεῖν τι may be put for ἱερουργόν τινος εἶναι (Galen, de Theriaca μυστη-ρίων ἱερουργόν), so 4 Macc. vii. 8 (v. l.) τοὺς ἱερουργοῦντας τὸν νόμον: Greg. Naz. ἱερουργεῖν σωτηρίαν τινός (see Fri. ad loc. from whom this note is taken).

ἡ προσφορά. With this use of sacrificial language, cf. xii. 1, 2. The sacrifices offered by the priest of the New Covenant were not the dumb animals as the old law commanded, but human beings, the great body of the Gentile Churches. Unlike the old sacrifices which were no longer pleasing to the Lord, these were acceptable (εὐπρόσδεκτος, 1 Pet. ii. 5). Those were animals without spot or blemish; these are made a pure and acceptable offering by the Holy Spirit which dwells in them (cf. viii. 9, 11). For the construction of προσφορά cf. Heb. x. 10 π. τοῦ σώματος 'I. Χρ.

17. ἔχω οὖν τὴν καύχησιν. The τήν should be omitted (see below). 'I have therefore my proper pride, and a feeling of confidence in my position, which arises from the fact that I am a servant of Christ, and a priest of the Gospel of God.' St. Paul is defending his assumption of authority, and he does so on two grounds: (1) His Apostolic mission, διὰ τὴν χάριν τὴν δοθεῖσάν μοι, as proved by his successful labours (vv. 18-20); (2) the sphere of his labours, the Gentile world, more especially that portion of it in which the Gospel had not been officially preached. The emphasis

therefore is on ἐν Χρ. Ἰ., and τὰ πρὸς τὸν θεόν. With καύχησιν cf. iii. 27, 1 Cor. xv. 31; with the whole verse, 2 Cor. x. 13 ἡμεῖς δὲ οὐχὶ εἰς τὰ ἄμετρα καυχησόμεθα . . . 17 ὁ δὲ καυχώμενος ἐν Κυρίῳ καυχάσθω.

The RV. has not improved the text by adding τήν before καύχησιν. The combination ℵ A L P, Boh., Arm., Chrys., Cyr., Theodrt. is stronger than that of B D E F G in this Epistle. C seems uncertain.

18. οὐ γὰρ τολμήσω κ.τ.λ. 'For I will not presume to mention any works but those in which I was myself Christ's agent for the conversion of Gentiles.' St. Paul is giving his case for the assumption of authority (καύχησις). It is only his own labour or rather works done through himself that he cares to mention. But the value of such work is that it is not his own but Christ's working in him, and that it is among Gentiles, and so gives him a right to exercise authority over a Gentile Church like the Roman.

With τολμήσω (ℵ A C D E F G L P, Boh. Harcl., etc.) cf. 2 Cor. x. 12; there seems to be a touch of irony in its use here; with κατειργάσατο 2 Cor. xii. 12, Rom. vii. 13, &c.; with λόγῳ καὶ ἔργῳ, 'in speech or action,' 2 Cor. x. 11.

19. ἐν δυνάμει σημείων κ.τ.λ.: cf. 2 Cor. xii. 12 τὰ μὲν σημεῖα τοῦ ἀποστόλου κατειργάσθη ἐν ὑμῖν ἐν πάσῃ ὑπομονῇ, σημείοις τε καὶ τέρασι καὶ δυνάμεσι: Heb. ii. 4 συνεπιμαρτυροῦντος τοῦ Θεοῦ σημείοις τε καὶ τέρασι καὶ ποικίλαις δυνάμεσι καὶ Πνεύματος Ἁγίου μερισμοῖς κατὰ τὴν αὐτοῦ θέλησιν: 1 Cor. xii. 28.

The combination σημεῖα καὶ τέρατα is that habitually used throughout the N. T. to express what are popularly called miracles. Both words have the same denotation, but different connotations. τέρας implies anything marvellous or extraordinary in itself, σημεῖον represents the same event, but viewed not as an objectless phenomenon but as a sign or token of the agency by which it is accomplished or the purpose it is intended to fulfil. Often a third word δυνάμεις is added which implies that these 'works' are the exhibition of more than natural power. Here St. Paul varies the expression by saying that his work was accomplished in the power of signs and wonders; they are looked upon as a sign and external exhibition of the Apostolic χάρις. See Trench, *Miracles* xci; Fri. *ad loc.*

There can be no doubt that St. Paul in this passage assumes that he possesses the Apostolic power of working what are ordinarily called miracles. The evidence for the existence of miracles in the Apostolic Church is twofold: on the one hand the apparently natural and unobtrusive claim made by the Apostles on behalf of themselves or others to the power of working miracles, on the other the definite historical narrative of the Acts of the Apostles. The two witnesses corroborate one another. Against them it might be argued that the standard of evidence was lax, and that the miraculous and non-miraculous were not sufficiently distinguished. But will the first argument hold against a personal assertion? and does not the narrative of the Acts make it clear that miracles in a perfectly correct sense of the word were definitely intended?

ἐν δυνάμει Πνεύματος Ἁγίου: cf. ver. 13, and on the reading here see below. St. Paul's Apostolic labours are a sign of commission because they have been accompanied by a manifestation of more

than natural gifts, and the source of his power is the Holy Spirit
with which he is filled.

This seems one of those passages in which the value of the text of B
where it is not vitiated by Western influence is conspicuous (cf. iv. 1). It
reads (alone or with the support of the Latin Fathers) πνεύματος without
any addition. אּ L P &c., Orig.-lat. Chrys. &c., add θεοῦ, A C D F G Boh.
Vulg. Arm., Ath. &c. read ἁγίου. Both were corrections of what seemed an
unfinished expression.

ἀπὸ Ἱερουσαλὴμ καὶ κύκλῳ μέχρι τοῦ Ἰλλυρικοῦ. These words
have caused a considerable amount of discussion.

1. The first question is as to the meaning of κύκλῳ.

(1) The majority of modern commentators (Fri. Gif. Mey-W.)
interpret it to mean the country round Jerusalem, as if it were καὶ
τοῦ κύκλῳ, and explain it to mean Syria or in a more confined
sense the immediate neighbourhood of the city. But it may be
pointed out that κύκλῳ in the instances quoted of it in this sense
(Gen. xxxv. 5; xli. 48) seems invariably to have the article.

(2) It may be suggested therefore that it is better to take it as
do the majority of the Greek commentators and the AV. 'from
Jerusalem and round about unto Illyricum.' So Oecumenius κύκλῳ
ἵνα μὴ τὴν κατ' εὐθεῖαν ὁδὸν ἐνθυμηθῇς, ἀλλὰ κατὰ τὰ πέριξ and to the
same effect Chrys. Theodrt. Theophylact. This meaning is exactly
supported by Xen. *Anab.* VII. i. **14** καὶ πότερα διὰ τοῦ ἱεροῦ ὄρους δέοι
πορεύε〜θαι, ἢ κύκλῳ διὰ μέσης τῆς Θρᾴκης, and substantially by Mark
vi. 6.

2. It has also been debated whether the words 'as far as Illyria'
include or exclude that country. The Greek is ambiguous;
certainly it admits the exclusive use. μέχρι θαλάσσης can be used
clearly as excluding the sea. As far as regards the facts the narrative of the Acts (τὰ μέρη ἐκεῖνα Acts xx. 2; cf. Tit. iii. 12) suggests
that St. Paul may have preached in Illyria, but leave it uncertain.
A perfectly tenable explanation of the words would be that if
Jerusalem were taken as one limit and the Eastern boundaries
of Illyria as the other, St. Paul had travelled over the whole of
the intervening district, and not merely confined himself to the
direct route between the two places. Jerusalem and Illyria in fact
represent the limits.

If this be the interpretation of the passage it is less important to
fix the exact meaning of the word Illyria as used here; but a passage
in Strabo seems to suggest the idea which was in St. Paul's mind
when he wrote. Strabo, describing the Egnatian way from the
Adriatic sea-coast, states that it passes through a portion of
Illyria before it reaches Macedonia, and that the traveller along it
has the Illyrian mountains on his left hand. St. Paul would have
followed this road as far as Thessalonica, and if pointing Westward
he had asked the names of the mountain region and of the peoples

inhabiting it, he would have been told that it was 'Illyria.' The
term therefore is the one which would naturally occur to him as
fitted to express the limits of his journeys to the West (Strabo vii.
7. 4).

The word Illyria might apparently be used at this period in two senses.
(1) As the designation of a Roman province it might be used for what was
otherwise called Dalmatia, the province on the Adriatic sea-coast north
of Macedonia and west of Thrace.   (2) Ethnically it would mean the
country inhabited by Illyrians, a portion of which was included in the Roman
province of Macedonia.   In this sense it is used in Appian, *Illyrica* 1, 7;
Jos. *Bell. Iud.* II. xvi. 4; and the passage of Strabo quoted above.

πεπληρωκέναι τὸ εὐαγγέλιον τοῦ Χριστοῦ: cf. Col. i. 25 ἧς ἐγενόμην
ἐγὼ διάκονος κατὰ τὴν οἰκονομίαν τοῦ Θεοῦ τὴν δοθεῖσάν μοι εἰς ὑμᾶς, πληρῶσαι τὸν λόγον τοῦ Θεοῦ. In both passages the meaning is to 'fulfil,'
'carry out completely,' and so in the AV. 'to fully preach.' In
what sense St. Paul could say that he had done this, see below.

20. οὕτω δὲ φιλοτιμούμενον κ.τ.λ. introduces a limitation of the
statement of the previous verses. Within that area there had been
places where he had not been eager to preach, since he cared only
to spread the Gospel, not to compete with others. οὕτω is explained by what follows. φιλοτιμούμενον (1 Thess. iv. 11; 2 Cor.
v. 9) means to 'strive eagerly,' having lost apparently in late Greek
its primary idea of emulation. See Field, *Otium Norv.* iii. p. 100,
who quotes Polyb. i. 83; Diod. Sic. xii. 46; xvi. 49; Plut. *Vit.
Caes.* liv.

ὠνομάσθη: 'so named as to be worshipped.' Cf. 2 Tim. ii. 19;
Isa. xxvi. 13; Amos vi. 10.

ἀλλότριον θεμέλιον. For ἀλλότριον cf. 2 Cor. x. 15, 16. St. Paul
describes his work (1 Cor. iii. 10) as laying a 'foundation stone':
ὡς σοφὸς ἀρχιτέκτων θεμέλιον ἔθηκα· ἄλλος δὲ ἐποικοδομεῖ: and so
generally the Church is built on the foundation of the apostles and
prophets (Eph. ii. 20).

21. ἀλλὰ καθὼς γέγραπται. St. Paul describes the aim of his
mission (the limitations of which he has just mentioned) in words
chosen from the O.T. The quotation which follows is taken
verbally from the LXX of Isa. lii. 15, which differs but not essentially from the Hebrew. The Prophet describes the astonish-
ment of the nations and kings at the suffering of the servant of
Jehovah. 'That which hath not been told them they shall see.'
The LXX translates this 'those to whom it was not told shall see,'
and St. Paul taking these words applies them (quite in accordance
with the spirit of the original) to the extension of the knowledge
of the true Servant of Jehovah to places where his name has not
been mentioned.

Verses 19-21, or rather a portion of them (ὥστε με . . . ἀλλά), are still
objected to by commentators (as by Lipsius) who recognize the futility of

the objections to the chapter as a whole. In a former case (xi. 8-10) the clumsiness of an excision suggested by Lipsius was noticed and here he has not been any happier. He omits ver. 20, but keeps the quotation in ver. 21, yet this quotation is clearly suggested by the preceding words οὐχ ὅπου ὠνομάσθη Χριστός. It would be strange if an interpolator were to make the sequence of thought more coherent.

The general objections to the passage seem to be—

(1) It is argued that St. Paul had never preached in Jerusalem, nor would have been likely to mention that place as the starting-point of his mission ; that these words therefore are a 'concession made to the Jewish Christians,' and hence that the chapter is a result of the same conciliation tendency which produced the Acts. Most readers would probably be satisfied with being reminded that according to the Acts St. Paul had preached in Jerusalem (Acts ix. 28, 29). But it may be also pointed out that St. Paul is merely using the expression geographically to define out the limits within which he had preached the Gospel ; while he elsewhere (Rom. xi. 26) speaks of Sion as the centre from which the Gospel has gone forth.

(2) It is asserted that St. Paul had never preached in Illyricum. There is some inconsistency in first objecting to the language of this passage because it agrees with that of the Acts, and then criticizing it because it contains some statement not supported by the same book. But the reference to Illyricum has been explained above. The passages of the Acts quoted clearly leave room for St. Paul having preached in districts inhabited by Illyrians. He would have done so if he had gone along the Egnatian way. But the words do not necessarily mean that he had been in Illyria, and it is quite possible to explain them in the sense that he had preached as far as that province and no further. In no case do they contain any statement inconsistent with the genuineness of the passage.

(3) It is objected that St. Paul could in no sense use such a phrase as πεπληρωκέναι τὸ εὐαγγέλιον. But by this expression he does not mean that he had preached in every town or village, but only that everywhere there were centres from which Christianity could spread. His conception of the duties of an Apostle was that he should found churches and leave to others to build on the foundation thus laid (1 Cor. iii. 7, 10). As a matter of fact within the limits laid down Christianity had been very widely preached. There were churches throughout all Cilicia (Acts xv. 41), Galatia, and Phrygia (Gal. i. 1 ; Acts xviii. 23). The three years' residence in Ephesus implied that that city was the centre of missionary activity extending throughout all the province of Asia (Acts xix. 10) even to places not visited by St. Paul himself (Col. ii. 1). Thessalonica was early a centre of Christian propaganda (1 Thess. i. 7, 8 ; iv. 10), and later St. Paul again spent some time there (Acts xx. 2). The Second Epistle to the Corinthians contains in the greeting the words σὺν τοῖς ἁγίοις πᾶσι τοῖς οὖσιν ἐν ὅλῃ τῇ Ἀχαίᾳ, showing that the long residence at Corinth had again produced a wide extension of the Gospel. As far as the Adriatic coast St. Paul might well have considered that he had fulfilled his mission of preaching the Gospel, and the great Egnatian road he had followed would lead him straight to Rome.

(4) A difficulty is found in the words 'that I may not build on another man's foundation.' It is said that St. Paul has just expressed his desire to go to Rome, that in fact he expresses this desire constantly (i. 5, 13 ; xii. 3 ; xv. 15), but that here he states that he does not wish to build on another man's foundation ; how then it is asked could he wish to go to Rome where there was already a church ? But there is no evidence that Christianity had been officially or systematically preached there (Acts xxviii. 22), and only a small community was in existence, which had grown up chiefly as composed of settlers from other places. Moreover, St. Paul specially says that it is for the sake of mutual grace and encouragement that he wishes to go there ; he

implies that he does not wish to stay long, but desires to press on further
westward (ver. 24).

THE APOSTLE'S PLANS.

XV. 22–33. *I have been these many times hindered from
coming to you, although I have long eagerly desired it. Now
I hope I may accomplish my wish in the course of a journey
to Spain. But not immediately. I must first take to Jerusalem the contributions sent thither by Macedonia and
Achaia—a generous gift, and yet but a just recompense for
the spiritual blessings the Gentile Churches have received
from the Jews. When this mission is accomplished I hope
I may come to you on my way to Spain* (vv. 22–29).

*Meantime I earnestly ask your prayers for my own
personal safety and that the gifts I bear may be received by
the Church. I shall then, if God will, come to you with
a light heart, and be refreshed by your company. May the
God of peace make His peace to light upon you* (vv. 30–33).

22. διὸ καί. The reason why St. Paul had been so far prevented
from coming to Rome was not the fear that he might build on
another man's foundation, but the necessity of preaching Christ in
the districts through which he had been travelling ; now there was
no region untouched by his apostolic labours, no further place for
action in those districts. ἐνεκοπτόμην : Gal. v. 7 ; 1 Th. ii. 18 ;
1 Pet. iii. 7.

τὰ πολλά, 'these many times,' i. e. all the times when I thought
of doing so, or had an opportunity, as in the RV. ; not, as most
commentators, 'for the most part' (Vulg. *plerumque*). πολλάκις,
which is read by Lips. with B D E F G, is another instance of
Western influence in B.

23. νυνὶ δὲ μηκέτι τόπον ἔχων, 'seeing that I have no longer
opportunity for work in these regions.' τόπον, as in xii. 19, q.v. ;
Eph. iv. 27 ; Heb. xii. 17, 'opportunity,' 'scope for action.' κλίμασι,
'tracts' or 'regions' (2 Cor. xi. 10 ; Gal. i. 21 ; often in Polybius).

ἐπιποθίαν does not occur elsewhere ; but ἐπιποθεῖν (Rom. i. 11 ;
2 Cor. v. 2 ; ix. 14 ; Phil. i. 8 ; ii. 26 ; 1 Th. iii. 6 ; 2 Tim. i. 4 ;
James iv. 5 ; 1 Pet. ii. 2) and ἐπιπόθησις (2 Cor. vii. 7, 11) are not
uncommon. On its signification, 'a longing desire,' see on i. 11.

ἱκανῶν : a very favourite word in the Acts of the Apostles (ix. 23 ;
xviii. 18, &c.). 'It is likely enough that St. Paul's special interest
in the Christian community at Rome, though hardly perhaps his

knowledge of it, dates from his acquaintance with Aquila and
Priscilla at Corinth.   This was somewhere about six years before
the writing of the Epistle to the Romans, and that interval would
perhaps suffice to justify his language about having desired to visit
them ἀπὸ ἱκανῶν ἐτῶν (a rather vague phrase, but not so strong as
the ἀπὸ πολλῶν ἐτῶν, which was easily substituted for it)' Hort,
Rom. and Eph. p. 11.

For ἐπιποθίαν δὲ ἔχων Western authorities (D F G) read ἔχω, an attempt
to correct the grammar of the sentence. ἱκανῶν, read by B C 37. 59. 71,
Jo.-Damasc., is probably right for πολλῶν, which is supported by all other
authorities and is read by R.V.

24. In this verse the words ἐλεύσομαι πρὸς ὑμᾶς, which are inserted
by the TR. after Σπανίαν, must be omitted on conclusive manuscript
evidence, while γάρ must as certainly be inserted after ἐλπίζω.
These changes make the sentence an anacolouthon, almost exactly
resembling that in v. 12 ff., and arising from very much the same
causes.   St. Paul does not finish the sentence because he feels that
he must explain what is the connexion between his visit to Spain
and his desire to visit Rome, so he begins the parenthesis ἐλπίζω γάρ.
Then he feels he must explain the reason why he does not start at
once ; he mentions his contemplated visit to Jerusalem and the
purpose of it.   This leads him so far away from the original
sentence that he is not able to complete it ; but in ver. 28 he
resumes the main argument, and gives what is the logical, but not
the grammatical, apodosis (cf. v. 18).

ὡς ἂν πορεύωμαι.   The ὡς ἄν is temporal : cf. Phil. ii. 23 ; 1 Cor.
xi. 34 : on this latter passage Evans, in *Speaker's Comm.* p. 328,
writes : 'When I come : rather *according as I come* : the presence of
the ἄν points to uncertainty of the time and of the event : for this
use comp. Aesch. *Eum.* 33 μαντεύομαι γάρ ὡς ἂν ἡγῆται θεός.'

προπεμφθῆναι : 1 Cor. xvi. 6, 11 ; 2 Cor. i. 16 ; need not mean
more than to be sent forward on a journey with prayers and good
wishes.   The best commentary on this verse is ch. i. 11 ff.

Lipsius again strikes out vv. 23, 24 and below in ver. 28 δι' ὑμῶν
εἰς τὴν Σπανίαν—a most arbitrary and unnecessary proceeding.
The construction of the passage has been explained above and is
quite in accordance with St. Paul's style, and the desire to pass
further west and visit Spain is not in any way inconsistent with
the desire to visit Rome.   The existence of a community there
did not at all preclude him from visiting the city, or from
preaching in it ; but it would make it less necessary for him to
remain long.   On the other hand, the principal argument against
the genuineness of the passage, that St. Paul never did visit Spain
(on which see below ver. 28), is most inconclusive ; a forger would
never have interpolated a passage in order to suggest a visit to
Spain which had never taken place. But all such criticism fails

absolutely to realize the width and boldness of St. Paul's schemes. He must carry the message of the Gospel ever further. Nothing will stop him but the end of his own life or the barrier of the ocean.

25. St. Paul now mentions a further reason which will cause some delay in his visit to Rome, and his missionary journey to Spain.

διακονῶν τοῖς ἁγίοις : cf. 2 Cor. viii. 4 τὴν κοινωνίαν τῆς διακονίας τῆς εἰς τοὺς ἁγίους. The expression 'ministering to the saints' has become almost a technical expression in St. Paul for the contributions made by the Gentile Christians to the Church at Jerusalem.

26. εὐδόκησαν implies that the contribution was voluntary, and made with heartiness and good-will: see on Rom. x. 1 (εὐδοκία); 1 Cor. i. 21 ; Gal. i. 15.

κοινωνίαν : of a collection or contribution 2 Cor. viii. 4 ; ix. 13 ἁπλότητι τῆς κοινωνίας εἰς αὐτοὺς καὶ εἰς πάντας and κοινωνεῖν Rom. xii. 13 ταῖς χρείαις τῶν ἁγίων κοινωνοῦντες.

πτωχούς : cf. Gal. ii. 10 μόνον τῶν πτωχῶν ἵνα μνημονεύωμεν. On the poor Christians at Jerusalem see James ii. 2 ff. ; Renan, *Hist. des Origines*, &c. vol. iv. ch. 3. In Jerusalem the Sadducees, who were the wealthy aristocracy, were the determined opponents of Christianity, and there must have been in the city a very large class of poor who were dependent on the casual employment and spasmodic alms which are a characteristic of a great religious centre. The existence of this class is clearly implied in the narrative at the beginning of the Acts of the Apostles. There was from the very first a considerable body of poor dependent on the Church, and hence the organization of the Christian community with its lists (1 Tim. v. 19) and common Church fund (ἀπὸ τοῦ κοινοῦ Ign. *Ad Polyc.* iv. 3) and officers for distributing alms (Acts vi. 1–4) must have sprung up very early.

27. εὐδόκησαν κ.τ.λ. St. Paul emphasizes the good-will with which this contribution was made by repeating the word εὐδόκησαν ; he then points out that in another sense it was only the repayment of a debt. The Churches of the Gentiles owed all the spiritual blessings they enjoyed to that of Jerusalem, 'from whom is Christ according to the flesh,' and they could only repay the debt by ministering in temporal things.

πνευματικοῖς ... σαρκικοῖς. Both are characteristically Pauline words. 1 Cor. ix. 11 εἰ ἡμεῖς ὑμῖν τὰ πνευματικὰ ἐσπείραμεν, μέγα εἰ ἡμεῖς ὑμῶν τὰ σαρκικὰ θερίσομεν ; σαρκικοῖς is used without any bad association.

ἐκοινώνησαν. The word κοινωνέω, of which the meaning is of course 'to be a sharer or participator in,' may be used either of the giver or of the receiver. The giver shares with the receiver by giving contributions, so Rom. xii. 13 (quoted on ver. 26) ; the receiver with the giver by receiving contributions, so here. The normal construction in the N. T. is as here with the dative : once (Heb. ii. 14) it is used with the genitive, and this construction is common in the O. T. (Lft. on Gal. vi. 6).

The contributions for the poor in Jerusalem are mentioned in Rom. xv. 26, 27; 1 Cor. xvi. 1–3; 2 Cor. ix. 1 ff; Acts xxiv. 17, and form the subject of the ablest and most convincing section in Paley's *Horae Paulinae*. Without being in any way indebted to one another, and each contributing some new element, all the different accounts fit and dovetail into one another, and thus imply that they are all historical. 'For the singular evidence which this passage affords of the genuineness of the Epistle, and what is more important, as it has been impugned, of this chapter in particular, see Paley's *Horae Paulinae*, chap. ii. No. 1.' Jowett, *ad loc.*, and for some further reff. see Introd. § 4.

28. ἐπιτελέσας ... σφραγισάμενος. St. Paul resumes his argument and states his plans after the digression he has just made on what lies in the immediate future. With ἐπιτελέσας (a Pauline word), cf. Phil. i. 6; it was used especially of the fulfilment of religious rites (Heb. ix. 6 and in classical authors), and coupled with λειτουργῆσαι above, suggests that St. Paul looks upon these contributions of the Gentile communities as a solemn religious offering and part of their εὐχαριστία for the benefits received.

σφραγισάμενος, 'having set the seal of authentication on.' The seal was used as an official mark of ownership: hence especially the expression 'the seal of baptism' (2 Cor. i. 22; Eph. i. 13; see on iv. 11). Here the Apostle implies that by taking the contributions to Jerusalem, and presenting them to the Church, he puts the mark on them (as a steward would do), showing that they are the fruit to the Church of Jerusalem of those spiritual blessings (πνευματικά) which through him had gone forth to the Gentile world.

εἰς τὴν Σπανίαν. It has been shown above that it is highly probable that St. Paul should have desired to visit Spain, and that therefore nothing in these verses throws any doubt on the authenticity of the chapter as a whole or of any portions of it. A further question arises, Was the journey ever carried out? Some fresh light is perhaps thrown on the question by Professor Ramsay's book *The Church and the Empire*. If his arguments are sound, there is no reason to suppose that if St. Paul was martyred at Rome (as tradition seems to suggest) he must necessarily have suffered in what is ordinarily called the Neronian persecution. He might have been beheaded either in the later years of Nero's reign or even under Vespasian. So that, if we are at liberty to believe that he survived his first imprisonment, there is no need to compress, as has been customary, the later years of his missionary activity.

It is on these assumptions easier to find room for the Spanish journey. Have we evidence for it? Dismissing later writers who seem to have had no independent evidence, our authorities are reduced to two, the Muratorian Fragment on the Canon, and Clement of Rome. We cannot lay much stress on the former; it is possible perhaps that the writer had independent knowledge, but it is certainly more probable that he is merely drawing a conclusion, and not quite a correct one, from this Epistle: the words are *sed et profectionem Pauli ab urbe ad Spaniam proficiscentis*. The passage in Clement (§ 5) runs as follows: Παῦλος ὑπομονῆς βραβεῖον ὑπέδειξεν, ἑπτάκις δεσμὰ φορέσας, φυγαδευθείς, λιθασθείς, κῆρυξ γενόμενος ἔν τε τῇ ἀνατολῇ καὶ ἐν τῇ δύσει, τὸ γενναῖον τῆς πίστεως αὐτοῦ κλέος ἔλαβεν, δικαιοσύνην διδάξας ὅλον τὸν κόσμον καὶ ἐπὶ τὸ τέρμα τῆς δύσεως ἐλθών, καὶ μαρτυρήσας ἐπὶ τῶν ἡγουμένων, οὕτως ἀπηλλάγη τοῦ κόσμου καὶ εἰς τὸν ἅγιον τόπον ἐπορεύθη. This passage is much stronger, and Lightfoot's note in favour of interpreting the words τὸ τέρμα τῆς δύσεως as meaning Spain is very weighty; but is it quite certain that a Jew, as Clement probably was (according to Lightfoot himself), speaking of St. Paul another Jew would not look upon Rome relatively to Jerusalem as the τέρμα τῆς δύσεως, 'the western limit'? We in England might for example speak of Athens as being in the Eastern Mediterranean. There is also some force in Hilgenfeld's argument that ἐλθών and μαρτυρήσας should be taken together. For these reasons the question whether St. Paul ever visited Spain must remain very doubtful.

29. πληρώματι : see on xi. 12. St. Paul feels confident that his visit to Rome will result in a special gift of Christ's blessing. He will confer on the Church a χάρισμα πνευματικόν, and will in his turn be comforted by the mutual faith which will be exhibited. Cf. i. **11, 12.**

It has been pointed out how strongly these words make for the authenticity and early date of this chapter. No one could possibly write in this manner at a later date, knowing the circumstances under which St. Paul actually did visit Rome. See also ver. 32 ἵνα ἐν χαρᾷ ἐλθὼν πρὸς ὑμᾶς διὰ θελήματος Θεοῦ συναναπαύσωμαι ὑμῖν.

The TR. reads with א° L &c., Vulg.-clem. Syrr. Arm., Chrys. Theodrt. εὐλογίας τοῦ εὐαγγελίου τοῦ Χρ. The words τοῦ εὐ. τοῦ should be omitted on decisive authority.

30. The reference to his visit to Jerusalem reminds St. Paul of the dangers and anxieties which that implies, and leads him to conclude this section with an earnest entreaty to the Roman Christians to join in prayers on his behalf. Hort (*Rom. and Eph.* pp. 42-46) points out how this tone harmonizes with the dangers that the Apostle apprehended (cf. Acts xx. 17-38, xxi. 13, &c.): 'We cannot here mistake the twofold thoughts of the Apostle's mind. He is full of eager anticipation of visiting Rome with the full blessing of the accomplishment of that peculiar ministration.

But he is no less full of misgivings as to the probability of escaping
with his life ' (p. 43).

διὰ τῆς ἀγάπης τοῦ Πνεύματος. That brotherly love which is one
of the fruits of the Spirit working in us (cf. Gal. v. 22). That
πνεῦμα is personal is shown by the parallelism with the first clause.

συναγωνίσασθαι. ' He breaks off afresh in an earnest entreaty to
them to join him in an intense energy of prayer, wrestling as it were '
(Hort, *op. cit.* p. 43). They will as it were take part in the contest
that he must fight by praying on his behalf to God, for all prayer
is a spiritual wrestling against opposing powers. So of our Lord's
agony in the garden: Luke xxii. 44; Matt. xxvi. 42. Cp. Origen
ad loc.: *Vix enim invenies, ut oranti cuiquam non aliquid inanis et
alienae cogitationis occurrat, et intentionem, qua in Deum mens diri-
gitur, declinet ac frangat, atque eam per ea quae non competit, rapiat.
Et ideo agon magnus est orationis, ut obsistentibus inimicis, et orationis sensum in diversa rapientibus, fixa ad Deum semper mens stabili
intentione contendat, ut merito possit etiam ipse dicere: certamen
bonum certavi, cursum consummavi.*

31. The Apostle's fear is double. He fears the attacks upon
himself of the unbelieving Jews, to whom more than any other
Christian teacher he was an object of hatred: and he is not certain
whether the peace-offering of the Gentile Churches which he was
bearing to Jerusalem would be accepted as such by the narrow
Jewish Christians at Jerusalem. How strong the first feeling was
and how amply justified the Acts of the Apostles show (Acts xx. 3,
22; xxi. 11).

In ver. 30 ἀδελφοί is omitted by B 76, Aeth., Chrys. alone, but perhaps
correctly. In ver. 31 ἡ δωροφορία for διακονία, and ἐν Ἱερουσαλήμ for εἰς Ἰ.
are instances of Western paraphrase shared by B (B D F G).

32. But the prayer that the Roman Christians offer for St. Paul
will also be a prayer for themselves. If his visit to Jerusalem be
successful, and his peace-offering be accepted, he will come to
Rome with stronger and deeper Christian joy. ' After the personal
danger and the ecclesiastical crisis of which the personal danger
formed a part' (Hort) he hopes to find rest in a community as yet
untroubled by such strife and distraction.

συναναπαύσωμαι, 'I may rest and refresh my spirit with you.'
Only used here in this sense (but later in Hegesippus *ap*. Eus.
H. E. IV. xxii. 2). Elsewhere it is used of sleeping together
(Is. xi. 6). The unusual character of the word may have been the
cause of its omission in B and the alteration in some Western MSS.
(see below).

There are several variations of reading in this verse:
(1) אַ A C, Boh. Arm., Orig.-lat. read ἐλθὼν . . . συναναπαύσωμαι with
some variation in the position of ἐλθών (after ἵνα א, Boh., Orig.-lat.; after
χαρᾷ A C agreeing in this with other authorities). All later MSS. with the

Western group read ἔλθω and insert καί before συναναπαύσωμαι. B is alone in having ἔλθω and omitting συναναπαύσωμαι ὑμῖν, but receives support in the reading of some Western authorities; D E read ἀναψύξω μεθ᾽ ὑμῶν, F G ἀναψύχω μ. ὑ., agreeing with most Latin authorities, *refrigerer vobiscum*.

(2) For διὰ θελήματος Θεοῦ (A C L P, Vulg. Syrr. Boh. Arm., Orig.-lat. Chrys. Thdrt.), ℵ Ambrst. have δ. θ. Ἰησοῦ Χριστοῦ, D E F G (with d e f g), fuld. Χριστοῦ Ἰησοῦ, B Κυρίου Ἰησοῦ. Lightfoot (*On a fresh Revision*, &c., pp. 106 ff.) suggests that the original reading was θελήματος used absolutely of the Divine will: cf. Rom. ii. 18; 1 Cor. xvi. 12. See also his note on Ign. *Eph.* § 20, *Rom.* § 1 (where some authorities add τοῦ Θεοῦ, others *domini*), Smyrn. §§ 1, 11. Elsewhere in St. Paul the expression always is θέλημα Θεοῦ, except once, Eph. v. 17 τὸ θέλημα τοῦ Κυρίου.

33. ὁ δὲ Θεὸς τῆς εἰρήνης: cf. ver. 5. St. Paul concludes his request for a prayer with a prayer of his own for them. ‘Peace,’ a keynote of the Epistle, is one of his last thoughts.

A F G and some minuscules omit ἀμήν. On the importance ascribed to this word by some commentators see the Introduction, § 9.

PERSONAL GREETINGS.

XVI. 1–16. *I commend to you Phoebe our sister. Receive her as becometh members of a Christian Church. For she has stood by many others, and myself as well* (vv. 1, 2).

Greet Prisca and Aquila. Greet all those whose names or persons I know, who are members of your community (vv. 3–16).

1. συνίστημι. The ordinary word for to ‘commend,’ ‘introduce’; see on iii. 5, a derivative of which appears in the phrase συστατικαὶ ἐπιστολαί (2 Cor. iii. 1; for its use in the later ecclesiastical writings see Suicer, *Thesaurus*). These letters played a very large part in the organization of the Church, for the tie of hospitality (cf. xii. 13), implying also the reception to communion, was the great bond which united the separate local Churches together, and some protection became necessary against imposture.

Φοίβην. Nothing is otherwise known of Phoebe, nor can we learn anything from the name. She was presumably the bearer of this letter.

διάκονον, ‘a deaconess.’ The only place in which this office is referred to by name in the N. T. (for 1 Tim. iii. 11, v. 3 ff. cannot be quoted). The younger Pliny (*Ep.* X. xcvi. 8) speaks of *ministrae: quo magis necessarium credidi ex duabus ancillis, quae ministrae dicebantur, quid esset veri et per tormenta quaerere.* They do not appear elsewhere to be referred to in any certain second-century writing; but constant reference to them occurs in the *Apostolic*

Constitutions, in the earlier books under the name of διάκονος (ii. 26; iii. 15), in the later of διακόνισσα (viii. 19, 20, 28). Of the exact relation of the 'deaconess' to the 'widows' (1 Tim. v. 3) it is not necessary to speak, as we have no sufficient evidence for so early a date; it is quite clear that later they were distinct as bodies, and that the widows were considered inferior to the deaconesses (*Apost. Const.* iii. 7); it is probable however that the deaconesses were for the most part chosen from the widows. That the reference to a 'deaconess' is in no sense an anachronism may be inferred both from the importance of διακονία in the early Church, which had quite clearly made it necessary for special male officials to be appointed, and from the separate and secluded life of women. From the very beginning of Christianity—more particularly in fact at the beginning —there must have been a want felt for women to perform for women the functions which the deacons performed for men. Illustrations of this need in baptism, in visiting the women's part of a house, in introducing women to the deacon or bishop, may be found in the *Apostolical Constitutions* (iii. 15, &c.). So much is clear. An office in the Church of this character, we may argue on *à priori* grounds, there must have been; but an order in the more ecclesiastical sense of the term need not have existed. διάκονος is technical, but need hardly be more so than is προστάτις in ver. 2. (The arguments of Lucht against the authenticity of portions of these two verses are examined very fully by Mangold, *Der Römerbrief und seine geschichtlichen Voraussetzung*, pp. 136 ff.)

τῆς ἐκκλησίας τῆς ἐν Κεγχρεαῖς. Cenchreae was the port of Corinth on the Saronic Gulf. During St. Paul's stay at Corinth that city had become the centre of missionary activity throughout all Achaia (cf. 2 Cor. i. 1), and the port towards Ephesus, a place where there must have been many Jews living, could easily be a centre of the Christian Church. Its position would afford particularly an opportunity for the exercise by Phoebe of the special duties of hospitality.

2. ἀξίως τῶν ἁγίων, 'in a manner worthy of the saints,' i. e. 'of the Church.' Not only to provide for her wants, but to admit her to every spiritual privilege as ' in the Lord.'

προστάτις, a 'succourer' or 'helper'; this almost technical word is suggested by παραστῆτε. It is the feminine form of προστάτης, used like the Latin *patronus* for the legal representative of the foreigner. In Jewish communities it meant the legal representative or wealthy patron: see Schürer, *Die Gemeinde-Verfassung*, &c., Ins. 31: ενθαδε κειτε | γαις προστατης | οσιος εζηςεν | ετη οβ εν ειρη | κοιμηςις ςοy, cf. also *C. I. G.* 5361. We also find the word used of an office-bearer in a heathen religious association, see Foucart, *Associations Religieuses*, p. 202, Ins. 20, line 34 (= *C. I. G.* 126) δοκιμαζέτω δὲ ὁ προστάτης καὶ ὁ ἀρχιερανιστὴς καὶ ὁ γραμματεὺς καὶ οἱ ταμίαι καὶ σύνδικοι. Here the expression suggests that Phoebe was a person of some wealth and position who was thus able to act as patroness of a small and struggling community.

3. Πρίσκαν καὶ 'Ακύλαν. So the MSS. here by preponderating authority for Πρίσκιλλα κ. 'A. Priscilla is a diminutive for Prisca, and both are Roman names.

In Acts xviii. 2 the reading is 'Ακύλαν ... καὶ Πρίσκιλλαν γυναῖκα αὐτοῦ, in ver. 18 Πρίσκιλλα καὶ 'Ακύλας; in 1 Cor. xvi. 19 'Ακύλας καὶ Πρίσκα (so א B M P, Boh., but A C D E F G, &c., Vulg. Syrr. Πρίσκιλλα); in 2 Tim. iv. 19 Πρίσκαν καὶ 'Ακύλαν (by preponderating authority). The fact that Prisca is so often mentioned first suggests that she was the more important of the two.

4. οἵτινες ... τὸν ἑαυτῶν τράχηλον κ.τ.λ. probably refers to some great danger which they had run on his behalf. It may have been the great tumult at Ephesus, although this was somewhat recent. If so the danger then incurred may have been the reason that they had left that city and returned for a time to Rome. The special reference to the Churches of the Gentiles perhaps arises from the fact that, owing to their somewhat nomadic life, they were well known to many Christian Churches.

Aquila and Priscilla.

The movements of Aquila and Priscilla have been considered to be so complicated as to throw doubts on the authenticity of this section of the Epistle, or to suggest that it was addressed not to the Church at Rome, but to the Church of Ephesus.

From Acts xviii. 1, 2 we learn that Aquila was a Jew of Pontus. He and his wife Prisca had been compelled to leave Rome in 52 A.D. by the decree of Claudius. They retired to Corinth, where they first became acquainted with St. Paul. With him they went to Ephesus, where they remained some time; they were there when the first Epistle to the Corinthians was written, and had a church in their house (ἀσπάζεται ὑμᾶς ἐν Κυρίῳ πολλὰ 'Ακύλας καὶ Πρίσκα σὺν τῇ κατ' οἶκον αὐτῶν ἐκκλησίᾳ 1 Cor. xvi. 19). This Epistle was written probably about twelve months before the Epistle to the Romans. In 2 Tim. iv. 19, written in all probability at least eight years later, they appear again at Ephesus.

Now, is not the life ascribed to them too nomadic? And is not the coincidence of the church in their house remarkable? The answer is that a nomadic life was the characteristic of Jews at that day, and was certainly a characteristic of Aquila and Priscilla (Lightfoot, *Biblical Essays*, p. 299, and Renan, *Les Apôtres*, pp. 96, 97, Zahn, *Skizzen*, p. 169). We know that although Aquila was a Jew of Pontus, yet he and his wife lived, within the space of a few years, at Rome, at Corinth, and at Ephesus. Is it then extremely improbable that they should travel in after years, probably for the sake of their business? And if it were so, would they not be likely to make their house, wherever they were, a place in which Christians could meet together? On à priori grounds we cannot argue against the possibility of these changes. Are there any positive arguments for connecting them with the Roman Church? De Rossi, in the course of his archaeological investigations, has suggested two traces of their influence, both of which deserve investigation.

(i) Amongst the older churches of Rome is one on the Aventine bearing the name of St. Prisca, which gives a title to one of the Roman Cardinals. Now there is considerable evidence for connecting this with the names of Aquila and Priscilla. In the *Liber Pontificalis*, in the life of Leo III (795–816), it is described as the 'titulus Aquilae et Priscae' (Duchesne, *Lib. Pont.* II. p. 20); in the legendary *Acts of St. Prisca* (which apparently date from the tenth century) it is stated that the body of St. Prisca was translated from the place on the Ostian road where she had been buried, and transferred to the church of St. Aquila and Prisca on the Aventine (*Acta Sanctorum*, Jan. Tom. ii. p. 187 *et deduxerunt ipsam ad urbem Romam cum hymnis et canticis spiritualibus, iuxta Arcum Romanum in ecclesia sanctorum Martyrum Aquilae et Priscae*), and the tradition is put very clearly in an inscription apparently of the tenth century which formerly stood over the door of the church (*C. Ins. Christ.* ii. p. 443):

> *Haec domus est Aquilae seu Priscae Virginis Almae*
> *Quos lupe Paule tuo ore vehis domino*
> *Hic Petre divini Tribuebas fercula verbi*
> *Sepius hocce loco sacrificans domino.*

Many later testimonies are referred to by De Rossi, but they need not here be cited.

For the theory that this church is on the site of the house of Prisca and Aquila, De Rossi finds additional support in a bronze diploma found in 1776 in the garden of the church bearing the name of G. Marius Pudens Cornelianus: for in the legendary Acts of Pudens, Pudenziana, and Praxedis, Priscilla is stated to have been the mother of Pudens (*Acta Sanct.* Mai. Tom. iv. p. 297), and this implies some connexion between the names of Aquila and Priscilla and the family of Pudens.

The theory is a plausible one, but will hardly at present stand examination. In the first place the name of Aquila and Priscilla (or Prisca) is not the oldest borne by the church; from the fourth to the eighth century it seems always to have been the *titulus S. Priscae* (see *Liber Pontificalis*, ed. Duchesne, i. 501, 517[45]), and although the origin of this name is itself doubtful, it is hardly likely that if the locality had borne the name of Aquila and Priscilla, that name would first have been lost and then revived. It is much more probable that the later name is an attempt to connect the biblical account with this spot and to explain the origin of the name of Prisca.

Nor is the second piece of evidence of any greater weight. The acts of Pudens and his daughters, supposed to be narrated by the person called St. Pastor, who was a contemporary of Pius the bishop and addressed his letters to Timothy, are clearly legendary, and little or no stress can be laid on the mention of Priscilla as the mother of Pudens. The object of the Acta is in fact to invent a history for martyrs whose names were known, and who were for some reason grouped together. But why were they thus grouped? The reason probably is given in the statement at the end, that they were buried in the cemetery of Priscilla. These names would probably be found in the fourth century in that cemetery, attached to graves close to one another, and would form the groundwork of the *Acta*. There may still be some connexion between the names, which may or may not be discovered, but there is not at present any historical evidence for connecting the *titulus St. Priscae* with the Aquila and Priscilla of the N. T. (see de Rossi, *Bull. Arch. Christ.* Ser. i. No. 5 (1867), p. 45 ff.)

(ii) A second line of argument seems more fruitful. The explorations of De Rossi in the *Coemeterium Priscillae*, outside the *Porta Salaria*, have resulted in the discovery that as the *Coemeterium Domitillae* starts from a burying-place of Domitilla and her family, so that of Priscilla originates in the burying-place of Acilius Glabrio and other members of the Acilian gens. This seems to corroborate the statement of Dio Cassius (lxvii. 14) that the

Acilius Glabrio who was consul with Trajan in A. D. 91 was a Christian and
died as such, and implies that Christianity had penetrated into this as into
other leading Roman families. Now the connexion with the subject immediately
before us is as follows. The same researches have shown that a name of
the females of the Acilian gens is Priscilla or Prisca. For instance, in one
inscription we read:

M' ACILIUS V . . . . .
C. V.
PRISCILLA . . C

Aquila was a Jew of Pontus: how then does it happen that his wife, if not
he himself, bore a Roman name? The answer seems to be suggested by
these discoveries. They were freedmen of a member of the Acilian gens,
as Clemens the Roman bishop was very probably the freedman of Flavius
Clemens. The name Prisca or Priscilla would naturally come to an adherent of the family. The origin of the name Aquila is more doubtful, but
it too might be borne by a Roman freedman. If this suggestion be correct,
then both the names of these two Roman Christians and the existence of
Christianity in a leading Roman family are explained.

Two other inscriptions may be quoted, as perhaps of interest. The first
is clearly Christian:

AQUILIAE PRISCAE IN PACE

The second C. I. L. vi. 12273 may be so. The term *Renata* might suggest
that it is but also might be Mithraic:

D. M.
AQUILIA · RENATA
QVAE · V · A · N . . .
SE · VIVA · POSVIT · SIBI
CVRANTE · AQVILIO   IVSTO
ALVMNO · ET · AQVILIO
PRISCO · FRATRE

The argument is not demonstrative, but seems to make the return of
Aquila and Priscilla to Rome, and their permanent connexion with the
Roman Church, probable. See De Rossi, *Bull. Arch. Christ.* Ser. iv.
No. 6 (1888-9), p. 129 *Aquila e Prisca et gli Acilii Glabrioni.*

Dr. Hort (*Rom. and Eph.* pp. 12-14), following a suggestion made by
Dr. Plumptre (*Biblical Studies*, p. 417), points out that it is a curious fact
that in four out of the six places in which the names occur that of the wife is
the first mentioned. He connects the name with the cemetery of St. Prisca,
and suggests that Prisca was herself a member of some distinguished Roman
family. He points out that only Aquila is called a Jew from Pontus, not
his wife. There is nothing inconsistent in this theory with that of the
previous argument; and if it be true much is explained. It may however be
suggested that for a noble Roman lady to travel about with a Jewish husband
engaged in mercantile or even artisan work is hardly probable; and that the
theory which sees in them freed members of a great household is perhaps
the most probable.

5. καὶ τὴν κατ' οἶκον αὐτῶν ἐκκλησίαν. There is no decisive
evidence until the third century of the existence of special buildings
used for churches. The references seem all to be to places in
private houses, sometimes very probably houses of a large size. In
the N.T. we have first of all (Acts xii. 12) the house of Mary, the
mother of John, where many were collected together and praying.
Col. iv. 15 ἀσπάσασθε τοὺς ἐν Λαοδικείᾳ ἀδελφούς, καὶ Νυμφᾶν, καὶ τὴν

κατ' οἶκον αὐτῶν ἐκκλησίαν: Philemon 2 καὶ τῇ κατ' οἶκόν σου ἐκκλησίᾳ:
besides 1 Cor. xvi. 19.   At a later date we have Clem. *Recog.* x. 71
Theophilus, domus suae ingentem basilicam ecclesiae nomine consecraret:
De Rossi, *Roma Sott.* i. p. 209 *Collegium quod est in domo Sergiae
Paulinae.*   So in Rome several of the oldest churches appear to
have been built on the sites of houses used for Christian worship.
So perhaps San Clemente is on the site of the house of T. Flavius
Clemens the consul (see Lightfoot, *Clement.* p. 94).

There is no reason to suppose that this Church was the meeting-
place of all the Roman Christians; similar bodies seem to be
implied in vv. 14, 15.   We may compare *Acta Iustini Martyris* § 2
(Ruinart) where however the speaker is of course intentionally
vague: *Quaesivit Praefectus, quem in locum Christiani convenirent.
Cui respondit Iustinus, eo unumquemque convenire quo vellet ac posset.
An, inquit, existimas omnes nos in eumdem locum convenire solitos?
Minime res ita se habet ... Tunc praefectus: Age, inquit, dicas,
quem in locum conveniatis, et discipulos tuos congreges.   Respondit
Iustinus: Ego prope domum Martini cuiusdam, ad balneum cogno-
mento Timiotinum, hactenus mansi.*

Ἐπαίνετος.   Of him nothing is known: the name is not an uncommon one and occurs in inscriptions from Asia Minor, *C. I. G.*
2953 (from Ephesus), 3903 (from Phrygia).   The following in-
scription from Rome is interesting, *C. I. L.* vi. 17171 DIS · MAN |
EPAENETI (*sic*) | EPAENETI . F | EPHESIO | T · MVNIVS | PRIS-
CIANVS | AMICO SVO.

ἀπαρχὴ τῆς Ἀσίας: i. e. one of the first converts made in the
Roman province of Asia: cp. 1 Cor. xvi. 15 οἴδατε τὴν οἰκίαν Στεφανᾶ,
ὅτι ἐστὶν ἀπαρχὴ τῆς Ἀχαίας, καὶ εἰς διακονίαν τοῖς ἁγίοις ἔταξαν ἑαυτούς.
On the importance of first converts see Clem. Rom. § xlii κατὰ χώρας
οὖν καὶ πόλεις κηρύσσοντες καθίστανον τὰς ἀπαρχὰς αὐτῶν, δοκιμάσαντες τῷ
πνεύματι, εἰς ἐπισκόπους καὶ διακόνους τῶν μελλόντων πιστεύειν.

This name caused great difficulty to Renan, 'What! had all the
Church of Ephesus assembled at Rome?' 'All' when analyzed is
found to mean three persons of whom two had been residents at
Rome, and the third may have been a native of Ephesus but is
only said to have belonged to the province of Asia (cf. Lightfoot,
Biblical Essays, p. 301).   How probable it was that there should
be foreigners in Rome attached to Christianity may be illustrated
from the Acts of Justin which were quoted in the note on an
earlier portion of the verse.   These give an account of the
martyrdom of seven persons, Justin himself, Charito, Charitana,
Euelpistus, Hierax, Liberianus, and Paeon.   Of these Justin we
know was a native of Samaria, and had probably come to Rome
from Ephesus, Euelpistus who was a slave of the Emperor was
a native of Cappadocia, and Hierax was of Iconium in Phrygia.
This was about 100 years later.

'Aσίας is supported by preponderating authority (אABCDFG, Vulg. Boh. Arm. Aeth., Orig.-lat. Jo.-Damasc. Ambrst.) against 'Aχαίας (LP &c., Syrr., Chrys. Theodrt.).

For the idea of illustrating this chapter from inscriptions we are of course indebted to Bishop Lightfoot's able article on Caesar's household (*Philippians,* p. 169). Since that paper was written, the appearance of a portion of vol. vi. of the *Corpus* of Latin Inscriptions, that, namely, containing the inscriptions of the city of Rome, has both provided us with more extensive material and also placed it in a more convenient form for reference. We have therefore gone over the ground again, and either added new illustrations or given references to the Latin *Corpus* for inscriptions quoted by Lightfoot from older collections. Where we have not been able to identify these we have not, except in a few cases, thought it necessary to repeat his references. A large number of these names are found in *Columbaria* containing the monuments and ashes of members of the imperial household during the first century : these special collections are kept together in the *Corpus* (vi. 3926-8397). There is also a very large section devoted to other names belonging to the *domus Augusti* (vi. 8398-9101). A complete use of these materials will not be possible until the publication of the *Indices* to vol. vi. For a discussion of the general bearing of these references, see Introduction, § 9.

6. Mαρίαν (which is the correct reading) may like Mαριάμ be Jewish, but it may also be Roman. In favour of the latter alternative in this place it may be noticed that apparently in other cases where St. Paul is referring to Jews he distinguishes them by calling them his kinsmen (see on ver. 7). The following inscription from Rome unites two names in this list, *C. I. L.* vi. 22223 D · M · | MARIAE | AMPLIATAE *cet.* ; the next inscription is from the household, ib. 4394 MARIAE · M · L · XANTHE | NYMPHE · FEC · DE · SVO.

ἥτις πολλὰ ἐκοπίασεν εἰς ὑμᾶς. This note is added, not for the sake of the Roman Church, but as words of praise for *Maria* herself.

Mαρίαν is read by A B C P, Boh. Arm. ; Mαριάμ by א D E F G L, &c., Chrys. The evidence for εἰς ὑμᾶς, which is a difficult reading, is preponderating (א A B C P, Syrr. Boh.), and it is practically supported by the Western group (D E F G, Vulg.), which have ἐν ὑμῖν. The correction εἰς ἡμᾶς is read by L, Chrys. and later authorities.

7. 'Aνδρόνικον: a Greek name found among members of the imperial household. The following inscription contains the names of two persons mentioned in this Epistle, both members of the household, *C. I. L.* vi. 5326 DIS · MANIBVS | C. IVLIVS · HERMES | VIX · ANN · XXXIII · M · V | DIEB · XIII | C · IVLIVS · ANDRONICVS | CONLIBERTVS · FEC | BENE · MERENTI · DE · SE: see also 5325 and 11626 where it is the name of a slave.

'Iουνίαν: there is some doubt as to whether this name is masculine, 'Iουνίας or 'Iουνιᾶς, a contraction of Junianus, or feminine Junia. Junia is of course a common Roman name, and in that case the two would probably be husband and wife ; Junias on the other hand is less usual as a man's name, but seems to represent a form of contraction common in this list, as Patrobas,

Hermas, Olympas. If, as is probable, Andronicus and Junias are included among the Apostles (see below) then it is more probable that the name is masculine, although Chrysostom does not appear to consider the idea of a female apostle impossible : ' And indeed to be apostles at all is a great thing. But to be even amongst these of note, just consider what a great encomium this is ! But they were of note owing to their works, to their achievements. Oh ! how great is the devotion of this woman, that she should be even counted worthy of the appellation of apostle ! '

τοὺς συγγενεῖς μου. St. Paul almost certainly means by ' kinsmen,' fellow-countrymen, and not relations. The word is used in this sense in ix. 3, and it would be most improbable that there should be so many relations of St. Paul amongst the members of a distant Church (vv. 7, 11) and also in Macedonia (ver. 21); whereas it is specially significant and in accordance with the whole drift of the Epistle that he should specially mention as his kinsmen those members of a Gentile Church who were Jews.

καὶ συναιχμαλώτους μου. Probably to be taken literally. Although St. Paul had not so far suffered any long imprisonment, he had certainly often been imprisoned for a short time as at Philippi, 2 Cor. xi. 23 ἐν φυλακαῖς περισσοτέρως ; Clem. Rom. ad Cor. v ἑπτάκις δεσμὰ φορέσας. Nor is it necessary that the word should mean that Andronicus and Junias had suffered at the same time as St. Paul; he might quite well name them fellow-prisoners if they had like him been imprisoned for Christ's sake. Metaphorical explanations of the words are too far-fetched to be probable.

οἵτινές εἰσιν ἐπίσημοι ἐν τοῖς ἀποστόλοις may mean either (1) well known to the Apostolic body, or (2) distinguished as Apostles. In favour of the latter interpretation, which is probably correct, are the following arguments. (i) The passage was apparently so taken by all patristic commentators. (ii) It is in accordance with the meaning of the words. ἐπίσημος, lit. ' stamped,' ' marked,' would be used of those who were selected from the Apostolic body as ' distinguished,' not of those known to the Apostolic body, or looked upon by the Apostles as illustrious ; it may be translated ' those of mark among the Apostles.' (iii) It is in accordance with the wider use of the term ἀπόστολος. Bp. Lightfoot pointed out (Galatians, p. 93) that this word was clearly used both in a narrow sense of ' the twelve ' and also in a wider sense which would include many others. His views have been corroborated and strengthened by the publication of the Didache. The existence of these 'Apostles,' itinerant Christian Evangelists, in Rome will suggest perhaps one of the methods by which the city had been evangelized.

οἳ καὶ πρὸ ἐμοῦ γεγόνασιν ἐν Χριστῷ. Andronicus and Junias had been converted before St. Paul : they therefore belonged to the earliest days of the Christian community; perhaps even they were of those who during the dispersion after the death of Stephen began almost immediately to spread the word in Cyprus and Syria (Acts xi. 19). As Dr. Weymouth points out (*On the Rendering into English of the Greek Aorist and Perfect*, p. 26) the perfect should here be translated 'were.'

> 'It is utterly amazing,' he writes, 'that in Rom. xvi. 7 οἳ καὶ πρὸ ἐμοῦ γεγόνασιν ἐν Χρ. is rendered in the RV. "who also have been in Christ before me." The English idiom is here simply outraged. What officer in our Navy or Army would not stare at the βάρβαρος who should say of a senior officer, "He has been in the Service before me"? "He was in the Navy before me" is the only correct English form. . . . The English mind fastens on the idea of time defined by "before me," and therefore uses the simple Past. . . . The *Greek* Perfect is correctly employed, because it is intended to convey, and does convey, the idea that they are still in Christ, while the English "have been" suggests precisely the contrary.'

8. Ἀμπλιᾶτος is the more correct reading for the abbreviated form Ἀμπλιᾶς which occurs in the TR. This is a common Roman slave name, and as such occurs in inscriptions of the imperial household. *C. I. L.* vi. 4899 AMPLIATVS | RESTITVTO · FRATRI | SVO · FECIT · MERENTI : 5154 C. VIBIVS · FIRMVS · C | VIBIO · AMPLIATO | PATRONO · SVO, &c., besides inscriptions quoted by Lft. But there is considerable evidence for connecting this name more closely with the Christian community in Rome. In the cemetery of Domitilla, now undoubtedly recognized as one of the earliest of Christian catacombs, is a chamber now known by the name of 'Ampliatus' owing to an inscription which it contains. This chamber is very early : pre-Christian in character if not in origin. The cell over which the name of Ampliatus is inscribed is a later insertion, which, from the style of its ornament, is ascribed to the end of the first or beginning of the second century. The inscription is in bold, well-formed letters of the same date. Not far off is another inscription, not earlier than the end of the second century, to members of apparently the same family. The two inscriptions are AMPLIAT[I] and AVRELIAE · BONIFATIAE | CONIVGI · INCOMPARABILI | VERAE CASTITATIS FEMINAE | QVAE · VIXIT · ANN · XXV · M · II | DIEB · IIII · HOR · VI | AVREL · AMPLIATVS CVM | GORDIANO · FILIO. The boldness of the lettering in the first inscription is striking. The personal name without any other distinction suggests a slave. Why then should any one in these circumstances receive the honour of an elaborately painted tomb? The most plausible explanation is that he was for some reason very prominent in the earliest Roman Church. The later inscription clearly suggests that there was a Christian family bearing this name ; and the connexion with Domitilla seems to show that here we have the name of a slave or freedman through whom Christianity had penetrated into a second great Roman household. See de Rossi, *Bull. Arch. Christ.* Ser. iii. vol. 6 (1881), pp. 57–74; *Athenaeum*

March 4, 1884, p. 289; the inscription is just referred to by Light-foot, *Clement.* i. p. 39.

9. Οὐρβανός: a common Roman slave name found among members of the household, *C. I. L.* vi. 4237 (quoted by Lft. from Murat. 920. 1) VRBANVS · LYDES · AVG · L · DISPENS | INMVNIS · DAT · HERMAE · FRATRI · ET | CILICAE · PATRI : cf. 5604, 5605, and others, quoted by Lft. (Grut. p. 589. 10, p. 1070. 1).

τὸν συνεργὸν ἡμῶν. Where St. Paul is speaking of personal friends he uses the singular τὸν ἀγαπητόν μου: here he uses the plural because Urbanus was a fellow-worker with all those who worked for Christ.

Στάχυν: a rare Greek name, but found among members of the imperial household : *C. I. L.* vi. 8607 D. M. | M. VLPIO · AVG · L | EROTI | AB · EPISTVLIS · GRAECIS | EPAPHRODITVS | ET · STACHYS | CAESAR · N̄ · SER | FRATRI · KARISSIMO · ET | CLAVDIA · FORMIANA | FECERVNT : cf. also inscriptions quoted by Lft.

10. Ἀπελλῆν. Again a name borne by members of the house-hold and by Jews: amongst others by the famous tragic actor. See the instance quoted by Lft. and cf. Hor. *Sat.* I. v. 100 *Credat Iudaeus Apella, non ego.*

τὸν δόκιμον: cf. 1 Cor. xi. 19; 2 Cor. x. 18; xiii. 7. One who has shown himself an approved Christian.

τοὺς ἐκ τῶν Ἀριστοβούλου. The explanation of this name given by Lft. bears all the marks of probability. The younger Aristo-bulus was a grandson of Herod the Great, who apparently lived and died in Rome in a private station (Jos. *Bell. Iud.* II. xi. 6; *Antiq.* XX. i. 2); he was a friend and adherent of the Emperor Claudius. His household would naturally be οἱ Ἀριστοβούλου, and would presumably contain a considerable number of Jews and other orientals, and consequently of Christians. If, as is probable, Aristobulus was himself dead by this time, his household would probably have become united with the imperial household. It would, however, have continued to bear his name, just as we find servants of Livia's household who had come from that of Maecenas called Maecenatiani (*C. I. L.* vi. 4016, 4032), those from the house-hold of Amyntas, Amyntiani (4035, cf. 8738): so also Agrippiani, Germaniciani. We might in the same way have *Aristobuliani* (cf. Lft. *Phil.* pp. 172, 3).

11. Ἡρῳδίωνα τὸν συγγενῆ μου. A mention of the household of Aristobulus is followed by a name which at once suggests the Herod family, and is specially stated to have been that of a Jew. This seems to corroborate the argument of the preceding note.

τοὺς ἐκ τῶν Ναρκίσσου, ʻthe household of Narcissus,ʼ ʻNarcis-siani.ʼ The Narcissus in question was very possibly the well-known freedman of that name, who had been put to death by Agrippina shortly after the accession of Nero some three or four

years before (Tac. *Ann.* xiii. 1; Dio Cass. lx. 34). His slaves
would then in all probability become the property of the Emperor,
and would help to swell the imperial household. The name is
common, especially among slaves and freedmen, cf. *C. I. L.* vi. 4123
(in the household of Livia), 4346, 5206 HELICONIS NARCISSI |
AVGVSTIANI | : 22875 NARCISSVS · AVG · LIB. Lft. quotes also
the two names Ti. Claudius Narcissus (see below), Ti. Iulius Narcissus from Muratori, and also the form Narcissianus, TI · CLAVDIO ·
SP · F · NARCISSIANO (Murat. p. 1150. 4). The following inscrip-
tion belongs to a somewhat later date : *C. I. L.* vi. 9035 D. M. |
T · FLAVIVS · AVG · LIB | NARCISSVS · FECIT · SIBI | ET · COELIAE ·
SP · FILIAE | IERIAE · CONIVGI · SVAE . . . , and lower down T
FLAVIVS · AVG · LIB · FIRMVS · NARCISSIANVS | RELATOR · AVC-
TIONVM · MONVMENTVM · REFECIT. See also 9035 a. (Lightfoot,
Phil. p. 173.)

Dr. Plumptre (*Biblical Studies*, p. 428) refers to the following interesting
inscription. It may be found in *C. I. L.* v. 154* being reputed to have come
from Ferrara. D. M. | CLAVDIAE | DICAEOSYNAE | TI · CLAVDIVS | NAR-
CISSVS | LIB. AEID. COIV | PIENTISSIMAE | ET FRVGALISSI | B. M. Tiberius
Claudius suggests the first century, but the genuineness of the Ins. is not
sufficiently attested. The editor of the fifth volume of the *Corpus* writes :
*Testimonia auctorum aut incertorum . . . aut fraudulentorum de loco cum
parum defendant titulum eum exclusi, quamquam fieri potest ut sit
genuinus nec multum corruptus.* The name *Dicaeosyne* is curious but is
found elsewhere *C. I. L.* iii. 2391; vi. 25866 : x. 649. There is nothing distinctively Christian about it.

12. Τρύφαιναν καὶ Τρυφῶσαν are generally supposed to have been
two sisters. Amongst inscriptions of the household we have
4866 D. M. | VARIA · TRYPHOSA | PATRONA · ET | M. EPPIVS ·
CLEMENS | : 5035 D. M. | TRYPHAENA | VALERIA · TRYPHAENA
| MATRI · B · M · F · ET | VALERIUS · FVTIANVS (quoted by Lft.
from *Acc. di Archeol.* xi. p. 375): 5343 TELESPHORVS · ET · TRY-
PHAENA, 5774, 6054 and other inscriptions quoted by Lft. Attention is drawn to the contrast between the names which imply
'delicate,' 'dainty,' and their labours in the Lord.

The name Tryphaena has some interest in the early history of the Church
as being that of the queen who plays such a prominent part in the story of
Paul and Thecla, and who is known to have been a real character.

Περσίδα. The name appears as that of a freedwoman, *C. I. L.* vi.
23959 DIS · MANIB | PER · SIDI · L · VED | VS · MITHRES | VXORI.
It does not appear among the inscriptions of the household.

13. Ῥοῦφον : one of the commonest of slave names. This Rufus
is commonly identified with the one mentioned in Mark xv. 21,
where Simon of Cyrene is called the father of Alexander and Rufus.
St. Mark probably wrote at Rome, and he seems to speak of
Rufus as some one well known.

τὸν ἐκλεκτὸν ἐν Κυρίῳ. 'Elect' is probably not here used in the technical sense 'chosen of God,'—this would not be a feature to distinguish Rufus from any other Christian,—but it probably means 'eminent,' 'distinguished for his special excellence,' and the addition of ἐν Κυρίῳ means 'eminent as a Christian' (2 Jo. 1 ; 1 Pet. ii. 6). So in English phraseology the words 'a chosen vessel' are used of all Christians generally, or to distinguish some one of marked excellence from his fellows.

καὶ τὴν μητέρα αὐτοῦ καὶ ἐμοῦ. St. Paul means that she had showed him on some occasion all the care of a mother, and that therefore he felt for her all the affection of a son.

14. Ἀσύγκριτον: the following inscription is of a freedman of Augustus who bore this name, *C. I. L.* vi. 12565 D. M. | ASYNCRETO | AVG · LIB · FECIT · FL | AVIA · SVCCESSA | PATRONO BENE | MERENTI. The name Flavia suggests that it is somewhat later than St. Paul's time.

Φλέγοντα. The inscriptions seem to throw no light on this name. The most famous person bearing it was the historian of the second century who is referred to by Origen, and who gave some information concerning the Christians.

Ἑρμῆν: one of the commonest of slave names, occurring constantly among members of the imperial household.

Πατρόβαν. An abbreviated form of Patrobius. This name was borne by a well-known freedman of Nero, who was put to death by Galba (Tac. *Hist.* i. 49 ; ii. 95). Lft. quotes instances of other freedmen bearing it: TI · CL · AVG · L · PATROBIVS (Grut. p. 610. 3), and TI · CLAVDIO · PATROBIO (Murat. p. 1329).

Ἑρμᾶς is likewise an abbreviation for various names, Hermagoras, Hermerus, Hermodorus, Hermogenes. It is common among slaves, but not so much so as Hermes. Some fathers and modern writers have identified this Hermas with the author of the 'Shepherd,' an identification which is almost certainly wrong.

καὶ τοὺς σὺν αὐτοῖς ἀδελφούς. This and the similar expression in the next verse seem to imply that these persons formed a small Christian community by themselves.

15. Φιλόλογος. A common slave name. Numerous instances are quoted from inscriptions of the imperial household : *C. I. L.* vi. 4116 DAMA · LIVIAE · L · CAS . . . | PHOEBVS · PHILOLOGI | quoted by Lft. from Gorius, *Mon. Liv.* p. 168 ; he also quotes Murat. p. 1586. 3, p. 2043. 2 ; Grut. p. 630. 1. He is generally supposed to be the brother or the husband of Julia, in the latter case Nereus, his sister Nerias, and Olympas may be their children.

Ἰουλίαν. Probably the commonest of all Roman female names, certainly the commonest among slaves in the imperial household. The following inscription is interesting : *C. I. L.* vi. 20416 D. M. | IVLIAE NEREI · F · | CLAVDIAE. The name Julia Tryphosa occurs 20715–7 in one case apparently in a Christian inscription.

Νηρέα. This name is found in inscriptions of the imperial household, *C. I. L.* vi. 4344 NEREVS · NAT · GERMAN | PEVCENNVS · GERMANICI | ANVS · NERONIS · CAESARIS. It is best known in the Roman Church in connexion with the Acts of Nereus and Achilleus, the eunuch chamberlains of Domitilla (see *Acta Sanctorum* May. iii. p. 2 ; *Texte und Untersuchungen*, Band xi. Heft 2). These names were, however, older than that legend, as seems to be shown by the inscription of Damasus (*Bull. Arch. Christ.* 1874, p. 20 sq. ; *C. Ins. Christ.* ii. p. 31) which represents them as soldiers. The origin of the legend was probably that in the catacomb of Domitilla and near to her tomb, appeared these two names very prominently ; this became the groundwork for the later romance. An inscription of Achilleus has been found in the cemetery of Domitilla on a stone column with a corresponding column which may have borne the name of Nereus : both date from the fourth or fifth century (*Bull. Arch. Christ.* 1875, p. 8 sq.). These of course are later commemorations of earlier martyrs, and it may well be that the name of Nereus was in an early inscription (like that of Ampliatus above). In any case the name is one connected with the early history of the Roman Church ; and the fact that Nereus is combined with Achilleus, a name which does not appear in the Romans, suggests that the origin of the legend was archaeological, and that it was not derived from this Epistle (Lightfoot, *Clement.* i. p. 51 ; Lipsius *Apokr. Apgesch.* ii. 106 ff.).

Ὀλυμπᾶς : an abbreviated form like several in this list, apparently for Ὀλυμπιόδωρος.

16. ἐν φιλήματι ἁγίῳ : so 1 Thess. v. 26 ; 1 Cor. xvi. 20 ; 2 Cor. xiii. 12 ; 1 Pet. v. 14 ἀσπάσασθε ἀλλήλους ἐν φιλήματι ἀγάπης. The earliest reference to the 'kiss of peace' as a regular part of the Christian service is in Just. Mart. *Apol.* i. 65 ἀλλήλους φιλήματι ἀσπαζόμεθα παυσάμενοι τῶν εὐχῶν. It is mentioned in Tert. *de Orat.* 14 (*osculum pacis*) ; Const. Apost. ii. 57. 12 ; viii. 5. 5 ; and it became a regular part of the Liturgy. Cf. Origen *ad loc.* : *Ex hoc sermone, aliisque nonnullis similibus, mos ecclesiis traditus est, ut post orationes osculo se invicem suscipiant fratres. Hoc autem osculum sanctum appellat Apostolus.*

αἱ ἐκκλησίαι πᾶσαι τοῦ Χριστοῦ : this phrase is unique in the N.T. Phrases used by St. Paul are αἱ ἐκκλησίαι τῶν ἁγίων, ἡ ἐκκλησία τοῦ θεοῦ, αἱ ἐκκλησίαι τοῦ θεοῦ, ταῖς ἐκκλησίαις τῆς Ἰουδαίας ταῖς ἐν Χριστῷ (Gal. i. 22), τῶν ἐκκλησίων τοῦ θεοῦ τῶν οὐσῶν ἐν τῇ Ἰουδαίᾳ ἐν Χριστῷ Ἰησοῦ, and in Acts xx. 28 we have the uncertain passage τὴν ἐκκλησίαν τοῦ Κυρίου or τοῦ Θεοῦ, where Θεός must, if the correct reading, be used of Χριστός. It is a habit of St. Paul to speak on behalf of the churches as a whole : cf. xvi. 4 ; 1 Cor. vii. 17 ; xiv. 33 ; 2 Cor. viii. 18 ; xi. 28 ; and Hort suggests that this unique phrase is used to express 'the way in which the Church of Rome was an object of love and respect to Jewish and Gentile Churches alike' (*Rom. and Eph.* i. 52).

WARNING AGAINST FALSE TEACHERS.

XVI. 17–20. *Beware of those breeders of division and mischief-makers who pervert the Gospel which you were taught. Men such as these are devoted not to Christ but to their own unworthy aims. By their plausible and flattering speech they deceive the unwary. I give you this warning, because your loyalty is well known, and I would have you free from every taint of evil. God will speedily crush Satan beneath your feet.*

May the grace of Christ be with you.

17–20. A warning against evil teachers probably of a Jewish character. Commentators have felt that there is something unusual in a vehement outburst like this, coming at the end of an Epistle so completely destitute of direct controversy. But after all as Hort points out (*Rom. and Eph.* pp. 53–55) it is not unnatural. Against errors such as these St. Paul has throughout been warning his readers indirectly, he has been building up his hearers against them by laying down broad principles of life and conduct, and now just at the end, just before he finishes, he gives one definite and direct warning against false teachers. It was probably not against teachers actually in Rome, but against such as he knew of as existing in other churches which he had founded, whose advent to Rome he dreads.

It has been suggested again that 'St. Paul finds it difficult to finish.' There is a certain truth in that statement, but it is hardly one which ought to detain us long. When a writer has very much to say, when he is full of zeal and earnestness, there must be much which will break out from him, and may make his letters somewhat formless. To a thoughtful reader the suppressed emotion implied and the absence of regular method will really be proofs of authenticity. It may be noted that we find in the Epistle to the Philippians just the same characteristics: there also in iii. 1, just apparently as he is going to finish the Epistle, the Apostle makes a digression against false teachers.

17. σκοπεῖν, 'to mark and avoid.' The same word is used in Phil. iii. 17 συμμιμηταί μου γίνεσθε, ἀδελφοί, καὶ σκοπεῖτε τοὺς οὕτω περιπατοῦντας in exactly the opposite sense, 'to mark so as to follow.'

διχοστασίαι: cf. Gal. v. 20. Those divisions which are the result of the spirit of strife and rivalry (ἔρις and ζῆλος) and which eventually if persisted in lead to αἱρέσεις. The σκάνδαλα are the hindrances to Christian progress caused by these embittered relations.

τὴν διδαχήν, not 'Paulinism,' but that common basis of Christian doctrine which St. Paul shared with all other teachers (1 Cor. xv. 1), and with which the teaching of the Judaizers was in his opinion inconsistent.

ἐκκλίνατε: cf. Rom. iii. 11. The ordinary construction is with ἀπό and the genitive (a) of the cause avoided ἀπὸ κακοῦ (1 Pet. iii. 11), or (b) of the person.

18. These false teachers are described as being self-interested in their motives, specious and deceptive in their manners. Cf. Phil. iii. 19 ὧν τὸ τέλος ἀπώλεια, ὧν ὁ θεὸς ἡ κοιλία, καὶ ἡ δόξα ἐν τῇ αἰσχύνῃ αὐτῶν, οἱ τὰ ἐπίγεια φρονοῦντες.

τῇ ἑαυτῶν κοιλίᾳ. These words do not in this case appear to mean that their habits are lax and epicurean, but that their motives are interested, and their conceptions and objects are inadequate. So Origen: Sed et quid causae sit, qua iurgia in ecclesiis suscitantur, et lites, divini Spiritus instinctu aperit. Ventris, inquit, gratia: hoc est, quaestus et cupiditatis. The meaning is the same probably in the somewhat parallel passages Phil. iii. 17-21; Col. ii. 20-iii. 4. So Hort (Judaistic Christianity, p. 124) explains ταπεινοφροσύνη to mean 'a grovelling habit of mind, choosing lower things as the primary sphere of religion, and not τὰ ἄνω, the region in which Christ is seated at God's right hand.'

χρηστολογίας καὶ εὐλογίας, 'fair and flattering speech.' In illustration of the first word all commentators quote Jul. Capitolinus, Pertinax 13 (in Hist. August): χρηστολόγον eum appellantes qui bene loqueretur et male faceret. The use of εὐλογία which generally means 'praise,' 'laudation,' or 'blessing' (cp. xv. 29), in a bad sense as here of 'flattering' or 'specious' language is rare. An instance is quoted in the dictionaries from Aesop. Fab. 229, p. 150, ed. Av. ἐὰν σὺ εὐλογίας εὐπορῇς ἔγωγέ σου οὐ κήδομαι.

19. ἡ γὰρ ὑμῶν ὑπακοή. 'I exhort and warn you because your excellence and fidelity although they give me great cause for rejoicing increase my anxiety.' These words seem definitely to imply that there were not as yet any dissensions or erroneous teaching in the Church. They are (as has been noticed) quite inconsistent with the supposed Ebionite character of the Church. When that theory was given up, all ground for holding these words spurious was taken away.

θέλω δὲ ὑμᾶς. St. Paul wishes to give this warning without at the same time saying anything to injure their feelings. He gives it because he wishes them to be discreet and wary, and therefore blameless. In Matt. **x.** 16 the disciples are to be φρόνιμοι and ἀκέραιοι: see also Phil. ii. 15.

20. ὁ δὲ Θεὸς τῆς εἰρήνης. See on xv. 13. It is the 'God of peace' who will thus overthrow Satan, because the effect of these divisions is to break up the peace of the Church.

συντρίψει: 'will throw him under your feet, that you may trample upon him.'

τὸν Σατανᾶν. In 2 Cor. xi. 14 St. Paul writes 'for even Satan fashioneth himself into an angel of light. It is no great thing therefore if his ministers also fashion themselves as ministers of righteousness.' The ministers of Satan are looked upon as impersonating Satan himself, and therefore if the Church keeps at peace it will trample Satan and his wiles under foot.

ἡ χάρις κ.τ.λ. St. Paul closes this warning with a salutation as at the end of an Epistle.

There is very considerable divergence in different authorities as to the benedictions which they insert in these concluding verses.

(1) The TR. reads in ver. 20 ἡ χάρις τοῦ Κυρίου ἡμῶν Ἰησοῦ [Χριστοῦ] μεθ' ὑμῶν.

This is supported by ℵ A B C L P, &c., Vulg. &c., Orig.-lat.

It is omitted by D E F G Sedul.

(2) In ver. 24 it reads ἡ χάρις τοῦ Κυρίου ἡμῶν Ἰ. Χ. μετὰ πάντων ὑμῶν. ἀμήν.

This is omitted by ℵ A B C, Vulg. codd. (am. fuld. harl.) Boh. Aeth. Orig.-lat.

It is inserted by D E F G L, &c., Vulg. Harcl. Chrys. &c. Of these F G L omit vv. 25–27, and therefore make these words the end of the Epistle.

(3) A third and smaller group puts these words at the end of ver. 27: P. 17. 80, Pesh. Arm. Ambrstr.

Analyzing these readings we find:

ℵ A B C, Orig.-lat. have a benediction at ver. 21 only.

D E F G have one at ver. 24 only.

L, Vulg. clem., Chrys., and the mass of later authorities have it in both places.

P has it at ver. 21, and after ver. 27.

The correct text clearly has a benediction at ver. 21 and there only; it was afterwards moved to a place after ver. 24, which was very probably in some MSS. the end of the Epistle, and in later MSS., by a natural conflation, appears in both.   See the Introduction, § 9.

GREETINGS OF ST. PAUL'S COMPANIONS.

XVI. 21–23. *All my companions—Timothy, Lucius, Jason, and Sosipater—greet you. I Tertius, the amanuensis, also give you Christian greeting. So too do Gaius, and Erastus, treasurer of Corinth, and Quartus.*

21–23. These three verses form a sort of postscript, added after

the conclusion of the letter and containing the names of St. Paul's
companions.

21. Τιμόθεος had been with St. Paul in Macedonia (2 Cor. i. 1):
of his movements since then we have no knowledge. The μου
with συνεργός is omitted by B.

Λούκιος might be the Lucius of Cyrene mentioned Acts xiii. 1.
Ἰάσων is probably the one mentioned in Acts xvii. 5-7, 9 as
St. Paul's host, and Σωσίπατρος may be the same as the Σώπατρος
of Acts xx. 4, who was a native of Berea. If these identifications
are correct, two of these three names are connected with Macedonia, and this connexion is by no means improbable. They had
attached themselves to St. Paul as his regular companions, or
come to visit him from Thessalonica. In any case they were
Jews (οἱ συγγενεῖς μου cf. ver. 7). It was natural that St. Paul
should lodge with a fellow-countryman.

22. ὁ γράψας. St. Paul seems generally to have employed an
amanuensis, see 1 Cor. xvi. 21; Col. iv. 18; 2 Thess. iii. 17, and
cf. Gal. vi. 11 ἴδετε πηλίκοις ὑμῖν γράμμασιν ἔγραψα τῇ ἐμῇ χειρί.

23. Γάϊος who is described as the host of St. Paul and of
the whole Church is possibly the Gaius of 1 Cor. i. 14. In all
probability the Christian assembly met in his house. Erastus
(cf. 2 Tim. iv. 20) who held the important office of οἰκόνομος τῆς
πόλεως, 'the city treasurer,' is presumably mentioned as the most
influential member of the community.

THE CONCLUDING DOXOLOGY.

XVI. 25-27. *And now let me give praise to God, who can
make you firm believers, duly trained and established according to the Gospel that I proclaim, the preaching which
announces Jesus the Messiah; that preaching in which
God's eternal purpose, the mystery of his working, kept
silent since the world began, has been revealed, a purpose
which the Prophets of old foretold, which has been preached
now by God's express command, which announces to all the
Gentiles the message of obedience in faith: to God, I say, to
Him who is alone wise, be the glory for ever through Jesus
Messiah. Amen.*

25-27. The Epistle concludes in a manner unusual in St. Paul
with a doxology or ascription of praise, in which incidentally all
the great thoughts of the Epistle are summed up. Although

doxologies are not uncommon in these Epistles (Gal. **i. 5**; Rom. xi. 36), they are not usually so long or so heavily weighted; but Eph. iii. 21; Phil. iv. 20; 1 Tim. i. 17 offer quite sufficient parallels; the two former at a not much later date. Ascriptions of praise at the conclusion of other Epp. are common, Heb. xiii. 20, 21; Jude 24, 25; Clem. Rom. § lxv; *Mart. Polyc.* 20.

The various questions bearing on the genuineness of these verses and their positions in different MSS., have been sufficiently discussed in the Introduction, § 9. Here they are commented upon as a genuine and original conclusion to the Epistle exactly harmonizing with its contents. The commentary is mainly based on the paper by Hort published in Lightfoot, *Biblical Essays*, p. 321 ff.

25. τῷ δὲ δυναμένῳ ὑμᾶς στηρίξαι: cf. Rom. xiv. 4 στήκει ἢ πίπτει· σταθήσεται δέ· δυνατεῖ γὰρ ὁ Κύριος στῆσαι αὐτόν. A more exact parallel is furnished by Eph. iii. 20 τῷ δὲ δυναμένῳ ... ποιῆσαι ... αὐτῷ ἡ δόξα. στηρίζω is confined in St. Paul to the earlier Epistles (Rom. i. 11; and Thess.). δύναμαι, δυνατός, δυνατέω of God, with an infinitive, are common in this group. We are at once reminded that in i. 11 St. Paul had stated that one of the purposes of his contemplated visit was to confer on them some spiritual gift that they might be established.

κατὰ τὸ εὐαγγέλιόν μου: Rom. ii. 16; 2 Tim. ii. 8; cf. also Rom. xi. 28 κατὰ τὸ εὐαγγέλιον. One salient feature of the Epistle is at once alluded to, that special Gospel of St. Paul which he desired to explain, and which is the main motive of this Epistle. St. Paul did not look upon this as antagonistic to the common faith of the Church, but as complementary to and explanatory of it. To expound this would especially lead to the 'establishment' of a Christian Church, for if rightly understood, it would promote the harmony of Jew and Gentile within it.

καὶ τὸ κήρυγμα Ἰησοῦ Χριστοῦ. The words κήρυγμα, κηρύσσειν occur throughout St. Paul's Epp., but more especially in this second group. (Rom. x. 8; 1 Cor. i. 21, 23; ii. 4; 2 Cor. i. 19; iv. 5; xi. 4; Gal. ii. 2, &c.) The genitive is clearly objective, the preaching 'about Christ'; and the thought of St. Paul is most clearly indicated in Rom. x. 8–12, which seems to be here summed up. St. Paul's life was one of preaching. The object of his preaching was faith in Jesus the Messiah, and that name implies the two great aspects of the message, on the one hand salvation through faith in Him, on the other as a necessary consequence the universality of that salvation. The reference is clearly to just the thoughts which run through this Epistle, and which marked the period of the Judaistic controversies.

κατὰ ἀποκάλυψιν μυστηρίου κ.τ.λ. Cf. 1 Cor. ii. 6, 7, 10 σοφίαν δὲ λαλοῦμεν ἐν τοῖς τελείοις ... Θεοῦ σοφίαν ἐν μυστηρίῳ, τὴν ἀποκεκρυμμένην, ἣν προώρισεν ὁ Θεὸς πρὸ τῶν αἰώνων ... ἡμῖν δὲ ἀπεκάλυψεν ὁ Θεὸς διὰ τοῦ Πνεύματος. Eph. iii. 3, 5, 6; Tit. i. 2, 3; 2 Tim. i. 9, 10, and for separate phrases, Rom. i. 16; iii. 21; xi. 25. This is the thought which underlies much of the argument of chaps. ix–xi, and is indirectly implied in the first eight chapters. It represents in fact, the conclusion which the Apostle has arrived at in musing over the difficulties which the problems of human history as he knew them had suggested. God who rules over all the aeons or periods in time, which have passed and which are to come, is working out an eternal purpose in the world. For ages it was a mystery, now in these last days it has been revealed: and this revelation explains the meaning of God's working in the past. The thought then forms a transition from the point of view of the Romans to that of the Ephesians. It is not unknown in the Epp. of the second group, as the quotation from Corinthians shows; but there it represents rather the conclusion which is being arrived at by the Apostle, while in the Epp. of the Captivity it is assumed as already proved, and as the basis on which the idea of the Church is developed. The end of the Epistle to the Romans is the first place where we should expect this thought in a doxology, and coming there, it exactly brings out the force and purpose of the previous discussion.

The passage κατὰ ἀποκάλυψιν down to γνωρισθέντος goes not with στηρίξαι but with κήρυγμα. The preaching of Christ was the revelation of the 'mystery which had been hidden,' and explained God's purpose in the world.

26. In this verse we should certainly read διά τε γραφῶν προφητικῶν. The only Greek MSS. that omit τε are DE, and the authority of versions can hardly be quoted against it. Moreover, the sentence is much simpler if it be inserted. It couples together φανερωθέντος and γνωρισθέντος, and all the words from διά τε γραφῶν to the latter word should be taken together. εἰς πάντα τὰ ἔθνη probably goes with εἰς ὑπακοὴν πίστεως and not with γνωρισθέντος.

διά τε γραφῶν προφητικῶν ... γνωρισθέντος. All the ideas in this sentence are exactly in accordance with the thoughts which run through this Epistle. The unity of the Old and New Testaments, the fact that Christ had come in accordance with the Scriptures (Rom. i. 1, 2), that the new method of salvation although apart from law, was witnessed to by the Law and the Prophets (μαρτυρουμένη ὑπὸ τοῦ νόμου καὶ τῶν προφητῶν Rom. iii. 21), the constant allusion esp. in chaps. ix–xi to the Old Testament Scriptures; all these are summed up in the phrase διὰ γραφῶν προφητικῶν.

The same is true of the idea expressed by κατ᾽ ἐπιταγὴν τοῦ αἰωνίου Θεοῦ. The mission given to the preachers of the Gospel is brought out generally in Rom. x. 15 ff., the special command to the Apostle is dwelt on in the opening vv. 1–5, and the sense of commission is a constant thought of this period. With regard to the words, αἰωνίου is of course suggested by χρόνοις αἰωνίοις: cp. Baruch iv. 8, Susanna (Theod.) 42 (LXX) 35. The formula κατ᾽ ἐπιταγήν occurs 1 Cor. vii. 6; 2 Cor. viii. 8, but with quite a different meaning; in the sense of this passage it comes again in 1 Tim. i. 1; Tit. i. 3.

We find the phrase εἰς ὑπακοὴν πίστεως in Rom. i. 5. As Hort points out, the enlarged sense of ὑπακοή and ὑπακούω is confined to the earlier Epistles.

The last phrase εἰς πάντα τὰ ἔθνη γνωρισθέντος hardly requires illustrating; it is a commonplace of the Epistle. In this passage still carrying on the explanation of κήρυγμα, four main ideas of the Apostolic preaching are touched upon—the continuity of the Gospel, the Apostolic commission, salvation through faith, the preaching to the Gentiles.

μόνῳ σοφῷ Θεῷ: a somewhat similar expression may be found in 1 Tim. i. 17, which at a later date was assimilated to this, σοφῷ being inserted. But the idea again sums up another line of thought in the Epistle—God is one, therefore He is God of both Jews and Greeks; the Gospel is one (iii. 29, 30). God is infinitely wise (ὦ βάθος πλούτου καὶ σοφίας καὶ γνώσεως Θεοῦ xi. 33); even when we cannot follow His tracks, He is leading and guiding us, and the end will prove the depths of His wisdom.

27. ᾧ ἡ δόξα κ.τ.λ. The reading here is very difficult.

1. It would be easy and simple if following the authority of B. 33. 72, Pesh., Orig.-lat. we could omit ᾧ, or if we could read αὐτῷ with P. 31. 54 (Boh. cannot be quoted in favour of this reading; Wilkins' translation which Tisch. follows is wrong). But both these look very much like corrections, and it is difficult to see how ᾧ came to be inserted if it was not part of the original text. Nor is it inexplicable. The Apostle's mind is so full of the thoughts of the Epistle that they come crowding out, and have produced the heavily loaded phrases of the doxology; the structure of the sentence is thus lost, and he concludes with a well-known formula of praise ᾧ ἡ δόξα κ.τ.λ. (Gal. i. 15; 2 Tim. iv. 18; Heb. xiii. 21).

2. If the involved construction were the only difficulty caused by reading ᾧ, it would probably be right to retain it. But there are others more serious. How are the words διὰ ᾽Ι. Χ. to be taken? and what does ᾧ refer to?

(1) Grammatically the simplest solution is to suppose, with Lid., that ᾧ refers to Christ, and that St. Paul has changed the construction owing to the words διὰ ᾽Ι. Χ. He had intended to finish 'to the only wise God through Christ Jesus be Glory,' as in Jude 25 μόνῳ Θεῷ σωτῆρι ἡμῶν, διὰ ᾽Ι. Χ. τοῦ Κυρίου ἡμῶν, δόξα,

μεγαλωσύνη, κ.τ.λ., but the words Ἰησοῦ Χριστοῦ remind him that it is through the work of Christ that all this scheme has been developed; he therefore ascribes to Him the glory. This is the only possible construction if ᾧ be read, but it can hardly be correct; and that not because we can assert that on *a priori* grounds a doxology cannot be addressed to the Son, but because such a doxology would not be in place here. The whole purpose of these concluding verses is an ascription of praise to Him who is the only wise God.

(2) For this reason most commentators attempt to refer the ᾧ to Θεῷ. This in itself is not difficult: it resembles what is the probable construction in 1 Pet. iv. 11, and perhaps in Heb. xiii. 21. But then διὰ Ἰ. Χ. becomes very difficult. To take it with σοφῷ would be impossible, and to transfer it into the relative clause would be insufferably harsh.

There is no doubt therefore that it is by far the easiest course to omit ᾧ. We have however the alternative of supposing that it is a blunder made by St. Paul's secretary in the original letter. We have seen that some such hypothesis may explain the impossible reading in iv. 12.

εἰς τοὺς αἰῶνας should be read with B C L, Harcl., Chrys. Cyr. Theodrt. τῶν αἰώνων was added in אADEP, Vulg. Pesh. Boh., Orig.-lat. &c., owing to the influence of 1 Tim. i. 17.

The doxology sums up all the great ideas of the Epistle. The power of the Gospel which St. Paul was commissioned to preach; the revelation in it of the eternal purpose of God; its contents, faith; its sphere, all the nations of the earth; its author, the one wise God, whose wisdom is thus vindicated—all these thoughts had been continually dwelt on. And so at the end feeling how unfit a conclusion would be the jarring note of vv. 17–20, and wishing to 'restore to the Epistle at its close its former serene loftiness,' the Apostle adds these verses, writing them perhaps with his own hand in those large bold letters which seem to have formed a sort of authentication of his Epistles (Gal. vi. 11), and thus gives an eloquent conclusion to his great argument.

INDEX TO THE NOTES

I. SUBJECTS.

Western Text, The, p. lxxi ff.
Wetstein, J. J., p. cv.
Weymouth, Dr. R. F., p. 424.
Wiclif, pp. 9; 175; 194.
Wordsworth, Dr. Christopher, p. cvii.

Works, pp. 57; 102; 275 ff.
Wrath of God, pp. 47; 117.

Zahn, Dr. Theodor, p. lxxxv
Ziegler, L., p. lxvi.

II. LATIN WORDS.

angustia, p. 57.
caritas, pp. 124; 375.
definitus, p. 8.
deputatus, p. 222.
destinatus, p. 8.
dilectio, pp. 124; 375.

iugulatio, p. 222.
mortificari, p. 222.
perficio, pp. 58; 124.
perpetro, p. 58.
pressura, pp. 57; 124
victima, p. 222.

III. GREEK WORDS.

[This is an Index to the Notes and not a Concordance; sometimes however, where it is desirable to illustrate a particular usage, references are given to passages which are not directly annotated in the Commentary. The opportunity is also taken to introduce occasional references to two works which appeared too late for use in the Commentary, *Notes on Epistles of St. Paul from unpublished Commentaries* (including the first seven chapters of the Romans) by Bp. Lightfoot, and *Bibelstudien* by G. Adolf Deissmann (Marburg, 1895). Some especially of the notes on words in the former work attain to classical value (ἀγαθός and δίκαιος, ἀνακεφαλαιοῦσθαι, ὀψώνιον), and the latter brings to bear much new illustrative matter from the Flinders Petrie and other papyri and from inscriptions. In some instances the new material adduced has led to a confirmation, while in others it might have led to a modification of the views expressed in the Commentary. We cannot however include under this latter head the somewhat important differences in regard to δικαιοῦν and καταλλάσσειν. Bp. Lightfoot's view of δικαιοῦν in particular seems to us less fully worked out than was usual with him.]

Ἀββᾶ, viii. 15.
ἄβυσσος, x. 7.
ἀγαθός, v. 7 (=Lft.); τὸ ἀγαθόν, xiii. 4; xiv. 16; xv. 2.
ἀγαθωσύνη, xv. 14.
ἀγαπᾶν, xiii. 8, 9.
ἀγάπη, v. 5, 8; xii. 9; xiii. 10; xv. 30; pp. 374 ff.: cf. Deissmann, p. 80 f.
ἄγγελος, viii. 38.
ἁγιασμός, vi. 19.
ἅγιος, i. 7; xi. 16; xii. 1, 13; xvi. 2, 14.

ἁγιωσύνη, i. 4.
ἀγνοεῖν, x. 3; xi. 25.
ἀγριέλαιος, xi. 17.
ἀδελφός, x. 1: cf. Deissmann, p. 82 f.
ἀδικία, i. 18, 29; iii. 5.
ἀδόκιμος, i. 28.
ἀδύνατος, viii. 3.
ἀΐδιος, i. 20.
αἷμα, iii. 25; pp. 91 f., 119.
αἰών, xii. 2.
ἀκαθαρσία, vi. 19.
ἀκοή, x. 16.
ἀκροατής, ii. 13.

κατηχεῖν, ii. 18.
καυχᾶσθαι, v. 3, 11.
  καυχᾶσαι, ii. 17.
καύχημα, iv. 2.
καύχησις, v. 3 ; xv. 17.
Κεγχρεαί, xvi. ς.
κήρυγμα, xvi. 25.
κηρύσσειν, x. 14, 15.
κίνδυνος, viii. 35.
κλάδος, xi. 16.
κληρονόμος, iv. 13, 14 ; viii. 17.
κλῆσις, xi. 29.
κλητός, i. 1, 6, 7 ; viii. 28 ; p. 18.
  κλητὴ ἁγία, p. 12 f.
κλίμα, xv. 23.
κοιλία, xvi. 18.
κοινός, xiv. 14.
κοινωνεῖν, xii. 13 ; xv. 27.
κοινωνία, xv. 26.
κοίτη, xiii. 13.
  κοίτην ἔχειν, ix. 10.
κοπιᾶν, xvi. 6.
κόσμος, ὁ, iii. 6 ; v. 12.
κρίνειν, κρίνεσθαι, iii. 4 ; xiv. 5, 13.
κτίσις, i. 20 ; viii. 19, 21, 39.
κύκλῳ, xv. 19.
κυριεύειν, vi. 9.
Κύριος, i. 4, 7 ; x. 12, 13 ; xii. 11 ;
  xiv. 8 ; xv. 6 ; p. 18.
κῶμος, xiv. 14.

λαλεῖν, iii. 19.
λαός, xi. 1.
λατρεία, ix. 4 ; xii. 1.
λατρεύειν, i. 9.
λάχανα, xix. 2.
λέγειν, iii. 19.
  ἀλλὰ λέγω, x. 18, 19.
  λέγω οὖν, xi. 1, 11.
λεῖμμα, xi. 5.
λειτουργεῖν, p. 20 : cf. Deissmann,
  p. 137 f.
λειτουργός, xiii. 6 ; xv. 16.
λόγια τά, iii. 2.
λογίζεσθαι, viii. 18 ; xiv. 14.
  λογίζεσθαι εἰς, ii. 26 ; iv. 3.
λογικός, xii. 1.
λογισμός, ii. 15.
λόγος, iii. 4 ; ix. 6.
λυπεῖσθαι, xiv. 15.
λύπη, ix. 2.

μακάριος, iv. 7, 8 ; xiv. 22.
μακαρισμός, iv. 6.
μακροθυμία, ii. 4.
Μαρία (Μαριάμ), xvi. 6 (v. l.).
μαρτυρεῖν, iii. 21 ; x. 2.

ματαιότης, viii. 20.
ματαιοῦσθαι, i. 21.
μάχαιρα, viii. 35.
μείζων, ix. 12.
μέλλειν, viii. 18.
μέλλων, ὁ, v. 14.
μέν, x. 1.
  μὲν οὖν, xi. 13 ; p. 324.
  μενοῦνγε, ix. 20 ; x. 18.
μένειν, ix. 11.
μεστός, i. 29 ; xv. 14.
μεταδιδόναι, xii. 8.
μεταμορφοῦσθαι, xii. 2.
  μεταξὺ ἀλλήλων, ii. 15.
μή, ii. 14 ; iii. 5 ; iv. 19 ; ix. 14 ;
  x. 19.
  μὴ γένοιτο, iii. 4 ; ix. 14 ; xi. 1,
  11.
μήπω, ix. 11.
μνεία, xii. 13 (v. l.).
μόνος, xvi. 26.
μόρφωσις, ii. 20.
μυστήριον, xi. 25 ; xvi. 25.

νεκρός, i. 4 (cf. Lft.) ; viii. 10 ; xi. 15.
  ἐκ νεκρῶν, vi. 13 (cf. Lft.).
νήπιος, ii. 20.
νικᾶν, iii. 4 ; xii. 21.
νομοθεσία, ix. 4.
νόμος, metaphorical use of, iii. 27 ; vii.
  21, 23 ; viii. 2 ; x. 31.
νόμος (sine artic.), ii. 12, 13, 14, 25 ;
  iii. 31 (cf. Lft.) ; iv. 13 ; v. 13 ;
  vii. 1 ; ix. 31 ; x. 4.
  νόμος, ὁ, ii. 13, 14 ; iii. 19 ; vii. 2,
  12.
νοῦς, i. 28 ; vii. 23 ; xii. 2.
νυνί, iii. 21.

ὁδηγός, ii. 19.
οἴδαμεν, ii. 2 ; viii. 22, 28.
οἰκοδομή, xiv. 19.
οἰκτείρειν, ix. 15.
οἰκτιρμός, xii. 1.
οἷος, ix. 6.
ὀκνηρός, xii. 11.
ὅλος, viii. 36.
ὁμοθυμαδόν, xv. 6.
ὁμοίωμα, vi. 5 ; viii. 3.
ὁμολογεῖν, ix. 9.
ὀνειδισμός, xv. 3.
ὄνομα, i. 5 ; p. 18.
ὀνομάζειν, xv. 20.
ὅπλον, vi. 13.
ὅπως ἄν, iii. 4.
ὀργή, ἡ ὀργή, i. 18 ; ii. 5, 8 ; iii. 5 ;
  xii. 19 ; xiii. 4.

πρωτότοκος, viii. 29.
πταίειν, xi. 11.
πτωχός, xv. 26.
πωροῦν, xi. 7.
πώρωσις, xi. 25.

ῥῆμα, x. 8, 17.
ῥίζα, xi. 16 ff. ; xv. 12.
ῥυόμενος, ὁ, xi. 26.
Ῥώμη, i. 7.

σαρκικός, xv. 27.
σάρκινος, vii. 14.
σάρξ, iii. 20; vi. 19 ; ix. 8 ; xiii. 14 ;
  p. 181.
  ἐν σαρκί, ἐν τῇ σαρκί, vii. 5 ; viii.
  3, 9.
  κατὰ σάρκα, i. 3 ; iv. 1 ; viii. 4,
  5 ; ix. 3, 5 ; p. 233 ff.
Σατανᾶς, xvi. 20 ; p. 145.
σεβάζεσθαι, i. 25.
σημεῖον, iv. 11 ; xv. 19.
σκάνδαλον, xi. 9 ; xiv. 13.
σκεῦος, ix. 21, 22.
σκληρύνειν, ix. 18.
σκοπεῖν, xvi. 17.
Σπανία, xv. 24, 28.
σπέρμα, ix. 7.
σπουδή, xii. 8, 11.
στενοχωρία, ii. 9.
στήκειν, xiv. 4.
στηρίζειν, i. 11 ; xvi. 25.
στοιχεῖν, iv. 12 (on τοῖς στοιχ. see
  Lft.).
συγγενής, ix. 3 ; xvi. 7, 10, 21.
συγκλείειν, xi. 32.
συγκληρονόμος, viii. 17.
συγκοινωνός, xi. 17.
συμμαρτυρεῖν, ii. 15 ; viii. 16 ; ix. 1.
σύμμορφος, viii. 29.
συμπαρακαλεῖσθαι, i. 12.
συμπάσχειν, viii. 17.
σύμφυτος, vi. 5.
συναγωνίζεσθαι, xv. 30.
συναιχμάλωτος, xvi. 7.
συναναπαύεσθαι, xv. 32.
συναντιλαμβάνεσθαι, viii. 26.
συναπάγεσθαι, xii. 16.
συνείδησις, ii. 15 ; ix. 1.
συνεργεῖν, viii. 28.
συνευδοκεῖν, i. 32.
συνθάπτεσθαι, vi. 4.
συνιστάναι, iii. 5 ; xvi. 1.
συνιῶν, iii. 11.
συντελεῖν, ix. 28.
συντέμνειν, ix. 28.
συντρίβειν, xvi. 20.

σύντριμμα, iii. 16.
συνωδίνειν, viii. 22.
συσταυροῦσθαι, vi. 6.
συσχηματίζεσθαι, xii. 2.
σφαγή, viii. 36.
σφραγίζειν, xv. 28.
σφραγίς, iv. 11.
σώζειν, σώζεσθαι, v. 9 ; viii. 24 ; xi
  26 : cf. Lft. p. 288.
σῶμα. vi. 6 ; vii. 4, 24 ; xii. 1.
Σωσίπατρος, xvi. 21.
σωτηρία, i. 16 ; x. 1 ; xi. 11.

ταπεινός, xii. 16.
τε γάρ, vii. 7.
τέκνον, viii. 14, 17 ; ix. 8 (cf. Deissmann, p. 164).
τέλος (= end), x. 4 ; (= toll), xiii. 7.
τί ἐροῦμεν, iii. 5.
  τί οὖν ; iii. 9 ; vi. 15 ; xi. 7.
  τί οὖν ἐροῦμεν ; iv. 1 ; vi. 1 ; vii.
  7 ; viii. 31 ; ix. 14, 30.
  ἀλλὰ τί λέγει ; x. 8 ; xi. 4.
τιμή, xii. 10.
τινές, iii. 3 ; xi. 17.
τὸ κατ᾽ ἐμέ, i. 15.
τολμᾶν, v. 7.
τολμηρότερον, xv. 15.
τόπος, xii. 19 ; xv. 23.
τοῦ with infin., vi. 6 ; vii. 3.
τράπεζα, xi. 9.
τράχηλος, xvi. 4.
τύπος, v. 14 ; vi. 17.

ὑβριστής, i. 30.
υἱοθεσία, viii. 15.
υἱός (of Christ; cf. Deissmann. p.166 f.),
  i. 4; viii. 29; (of man), viii. 14.
ὑμέτερος, xi. 31.
ὑπακοή, i. 5 ; v. 19 ; xvi. 19.
ὑπακούειν, x. 16.
ὕπανδρος, vii. 2.
ὑπάρχειν, iv. 19.
ὑπερεντυγχάνειν, viii. 26.
ὑπερέχειν, xiii. 1.
ὑπερήφανος, i. 30.
ὑπερνικᾶν, viii. 37.
ὑπερπερισσεύειν, v. 20.
ὑπερφρονεῖν, xii. 3.
ὑπό, iii. 9.
ὑπόδικος, iii. 19.
ὑπόλειμμα, ix. 27.
ὑπομένειν, xii. 12.
ὑπομονή, v. 3.
ὑποτάσσειν, ὑποτάσσεσθαι, viii. 20 ; x.
  3 ; xiii. 1.
ὑστερεῖσθαι, iii. 23.

G g